General equilibrium models for development policy

General equilibrium models for development policy
A World Bank Research Publication

KEMAL DERVIŞ
The World Bank
Washington, D.C.

JAIME DE MELO
Georgetown University
Washington, D.C.

SHERMAN ROBINSON
The World Bank
Washington, D.C.

WITH A FOREWORD BY HOLLIS CHENERY

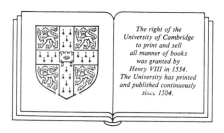

The right of the
University of Cambridge
to print and sell
all manner of books
was granted by
Henry VIII in 1534.
The University has printed
and published continuously
since 1504.

CAMBRIDGE UNIVERSITY PRESS

Cambridge
London   New York   New Rochelle
Melbourne   Sydney

Published by the Press Syndicate of the University of Cambridge
The Pitt Building, Trumpington Street, Cambridge CB2 1RP
32 East 57th Street, New York, NY 10022, USA
296 Beaconsfield Parade, Middle Park, Melbourne 3206, Australia

First published 1982

Printed in the United States of America
Reprinted 1984

Library of Congress Cataloging in Publication Data
Dervis, Kemal.
General equilibrium models for development
policy.
(A World Bank research publication)
Bibliography: p.
Includes index.
1. Economic development – Mathematical models.
2. Economic policy – Mathematical models.
3. Underdeveloped areas – Mathematical models.
4. Equilibrium (Economics) I. Melo, Jaime de.
II. Robinson, Sherman. III. Title. IV. Series.
HD75.5.D47   338.9′00724   81–12307
ISBN 0 521 24490 0 hard covers   AACR2
ISBN 0 521 27030 8 paperback

Contents

v

Part V. Income distribution and multisector planning models

Part VI. Methodological appendixes

Tables and figures

Tables

x

Figures

Foreword

The analysis of development policy has evolved through the interactions between development theories and their application to varied countries and problems. This process has been facilitated by the rapid accumulation of information on developing economies and the better identification of constraints on the development process and the policy instruments available to governments. In the course of this evolution there has been a shift in emphasis away from planning techniques to models that can simulate the functioning of mixed economies in which policies are implemented largely through market mechanisms.

The heart of the development problem is the relation among resource allocation decisions in different sectors of the economy. Early formulations of this problem were based on simple extensions of the Leontief input–output system. These led to the accumulation of data on the relations among economic sectors, which has in turn made possible the formulation of more complex analytical systems. In this way, general equilibrium models that were being tested only in experimental forms ten years ago have evolved into tools that can be used in a variety of practical applications.

The work of Derviş, de Melo, and Robinson represents a substantial advance in this direction, both in the systematic formulation of computable general equilibrium models and in their application to the policy problems of individual countries. The authors' theoretical approach has been refined in a series of applications to problems ranging from the response to rising energy prices to long-term structural change and income distribution. As a result of extensive testing of alternative methods, they are able to show the advantages and limitations of more complex general equilibrium formulations in comparison to simpler forms of interindustry analysis.

The present work is one of a series of studies supported by the World Bank research program that are designed to contribute to the methodology and use of policy analysis.

HOLLIS CHENERY
Vice-president, Development Policy
The World Bank

Preface

Recent years have seen a great deal of effort focused on building applied general equilibrium models to support the formulation and conduct of economic policy in developing countries. This work is in the tradition of the earlier input–output and linear programming "planning models" pioneered in the 1950s and 1960s by Leontief, Chenery, and others. The more recent work focuses explicitly on the mixed-market nature of most developing economies. Instead of describing the problem from the point of view of a planner able to determine economic quantities as part of a centrally determined optimal plan, the emphasis has shifted to modeling the market mechanism, including special institutional features and distortions, as it operates in actual, always partially decentralized, economies.

Our basic objective in this book is to present the theoretical structures underlying these applied models and hence to clarify their relationship to economic theory, particularly general equilibrium, growth, and trade theory. We thus attempt to establish a more structured framework for the applied model builder, analyzing the various stages of multisector model building from static input–output models with fixed prices to dynamic computable general equilibrium models with endogenous price determination and an elaborate treatment of trade and income distribution. Paralleling the theoretical discussion, we present a series of empirical applications that illustrate how applied general equilibrium models can be used in policy analysis. Our particular applications are concerned with questions of growth and structural change, the choice of foreign exchange regime, and the impact of different development strategies on the distribution of income.

Our collaboration over the years has greatly benefited from the facilities and support of a number of institutions. In the early phases, the Research Program in Development Studies at Princeton University provided a congenial atmosphere and generous support. The presentation of the material has also benefited from student reactions to courses taught at Georgetown, Johns Hopkins, Princeton, and Middle East Technical Universities. Some of our work was financially supported by the Agency for International Development. However, the bulk of the study was completed at the World Bank, which provided much of the stimulus for our work. In particular, two research projects at the Bank have provided the material for most of the empirical applications: (1) "A Comparative Study of the Sources of Industrial Growth and Structural Change" (World Bank reference RPO 671-32) and (2) "The Sources of Growth and Productivity Change: A Comparative Analysis" (RPO 671-79).

Hollis Chenery and Larry Westphal have, over the past few years, provided inspiration, criticism, and sustained encouragement. Their support was always available when it was most needed. In addition, we owe a general intellectual debt to Hollis Chenery. Indeed, much of what we have done can be seen as an attempt to pull together and build on the various strands of his work on multisector models over the past twenty years.

Throughout the drafting we have profited from the comments and criticisms of a number of colleagues. In particular, we would like to thank Irma Adelman, Bela Balassa, Michael Bruno, Merih Celasun, Shanta Devarajan, Peter Dixon, Vinod Dubey, Alan Gelb, Victor Ginsburgh, Wafik Grais, Timur Kuran, Thomas McCool, Martha de Melo, Joan Nelson, Graham Pyatt, Lance Taylor, Laura Tyson, Jean Waelbroeck, and Adrian Wood. We owe a special debt of gratitude to Anne Krueger, who read the entire draft of the book. Her queries and suggestions, both on substance and exposition, have greatly improved the product. Murat Köprülü, Maria Kutcher, Jeffrey Lewis, and Narayana Poduval have supported our work through their exceptionally skillful and dedicated research assistance. For their help and patience in typing the various drafts of the manuscript, we thank Nenita Bencio, Isabelle Kim, Robert Kisch, and Kim Tran. From Cambridge University Press we have had both encouragement and substantive support. Finally, we owe an enormous debt of gratitude to our wives, Neslihan, Martha, and Barbara, who have tolerated the inordinate demands on our time over the past few years. This book could not have been written without the support of all those teachers, colleagues, friends, and family mentioned above. The responsibility for the views expressed herein, including any errors, remains, of course, solely ours.

KEMAL DERVIŞ
JAIME DE MELO
SHERMAN ROBINSON

CHAPTER 1

Introduction

1.1 Introduction

Currently developed countries required a century to industrialize. This transformation, which Kuznets (1966) calls "modern economic growth," involves large and systematic shifts in the structure of production, demand, employment, investment, and trade. Today, some fast-growing developing countries are achieving a similar transformation in a quarter of a century. Both the speed and systematic nature of this transformation implies that sectors cannot be considered in isolation from one another. Bottlenecks arise, and it is necessary to view the economy at a sufficiently disaggregated level to reflect important differences in production and trade structures. Furthermore, this complex transformation process depends jointly on both domestic policies and external events, including changes in international prices and access to markets in developed countries. Structural adjustment to external events is an important feature of development policy.

In understanding and managing structural change, multisector models have provided an especially useful framework. Such models incorporate production at a level of aggregation that permits the analysis of structural change and also captures the essential interdependent nature of production, demand, and trade within a general equilibrium system. Whereas the earlier input–output models could capture only very simple general equilibrium relationships, more recent models are able to incorporate market mechanisms and policy instruments that work through price incentives. In virtually all modern countries, development takes place within the structure of a mixed-market economy, so it is important for models to capture the relevant market mechanisms.

This book concerns the application of multisector, general equilibrium models. The more theoretical chapters aim to provide the reader with an understanding of the nature of these models and their links to economic theory. The chapters devoted to cross-country applications show how multisector models can capture the diversity in economic conditions across countries and how this diversity can affect a country's development strategy. The chapters devoted to applications within par-

1

ticular countries show how applied general equilibrium analysis can contribute to policy debate and to a better understanding of how different policies affect economic performance.

1.2   Theory, models, and policy analysis

In policy analysis, there is a gap between the realm of pure theory, trade and growth theory in particular, and the real world that faces the policy maker and planner. When it comes to policy debate and policy formulation, more is needed than the qualitative insights that pure theory can yield. Although theoretical reasoning and the insights gained from simplified abstract models must provide the starting point, more elaborate and "realistic" analysis is also required. Intelligent policy debate and policy formulation requires knowledge of the quantitative significance of the various mechanisms analyzed by theory. Furthermore, indirect effects of policies may escape intuition and thus the attention of theorists, whereas empirical modeling can reveal their presence and importance. Finally, sensitivity tests are needed to clarify the role of key behavioral assumptions or important parameter values. Models simple enough for analytic solution can seldom provide the framework for such analysis.

Empirical general equilibrium models that can be solved numerically are thus useful to provide a bridge between the theorist, the planner, and the practical policy maker. Theorists will be able to recognize in their specification the fundamental structure of simpler theoretical models and will be able to relate the functioning of the applied models to known theorems and analytical results. Policy makers, on the other hand, will be able to recognize in the questions addressed by the models some of the real-world policy dilemmas they face. Constructive debate can focus on particular behavioral assumptions, a particular sector, or a particular set of parameter values. Disagreements and differences in policy recommendations can be traced back to specific behavioral assumptions, empirical estimates, or fundamental differences in normative goals.

This book focuses on models that are flexible and detailed enough to accommodate various aspects of the reality of developing countries but that also remain close to pure economic theory. This general approach determines, to a great extent, both the strengths and weaknesses of the resulting models as tools of analysis and planning. Mainstream economic theory provides a powerful framework of analysis and the only really systematic accumulation of useful taxonomies and formal results. Important aspects of reality still defy formal economic analysis, however, and development problems in particular do not always fit into the established neoclassical framework.

It must be stressed that different general equilibrium models may focus on different kinds of economy-wide consistency. Malinvaud recently made the point very well: "The type of consistency that is assumed to exist between individual decisions is specific to each equilibrium theory. For the study of (Keynesian) employment it can only be a short-run consistency which will be quite different from the long-run consistency that one will want to consider when studying, for instance, industrial structure" (Malinvaud, 1977). A multisector, general equilibrium model need not always conform to Walrasian theory. Indeed, we specify various forms of general equilibrium models with rationing of foreign exchange and persistent excess demands in some important markets. Although the equilibrium described may not be Walrasian, neoclassical resource allocation theory remains the fundamental framework of analysis.

The models in this book are structural models designed for policy analysis and cannot be used to make unconditional projections or forecasts. They thus stand in stark contrast to the large, temporally disaggregated, macroeconomic forecasting models whose econometric specification relies heavily on lagged endogenous variables and reduced-form equations to capture the role of expectations and frictions in the economy. In such models, however, it is often difficult to trace the causal mechanisms at work. A major advantage of the applied general equilibrium models presented here is that the mechanisms driving them are clear and (when properly formulated) easy to grasp because their structure is rooted in received theory. We have made a conscious effort throughout the presentations and applications in this book to make the mechanisms governing the models as transparent and simple as possible, given the focus at hand. We believe that transparency is a key characteristic that an empirical general equilibrium model must have if it is to provide a framework for policy analysis.

Consider, for example, a disagreement about the appropriateness of a major devaluation in a country facing a foreign shortage. Do those who oppose devaluation oppose it because they believe in low export demand elasticities and/or low substitution elasticities between domestic and imported goods? If so, are they primarily worried about an adverse terms-of-trade effect? Is it that supply elasticities are thought to be very low? If so, in which sectors and for what reasons? Is the problem more macroeconomic, with the price level seen tied to the exchange rate by strong cost-push factors that make a real devaluation impossible? Or, yet another possibility, is the whole problem that the opposition to exchange-rate adjustment is based on income distribution considerations? If so, who stands to gain or lose from a devaluation? Theory and intuition can provide only limited help in settling such questions. What is needed is an economy-wide framework that permits an explicit specification of an economy's operation where each of these views can be evaluated.

The focus of multisector, general equilibrium models is traditionally on issues of medium-term planning. Development policy is also concerned with issues of short-term macro management, on the one hand, and with issues of project analysis on the other. Although these two policy areas are largely outside the scope of the discussion in this book, it is very important to understand how multisector models "fit" in the continuum of tools of policy analysis. In order to describe the role of multisector, general equilibrium models in the analysis of development policy issues, we present here a stylized picture of how policy formulation is undertaken in an economy. This stylized description will serve to place planning models within both an analytic and policy context.

1.3   Multisector models and development policy

Consider a hypothetical developing country in which policy formulation is carried on in three different types of ministries: the Ministry of Finance, the Ministry of Planning, and a variety of "sectoral" ministries (industry, agriculture, health, etc.). What are the concerns of these different ministries? What are the different policy instruments they control? What is the behavior of the economic agents who will respond to the policies of these ministries? What are the different analytic and data frameworks in which policy formulation occurs? In the discussion that follows, the distinctions between the "finance," "planning" and "sectoral" ministries are exaggerated in order to highlight the particular role of the Ministry of Planning and the use of multisector models.

In our hypothetical economy, the Ministry of Finance is concerned with relatively short-run issues that can be placed under the broad heading of "stabilization policy." Concern is focused largely on various nominal flow-of-funds balances in the economy, in particular, the balance of payments, the government accounts and the savings–investment balance. The problems that provide the central focus of analysis include the level of foreign debt, inflation, government revenue, the aggregate level of economic activity, "Keynesian" unemployment, and perhaps the distribution of income to broadly defined factors of production (labor, capital).

The analytic framework on which policy analysis of these problems is based is that of macroeconomic models in the "Keynesian" and/or "monetarist" traditions. The important variables included in such analysis are the government deficit, the money supply, the components of aggregate demand, the volume of credit, interest rates, nominal wages and profits, and the exchange rate – all typical variables included in econometric macromodels. The national income and product accounts provide both the data base and the underlying conceptual framework for policy analysis at the macroeconomic level.

The Ministry of Planning is concerned with the medium to long run and with issues that might be placed under the broad heading of "development strategy." The focus is on real variables such as the growth and structure of production, employment, and investment. Factors such as capital accumulation, rural–urban migration, labor force growth, productivity change, trade structure, investment allocation, real resource transfers through the foreign sector, and broad changes in the structure of demand as a result of income growth reflect the important forces at work. These factors largely determine the nature of the development process in a country and must provide the central focus of an analysis of different development strategies.

Given the focus on the medium to long term, the Ministry of Planning is concerned largely with problems that will affect the structure and pace of growth. Particularly in the semi-industrial countries that are undergoing rapid structural change and are heavily dependent on imported inputs, policy makers in the Ministry of Planning are concerned with trade and industrialization strategies. Is a more open development strategy with a larger role for foreign trade more conducive to growth and industrialization than an import-substituting development strategy? While the Ministry of Finance is concerned with foreign debt, the balance of payments, and absorption, the Ministry of Planning is concerned with the relationships among trade policy, growth, and industrial structure.

Historically, planners in socialist as well as in some developing countries worked within the environment of a command economy. They were thus able to ignore the market system and to rely largely on command instruments. Production targets, investment allocation, intermediate inputs, and even labor were allocated directly in physical terms without much concern with the underlying value flows and market incentives. Most countries today, however, including the postreform Eastern European countries, work within the environment of a mixed economy in which the market plays a central role. The exchange rate, taxes, tariffs, subsidies, and other policy variables that affect relative prices and incentives through the market mechanism have become more important than command policies in modern mixed economies, developed and underdeveloped.

Given the prevalence of the market mechanism, a major focus of policy analysis in the Ministry of Planning is to explore the relationship between different policies and policy packages on the one hand and, on the other, the market responses to them. It is crucial to understand how incentive policies affect the allocation of resources and the structure of growth. Wages, prices, and the exchange rate are viewed not in terms of their impact on the aggregate flow of funds and the various macro balances but in terms of their impact on relative factor returns across sectors and by type of factor (labor by skill and sector, capital by sector, etc.). The Ministry of Finance is concerned with inflation and balancing the nominal flow of funds; the Ministry of Planning is concerned with relative prices, real incomes, and the structure of employment.

The analytic framework on which policy analysis is based in the Ministry of Planning is, explicitly or implicitly, that of an economy-wide, multisector model. The core around which all such applied models are built is the input–output model pioneered by Leontief. The essence of input–output analysis is that it captures the crucial element of the interrelatedness of production arising through the flow of intermediate goods among sectors. Even with its assumptions of linearity and cost-determined prices independent of demand, the simplest input–output model nonetheless represents a powerful tool for applied general equilibrium analysis. But the major challenge that led to this book is to extend multisector planning models to include in a realistic manner the feedbacks through the price mechanism that achieve equilibrium between the independently pursued optimizing behavior of suppliers and demanders of products. The essence of multisector policy analysis is to capture this interdependence. Whereas the Ministry of Finance bases its policy analysis on Keynesian and/or monetary theories of macroeconomics, the Ministry of Planning bases its analysis on general equilibrium theory. A "sector" may be defined in a variety of ways, and "multisector" may refer to as few as two, but the underlying theory is essentially microeconomic in spirit. Walras rather than Keynes is the patron saint of multisector analysis.

The accounting framework that underlies multisector analysis is that of the input–output accounts. Through the more complete "System of National Accounts" (SNA), the input–output and national income and product accounts have been integrated into a single general framework. The more recent interest in income distribution and the flow of funds among "institutions" defined more broadly than in the SNA has led to the development of a yet more general social accounting framework. All these systems provide a complete and consistent picture of the "circular flow" in an economy. Even without the apparatus of a fully specified formal model, such accounting systems provide a powerful tool of analysis because they focus on the interrelationships among the different "actors" in the economy and impose the requirement that all real and nominal flows must be consistent. Such a "consistency check" can often reveal problems both with the data and with the economic assumptions underlying policy analysis. Indeed, it can be argued that the major usefulness of applied general equilibrium models is not in their particular empirical results, which may quickly become outdated, but in the fact that they force policy makers to analyze the implications of policy choices within a consistent analytic and information framework.

The final agencies of policy formulation and implementation in our hypothetical economy are the various sectoral ministries. These ministries are also concerned with the medium to long run, but focus on individual projects and investment analysis at the subsector level. They are concerned with problems of analyzing the technical feasibility and social profitability of individual investment projects. The underlying analytic framework is that of partial equilibrium theory, especially the theory of benefit–cost analysis. They also may rely on quite sophisticated models of the production technology in specific subsectors. But these would be sector, not economy-wide, models, and their consideration is outside the scope of this study.

The analytical base for, and the nature of, policy analysis in each of the different ministries is presented in the preceding discussion as being quite distinct and independent. Of course, such separation cannot be achieved either in theory or in practice. For example, consider the relations between the sectoral ministries and the Ministry of Planning. The determination of appropriate shadow prices, especially of key factors such as foreign exchange, labor, and capital, really cannot be done in a partial equilibrium framework. Also, if important projects are large enough, it is necessary to consider explicitly their impact on the rest of the economy, and a general equilibrium framework is required.

The relations between the Ministries of Finance and Planning are often strained, both at the policy-making and research levels. The distinction between the short and medium term can be quite blurred in practice, and it is often the case that short-run stabilization problems will have a lasting impact on a country's development strategy and on the pace and structure of growth in the medium term. This conflict is nowhere more evident than in the area of trade policy, especially with regard to the exchange rate. On the one hand, the Ministry of Finance sees the exchange rate as an instrument of stabilization policy whose major impact is on macro balances, inflation, and absorption. On the other hand, the Ministry of Planning is concerned with the structure of incentives and views changes in the exchange rate as having important effects on the structure of production between tradables and nontradables and between exports and import substitutes. Other areas of potential conflict between the two ministries concern the long-run structural implications of different short-run stabilization packages. The problem here is one of time horizon and the potential trade-offs between policies for demand management and policies affecting growth, structural change, and income distribution in the longer term.

Consider, for example, the case of countries attempting a transition toward a more liberalized trade regime while also liberalizing domestic financial markets under strong inflationary pressures. The liberalization of domestic financial markets tends to increase real returns on domestic financial assets. During the period of portfolio adjustment, the real exchange will appreciate relative to what it would have been in the absence of financial liberalization, to the distress of those in the planning ministry who seek a higher and more stable real exchange rate to expand and diversify exports.

Although there are times when coordination is difficult because of conflicts and problems of overlap, both in goals and policy analysis, between the two ministries, it is nonetheless true that the differences in time horizon and policy focus lead to different theoretical and policy concerns. To say that "the long run is simply a series of short runs" is temporally tautological but analytically untrue. Concern with medium- and long-term development strategies and their impact on growth, structural change, and income distribution requires quite a different set of tools for theoretical and policy analysis than a concern with short-term issues. The two approaches can be complementary and are certainly not independent, but they are nonetheless distinct.

This book is concerned with models and their theoretical underpinnings that support the sort of policy analysis that is the concern of the Ministry of Planning. The problems of overlap with the concerns of the Ministry of Finance or of the sectoral ministries appear in a number of ways – for example, in the areas of exchange rate policy and tax policy – and we consider them as they arise. However, we have made a determined effort to focus on issues of trade policy, industrial strategy, growth, and income distribution, and so do not discuss in any detail the quite different analytical apparatus needed to analyze problems of short-run macro management and stabilization, or problems of sectoral planning and project appraisal.

1.4   Chapter outline

The book is divided into five substantive parts. After the introduction, the three chapters in Part I introduce the input–output system and the linear models based on it. This part sets the stage for the discussion of the more complex nonlinear, price endogenous models by presenting in the context of relatively simple linear models a number of concepts and mechanisms that are common to all general equilibrium models. The empirical applications in this part focus on fundamental properties of growth and structural change and provide a comparative benchmark for the later applications.

The basic input–output model is presented in Chapter 2. The discussion emphasizes the treatment of imports and provides a basis for understanding the treatment of trade in the later nonlinear models. The dynamic input–output model is discussed in a way that emphasizes the nature of dynamic equilibrium embodied in such models. The dynamic model is seen as a useful tool for analyzing long-run equilibrium growth paths in a framework in which capital accumulation is the only serious constraint to growth. The implicit price system embodied in the input–output model is also discussed with an emphasis on the nature of the assumptions required to generate a sensible cost–price system.

The introduction of inequality constraints in the context of linear programming models extends considerably the restricted domain of choice in input–output models. Chapter 3 discusses the basic structure of a dynamic linear programming planning model and considers both its strengths and weaknesses as a tool for policy analysis. The treatment of trade – the "make-or-buy" decision – provides a major focus of the discussion and illustrates well the inherent limitations of linear models, even optimizing ones, as tools for policy analysis. The chapter also discusses the role of "shadow prices" and their relation to market prices, and indicates the need for a nonlinear specification if the prices generated by a planning model are to be interpreted as reflecting prices generated by the interaction of market forces. The chapter closes with a brief discussion of the difficult problem faced by all optimizing models that arises from the need to impose terminal conditions.

Chapter 4 presents two empirical applications of input–output models. The first uses a comparative-static, input–output framework to analyze the nature of growth and structural change in a sample of eight countries for which comparable data are available. The analysis provides a comparative benchmark for analyzing the historical experience of different countries and the projected experience generated by multisector models applied to particular countries. The analysis focuses on the relative contributions to growth and structural change of domestic demand expansion, export expansion, import substitution, and changes in inter-industry relations. The second empirical application uses a dynamic input–output model to explore the role of trade in determining the structure of growth in South Korea during the 1963–73 period. Although it is quite simple, the model does capture some important features of long-run growth arising from the interaction between the changing sectoral structure of demand and sectoral differences in factor requirements.

Part II presents the nonlinear, price endogenous computable general equilibrium (CGE) models and represents the methodological core of the book. Chapter 5 presents, block by block, the components of a CGE model for a closed economy. Prices play a crucial role in these models and are solved so as to "clear markets" in the model economy. They are thus determined endogenously so as to equilibrate the results of individual optimizing behavior by a number of actors, for example, producers, owners of factors of production, households, and government. The chapter discusses all the major features of such models, including alternative functional forms for the various behavioral relations, the nature of market-clearing and excess-demand functions, alternative price-normalization rules, the treatment of investment, and strategies for solving the system empirically. The chapter concludes with a discussion of the nature of a time-recursive dynamic model and of the components of a "between-period" intertemporal model.

Chapter 6 opens the core CGE model to foreign trade, starting with a discussion of the role of the exchange rate in general equilibrium models, including both traded goods and nontraded goods. The discussion focuses on the nature of changes in the equilibrium exchange rate under different price-normalization rules, a topic that has been subject to much confusion and misinterpretation in the literature. The remainder of the chapter is devoted to a discussion of the introduction of trade-policy instruments in a CGE model and a review of concepts from the pure theory of trade that are needed for an understanding of the applications in later chapters.

Chapter 7 explores how one can add considerable realism in the specification of foreign trade in a CGE model by introducing product differentiation between domestically produced and foreign commodities. This extension of the basic model provides a framework that can be used to explore important problems concerning development economics. The extended model falls between the extremes of the theoretical trade models, which exaggerate the ease with which domestic and foreign goods can be substituted for one another, and of the two-gap models, which allow for no substitution whatsoever. The implications of this formulation for the analysis of the impact of policy incentives on resource allocation are profound. No longer are models constrained by the traditional specification in which prices of tradables are determined outside of the model and prices of nontradables are determined endogenously. Instead, there is a continuum characterized by different degrees of "tradability," and the domestic price system in the model acquires a realistic degree of autonomy.

The two chapters in Part III are devoted to an examination of the microeconomic price and quantity linkages at work in the CGE model presented in Chapter 7 and of the resulting macroeconomic implications. These chapters also explore the sensitivity of the model results to systematic variation in key foreign trade parameters. Chapter 8 presents a quantitative microeconomic investigation of the effects of changes in tariffs and subsidies on resource allocation, followed by an analysis of the sensitivity of exchange-rate adjustments to variations in trade elasticities. There is also a discussion of the nature and usefulness of calculations of effective rates of protection and domestic resource costs in a model featuring product differentiation. Finally, there is a comparison between resource-pull calculations based on partial equilibrium assumptions and those arising from the general equilibrium model.

Chapter 9 provides a macroeconomic analysis of alternative adjustment mechanisms open to a developing country facing a sizable shortfall in foreign exchange receipts. Three adjustment mechanisms are modeled: devaluation, premium rationing, and fixed-price rationing. In the case of devaluation, adjustment directly affects both exports and imports. Premium rationing, which is effectively equivalent to a general increase in tariffs, places the direct burden of adjustment on the import side. Fixed-price rationing, which is equivalent to perfect import licensing, yields significant rents to importers and spreads the burden of adjustment quite differently from premium rationing. The chapter also considers the real resource costs associated with attempts by users of imports to garner the rents associated with the two rationing schemes. A stylized model is presented of the empirical costs of these "rent-seeking" activities.

Part IV presents an application of a model incorporating the specification of trade developed in Parts II and III to the policy problems of the Turkish economy. In the late 1970s, Turkey was a striking example of an economy constrained by a severe shortage of foreign exchange. The crisis emerged in 1977, causing economic stagnation after decades of fairly rapid growth and threatening the fabric of Turkish society.

Chapter 10 provides a careful analysis of the sources of this crisis. The CGE modeling framework is used for a historical decomposition analysis, first of the total change in the equilibrium exchange rate between 1973 and 1977, and second, of the total change in the level of absorption or real income during the same period. The model is used to carry out counterfactual experiments designed to isolate the effect of specific causal factors, such as the quadrupling of oil prices in 1974, on the equilibrium exchange rate and real income in Turkey. An important conclusion that emerges from the analysis is that simplistic purchasing-power-parity computations can be very misleading in evaluating the magnitude of required exchange-rate adjustments. Changes in the real sphere of the economy, including changes in real resource transfers from abroad and changes in the terms of trade, may at times be more important than differential inflation rates in determining the extent of disequilibrium.

Chapter 11 turns to a forward-looking planning exercise for Turkey of a kind more familiar from the literature on multisector planning models. What distinguishes planning with a CGE model from the planning exercises carried out with the traditional linear models, however, is the explicit link between policy instruments and the characteristics of the growth paths generated by the CGE model. In this case, government policies on the exchange rate and trade incentives, working through the price system, determine not only the overall pace of economic growth but its sectoral pattern and the relative importance of export expansion, import substitution, and domestic demand expansion in the growth of total demand. A link is thus established between the descriptive-historical sources of growth presented in Chapter 4 and a forward-looking policy-planning exercise. This link is very useful not only in allowing a degree of understanding of the implications of a particular policy package but also in comparing a projected growth path with historical experience both in the same and in different countries.

In Part V, we turn to a consideration of the use of planning models in analyzing the relationships among policy regimes, development strategies, and the distribution of income. Chapter 12 starts out with a discussion of the variety of approaches to considering the distribution of income in economics and of the many theoretical problems involved. The theory of income distribution is much less well developed than, say, trade theory, and it is thus much harder to agree on what are the major forces that should be captured in an empirical model. We discuss different approaches that have been used to model distributional mechanisms and briefly review past work with CGE models in this area. A certain degree of modesty and a willingness to consider a variety of approaches seem called for. The chapter then discusses a number of technical problems involved in expanding the CGE model framework to include distributional mechanisms and to generate various distributions.

Finally, Chapter 13 presents an application in which the expanded CGE model discussed in Chapter 12 is used to explore the impact of external shocks and of the resulting trade-policy adjustments on the distribution of income among socioeconomic groups. The selected policy regimes include devaluation, premium rationing, and premium rationing with a fixed real wage for unskilled labor. Rather than basing the model on the historical, political, and economic circumstances that have surrounded a particular country, we have sought to investigate how a common policy event might be transmitted differently in alternative environments. This is done by considering three archetype economies and subjecting them to the same set of policy reactions to an identical shock originating from the external sector. The effects of these alternative adjustment mechanisms on the distribution of income are contrasted for an open primary exporter, an open manufacturing exporter, and a relatively closed economy dependent on key intermediate and capital goods imports.

By investigating quantitatively the links among the structure of the economy, policy choice, and the distribution of income, it is possible to illustrate how the struggle among socioeconomic groups to improve their relative position ultimately determines the choice of government policy. The chapter concludes with a comparison of the different adjustment mechanisms across the three archetype economies based on different measures of political power. The analysis indicates how initial conditions, social structure, and relative political power affect the economic feasibility of alternative structural adjustment mechanisms and the political feasibility of alternative policy packages.

PART I

Linear models

CHAPTER 2

Input–output models

2.1 Introduction

From the earliest work on input–output analysis, multisector planning models have been based largely on a mathematical structure of linear functions. It is only quite recently, in the last five to ten years, that it has become possible to specify and implement models making extensive use of nonlinear functions in a general equilibrium framework. Although assumptions of linearity are quite strong, linear models have been widely used and provide a general equilibrium framework that highlights a wide variety of important theoretical issues. In this chapter and the next, we present a survey of traditional input–output and linear programming models. Our survey is not exhaustive, but focuses on the essential economic and mathematical properties of these models. We try to concentrate on those aspects of linear planning models that are relevant to the development of the new generation of nonlinear general equilibrium models that constitute the main focus of this book.

In the next section, we describe the accounting framework, economic assumptions, and mathematical structure of the static input–output model that has provided the starting point for all multisector planning models. We then discuss the dynamic input–output model, focusing on the role of capital accumulation and the nature of intertemporal equilibrium. Finally, we describe the use of input–output models for the planning and analysis of consistent price systems. Linear programming models are discussed in Chapter 3.

2.2 The static input–output model

Accounts and models

Underlying any economic analysis, there is – implicitly or explicitly – a set of economic accounts. In the history of economics, the development of new methods of accounting has been a necessary part of the development of new theories and models. In the area of macro modeling, the accounting framework was given by the national income and product

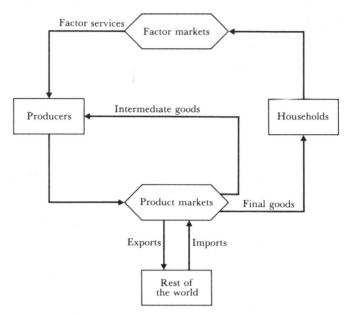

Figure 2.1. Economy-wide circular flow.

accounts whose modern development is associated with economists such as Simon Kuznets. In the field of multisector planning, the starting point has been the system of input–output accounts whose development is largely due to the pioneering work of W. Leontief.

There are three features of an accounting system that are useful to examine when viewing it as a framework for economy-wide analysis or modeling. First, what are the economic institutions or "actors" that are included? Second, what are the markets that are explicitly or implicitly included? Finally, what are the behavioral or technical assumptions that underlie the accounts? As an example, consider Figure 2.1, which depicts a very simple view of the "circular flow" in an economy. Excluding foreign trade, there are only two sets of actors, "producers" taking in inputs and delivering products and "households" taking in products and delivering factor services. There are also only two markets: factor markets and product markets. However, in the product markets there are two sets of customers. Producers not only deliver final goods to households, but also intermediate goods to other producers. The inclusion of intermediate goods is a major focus of the input–output accounting system, permitting the analysis of both the structure of gross production and of interindustry linkages. National income and product accounts are not concerned with intermediate goods, and the accounts net them out. Macro models, in turn, tend to leave them out.

The arrows in Figure 2.1 indicate the flow of real goods and services in the system. For each arrow there corresponds an arrow in the opposite direction, which indicates a money flow of payments for the real goods and services. It is a matter of the questions under analysis and of convenience whether one wishes to look at the counterclockwise flow of real goods and services or the clockwise flow of money payments for the real flows, although – as discussed later – there are conceptual problems in reconciling real and nominal accounts.

The accounting framework that corresponds to Figure 2.1 provides an extremely simple view of the economy. There are only two sets of actors whose behavior must be considered – producers and households – and only two kinds of markets – those for products (both intermediate and final) and factors. There is no consideration of the role of other important institutions such as government, the banking system, and so on. Even so, this system underlies a lot of input–output-based planning models and provides the basic framework for the analysis of static and dynamic input–output models. Note that foreign trade is seen simply as a source of supply of and demand for goods in the product markets. In a multisector accounting framework, there are a variety of ways of treating foreign trade, especially imports, which reflect quite different views of its role in the economy. In this and later chapters, we explore in some detail different ways of treating trade both in the economic accounts and in the models based on them. Indeed, the nature and significance of foreign trade, and how best to include it in planning models, constitute a major theme of this book.

Table 2.1 provides an example of a seven-sector input–output table that provides a snapshot summary of the circular flow depicted in Figure 2.1. The table is for Turkey in 1973 and is an aggregation of a more detailed 64-sector table that underlies the model discussed in Chapters 10 and 11. Each entry in the table reflects the flow of goods from the row sector to the column sector. Thus, for example, row (1) reflects the deliveries from the agricultural sector to all other sectors and to final demand. Regardless of sector, all flows are measured in (American) billions of Turkish lira (TL), so the entries also represent a nominal payment by a column sector to a row sector. For example, entry (1, 2) indicates that agriculture delivers 28.9 billion TL worth of agricultural products to the processed food sector or, equivalently, that the processed food sector pays the agricultural sector 28.9 billion TL.

It is possible to go from the input–output accounts to the national income and product accounts, although there are some conventions involved. Total value added at factor cost is equal to 138.1 + 137.1 = 275.2 billion TL. To get total value added at market prices, indirect taxes (18.9) are added, yielding 294.1 billion TL. This number also

Table 2.1. Input–output table for Turkey, 1973 (billion TL)

	Intermediate flows								Final demand						
	Agriculture goods (1)	Consumer goods (2)	Intermediate goods (3)	Capital goods (4)	Construction (5)	Infrastructure (6)	Service (7)	Sum (1–7) (8)	Consumption (9)	Investment (10)	Exports (11)	Imports (12)	Tariffs (13)	Net final demand (14)	Total domestic supply (15)
Agriculture (1)	18.0	28.9	0.7	0.0	0.0	0.4	0.4	48.4	55.8	−1.0	2.1	1.0	0.2	55.7	104.1
Consumer goods (2)	1.5	16.3	0.9	0.2	2.1	0.1	3.5	24.6	50.5	0.7	12.1	0.8	0.3	62.2	86.8
Intermediate goods (3)	4.4	4.8	27.7	5.6	9.1	10.5	2.2	64.3	23.7	1.5	2.5	16.0	7.2	4.5	68.8
Capital goods (4)	0.4	0.1	0.4	6.5	1.2	3.0	0.1	11.7	10.5	23.0	0.1	13.8	4.0	15.8	27.5
Construction (5)	0.0	0.0	0.0	0.0	0.0	0.0	0.0	0.0	0.5	29.3	0.0	0.0	0.0	29.8	29.8
Infrastructure (6)	1.4	3.3	4.1	0.8	1.1	2.0	2.1	14.8	40.2	1.7	4.3	0.8	0.0	45.4	60.2
Service (7)	4.1	7.6	6.5	2.3	1.9	3.2	6.3	31.9	74.0	3.1	4.9	1.3	0.0	80.7	112.6
Sum (1–7) (8)	29.8	61.0	40.3	15.4	15.4	19.2	14.6	195.7	255.2	58.3	26.0	33.7	11.7	294.1	489.8
Indirect tax (9)	0.7	5.7	3.4	0.8	0.1	2.1	6.1	18.9							
Labor (10)	44.6	10.7	8.7	3.9	8.7	8.8	52.7	138.1							
Capital (11)	29.0	9.4	16.4	7.4	5.6	30.1	39.2	137.1							
Sum (9–11) (12)	74.3	25.8	28.5	12.1	16.4	41.0	98.0	294.1							
Total expenditure (13)	104.1	86.8	68.8	27.5	29.8	60.2	112.6	489.8							

Note: "Net final demand" equals columns (9) + (10) + (11) − (12) − (13); "total domestic supply" equals columns (8) + (14).

equals aggregate net final demand, which is the sum of consumption, investment, and exports, minus imports (including tariffs). However, in the standard national accounts, GDP is defined net of imports valued in border prices (in domestic currency) rather than in domestic market prices. Thus, GDP equals total value added in market prices plus tariffs: $294.1 + 11.7 = 305.8$ billion TL.

In our table, imports have been treated as an alternative source of supply of goods classified by the input–output sectors. The intermediate and final demand flows thus already include imports, which then have to be subtracted to calculate total domestic supplies. A different approach that is also commonly used is to treat imports as a nonproduced input analogous to capital and labor. Instead of a column, imports appear as a row along with payments for indirect taxes and factors of production. In this case, the intermediate and final demand flows [rows (1) to (7)] refer only to payments for domestic goods. These alternative treatments of imports in the accounts reflect different views of the nature of imports. In the first approach, imports are viewed as "competitive," as an alternative source of supply to domestic production. In the second, they are viewed as "noncompetitive," as another input that is not produced in the economy. The two approaches are not mutually exclusive; some tables classify part of imports as competitive and part as noncompetitive. The implications of these different treatments for planning models are significant. Below we discuss in detail alternative specifications and in later chapters we shall see how to achieve a synthesis of the two extreme approaches.

Material balance equations

The input–output accounts in Table 2.1 can, with some very strong assumptions, form the basis of an economy-wide general equilibrium model that focuses on production. The essential assumptions are that: (1) each sector or "activity" produces only one output; and (2) inputs are required in fixed proportions to output in each sector. The second assumption implies that there are constant returns to scale in production.

To move from the nominal input–output accounts to a real model, we must first separate prices and quantities in the accounts. Define the following variables:

X_{ij} = flow of intermediate goods from sector i to sector j
X_i = production in sector i
P_i = the price of output in sector i

F_i = final demand for sector i

a_{ij} = intermediate requirements from sector i per unit of output of sector j

Ignoring exports and imports for the moment, the rows of the nominal input–output accounts can be written as

$$P_i X_i = \sum_j P_i X_{ij} + P_i F_i \qquad (2.2.1)$$

Assuming a fixed coefficient technology, the input–output coefficients are constant and are given by

$$a_{ij} = \frac{X_{ij}}{X_j} \qquad (2.2.2)$$

In any given year, the ratio of nominal intermediate flows to nominal output is given by

$$\frac{P_i a_{ij}}{P_j} = \frac{P_i X_{ij}}{P_j X_j} \qquad (2.2.3)$$

Given a base-year table (such as Table 2.1), it is convenient to define the units of real flows such that all prices equal one. In this case, Eqs. (2.2.2) and (2.2.3) are the same. The coefficient a_{ij} is defined as a Turkish lira's worth of input from sector i required to produce a lira's worth of output in sector j in base-year (1973) prices and is computed directly from the nominal input–output accounts table. Note that coefficients computed from Eq. (2.2.3) for different years (or countries) in which relative prices are different cannot be compared, because units of real outputs are different.

Dividing by the price and using the input–output coefficients, Eq. (2.2.1) can be written as

$$X_i = \sum_j a_{ij} X_j + F_i \qquad (2.2.4)$$

This is the basic material balance equation of the input–output model. In matrix notation, it is

$$X = AX + F \qquad (2.2.5)$$

or, solving for X,

$$X = (I - A)^{-1} F \qquad (2.2.6)$$

Equation (2.2.6) constitutes the "solution" of the static input–output model. Given exogenously specified final demand, the equation can be used to determine production requirements necessary to satisfy the demand.

A great deal of the literature has been concerned with the properties of the inverse matrix $(I - A)^{-1}$. The coefficient matrix A, derived from an empirical input–output table, will always have the property that all column sums of coefficients will be strictly less than one. This property plus the fact that all the coefficients are greater than or equal to zero suffices to prove that all the elements in the inverse matrix are greater than or equal to zero and that the inverse can be written in the form of a converging series expansion. We have

$$I + A + A^2 + \ldots + A^n \simeq (I - A)^{-1} \qquad (2.2.7)$$

where the approximation becomes very close as n gets larger. In practice, $n = 5$ or 6 gives a good enough approximation to the Leontief inverse $(I - A)^{-1}$. An economy whose input–output coefficients satisfy the properties required for convergence of the matrix series is called "viable."[1] For such a system we can rewrite Eq. (2.2.6) in the form

$$X = (I + A + A^2 + \ldots)F = F + AF + A^2F + \ldots \qquad (2.2.8)$$

This underlines the basic nature of the material balance problem. Starting from a vector of final demand F, one computes the successive rounds of input requirements that arise in the attempt to satisfy the exogenous F vector. When this process converges, one has reached a general equilibrium solution in the productive sphere of the economy. The most important result of the fact that the inverse matrix is non-negative is that it appears possible to deliver any vector of non-negative final demands. That is, there exists a non-negative gross production vector to satisfy both any specified final demand and induced intermediate demand. Whether this gross production vector is feasible from the point of view of installed capacity and/or primary factor requirements is a separate question that the material balance equations do not address.

Equation (2.2.6) can be used to provide a consistency framework for a planning exercise. Given final demand targets, the Leontief inverse $(I - A)^{-1}$ allows calculation of the implied targets for sectoral production, which can then be evaluated for "reasonableness," perhaps by comparing them with projected sectoral capacities. Unless the economy is a command economy in which sectoral outputs are set by the government, the input–output model contains no policy variables. However,

---

[1] The mathematical properties of the input–output system are discussed in the appendix to this chapter.

even the simple material balance equation is a powerful tool for policy analysis, because it embodies the requirement for economy-wide consistency of sectoral production plans.

There are a number of extensions of the simple input–output model, without moving to dynamic models, that exploit its consistency properties and make it a useful tool for policy analysis. For example, one can use the inverse to calculate "multipliers" that give the impact on endogenous variables of shifts in exogenous elements of final demand. These exercises in what might be called "identity-based" planning are clearly useful precisely because they force policy makers to work within the context of a consistent system, even if such models have very little behavioral content.

In Chapter 4 we shall describe an example of such an approach that focuses on the impact of domestic demand expansion, export expansion, import substitution, and changes in the input–output coefficients on growth and structural change. Before presenting such applications to trade-related questions, we first must consider in some detail how the simple input–output model discussed above can be adapted to include foreign trade.

Foreign trade

Considering the significance of trade in most currently developing countries, it is important to include imports and exports explicitly in the input–output model. A standard and perhaps the simplest approach is to assume that imported and domestic goods are the "same"; that is, they are perfect substitutes in all uses. It is then possible to rewrite the material balance equation, differentiating among different categories of supply and demand:

$$X + M = AX + F + E \tag{2.2.9}$$

where the new variables are

M = import vector
F = domestic demand vector
E = export vector

Solving for X,

$$X = (I - A)^{-1}(F + E - M) \tag{2.2.10}$$

Equation (2.2.10) is the same as Eq. (2.2.6) except that $F + E - M$ is the net demand for domestically produced goods.

The problem with the formulation in Eq. (2.2.10) is that for some sectors the net final demands might well be negative. In developing countries, imports of intermediate goods such as chemicals, petroleum, or basic metals often exceed final demand, thus yielding negative net final demands. The question being asked is this: What are the domestic production requirements for a sector given that final demand is a net supplier rather than a demander of the good? The question is certainly reasonable, but it raises the theoretical possibility that the application of Eq. (2.2.10) will yield a negative domestic production in some sectors. A negative X_i implies running the production process in reverse, taking in the product and delivering its component parts (including primary factors) to the rest of the system, which is not reasonable.

One solution to this problem is used by Chenery and Clark (1959), who make a crucial behavioral assumption and recast the problem in terms of total supply and demand. The behavioral assumption is that the ratio of imports to domestic production is fixed by sectors:

$$\mu_i = \frac{M_i}{X_i} \geq 0$$

Define a diagonal matrix of import ratios,

$$\hat{\mu} = \begin{bmatrix} \mu_1 & & 0 \\ & \cdot & \\ & \cdot & \\ & \cdot & \\ 0 & & \mu_n \end{bmatrix}$$

and a variable for total supply, $Q = X + M$. Then

$$Q = X + M = X + \hat{\mu}X = (I + \hat{\mu})X$$

Therefore,

$$X = (I + \hat{\mu})^{-1}Q \tag{2.2.11}$$

Now,

$$Q = AX + (F + E) = A(I + \hat{\mu})^{-1}Q + (F + E)$$

and hence

$$Q = (I - A^*)^{-1}(F + E) \tag{2.2.12}$$

where

$$A^* = A(I + \hat{\mu})^{-1}$$

Note that

$$(I + \hat{\mu})^{-1} = \begin{bmatrix} \dfrac{1}{1 + \mu_1} & & & 0 \\ & \cdot & & \\ & & \cdot & \\ & & & \cdot \\ 0 & & & \dfrac{1}{1 + \mu_n} \end{bmatrix}$$

and hence $a_{ij}^* = a_{ij}/(1 + \mu_j)$. Because $\mu_j \geq 0$, the effect is to divide (and hence reduce or at least not increase) the elements in each column of A by one plus the import ratio for that sector. Thus, the coefficients a_{ij}^* give the intermediate inputs from sector i required per unit of total supply of sector j.

The new matrix A^* is well behaved in the sense that it satisfies the requirements for the system to be viable and the new final demand vector $(F + E)$ will never have negative elements. However, exports and imports are still assumed to be perfect substitutes in the sense that they are added together to get total supply, and there is no particular reason for assuming a fixed ratio between imports and domestic production.

A polar opposite approach is to treat imports as completely different from domestically produced goods. In this case, imports are "noncompetitive" and are treated in the model like a nonproduced primary input. They thus do not appear in the material balance equations and their treatment in the input–output accounts must also be changed, as discussed in the previous section on accounting. The column that specifies imports by sector of origin must be deleted and replaced by a row that specifies imports by sector of destination. The intermediate flows matrix must also be redefined to exclude imports, because conceptually noncompetitive imports do not have the same units as domestic production and the two cannot be added together. Although it is possible to differentiate noncompetitive imports by sector, just as it is possible to differentiate among types of labor, they should never be aggregated with domestic production even if the sectoral classification happens to be the same. Some countries in fact split imports, including both a column of competitive imports and a row of noncompetitive imports in the input–output table.

Both polar treatments seem too extreme because, even if both are used in the same table, they require every import to be classified as either purely competitive or purely noncompetitive. In the models discussed in this book, we generally use a different approach that keeps the treatment of imports separate from the treatment of domestically produced goods, but does not require that they be classified as either purely competitive or purely noncompetitive. The accounting framework for the approach is presented later, and its theoretical properties are discussed in some detail in Chapter 7. In this section we use the superscript d to denote domestically produced goods and the superscript m to denote imported goods to highlight the distinction between them. Variables without a superscript represent a composite mix of imported and domestic goods. In the accounts, the composite entries have a nominal value equal to the sum of the values of imported and domestic goods. Define the following variables:

X^d = domestic production vector
V = intermediate demand vector (composite of imported and domestic goods)
F = domestic final demand vector (composite of imported and domestic goods)
E^d = export vector of domestic goods
M^m = import vector
A = input–output coefficients matrix such that a_{ij} is composite intermediate demand of sector i per unit of domestic output in sector j. As in the standard model, $V = AX^d$.

Now make a behavioral assumption similar, but not identical, to that made by Chenery and Clark. Assume that the ratio of domestic demand for domestically produced goods to total domestic demand is fixed by sectors. These domestic demand ratios are given by

$$d_i = \frac{X_i^d - E_i^d}{F_i + V_i} \tag{2.2.13}$$

Defining a diagonal matrix $\hat{D}$ of the d_i parameters, the material balance equation for domestic goods is given by

$$X^d = V^d + F^d + E^d \tag{2.2.14}$$

where $V^d = \hat{D}V$ and $F^d = \hat{D}F$.

Noting that $V = AX^d$, the material balance equation can be written as

$$X^d = (I - \hat{D}A)^{-1}(\hat{D}F + E^d) \tag{2.2.15}$$

or

$$X^d = (I - A^d)^{-1}(F^d + E^d)$$

where $A^d = \hat{D}A$.

Note that imports do not appear in Eqs. (2.2.13) and (2.2.14) and that each of the vectors has units of domestic sectoral production. The input–output matrix A^d has units of domestically produced inputs per unit of domestic production. Because F and V include the value of imports whereas $X^d - E^d$ do not, it will always be true of empirical matrices that $0 < d_i \leq 1$ for all sectors and $A_{ij}^d \leq A_{ij}$ for all i and j. Thus the A^d matrix will be well behaved and the system will be viable. The final demand vector $(F^d + E^d)$ will also always be non-negative.

The definition of d_i in Eq. (2.2.13) embodies two behavioral assumptions that will be discussed in more detail in Chapter 7. First, imports are assumed to be used only in the domestic economy and are not directly embodied in exports. That is, exports consist only of domestically produced goods, not a composite of domestic and imported goods. Note that exports *indirectly* embody imports through intermediate goods required for their production, but that the indirect effect works only through the input–output matrix and hence exports are measured in units of domestic output. The effect of this assumption is that the numerator in Eq. (2.2.13) is *domestic* demand for domestic production rather than total demand (X^d), and the denominator does not include exports.

The second assumption embodied in Eq. (2.2.13) is that the d_i ratio is the same for all categories of demand for sector i. One might, for example, assume instead that the domestic demand ratio for a given sector for intermediate use is different from the ratio for final use. Such a generalization is not difficult to accommodate. The d vector is replaced by a matrix with a different ratio for every element in the input–output table, including the domestic final demand columns.[2]

Corresponding to the domestic demand ratio is an import demand ratio. Define it as a ratio to domestic demand for domestically produced goods, an approach very close to that of Chenery and Clark. Then it is defined as

$$m_i = \frac{M_i^m}{X_i^d - E_i^d} \tag{2.2.16}$$

Starting from the material balance equation for domestic goods, one can calculate the corresponding balance equation for imports:

$$M^m = \hat{M}(X^d - E^d) \tag{2.2.17}$$

where $\hat{M}$ is a diagonal matrix of the m_i coefficients.

[2] See Syrquin (1976) for an input–output model incorporating the general approach and also the discussion of trade in the dynamic input–output model.

The two sets of material balance equations (2.2.14) and (2.2.17) can be treated completely separately. Note that if the variables are measured in nominal terms, the sum of the two equations replicates the nominal input–output accounts. Indeed, if the coefficients d and m are estimated from a consistent set of nominal accounts, it will be true that, for all sectors,

$$m_i = \frac{1}{d_i} - 1 \qquad (2.2.18)$$

Although Eq. (2.2.18) must hold if the ratios are computed from consistent nominal data, it certainly need not hold if they are measured in different units. Conceptually, for example, it might make sense to express Eq. (2.2.17) in different units from Eq. (2.2.14). In Chapter 7 we present a more general formulation in which domestically produced and imported goods are specified as imperfect substitutes with a known elasticity of substitution. In this case, the d and m parameters are related and both are functions of relative prices of domestic and imported goods, but Eq. (2.2.18) does not hold in general.

Equations (2.2.15) and (2.2.17) can provide the basic framework for a consistency planning exercise including foreign trade. The planner can start with a set of final domestic demand and export projections. He can then postulate a vector of domestic use ratios d_i and a vector of import coefficients m_i and derive total domestic production requirements by premultiplying $(\hat{D}F + E^d)$ by $(I - \hat{D}A)^{-1}$ as shown in Eq. (2.2.15). Finally, by premultiplying the resulting $(X^d - E^d)$ vector by $\hat{M}$, it is possible to obtain the levels of sectoral imports consistent with domestic production and final demands. The planner can then compare the X^d vector with existing production capacities and compare the sum of sectoral imports with the sum of sectoral exports and exogenous foreign exchange flows to evaluate the feasibility of the proposed plan.

The simple model described above has also been used for a historical cross-country analysis of the sources and composition of economic growth. In Chapter 4 we shall describe this approach pioneered and developed by Hollis Chenery and summarize some of the interesting empirical results obtained recently by applying the basic material balance identity (2.2.15) to a group of countries at different points in time.

Direct and indirect factor requirements

Another set of problems that has been analyzed with the simple static input–output model has been concerned with primary factor requirements and factor intensities. As we have already stressed, the Leontief inverse itself does not take into account the primary factor requirements of the production process. But it is easy to extend input–output models to include an analysis of primary factor requirements. Consider, for example, labor, and assume that l_i units of labor are required per unit of domestic production, X_i^d. Then if a domestic production vector X^d has been derived from an exogenous projection of final demand and exports, we can compute the total employment requirement implicit in the final demand and export projection.

$$\tilde{L} = LX^d = L(I - A^d)^{-1}(F^d + E^d) \tag{2.2.19}$$

where L is the row vector of labor coefficients and $\tilde{L}$, a scalar, gives us the total demand for labor derived from $F^d + E^d$. This can be contrasted to an independent labor supply projection to test the feasibility of the plan from the point of view of labor availability. The same kind of exercise can be repeated for other primary factors or for different skill categories of labor.

Beyond such overall feasibility checks, the framework we have described also allows us to analyze sectoral final demand in terms of the total, direct and indirect, primary factor requirements that it implies. Consider, for example, an expansion of exports from sector j and its effect on the demand for labor. Linearity allows us to recast Eq. (2.2.19) in incremental form so that we have (where Δ means "change in")

$$\Delta\tilde{L} = L(I - A^d)^{-1}(\Delta F^d + \Delta E^d) \tag{2.2.20}$$

Assuming that $\Delta F_i^d = 0$ for all i and $\Delta E_i^d = 0$ for all $i \neq j$, we get

$$\Delta\tilde{L} = \sum_{i=1}^{n} l_i r_{ij}^d \Delta E_j \tag{2.2.21}$$

where r_{ij}^d are the elements of the domestic inverse.

Define $L^* = L(I - A^d)^{-1} = L(I + A^d + A^{d^2} + A^{d^3} + \dots)$ as the total labor requirements vector whose elements

$$\sum_{i=1}^{n} l_i r_{ij} = l_j^*, j = 1, \dots, n$$

give the total, direct and indirect, employment effect of a unit expansion in exports or domestic final demand in the various sectors distinguished by the model. Thus expanding exports of transport equipment not only requires more labor employed in the transport equipment sector, but also more domestic production of metals and metal products and therefore more employment in the metal industries. Expanded production in the metal industries may require an increased output from the mining sector and perhaps in turn from the transportation equipment sector itself, leading to further employment requirements. The L^* tells us the end result of this process. If $l_j^* = 10$ while $l_i^* = 5$, a unit of final demand is twice as "labor intensive" in its total effect in sector j than it is in sector i. It is important to stress that this may be so even though l_j may be smaller than l_i; a particular production process may use very little labor directly but use intermediate inputs that must be produced by very labor-intensive processes. Thus, if one wants to evaluate the labor intensity of particular elements of final demand, it is very important to look at total requirements and not just at the direct or first-round requirements observed in a single sector's production process.

Leontief himself used this distinction and the L vector of total requirements to test whether American exports were relatively capital intensive when compared to import-competing activities and found the result, paradoxical from the point of view of Heckscher-Ohlin trade theory, that American exports were relatively labor intensive (see Leontief, 1953). A massive amount of similar empirical work for many countries has been carried out following the publication of Leontief's paradox, testing the basic trade-theory hypothesis that a country will export commodities that use intensively the factor with which it is relatively well endowed. The basic model used in all this research is the static input–output model. The empirical results varied, but it is now generally accepted that the Heckscher-Ohlin theory can be broadly validated if production factors are defined carefully and are further disaggregated to distinguish, in particular, between skilled and unskilled labor and between capital and natural resources. Be that as it may, these attempts at testing the basic tenets of neoclassical trade theory provided a major field of application for the static input–output model, quite apart from its use as a planning tool. They provide a good illustration of the important distinction that must be made between the direct and total factor requirements of elements of final demand.

2.3   The dynamic input–output model

A one-sector model

So far no particular distinction has been made between investment and consumption inside the final demand vector F. Because presumably investment is undertaken to allow continued or greater consumption in the future, investment demand should be a derived demand rather than exogenously set with consumption. The characteristic feature of the dynamic input–output model is that it endogenizes investment and considerably extends the requirement of consistency beyond the static material balance equations.

The mathematical properties of the dynamic input–output model have been much studied in the last thirty years. However, to understand how dynamic input–output models work and what are their crucial assumptions, it is very important to distinguish the major economic features of the models from their formal mathematical properties. In particular, it is important to understand the behavioral assumptions and the nature of equilibrium that are implicitly incorporated in such a model.

To bring out some of the characteristics of the dynamic model and to introduce the use of difference and differential equations, it is useful to start with a one-sector model. The model is very much in the spirit of the standard Harrod-Domar model, although it is presented as a kind of planning model. The following discussion makes two important points. The first is that the economy cannot grow faster than a maximum rate determined by technology. The second is that unless the economy happens in the base period to be on a long-run equilibrium growth path, the dynamic model becomes unstable and eventually generates negative output. It is convenient to present the one-sector model in continuous time and use differential equations. The important points being made carry over to a discrete-period model specified in terms of difference equations.

The behavior of the model is given by three equations:

$$C(t) = C_0 e^{gt} \tag{2.3.1}$$
$$Y'(t) = \sigma Z(t) \tag{2.3.2}$$
$$Y(t) = C(t) + Z(t) \tag{2.3.3}$$

The first equation states that consumption C must grow at the rate g from a value of C_0 in time zero. In terms of economic planning, it represents the target path that planners wish to achieve. The value C_0 in the base year is assumed given. The target growth rate g is also assumed given, but one purpose of a planning exercise would be to explore the properties of the system with different values of g.

Equations (2.3.2) and (2.3.3) describe the technology and overall resource constraint of the system. Equation (2.3.2) is the familiar Domar investment equation, stating that the change in output Y' equals a fixed coefficient times investment. The parameter σ is the incremental output–capital ratio (the inverse of the usual incremental capital–output ratio, or ICOR) and is usually assumed to be less than one. Equation (2.3.3) is the standard income identity and states that output equals consumption plus investment and thus the economy is closed.

Substituting Eq. (2.3.2) into Eq. (2.3.3) yields the following differential equation:

$$Y' - \sigma Y = -\sigma C(t) \tag{2.3.4}$$

Defining the rate of investment (and hence saving) as $s = Z/Y = (Y - C)/Y$, then from Eq. (2.3.4) the rate of growth of output is

$$\frac{Y'}{Y} = \sigma s \tag{2.3.5}$$

The growth rate σs is Harrod's "warranted rate," which he assumed to be constant because in his model the savings rate is a fixed parameter. In this model, however, it is not assumed fixed and hence the warranted rate need not be constant.

Equation (2.3.1) is a first order linear differential equation and its general solution can be written in the following general form:

$$Y(t) = AH(t) + Y^*(t) \tag{2.3.6}$$

where A is an arbitrary constant that will depend on initial conditions, $AH(t)$ is the general solution of the associated homogeneous differential equation $Y' - \sigma Y = 0$, and $Y^*(t)$ is a particular solution that satisfies Eq. (2.3.4) without regard to initial conditions.[3] Mathematically, the solution of the homogeneous equation is straightforward, yielding, in this case,

$$H(t) = e^{\sigma t} \tag{2.3.7}$$

Finding a particular solution is usually more difficult and involves solving an integral that depends on the functional form of the nonhomogeneous term, in this case $-\sigma C(t)$. Given the specification of $C(t)$ in Eq. (2.3.1), particular solutions for Eq. (2.3.6) are

$$Y^*(t) = \frac{\sigma C_0}{\sigma - g} e^{gt} \qquad g \neq \sigma \tag{2.3.8}$$

$$Y^*(t) = -\sigma C_0 t e^{gt} \qquad g = \sigma \tag{2.3.9}$$

For a mathematician, the problem is solved.[4] One need only substitute in some initial condition $Y(0) = Y_0$, calculate the constant, and Eq.

---

[3] For the general first-order linear differential equation, $Y'(t) + aY(t) = b$, where a and b may both be functions of time, the functions $H(t)$ and $Y^*(t)$ are $H(t) = \exp(-\int a \, dt)$ and $Y^*(t) = [\exp(-\int a \, dt)] \int b \exp(\int a \, dt) \, dt$, where $\exp(x) = e^x$. See Kaplan (1958).

[4] Note, however, that if $g > \sigma$, output is negative.

(2.3.6) is completely specified. However, it is possible to express Eq. (2.3.6) in an alternative form that is economically quite interesting.

Assume that an initial condition $Y(0) = Y_0$ is given. Then the general solution of the first-order linear differential equation (and also of the analogous first-order linear difference equation) can always be written as[5]

$$Y(t) = [Y_0 - Y^*(0)]H(t) + Y^*(t) \qquad (2.3.10)$$

Although mathematically not especially interesting, Eq. (2.3.10) is a useful formulation for various economic applications. Consider the particular solution $Y^*(t)$. If its value in the initial period, $Y^*(0)$, happens to equal the initial value of Y, Y_0, then the solution time path of $Y(t)$ equals that of $Y^*(t)$ because the first term in Eq. (2.3.10) is always zero.

In the growth model presented earlier, and in the dynamic input–output model discussed later, the particular solution can be interpreted as a special kind of equilibrium growth path. It represents an equilibrium growth path because it satisfies the equilibrium conditions embodied in the differential equation. However, it is special because it will not satisfy the differential equations for any choice of initial conditions. We shall refer to it as a "target equilibrium" (or, alternatively, as a "target function" or "target path").

The first term in Eq. (2.3.10) will be referred to as the "adjustment function." It shows how, at every point in time, the target equilibrium must be adjusted in order that the system satisfy the differential equation given that it did not start from the right initial condition. It is tempting to view the adjustment function as describing how the system

---

[5] To see this, note that in the general solution shown in footnote 3, the particular solution can always be written as $Y^*(t) = H(t) D(t)$, where $H(t)$ is the solution of the homogenous equation and $D(t)$ is an arbitrary function depending on the form of $C(t)$ (or b in footnote 3). Thus,

$$Y(0) = A H(0) + H(0) D(0) = Y_0$$

$$A = \frac{Y_0}{H(0)} - D(0)$$

and from (2.3.6), noting that $H(0) = 1$,

$$Y(t) = \left[\frac{Y_0}{H(0)} - D(0) \right] H(t) + Y^*(t)$$

$$= [Y_0 - H(0) D(0)] \frac{H(t)}{H(0)} + Y^*(t)$$

$$= [Y_0 - Y^*(0)] H(t) + Y^*(t)$$

behaves when it is "out of equilibrium." This view is correct only in a very special sense. There are two kinds of equilibria embodied in the solution of the differential equation; the first describes equilibrium intertemporal linkages and the second adds to the first a set of initial conditions. The adjustment function describes how the system adjusts to satisfy the intertemporal conditions when the initial conditions are not right.

Returning to the one-sector model, assume for the moment that $g \neq \sigma$ and substitute (2.3.7) and (2.3.8) into (2.3.10) to get the general solution

$$Y(t) = \left(Y_0 - \frac{\sigma C_0}{\sigma - g} \right) e^{\sigma t} + \frac{\sigma C_0}{\sigma - g} e^{gt} \qquad (2.3.11)$$

where

$$Y^*(0) = \frac{\sigma C_0}{\sigma - g} \quad \text{and} \quad H(0) = 1$$

Consider first the case where $g > \sigma$. The target equilibrium starts out negative and keeps going down, while the adjustment function starts out positive (if $Y_0 > 0$). However, even if $Y(t)$ starts out positive, it must go negative eventually, because with $g > \sigma$ the absolute value of the target equilibrium must eventually exceed that of the adjustment function. The problem is that, as can be seen from Eq. (2.3.5), the maximal attainable growth rate is σ, which is achieved when the savings rate equals one. The economy cannot physically grow faster than σ, so any target equilibrium rate larger than σ is infeasible. Substituting in Eq. (2.3.9), it is clear that $g = \sigma$ is also infeasible.

Next, consider a special case in which the savings rate in the initial period is such that the warranted growth rate in Eq. (2.3.5) happens to equal the target equilibrium rate. In this case,

$$s_0 = \frac{Y_0 - C_0}{Y_0} \quad \text{and} \quad g = \sigma s_0$$

The term $Y_0 - Y^*(0)$ in the adjustment function becomes

$$Y_0 - Y^*(0) = \frac{Y_0(\sigma - \sigma s_0) - \sigma C_0}{\sigma - \sigma s_0}$$

$$= \frac{\sigma Y_0(1 - s_0) - \sigma C_0}{\sigma - \sigma s_0}$$

$$= \frac{C_0 - C_0}{1 - s_0} = 0$$

Thus, if in the initial period the warranted rate of growth happens to equal the target equilibrium rate, the economy will follow the target path with consumption, output, and investment all growing at the rate g.

As with the Harrod-Domar model, the target equilibrium path is unstable in that if the economy does not start with $g = \sigma s_0$, it will never achieve the target path. If $Y_0 \neq Y^*(0)$ and $\sigma > g$, then the adjustment function will eventually dominate the model dynamics. The instability properties of the Harrod-Domar model are well known and much studied. It turns out that with quite reasonable changes in specification, the adjustment function will yield smooth convergence to the target path. For example, viewing the parameter σ in Eq. (2.3.2) as technologically fixed is a very strong assumption. If one assumes a neoclassical production function with a variable σ, the instability of the Harrod-Domar model disappears (see Solow, 1956). Alternatively, one might view σ as arising from an accelerator theory of investment. In this case, a more realistic specification might be a distributed lag accelerator, which leads to higher-order differential equations with, usually, a tendency toward stability.

For different, but analogous, reasons, the adjustment function in the multisector model also generally yields an unstable solution.[6] We would argue that for planning purposes where the focus is on the medium term, too much attention has been paid to the adjustment function, which imposes short-term constraints on a long-run model, and not enough to the target equilibrium. The dynamic input–output model application in Chapter 4 will take a long-run view and concentrate on the alternative target equilibrium growth paths. In the one-sector model presented above, one might assume that there is a long-run tendency for the incremental output–capital ratio σ to be constant, although it may well vary in the short run. Thus, one might argue that the adjustment function is unrealistic but that the target equilibrium is a valid reflection of long-run trends. This general view of the distinction between the target equilibrium and the adjustment function will be developed in more detail in the context of the multisector model.

The multisector model

In the static input–output model, all the components of final demand are treated as exogenous. The dynamic model treats investment demand

---

[6] For a comparison of the stability properties of the one-sector and multisector models, see the appendix to this chapter.

as endogenous and incorporates two fundamental assumptions about technology and capital. First, as in the one-sector model, there are assumed to be fixed incremental capital–output ratios by sectors. Second, sectoral capital stocks have a fixed compositional structure (by sector of origin).

These assumptions imply the following relationships, switching now to discrete time:

$$\Delta K_i = k_i \, \Delta X_i \tag{2.3.12}$$

where

$$
\begin{aligned}
\Delta K_i &= K_i(t+1) - K_i(t) \\
\Delta X_i &= X_i(t+1) - X_i(t) \\
K_i &= \text{capital stock in sector } i \\
\Delta K_i &= \text{investment by sector of destination} \\
k_i &= \text{incremental capital–output ratio for sector } i \\
X_i &= \text{output in sector } i \\
t &= \text{time variable with only integer values}
\end{aligned}
$$

The translation of investment by sector of destination into a demand for investment goods by sector of origin is given by

$$Z_i(t) = \sum_j s_{ij} \, \Delta K_j(t) \tag{2.3.13}$$

where Z_i = investment by sector of origin and s_{ij} = proportion of capital stock in sector j originating in sector i. Note that $\sum_i s_{ij} = 1$ for all j.

The assumption of a constant composition of capital in each sector is crucial, because it implies that the capital stock in each sector is a well-defined aggregate of various commodities. In contrast, the economy-wide capital stock is an ambiguous concept, because the commodity composition of capital differs across sectors. In this sense, capital is heterogeneous and cannot be aggregated across sectors.

Define a capital coefficients matrix B such that

$$b_{ij} = s_{ij} k_j \tag{2.3.14}$$

Equations (2.3.12) and (2.3.13) can be combined into the matrix equation

$$Z(t) = B \, \Delta X = B[X(t+1) - X(t)] \tag{2.3.15}$$

Adding C as a final demand in the input–output material balance equations yields the fundamental balance equation of the dynamic model:

$$X(t) = AX(t) + B[X(t+1) - X(t)] + C(t) \tag{2.3.16}$$

Writing the equation in recursive form and solving for $X(t + 1)$ yields[7]

$$X(t + 1) = [B^{-1}(I - A + B)] X(t) - B^{-1}C(t) \qquad (2.3.17)$$

In Eq. (2.3.17), the inverse of the capital coefficients matrix is assumed to exist. In fact, because many sectors do not produce capital goods, the S and hence B matrices will have a number of zero rows and will be singular. However, it is always possible to reduce the system to an order equal to the number of capital goods-producing sectors and work with this reduced form (see Kendrick, 1972). Alternatively, one can assume that every sector requires inventory investment and incorporate the inventory coefficients into the B matrix.[8] In any case, the complication is usually ignored for expository purposes and B^{-1} is simply assumed to exist.

As it stands, Eq. (2.3.17) can be used to "solve" the dynamic model in the sense of being able to be used to generate a series of $X(t)$ vectors. Given a value of X_0 and a series of known target consumption vectors $C(t)$, Eq. (2.3.17) is simply used as a recursion formula. Given X_0 and $C(0)$, one solves for $X(1)$. Given $X(1)$ and $C(1)$, one gets $X(2)$, and so forth. Early work with the model used this approach and, not surprisingly, uncovered problems of stability. Starting from an initial output vector (X_0), the mode, after a very few periods, generates output vectors with negative elements.

To analyze the stability properties of the dynamic model, it is useful to write out the general solution of the difference equation in the same form as that for the first-order linear differential equation discussed earlier. Like the solution of the differential equation, the solution of the difference equation can always be written as the sum of an adjustment function and a target function. For Eq. (2.3.17), the general solution given an initial output vector X_0 is

$$X(t) = [B^{-1}(I - A + B)]^t [X_0 - X^*(0)] + X^*(t) \qquad (2.3.18)$$

where $X^*(t)$ is the target equilibrium (the particular solution) and the first term is the adjustment function. As in the differential equation case,

---

[7] Note the similarity between Eq. (2.3.17) and Eq. (2.3.4) for the one-sector model. The parameter σ in the one-sector model is the output–capital ratio, whereas the elements of B are capital–output ratios – hence the appearance of the inverse of B in Eq. (2.3.17).

[8] If inventory investment is given by $Z^{(2)} = H \Delta X$, then adding $Z^{(2)}$ as a final demand in the dynamic equation results in $B + H$ appearing whenever B appeared formerly. If inventories are always assumed to be held in the form of final goods, H is a diagonal matrix. If inventories are held also in the form of stocks of inputs, H is no longer diagonal. In any case, it is of full rank.

the adjustment function is the general solution of the homogeneous differential equation with $X^*(t) \equiv 0$.

It is the properties of the adjustment function that determine the stability properties of the general solution. The mathematical properties of this function are discussed in the appendix to this chapter. It is important to stress, however, that these mathematical properties reflect the economic assumptions embodied in the dynamic equation, and it is therefore important to analyze these assumptions closely before embarking on a purely mathematical analysis of the equation system. Start from the basic dynamic equation (2.3.16) and consider how the investment process works given an initial output vector X_0.

From the material balance equation, given production X_0 and consumption $C(0)$, the amount of production in each sector available for use as investment is given by

$$Z(0) = X_0 - AX_0 - C(0) \tag{2.3.19}$$

For the strict equality to be satisfied, all of this sectoral production *must* be used for investment. From Eq. (2.3.13), $Z(t) = S \, \Delta K(t)$ and hence the unique vector of changes in sectoral capital stocks that will use the available investment goods is given by

$$\Delta K(0) = S^{-1} Z(0) \tag{2.3.20}$$

Given $\Delta K(0)$, output in year 1 is given by

$$X(1) = X_0 + \hat{K}^{-1} \Delta K(0) \tag{2.3.21}$$

where $\hat{K}$ is the diagonal vector of sectoral capital–output ratios. Given $X(1)$, the process is repeated for the next period.

The problem arises because in Eq. (2.3.20) some of the elements of the inverse of the capital proportions matrix S^{-1} will generally be negative. This implies that some elements of ΔK may be negative. Given the structure of sectoral production available for investment embodied in Z, it may well be necessary to dissolve capital stock in some sectors into their sectoral components in order to achieve the required balance of demand for investment by sector of origin such that all available investment goods are used. Once the system starts dissolving sectoral capital, from Eq. (2.3.21) it can be seen that those sectors will very quickly tend to generate negative output.[9]

---

[9] Note that the mechanism yielding instability in this model depends on multisector relationships and is quite different from the mechanism at work in the one-sector model. The relationship between the different mechanisms and the stability properties of the multisector model are discussed rigorously in the appendix to this chapter.

Once the mechanism we have described is understood, it is clear that in general one cannot expect the model to behave reasonably. On the contrary, empirical models almost always tend to dissolve capital in some sectors and quickly generate negative sectoral output. The investment behavior implied in the adjustment function is nonsensical: Invest whatever is left over in every sector and never leave a stock unused. The model derives its historical starting point X_0 by implicitly assuming that capital in the base period is strictly nonshiftable, but then happily proceeds to dissolve sectoral capital stocks in order to accommodate the initial sectoral production dynamically.

As long as an arbitrary initial condition is imposed on the dynamic input–output model and the system is also constrained to be always operating at full capacity, then it seems clear that the system cannot yield reasonable results. Indeed, in a sense, the two assumptions are contradictory. Full capacity in all periods and sectors implies some sort of long-run equilibrium, whereas arbitrary initial conditions reflect historical conditions that include transitory features. The multisector model also displays the same sort of knife-edge feature as the one-sector model: Once off the equilibrium path, the model will not return to it.

The instability properties of the forward-running model have generated a great deal of literature and a number of suggestions on how to fix the problem. Most of the suggestions involve loosening the extreme assumption that the economy work at full capacity in every period and sector. They thus work with the adjustment function directly, attempting to make it more flexible or "realistic" (see Leontief, 1953; Bergsman and Manne, 1966; Gupta, 1977). An example of such an approach is a recent contribution by Leontief that suggests a reformulation of the adjustment function (Leontief, 1970). His idea is to run the system backwards instead of forwards, with the same target consumption path $C(t)$ but specifying an arbitrary terminal output vector X_T. Adopting this approach, $X(0)$ is solved endogenously and X_T takes its place as the arbitrary boundary condition. A quite different investment theory is implied. The problem now is to determine an output and investment sequence $X(t)$, $Z(t)$, $t = 0, \ldots, T - 1$ such that the system can deliver the target consumption sequence $C(t)$, $t = 1, \ldots, T$ and accumulate the required capital to produce the specified terminal output vector X_T. Can this approach be expected to yield more reasonable results?

The general solution of the backward-running model is given by

$$X(t) = [(I - A + B)^{-1}B]^{T-t}[X_T - X^*(T)] + X^*(t) \quad (2.3.22)$$

which can be compared to the solution of the forward-running model from Eq. (2.3.18):

$$X(t) = [B^{-1}(I - A + B)]^t[X_0 - X^*(0)] + X^*(t)$$

Note that $(I - A + B)^{-1}B$ is the inverse of $B^{-1}(I - A + B)$. Mathematically, the adjustment function in the backward-running model is, in a sense, the reciprocal of that in the forward-running model. If this were a one-sector model, instability in the forward-running model would imply that the backward-running model was stable. However, in a multisector model this conclusion does not follow.

The best that can be said is that, given the fundamental properties of the A and B matrices, the model will have what has been referred to as a "dual stability" property. If the backward-running model is stable, then the forward-running model is unstable, and vice versa. However, both models may be unstable.[10] Thus, if the forward-running model is unstable, the backward-running model may be stable, but need not be.

Although much of the literature has focused on the stability properties of the adjustment function, not enough attention has been paid to the target equilibrium path – the particular solution $X^*(t)$. Even if either the forward- or backward-running model is stable in the sense that the adjustment function does not force the system to dismantle capital and run production processes in reverse, the short-run investment theories they incorporate are nonetheless both quite unrealistic.

Notice that in the general solutions of the forward- and backward-running models – Eqs. (2.3.18) and (2.3.22) – whereas the adjustment functions differ, the target equilibrium function is the same. However, even if the adjustment function is stable, there is no guarantee that the system will converge to the target equilibrium path. In most empirical applications it will not because, loosely speaking, convergence requires that for all sectors, the target growth rate exceed the corresponding rate from the adjustment function, a most unlikely occurrence.[11]

The target function is interesting in its own right precisely because it can be interpreted as a long-run equilibrium path that satisfies the equilibrium intertemporal linkage conditions and produces the desired sequence of consumption vectors. Whether or not $X^*(0)$ is consistent with the base-year initial production vector X_0 is a question that can be

[10] The theorem is formally analogous to the "dual stability" theorem proved by Jorgenson for price–quantity equations in the dynamic Leontief model. See the appendix to this chapter for further discussion. The requirements of full capacity use at all times combined with an arbitrary consumption path may yield negative outputs just as is the case in the forward-looking model, although the implicit investment theory is somewhat more reasonable when the model is run backward.

[11] See the appendix to this chapter for a further discussion. Stability in this sense is analogous to that in the one-sector model.

explored separately. One might well argue that a planning model should be concerned only with the target equilibrium path, and treat as a completely separate policy problem how to move the economy onto the target path. Certainly one would not put a great deal of credence in the very unrealistic investment behavior embodied in the adjustment function, and the various attempts so far to make the adjustment function behave have not yet resulted in a satisfactory theory of short-run investment behavior.

In the next section, we shall discuss different target equilibrium functions given different assumptions about how target consumption grows. We shall also discuss the notion of the feasibility of such target paths.

Target equilibrium paths

The target equilibrium is a particular solution to the basic difference equation (2.3.17) and depends on both the technology of production and growth as reflected in the A and B coefficient matrices and on the target consumption path $C(t)$.[12] It does not, however, depend on initial (or any boundary) conditions and hence can be seen as a long-run equilibrium path.

In order to bring out the sole dependence of the target function on the consumption path $C(t)$, it is useful to recast the basic difference equation in terms of changes in $C(t)$. This can be done by using the algebra of operators. Define a matrix of difference operators $\hat{\Delta}$, which is simply a diagonal matrix of the difference operator:

$$\hat{\Delta} = \begin{bmatrix} \Delta & & & 0 \\ & \cdot & & \\ & & \cdot & \\ & & & \cdot \\ 0 & & & \Delta \end{bmatrix}$$

In this notation, $\Delta X(t)$ is written as the product of the operator matrix $\hat{\Delta}$ and the vector $X(t)$. The advantage of using the operator approach is that we can treat $\hat{\Delta}$ separately from the $X(t)$ vector and perform algebraic operations with it.[13]

Using the operator notation, the basic difference equation of the dynamic model, Eq. (2.3.16), can be written as

[12] The derivation of particular solutions for the open dynamic input model are given by Stone and Brown (1962), Mathur (1964). See also Woods (1978).

[13] $\hat{\Delta}$ is not, however, the same as a matrix of numbers – it can only be treated in an analogous manner. See Allen (1960, app. A), for a discussion of the algebra of operators.

$$X(t) = RB\,\hat{\Delta}X(t) + RC(t) \tag{2.3.23}$$

where $R = (I - A)^{-1}$. Solving for $X(t)$, one gets

$$X(t) = (I - RB\,\hat{\Delta})^{-1}RC(t) \tag{2.3.24}$$

Writing this equation as a series expansion,

$$X(t) = [I + RB\,\hat{\Delta} + (RB\,\hat{\Delta})^2 + \dots]RC(t) \tag{2.3.25}$$

Because R and B are assumed not to vary over time, it follows that $\hat{\Delta}RC(t) = R\,\hat{\Delta}C(t)$ and Eq. (2.3.25) can be written as

$$X(t) = R[I + BR\hat{\Delta} + (BR)^2\,\hat{\Delta}^2 + \dots]C(t) \tag{2.3.26}$$

If Eq. (2.3.26) is multiplied out, it can be seen that the initial difference equation in ΔX has now been expressed as a function of successive differences of $C(t)$. Thus, Eq. (2.3.26) is a general representation of the target equilibrium as a function only of the target consumption path, $C(t)$. We shall consider two special cases.

Assume that consumption in each sector grows at a constant compound rate g_i, which can vary across sectors. Then $\hat{\Delta}C(t) = \hat{G}C(t)$, where $\hat{G}$ is the diagonal matrix of sectoral growth rates. Equation (2.3.26) becomes

$$X^*(t) = R[I + BR\hat{G} + (BR)^2\hat{G}^2 + \dots]C(t) \tag{2.3.27}$$

where $X^*(t)$ replaces $X(t)$ to denote that this is a target equilibrium, and

$$C(t) = (I + \hat{G})^t C_0 \tag{2.3.28}$$

Define the infinite sum

$$Q = \sum_{k=1}^{\infty} (BR)^k \hat{G}^k \tag{2.3.29}$$

and Eq. (2.3.27) becomes

$$X^*(t) = RC(t) + RQC(t) \tag{2.3.30}$$

In Eq. (2.3.20), the first term $RC(t)$ gives the production requirements every year if there were no investment requirements. The term $QC(t)$ gives the investment required to sustain the specified growth, and $RQC(t)$ gives the total output required to produce the necessary investment.

Given the assumption of constant sectoral growth rates, Eqs. (2.3.28), (2.3.29), and (2.3.30) define the target equilibrium. The matrix Q can be solved numerically by simply adding terms in the series expansion until it converges.[14] Given the initial consumption vector C_0 and the specified sectoral growth rates, $C(t)$ is given and hence all the right-hand terms in Eq. (2.3.30) are specified.

Viewing the target equilibrium as an economic plan raises questions about its "reasonableness." Examining the reasonableness of the target equilibrium has two components: (1) internal consistency and (2) feasibility. In discussing these properties, it is convenient to work with a somewhat simpler model. Instead of assuming that sectoral consumption grows at different rates, assume that consumption in all sectors grows at the same rate g. Thus $g_i = g$ for all sectors. In this case, the infinite sum in Eq. (2.3.29) has a simple representation,

$$I + Q = (I - gBR)^{-1} \tag{2.3.31}$$

and hence, from Eq. (2.3.30),

$$X^*(t) = R(I - gBR)^{-1}C(t)$$

The term on the right can be simplified (after a little algebra) as

$$X^*(t) = (I - A - gB)^{-1}C(t) \tag{2.3.32}$$

First, consider the internal consistency of the target equilibrium. Given that the economy is viable, $(I - A)^{-1}$ is a non-negative matrix, and it is clear that there exist values of $g > 0$ such that $(I - A - gB)^{-1}$ is also non-negative. It is also true that there is some maximum value of g beyond which the inverse matrix has negative elements and hence, for some t, the target equilibrium is inconsistent because elements of $X^*(t)$ go negative.[15] Thus, to be internally consistent, the model will allow only a certain range of growth rates.

Internal consistency is a rather weak test of reasonableness because, for actual empirical models, the maximum internally consistent growth rate is usually very large, much larger than observed sectoral growth rates. However, although it is easy to define what is meant by an internally consistent target path – that it satisfies the difference equation and yields non-negative output – it is much harder to define what is meant by a "feasible" target path.

One notion of feasibility that might be termed "base-year feasibility" is that the initial target output vector $X^*(0)$ must be inside the base-

[14] The question of whether it converges will be discussed later. There does not appear to be any simple algebraic representation of the series expansion in Eq. (2.3.29).

[15] The restriction on g is that the modulus of the dominant root of the matrix $(A + gB)$ must be smaller than one.

year production possibility frontier of the economy. If factors of production are assumed to be completely nonshiftable in the base year, then base-year feasibility implies that $X^*(0) \leq X_0$. Although the assumption of nonshiftability seems rather extreme, the definition of a short-run production possibility frontier along which the economy can move in order to get onto the target path represents a difficult analytical problem.

One simple approach is to define the frontier by the "distance" of the base-year production vector from the origin, $\|X_0\|$. For a Euclidean measure of distance, this approach implies that the short-run production possibility frontier is a section of sphere in the positive orthant.[16] The initial target output vector is considered to be feasible if it falls within the sphere $\|X^*(0)\| \leq \|X_0\|$.

Alternatively, one might take a more heuristic approach and define as feasible any initial target vector that is less than some specified "distance" from the actual base-year production vector. One might also specify the starting point of the plan period some time after year 0. Then the feasible distance measure is given by $\|X_0 - X^*(\tau)\| < \delta$, where τ is the starting period and δ is a small number. How the economy is to move in τ periods from X_0 to the initial target production vector $X^*(\tau)$ is considered to be a transition problem that must be considered separately. The problem of planning the transition from a historical capital stock and structure of production to a desired equilibrium allocation is thus left open by the model.

A dynamic input–output model implicitly includes a complete set of macroeconomic accounts in real terms. These accounts can be used to analyze what might be called "macroeconomic feasibility." As shown in the application in Chapter 4, at the macro level, changes in the balance of trade (defined in real terms), investment, and hence required savings are important variables in considering the feasibility of the target path.[17] Before turning to a discussion of prices in input–output models, it is

[16] There is a variety of such distance measures, or "norms." See the appendix to this chapter for a brief discussion of such measures.

[17] The notion of "feasibility" is presented in a later section and further discussed in the appendix to this chapter. In an empirical application, the trade-offs among the various criteria for feasibility are complex. Either lowering the target growth rates or lowering the target base-year values of sectoral consumption will yield lower values of $X^*(0)$ and hence improve base-year feasibility. On the other hand, lowering initial consumption raises the base-year savings rate, which is potentially macroeconomically infeasible. Given C_0, the higher the growth rate, the higher the implied savings rate. In an actual application, the model can be used to explore some of the trade-offs empirically.

worthwhile to spend some time exploring selected extensions to the basic model that will turn out to be useful for the exposition in later chapters.

Extensions of the model: technological change and foreign trade

In the derivation of the target functions, technology was assumed fixed in that the A and B coefficients did not change over time. Although this is acceptable for a reasonably short period, these assumptions are clearly empirically incorrect for longer time periods in most countries, developing or developed. It is possible to assume that both the A and B matrices change over time, but at the cost of complicating the solution problem. Several approaches have been tried.

Clopper Almon, in his work on the United States, has generalized the solution approach to include changes in technology (see Almon, 1967). He assumes that the consumption path $C(t)$ can be approximated by polynomials in time and also allows the A and B matrices to change over time. The target function can no longer be represented analytically, but Almon has developed various techniques for solving it numerically. Adelman and co-workers, in a model used for the second Korean five-year plan, specified the target consumption path explicitly, allowed for changes in the input–output coefficients over time, and numerically solved for the target equilibrium path using an iterative technique (see Adelman, 1969). In Cambridge, England, a number of models of the British economy have been built under the general supervision of Richard Stone. The earliest of these specified differential constant sectoral growth rates (as discussed above), and much of the later work has been concerned with the treatment of changes in technology.[18] We shall not discuss these empirical applications further here, but it is worth noting that they represent excellent examples of the application of the general approach of seeking a target equilibrium solution.

Foreign trade can be included in the dynamic model exactly as it was introduced in the static model. Exports can be considered as a distinct final demand category, and imports can be computed using fixed coefficients as discussed in the previous section on the static input–output model. We shall present a slightly more general specification of import coefficients in which the treatment above is a special case.[19]

---

[18] See Stone (1970). The earliest model is described in Stone and Brown (1962).

[19] See Robinson and Song (1972), which describes the general technique, including the solution approach discussed earlier, for a model of Korea.

Assume that import coefficients are differentiated by type of demand. That is, the ratio of imports to total demand differ by use: consumption, investment, and intermediate goods demand. Thus, total import demand is given by

$$M^m(t) = A^m X(t) + \hat{M2} Z(t) + \hat{M3} C(t) \qquad (2.3.33)$$

where

A^m = matrix of intermediate import demand coefficients
$\hat{M2}$ = diagonal matrix of imported investment coefficients
$\hat{M3}$ = diagonal matrix of imported consumption coefficients
M^m = vector of imports
C = vector of final demands, excluding exports and investment (includes private and government consumption)

The fundamental balance equation of the dynamic model, Eq. (2.3.16), can be rewritten in terms of domestically produced goods:

$$X^d(t) = A^d X^d(t) + B^d \Delta X^d(t) + F^d(t) \qquad (2.3.34)$$

where the variables are the same as those used in Eq. (2.3.16) except that A^d is the matrix of domestic input–output coefficients, B^d is the matrix of domestic capital coefficients, and $F^d = C^d + E^d$, domestic consumption demand plus exports.

If the domestic demand ratios are the same for all categories of demand (as discussed in the static model), then $A^d = \hat{D}A$, $B^d = \hat{D}B$, and $C^d = \hat{D}C$.

If base-year data are used to estimate the various import coefficients (A^m, $\hat{M2}$, and $\hat{M3}$) and they are not assumed to be the same across categories of demand, then the domestic coefficient matrices are given by $A^d = A - A^m$ and $B^d = (I - \hat{M2})B$, and domestic final demand by $F^d = (I - \hat{M3})C + E^d$. In either case, the dynamic model is exactly the same as before, starting from Eq. (2.3.34) instead of (2.3.16).

The inclusion of foreign trade in the dynamic model adds a new dimension to the question of the macroeconomic feasibility of the target path: the balance of payments. Both components of target final demand – exports and consumption – must be specified exogenously. Imports will be determined endogenously from Eq. (2.3.33). The balance of trade (in real terms) will thus be determined endogenously and, like the aggregate savings rate, should be considered in an analysis of the macroeconomic feasibility of the target equilibrium. In Chapter 4 we shall present an illustrative application of the dynamic input–output model to the problems of growth and trade strategy in Korea.

2.4   Relative prices and input–output models

Production prices and the factor price frontier

Input–output techniques were originally developed to analyze and help achieve overall consistency of production plans in an economy. The units used to measure output in each sector can be arbitrary (e.g., tons, bushels), although in practice they are determined by what could be bought by a unit of currency at the base-year prices that happened to prevail when the input–output table was constructed. Prices need not appear explicitly in either the static or dynamic version of the model discussed previously.

The input–output approach has also been used, however, to analyze the consistency of commodity prices and value flows that accompany physical transactions in an economy. In Eastern Europe, for example, input–output models were constructed during the 1960s with the explicit objective of reforming the price systems ruling in these economies. In the West, the input–output model has been instrumental in a reexamination of some fundamental value-theoretic questions that date back to Ricardo and Marx. In this section we discuss briefly the use of input–output models in the analysis of prices and values.

The fundamental principle underlying the construction of price systems based on input–output models is that commodity prices reflect production costs and certain mark-up rates over cost that determine the relative profitability of different sectors. Although it is possible to construct various forms of mark-up pricing models, we concentrate on one most closely in accord with general equilibrium theory and most often discussed in the literature, where commodity prices reflect production costs inclusive of profit margins on capital advances. We have

Value of output = value of intermediate inputs + wage costs + profits

We assume here a closed economy, a standard assumption in the literature on "production prices." Imports can be thought of as noncompetitive and incorporated in intermediate input costs, or, alternatively, they could constitute a fourth, separate component of cost.

The value balance equations, dual to the material balance equations, have the following form:

$$P_j X_j = \sum_{i=1}^{n} a_{ij} P_i X_j + W_j l_j X_j + R_j \sum_{i=1}^{n} s_{ij} P_i k_j X_j \qquad (2.4.1)$$

where P_j and P_i are commodity prices, W_j is the wage rate in sector j, and R_j is the profit rate on the value of capital installed in sector j. The value of a "unit" of capital is given by $\Sigma_{i=1}^{n} s_{ij} P_i$, where the s_{ij} are the capital composition coefficients. Because $b_{ij} = s_{ij} k_j$, we can rewrite (2.4.1) as

$$P_j X_j = \sum_{i=1}^{n} a_{ij} P_i X_j + W_j l_j X_j$$

$$+ R_j \sum_{i=1}^{n} b_{ij} P_i X_j \qquad j = 1, \ldots, n \quad (2.4.2)$$

Dividing through by X_j, we can rewrite the value balance equations in the form of price-equals-unit-cost equations:

$$P_j = \sum_{i=1}^{n} a_{ij} P_i + W_j l_j + R_j \sum_{i=1}^{n} b_{ij} P_i \qquad j = 1, \ldots, n \quad (2.4.3)$$

Note that we have implicitly assumed that a commodity has the same price whether it is an input or an output in the system. We are thus dealing with a system where relative prices are restricted to remain constant over time, as would be the case on some steady-state growth path. This is a very important restrictive feature of this kind of input–output-based price system and should be kept firmly in mind.

Next make the "Marxian" assumption, taken over by neoclassical theory, that wage rates and profit rates are equalized across sectors throughout the economy, so that we have $W_j = W$ and $R_j = R$, all j. We can then assemble Eq. (2.4.3) in the following matrix form (where P is a row vector):

$$P = PA + RPB + WL \qquad (2.4.4)$$

where A and B are the familiar material input and capital coefficients matrices and L is a row vector of labor coefficients; R and W are scalars. Rearranging, we get

$$P[I - A - RB] = WL \qquad (2.4.5)$$

We can therefore solve for P:

$$P = WL[I - A - RB]^{-1} \qquad (2.4.6)$$

Or, on the assumption that the series converges,

$$P = WL[I + (A + RB) + (A + RB)^2 + \ldots] \qquad (2.4.7)$$

Note that W, the wage rate, determines the level of prices without affecting their relative structure. Because it is only relative prices that we are discussing here, we can set $W = 1$ without loss of generality and use the wage as our numéraire. The system is then determinate for any given value of R. In particular, if $R = 0$, there are no profits in the economy and we have

$$P = L[I - A]^{-1} = L[I + A + A^2 + \ldots] = L^* \qquad (2.4.8)$$

which would make relative prices exactly equal (proportional if $W \neq 1$) to total direct and indirect requirements of labor per unit of final demand. Thus, with $R = 0$, the input–output model leads to a labor-theory-of-value price system with prices proportional to labor costs.

With positive profits in the economy, the price system based on production costs computed from (2.4.7) will no longer yield prices proportional to labor costs except in the unlikely event that each sector requires labor and capital in the same proportions (Marx's equal organic composition of capital assumption). In general, prices will reflect a weighted average of labor and capital costs, with the weighting determined by the magnitude of R. As R increases, the RB component of the series expansion will tend to dominate. It is important to stress, however, that the RB terms also are premultiplied by L, so that capital can be viewed as indirect or "dated" labor and R can be seen as determining the relative value of "past" labor that went into the production of capital goods in contrast to "present" labor that produces current intermediate goods and output.

There is clearly a maximum value of R beyond which the profit rate cannot rise. The value R_{max} is reached when the matrix $[I - A - RB]$ becomes singular. For $R = R_{max}$, all of net production has to go to capital, so

$$PX - PAX = R_{max}BX \qquad (2.4.9)$$

and therefore

$$P[I - A - R_{max}B] = 0 \qquad (2.4.10)$$

implying that $W = 0$. The profit rate reaches its maximum value when the wage rate declines to zero. Note that this also implies that the dominant characteristic root of $[A + RB]$ has reached unity.[20]

Any value of R between 0 and R_{max} gives rise to a well-defined vector of relative commodity prices. Examination of (2.4.7) shows clearly that *all* prices P_i will be monotonically increasing functions of the profit rate R. Therefore, the real wage, however defined in terms of commodity weights, is a monotonically decreasing function of the profit rate. This fundamental inverse relationship between the real wage and the profit

---

[20] See the appendix for a formal mathematical discussion. Note the mathematical similarity to the dynamic input–output model.

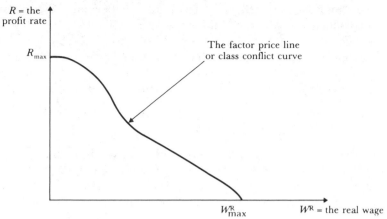

Figure 2.2. The factor price line.

rate is usually called the factor price line, and we illustrate it in Figure 2.2.

We have assumed a closed economy and ignored imports and exports. It is possible to introduce noncompetitive imports into the system without altering its fundamental characteristics. One simply adds a row of import requirements, and their cost becomes part of production cost in each sector. What would completely alter the nature of the system, however, would be to introduce competitive imports and exports and allow exogenous world prices to determine relative domestic prices. Causality in input–output-based price models always runs from domestic factor prices to commodity prices. This implies noncompetitive imports and/ or domestic markets insulated from world markets by appropriate tariffs and trade restrictions that allow domestic prices to be determined independently of world prices.

It is clear that for each distinct set of A and B matrices (i.e., technologies), one could derive a different factor price line. Profit maximization will always lead onto the outermost factor price line, so that in a model with many alternative technologies, one can concentrate on the envelope of all these curves, called the factor price frontier.[21] There is a vast literature on the shape of the factor price frontier and on whether or not it is possible to rank technologies in order of appearance on the frontier as R increases from zero toward R_{max}. The literature on capital

[21] This result is often called, rather confusingly, the "nonsubstitution theorem." As long as the real wage is fixed at a particular level, production techniques and relative prices will also be fixed, irrespective of demand conditions. See, for example, Morishima (1977).

theory and the reswitching of techniques is beyond the scope of this book, which focuses on planning models, and the interested reader is referred to the excellent survey by Harcourt (1972). Suffice it here to note that the input–output model has provided a very useful framework for the analysis of basic value-theoretic questions that have divided the economics profession from the time economics emerged as a science.

Multichannel price systems

Before concluding this section on prices, it is worth providing an example of the so-called multichannel price systems, based on the input–output model, which served as models for price reform in Eastern Europe. We briefly describe a system implemented in Czechoslovakia during the days preceding the famous Spring of Prague, in 1968 (see Sekerka, Kyn, and Hejl, 1970). These attempts at reform reflected the need to introduce some uniformity into the various mark-up and profit rates implicit in the centrally administered price systems so as to allow the identification of sectors with abnormally high or low profitabilities and facilitate the use of performance criteria based on profitability notions. The following consistency framework was proposed in Czechoslovakia:

$$P = (1 + v)PA + \rho PB + \mu PC \tag{2.4.11}$$

where A and B are the familiar material input and capital coefficient matrices and C is a labor consumption matrix reflecting a fixed proportions consumption basket of labor in each sector. Prices in such a system cover costs of materials and lead to income or surplus formation as a sum of three components: the first proportional to material cost, the second to capital, and the third to the expenditure of labor. The prices are referred to as multichannel prices when the parameters v, ρ, and μ are all positive. The parameter ρ is analogous to the profit rate R, μ is a kind of wage rate, and v is a charge for working capital (including depreciation).

Rewriting (2.4.11) in eigenvalue form, we get

$$P = P[(1 + v)A + \rho B + \mu C] \tag{2.4.12}$$

Note that the distribution parameters v, ρ, and μ are mutually bound by the condition that the matrix $[(1 + v)A + \rho B + \mu C]$ has a unit eigenvalue that is also its dominant characteristic root. Any increase in one of the parameters must imply a decrease in at least one of the others, because we now have a kind of three-dimensional factor price line.

In Czechoslovakia this multichannel price model formed the conceptual basis of a sweeping price reform affecting 25,000 groups of products; after some experimentation and debate, ρ was set at 0.06, μ at 0.22, and ν at zero. Future matrices and parameters were estimated. In Hungary the same basic construct was used to prepare the ground for the 1968 reform (see Brody, 1970). In contrast to Czechoslovakia, however, only a relatively small fraction of prices was actually fixed centrally. The system also allowed for differences in ρ by sector reflecting investment priorities, which, of course, destroys the mathematical simplicity of the model.

It must be stressed that in practice these production price systems have not had a very long practical life. They are long-term equilibrium constructs, and the equation of marginal to average cost raises fundamental difficulties in using them for applied price-planning exercises. It is possible to extend the basic framework to out-of-steady-state situations where relative prices change over time, but the model then loses its appealing simplicity. What is perhaps even more important is that the causality implicit in these price systems may need to be reversed when analyzing economies open to foreign trade, where world prices may have a determining influence on domestic prices in a large portion of the economy. Although their practical usefulness is therefore quite limited, it is instructive to keep these production price models in mind as representing one extreme among the many alternative ways planners and policy makers have approached the problem of relative price determination. Elements of the production price concept remain valid in many of the very different models we shall discuss throughout the book.

2.A Mathematical appendix

In this appendix we gather together some of the mathematical properties of semipositive matrices that relate to the static and dynamic input–output models.[22] In particular, we consider (1) the viability of the static model and (2) the stability of the dynamic model. There are a variety of ways to approach these questions. We shall start from the notion of the diagonalization of a matrix.

Diagonalization

Consider the homogeneous equation

$$(A - \lambda I)X = 0 \tag{2.A.1}$$

---

[22] A good textbook on the mathematics of multisector models is Woods (1978). See also Lancaster (1968) and Burmeister and Dobell (1970).

where A is an $(n \times n)$ matrix, X is a vector, and λ is a scalar. This system has a nontrivial solution if and only if the determinant

$$|A - \lambda I| = 0 \qquad (2.A.2)$$

Given A, Eq. (2.A.2) is a polynomial in λ. The n roots of this polynomial are called eigenvalues, latent roots, or characteristic roots. For any root λ_k,

$$(A - \lambda_k I)X^k = 0 \qquad (2.A.3)$$

where X^k is the solution vector. X^k is known as an eigenvector (or latent vector, or characteristic vector) and is determined only up to a scalar multiplier. Usually, it is convenient to scale the eigenvectors so that

$$\sum_i (X_i^k)^2 = 1 \qquad (2.A.4)$$

Consider a matrix V whose columns are the eigenvectors X^k and a diagonal matrix Λ such that $\Lambda_{kk} = \lambda_k$, where the kth eigenvalue on the diagonal corresponds to the kth column of V. Equation (2.A.3) can now be written in matrix terms:

$$AV = V\Lambda \qquad (2.A.5)$$

Assume that the roots λ_k are all distinct.[23] In this case all the eigenvectors are linearly independent and hence V^{-1} exists. We can then write

$$A = V\Lambda V^{-1} \qquad (2.A.6)$$

The matrix of eigenvectors is said to "diagonalize" the matrix A because

$$V^{-1}AV = \Lambda \qquad (2.A.7)$$

Consider the matrix A^n, where n is a rational number. Then it can be shown that:
1. If A has characteristic roots λ_k, then A^n has characteristic roots $(\lambda_k)^n$.
2. The eigenvectors of A^n are the same as those of A. Thus

$$V^{-1}A^n V = \Lambda^n \qquad (2.A.8)$$

[23] In economics problems, it is usually reasonable to assume that the eigenvalues are distinct because, if there are repeated roots, the matrix can be perturbed by an arbitrarily small number to yield a new matrix with distinct roots.

The diagonalization of a nonsymmetric matrix A, and especially of powers of A as shown in Eq. (A.2.8), is important in demonstrating important theoretical results. Although A can be any matrix with distinct characteristic roots, input–output analysis is concerned with "semipositive" matrices. The next section states some important properties of this type of matrix.

Semipositive matrices

A "semipositive" matrix is a matrix with only non-negative numbers ($a_{ij} \geq 0$ for all i and j) and with at least one positive entry in every row and column. If all the elements are strictly greater than zero, the matrix is called "positive" ($a_{ij} > 0$ for all i and j). A semipositive matrix is "indecomposable" if its rows and columns cannot be permuted (remembering that the row and column indices are not independent) so as to create a block triangular matrix (see Dorfman, Samuelson, and Solow, 1958). A positive matrix is, of course, always indecomposable.

We list below, without proof, a number of properties of semipositive matrices. Most of them are contained in what is loosely called the Perron–Frobenius theorem. Given that A is a semipositive matrix, then:

1. The matrix A has a dominant eigenvalue λ^* that is real and non-negative. If A is indecomposable, λ^* is positive. Dominance is defined in property 3.

2. Associated with λ^* is a semipositive eigenvector $X^* \geq 0$. If A is indecomposable, then $X^* > 0$ and no other characteristic root has an associated non-negative eigenvector.

3. The modulus of λ^*, denoted $|\lambda^*|$, is greater than or equal to the modulus of any other root.[24] If the matrix A is positive, the inequality is strict; that is, $|\lambda^*| > |\lambda^k|$ for all other k.

4. For any number $\mu > \lambda^*$, the matrix $(\mu I - A)$ is nonsingular and $(\mu I - A)^{-1}$ is semipositive. If A is indecomposable, $(\mu I - A)^{-1}$ is a positive matrix.

5. $\partial \lambda^* / \partial a_{ij} \geq 0$ for all i and j. For indecomposable matrices, the inequality is strict. That is, increasing the value of any element in the matrix cannot decrease the dominant eigenvalue (and will increase it for an indecomposable matrix).

There are various theorems that serve to determine bounds on the characteristic roots of a matrix. In considering these theorems, it is use-

---

[24] The modulus of a real number is just its absolute value. The modulus of a complex number $a + bi$ is given by $|a + bi| = +\sqrt{a^2 + b^2}$, and thus depends on both the real and imaginary parts.

ful to start from the notion of a "norm" of a matrix.[25] For a vector, the "norm" is defined as a general measure of length. The usual Euclidean measure of length is one kind of norm. For a vector X, the Euclidean norm is given by

$$\|X\|_E = \left[\sum_i X_i^2 \right]^{1/2} \tag{2.A.9}$$

There are two other common norms, which we shall call L and M and which are defined as[26]

$$\|X\|_M = \max_i |X_i| \tag{2.A.10}$$

$$\|X\|_L = \sum_i |X_i| \tag{2.A.11}$$

Consider the problem discussed in the text of determining the feasibility of the initial period of a target equilibrium, $X^*(0)$. It was suggested that $X^*(0)$ be considered to be base-year feasible if it is no further "distance" from the origin than actual production in the initial year. Using the norm to represent the measure of "distance," base-year feasibility implies that

$$\|X^*(0)\| \leq \|X_0\| \tag{2.A.12}$$

In this context, different norms have quite different economic interpretations. The Euclidean norm implies that the short-run production possibility frontier is a section of a sphere centered on the origin. The L norm states that the sum of production (in base-year prices if a value measure of output is used) is the appropriate measure and hence that the production possibility frontier is a hyperplane in the positive orthant – a straight line if there are only two sectors. In fact, the L norm defines the largest cube that can be circumscribed by any sphere defined by the Euclidean norm. The M norm implies that the frontier is a cube with the dimensions of the largest sectoral output. It is thus the smallest cube in which any sphere defined by the E norm can be inscribed.

The vector norms we have used so far can be generalized to matrices.

---

[25] Vector and matrix norms are not much used in economics. For a brief treatment, see Almon (1967) or Woods (1978). For a mathematical treatment, see Stewart (1973).

[26] These definitions follow Almon (1967); L stands for the mathematician Lebesgue. In some books, these are called L_1 and L_2 norms. See also Nikaido (1968).

One definition of a norm of a matrix A is the smallest number $\|A\|$ such that

$$\|AX\| \leq \|A\| \, \|X\| \tag{2.A.13}$$

for any vector X.[27] Intuitively, the norm of A is the maximum relative "distance" that multiplication by A extends any vector X, where the definition of "distance" depends on the type of norm. For the M norm,

$$\|A\|_M = \max_i \sum_j a_{ij} \tag{2.A.14}$$

That is, it equals the maximum row sum of absolute values. For the L norm,

$$\|A\|_L = \max_j \sum_i a_{ij} \tag{2.A.15}$$

That is, it equals the maximum column sum of absolute values.

The various approaches that have been used in the economics literature to prove that an input–output system is viable [i.e., that $(I - A)^{-1}$ is non negative] all make use of norms, even if not explicitly defining them.[28] They essentially make use of various properties of an input–output matrix to establish that the modulus of the largest eigenvalue of the coefficient matrix is less than one. However, there is a general theorem establishing an inequality between the norms and eigenvalues of a matrix. The theorem states that for any matrix A, the moduli of the eigenvalues are all bounded by any (consistent) norm of the matrix (see Stewart, 1973, p. 270):

$$|\lambda| \leq \|A\|$$

For an input–output matrix that is based on a consistent set of accounts, the elements of A are all non-negative and the column sums are all less than one because each sector has at least some value-added (nonproduced inputs). Therefore, for an input–output matrix,

$$\|A\|_L < 1$$

[27] Under this definition, the matrix norm $\|A\|$ is consistent. That is, $\|AB\| \leq \|A\| \, \|B\|$ for any conformable matrices A and B. There are more general definitions, but this one will suffice for our purposes.

[28] For example, McKenzie's (1960) treatment of a dominant diagonal matrix relies on properties of the M norm. The proofs in Lancaster (1968) are especially clear. The Hawkins-Simon conditions are subsumed under the conditions for a dominant diagonal matrix. Woods (1978) has an interesting treatment that starts from the Hawkins-Simon conditions.

Thus, for the input–output matrix, $|\lambda| < 1$. For a semipositive inde-composable matrix, it is possible to strengthen the theorem. First, note that for such a matrix, the dominant eigenvalue λ^* is real and positive, so that $|\lambda^*| = \lambda^*$. In this case, λ^* can be shown to be bounded from above and below, and such matrices have the following properties:

6. If A is semipositive and indecomposable, the dominant eigenvalue is strictly bounded from above by $\|A\|_L$ and from below by the mini-mum column sum of absolute values. That is, $S < \lambda^* < \|A\|_L$, where S is the minimum column sum. If $S = \|A\|_L$, then $\lambda^* = \|A\|_L = S$. Similar bounds hold for $\|A\|_M$.

Given that $\|A\|_L < 1$, then $\lambda^* < 1$. Actually, given property 6, the inequality on λ^* can be proven with somewhat weaker conditions. We require only that $\|A\|_L \leq 1$ and $S < 1$. Thus, all column sums but one can equal 1.

Viability of an input–output system

For any actual input–output matrix, we have thus shown that $\lambda^* < 1$. From property 4, set $\mu = 1 > \lambda^*$, and it follows that $(I - A)^{-1}$ is positive (semipositive if A is decomposable). Thus the system is viable.[29] The condition that $\lambda^* < 1$ is also sufficient to prove that the multiplier series (the series representation of the inverse) converges.

Consider the series $R(k)$,

$$R(k) = I + A + \ldots + A^k \tag{2.A.16}$$

and the product

$$(I - A)R(k) = I - A^{k+1} \tag{2.A.17}$$

The limit of $R(k)$ as k goes to infinity is equal to $(I - A)^{-1}$ if and only if $\lim_{k \to \infty} A^k = \emptyset$.

Now diagonalize R in Eq. (2.A.16). From Eq. (2.A.8),

$$V^{-1}RV = I + \Lambda + \Lambda^2 + \ldots + \Lambda^k \tag{2.A.18}$$

Each of the components of the series is of the form $(1 + \lambda_i + \lambda_i^2 + \ldots)$ and these converge if $|\lambda_i| < 1$, which is true because the largest root is strictly less than one. Thus the multiplier series converges if the system is viable.

[29] The inequality $\lambda^* < 1$ also holds for any matrix that differs from A by only a change of units. See Fisher (1965).

Stability of the dynamic system

The equations of the forward-running dynamic model can be written as

$$X(t) = D^t[X_0 - X^*(0)] + X^*(t) \tag{2.A.19}$$

where $D = B^{-1}(I - A + B)$. Diagonalize D:

$$D = V\Lambda V^{-1} \tag{2.A.20}$$
$$D^t = V\Lambda^t V^{-1} \tag{2.A.21}$$

The adjustment function will thus be a weighted sum of the eigenvectors in V with the weights given by the vector $\Lambda^t V^{-1}[X_0 - X^*(0)]$.

If the vector $X_0 - X^*(0)$, or just X_0 for the homogeneous equation, is proportional to one of the eigenvectors in V, then $V^{-1}[X_0 - X^*(0)]$ will have zeros in every entry except the one corresponding to that eigenvector. In this case, the adjustment function will expand along the direction given by the one eigenvector.

If, as one would usually expect, $V^{-1}[X_0 - X^*(0)]$ has no zero elements, then eventually the weights will be dominated by the Λ^t terms. As t becomes large, the adjustment function will expand in the direction of the eigenvector associated with the largest eigenvalue (in modulus). Questions of stability or consistency of the adjustment function thus all depend on the properties of the largest eigenvalue and its associated eigenvector.

The backward-running model can be written as

$$X(t) = (D^{-1})^{T-t}[X_T - X^*(T)] + X^*(t) \tag{2.A.22}$$

From Eq. (2.A.8), we have that the eigenvalues of D^{-1} are given by Λ^{-1} and the associated eigenvectors are unchanged. Thus, the properties of the backward-running adjustment function are related to those of the forward-running model.

Consider the D matrix. It can be written as

$$D = I + B^{-1}(I - A) \tag{2.A.23}$$

The inverse of the second term is $(I - A)^{-1}B$. This matrix will be positive and hence will have a dominant positive real eigenvalue, μ^*, with an associated positive eigenvector.[30] Furthermore, no other eigenvector is positive. Now $1/\mu^*$ is an eigenvalue of $B^{-1}(I - A)$, and so there exists one balanced growth path for the adjustment function with

[30] If A is indecomposable, $(I - A)^{-1}$ is positive. B is semipositive, hence their product is positive.

all sectors having positive outputs and the system expanding at the rate $1 + 1/\mu^*$. The remaining question is whether this path is the dominant one.

Given that μ^* is the dominant eigenvalue of $(I - A)^{-1}B$, then all other eigenvalues of $B^{-1}(I - A)$, call them λ_i, will be greater in modulus than $1/\mu^*$. If the value of $(1 + 1/\mu^*)$ does not dominate the values of $(1 + \lambda_i)$ for the other roots, then the system will not generally stay on the positive balanced growth path and must therefore eventually generate negative outputs for some sectors.

At first glance, it would seem that because $|\lambda_i| > (1/\mu^*)$, the system *must* be unstable. However, this is not true because what must be compared is the modulus of $1 + \lambda_i$ relative to $1 + 1/\mu^*$. Define $\lambda^* = 1/\mu^*$ and note that λ^* is real, so that $|1 + \lambda^*| = 1 + \lambda^*$. However, for the other roots, $|1 + \lambda_i| \leq 1 + |\lambda_i|$, and we cannot prove any relationship between $|1 + \lambda_i|$ and $|1 + \lambda^*|$.

Although we cannot prove that the forward- or backward-running models are either stable or unstable, there is a "dual stability" relationship between the two models.[31] Given that the eigenvalues for the backward-running model are the reciprocals of those for the forward-running model, the same root cannot be dominant in both models. Because the positive eigenvector is unique, if the forward-running model happened to be stable, the backward-running model would not be – and vice versa. However, both could be unstable.

Note finally that the adjustment function will never be stable in the sense that $t \overset{\lim}{\to} \infty \; D^t = \emptyset$. Thus, the only way that the general solution $X(t)$ will approach the target equilibrium path $X^*(t)$ is if the target path dominates the adjustment path. This will happen only if all the roots of D are appropriately small, a very unlikely occurrence because the roots of the adjustment function represent the maximum rate of growth the system can achieve assuming that there is no consumption.[32]

A comparison of the one-sector and multisector models

The analysis in the previous section is also useful to bring out the differences and similarities between the one-sector and multisector models.

---

[31] Although the theorem has never been stated in this form, it is formally analogous to the dual stability theorem for price and quantity equations conjectured by Solow and proved by Jorgenson. For a discussion, see Burmeister and Dobell (1970).

[32] Speaking loosely, $(1 + \lambda_i)$ for all λ_i including λ^* must be less than the sectoral rates of expansion of $X^*(t)$.

As discussed in the text, there are many similarities between the two models, although the mechanisms that underlie their instability properties are quite different. It is revealing to explore the assumption required to have the same mechanisms.

First, assume that both the A and B matrices are diagonal. Then there is no sectoral interdependence through intermediate input requirements and each sector uses only its own output as capital input. In this case, the sectors are entirely independent and the multisector model can be seen as a collection of independent one-sector models. In this case the B matrix is certainly of full rank and the capital composition matrix (S) is just the identity matrix, so its inverse will, of course, have no negative elements.

Second, assume that the A and B matrices are not diagonal, but that all the columns of the S matrix are the same. There is interdependence through demand for intermediate inputs and sectoral capital is made up of goods from different sectors, but the sectoral composition of capital by sector of origin is the same for all sectors (of destination). In this case, the rank of the B matrix is one, even if incremental capital-output ratios differ across sectors, and the notion of an aggregate capital stock in the economy is well defined.

Consider the adjustment function of the forward-running model, Eq. (2.A.19). As discussed above, the inverse of the second term of the D matrix in Eq. (2.A.23) is $(I - A)^{-1}B$. This matrix is positive and hence has a dominant positive real eigenvalue with an associated positive eigenvector. However, if the B matrix is of rank one, then $(I - A)^{-1}B$ is also of rank one and hence the dominant eigenvalue is also unique. Thus there is only one balanced growth path and it has positive output in every sector. With no variation in the sectoral composition of capital, there is no possibility of having the adjustment function generate a solution path with negative sectoral output.[33]

The model with the same composition of capital across sectors is the multisector analogue of the one-sector model. The question of stability in both models reduces to a comparison of the single growth rate generated by the adjustment function with that from the target equilibrium. In both models, the growth rate generated by the adjustment function is the maximum that the economy could achieve, because it involves investing all output, with no consumption. Thus, unless the economy happens to start on the target path, the dynamics will be dominated by the adjustment function.

[33] Unless the constant in Eq. (2.A.19), $X_0 - X^*(0)$, is negative. That is, the target equilibrium is in some sense not base-year feasible.

CHAPTER 3

Linear programming models

3.1 Introduction

Input–output models are consistency models that do not have an endogenous mechanism of choice among alternative feasible scenarios. Linear programming introduces a great deal of flexibility into the basic linear input–output structure by allowing inequality constraints and introducing the explicit maximization of a planner's preference function into economy-wide planning models. Maximization implies the possibility of choice, which in turn implies that the feasible set defined by the mathematical relations constituting the planning model contains many alternative solutions. It is therefore the introduction of inequality constraints and the ability to deal systematically with these constraints that is the fundamental characteristic of linear programming (LP) models.

Many of the problems that arise in the context of the input–output models we have discussed are related to the formulation of the basic constraints as strict equalities. If a sector has a certain amount of capital installed, all of it *must* be used to produce output. If a certain ratio of imports to domestic production is observed, that ratio becomes a fixed coefficient and there is no endogenous make-or-buy choice that the model can simulate. We discussed the difficulties this created for the dynamic input–output model. In contrast, LP models can allow endogenous choice of capacity utilization and endogenous determination of how much of a good will be imported or exported.

The linear programming framework has been and continues to be used both for economy-wide and more microeconomic, sector-focused planning exercises. The great flexibility of the LP framework, because one is always able to add specific inequality constraints reflecting particular features of the economy, also implies that there are very many different variants of linear programming models. In fact, their flexibility is both their chief virtue and their chief vice. Virtue, because one can generally add and subtract equations and constraints from a given model, depending on particular circumstances and perceived constraints, without upsetting the overall consistency of the system or the ability to obtain a solution. Vice, because the ad hoc constraints may reflect no

62

more than the prior biases of model builders and it is often unclear whether important features of a solution path are due to the fundamental nature of the technology and the objectives specified or to a superstructure of additional constraints imposed on the system.

The objective of this chapter is to outline the essential "core" structure of economy-wide linear programming models used for development planning purposes. We shall not dwell on the many variants that can be developed from the basic core, but focus in particular on how the interactions among domestic capacity utilization, investment, and trade are specified.[1] In Section 3.2 we present the basic structure of a linear programming model. Section 3.3 discusses shadow prices and duality. In Section 3.4 we discuss in greater depth the notion of comparative advantage and the mechanism determining the direction and volume of trade in linear programming models. Finally, in Section 3.5, we discuss the difficult problem of terminal conditions.

3.2 Basic structure of a dynamic linear programming model

Any LP model, however large, can be formulated compactly in a simple form:

Objective function	Constraints	Non-negativity conditions
Max αX	Subject to $MX \leq B$	$X \geq 0$

$$(3.2.1)$$

The vector α, the matrix M, and the vector B are to be considered as given data. The feasible set $S = \{X \mid MX \leq B, X \geq 0\}$ must be bounded and nonempty for the solution of the program to yield an optimal vector X^* that satisfies the conditions[2] $X^* \in S$ and $\alpha X^* \geq \alpha X$ for all $X \in S$.

The great attraction of linear programming models has been that once they are in the form given in (3.2.1), their solution is routine and

---

[1] For comprehensive surveys of linear programming models, see Manne (1974) and Taylor (1975). See also Srinivasan (1975) for a discussion of the role of foreign trade.

[2] As we shall indicate in our discussion of the duality theorem, in some cases it may be more appropriate to minimize the objective function. This need not affect the discussion because, with the feasible set unchanged, it does not matter at all whether we maximize αX or minimize $-\alpha X$; the optimal solution will be the same. We shall therefore always cast the discussion in terms of the maximization problem.

the economist need not be concerned with solution methods.[3] The solution is achieved by the simplex method or its variants, a purely mathematical technique. No information on the substantive economic content of the problem need be communicated to the programmer: Knowledge of the numbers contained in α, M, and B is entirely sufficient for the solution algorithm to proceed. There can be a neat division of labor between the economist-planner concentrating on generating the entries into α, M, and B and the programmer, who is interested simply in solving a maximization problem numerically.

A second important feature of linear programming models that has made these models so attractive to the development planner derives from the duality theorem and the existence of multipliers that can often be interpreted as "prices" in the traditional microeconomic sense of the term. A "primal" problem of the form

$$\text{Max } \alpha X \qquad \text{subject to } MX \leq B \qquad X \geq 0 \qquad (3.2.2)$$

has a "dual" of the form

$$\text{Min } \lambda B \qquad \text{subject to } \lambda M \geq \alpha \qquad \lambda \geq 0 \qquad (3.2.3)$$

where the dual variables λ_i are conceptually very close to the Lagrangean multipliers of classical optimization theory. These multipliers can be interpreted as scarcity indicators or "prices," and linear programming thus leads to planning models that deal not only with purely quantitative aspects but also with the "value" or price implications of alternative solutions. It is this feature of linear programming models that has led to the claim that LP models are at least first approximations to computable general equilibrium models of market economies.

We shall present, in the form of equation groups, the basic structure of the kind of linear programming models that have been used to explore alternative growth paths for a developing economy and ways to help steer it onto a feasible path that is considered optimal by the economic planner. The models are called dynamic because they extend over time and are indecomposable or nonrecursive. We do not separately discuss the "static" one-period models because they are essentially a special, simpler case of the dynamic models.

The technology is of the input–output type, and each product is producible by a single fixed-coefficients activity. Capital is treated exactly as it is in dynamic input–output analysis with the exception that one does not insist on full-capacity use. Everything is measured in constant,

---

[3] For very large models, however, it can be difficult to generate the M matrix from the parameters of the individual equations.

unit, base-year prices. Following is the core of the equation system characterizing a typical linear programming planning model. As usual, subscripts i and j refer to the sectors of origin and destination and t refers to the time period. There are n sectors and T time periods.

The objective function

$$\text{Max} \sum_{t=1}^{T} \left(\frac{1}{1+\rho}\right)^t C_t + \sum_{i=1}^{n} \overline{U}_{iT+1} K_{iT+1} \qquad (3.2.4.)$$

What is maximized is the discounted sum of aggregate consumption (C_t) over the T years of the planning period plus the value of the terminal capital stock left over at the end of the planning period. The terminal values $\overline{U}_{it+1}$ are given exogenously, whereas the terminal capital stocks are determined endogenously.[4] The discount rate ρ is constant over time and expresses the social rate of time preference.

Material balance equations

$$M_{it} + X_{it} \geq \sum_{j=1}^{n} a_{ij} X_{jt} + \sum_{j=1}^{n} s_{ij} Y_{jt} + q_{it} C_t + E_{it} \qquad (3.2.5)$$

The variables are $(i = 1, n$ and $t = 1, T)$

M_{it} = competitive imports by sector of origin
X_{it} = production levels by sector of origin
Y_{jt} = investment levels by sector of destination
E_{it} = exports by sectors of origin
C_t = aggregate consumption
a_{ij} = input–output coefficients
s_{ij} = capital-composition coefficients
q_{it} = consumption-composition coefficients

The supply of each domestically producible commodity is made up of production X_{it} and imports M_{it}, whereas the right-hand side of (3.2.5) represents total demand.

The treatment of consumption differs from that in input–output analysis. Consumption by sector of origin is linked to aggregate consumption by consumption composition coefficients q_{it}:

$$C_{it} = q_{it} C_t \qquad (3.2.6)$$

[4] See later discussion of terminal conditions.

Thus, $q_{it}C_t$ takes the place of C_{it} in the material balance equations, and in any one year we deal with only one, aggregate, consumption variable. The q_{it} coefficients must sum to one in every year (Σ $q_{it} \equiv 1$, $t = 1$, T), and q_{it} represents the share of the ith sector in total consumption in year t. These shares may be changed exogenously over time, reflecting the changing composition of consumption in a growing economy. They are, however, exogenous, and therefore the composition of consumption does not change in these models, no matter what else happens in the economy. No endogenous substitution mechanism exists that links the structure of consumption directly to changes in relative production costs and relative prices. Interpreting this specification from the point of view of neoclassical utility theory, we can say that utility functions are assumed to be rectangular.[5]

It is possible to make the opposite assumption and assume linear utility curves. In that case the objective function would become $\Sigma\Sigma_{ti}^{Tn}$ $[1/(1 + \rho)]^tC_{it}$, and the sectoral consumption levels (C_{it}) would appear directly in the material balance equations. Different categories of consumption goods would be perfect substitutes. Unfortunately, the more reasonable treatment of different consumption goods as imperfect substitutes is very hard to introduce into the LP format. Simple linearity requires either linear or rectangular indifference curves.

The treatment of investment is exactly as in dynamic input–output models. The same is true, of course, for intermediate demand. Imports and exports, on the other hand, can now, in principle, be treated as fully endogenous, greatly extending the region of the feasible set and adding a lot of choice to the model. As we shall see, however, unrestricted endogenous choice may lead to unrealistic specialization and is not always desirable.

Capacity constraints

$$k_i X_{it} \leq K_{it} \tag{3.2.7}$$

Here k_i and K_{it} represent the sectoral capital–output ratios and the sectoral capital stocks. Sectoral production is thus constrained by the availability of capital installed in a particular sector. Capital is nonshiftable and sector specific in the short run. It is often more realistic to differ-

---

[5] Note that although products are consumed in fixed marginal proportions, it is not necessary to restrict the marginal and the average consumption propensity for a commodity to be equal. One need only add an "intercept" term $q_{it}(\Sigma_i \bar{q}_{it} = 0)$. The elasticity of demand with respect to expenditure is $q_{it}/[q_{it} + (\bar{q}_{it}/C_t)]$.

entiate between average and incremental capital–output ratios. Redefining the k_i as "marginal" capital–output ratios, we could write

$$k_i(X_{it} - \overline{X}_{io}) \leq K_{it} - \overline{K}_{io} \tag{3.2.7a}$$

$\overline{X}_{io}$ and $\overline{K}_{io}$ represent initial output and capital stock levels, and capacity limitations are now governed by increments to capital stocks and incremental capital–output ratios. Note that there is no "base-year feasibility" problem. An initial vector of sectoral capacities is given, but it may or may not be fully utilized.

Investment or capital updating equations

$$K_{it+1} = K_{it}(1 - dp_i) + Y_{it} \tag{3.2.8}$$

Here, dp_i is the proportion of the capital stock that depreciates in one year. Total investment is made up of net investment Y_{it} and replacement investment $dp_i K_{it}$. Note that we again assume a uniform one-year gestation lag: Investment in year t does not affect capacity in the same year but only capacity in the year $t + 1$. It is not difficult to build more general and flexible lag structures into the linear programming models. But, largely because of data limitations, this has not been general practice.

Foreign exchange constraints

$$\sum_{i=1}^{n_1} PW_{it} M_{it} + \overline{PW}_{ot} M_{ot} \leq \sum_{i=1}^{n_1} PW_{it} E_{it} + \overline{F}_t \tag{3.2.9}$$

We have, in addition to variables already defined,

PW_{it} = the dollar prices of competitive imports and exports
PW_{ot} = the dollar price of noncompetitive imports
M_{ot} = noncompetitive imports

$\overline{F}_t$ = net foreign capital inflow expressed in dollars
n_1 = the number of tradable sectors, assumed to be the first n_1 sectors distinguished in the model

The foreign exchange constraint restricts the foreign exchange that can be spent on imports in any given year to be less than or equal to foreign exchange revenue generated in that year through exports and capital inflows. Noncompetitive imports, M_{ot}, are either exogenous or linked to output and/or investment levels by fixed coefficients:

$$M_{ot} = \sum_{j=1}^{n} a_j^o X_{jt} + \sum_{j=1}^{n} s_j^o Y_{jt} \qquad (3.2.10)$$

where a_j^o and s_j^o represent the ratio of noncompetitive imports to output and investment. For simplicity we shall assume that $a_j^o = 0$, so that the only noncompetitive imports are investment goods.

The world dollar prices of traded goods are assumed fixed, implying the small-country assumption. Note that implicit in the PW_{it} is the base-year exchange rate, because the M_{it} and the E_{it} are expressed in unit base-year prices.[6]

The year-by-year form of the foreign exchange constraint may be unduly restrictive. The availability of reserves to absorb or cushion short-run surplus or deficits should allow a more flexible foreign exchange constraint that requires equilibrium only over the period as a whole:

$$\sum_{t=1}^{T} \sum_{i=1}^{n_1} PW_{it} M_{it} + \sum_{i=1}^{T} PW_{ot} M_{ot} \leq \sum_{t=1}^{T} \sum_{i=1}^{n_1} PW_{it} E_{it} + \sum_{t=1}^{T} \overline{F}_t \qquad (3.2.11)$$

The last term should be interpreted as the net borrowing capacity over the period. For simplicity, we have left out an explicit treatment of debt management and interest payments.

As is discussed in greater detail later, it is a difference between world prices PW_{it} and the pretrade domestic commodity transformation rates that leads our model to trade, exactly in the spirit of neoclassical trade theory. The profile of trade generated by a model that does not include any further restrictions on exports and imports is often extremely unrealistic, however. The assumption that a country can export ever greater amounts of a commodity at constant prices is often not met in reality. Furthermore, on the import side, the linearity of the underlying technology will tend to lead to specialization. This will not happen immediately, because capital stocks are sectorally fixed in the short run and all goods will normally be produced. But in the longer run, investment will occur in the least-cost sectors and lead to unrealistically high levels of imports in the higher-cost sectors. To obtain a more reasonable pattern of trade, most models include upper bounds on exports to pre-

---

[6] In practice, PW_i will differ between imports and exports because of transportation margins and other factors. These can be incorporated into the world price system exogenously.

vent extreme specialization. Because these bounds are essentially arbitrary, they greatly reduce the attractiveness of the model as a device for endogenously generating the structure of production. Unfortunately, such "ad hoc" constraints are, in practice, unavoidable if an essentially nonlinear world is to be fitted into a linear framework.[7]

Labor constraints

$$\sum_{j=1}^{n} l_{sjt} X_{jt} \leq \overline{L}_{st} \tag{3.2.12}$$

Distinguishing different skill categories or types of labor limited in supply further restricts the feasible set. The supply of labor is usually assumed to grow exogenously and, in general, no allowance is made for substitutability between labor categories. These rigid features can be modified to incorporate some substitution between labor categories by introducing labor-downgrading activities allowing workers within high skill categories to substitute, on a one-to-one basis, for workers with lower skill categories.[8]

Summary

The equations just given constitute the essential core of most dynamic linear programming models. It is extremely useful to summarize them in a simplex tableau that exhibits in compact form the structure of the model. Table 3.1 is obtained from this equation system, transforming the $\geq$ inequalities into $\leq$ relations by multiplying through by -1, and ordering the primal variables by sector and time period to bring out the almost time-recursive structure of the model. Table 3.1 fully summarizes an illustrative n-sector, three-time-period model.

In Table 3.1, each column contains the parameters appearing in front of the vector of primal variables that constitute the column heading. The column appearing on the right-hand side of the inequality signs gives the exogenous B vector.[9] The rows of the tableau reflect the constraint system. To each row we have attached a shadow multiplier. Finally, the

---

[7] The specialization problem and the mechanism that determines the direction and pattern of trade is discussed further below.

[8] See, for example, Blitzer (1975). Alternatively, one could have different outputs for different classes of workers.

[9] The B vector here should not be confused with the capital coefficients matrix $B = S\hat{K}$.

Table 3.1. *Detailed coefficients tableau for dynamic linear programming model*

	X_1	Y_1	M_1	E_1	C_1	X_2	Y_2	M_2	E_2	C_2
MBAL1	$-(I-A)$	S	$-I^{n_1}$	$+I^{n_1}$	Q_1					
CAP1	$\hat{K}$									
INV1		$-I$								
LAB1	L_t°									
BOP1			$PW_1\hat{S}_1$	PW_1	$-PW_1$					
MBAL2						$-(I-A)$	S	$-I^{n_1}$	$+I^{n_1}$	Q_2
CAP2						$\hat{K}$				
INV2							$-I$			
LAB2						L_2°				
BOP2								$PW_2\hat{S}_2$	PW_2	$-PW_2$
MBAL3										
CAP3										
INV3										
LAB3										
BOP3										
OBJ. FUNC.				$\left(\dfrac{1}{1+\rho}\right)$					$\left(\dfrac{1}{1+\rho}\right)^2$	

last row contains the vector α, whose elements are the weights appearing in the objective function. The tableau is thus a complete representation of our linear program. Provided that actual numerical values are assigned to the elements of M, B, and α, it contains all the information needed to solve the program. The matrices, vectors, and scalars that appear inside the tableau are the following:

I = identity matrix of order $n \times n$
I^{n_1} = identity matrix of order $n_1 \times n_1$ (n_1 = number of tradables)
A = input–output matrix
S = capital composition matrix
$\hat{S}$ = diagonal noncompetitive import requirements matrix
PW_{it} = world price vectors
Q_t = consumption shares vectors
$\hat{K}$ = diagonal matrix of capital–output ratios
$\hat{DP}$ = diagonal matrix of depreciation rates
L_t = labor coefficients matrix
$\overline{U}_{T+1}$ = terminal capital price vector
ρ = social rate of discount

The fact that we have allowed time superscripts for the world price and consumption shares vectors and for the labor coefficients matrix reflects the possibility of allowing exogenous changes in these parame-

K_2	X_3	Y_3	M_3	E_3	C_3	K_3	K_4			
								$\leq$		P_1
								$\leq$	$\bar{K}_1$	RN_1
								$\leq$	$(I - \hat{DP})\,\bar{K}_1$	U_1
								$\leq$	$\bar{L}_1$	W_1
								$\leq$	F_1	SR_1
$-I$								$\leq$		P_2
$-(I - \hat{DP})$								$\leq$		RN_2
						$+I$		$\leq$		U_2
								$\leq$	$\bar{L}_2$	W_2
								$\leq$	$\bar{F}_2$	SR_2
	$-(I - A)\,S$		$-I^{n1}$	$+I^{n1}$	Q_3			$\leq$		P_3
	$\hat{K}$					$-I$		$\leq$		RN_3
	$-I$					$-(I - \hat{DP})$	$+I$	$\leq$		U_3
	L_3°							$\leq$	$\bar{L}_3$	U_3
	$PW_3\,\hat{S}_3$	PW_3	$-PW_3$					$\leq$	$\bar{F}_3$	SR_3
				$\left(\dfrac{1}{1+\rho}\right)^3$			$\bar{U}_4$			

ters over time. Projections of prospective changes in the terms of trade, in the structure of consumption, and in the productivity of labor should form an integral part of the planning exercise. In principle, of course, all other parameters could also be changing over time. Most often they are assumed constant.

Once the model is expressed in tableau format, its solution becomes routine. By starting from an initial basic feasible solution, the simplex algorithm progressively achieves higher and higher values for the objective function by moving from extreme point (feasible basic solution) to extreme point of the feasible set until finally an optimal solution is achieved. Thanks to linearity of both the constraint equations and the objective functions, only extreme points need be examined for optimality. The optimal solution will yield the combination of primal activities that maximizes the objective function. It will also lead to "optimal" values for each of the dual multipliers attached to the rows of our problem. We now turn to a discussion of these multipliers.

3.3 Shadow prices in linear programming models

The existence of "shadow multipliers" that accompany the optimal solution of a constrained optimization problem is one of the most fundamental results of advanced optimization theory. Linear programming constitutes a special case of the general constrained optimization problem, and the dual variables are a special case of the class of multipliers that accompany optimal solutions in general. As a general rule, it may be stated that these shadow multipliers measure the "importance" of the constraint to which they are attached.

We shall not dwell on the mathematical theory of constrained optimization or on the existence proofs. The interested reader is referred to the vast literature on the subject (see Kuhn and Tucker, 1956; Karlin, 1959; Gale, 1960; Hadley, 1962). We shall simply restate some of the central theorems and discuss them insofar as they are important for an understanding of the shadow price system generated by dynamic linear programming models.

Consider the following pair of linear programs:

$$\text{Max } f(X) = \alpha X \qquad MX \leq B \qquad X \geq 0 \qquad \text{(primal)} \qquad (3.3.1)$$
$$\text{Min } g(\lambda) = \lambda B \qquad \lambda M \geq \alpha \qquad \lambda \geq 0 \qquad \text{(dual)} \qquad (3.3.2)$$

The duality theorem states that for a vector X^*, feasible for the primal, to be optimal, it is necessary and sufficient that there exists a feasible dual vector λ^* such that

$$\lambda^*(MX^* - B) = 0 \qquad (3.3.3)$$
$$(\lambda^*M - \alpha) X^* = 0 \qquad (3.3.4)$$

λ^* will also be the optimal vector for the dual. Equations (3.3.3) and (3.3.4) together constitute the complementary slackness conditions. They can be decomposed into the following conditions:

$$\lambda_i^* > 0 \Rightarrow \sum_{j=1}^{n} M_{ij}X_j^* - B_i = 0 \qquad (3.3.5)$$

$$\sum_{j=1}^{n} M_{ij}X_j^* - B_i > 0 \Rightarrow \lambda_i^* = 0 \qquad (3.3.6)$$

$$X_j^* > 0 \Rightarrow \sum_{i=1}^{n} \lambda_i^*M_{ij} - \alpha_j = 0 \qquad (3.3.7)$$

$$\sum_{i} \lambda_i^*M_{ij} - \alpha_j > 0 \Rightarrow X_j^* = 0 \qquad (3.3.8)$$

The duality theorem states that whenever a constraint in one of the problems is not binding (i.e., carries the $<$ or $>$ sign at optimum), the corresponding variable in the dual problem has a zero value. Thus, when the dual multiplier of a row in a linear program is zero at the optimum, the constraint embodied in that row is not really binding: It could be taken out of the problem without affecting either the value of the objective function or the optimal mix of activities. If, for instance, the available supply of labor of a given skill category cannot be used, the corresponding labor constraint is not binding. If the supply of that category of labor were increased by a small amount, it would also remain unused, and would therefore not lead to an improvement in the value of the objective function. Likewise, if a small amount of labor of that skill category were taken away from the economy, it still would not affect the objective function or optimal solution, because that labor had been unused to start with.[10]

In general, when the columns of the M matrix can be interpreted as representing the input requirement vectors of productive activities, the B vector can be interpreted as representing fixed input supplies, and the α vector as objective value weights, the duality theorem naturally leads to interpretation of the dual multipliers as input "prices." Equation (3.3.5) then states that only fully used inputs can carry positive prices, whereas (3.3.7) states that only activities that do not make a loss would actually be run at positive levels.

It can also be shown that, provided that the set of activities selected at optimum is not changed by an increment in one of the elements of the B vector, the following equality holds:

$$\frac{\Delta f^*(x)}{\Delta B_i} = \lambda_i^* \tag{3.3.9}$$

where ΔB_i represents a small increase in the availability of input i. This leads to a small increase in the value of the objective function given by $\Delta f^*(x)$. The ratio of $\Delta f^*(x)$ to Δb_i is thus the marginal value productivity of input i and is equal to the shadow price λ_i of the input in question. It is therefore natural to think of the dual multipliers as sharing many of the properties of competitive equilibrium prices. Similar to the latter, they are signals of relative scarcity that can be extremely helpful to planners' decision making. But, as we shall argue extensively, the fact that the dual multipliers share the "marginal productivity" content of competitive equilibrium prices should not automatically be taken to imply that they also share all other properties of equilibrium prices.

Returning to the basic dynamic planning model introduced in Section 3.2, it gives rise to a set of optimal dual multipliers, one for each row, and the relations between these dual variables and the variables of the primal obey the complementary slackness conditions of the duality theorem. Below we discuss, one by one, the dual constraint system of the form $\lambda M \geq \alpha$ given in Table 3.1. The names of the dual variables are given in the last column.

[10] See Bruno (1966) for a programming model with several skill categories. Also see his discussion of how to overcome inflexibilities in such a model.

Cost equations (columns X_t)

$$P_t(I - A) + RN_t\hat{K} + \hat{W}_tL_t \geq 0 \qquad (3.3.10)$$

or

$$P_tA + RN_t\hat{K} + \hat{W}_tL \geq P_t$$

For any one equation i, we have

$$\sum_{i=1}^{n} P_{it}a_{ij} \quad + RN_{it}K_i + \sum_{s=1}^{n} W_{st}l_{ist} \geq P_{jt}$$

Intermediate	+ capital	+ labor	$\geq$ unit price
costs	costs	costs	

Thus P_{it} can be interpreted as commodity prices, RN_{it} as capital rentals, and W_{st} as wages for the various categories of labor. The duality theorem ensures that production costs will exactly equal prices for all goods that are actually produced. Whenever the strict inequality holds, the corresponding goods will simply not be produced. The shadow prices can thus be interpreted as competitive output and input prices.

The price of capital goods (columns Y_t)

$$P_tS - U_t + SR_tPW_iS_t^o \geq 0 \qquad (3.3.11)$$

Taking any one of the equations, we have

$$\sum_{i=1}^{n} P_{it}S_{ij} + SR_tPW_{it}S_{it}^o \geq U_{jt}$$

Production cost	$\geq$ market value
of capital goods	of capital goods

These equations are simple aggregation equations. Capital stocks are composite commodities, and their production costs simply reflect the prices of the individual components weighted by the shares of these components. Whenever the cost of assembling capital exceeds its market value, no capital accumulation will take place.

Tradable commodity price equations (columns M_t and E_t)

$$-P_t^{n_1} + SR_tPW_t \geq 0 \qquad (3.3.12)$$
$$P_t^{n_1} - SR_tPW_t \geq 0 \qquad (3.3.13)$$

Taking any one of the equations for tradable commodities, Eqs. (3.3.12) and (3.3.13) together imply ($i = 1, n_1$)

$$P_{it} = SR_t PW_{it}$$
Domestic = shadow price of foreign   (3.3.14)
price   exchange times world price

For tradable commodities, relative domestic shadow prices are thus entirely determined by relative world prices. Domestic relative prices are fixed and equal. This equality reflects the "efficiency" of the optimal solution. Efficiency requires the equalization of domestic and foreign marginal transformation rates except when goods are not produced domestically. Any difference between the rates of transformation through trade given by the world price ratios and the domestic transformation ratios given by the ratios of domestic prices would imply an inefficient allocation of resources and thus would certainly be suboptimal. The equality between relative domestic shadow prices and world prices simply reflects this efficiency requirement.[11]

Value composition equation (columns C_t)

$$P_t Q_t \geq \left(\frac{1}{1 + \rho} \right)^t \tag{3.3.15}$$

For any one of these equations, we have

$$\sum_{i=1}^{n} P_{it} q_{it} \geq \left(\frac{1}{1 + \rho} \right)^t$$

These equations can be thought of as normalization equations determining the price "level," defined to be a weighted average of the individual prices, the weights being given by the consumption shares. Assuming positive consumption shares every year, the equality will hold strictly. In every year the price level will be equal to the weight aggregate consumption has in the intertemporal objective function. Because this weight is declining over time due to a positive discount rate ρ, the price level will also be declining at the same rate. For two adjacent periods, t and $t + 1$, we shall have

[11] Note, furthermore, that if all goods are tradable, the *level* of domestic prices is determined entirely by the value of SR_t. As we shall show, in a model containing only tradables, the shadow exchange rate is not really a relative price but simply a conversion factor from foreign exchange units to domestic commodity units.

$$\frac{\sum_{i=1}^{n} P_{it}q_{it}}{\sum_{i=1}^{n} P_{it}q_{it}} = \frac{[1/1 + \rho]^{t}}{[1/1 + \rho]^{t+1}} = 1 + \rho$$

It is interesting to note that in a model where all commodities are tradable and where imports, domestic goods, and exports are perfect substitutes in any particular sector, changing $\bar{F}_{t}$ will *not* affect the value of SR_{t}. It is easy to see this if one remembers that $SR_{t} = \Delta f^{*}(X_{t})/\Delta F_{t}$.

First note that the shadow price SR_{t} can never be zero because it is always possible to use foreign resources to purchase goods from abroad and consume them in the required ratio. SR_{t} is always positive and describes how foreign resources can be converted into domestic utility. Given world prices and a particular domestic utility scale, the ratio $\Delta f_{t}^{*}/\Delta F_{t}$ is determinate and independent of what else goes on in the system and in particular independent of the initial value of F_{t}. The value of an additional dollar is always at least equal to the utility of the goods that can be purchased with it at fixed prices. Could it, however, be greater than that utility? The answer in our simple model is negative, because if it were, it would pay to restrict imports or expand exports until the equality is reestablished. Because in our simple model there are no constraints preventing such a reallocation, the equality will always hold. This underlines the nature of the exchange rate in a model where all commodities are fully tradable and world prices are fixed: It simply reflects the scale of the utility function. The situation is more complicated if there are upper bounds on exports or if the objective function is nonlinear and there are nontradable commodities. With nontradables, the shadow price of foreign exchange will reflect the relative scarcity of tradables with respect to nontradables. If, moreover, there are exogenous constraints on exports, the small-country assumption breaks down and the domestic shadow price system is no longer a simple reflection of world prices.

Assuming for the moment that all goods are tradable, that world prices are constant, and that consumption shares do not vary with time, we could write

$$\frac{\sum_{i=1}^{n} SR_{t}PW_{it}q_{i}}{\sum_{i=1}^{n} SR_{t+1}PW_{it+1}q_{i}} = \frac{SR_{t}\left(\sum_{i=1}^{n} PW_{it}q_{i}\right)}{SR_{t+1}\left(\sum_{i=1}^{n} PW_{it}q_{i}\right)} = 1 + \rho$$

and therefore

$$SR_t = (1 + \rho)SR_{t+1} \qquad (3.3.16)$$
$$P_{it} = (1 + \rho)P_{it+1} \qquad (3.3.17)$$

and for new capital goods that are actually being produced,

$$U_{it} = (1 + \rho)U_{it+1} \qquad (3.3.18)$$

Thus, under the assumptions made, all prices would actually be falling at an identical rate ρ equal to the rate of time preference exogenously given to the model.

The story is usually not quite as simple, because not all goods are tradable, parameters change, and in some sectors there will be no new investment. Nevertheless, the fundamental value theory embodied in the shadow prices of linear programs and the role played by the discount rate is well illustrated by these equations.

Profit rate equations (columns K_i)

$$U_t - RN_{t+1} - (I - \hat{DP})U_{t+1} \geq 0 \qquad (3.3.19)$$

It can safely be assumed that capital stocks will never be zero, so the equality holds strictly. Taking any one of the equations in (3.3.19) and dividing by $U_{it} + 1$, we get

$$\frac{U_{it} - U_{it+1}}{U_{it+1}} = \frac{Q_{it} - dp_i U_{it+1}}{U_{it+1}} \qquad (3.3.20)$$

The numerator in (3.3.20) can be interpreted as the rental value of a unit of capital net of depreciation. The rental rate is RN_{it}, but the owner must deduct from this rent the depreciation loss suffered, $dp_i U_{it+1}$. From (3.3.18) we have $U_{it} = (1 + \rho)U_{it+1}$. Replacing this into (3.3.20), we get

$$\frac{(1 + \rho)U_{it+1} - U_{it+1}}{U_{it+1}} = \rho \qquad (3.3.21)$$

Therefore, we may write

$$\rho = \frac{RN_{it} - d_i U_{it+1}}{U_{it+1}} = \frac{\text{profit}}{\text{value of investment}} = R_i \qquad (3.3.22)$$

where R_i is the profit rate, the "per-unit" return on capital in sector i.

We see that under our assumptions prices are falling at the rate ρ and the profit rates in every sector are equated to this common rate of decline in the price level. If we let world prices change and if the consumption shares do not remain constant over time, the story loses some of its simplicity. Relative prices may now change, and although the price level will still decline at a constant rate, the individual shadow prices will not necessarily all decline at the same rate. But the fundamental trends and relationships remain.

Shadow prices and "market" prices

The shadow price system emerging from a dynamic linear programming model shares many of the properties of an intertemporal competitive equilibrium price system à la Malinvaud-Debreu. In general equilibrium theory, the speed of the decline of "prices" is determined by the interaction of productivity and thrift. The prices we refer to are "present-value" prices, prices that describe what must be paid today for delivery of a good in some future time period in a world of no uncertainty and perfect futures markets. They are, just like the shadow prices of linear programming, measuring marginal intertemporal transformation rates between commodities. But because in our model we have a constant, fixed discount rate with no diminishing returns in the intertemporal utility function, it is the productive sphere of the economy that must adjust until the return on investment equals the constant rate of time preference. In the dynamic LP model, it is "thrift" alone that determines the profit rate, with productivity adjusting to the exogenously set ρ. This unidirectional causation is, of course, due to the rigid linearity in the objective function and could be altered by building diminishing returns into the objective function. From this discussion, it is obvious that increasing ρ will increase the implicit profit rate. In order to be undertaken, investment will have to be "more profitable." With labor and other complementary factors fixed, this will in general lead to less investment than would have been optimal with a lower ρ.

There is, however, a more important difference between the shadow price system emerging from a dynamic linear program and competitive equilibrium prices. Equilibrium prices are prices at which the demand and supply decisions of many independent economic actors maximizing their profits and utilities given initial endowments are reconciled. A major requirement for an equilibrium price system is that each actor remains within a budget constraint. Input prices must be such that the incomes generated by these factor prices lead to a vector of commodity demand that exactly matches the vector of commodity supply. It is true that the total value of inputs in our linear programming problem will equal the total value of final output (i.e., consumption plus terminal capital stocks), because the duality theorem ensures that the objective function of the dual will equal, at optimum, the objective function of the primal. Thus an *overall* budget constraint is satisfied. Nothing guarantees, however, that the budget constraints of the individual actors or groups of actors in the economy are satisfied. The essence of the general equilibrium problem is the reconciliation of maximizing decisions made separately and independently by various actors in an economic system. This essential problem is absent from the standard linear programming exercise, where the central planner is the only maximizing actor.

Another related problem arises when one attempts to go from the shadow prices of a linear programming model to the market-clearing prices of general equilibrium theory. The latter can accommodate all kinds of distortions, such as taxes and tariffs or monopolistically fixed factor prices. Assume, for example, that there are *ad valorem* taxes in the system. Because the dual price system is not known except as a by-product of the solution of the primal problem, it is not possible to incorporate such taxes into the primal equation system. To do so would necessitate the introduction of endogenous price variables into the primal system that would have to be multiplied by the endogenous quantity variables, and that would destroy the linearity of the system. It is this inability to multiply price times quantity in the constraint set that constitutes the fundamental difficulty for attempts at using linear programming models to simulate the decentralized market mechanism.

The preceding discussion should not be taken to imply that one cannot transform the standard linear programming approach to approximate more closely the workings of decentralized markets. The basic difficulty that must be overcome is that the shadow prices that determine income, and that should therefore influence behavior, have no feedback effect on the "primal" prices, which are taken as given in the objective function. This kind of feedback, so essential to general equilibrium theory, is absent from the standard linear programming approach. It is possible, however, to build such a feedback into linear programming by formally iterating between the shadow price system and the primal weights in the objective function until additional nonlinear behavioral constraints are satisfied.[12] The problem with this approach is that the convergence of the iterations constitutes an important computational

---

[12] See, for example, Dixon (1975), Ginsburgh and Waelbroeck (1980), and Manne, Chao, and Wilson (1978). For a more general discussion of decentralized planning, see Heal (1973).

problem requiring nonlinear solution techniques. Thus the chief attraction of linear programming, routine numerical solution, disappears. Given that the ability to use routine linear solution methods is lost, it is not clear why linearity should be preserved on the production side of the model. It can, of course, be preserved, and we shall argue in Chapter 5 that it is always possible to embed a linear programming model of production in a nonlinear general equilibrium model of an economy. But the model taken as a whole then ceases to be a linear programming model.

3.4   Comparative advantage and trade policy in linear programming models

Comparative advantage and the direction of trade

It is easy to see that the trade activity columns M_{it} and E_{it} greatly extend the feasible set and therefore the amount of endogenous choice possible in a linear programming model. An optimal solution is always a basic feasible solution or extreme point of the feasible set. The trade activities increase the dimensionality of the primal problem and the number of possible basic solutions. Note, however, that for any given i and t, non-zero E_{it} and M_{it} cannot both be part of the same basic solution. The activity coefficients of one are the negative of the other, and the resulting basis would have linearly dependent columns. This reflects the fact that two-way trade does not make sense in our model. Because the commodity imported and the commodity exported are identical, exporting ten units of a commodity and importing five units of the same commodity is equivalent to exporting five and importing none. It is only the latter kind of solution that the linear programming model will ever generate. One is, of course, free to think of trading activities as net imports and exports, but given the underlying assumption of perfect substitutability in use, there is never any reason for two-way trade in this kind of model.[13]

What determines the direction of trade? Let us for a moment think of our linear programming model as one of a closed economy. In that case the foreign trade activity columns, E_{it} and M_{it}, and the balance-of-payments constraint rows, SR_t, disappear from the tableau. This

---

[13] This same problem arises in all economic models that treat each particular category of goods as homogeneous and also ignore transport costs. Chapter 7 shows how one can accommodate two-way trade by relaxing the assumption of perfect homogeneity between domestically produced and foreign goods.

changes the relationship between the number of variables and the number of constraints: There will be fewer primal variables relative to primal constraints and more dual variables relative to dual constraints. In other words, closing the economy to foreign trade restricts choice in quantity space but frees the dual variables. Whereas production and investment activities become tightly constrained by existing capacities and consumption requirements, relative prices are no longer tied to exogenous world prices.

Let us denote the material balance shadow prices that would be associated with a closed-economy solution by P_{it}^C. If we now open the economy to trade by introducing the exogenous world prices, PW_{it}, and denote the shadow price of foreign exchange by SR_t, there are, for any sector and any time period, three possibilities:

1. $P_{it}^C > SR_t PW_{it}$
2. $P_{it}^C < SR_t PW_{it}$
3. $P_{it}^C = SR_t PW_{it}$

In case 1, the pretrade domestic price is greater than the world price converted into a domestic price by the shadow exchange rate. When the economy is opened to trade, the production of commodity i in period t must fall until $P_{it} = SR_t PW_{it}$ [see Eq. (3.3.14)]. If it is not possible to reduce domestic production costs to the level of world prices, the commodity in question will not be produced at all.[14]

The opposite will occur in case 2, where the pretrade domestic price is lower than the world price. Production will expand until domestic costs rise to the level of world prices. Note that, contrary to case 1, the strict inequality cannot persist at the optimum solution. When a commodity is actually produced, the domestic price will always equal the world price. If this equality is not satisfied, it would pay to expand domestic production for exports, and if it is no longer possible to move additional resources into such an activity, then the existing resources will derive their shadow value from the value of a marginal unit of exports.

The last case (3) refers to the possibility of equality between pretrade and post-trade shadow prices. In this special case domestic production would neither expand nor contract as a consequence of trade.

Figure 3.1 illustrates the mechanisms at work in the case of a simple two-sector, one-period model with no intermediate inputs and no exog-

---

[14] Note, however, that as one moves away from the zero trade situation in one market, the direction of inequality may change from the initial situation for some other goods.

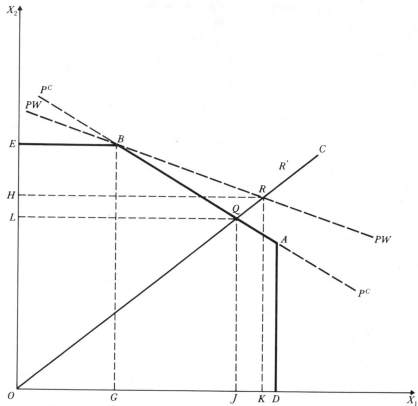

Figure 3.1. Production and trade in a simple linear programming model.

enous flow of foreign resources. The feasible set is given by $OEBAD$, where OD is capacity in sector 1, OE is capacity in sector 2, and the line BA reflects an economy-wide labor constraint. OC is the fixed proportions domestic consumption ray that cuts the boundary of the feasible set at Q on the segment BA. Note that in this simple example the slope of the domestic shadow price line will coincide with the slope of the labor constraint line BA. There will be excess capacity in both sectors, leading to zero rental values, and production costs in both sectors will consist of labor costs only. Domestic prices will be labor value prices, and production and consumption will take place at point Q.

When we open this economy to trade, a world price line $PWPW$ appears extending the feasible consumption set facing our economy to the entire triangle lying below the world price line. Production will now be at point B and consumption will be at point R, well above Q, and relative domestic shadow prices will coincide with world prices. Production of X_2 expands with labor moving out of sector 1 into sector 2 until the capacity limit given by the fixed installed capital stock is reached in sector 2. Note that at that point the marginal productivity of labor is determined entirely by the world price of the first commodity. With sector 2 producing at the limit of its capacity, an additional unit of labor would lead to a marginal increase of production in sector 1 alone. We have

$$P_1 = Wl_1 = SR \, PW_1 \quad \text{and} \quad P_2 = RN_2 k_2 + Wl_2 = SR \, PW_2 \qquad (3.4.1)$$

because $RN_2 = 0$. Remembering that $W^C l_2 / W^C l_1 = P_2^C / P_1^C$, we can summarize the situation as follows:

$$\frac{P_2^C}{P_1^C} = \frac{l_2}{l_1} < \frac{PW_2}{PW_1} = \frac{RN_2 k_2 + Wl_2}{Wl_1} = \frac{P_2}{P_1} \qquad (3.4.2)$$

Our simple economy has a *comparative* advantage in sector 2 in the sense that the pretrade *ratio* of sector 2 costs to sector 1 costs is lower than the world price ratio. As a result, trade leads to an expansion of production in sector 2 from OL to OE (LE) and to exports from this sector given by EH. The difference between OH and EH, OH, is consumed at home. On the other hand, production in sector 1 contracts from OJ to OG. The (negative) difference between domestic production OG and domestic consumption OK (GK), is imported from abroad in exchange for exports LE. The terms of trade LE/GK reflect the world price ratio as given by the slope of $PWPW$. Introducing an exogenous flow of net foreign resources would generate a parallel outward shift of the world price or budget line, not otherwise altering the picture, but allowing consumption at a point such as R' rather than at R.

The basic mechanisms determining the direction of trade remain unaltered when we go from the simple two-sector static model illustrated in Figure 3.1 to a multisector, multiperiod model with nontradables and intermediate goods. We can still start by visualizing a closed-economy model with associated shadow price P_{it}^C. The direction of trade will be determined as before by the relationship of P_{it}^C to PW_{it}. Although the basic mechanisms at work are the same, the introduction of a great number of tradable sectors does create some problems for linear programming models because the basic linearity of the model will lead to extreme specialization and corner solutions. This tendency would be quite explicit if, instead of having sector-specific capacity constraints, we were to treat capital as mobile across sectors. In that case, resources could be shifted to the lowest-cost sectors and output expanded without hitting the rigid ceiling given by sectorally fixed capital stocks. As a result, fewer commodities would be produced but in greater quantities, and more would be exported and imported. As Samuelson (1953) has shown, when factors are mobile across sectors and there are constant returns to scale, the number of commodities produced at home will not exceed the number of factors constraining economy-wide production. Because world prices are given and equality is required among world prices, domestic prices, and production costs, there is for each commodity produced a price-equals-cost equation where price is given and cost is determined by, in our case, fixed input coefficients and the shadow prices of factors. If there are m factors and n commodities with $n > m$, we would have n linear equations in only m unknown factor prices and the system would therefore be overdetermined. With only m of the n commodities actually produced, we can drop the $n-m$ other equations for those sectors where production cost would exceed price. We thus are back to a consistent system with only as many goods produced as there are endogenous factor prices.

In the model we have described, capital is sectorally fixed so that each sector has a sector-specific scarce factor with its "own" shadow price reflecting the constraining effects of installed capacity. But new investment can move to any sector, so there is a more subtle, dynamic tendency to specialize in multisector linear programming models. Incremental capacity will be built in sectors where it is least costly relative to the benefit of doing so as determined by the fixed world price of output. The principle is clearly valid, but what the linear specification neglects is the likelihood of gradually increasing costs of new capacity installation. Furthermore, as we shall discuss in great detail in later chapters, the notion of perfect substitutability between domestic and foreign goods, on which the whole formulation rests, is itself questionable.[15]

Turning our attention from the number of sectors to the number of periods, it must be realized that it is perfectly possible for $P_{it}^C > PW_{it}$ for some time periods and $P_{it}^C < PW_{it}$ for others. In a multiperiod linear programming model the notion of comparative advantage gains a dynamic dimension, and the model will generate a pattern of investment and trade that fits the underlying shifts in comparative advantage and resource availabilities. In particular, the investment criteria implicit in a dynamic linear programming model will not be the simplistic rules suggested by static comparative advantage notions. For example, if the

---

[15] Note that this latter problem is quite independent and distinct, in itself, from the problems associated with a fixed-coefficients, linear technology.

terms of trade are expected to move against textiles and clothing and in favor of machinery and metal products, the model will start building capacity in these sectors early in the plan period, at a time when the static configuration of prices may not warrant such investment. The model will compare, on the margin, the cost of foregoing consumption and/or investment early in the plan period to the benefit of greater consumption and/or investment later in the plan period.[16] The magnitude of the discount rate will therefore have a very important impact on how far resource allocation and investment will deviate from the rules of static comparative advantage. It must be stressed, however, that the dynamic allocation rules implicit in an optimizing multiperiod model still require that any activity undertaken break even when evaluated in the associated shadow prices. No activity will run at a loss in any period and then show positive profits in future periods. The solution shadow prices will anticipate and reflect the underlying shifts in comparative advantage and, just as would be the case with perfect futures markets, the changes in world prices, technology, or tastes that are foreseen in the future will determine the shadow prices of the present.

It is clear that the optimality of the resulting production and investment pattern depends on the accuracy of the world price and technology parameter forecasts that are given to the model exogenously. Dynamic allocation rules are superior to static allocation rules only if the forecasts on which they must be based have a fair degree of accuracy. Nevertheless, it is important to stress that multiperiod linear programming models are not tied to purely static notions of allocation but can be used to analyze the impact of dynamic changes in world prices and resource availabilities on optimal patterns of investment and trade.

Trade policy in a linear programming framework

So far we have repeatedly stressed the requirement of equality between relative domestic and world prices and have shown how the dual equations would enforce this equality for the model presented. In an economy with tariffs, however, it is clear that the existing tariff-ridden market prices will not be proportional to world prices but will reflect the structure of tariffs. In the market, we shall have

$$P_i = (1 + tm_i)PW_iSR \tag{3.4.3}$$

[16] Westphal (1971) provides a good example of this kind of behavior in an integer programming model that captures economies of scale as well as problems of investment timing.

where tm_i is the *ad valorem* tariff rate, instead of $P_i = PW_iSR$, as given by (3.3.14).

This difference provides a very good example of why one must be careful when interpreting shadow prices as market prices. In an economy with tariffs, for that reason alone, market prices will differ from the shadow prices generated by our linear programming model.

Could one not alter the model so as to incorporate tariffs in the shadow price system? For example, if we define tariff-augmented world prices $PW'_i = PW_i(1 + tm_i)$ and use them in lieu of PW_i, we get

$$P_i = PW'_iSR = (1 + tm_i)PW_iSR$$

and the domestic shadow prices would reflect the existing tariff structure. But if we used PW' instead of PW, we would imply, in the balance-of-payments equation, that the country actually trades at PW' prices instead of the correct world prices PW. The balance-of-payments constraint would no longer reflect the conditions prevailing on world markets. Thus, by forcing shadow prices to equal market prices, we transform the feasible set characterizing the economy to an artificial one that does not reflect actual constraints as they exist in reality. This kind of contradiction between market prices and shadow prices is not easily bridged, although there are various more-or-less cumbersome devices by which an imperfect compromise can be achieved.[17]

If the analysis of optimal and efficient solutions is our only objective, the fact that shadow prices do not equal market prices may not be too disturbing. But whenever linear programming models are used to analyze the actual workings of market economies where behavior is responsive to the tariff-ridden and otherwise imperfect market prices, great difficulties arise. It is not possible, for example, to use the linear programming model outlined above in a consistent fashion to explore the effects of alternative tariff structures on resource allocation and growth in an economy. All we can say is that the dual shadow prices are appropriate indicators of scarcity given the chosen objective function, world prices, and the technological and resource constraints specified in the economy. Although the dual solution may yield important insights into the underlying structure of comparative advantage and its evolution over time, it cannot be used as a laboratory to test the effect of alternative trade and protection policies that work by altering relative market prices

[17] For example, while no solution has been found for *ad valorem* tariffs, it is possible to model specific tariffs by attaching a tariff payment activity to each import activity. For details see Evans (1972).

and the incentives affecting the behavior of decentralized economic agents.

3.5   The problem of terminal conditions

There has been a continuing interest in infinite horizon growth models in the theoretical literature.[18] Applied planning models, however, cannot easily accommodate an infinite horizon, if only for computational reasons. Also, to project such variables as technological coefficients or world prices decades into the future would not make much sense. Planning models therefore cover a limited number of years. This means that there is no explicit analysis of what is to happen after the terminal year of the plan. What links the post-terminal period to the period covered by the planning model is the amount and sectoral distribution of productive capacity generated by the investments undertaken. Just as the historically given initial capacities constrain production and consumption during the period explicitly analyzed by the model, the terminal capacity we leave for future years at the end of plan period will constrain what can be done after year T.

In our presentation so far, we dealt with this problem by attaching explicit and exogenous value weights to terminal-year capital stocks and by adding the "value" of terminal capital stock to the discounted sum of consumption in the objective function. Provided that the terminal-year value weights are accepted, this formulation allows the simplest and purest presentation of the dual equations and shadow prices. The analogy with an intertemporal market price system enjoying perfect foresight, notably regarding terminal-year prices, is as close as it can become in a linear programming framework. Unfortunately, neither planners nor markets enjoy perfect foresight, and the terminal-year capital stock prices, $\overline{U}_{T+1}$, are found to reflect a rather arbitrary judgment. For tradable capital goods, they can of course be set equal to projected world prices appropriately discounted. But for nontradables, we do not have this option.

Two general issues arise in the context of terminal-year weights. The first concerns the *level* of terminal-year prices. The higher these prices, the more weight terminal capital stock acquires in the objective function at the expense of consumption. We could, for example, set these terminal weights at so high a level that all efforts during the plan period

---

[18] See, for example, Chakravarty (1969). See also Taylor (1975) for a somewhat different discussion of many of the issues considered in this section.

would be devoted to building up the capital stock, with no consumption allowed at all. Thus it is the explicit or implicit weight accorded to terminal-year capital stock that determines, jointly with the discount rate applied to consumption, the balance between consumption and investment during the plan period.

An alternative and perhaps more practical way of ensuring an adequate terminal capital stock to be bequeathed to future generations is to require a certain minimum average annual growth in the base-year price-weighted sum of sectoral capital stocks. We would then take terminal capital stocks out of the objective function, but add the following constraint to the system:

$$\sum_{i=1}^{n} K_{it} \geq (1 + g_k)^{t-1} \sum_{i=1}^{n} K_{i1} \qquad t = 2, T \qquad (3.5.1)$$

This guarantees that the economy-wide capital stock will grow on average at least at the rage g_k measured in constant base-year prices. Investment will have to be sufficient to allow such growth, and the interests of future generations will be taken into account, with potential welfare in post-terminal periods depending on the magnitude of the target growth rate.

It is not only, however, the overall level of terminal capacity that must be considered. The sectoral distribution of capacity also matters and affects the feasibility of alternative growth paths in the post-terminal period. As already noted, for the tradable portions of capital stock, it is possible to derive relative terminal-year weights from the relative world prices that are projected for the terminal year. But this leaves open the question of relative weights to be accorded to the nontradable elements in sectoral capacities (buildings plus structures) and in particular the question relating to the relative price of tradables with respect to nontradables. One solution that has often been proposed is to define some kind of "turnpike" or steady-state growth path on which the economy is supposed to travel after the terminal year, and to impose the initial conditions necessary for this target path as terminal conditions of a linear programming model. The solution of the linear program would thus constitute an "optimal" transient path toward some kind of long-run equilibrium solution. It is possible, for example, to take the target equilibrium path of a dynamic input–output model defined and discussed in Section 2.3, and treat it as a long-run equilibrium path. We had

$$X^*(t) = RC(t) + R \sum_{k=1}^{\infty} (BR)^k \hat{G}^k C(t) \qquad (2.3.30)$$

where R was the Leontief inverse $(I - A)^{-1}$, B was the capital coefficients matrix, and $\hat{G}$ was a diagonal matrix of target growth rates of final demand. We stressed in our discussion of input–output models that nothing guaranteed the base-year feasibility of X_i^*. For base-year feasibility we would have to have

$$K(b) = \hat{K}X^*(b) \tag{3.5.2}$$

where $\hat{K}$ is the diagonal matrix of capital–output ratio and b refers to the base year of the target equilibrium path. Now instead of treating the initial year of the target equilibrium path as the first year of our plan, we could treat it, say, as year 5. But year 5 would also be the terminal year T of a linear programming model designed to get the economy from year 1 to year 5 in such a way that it maximizes consumption in the interim while generating exactly the amount of sectoral capacity needed to put it onto its target equilibrium path in period 5. We would have initial and terminal conditions of the form

$$K_{i1} = \overline{K}_{i1} \tag{3.5.3}$$
$$K_{i5} = k_i X_{i\,b}^* \tag{3.5.4}$$

where $\overline{K}_{i1}$ reflects, as usual, historically given current installed capacities, but K_{i5} is the capital stock derived from the base-year requirements of the target equilibrium path.

This way of handling the terminal conditions problem would be very attractive for a closed economy but, with trade, it is not really a good solution. As we saw in Chapter 2, to define a Stone-Almon target equilibrium path for an open economy, it is necessary to specify exogenous export growth rates and exogenous import coefficients. The terminal capital stocks that we would impose would therefore be dependent on these exogenous trade parameters and coefficients. This would seem to negate the whole purpose of dynamic linear programming models, which we saw to be the exploration of the structure and shifting pattern of comparative advantage. Linear programming models should help us find optimal export growth rates and import patterns. If we were to impose these on an LP model in the form of terminal conditions, we would fail to meet the challenge and would in fact transform the LP model into no more than a device to generate base-year feasibility for a dynamic input–output model.

A more useful and reasonable way to approach the terminal conditions problem is to admit that the future is essentially open ended and hard to predict, and hence that our confidence in the guidelines generated by a planning model diminishes as the planning horizon extends into the future. It may therefore be best to use terminal capital stock weights and set up a model with, for example, a ten- or fifteen-year horizon, but use only the first five years of the solution to generate a five-year plan. By ignoring periods close to the terminal year, we can reduce the necessarily arbitrary influence terminal conditions will always have on the solution path. Such a "rolling plan" approach, where only the solution for the first few years of a much longer-run plan is effectively used, constitutes probably the most reasonable though time-consuming solution to the terminal conditions problem. In that way, we let the model endogenously generate the optimal production and trade patterns that correspond to the exogenous information we are projecting, but we always stand ready to revise this information and do not trust the model's solution too far into an uncertain future. This approach is a good and robust prescription that holds not only for linear programming models, but for all planning models and, indeed, for rational behavior in general.

CHAPTER 4

Growth and structural change: an input–output analysis

4.1 Introduction

The basic interindustry model discussed in Chapter 2 provides the core around which much of the rest of the book is organized. In spite of its simplicity and at times awkward rigidity resulting from the use of fixed coefficients on both the demand and supply sides, the input–output model provides an indispensable framework highlighting the interdependence of the various productive sectors of an economy. The nature of this interdependence, and the sectoral structure of an economy, changes with development and rising per capita income. In this chapter, we focus on the nature of the structural transformation and its dependence on particular development strategies, using first the static and then the dynamic input–output model as our framework for analysis.

In their analysis of patterns of structural change in a sample of some 100 countries, Chenery and Syrquin (1975) classified universal development processes related to the level of income into three broad categories: accumulation processes (e.g., investment, education), demographic and distribution processes (demographic transition, income distribution, labor allocation), and resource allocation processes (e.g., structure of demand, production, and trade). Most of the processes describing the transition from a primary economy to an industrial one can be approximated by a logistic curve with asymptotes at low and high levels of income. For instance, the share of industry starts at around 10 percent of GDP at low levels of per-capita income, rises quickly in the middle range, and finally levels off at around 30 percent for income levels above $1,000 (in 1970 prices).

In addition to these universal processes, a particular country's development pattern is influenced by other factors such as market size and natural resources. In fact, it is the differences among countries, including differences in policy regimes, that make intercountry comparisons interesting for policy analysis. On the one hand, planners can gather information about what Kornai (1972) calls "international mainstreams" from average patterns of development derived from studying a large cross section of countries. See, for example, Chenery and Syrquin (1975). On the other hand, by a careful comparison of a small

91

selection of countries, the planner can explore the possible range of variation in structural change and its relation to the variety of initial conditions, institutional environments, and government policy regimes.

Of the broad processes we have mentioned, the input–output model is most useful for analyzing resource allocation and structural change. The two applications in this chapter focus on these issues. The first application is based on the static input–output model. By comparative statistics, it provides a decomposition of the changing demand patterns for a sample of eight countries and shows how structural change results from the interactions among the changing pattern of demand, technical change, and trade policies reflected in varying degrees of import substitution and export expansion.

The second application uses the dynamic input–output model developed in Section 2.3. It is a case study of Korea, one of the countries included in the first application. In comparison with other countries, Korea has achieved a significant rate of structural change led by a very large contribution of export expansion. With the dynamic input–output model, we investigate what would have been the likely consequences for Korea's economy, in terms of both capacity and structure, had it achieved a much lower rate of export expansion, that is, one similar to other comparable developing countries.

This second application introduces the first of a number of sets of counterfactual experiments presented in this book that illustrate how planning models can be used for policy analysis and formulation. Naturally, because the model underlying these experiments is extremely simple, the direct policy content of these experiments is rather limited, as there is no explicit consideration of the necessary policy instruments to carry out the counterfactual experiments. However, even such a simple model does capture some of the important forces at work in an interdependent economy, and the results show that there is much to be gained by working within a framework that imposes intersectoral consistency.

4.2   Sources of industrial growth and structural change: a cross-country comparison[1]

Different countries have followed different growth paths, determined partly by initial conditions and resource endowments, partly by government policies. Some have emphasized import substitution, others have successfully promoted exports. In some there appear to have been successive phases. To what extent can one generalize from past experience?

[1] The discussion in this section is based on Kubo and Robinson (1979).

How important have export expansion and import substitution been in the process of industrialization? What has been the role of changes in input–output coefficients? Are there lessons or guidelines to be derived from the past?

This first application shows how the static input–output model presented earlier can be used as a tool to disentangle the relative contributions to growth and structural change of different components of changes in final demand. In the application, we decompose changes in sectoral output into four sources: domestic demand growth, export expansion, import substitution, and change in input–output coefficients. Following a brief description of the methodology, we turn to an analysis of calculations of growth contributions in eight selected countries. These countries represent a wide range of initial conditions and development strategies. The decompositions help us describe some basic characteristics of the process of industrialization and allow some inferences in the relationship among industrial policies, changes in industrial structure, and economic performance.

Methodology

The original development of the decomposition methodology we shall describe is due to Chenery (1960) and Chenery, Shishido, and Watanabe (1962). Our presentation follows the extension by Syrquin (1976).

From Section 2.2, the material balance equations for the supply of and demand for domestically produced goods can be written as

$$X_i = d_i(F_i + V_i) + E_i \tag{4.2.1}$$

where (dropping the d superscripts)

X_i = domestic production in sector i
d_i = ratio of domestic demand for domestically produced goods to total domestic demand, as in Eq. (2.2.13)
F_i = final demand
V_i = intermediate demand
E_i = exports

In matrix notation, the material balance equation is given in Eq. (2.2.15). Repeating it here, without the superscripts,

$$X = (I - \hat{D}A)^{-1}(\hat{D}F + E) \tag{4.2.2}$$

where $\hat{D}$ is a diagonal matrix of the d_i ratios, A is the matrix of input–output coefficients, and X, F, and E are vectors. The matrix $\hat{D}A$ is the matrix of domestic goods input–output coefficients.

Denoting the change in a variable by Δ $[\Delta X = X(t + 1) - X(t)]$, the change in total domestic demand can be written (after some algebraic manipulation) as

$$\Delta X = R_1\hat{D}_1(\Delta F) \qquad \text{domestic demand expansion}$$
$$+ R_1(\Delta E) \qquad \text{export expansion}$$
$$+ R_1(\Delta \hat{D})(F_2 + V_2) \qquad \text{import substitution}$$
$$+ R_1\hat{D}_1(\Delta A)X_2 \qquad \text{change in input–output coefficients}$$

$$(4.2.3)$$

where $R_1 = (I - \hat{D}_1 A_1)^{-1}$ and the subscripts 1 and 2 refer to time periods. This equation gives the basic decomposition of the change in sectoral output into different sources (i.e., ΔF, ΔE, $\Delta \hat{D}$, and ΔA).

The first two terms on the right-hand side are the changes in gross output induced by expansion of domestic demand and exports. The third term measures the effects of import substitution on production, captured by the changes in domestic supply ratios. Finally, the last term shows the effect of changes in input–output coefficients, which represents widening and deepening of interindustry relationships over time brought about by the changing mix of intermediate inputs. It is caused by the changes in production technology as well as by substitution among various inputs (perhaps produced by changes in relative prices), although we cannot separate these two effects.

The above equation decomposes the first difference in output into various causal factors. It is of greater value than would be a direct decomposition based on Eq. (4.2.1), because it also explains the growth of intermediate demand, which would be left out in a direct decomposition. Because this equation decomposes the total change in output, it is referred to as the first difference formulation and is most suitable for identifying the major "engines" of sectoral growth. A second approach, called the deviation formulation, which decomposes the sources of sectoral deviations from balanced growth, is described later.

A few points are worth noting about the decomposition equation. First, import substitution is defined sectorally as arising from changes in the ratio of imports to total demand.[2] This specification implicitly assumes that imports are imperfect substitutes for domestic goods, because the source of supply constitutes an integral part of the economic structure. It differs conceptually from the treatment by Chenery et al. (1962), where imports are considered as perfect substitutes for domestic

---

[2] There is an extensive literature on the appropriate definition of import substitution in a multisector model. See, for example, Desai (1969), Eysenback (1969), Fane (1971, 1973), and Morley and Smith (1970).

goods and both are lumped together without distinction in final and intermediate demand and hence in the input–output material balance equation. As discussed in Section 2.2, our approach allows imports and domestically produced goods to be treated separately. Under the definition used here, the aggregate contribution of import substitution to growth is sensitive to the level of sectoral disaggregation. For example, it is possible to have positive import substitution in every sector but have the ratio of total imports to total demand increase because of changes in the sectoral composition of demand.

Second, note that the effect of changes in input–output coefficients includes changes in the total coefficients and does not separately distinguish between imported and domestically produced goods. Thus, the input–output coefficients may remain constant ($\Delta A_{ij} = 0$) and hence the last term in (4.2.3) will be zero even though there are changes in domestic supply ratios (which result in changes in DA or A^d). Changes in technology are defined as changes in the total coefficients, whereas any changes in the intermediate domestic supply ratios are included in the import substitution term.

Third, each term in the decomposition is multiplied by elements of the Leontief domestic inverse. It therefore captures both the direct and indirect impact of each causal factor on gross output, taking into account the linkages through induced intermediate demand.

Finally, note that there is an index number problem implicit in the decomposition equation because the decomposition can be defined either using the terminal-year structural coefficients and initial-year volume weights or using the initial-year structural coefficients and the terminal-year volume weights [as in (4.2.3)]. The two versions are analogous to Paasche and Laspeyres price indices. In the analysis that follows, both indices have been computed separately for the decomposition in each period and averages of the two are presented.

To analyze the causes of changes in the composition of output, it is useful to examine deviations from proportional growth. Define the deviation from proportional growth of output of sector i as $\delta X_i^2 = X_i^2 - \lambda X_i^1$, where λ is the ratio of total gross national product (GNP) in period 2 to GNP in period 1. After expressing the material balance equation in deviation form, one can explain the nonproportional growth in output in an analogous fashion to (4.2.3) as

$$
\begin{aligned}
\delta X = \ &R_1 \hat{D}_1\, \delta F & &\text{domestic demand expansion}\\
&+ R_1\, \delta E & &\text{export expansion}\\
&+ R_1\, \Delta\hat{D}(F_2 + V_2) & &\text{import substitution}\\
&+ R_1 \hat{D}_1\, \Delta AX_2 & &\text{change in input–output coefficients}
\end{aligned}
$$

$$(4.2.4)$$

In this formulation deviations (δ) replace increments (Δ), whereas the last two terms measuring import substitution and technological change are identical with (4.2.3). Note that because the sum of deviations from proportional demand growth is zero, the demand terms combine Engel and relative price effects. Moreover, because the magnitude of δX_i is usually much smaller than ΔX_i, and because the import substitution and technical change effects are the same, the relative importance of domestic demand in the deviation formulation is considerably lessened. This formulation is useful for explaining structural changes in production.

Analysis of growth and structural change[3]

We now turn to an examination of the pattern of growth and structural change in a group of eight countries: Korea, Taiwan, Japan, Turkey, Mexico, Norway, Colombia, and Israel. As can be seen from Table 4.1, the countries vary widely in size, income, and involvement in foreign trade. At one extreme, Israel and Norway, with populations in the 1950s of 2.0 million and 3.4 million, respectively, are the smallest countries in the group. Yet in the initial time period, their income per capita was already above $1,000 (US$ 1970), and they had undergone much of the structural transformations that accompany industrialization. At the other extreme in the group, Korea and Taiwan started out with incomes per capita of $131 and $203, respectively.

The group also shows a great deal of diversity in the area of foreign trade, with Norway maintaining a ratio of exports to GDP of around 40 percent and Turkey never exceeding 8 percent. It can also be seen from Table 4.1 that Turkey, Mexico, and Colombia had quite low ratios of manufacturing exports to GDP throughout the period, whereas Japan had steadily high ratios. Korea, Taiwan, Israel, and Norway had increasing shares of manufactured exports, with Korea and Taiwan showing the most dramatic change.

The great diversity in the group of countries presented here reflects a wide range of initial conditions relating to factor endowments, natural resources, internal market size, and policy-making environments. What,

---

[3] The results described here are based on an ongoing research project at the World Bank titled "A Comparative Study of the Sources of Industrial Growth and Structural Change" (RPO 671-32). The project members are Hollis Chenery, Yuji Kubo, Sherman Robinson, Moises Syrquin, and Larry Westphal. Individual country authors are Bela Balassa (Norway), Merih Celasun (Turkey), Mordechai Fraenkel (Israel), Kwang Suk Kim (Korea), Shirley Kuo (Taiwan), Jaime de Melo (Colombia), Moises Syrquin (Mexico), and Tsunehiko Watanabe and Yuji Kubo (Japan).

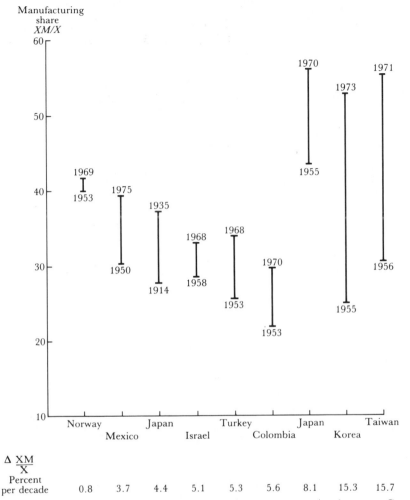

Figure 4.1. Structural change: manufacturing output/total output. Countries are arrayed in increasing order of the decadal change in the manufacturing share in total output, $\Delta(XM/X)$ per decade.

then, are the commonalities, or "mainstreams" within this diversity? What can we say about the rate at which, and the way in which, structural change takes place in this group of countries during the course of industrialization? To what extent have changes in foreign trade participation helped or hindered the effects of behavioral constraints in achieving the transformations that accompany industrialization?

Figure 4.1 ranks the eight countries by decadal rates of change in the ratio of manufacturing gross output (XM) to total output (X). For

Table 4.1. *Comparative economic indicators*

| | Population | | Per capita GNP | | Ratios (%) to GNP in current prices | | | | | |
	Number (million)	Average annual growth rate (%)	Level (US$, 1970)	Average annual growth rate (%)	Primary exports	Manufactured exports	Total exports[a]	Gross domestic investment	Primary value added	Manufacturing value added[b]
Korea										
1955	21.4	—	131	—	0.7	0.2	1.7	12.0	48.1	13.1
1963	27.0	2.8	149	1.6	1.3	1.2	4.8	18.6	46.8	16.9
1970	31.4	2.2	250	7.7	2.4	8.7	14.8	27.3	32.4	25.5
1973	32.9	1.6	323	8.9	4.1	24.3	31.7	26.0	28.8	29.7
Taiwan (ROC)										
1956	9.2	—	203	—	8.9	0.9	9.0	15.9	29.8	24.3
1961	11.0	3.6	231	2.6	6.0	5.1	12.8	19.8	29.3	25.4
1966	12.8	3.1	305	5.7	8.2	8.7	20.6	23.1	24.2	29.8
1971	14.8	2.9	426	6.9	6.0	24.6	36.8	26.1	14.8	39.3
Japan										
1955	89.0	—	500	—	1.3	9.1	10.7	24.7	25.0	26.5
1960	94.1	1.1	753	8.5	1.0	8.4	11.1	33.7	15.1	38.2
1965	98.8	1.0	1,159	9.0	0.5	8.9	10.8	32.9	10.7	37.9
1970	104.3	1.1	1,897	10.4	0.4	9.4	11.2	39.4	7.2	43.2

Turkey									
1953	22.8	—	239	6.9	0.3	7.8	12.4	51.1	12.1
1963	29.7	2.7	319	5.1	0.3	5.5	15.4	40.7	19.0
1968	33.5	2.4	377	4.1	0.3	5.3	18.0	32.3	24.4
1973	38.3	2.7	461	5.6	1.5	7.6	19.0	31.0	24.5
Mexico									
1950	26.3	—	380	n.a	n.a	14.1	13.5	20.3	24.6
1960	36.0	3.2	479	4.7	1.6	11.3	20.1	17.5	26.7
1970	50.4	3.4	670	2.1	1.6	8.1	19.6	12.7	30.9
Colombia									
1953	12.5	—	274	14.7	0.2	15.6	15.3	40.4	18.0
1966	18.4	3.0	330	8.6	1.0	12.1	20.4	32.4	22.4
1970	20.6	2.9	369	9.9	1.2	14.2	21.5	30.7	23.0
Israel									
1958	2.0	—	1,067	4.1	4.7	11.5	28.1	13.0	31.7
1965	2.6	3.6	1,587	4.4	10.6	18.9	28.1	8.2	36.3
1968	2.7	2.3	1,759	5.1	14.6	27.3	22.6	7.9	33.4
Norway									
1953	3.4	—	1,171	9.9	9.1	28.1	29.5	15.5	35.0
1961	3.6	0.9	2,028	6.4	12.3	29.7	31.1	9.9	32.6
1969	3.9	0.8	2,769	5.0	17.2	21.2	25.0	6.2	34.0

*Merchandise exports plus exports of nonfactor services.

*Includes construction.

Sources: (1) Comparative data compiled for "Patterns of Industrial Development," Research project, World Bank. (2) *World Tables 1976*, World Bank. (3) Background data for Chenery and Syrquin (1975).

instance, for Mexico, the share of manufacturing output in total output increased, on average, by 3.7 percentage points per decade. A glance at Figure 4.1 indicates clearly that in terms of both structure and rates of structural change, the eight countries fall into two very distinct groups: the Asian group and the rest. Thus Japan (in the period 1955–70), along with Korea and Taiwan, achieved both a much higher share of manufacturing output and a much higher rate of structural change than any other country in the group. It is remarkable indeed that the average decadal increase in the share of manufacturing output in the slowest changing country in this group, namely, Japan, was 8.1 percentage points, almost double the change in share of the fastest-changing country in the other group, Colombia (5.3 percentage points).[4]

Figure 4.1 also brings out a number of interesting additional features. First, Korea and Taiwan appear to be catching up in terms of structure with Japan. Both start at about the same time with a substantially lower share of manufacturing output, yet fifteen years later they have both managed to achieve virtually the same structure as Japan. In attempting to understand this remarkable achievement, one can only speculate about the relative role of universal factors such as access to a common technology and of the particular political and geographical position of these countries which, for example, enabled them to receive unusually high levels of foreign assistance per capita. Second, there is the difference between prewar and postwar Japan. Prewar Japan achieved a change in structure very similar to that achieved by Mexico in the postwar period. It is impossible to isolate the impact of the war and other special circumstances in explaining the difference in rates of structural change between the two periods. Finally, for most countries in both groups, the ones that have the lowest initial share of manufacturing in gross output achieve the greatest rates of structural change. Thus, in a sense, the "catching-up" phenomenon among the Asian group carries over to the other countries as well.[5]

The pattern of rapid expansion in manufacturing and relative decline in primary production is also reflected in Table 4.2 by the differential rates of output growth (column 1) as well as by the output deviations from balanced growth (column 2), which are expressed as percentages

---

[4] These rates are generally quite high. See Robinson (1972) for an econometric study of growth and aggregate structural change in a sample of thirty-nine developing countries.

[5] It is interesting to compare this general "catching-up" phenomenon with Gerschenkron's analysis of the role of relative backwardness in European economic history. See Gerschenkron (1952).

of the change in aggregate gross output.[6] Because the output deviations do not depend on currency units, the figures are comparable across countries. They confirm the results of Figure 4.1 and indicate that structural change in production proceeded most rapidly in Korea and Taiwan and least rapidly in Israel and Norway.

The decomposition methodology we have presented allows us to determine the contributing factors on the demand side to structural change for the group of countries. Keep in mind, however, that the observed final demand vectors in this simple interindustry model reflect both income effects (different elasticities) and shifts in relative prices. Thus, we are measuring ex post demands that are the result of the interaction of demand and supply factors.

The sources of differential output growth in the primary, manufacturing, and services sectors are reported in columns 3–6 of Table 4.2. The output deviations and their decomposition into separate sources are expressed as percentages of the change in aggregate gross output. The separate elements of the decomposition thus add up to column 2 for each sector. The results of the decomposition provide important insights about the underlying patterns of structural change, especially for the primary and manufacturing sectors.

In virtually all countries, the relative decline in primary production is caused mainly by the compositional shift of domestic demand, presumably due largely to the low income elasticity of demand for primary products and the high elasticity for most manufacturing products. Changes in input–output coefficients also reduce the demand for primary products in almost all countries and increase the demand for manufactured goods. The effects of changes in input–output coefficients are thus important and, together with changes in the composition of demand, account for more than 75 percent of the relative decline in primary production in all countries except Norway and Mexico (about 50 percent).

For the manufacturing sector, there is much greater variation among the eight countries. In Korea and Taiwan, the significant deviation of manufacturing output from balanced growth is due largely to the rapid expansion of exports, which accounts for more than 70 percent of the

---

[6] The decomposition has been applied using input–output tables for a number of years in each country. The tables for each country have been deflated so that the accounts are in comparable real terms for all periods within each country. The tables for all countries have been aggregated to a comparable twenty-four-sector level, and the decomposition methodology has been applied at that level in every country.

Table 4.2. *Sources of output deviation from balanced growth (% of change in aggregate gross output)*

	Average output growth rate (%)	Output deviation (%)	Sources of output deviation			
			Domestic demand expansion (%)	Export expansion (%)	Import substitution (%)	Changes in input–output coefficients (%)
Korea (1955–73)						
Primary	5.7	−11.3	−7.7	1.8	−2.3	−3.1
Manufacturing	15.8	27.5	4.7	21.1	1.4	0.2
Services	10.3	4.6	0.9	4.3	0.2	−0.7
Taiwan (1956–71)						
Primary	7.1	−7.6	−4.2	1.5	−2.7	−2.2
Manufacturing	16.2	28.2	0.7	20.1	3.5	3.9
Services	9.7	−2.0	−4.5	3.5	0.1	−1.2
Japan (1955–70)						
Primary	2.2	−7.6	−3.2	−0.2	−1.9	−2.4
Manufacturing	13.3	12.6	5.0	2.8	−1.2	5.9
Services	11.4	1.0	−1.0	1.2	−1.0	1.7
Turkey (1953–73)						
Primary	2.5	−18.1	−11.5	−2.1	0.2	−4.7
Manufacturing	8.1	17.2	4.6	4.5	2.4	5.8
Services	6.7	9.0	3.6	2.1	0.2	3.1

Mexico (1950–75)						
Primary	4.8	−5.8	−2.3	−2.6	−0.2	−0.7
Manufacturing	7.7	10.1	3.5	−0.2	4.3	2.5
Services	6.4	1.0	0.5	−0.5	0.6	0.5
Colombia (1953–70)						
Primary	4.5	−3.7	−7.9	3.8	0.3	0.1
Manufacturing	8.1	16.1	1.4	1.4	7.8	5.6
Services	5.5	1.9	−0.8	1.2	0.4	1.0
Israel (1958–68)						
Primary	6.8	−4.4	−4.7	1.0	0.0	−0.7
Manufacturing	12.3	6.8	−2.7	7.5	−0.6	2.5
Services	10.2	−3.2	0.2	4.9	−4.2	−4.1
Norway (1953–69)						
Primary	2.5	−4.7	−3.1	0.0	−2.0	0.4
Manufacturing	5.2	7.8	−1.6	12.6	−9.2	6.0
Services	4.8	6.2	−0.8	9.3	−3.1	0.8

Notes: Column 1 shows the average annual growth rates at sectoral gross output.
Sectoral output deviations and the sources of growth contributions are expressed as percentages of the change in aggregate gross output over all sectors during the specified period in each country.
For each subperiod, columns 3–6 add up to column 2.
Results for Mexico, Colombia, and Israel are preliminary.

deviation, with all other factors playing a minor role. Thus, the rapid structural change experienced in these two countries is attributable to their export-led, outward-looking industrial development strategies adopted since the early 1960s. Japan also adopted various export promotion schemes in the postwar period with fairly restrictive import controls. The fact that the export expansion effect was not as pronounced as in Korea and Taiwan is due to the much larger size of Japan's domestic market relative to exports, which also accounts for the importance of domestic demand expansion in its industrial growth.

In contrast, the manufacturing expansion in Colombia and Mexico depends very little on export expansion. Instead, import substitution played the most important role (about 45 percent) in the overall expansion of manufacturing production, which is reinforced by the effect of changes in input–output coefficients. Thus, the development experience in these countries reflects their import-substitution-oriented, inward-looking development strategies. Turkey, with the effects of import substitution and changes in input–output coefficients accounting for half the manufacturing output deviation, may be classified in this group, although import substitution played a more limited role than in the other two countries. It is not surprising to observe a sizable effect of changes in input–output coefficients in these countries, as import substitution often requires introduction of new technologies, although this is not specific to the countries that adopted an import-substitution strategy.

Finally, Norway and Israel, the two smallest and most developed countries in the sample at the outset, show a different pattern of manufacturing growth. On the one hand, both countries had achieved major structural transformation prior to the period under study.[7] On the other hand, with relatively small domestic markets, both countries pursued more open development strategies. For both countries, export expansion and changes in input–output coefficients more than offset the small domestic demand growth and increased dependence on imports reflected in negative import substitution. In particular, in Norway, rapid export expansion is associated with a significant increase in import dependence reflecting increased specialization and openness resulting from a liberal trade policy. In turn, as the main exports are manufactured products, the significant effect of changes in input–output coefficients for the man-

---

[7] For an interesting account of the significant amount of structural change undergone by Israel during the period 1948–51, see Pack (1971). His chapter 3 documents the compositional change of output in the economy using a similar decomposition methodology.

ufacturing sector can be viewed as reflecting technological changes required to meet international competition.

Two important observations emerge from this brief examination of the patterns of changes in output composition across countries. First, with regard to the primary sector, there is much uniformity across countries, reflecting the leading role of the universal factors mentioned earlier. Second, the great diversity of sources of structural change in the manufacturing sector indicate the importance of initial conditions and particular factors as well as the important role of development policy in altering the relative contribution of trade as a source of structural change. Therefore, it is useful to examine further the sources of growth within manufacturing.

Trade strategy and growth in the manufacturing sector

Although the analysis of structural change for the whole period in each country reveals different patterns of growth, particularly for manufacturing, it conceals a considerable variation in the relative importance of causal factors over time. In order to bring out this variation, we examine, period by period, the sources of growth in the manufacturing sector. For this purpose, we switch from the deviation formulation [Eq. (4.2.4)] to the first difference formulation [Eq. (4.2.3)], which is better suited to measure the relative contribution of the various factors to sectoral growth.

Table 4.3 presents the sources of growth in manufacturing production for the different periods, given the benchmark years determined by the availability of input–output tables. Columns 2–5 express the sources of growth contributions for the manufacturing sector as percentages of the change in total manufacturing output over the period.

As explained above, the contribution of domestic demand expansion increases when the contributions to growth are expressed in first difference form. Thus, in all countries, a large proportion of the increase in manufacturing output is induced by growth in domestic final demand. As one would expect, given the differences in the size of the domestic market, the relative contribution of domestic demand expansion is generally greater in large countries such as Japan, Turkey, and Mexico and smaller in Taiwan, Norway, and Israel. The existence of economies of scale in key manufacturing sectors such as chemicals implies that countries with small internal domestic markets must engage in relatively more international trade than larger countries in order to expand their effective market size.

Table 4.3. *Sources of change in manufacturing production*

	Average annual growth rate (%)	Sources (%)			
		Domestic demand expansion	Export expansion	Import substitution	Changes in IO coefficients
Korea					
1955–63	10.4	57.3	11.5	42.2	−11.0
1963–70	18.9	70.1	30.4	−0.6	0.1
1970–73	23.8	39.0	61.6	−2.5	1.8
Taiwan (ROC)					
1956–61	11.2	34.8	27.5	25.4	12.3
1961–66	16.6	49.2	44.5	1.7	4.6
1966–71	21.1	34.9	57.0	3.8	4.3
Japan					
1914–35	5.5	69.9	33.6	4.7	−8.2
1935–55	2.8	70.9	−7.1	15.5	20.7
1955–60	12.6	76.2	11.9	−3.4	15.2
1960–65	10.8	82.3	21.7	−0.3	−3.7
1965–70	16.5	74.2	17.6	−1.4	9.6
Turkey					
1953–63	6.4	81.0	2.2	9.1	7.7
1963–68	9.9	75.2	4.5	10.4	9.9
1968–73	9.7	68.2	21.0	−1.6	12.3
Mexico					
1950–60	7.0	71.8	3.0	10.9	14.4
1960–70	8.6	86.1	4.0	11.0	−1.0
1970–75	7.2	81.5	7.7	2.6	8.2
Colombia					
1953–66	8.3	60.3	6.8	22.1	10.8
1966–70	7.4	75.5	4.7	4.3	15.5
Israel					
1958–65	13.6	58.9	26.2	9.8	5.2
1965–68	9.4	68.7	54.8	−27.7	4.2
Norway					
1953–61	5.1	64.3	37.3	−15.9	14.4
1961–69	5.3	50.6	58.8	−19.4	10.0

Notes: Column 1 shows the average annual growth rates of total manufacturing gross output. The sources of growth contributions in columns 2–5 are expressed as percentages of the change in total gross manufacturing output, and add up to 100% except for rounding errors.

Results for Mexico and Israel are preliminary.

Beyond the difference in trade orientation dictated largely by the particular factors that account for different initial conditions between countries, Table 4.3 shows that in most countries there is a period that is marked by a sizable effect of import substitution on manufacturing output growth. In Korea and Taiwan, this period corresponded to their early phase of industrialization, from the mid-1950s to the early 1960s. In Japan, the period was dominated by postwar reconstruction. However, after these particular subperiods, import substitution was insignificant as a source of manufacturing output growth. In Turkey, Mexico, and Colombia, the import-substitution phase continued for an extended period of 13–20 years. Although the choice of benchmark years precludes exact estimates, the period from the early 1950s through the late 1960s was one of important import substitution in these countries. The importance of import substitution declined dramatically thereafter.

In the three Asian countries, the import-substitution period was followed by periods where export expansion became very important. In particular, in Korea and Taiwan, this factor alone accounted for more than half of the growth of manufacturing in the final subperiod and, in Japan, 18–22 percent between 1960 and 1970. The increased importance to manufacturing growth of export expansion in these countries reflects the shift in emphasis of their governments' trade and industrial policies away from encouraging domestic industries to import substitutes through restrictive import measures to promoting exports through various incentive policies. The important point to note is that these policies were very successful, as shown in the sources of growth decompositions. Behind these successes, however, there was a period of extensive import substitution and technological improvements through which domestic industries developed and strengthened international competitiveness. In fact, without this preparatory stage, the successful industrialization led by export expansion in these countries might not have been possible.

In Mexico and Colombia, the relative importance of exports to manufacturing growth did not increase much after the import-substitution phase. In Turkey, the export expansion effect accounted for 21 percent of the growth of manufacturing output between 1968 and 1973 (and 16.3 percent for total gross output), due mainly to the devaluation of its currency and favorable export market conditions during this period. The growth of manufacturing production in these countries, however, was generally much slower than that of the Asian countries during their export promoting phases. The failure of export expansion to contribute more to the growth of manufacturing may be attributed to the prolonged protection of domestic industries, which left them unable to compete in international markets, or to the absence of export incentives.

Norway and Israel show a different pattern from the above two groups. In these countries, export expansion played an important role in manufacturing output growth, but the dependence on imports increased substantially at the same time (except for 1958–65 in Israel). The sizable effect of the changes in input–output coefficients in these countries may reflect technological change in response to international competition. The significant effect of export expansion and the increased dependence on imports show that these countries were rapidly liberalizing trade and moving toward more open development strategies.

The particular trade strategy followed by a country is the outcome of a combination of several contributing elements reflected in the decomposition of final demand discussed above, including resource endowments, policy regimes, and external influences. Various combinations of these elements result in a particular trade strategy. The analysis of the contributions to growth by time periods allows us to develop a typology that can then be used to cluster countries into groupings according to the role of export expansion (EE) and of import substitution (IS) in accounting for total manufacturing growth. The resulting typology of trade strategies is reported in Table 4.4.

Table 4.4 divides up the sample of countries by time periods (indicated in parentheses) according to the percentage contribution of import substitution and export expansion to manufacturing growth. Import substitution is measured along the horizontal axis and export expansion along the vertical axis. As indicated in the table, within each cell, episodes are listed in increasing order of export expansion to growth.

What is remarkable, as we have seen earlier, is that both Korea and Taiwan managed to catch up in terms of production structure with the other countries in the sample. The clustering in Table 4.4 brings out clearly that these are also the countries that stand out in terms of the contribution of export expansion to growth in the manufacturing sector. However, Korea and Taiwan are also the only countries that had a period since 1950 where import substitution contributed well over a third of manufacturing growth. These countries are thus at both extremes of the spectrum ranging from import substitution to export expansion. Finally, note that there are three periods (for Israel and Norway) that could be termed significant "trade liberalization" or "foreign exchange constraint relaxation" episodes in the sense that export expansion was coupled with negative import substitution.

In addition to a clustering of countries according to the contribution of import substitution and export expansion to growth, it is also possible

Table 4.4. *Typology of trade strategies: the role of export expansion and import substitution in total manufacturing growth (countries and periods)*

Export expansion (%)	Import substitution (%)				
	−28 to −16	−6 to +6	6 to 12	22 to 42	Row sum
2 to 8		Col (2) Mex (3)	Tur (1) Mex (1) Mex (2) Tur (2)	Col (1)	7
12 to 28		Jap (2) Jap (4) Tur (3) Jap (3)	Isr (1)	Kor (1) Tai (1)	7
30 to 62	Nor (1) Isr (2) Nor (2)	Kor (2) Jap (1) Tai (2) Tai (3) Kor (3)			8
Column sum	3	11	5	3	22

Notes: Within column categories, episodes are listed in increasing order of the contribution of export expansion to growth. Numbers in parentheses refer to time periods, earliest first, as shown in Table 4.3.
Source: Table 4.3 (excludes Japan 1935–55).

to see from Table 4.4 whether export expansion has either preceded import substitution, or, on the contrary, succeeded the establishment of a domestic market, as would be argued by those who view sales on the domestic market as a prerequisite for successful exports of manufactures. It is apparent from Table 4.4 that import substitution has preceded export expansion in all countries in the sample for which domestic demand expansion alone was not the main contributing factor to manufacturing growth. Although these patterns partly reflect the change in attitude toward the appropriate role of trade policies for industrialization that evolved during the 1960s, they also lend support to the view that the experience gained from sales on the domestic market is a prerequisite for successful exports of manufactures.

To summarize, we observe that within the wide range of initial conditions represented by the group of eight countries, there is a combination of uniformity and diversity in the patterns of growth and structural change. On the one hand, there is regularity in the factors contributing to structural change in Agriculture (and to a lesser extent in Services). Structural change comes mainly from changes in domestic demand expansion due to the compositional shifts in demand associated with rising income. There is also some uniformity in the rates at which structural change takes place reflected in a general "catching-up" phenomenon as the latecomers manage to shift resources into manufacturing more rapidly. These trends would seem to represent the universal mainstreams.

On the other hand, there is also diversity reflecting the influence of a combination of different initial conditions (market size, resource endowments, etc.) and different government policies. Thus, we find that the range of variation between periods in the contribution to growth of import substitution and export expansion is great within manufacturing compared with the contribution of domestic demand expansion. This is the case both within and across countries, suggesting the important role of trade strategies in the process of industrialization. From the analysis of the typology of trade strategies, it appears that the countries that achieved the sequential combination of a large contribution to growth of import substitution followed by a large contribution of export expansion have achieved the highest rates of growth and structural change. One should, however, interpret these observations cautiously, because the sample of countries is small.

Korea, along with Taiwan, belongs to the small group of countries that have managed to depart successfully from international mainstreams. In the next application, we briefly discuss the policies and external factors that led Korea to the dramatic change in trade strategy observed here. We then use a dynamic input–output model to investigate how a more inward-looking development strategy, more in line with other countries, would have affected the rate of growth and the pattern of structural change.

4.3   Trade strategy, structural change, and growth: analysis with a dynamic input–output model of Korea

The cross-country comparisons just presented reveal both the uniformities and differences characterizing the process of industrialization. When using the Chenery-Syrquin decomposition methodology, the overall growth rate of the economy is always taken as given and it is the composition of growth that is analyzed. Consideration of the results, however, naturally leads one to ask what kind of links there are between the composition of growth and the overall magnitude of the growth rate. Is a high percentage share of export expansion associated with more rapid economy-wide growth, or is it, on the contrary, import substitution that leads to more rapid growth?

It is not really possible to answer these questions adequately within the framework of input–output-type models. The fixed coefficients assumptions impose too stringent constraints on the analysis, and the models do not specify how policy variables interact with quantities produced and traded.[8] As we shall argue, nonlinear general equilibrium models can provide a more useful framework of analysis for questions of trade and growth, and much of this book is concerned with such analysis. However, it is instructive to explore how useful a simple dynamic input–output model that captures some important mechanisms can be in exploring the link between the pace and composition of growth. We take Korea as an example and compute alternative growth paths, adapting the dynamic input–output model described in Section 2.3. The basic run, or reference path, attempts to be close to the path actually followed by Korea between 1963 and 1973, a period characterized, as we have seen, by dramatic export expansion. The other experiments are characterized by a much smaller role of exports. In discussing the differences between the growth paths, we illustrate some of the strengths and weaknesses of dynamic input–output models as tools for analysis of questions of trade strategy and growth.

The experiments and the base run simulated growth path: 1963–73

The cross-country comparisons presented in Section 4.2 reveal the phenomenal rates of growth and structural change achieved by Korea, particularly over the period 1963–73.[9] The turning point came around 1965 during a period of trade liberalization and other important monetary and fiscal reforms. By maintaining the exchange rate near the free-trade level and granting exporters free access to imported inputs along with explicit export subsidies, the government provided on average roughly equal incentives to production for export and for domestic sales within the manufacturing sector. However, Korea's policy was not one of neutral free trade. Indeed, incentive policies discriminated against agriculture and, within manufacturing, the less efficient manufacturing sectors received higher-than-average subsidies. However, and most

---

[8] It is, however, possible to introduce ad hoc changes in crucial coefficients such as import coefficients. This would allow a partial treatment of the questions raised above. See Chenery and Bruno (1962) for such an application.

[9] For a more complete description of Korean economic performance, see Cole and Lyman (1971) or Frank, Kim, and Westphal (1975). This summary draws on Westphal (1978), and Adelman and Robinson (1978).

important, policy makers prevented the emergence of a home-market bias by providing incentives for export sales. These incentive policies were largely responsible for the unusually high contribution of export expansion to manufacturing growth observed in Table 4.3. Moreover, there was a further contribution of exports to growth as a result of the increased efficiency resulting from exporting in line with Korea's comparative advantage.

There were, however, other factors that contributed to the outward-looking development strategy that Korea pursued after 1965. First, Korea benefited from unusually high levels of foreign assistance during the 1950s and early 1960s, followed by substantial foreign capital inflows from all sources thereafter. Thus, between 1960 and 1975, about 40 percent of total investment was financed from abroad. After the mid-1960s, the large magnitude of these inflows was chiefly in response to Korea's export performance. Second, Korea also benefited from favorable initial conditions reflected in a relatively egalitarian distribution of assets and from a culture that places a high value on education, resulting in one of the highest literacy rates in the world. Third, Korea's export performance benefited directly from institutional incentives whereby the government put pressure on all industries, including "infants," to export (see Westphal, 1978; pp. 375-6).

With the linear models developed in Chapters 2 and 3, we cannot model explicitly the crucial role played by policy incentives on the rate of growth of the economy and therefore have to assume that they are in some way subsumed in the analysis. However, we can use the dynamic input–output model to generate alternative long-run equilibrium growth paths and thereby attempt to examine the interesting counterfactual question: What would have been the impact on growth and structural change if Korea had pursued a more inward-looking development strategy and, as a consequence, exports had grown at half the rate they did over the period 1963-73?

The base run (or reference path), to be discussed shortly, will be contrasted with the following two experiments reflecting variants of an inward-looking development strategy. In the first experiment (A-1), the rate of growth of exports in each sector is cut in half. In addition, the sectoral import coefficients are reduced uniformly so as to achieve the same cumulative trade balance, or foreign capital inflow, over the eleven-year period and hence capture the resulting decline in foreign exchange earnings that Korea would have had available to spend on imports. Thus, the experiment assumes both a reduction in exports and reduced imports so as to maintain the historical volume of foreign capital inflow. If Korea had achieved a much lower growth of exports, it is probably unreasonable to assume that it could have maintained the same cumulative level of foreign capital inflow. Thus, in experiment A-2, we maintain all the assumptions of A-1 except that we also cut cumulative foreign capital inflow in half.

It is important to emphasize some special features of the experiments. First, note that the model has no mechanism such as policy incentives to *induce* import substitution. Second, there is no import substitution *along* any one of the growth paths. The import coefficients are constant along the base-run growth path and are also constant, but reduced proportionately, in both experiments.[10] As we shall see, this assumption of fixed import coefficients is a serious limitation for the model as a practical tool for historical simulation. Because import coefficients are reduced in the base year and export demand is only reduced starting the second period, supply in the base year has in effect been reduced whereas demand has remained constant.

To make the model solution values for gross output feasible in the base year, aggregate base-year consumption is reduced and the growth rate of consumption is raised so as to achieve the same terminal-year consumption vector as in the base run.[11] As a result of these adjustments, the cumulative consumption achieved over the ten-year period with the two experiments is between 3% and 5% less than that achieved under the base-run growth path (see Table 4.7). Notwithstanding this small difference in the values of the integral of consumption, the welfare implication of a comparison between the experiments and the base run are expressed in terms of differences in capacity available for postplan growth.

To summarize, let us describe briefly the data base used for the model and the base-run growth path. The data base for the dynamic input–output model applied to Korea consists of the following: a domestic input–output coefficient matrix (A^d) for 1963, a diagonal matrix of import demand coefficients for intermediate and final demand (consumption + investment), all for 1963, a capital composition coefficients matrix (B) for 1968, and sectoral growth rates for consumption demand and export demand based on observed rates for the period 1963–73. Sectoral incremental capital–output ratios ($\hat{K}$) are based on comparative data on real sectoral investment and output for 1963, 1968, and 1973. Finally, labor coefficients are derived from the 1973 input–output table. All the data, including the input–output table, are in real terms, in 1968 prices.[12]

---

[10] Import coefficients are reduced to 61% of their values for A-1 and 45% of their values for A-2.

[11] See Chapter 2 for the definition of base-year feasibility.

[12] The data are from the World Bank research project, "A Comparative Study of the Sources of Industrial Growth and Structural Change" (RPO 671-32).

Table 4.5. *Actual and base run*

		Actual[a]	Base run
Investment/GDP (%)	1963	16.9	17.9
	1973	24.0	26.1
Exports/output (%)	1963	3.2	3.1
	1973	15.5	16.8
Imports/supply (%)	1963	12.4	12.6
	1973	18.5	14.6

[a]Export and import ratios are from input–output data. The investment ratio is based on national accounts.

Equipped with these parameters, the model determines endogenously sectoral outputs, imports, labor requirements, and investment by sector of origin and destination. With such an assortment of data from various years coupled with fixed incremental capital–output ratios (ICORs), fixed input–output coefficients, fixed capital coefficients, and fixed import coefficients, how good an approximation to Korea's pattern of growth is achieved by this model?

The base run against which experiments will be compared is designed to reflect as closely as possible what actually occurred in the 1963–73 period. It can be seen from Table 4.5 that the base run performs rather well in terms of the investment rate and total output (and hence the share of exports in total output) in both the initial and the terminal years. Where it is weak is on the import side: The model predicts an import share of 14.6% in 1977 whereas the actual share was 18.5%. The model badly underestimates the growth rate of imports which, of course, is due to the assumption of fixed import coefficients. Therefore the model overestimates the improvement in the balance of trade and the growth of GDP, and underestimates the growth of total absorption. It would thus appear, at least in the case of a country growing rapidly and experiencing substantial change in trade policies, that macroeconomic (and sectoral) projections based on the assumption of fixed import coefficients are likely to be substantially biased.[13]

[13] Another check on the base run is to see whether it is base-year feasible. Using the norm measures presented in Chapter 2 and illustrated below, indicates that gross production given by the model in the base year is within 2.5% of the actual aggregate production and that the deviation in the model's structure of production from the actual structure in 1963 is 5.5% of base-year production.

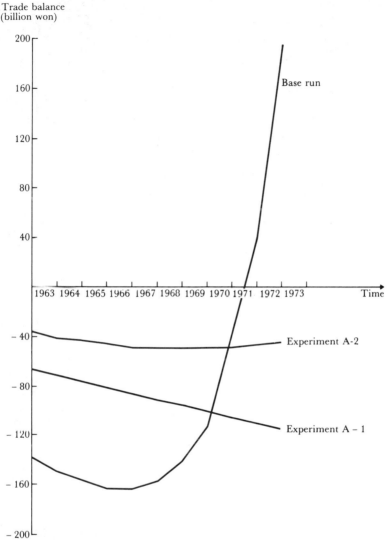

Figure 4.2. Time path of the trade balance under different experiments.

Capacity consequences of an inward-looking strategy

We now turn to a comparison of the base run with the two experiments. Figure 4.2 describes the year-to-year changes in the balance of trade net of trade taxes for the base run and each experiment. By design, the integrals of the curves for the base run and experiment A-1 are equal,

Table 4.6. *Structure of trade in the base year and output structure in the terminal year*

	Composition of imports (%) (1)	Import coefficient (2)	Composition of exports (%) (3)	Export growth rates (4)	Labor coefficient (5)	Capital coefficient (ICOR) (6)	Output composition (%)		
							Base run 1973 (7)	Experiment A-1 1973 (8)	Experiment A-2 1973 (9)
Agriculture	26.5	0.111	8.1	22.0	3.53	1.20	16.9	21.0	20.4
Mining	1.1	0.080	12.0	4.3	1.40	0.42	1.9	2.0	2.1
Food processing	3.5	0.050	8.1	22.3	0.31	0.19	9.5	11.9	11.5
Light industry	9.8	0.082	26.0	43.2	0.66	0.35	23.7	18.6	18.4
Heavy industry	36.3	0.387	13.0	36.2	0.32	0.54	10.3	10.8	11.8
Machinery	20.8	0.504	2.5	65.5	0.43	0.19	7.7	5.5	6.2
Social overhead	0.6	0.008	18.9	26.0	1.01	1.50	13.6	12.0	12.0
Services	1.4	0.011	12.4	28.9	2.35	1.40	16.4	18.2	17.6
Sum or average	100.0	0.140	100.0	35.4	1.40	0.72	100.0	100.0	100.0

Notes: (1) Units of labor coefficients are 1,000s workers per billion won (1968 prices). Data from 1973 input–output table. (2) Capital coefficients are sectoral incremental capital–output ratios. They are estimated from sectoral capital stock, investment, and production data. (3) Export growth rates are for 1963 to 1973.

reflecting the same cumulative balance of trade. Although the base run overestimates the balance-of-trade surplus achieved by Korea, it approximates well enough the dramatic changes that actually took place for the experiments selected here. Because exports are growing exponentially while imports are reduced linearly, the balance of trade must eventually improve. From Figure 4.2 it is evident that, in Experiment A-1, the time period is not long enough to show an improvement in the trade balance. However, particularly in Korea, where the indirect import content of exports is high, one could argue that in fact export growth would decline with a fall in imports. To explore this relationship we need the more elaborate models developed later where both imports and exports are determined endogenously and are responsive to changes in relative prices.

Table 4.6 describes the composition of trade in the base year, along with the key parameters in the model that determine the differences in output composition in the terminal year reported in columns 7–9 of that table. Because the model is demand driven with fixed sectoral ICORs (column 6), the effects of the experiments arise from the changes in the sectoral structure of demand interacting with differences in sectoral capital coefficients. In general, exports are concentrated in the manufacturing sectors with low capital coefficients, whereas imports are concentrated in sectors with relatively high ICORs. The total (direct plus indirect) effects of shifting toward an inward-looking strategy is to favor the expansion of sectors with high ICORs. This can be seen by a comparison of the composition of output in 1973 between the base run (column 7) and the two experiments (columns 8 and 9): Agriculture and Services, which have the highest ICORs in the economy, are the sectors that must expand to meet the needs of an inward-looking strategy. Sectoral differences in ICORs provide the crucial mechanism determining the basic results.

Given that cumulative consumption in the two experiments is close to that in the base run, a change in structure that raises the average ICOR over time must lead to a decline in the growth of capacity. In the model, this decline in capacity is reflected in lower gross output in the terminal year. Table 4.7 indicates that by 1973 the macroeconomic effects of the change in the structure of the economy are quite substantial. A development strategy emphasizing sectors with high ICORs leads to lower gross output (column 2) and lower GDP (column 3).

With productive capacity growing more slowly, investment also grows at a lower rate in both experiments. Note, however, the difference between A-1 and A-2: When imports are further squeezed to reduce the foreign capital inflow deficit (A-2), capacity (i.e., gross output) and

Table 4.7. *Macroeconomic indicators: ratios to base-run values (%)*

	ICOR	Gross output	GDP	Consumption	Investment	Exports	Imports
1963							
Experiment A-1	100.0	101.5	99.8	93.0	86.3	100.0	60.0
Experiment A-2	100.0	102.9	100.2	89.0	90.9	100.0	44.7
1973							
Experiment A-1	109.7	74.7	76.8	100.0	53.6	22.3	44.1
Experiment A-2	108.3	79.2	80.7	100.0	58.8	22.3	34.4
Cumulative, 1963–73							
Experiment A-1		86.1	89.7	97.0	66.2	35.8	51.2
Experiment A-2		89.7	92.5	95.3	71.5	35.8	39.2

Table 4.8. *Production in 1963 and 1973, distance measures from base run*

	1963		1973	
	Experiment A-1	Experiment A-2	Experiment A-1	Experiment A-2
Distance from base run	6.0	9.3	30.4	27.2
Distance along PF	6.0	9.3	19.5	18.5
Distance from PF	−0.3	−0.3	−25.4	−21.7
Distance from Experiment A-1	0.0	0.0	3.5	4.8

Notes: Distances are measured by Euclidean norms (*E* norm in the appendix to Chapter 2) and are expressed as a percent of the base-run norm of total production in 1963 and 1973. PF = production frontier. It is defined by the norm of base-run production.

GDP are higher in the terminal year. This result is due to the fact that consumption is lower in the base year in Experiment A-2. This in turn allows for greater cumulative investment over the plan period, which explains why gross output and GDP are higher under A-2.

The distance measures presented in Chapter 2 provide aggregate measures of the extent of structural change and the reduction in capacity resulting from an inward-looking strategy. The total distance from the base run is decomposed into two parts: (1) the distance along the production frontier (PF) that reflects differences in the structure of output, and (2) the distance from the PF that reflects differences in capacity. Table 4.8 gives the distances from the base run of the two experiments, and the results for Experiment A-1 in 1973 are also plotted in Figure 4.3. The difference in the structure of production in the two experiments in 1973 is quite large, but somewhat less in absolute magnitude than the change in capacity.

The cost of pursuing a development strategy emphasizing expansion in sectors with high ICORs can be quite substantial. For the counter-factual experiments with Korea, an inward-looking strategy yields, within a decade, an economy with 22–25 percent less capacity to produce than in the base run simulating the outward-looking strategy pursued by Korea.

In addition to the unfavorable impact on capacity, an inward-looking strategy would also have detrimental effects on employment. Table 4.9 indicates that total employment is much lower in 1973 in the two experiments, equaling 82.1 and 85.5 percent of the base-run value.[14]

[14] Employment is calculated by the fixed labor–output ratios given in Table 4.6.

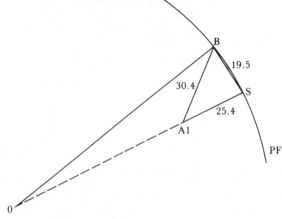

Figure 4.3. Experiment A-1: comparison of 1973 production to base run. B, base run; A1, Experiment A; S, projection to PF; PF, production frontier.

Table 4.9. *Decomposition of employment deviation from base run, 1973*

	Total employment		Manufacturing employment	
	Experiment A-1	Experiment A-2	Experiment A-1	Experiment A-2
Percent deviation from base run	−17.9	−14.5	−35.0	−30.7
Deviation due to lower output	−25.4	−21.7	−34.1	−29.6
Deviation due to change in output structure	7.5	7.2	−0.9	−1.1

Although the model is too aggregated in the manufacturing sector for a serious analysis of the effects of development strategy on employment, it is interesting to look at the decomposition of the change in total employment into its two components: the change due to the fact that total output is lower and the change due to differences in the structure of production. The decomposition is calculated by attributing to "lower output" the change in employment required to achieve the base-run level of aggregate output (defined by the Euclidean norm), but with the structure of output as in the experiment. The residual change in output is thus due to differences in the structure of production.

The conventional wisdom about Korea is that by promoting labor-intensive exports, the economy achieved greater employment. Such reasoning can be misleading, however, if one overlooks the source of increase in employment due to the increased aggregate output resulting from export-led growth. In terms of total employment, changes in the structure of total production that accompany a drastic reduction in exports actually increase employment because Agriculture and Services are, by far, the most labor-intensive sectors (see Table 4.6, column 5). Within the manufacturing sector, the change in structure that accompanies a reduction of exports does lead to a slight fall in manufacturing employment, but the effect is tiny compared to the impact of the reduction in manufacturing output. Note that indirect effects are important, because the change in the structure of gross output within manufacturing is much less than the change in the structure of final demand. A more disaggregated analysis would probably qualify these rather extreme results, because most Korean exports are in fact concentrated in a few subsectors within light industry. However, the predominance of the total output effect would undoubtedly remain, even in a more disaggregated model.

What emerges from this analysis is the important role of the composition of demand on growth. Although the simple dynamic input–output model used here is too rigid to be used as a projection model, it is useful to illustrate the benefits in terms of growth and employment of encouraging expansion of sectors with low capital coefficients and high labor output ratios, a seemingly obvious observation often disregarded by policy makers. The experiments also demonstrate that differences in structure between sectors and indirect linkages captured within the interindustry framework do matter.

In addition to the macroeconomic results we have discussed, it is important to examine the changes in production structure, export shares, and import shares that are part of the experimental results to see if they appear unrealistically extreme. We therefore turn briefly to an examination of results at the sectoral level, using the sources of growth decomposition methodology to permit comparison with the experience of other countries.

Comparison of sources of growth

Table 4.10 presents the sources of growth decomposition for total output and for three aggregated sectors: primary, manufacturing, and services. The change in output from the base run in 1963 to the terminal year (1973) in the base run and in the two experiments is decomposed or allocated to four "sources" due to changes in consumption, investment, exports, and import substitution. Note that because import coefficients

Table 4.10. *Korea: sources of growth decomposition, 1963–73 (%)*

Output	Growth rate	Output share		Sources of growth			
		1963	1973	Consumption	Investment	Export expansion	Import substitution
Total							
Actual data[a]	15.8	100.0	100.0	48.0	18.8	38.3	−3.6
Base run	14.5	100.0	100.0	41.0	18.9	40.1	0.0
Experiment A-1	11.2	100.0	100.0	65.1	13.8	11.4	9.7
Experiment A-2	11.8	100.0	100.0	60.9	15.1	10.7	13.3
Primary							
Base run	8.3	32.6	18.8	60.4	7.4	32.2	0.0
A-1	7.3	32.6	22.9	75.2	4.5	8.3	12.0
A-2	7.8	32.6	22.6	70.9	5.0	7.8	16.3
Manufacturing							
Base run	18.3	36.9	51.2	35.1	14.4	50.5	0.0
A-1	13.9	36.9	46.8	61.4	11.5	14.5	12.6
A-2	14.8	36.9	47.8	56.6	13.0	13.3	17.1
Services							
Base run	14.3	30.5	30.0	43.0	32.8	24.2	0.0
A-1	11.1	30.5	30.3	65.6	23.1	8.0	3.3
A-2	11.5	30.5	29.6	62.5	25.2	7.7	4.6

[a]Changes in input–output coefficients contributed −1.6% in the actual data. The contribution is zero in all experiments, because fixed input–output coefficients are specified in the model.

are fixed within each run, the contribution of import substitution in the base run is zero. It is positive for the two experiments because their terminal-year values are being compared to the base-run initial year. A fifth source, changes in input–output coefficients, is zero in all the runs because the model assumes unchanging input–output coefficients.

The first row of the table presents the decomposition of actual growth in the 1963–73 period. Note that, as discussed earlier, import coefficients increased over the period, yielding a negative contribution (-3.6 percent) of import substitution to total change in output. The contributions of the expansion of investment and exports are quite close to the corresponding values in the base run, indicating again that, except for the change in import coefficients, the base run is quite close to the actual data.

The decomposition reflects clearly the results of the experiments. The role of import substitution is quite large in both. Comparing the results to those from other countries presented earlier, they imply a contribution of import substitution to output change comparable to that which occurred in Taiwan, Japan, Turkey, or Mexico during their import-substitution phases. The contribution is also much less than occurred in Korea in the 1955–63 period. Thus, at the aggregate level, the implied role of import substitution in the two experiments is not out of line with historical experience in Korea and other countries, although no country has had such a large contribution over such a prolonged period as implied by the experiments.

However, when we turn to an analysis of the individual sectors, more serious questions about feasibility appear. Table 4.11 compares for 1973 the structure of imports across experiments with the actual data along with the accompanying ratios of imports to total supply on the domestic market. The composition of imports in the two experiments does not change very much from the base run, except for agriculture and machinery. However, the import ratios fall dramatically compared to the base run, especially in the heavy industry and machinery sectors.

Figure 4.4 shows the contributions of domestic demand expansion (consumption plus investment), export expansion, and import substitution to total output change in three sectors: light industry, heavy industry, and machinery. The decline in the role of exports, especially in light industry, is quite dramatic. There is a corresponding increase in the role of import substitution, although even in heavy industry and machinery it does not completely offset the decline in exports. However, in those two sectors in the experiments, import substitution accounts for about 20–30 percent of the total change in output.

Given the structure of imports, if Korea had pursued a development

Table 4.11. *Structure of imports in 1973*

Sector	Composition of imports (%)				Import ratios (%)[a]			
	Actual	Base run	Experiment A-1	Experiment A-2	Actual	Base run	Experiment A-1	Experiment A-2
Agriculture	15.5	14.3	18.0	17.2	18.2	11.1	6.8	5.0
Mining	1.5	1.1	1.1	1.2	24.1	8.0	4.9	3.6
Food processing	2.9	3.3	4.4	4.2	5.3	5.0	3.1	2.3
Light industry	16.1	10.0	10.5	10.2	18.5	8.2	5.0	3.7
Heavy industry	29.9	36.2	37.3	37.9	31.1	38.7	23.8	17.5
Machinery	32.6	33.2	26.6	27.3	58.8	50.4	31.0	22.7
Social overhead	1.2	0.7	0.7	0.7	1.9	0.8	0.5	0.4
Services	0.3	1.2	1.4	1.4	0.3	1.1	0.7	0.5

[a]Ratio of imports to total supply to domestic market (production + imports − exports).

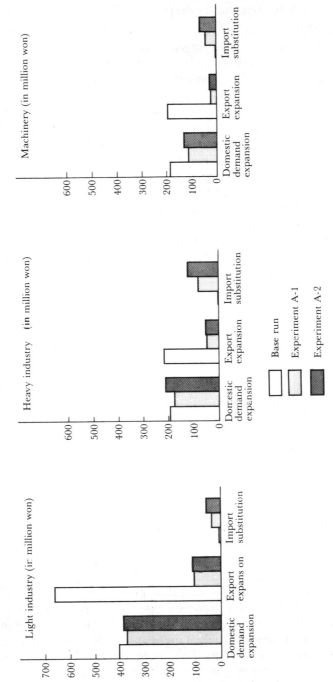

Figure 4.4. Sources of growth for light industry, heavy industry, and machinery.

strategy in the 1963–73 period based on continued import substitution, it would have involved major import substitution in agriculture, heavy industry, and/or machinery. The magnitude of the required import substitution, especially in heavy industry and machinery, would have been quite large, and it is not clear that Korea could have done it successfully in the middle 1960s. The model, of course, overstates the ease of achieving import substitution because, even though imports are determined by fixed coefficients, they are assumed to be perfect substitutes for domestically produced goods. In fact, especially in sectors such as heavy industry and machinery, quality differentials between domestic and imported goods are very important, and the nature of the relevant production technologies is often quite different. The difficulties and costs of achieving significant import substitution in such sectors before the economy has reached an appropriate level of development are quite large. These costs will be evaluated explicitly with the more complex models developed later, where import substitution is linked directly to changes in trade policy.

4.4   Conclusion

The comparison of the sources of growth and structural change across eight countries reveals a great deal of diversity in the relative contribution to growth of various components of final demand, particularly with regard to export expansion and import substitution. In addition to affecting the composition of growth, differences in the structure of final demand have an impact on the rate of growth.

Whereas the static input–output model can be used to decompose the sources of growth and structural change, the dynamic input–output model provides a useful framework for exploring the implications for growth of changes in the sectoral patterns of final demand. The model captures some of the major forces at work, namely, differences in sectoral capital and labor coefficients and in the sectoral composition of capital.

Some of the weaknesses of the dynamic input–output model, such as the assumption that the various coefficients are fixed over time, can be altered without changing the essential properties of the model. For example, it is relatively easy to specify exogenous time trends for various parameters such as import coefficients, which greatly improves the ability of the model to track actual changes at the cost of complicating the solution procedure somewhat. The basic dynamic properties of the model, however, are largely unaffected by such changes. Other changes, such as relaxing the rigidities of the fixed-coefficient specification by introducing choice and inequality constraints, require extending the model to a linear programming framework. As we have discussed in detail, such an extension has benefits and costs. The model becomes a somewhat more flexible tool, but there are still important rigidities that affect model behavior and, indeed, become more important in an optimizing model because they generally lead to rather extreme behavior.

A major weakness of both dynamic input–output and linear programming models is the fact that they do not include variables that reflect the major policy instruments governments typically use in mixed-market economies to affect the composition of final demand. Even in modern socialist countries, and certainly in all mixed economies, governments rely heavily on incentive policies that work through the market mechanism. Policies such as indirect taxes, subsidies, exchange-rate manipulation, and direct controls over some prices all affect the economy through their effects on prices and costs in various markets. The linear models do not provide an adequate framework for exploring the impact of policies that work through such mechanisms. Although much can be done with linear programming models, and there is a large literature in this area, we feel that for medium-term planning designed to be directly useful to the policy maker, it is more fruitful to abandon linear models and work within the framework of nonlinear general equilibrium models. The development and empirical implementation of such models is the central concern of the rest of this book.

PART II

Computable general equilibrium models

CHAPTER 5

A CGE model for a closed economy

5.1   Introduction

Multisector, economy-wide mathematical models have now been used for more than two decades as tools of development planning. Although the more sophisticated dynamic programming models have not yet significantly crossed academic boundaries, most developing countries have extended their national accounting effort to include input–output transaction tables. Indeed, many countries had by the early 1970s adopted some form of input–output analysis as the basic framework for their formal planning exercises. There is no doubt that the techniques of development planning have acquired a wide field of potential real-world application.

Given their theoretical structure, input–output and linear programming models seem best suited to a situation in which a central authority fully in control of the various quantity variables in the system, but subject to various technological and physical constraints, has to make consistent or optimal decisions. They are constructs that best reflect a pure command economy and, indeed, input–output analysis has often been used to "solve" the famous problems of material balancing in the productive sphere of a centrally planned economy. The Soviet economist Kantorovich perceived in a programming approach a clear link between centralized planning and the scarcity price concept of neoclassical economy theory, whereas Dantzig developed linear programming as a tool for optimal central decision making in a variety of settings.

The standard formulation of these models does not appear well suited to situations where many agents independently maximize their own welfare functions and jointly but inadvertently determine an outcome that can be affected only indirectly by the planner or policy maker. With very few exceptions, the countries of the world – including postreform Eastern Europe – are characterized by mixed economic systems in which a great deal of economic activity is not under the direct control of policy makers. In these countries, autonomous decision making by various economic "actors" and market mechanisms have an important impact on resource allocation. Linear programming and input–output

131

models usually do not contain variables that can be considered to be instruments controlled by policy makers in such market economies. Although policy makers can benefit from the consistent economy-wide picture provided by the models, they cannot easily relate the computed variables to any actual policy decisions.

In practice, applications of linear models to developing countries have always involved a number of compromises and ad hoc extensions to the basic model in order to make the models more realistic and useful in an applied setting.[1] Some modifications have sought to capture indirectly the presumed effects that policy changes would have on endogenous variables. For example, the impact on import coefficients of the rise in the relative price of imports due to a tariff can be specified exogenously and so be fed back into the model. Other modifications represent attempts to capture nonlinearities by imposing various constraints and/or piecewise linear functions. None of these modifications, however, addresses the essential problem that the models do not directly incorporate the sorts of price-incentive variables that represent the essential tools of planners and policy makers in mixed economies.

In order to achieve greater policy relevance, it is clear that the fiction of a central command economy must be abandoned in the very specification of the model and be replaced by a framework in which endogenous price and quantity variables are allowed to interact so as to simulate the workings of at least partly decentralized markets and autonomous economic decision makers. Such price endogeneity and general equilibrium interaction cannot be achieved using the standard linear programming formulation. The crucial difficulty lies in the fact that economic behavior and relations such as budget constraints, consumption functions, and saving functions must be expressed in current endogenous factor and commodity prices. But the standard primal constraint equations of a linear program cannot include the "shadow" prices that result as a by-product of the maximization. Or, to put it differently, one cannot in general expect that the resource allocation and production structure determined by the solution of a linear program is consistent with the incomes and budgets that result from its dual solution. Indeed, if factor prices have any impact on the structure of demand, the quantities supplied that are the outcome of the primal solution will in general not equal the quantities demanded that are implied by the dual solution.

In this chapter we introduce a class of models, which we call computable general equilibrium (CGE) models, that incorporate the fun-

---

[1] For examples of flexible linear models in particular applications, see Bruno (1966); Stone (1970); Chenery (1971); Evans (1972); and Goreux (1977).

damental general equilibrium links among production structure, incomes of various groups and the pattern of demand. Section 5.2 illustrates the "budget constraint problem" within the basic linear programming framework familiar from Part I. Section 5.3 describes the basic structure of a one-period CGE model. Sections 5.4 and 5.5 relate the CGE modeling methodology to social accounting by collecting the model equations into a kind of statistical picture of the workings of an economy. The grouping of equations in Section 5.5 leads to a brief discussion of the various solution strategies that can be used to obtain numerical solutions to CGE models. In Section 5.6 we turn to the problem of dynamic specification and the treatment of different time periods. Throughout this chapter, we shall be abstracting from problems of foreign trade and treat the economy as closed in order to outline more easily the basic nature of a CGE model. In Chapters 6 and 7 we discuss foreign trade in great detail and extend the model presented in this chapter to include foreign trade and trade policy variables.

5.2   Optimal solutions and market solutions

In Chapter 3 we discussed in an informal and general way the difference between the solution of a linear programming problem and the general equilibrium solution of a system of equations representing the decentralized interaction of various agents in a market economy. In this section we shall be more precise in describing the difference and analyzing the fundamental difficulty of obtaining a general equilibrium solution in a LP framework.

It is convenient to discuss the problem using the basic material balance equations that form the core of any planning model. For simplicity we consider the case of a closed economy. In equilibrium we must always have

$$X_i = \sum_j a_{ij}X_j + C_i \tag{5.2.1}$$

where X_i denotes gross sectoral output, C_i represents final consumption, and the a_{ij} are the familiar input–output coefficients determining intermediate demand. In a market economy the relative prices of commodities and factors will have a determining influence on the vector of outputs supplied $X = [X_1, \ldots, X_n]$, and final demands $C = [C_1, \ldots, C_n]$. Assume for the moment that the productive sphere of the economy is characterized by linear coefficients activities, and denote by H_{oi} ($i = 1, \ldots, m$) the various resources, fixed in supply during the period considered, that limit productive capacity. The production activities are characterized by the usual commodity input coefficients a_{ij}, supplemented by resource input coefficients h_{ij}. Given an arbitrary commodity price system P_i ($i = 1, \ldots , n$), it is clear that the problem for the productive sphere of the economy is

$$\text{Max:} \quad \sum_i PN_iX_i$$

$$\text{Subject to:} \quad \sum_i h_{sj}X_i \leq \overline{H}_s \qquad (5.2.2)$$

$$X_i \qquad \geq 0$$

where PN_i is the net price or per-unit value added, defined as

$$PN_i = P_i - \sum_j a_{ji}P_j \qquad (5.2.3)$$

Associating a "producer" or "firm" with each productive activity, the solution of this program is consistent with what would be achieved by a market process in which the n autonomous "firms" would attempt to maximize profits bidding for the scarce factors that themselves must be considered as mobile between activities and offering their services to the highest bidder. The shadow prices that the dual solution of the programming problem assigns to the scarce resources would in fact correspond to the values the market would assign to them. If we denote these resource prices by W_i, the duality theorem also guarantees that total factor income equals total net product value; that is,

$$\sum_s W_s\overline{H}_s = \sum_i PN_iX_i \qquad (5.2.4)$$

Summarizing, we see that to each price vector $(P_1, \ldots , P_n)$ corresponds a linear programming solution that associates outputs $(X_1, \ldots , X_n)$ and factor prices $(W_1, \ldots , W_m)$ with the price vector. We can regard the relationship between the price vector and the elements of the output vector as a vector supply function of the form

$$X^S = X(P_1, \ldots , P_n) \qquad (5.2.5)$$

Note that because the feasible set defined by the input use and non-negativity constraints is bounded, any price vector will lead to a solution of the linear program. It is true, however, that an arbitrary positive price vector may lead to a value-added vector with negative components. We must therefore assume that the only "allowable" price vectors will be those such that $P_i - \sum_j a_{ji}P_j \geq 0$ for all i and return to the problem later.

Another problem relates to the uniqueness of the supply response. When the price hyperplane is tangent to a facet of the feasible set, the linear program will have a non-unique solution, and more than one vector of output supplies will be consistent with a given price vector. This does not create any fundamental problem: One simply has to redefine the supply functions as supply correspondences. We shall occasionally use the term "function" more loosely to include point-to-set mappings.

Now consider the demand side of this simple market economy. We shall assume that all resources and factors $\overline{H}_{oi}$ are owned by households that use the income derived from letting firms use their resources to demand the commodities produced for final consumption. Each category of households, q, will have a system of expenditure equations that relate quantities demanded C_{iq}^D, to household incomes and commodity prices. Let us denote the income of household category or socioeconomic group q by Y_q. It is clear that no matter how resource ownership is distributed, Y_q will be a linear homogeneous function of resource rental prices (W_1, $\ldots$, W_m). The consumer demand functions are of the form

$$C_{iq}^D = g_{iq}(P_1, \ldots, P_n, Y_q) \tag{5.2.6}$$

where C_{iq}^D is the amount of commodity i demanded by household category q, g_{iq} expresses the form of the demand functions, and Y_q is determined by exogenous ownership shares and resource rentals. Aggregating over groups, we obtain market demand functions of the form

$$C_i^D = \sum_q C_{iq}^D = \sum_q g_{iq}(P_1, \ldots, P_n, Y_q) \tag{5.2.7}$$

To consumer demand, we must add intermediate demand by firms:

$$V_i^D = \sum_j a_{ij}X_j^S \tag{5.2.8}$$

Together, consumer and intermediate demand constitute total demand for the various products produced in the system:

$$X_i^D = C_i^D + V_i^D \tag{5.2.9}$$

But resource rentals (i.e., factor prices), and therefore incomes, are themselves determined by the solution of the linear program, which of course depends on the initial choice of commodity prices. The price vector $(P_1, \ldots, P_n)$ is thus seen to lead to a supply solution $(X_1^S, \ldots, X_n^S)$ via the linear program and to a demand solution $(X_1^D, \ldots, X_n^D)$ via the demand functions derived from the preferences and budget constraints of the various household categories. We have the vector functions

$$(P_1, \ldots, P_n) \left\langle \begin{array}{l} X^S = X(P_1, \ldots, P_n) \\ \\ X^D = D(P_1, \ldots, P_n) \end{array} \right.$$

where the X and the D are the aggregate market supply and demand functions, respectively, the former determined by the linear programs and the latter representing the sum of consumption and intermediate demands, taking account of the fact that consumer incomes are themselves functions of the initial price vector.

Our basic material balance equation requires that $X_i^S = X_i^D$ for all i. Clearly, it would be pure coincidence if this equality were satisfied for an arbitrary price vector $(P_1, \ldots, P_n)$. In general, we shall have $X_i^S \neq X_i^D$. Rewriting the equilibrium requirement in a form exactly analogous to input–output analysis, we have

$$X_i^S = C_i^D + V_i^D = X_i^D \tag{5.2.10}$$

where X_i^S can be interpreted as gross supply functions associating production levels with commodity prices, V_i^D are the intermediate demand functions derived from the gross supply functions, and C_i^D are the final demand functions. We now see how the solution problem reduces to that of finding a set of commodity prices (weights in the objective function of the linear program) such that the supply decisions made by firms exactly match the demand decisions made by households whose incomes are determined by the shadow prices emerging from the linear program.

This general equilibrium or fixed-point problem is clearly a much more subtle one than that faced by input–output analysis or standard economy-wide programming models. In the former the solution is very simple and we simply have the familiar input–output matrix equation: $X = (I - A)^{-1}\overline{C}$.

For linear programming models the solution is a little more difficult to obtain. Given certain exogenous preference weights in the objective function, X is obtained by "solving" the productive sphere of the economy. But the final demand vector is not linked to the factor incomes implicit in the solution, and there is therefore no feedback mechanism that would require an adjustment in prices. The simple model outlined above did, however, include such a feedback.

Generalizing, we shall define a computable general equilibrium (CGE) model to be one that includes this basic feedback. These models are also sometimes called price-endogenous models because all prices must adjust until the decisions made in the productive sphere of the economy are consistent with the final demand decisions made by households and other autonomous decision makers. General equilibrium feedback mechanisms and autonomous decision making are the concepts that must be stressed. This does not imply that the CGE framework insists on perfectly competitive models and instantaneous market clearing, or that it can handle only very limited government intervention. On the contrary, imperfectly competitive behavior, quantity or price adjustment lags, and widespread government intervention are compatible with the CGE framework. But the CGE approach does stress horizontal interaction among economic agents, suboptimizing autonomous behavior, and the workings of market-clearing processes. It is essentially applied general equilibrium analysis and is much better suited to planning and policy analysis in mixed-market economies than to planning in highly centralized systems, be they whole economies or individual corporations.

Although the fundamental notion of general equilibrium we have described goes back to Walras, the empirical implementation of general equilibrium models really starts with Johansen's path-breaking model of the Norwegian economy.[2] Johansen linearized the general equilibrium model (in logarithms) and so was able to solve it by simple matrix inversion, yielding growth rates of the endogenous variables. Since then, there have been advances in solution methods that permit CGE models to be solved directly for the levels of all the endogenous variables and so permit model specifications that cannot easily be put into log-linear form. As advances have been made in solution algorithms, computing power, and data availability, there has been a proliferation of empirical general equilibrium models in the last ten years.

The existing models fall into four general categories according to the problems on which they focus. First, there are a number of models of developing and developed countries that focus on issues of international trade, growth, economic structure, and/or income distribution.[3] Second, there are a number of models of developed countries that focus on issues in the theory of public finance (see Shoven and Whalley, 1974; Fullerton, King, Shoven, and Whalley, in press). Third, there are a few multicountry, international trade models that explore issues concerning the

---

[2] See Johansen (1960). See also Chenery and Uzawa (1958), and Chenery and Raduchel (1971), who present small, nonlinear demonstration models.

[3] See Taylor and Black (1974) (Chile); Derviş (1975) (Turkey); de Melo (1977) (Colombia); Dixon, Parmenter, Ryland, and Sutton (1977) (Australia); Whalley (1977) (Great Britain); Adelman and Robinson (1978) (Korea); Celâsun (1978) (Indonesia); Derviş and Robinson (1978) (Turkey); Ahluwalia and Lysy (1979) (Malaysia); de Melo (1979) (Sri Lanka); Eckaus, McCarthy, and Mohieldin (1979) (Egypt); de Melo and Robinson (1980) (Colombia); Feltenstein (1980) (Argentina), Lysy and Taylor (1980) (Brazil); and Dungan (1980) (Canada).

volume and direction of trade and its impact on particular regions (see Petri, 1976; Ginsburgh and Waelbroeck, 1978; Deardorff and Stern, 1979). Finally, there has been some work both with single-country and multicountry models focusing on energy (see Hudson and Jorgenson, 1978; Manne, Kim, and Wilson, 1980). In this book, we focus on models of developing countries and on issues of resource allocation, growth, structural change, foreign trade strategies, and the impact of different strategies on the distribution of income.

There are two remaining tasks for this chapter. The first is to provide a more detailed presentation of a streamlined CGE model, emphasizing the core equations and establishing the framework that will form the basis of discussions of foreign trade and income distribution in following chapters. This is done in Sections 5.3 to 5.5, and the presentation will abstract from specific functional forms, with the exception of the assumption of a Leontief technology for intermediate and capital goods, which has been a basic assumption of the linear models of Chapters 2 and 3 and which has so far been maintained in most nonlinear CGE models. The resulting model is quite neoclassical in spirit. It is also static and leaves aside dynamic considerations and the whole problem of imperfect adjustment. Consideration of these issues is the second task for this chapter and will be covered in Section 5.6, where the problems of equilibrium and intertemporal linkages will be reviewed in some detail. We shall also consider some important non-neoclassical characteristics of developing countries that must be incorporated into CGE planning models if they are to be useful tools for policy analysis.

5.3   The basic structure of a CGE model

So far we have presented the fundamental "feedback" problem faced as soon as one models the decentralized interaction of autonomous producers and consumers. A simple linear program was used to describe the supply side of the economy, and we ignored government activity and investment. The problem of overall equilibrium was posed but not solved. In this section we shall discuss the basic structure and equations of a somewhat more complete closed-economy CGE model, which can be thought of as a core model underlying the whole family of models that have been built using the same basic approach. A discussion of the implicit accounting framework follows in Section 5.4, and a summary of the complete model and alternative solution strategies are briefly discussed in Section 5.5.

A few notational rules will be generally observed in this and the following chapters. Italic capital letters without bars are endogenous variables. All other characters denote predetermined variables. There are n sectors, m labor categories, and capital; the corresponding subscripts are i, j for sectors and s for labor categories. Superscripts D and S are used to distinguish quantities demanded from quantities supplied.

Factor markets and supply of commodities

In the typical CGE model, each commodity distinguished in the economy is associated with a production sector, very much in the tradition of input–output analysis. Indeed, the sectors are usually defined by an input–output table. In the linear models presented in Chapter 2, a fixed-coefficients technology was specified for intermediate inputs, capital composition, and nonproduced primary factors. Although it is by no means necessary, existing CGE models have often retained the assumptions of fixed coefficients for intermediate technology and the composition of capital goods. In contrast, the production technology for primary factors is described by a neoclassical production function that allows smooth substitution among several factor inputs. The degree of substitutability is governed by the elasticities of substitution specified. It would be quite feasible and certainly compatible with the basic modeling approach to specify sets of alternative linear production activities instead of neoclassical production functions. But production functions have usually been preferred to activity analysis representations of the technology because they require a much more moderate data-collection effort. The really important question in this context relates to the degree of substitutability one believes ought to be specified. For most purposes in economy-wide modeling, it can reasonably be argued that the use of CES production functions with realistic substitution elasticities will capture most of the interactions one wants to analyze. Given the necessity of aggregating sectors in any applied economy-wide model into a relatively small number, it should be made quite clear that the production functions are only very rough representations of actual technical production processes. But they constitute an extremely flexible and convenient tool, and their careful use at the sectoral level is unlikely to distort seriously the representation of the underlying technology. Rather than using a linear programming specification, we shall therefore use neoclassical production functions throughout remaining applications.

Sectoral gross outputs are related to inputs according to a two-level production function that can be written generally as

$$X_i = f_i(\overline{A}_i, \overline{K}_i, L_i^a, V_i^a) \tag{5.3.1}$$

where

X_i = sectoral output

$\overline{A}_i$ = a shift parameter that will dynamically reflect disembodied technical progress

$\overline{K}_i$ = the stock of the aggregate capital good assumed to be fixed by sectors

L_i^a = an aggregation of labor inputs

V_i^a = an aggregation index of intermediate inputs

The parameter $\overline{A}_i$ is constant within a period and depends on the units in which output and inputs are measured. The sectoral capital stock $\overline{K}_i$ is assumed fixed within each period. A unit of sectoral capital stock is assumed to consist of fixed proportions of different investment goods (construction, machinery, etc.), with the proportions varying among sectors, exactly as in dynamic input–output models.

Because we choose to assume a Leontief input–output technology for intermediate inputs, we need not specify a separate aggregation function for an intermediate-goods aggregate. Given that both the shares among different intermediate inputs in a sector and the ratios of intermediate inputs to output are fixed, we can write the demands for intermediate inputs directly:

$$V_{ij} = a_{ij}X_j \tag{5.3.2}$$

where a_{ij} are the input–output coefficients. We can then aggregate intermediate demands to get total intermediate demand by sector of origin:

$$V_i = \sum_j V_{ij} = \sum_j a_{ij}X_j \tag{5.3.3}$$

The use of fixed coefficients obviates the need for a separate aggregation function to define V_i^a and, in this case, the variable is not required. If we had wished to specify substitution possibilities among intermediate goods or among aggregate intermediate goods and labor and capital, then a separate aggregation function for intermediate goods would be required.

The sectoral labor input is assumed to be an aggregation of labor of different skill categories. The function will be represented by the equation (with m types of labor)

$$L_i^a = L_i^a(L_{i1}, \ldots, L_{im}) \tag{5.3.4}$$

In all applications, this aggregation is given by either a CES or Cobb-

Douglas function with a single elasticity of substitution among all labor categories.

To summarize, the production technology exhibits a number of special characteristics. It is a CES or Cobb-Douglas function of aggregate capital and aggregate labor. Capital is a fixed-coefficient aggregation of investment goods. Labor is a CES or Cobb-Douglas aggregation of labor of different skill categories. The production function is thus a two-level function. Intermediate goods are required according to fixed coefficients and so can be treated separately.

In terms of modern neoclassical production functions, this specification of production technology seems cumbersome and even raises some problems in proving the existence of an equilibrium solution that are considered in the next section. Mathematically, specifying Eq. (5.3.1) as a generalized or multilevel CES function would have been more consistent. There are, however, a number of advantages to this specification. First, retaining a number of the assumptions underlying linear models facilitates exposition and comparisons between the CGE and earlier models. We have extended the earlier specification in those areas where it is necessary for an adequate specification of a model designed to capture price-sensitive general equilibrium market interactions. Second, specifying more elaborate production functions leads to a proliferation of parameters that must be estimated. Parameter estimation has always been a difficult problem in economy-wide planning models, and one must always consider the trade-offs between adequate econometric estimation and adequate structural specification. This specification requires a minimum of additional parameter estimation beyond that already required for linear planning models. Finally, the particular simplifications used here seem to be empirically reasonable for the levels of aggregation, the types of issues, and time horizons usually considered.

The judgments underlying the model choices are all subject to revision as more information and experience are acquired. Given more data and a higher level of disaggregation, one might well wish to use different specifications of technology. One certainly need not be restricted to CES functions. Given the data and the appropriate focus on problems, one might specify activity analysis or translog functions, or estimate cost functions directly. The CGE framework is flexible enough to incorporate a wide variety of specifications of production technology.

In addition to the specification of technology, the basic model also incorporates important assumptions about factor mobility. Usually, it is reasonable to assume that the amount of capital in each sector is fixed at the beginning of the period being modeled. This implies that current investment will add to capacity only in future periods, which seems realistic. For some purposes, however, it may be better to leave sectoral capital stocks as endogenous variables. Assume, for instance, that one is interested simply in finding an equilibrium configuration for some future year without actually modeling the path leading to this configuration. Then it is sensible to allow the model to determine sectoral capital stocks endogenously. It might be possible to find, with a separate "transition path" model, a sequence of investment allocations that would lead to the terminal capital configuration.

Most often, however, CGE models are run forward in time from given initial conditions, and the most important of these initial conditions is given by the capacity installed in the various sectors in the base year. We shall therefore, unless otherwise specified, assume fixed sectoral capital stocks.

The specification of the production set of the economy is incomplete without a set of factor availability constraints. Writing them in the form of excess demand functions for labor, we have

$$\sum_i L_{is} - \bar{L}_s = 0 \tag{5.3.5}$$

where $\bar{L}_s$ denotes the fixed supplies of the various categories of labor.[4]

To distinguish the net production possibility set from the gross production possibility set $X = X(X_1, \ldots, X_n)$, denote the net production of sector i by $X_i^N = X_i - \Sigma_j a_{ij}X_j$. The resulting net production possibility set is strictly convex if the gross production possibility set is strictly convex and the Hawkins-Simon conditions are satisfied.[5] Convexity is achieved if either capital stocks are fixed or capital stocks are mobile and none of the sectors has the same factor intensity. The net production possibility set will be "flatter" than the gross production possibility set and completely contained within it, except at the boundaries. The degree of convexity is of course increased when the number of sectorally fixed factors increases, because this assumption amounts to specifying decreasing returns to scale to the variable factors of production.

The specification of the production possibility set is the first step in specifying the supply side of the economy. It should be noted that the "production possibility set" is a strictly technical description of attainable combinations of outputs. It should be distinguished from the "transformation set," which includes, in addition, various assumptions

---

[4] In principle, one could generalize to let the $\bar{L}_s$ include natural resources.
[5] See the appendix to Chapter 2 for further discussion of these conditions.

about market behavior. The nature of these additional assumptions will be considered later in this chapter and in the next.

If we were interested in specifying and maximizing a central objective function, ignoring market behavior and the feedback from factor prices to commodity demands, then we could treat the system as a nonlinear program and maximize the objective function subject to the production possibility set and the appropriate non-negativity restrictions. The problem is a nonlinear generalization of the linear programming maximization problem presented in Section 5.2. Exactly as in the linear programming case, there will correspond to each net price vector (the weights in the objective function) a solution on the boundary of the net production set. Conversely, at each point on the boundary of the production set, there exists a net price vector (i.e., a separating hyperplane) that will make the point the solution to the maximization problem.

Rather than viewing the problem as a programming problem, one can specify the behavior of firms in the economy and add an explicit description of the workings of factor markets. Under the assumption of perfect competition in both factor and commodity markets, the supply response will be the same whether we treat the production side of the economy as a programming problem or as a decentralized market. If we drop the assumption of perfect competition, the supply functions will no longer be the same and we must replace the production possibility frontier with a transformation set.

Each sector in the economy is treated as made up of many similar firms maximizing profits and bidding for the scarce factors. The assumption of perfect competition in product markets amounts to assuming that firms take commodity prices as given. Under these circumstances, one can treat each sector as one large price-taking firm. The aggregate sectoral profit functions are given by

$$\Pi_i = P_i(1 - td_i)X_i - \sum_j P_j a_{ji} X_i - \sum_s W_s L_{is} \qquad (5.3.6)$$

where W_r is the wage of labor of type s and td_i is the indirect tax rate. Although the primary concern in this simple model is not with policy formulation, the inclusion of a government sector leads naturally to the inclusion of indirect and direct taxes in the system.

The profit equation can be rewritten as

$$\Pi_i = PN_i X_i - \sum_s W_s L_{is}$$

where

$$PN_i = P_i(1 - td_i) - \sum_{j=1}^{n} P_j a_{ji} \tag{5.3.7}$$

is the net price or value-added coefficient, this time net of indirect taxes. Labor demands are given by

$$PN_i \frac{\partial X_i}{\partial L_i^a} \frac{\partial L_i^a}{\partial L_{is}} = W_s \tag{5.3.8}$$

These are the familiar conditions that wages equal the value of the marginal products of different labor types.[6] These equations give the demand functions for labor by sectors and may be written as

$$L_{is} = F_{is}(W_1, \ldots, W_m, PN_1, \overline{K}_i) \tag{5.3.9}$$

Depending on the production function used, these $n \cdot m$ equations (one for each sector and each labor category) may be solved directly or by numerical methods. Should a neoclassical specification requiring full employment of all categories of labor be adopted, then the resource constraints will be binding and the wage for each labor category will adjust until the sum of sectoral demands for each category equals the fixed supply of that category.

In many applications, however, a specification where the supply of labor of certain categories is a function of the wage rate is preferred. In the extreme case, labor is in infinitely elastic supply at a fixed real wage given by

$$W_s = \overline{W}_s \sum_i P_i \Omega_i^W \tag{5.3.10}$$

where the Ω_i^W are weights in the price index that define the real wage $\overline{W}_s$. This formulation creates no complication because with fixed capital stocks the transformation set will still be strictly convex.[7] If this formulation is adopted for certain categories of labor, the resource constraints become side equations giving the total possible employment of labor in the economy, and the wages in the labor demand equation become a fixed argument along with capital stocks.

---

[6] It is straightforward to introduce fixed distortions such that labor of the same skill category is paid differently depending on its sector of employment. The implications of such an extension are discussed in Chapter 6, and are in fact used in most of the applications.

[7] If capital stock were mobile across sectors, the transformation curve would contain linear segments. We also rule out the unlikely case of equal factor intensities across sectors.

Whether a neoclassical or fixed-wage specification is adopted creates no difficulty because capital – assumed to be fixed during the period considered – plays the role of a constant, sector-specific factor. Given the ensuing diminishing returns to labor and the general continuity properties of neoclassical production functions, solving for a given set of positive net prices and wages will never constitute a theoretical problem. The payments to capital in each sector are defined residually after payments for labor and intermediate inputs. Total factor payments will therefore, by definition, equal total value added generated.

Given an arbitrary vector of allowable commodity prices leading to a non-negative vector of net prices, each sector will maximize profits subject to its capital stock, its technology, and the wages of the various types of labor. For neoclassical production functions, the marginal productivity curves are strictly concave and the solution will in fact be unique. Substituting the solution values of L_{is} into the labor aggregation and production functions will yield a unique vector of outputs $(X_1^S, \ldots, X_n^S)$ that constitutes the supply vector associated with a given price vector $(P_1, \ldots, P_n)$.

In the case where wages are not fixed, we simply add the m factor exhaustion equations to the system defining the supply response of the economy. We then have $n \cdot m + m$ equations to be solved for the $n \cdot m + m$ variables, L_{is} and W_s. Again, strict convexity guarantees a unique solution so that we obtain a set of well-behaved numerical supply functions of the form

$$X^S = X(P_1, \ldots, P_n) \tag{5.3.11}$$

that associate a vector of output supplies with each allowable price vector. It will usually not be possible to write them out explicitly, but they can be obtained numerically.

As a by-product of computing sectoral supplies associated with a given price vector by solving factor markets, we obtain factor incomes including the residual value added accruing to capital. We are thus ready to move on to the demand side of the system.

Income generation and demand for commodities

The decision-making units that determine the demand for commodities are the various categories of households, which demand consumer goods; the government, which also demands consumer goods; and the firms themselves, which demand intermediate goods and capital goods. For simplicity, we shall assume in this chapter that each household category is characterized by a single type of factor that it owns and supplies.

Thus there will be $m + 1$ categories of households, the first m categories supplying the different kinds of labor distinguished in the discussion of factor markets and the last category being the owners of capital who receive the residual value added. Again for simplicity, assume that the government does not own any capital and receives its income only through direct and indirect taxes. Given these simplifying assumptions, one can write

$$Y_s = \sum_i W_s L_{is}(1 - t_s) \tag{5.3.12}$$

$$Y_k = \left(\sum_i PN_i X_i - \sum_i \sum_s W_s L_{is} \right)(1 - t_k) \tag{5.3.13}$$

$$Y_g = \sum_s \frac{t_s}{1 - t_s} Y_s + \frac{t_k}{1 - t_k} Y_k + \sum_i td_i P_i X_i \tag{5.3.14}$$

where Y_s ($s = 1, m$), Y_k, and Y_g represent the net incomes of the $m + 1$ household categories and the government, and t_s and t_k are the direct average tax rates applying to the different groups and are assumed to be independent of the level of income. Note that by definition we always have

$$\sum_s Y_s + Y_k + Y_g = \sum_j P_j X_j - \sum_j \sum_i P_i a_{ij} X_j \tag{5.3.15}$$

so that total income generated in the system always equals total national product at market prices.

The government and the capitalist and labor households must now decide how to spend their incomes. Following a convenient if not theoretically very satisfying practice, assume that, prior to any consumption decisions they make, the various household groups and the government decide on the proportion of their income that will be saved. Total saving, denoted by TS, is withdrawn from the system and may be written as follows:

$$TS = \sum_s \hat{S}_s Y_s + \hat{S}_k Y_k + \hat{S}_g Y_g \tag{5.3.16}$$

This leaves each spending group with a reduced amount of income to be spent on consumer goods. We have

$$C_{is}^D = C_{is}[P_1, \ldots, P_n, (1 - \hat{S}_s)Y_s] \tag{5.3.17}$$
$$C_{ik}^D = C_{ik}[P_1, \ldots, P_n, (1 - \hat{S}_k)Y_k] \tag{5.3.18}$$
$$C_{ig}^D = C_{ig}[P_1, \ldots, P_n, (1 - \hat{S}_g)Y_g] \tag{5.3.19}$$

where C_{is}^D, C_{ik}^D, and C_{ig}^D are the amounts of consumer good i demanded by labor of type s, capitalists and the government, respectively.

This leads to the aggregate demand functions,

$$C_i^D = \sum_s C_{is}[P_1, \ldots, P_n, (1 - \hat{S}_s)Y_s] + C_{ik}[P_1, \ldots, P_n, (1 - \hat{S}_k)Y_k]$$
$$+ C_{ig}[P_1, \ldots, P_n, (1 - \hat{S}_g)Y_g] \tag{5.3.20}$$

Note that one need not in practical applications insist that these demand functions be derived from explicit utility functions. They are, however, required to be homogeneous of degree zero in prices and incomes. In most empirical applications, the estimated demand equations are usually derivable from additively separable utility functions. This assumption simplifies the problem of parameter estimation, but is limiting. For example, there can be no specific substitution effects and no inferior goods.[8] At this point, we shall simply require that the demand functions be continuous and "well behaved" so that to each set of prices and associated incomes we can associate a unique vector of consumption demands. What cannot be ruled out when there is more than one group of consumers is that the same vector of consumption demands recurs for different sets of prices.

Because factor incomes are fully determined by the set of commodity prices one initially gives to the system, one can write the consumption function more simply as a vector function:

$$C^D = C(P_1, \ldots, P_n) \tag{5.3.21}$$

It is understood that behind the equation lies the solution of factor markets as well as the various equations defining disposable incomes. Fundamentally, however, there is a simple chain of causality leading from the price vector to the vector of consumption demands, and it is this chain that is represented by Eq. (5.3.21).

To close the model, it remains to discuss what happens to the total savings withdrawn from the flow of funds. Assume that all savings are spent on investment goods. Denoting by $\overline{H}_i$ the share of investment going to sector i,

$$\overline{H}_i = U_i \frac{\Delta K_i}{TS} \tag{5.3.22}$$

and therefore

$$\Delta K_i = \overline{H}_i \frac{TS}{U_i} \tag{5.3.23}$$

---

[8] For a recent survey of empirical demand analysis, see Brown and Deaton (1972). Note also that one could include the savings decision as not being separable. See, for example, Lluch (1973).

where U_i denotes the price of capital and ΔK_i is real investment in sector i. The shares of $\overline{H}_i$ will for the moment be assumed to be predetermined. We shall discuss the problem of their determination extensively in Section 5.6.

Because capital in each sector is again simply a fixed-proportions composite commodity, the price of capital is, as in input–output models, the weighted average of its components:

$$U_i = \sum_j s_{ji} P_j \qquad (5.3.24)$$

where s_{ji} are the shares in the capital composition matrix. The sectoral capital accumulations ΔK_i are therefore uniquely determined by the price system, which uniquely determines the capital prices U_i and total savings TS. It remains to translate the sectoral pattern of capital accumulation into demands for investment goods by sector of origin. This is achieved by using the elements of the capital composition matrix. Letting Z_i denote total investment demand by sector of origin, we have, just as in a dynamic input–output model,

$$Z_i = \sum_{j=1}^{n} s_{ij} \Delta K_j \qquad (5.3.25)$$

It is again possible to write investment demands Z_i as a function of the initial price vector only, because a unique causal chain leads from the P_i to the Z_i. One can therefore write the vector function,

$$Z = Z(P_1, \ldots, P_n) \qquad (5.3.26)$$

in similar fashion to the consumer demand equations.

Excess demand equations for commodities

We thus have the following situation, where X^S and X^D are vector equations:

$$(P_1, \ldots, P_n) \Big\langle \begin{array}{l} X^S = X(P_1, \ldots, P_n) \\ X^D = D(P_1, \ldots, P_n) \end{array}$$

and the components of demand are given by

$$X_i^D = C_i^D + Z_i + V_i \qquad (5.3.27)$$

The problem faced is almost exactly analogous to the simpler one already discussed in the introductory section. A solution to the general equilibrium model is given by a price vector $(P_1, \ldots, P_n)$ such that excess demands equal zero in all sectors:

$$EX_i = X_i^D - X_i^S = 0 \qquad (5.3.28)$$

The excess demand functions have a number of important properties. First, they are homogeneous of degree zero in all prices. To see the homogeneity property, first consider the factor market equations. Doubling all prices implies doubling all net prices. Thus, doubling all wages W_s in Eq. (5.3.8) and leaving the labor allocations L_{is} unchanged will not affect the equalities, and thus the same factor allocation and factor prices will remain a solution to the marginal productivity equations. Because value added has doubled and wage incomes have doubled, the residual capital incomes must also double. While incomes have doubled in nominal terms, the sectoral supplies X_i^S have remained constant after the proportional increase in all prices; $X(P_1, \ldots, P_n)$ is unaffected by price changes.

Turning to the demand side, $D(P_1, \ldots, P_n)$ will also remain unaffected by a proportional change in all prices. As we have already noted, all incomes will change proportionately with prices. Relative prices and real incomes have remained constant, and therefore consumption demands will remain unchanged. The price of composite capital goods – Eq. (5.3.24) – also doubles, and hence the demand for real composite capital goods by sector of destination — Eq. (5.3.23) – does not change, because both the numerator and the denominator have doubled. Thus, in Eq. (5.3.25), the demand for investment goods by sector of origin will also remain unchanged. Finally, gross output remaining constant, the intermediate demands by producers will also remain unchanged. Hence neither $X(P_1, \ldots, P_n)$ nor $D(P_1, \ldots, P_n)$ is affected by proportional price changes, and the excess demand equations (5.3.28) are indeed homogeneous of degree zero in all prices and wages. This means that if a vector $(P_1, \ldots, P_n)$ constitutes a solution to the system of n excess demand equations, any vector $\lambda(P_1, \ldots, P_n)$ proportional to it $(\lambda > 0)$ will also constitute a solution. There seems to be an infinite number of solutions to a system of n equations in n unknowns.

In fact, the second important property of the excess demand equations is that they are not independent. For any allowable price vector $(P_1, \ldots, P_n)$, the following identity, known as Walras's law, holds:

$$\sum_i P_i(X_i^D - X_i^S) \equiv 0 \qquad (5.3.29)$$

To see that Walras's law always holds, it is sufficient to remember that $\sum_i P_i X_i^D = \sum_i P_i X_i^S$, the total value of output, and $\sum_i P_i X_i^D =$

$\Sigma_i \, P_i C_i^D + \Sigma_i \, P_i V_i + \Sigma_i \, P_i Z_i$, the total value of expenditures. Noting that $V_i = \Sigma_{i=1}^n a_{ij} X_j$ and subtracting $\Sigma_{i=1}^n P_i V_i$ from both D and X in the excess demand equation, Walras's law reduces to the requirement that

$$\sum_i PN_i X_i + \sum_i P_i td_i X_i \equiv \sum_i P_i C_i + \sum_i P_i Z_i \qquad (5.3.30)$$

or

$$\sum_s Y_s + Y_k + Y_g \equiv \sum_i P_i C_i + \sum_i P_i Z_i \qquad (5.3.31)$$

Because each spending unit's demands are subject to a budget constraint which says that outlays must equal income, it is clear that such a budget constraint also holds in the aggregate and (5.3.31) will hold not only at equilibrium, but *for all allowable price vectors*. There are thus only $(n - 1)$ independent excess demand equations to determine $(n - 1)$ relative price ratios.

Normalization, the price level, and macroeconomics

In pure general equilibrium theory, one can leave matters at this point. In practice, a CGE model must usually arrive at some way of determining an absolute price level as well as relative prices. A wide variety of price-normalization equations have been used. Johansen, in his path-breaking (1960) study, fixed the wage of labor and thus expressed all prices in terms of wages. One could alternatively fix the price of any one commodity and express all prices in terms of this numéraire commodity. Indeed, one could normalize around virtually any nominal magnitude in the model economy, because it will not affect any of the real variables.

When using such models as tools of policy analysis and formulation, it is best to use a price-normalization rule that provides a "no-inflation" benchmark against which all price changes are relative price changes. The equation used will be of the form

$$\sum_i P_i \Omega_i = \overline{P} \qquad (5.3.32)$$

where the Ω_i are weights defining the index $\overline{P}$ that one wants to hold constant. The index may be updated over time to reflect projected changes in, for example, the wholesale price index or some other index of aggregate prices.

With the price normalization, the formal presentation of the core equations of a CGE model is complete. However, the discussion of price normalization focuses attention on macroeconomic aspects of the model and raises what is perhaps the most controversial issue in the field of general equilibrium modeling, the inclusion of monetary mechanisms. Given the current state of theory in this area, essentially two options are open to the model builder.

First, the normalization rule can be seen as no more than the choice of a numéraire and the model remains a barter model, similar to the theoretical models of real growth or real trade theory. This option is consistent with the treatment in input–output and linear programming models, which have never tried to incorporate money in any way. The advantage of this option is that it is simple and preserves a close relationship between the new generation of CGE models and both the linear models discussed in Part I and the theoretical models of growth and trade theory. It precludes, however, any model-based policy analysis of macro or monetary issues. We cannot, for example, use such a model to analyze the causes of inflation or endogenously project the price level.

The second option is to add a macromonetary superstructure that interacts with the multisector general equilibrium model. One can, for example, attach monetary behavior equations to the model and attempt to capture the demand for and supply of financial assets and the interaction between money and the real sphere of the economy. Such an approach, in which the price level is determined endogenously, has the great advantage of extending the field of application of CGE models from the analysis of problems of industrial strategy, protection, and trade policy to problems of inflation, "Keynesian" imbalances between aggregate supply and demand, and short-run stabilization policy.

In this book, we have essentially chosen the first option and have not attempted to extend the essentially microeconomic, general equilibrium structure of the nonlinear CGE models to include money-holding and macroeconomic behavior. With the exception of the application to Turkey in Part IV, money never appears explicitly, and even then it remains quite "neutral," providing only a simple transfer mechanism to close the flow-of-funds accounts. We have chosen to concentrate our efforts on the resource allocation issues, with particular emphasis on the problems of adequately modeling foreign trade. In all the models we shall present, the aggregate price level is explicitly treated as exogenous and, implicitly, problems relating to its determination are treated as separable from problems relating to the determination of relative prices and incentives. We shall see that this separability is not always easy to preserve and, ultimately, it will no doubt have to be abandoned.

Our choice is based on our perception of the need to proceed in steps and on our desire to make the models presented quite transparent by remaining close to well-understood and established theory. The interaction between money and the real sphere of the economy is still a very difficult area of theory – as the largely unresolved literature on including money in a general equilibrium model and on the micro foundations of Keynesian macroeconomics attests. We feel that interweaving a simplistic and ad hoc macro money model with the microeconomic general equilibrium model may often detract from the usefulness of the latter as a planning tool focusing on multisector issues of growth, resource allocation, and structural change. Such issues have traditionally been a central focus of multisector planning, and we have maintained that focus in our work. It should be emphasized, however, that we do *not* feel that efforts to integrate a macro model with a multisector planning model are ill advised or premature. On the contrary, there is a great challenge in such work that must be met, and the rewards are potentially great.[9]

A case can be made for the realism of our implicit assumption that there can be a certain "separation" between analysis of microeconomic incentives, industrial strategy, and trade questions on the one hand and macroeconomic stabilization problems on the other. For example, this view has been eloquently argued by Krueger (1979). There are certainly many examples of CGE models that remain within the framework of what are essentially barter models.[10] There are also a few examples of CGE models that have extended the basic general equilibrium model to include some specification of money-holding behavior and/or macroeconomic relationships (see Adelman and Robinson, 1978; Ahluwalia and Lysy, 1979; Lysy and Taylor, 1980). Lance Taylor is probably the most persistent advocate of the importance of specifying the impact of macroeconomic "closure" rules and inflation on microeconomic variables and, in particular, on the distribution of income.[11] Although part of these differences in emphasis and approach reflect real differences in views on how economies work, part is also due simply to different time horizons. Taylor, for example, is often concerned with the very short run, and there is general agreement that money is much less "neutral" and hence more important in the short run compared to the medium-term horizon of most multisector planning models. Much depends on the specific purpose of a particular model-building effort.

[9] For a recent attempt at such an integration starting from an econometric macroeconomic model of Canada, see Dungan (1980).

[10] See, for example, Johansen and associates (1960, 1968); Derviş (1975); Petri (1976); Whalley (1977); de Melo (1978b); Ginsburgh and Waelbroeck (1978).

[11] See Taylor (1979). These "structuralist" issues are discussed in Chapter 12.

At this point, the presentation of the model is complete. In the next section we shall provide a summary listing of the model equations and discuss how they incorporate the "circular flow" in an economy by tying them into a social accounting matrix framework.

Before concluding this section, however, it is reasonable to ask if, in fact, a solution exists and, if so, whether or not it is unique. Most applied model builders, in contrast to theorists, have not worried too much about general existence problems. After all, a solution is numerically computed and an existence proof may appear unnecessary. The models are always quite well behaved and, given that very general existence proofs have been established for theoretical models of which CGE models form a rather well-behaved subset, it is reasonable to expect that nonexistence problems will not arise in practice. Nevertheless, it is worthwhile to examine briefly the existence problem for the core model and sketch the basic reasoning of an existence proof. We shall do this next, and use some set and matrix notation that are unique to the next section and that deviate slightly from our standard notation conventions. The reader who is either familiar with or not interested in existence proofs can proceed to Section 5.4.

Sketch of an existence proof[12]

Consider the set of "allowable" price vectors such that net prices are non-negative. Define this set as $P^s = \{P | (P - PA) \geq 0, P \geq 0\}$.

Provided that the input–output matrix is productive, P^s is nonempty, and it is clear that it is a convex cone. For if $P \in P^s$, $\lambda P \in P^s$ for all $\lambda \geq 0$ and if $P^1 \in P^s$ and $P^2 \in P^s$, $\lambda P^1 + (1 - \lambda)P^2 \in P^s$. Figure 5.1 describes the set P^s in a two-sector model. The two rays through the origin, R_1 and R_2, reflect the condition of non-negative net prices (value added) in sectors 1 and 2. The Hawkins-Simon (or productiveness conditions) guarantee that the slope of R_1 is greater than the slope of R_2 and that both slopes are positive:

$$(1 - a_{11})(1 - a_{22}) - a_{12}a_{21} > 0 \Rightarrow \frac{1 - a_{11}}{a_{21}} > \frac{a_{12}}{1 - a_{22}}$$

and

$$(1 - a_{11}) > 0 \Rightarrow \frac{1 - a_{11}}{a_{21}} > 0$$

$$(1 - a_{22}) > 0 \Rightarrow \frac{a_{12}}{1 - a_{22}} > 0$$

---

[12] The discussion of this section follows closely the treatment in Dorfman et al. (1958).

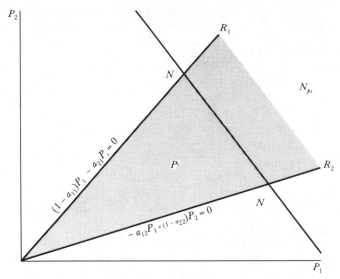

Figure 5.1. The cone of allowable prices in a two-sector model.

Each ray passes through the origin and therefore defines two half-spaces that are convex cones. The intersection of the two half-spaces defined by the inequalities is itself the convex cone of allowable prices. Note finally that the boundaries of the allowable set (i.e., the two rays R_1 and R_2) are constituted by points for which either PN_1 or PN_2 equals zero. For any non-negative net price vector PN, there exists a vector $P = PN(I - A)^{-1}$ in the allowable set.

We must now add the restriction that prices satisfy the normalization rule so that we define a new "normalized" allowable set $^nP^s$ such that $^nP^s = \{P|(P - PA) \geq 0, P > 0, \Sigma_i \, P_i\Omega_i = \overline{P}\}$. Clearly the set $^nP^s$ is a closed interval of the form NN shown in Figure 5.1. The equilibrium price vector must be contained in that closed interval that itself constitutes a closed, bounded, and convex set.

Let us now consider the following mapping from $^nP^s$ into itself. Take any price vector $P \in {}^nP^s$. Use it to solve for the production side of the economy and obtain factor prices and household and government incomes. Feeding these incomes into the demand side, obtain a net demand vector $XN^D = (XN_1^D, \ldots, XN_n^D)$ by subtracting intermediate demands from total gross demands. Scale this vector up or down by a scale factor λ_1, until it is situated on the boundary of the net production set X^N. There will exist a separating hyperplane at that point which defines a non-negative vector of net prices $PN = (PN_1, \ldots, PN_n)$ that would lead profit-maximizing firms (or a central planner) to the scaled point $\lambda_1 \cdot XN^D$. This vector of net prices is arbitrary up to a multiplicative constant, so it is possible to scale PN with a second scaling factor λ_2 such that $P = PN(I - A)^{-1} \in {}^nP^s$. These steps define a mapping from ${}^nP^s$ into itself. Using a theorem on the continuity properties of optimal solutions (see Debreu, 1959, sec. 1.8k), one can establish that the mapping satisfies the continuity properties required for fixed-point theorems. In this case, characterized by strict convexity of the production set, every step of the mapping constitutes a point-to-point mapping, and the entire mapping is therefore a continuous point-to-point mapping of a compact convex set into itself. One can therefore appeal to Brouwer's fixed-point theorem and claim that there exists at least one vector P^e such that $P^e = M(P^e)$, where $M(P)$ defines the mapping of ${}^nP^s$ into itself. By using Walras's law, one can then show that the two scaling factors used in the mapping must equal unity at the fixed point because the total value of net output must equal the sum of all incomes. At that point, when $P = P^e$, $\lambda_1 = \lambda_2 = 1$, and the supply decisions of firms will be consistent with the demand decisions of households and of the government. This argument establishes the general existence of an overall equilibrium solution to the basic CGE model. The fixed point discussed above cannot in the general case be show to be unique. If one were to assume a single decision maker on the demand side, the convexity of preferences leading to the weak axiom of revealed preference would imply uniqueness of equilibrium.[13] But the weak axiom need not hold in the general case when there is more than one category of demanders because as prices change, the distribution of income changes and the weak axiom no longer follows from the assumption of well-behaved individual utility functions: Equilibrium may therefore not be unique. In practice, none of the CGE models built so far seems to suffer from nonuniqueness.[14] It appears that changes in the community indifference map due to shifts in income distribution are never enough to create a uniqueness problem.[15] Whether this result will continue to hold for all kinds of CGE models remains an open question.

5.4 CGE models and social accounts

In this section, we discuss the CGE model in terms of the kind of statistical "picture" it provides of the workings of an economy. As an

[13] Arrow and Hahn (1971) provide a thorough treatment of existence and uniqueness in competitive general equilibrium analysis.

[14] Indeed, even models that violate the homogeneity assumptions have been solved empirically with no apparent problems.

[15] See Kehoe (1980) for a discussion of how to determine uniqueness properties in a class of general equilibrium models. In unpublished work he has constructed an interesting example of a model with multiple equilibria.

Table 5.1. *Structure of a social accounting matrix for Turkey, 1973*

Receipts	Expenditures — Activities (1)	Commodities (2)	Factors: Labor (3)	Factors: Capital (4)	Institutions: Households (5)	Institutions: Government (6)	Capital account (7)	Rest of world (8)
Activities (1)		Domestic commodity supplies				Export subsidy		Exports
Commodities (2)	Intermediate inputs				Private consumption	Government consumption	Investment	
Factors: Labor (3)	Wages							
Factors: Capital (4)	Rentals							
Institutions: Households (5)			Labor income	Capital income		Transfers		Capital inflow
Government (6)	Indirect taxes	Tariffs			Direct taxes			
Capital account (7)					Private saving	Government saving		
Rest of world (8)		Imports				Reserve accumulation		
Totals (9)	Total costs	Total absorption	Factor income	Factor income	Household income	Government expenditure	Investment	Foreign exchange inflow

organizing framework, we use the device of a social accounting matrix (SAM), which presents in one unified set of accounts a picture of the "circular flow" of a market economy. The SAM provides a consistent picture of the flow-of-funds accounts of the separate institutions or "actors" in the economy that one may wish to distinguish. There are a number of variations in the accounting conventions used in the construction of SAMs (see United Nations Statistical Office, 1975). Table 5.1 gives one such example, and Table 5.2 implements it with the same data for Turkey that are given in the input–output table presented in Chapter 2. In contrast to the input-output table, the SAM is a square matrix and the corresponding row and column sums are equal. The defining characteristic of a SAM is that each row and column reflects a separate account for which expenditures and receipts must balance. The focus is thus on the nominal flow of funds, with the rows representing receipt accounts and the columns expenditure accounts.

The SAM given in Tables 5.1 and 5.2 is designed to reflect the "view" of the economy that is embodied in the core CGE model we have outlined. For completeness, we have added a rest-of-the-world column, although the model presented in this chapter is that of a closed economy. An understanding of the particular conventions we have used in the SAM helps in understanding the structure of the core model, and its extensions that will be discussed in later chapters.

First, note that there is a distinction made in the SAM between "activities" and "commodities." The accounts of "activities" correspond to the producing sectors in the input–output accounts. For example, the interindustry flows in the input–output table have been aggregated into a single entry (195.7 billion TL) in the SAM: row 2, column 1, or entry (2, 1). The entries in column 1 of the SAM correspond to the aggregation of the sector accounts in the input output table (column 8 in Table 2.1)[16]

The "commodity" accounts combine domestic supply with imports to yield total supply to the domestic market, or absorption. From Table 2.1, total absorption can be defined as domestic supply plus imports (including tariffs) minus exports: $489.8 + 33.7 + 11.7 - 26.0 = 509.2$ billion TL, which is exactly the total of the "commodity" account (row and column 2) in the SAM.[17]

---

[16] Total expenditure by activities in the SAM is 489.8 billion TL and equals the sum of sectoral expenditure in the input–output table, entry (13, 8), Table 2.1.

[17] Note that the commodity account "pays" tariffs because all market prices are defined as prices to the buyer.

Table 5.2. *A social accounting matrix for Turkey, 1973 (billion TL)*

Receipts	Expenditures		Factors		Institutions				
	Activities (1)	Commodities (2)	Labor (3)	Capital (4)	Households (5)	Government (6)	Capital account (7)	Rest of world (8)	Total receipts (9)
Activities (1)		463.8				1.5		24.5	489.8
Commodities (2)	195.7				224.7	30.5	58.3		509.2
Factors:									
Labor (3)	138.1								138.1
Capital (4)	137.1								137.1
Institutions:									
Households (5)			138.1	137.1				19.7	294.9
Government (6)	18.9	11.7			23.5				54.1
Capital account (7)					46.7	11.6			58.3
Rest of world (8)	33.7					10.5			44.2
Total expenditures (9)	489.8	509.2	138.1	137.1	294.9	54.1	58.3	44.2	

The separation of the "activity" and "commodity" accounts is important in a modeling framework because activities are assumed to consist of producers who are behaviorally distinct in the models. The real counterpart to the monetary flows in row 1 of the SAM is the delivery of domestically produced goods to various demanders. The "commodity" account corresponds to the domestic market for all products, with supplies coming from producers and imports. Note that exports are not included in the "commodity" accounts but are sold directly to the "rest of the world" by producers ("activities").[18] Thus exports and imports are not treated symmetrically, a distinction that will reappear in later chapters.

The factor accounts indicate payments for factors of production (rows 3 and 4) and the distribution of factor income to the institutions we chose to distinguish (columns 3 and 4). In the SAM presented here, these accounts are very simple, with all of factor income (labor and capital) accruing to "households." The "households" are here the various "categories" of labor and the "capitalists" that earn the difference between value-added and labor income [see Eqs. (5.3.12–14)]. In the core CGE model, there is therefore no real distinction between "factors" and "institutions" except that the incomes of "households" differ from the incomes of the corresponding factors because of transfers received from, and taxes paid to, the government. Thus, the factor accounts act as transfer accounts, channeling wages and rentals from producers to "households." In models that focus on the distribution of income, the mapping from factor incomes to "institutions" needs to be much better developed to reflect the complexities of the distributional process. These issues will be discussed in greater detail in Chapter 12.

Along with producers, the "institutions" (households and government) represent the major economic actors in the system whose behavior provide much of the focus of the models we shall develop. In the accounts shown in this table, "enterprises" do not appear as a separate institution because they are not treated as behaviorally distinct from producers (activities). This simple treatment, which is reflected in the model of Turkey discussed in Part IV, is reasonable given the issues on which the model focuses, but should be expanded in models concerned more with income distribution, savings mechanisms, and/or taxation. Such an expanded treatment is given in Chapter 12.

"Households" and "government" accounts are treated separately,

---

[18] In the SAM, total exports in domestic prices include subsidies, entry $(1, 7)$ and so equal $24.5 + 1.5 = 26.0$ billion TL. This is the total shown for the export column in the input–output table, Table 2.1, entry $(8, 11)$.

Table 5.3. *The structure of a macroeconomic SAM*

	Activities	Institutions	Capital account	Rest of world
Activities	Domestic intermediates	Domestic consumption	Domestic investment	Exports
Institutions	Value added			
Capital account		Domestic saving		Net foreign saving
Rest of world	Intermediate imports	Consumer imports	Investment imports	
Column sum	Total costs	Value added	Total saving	Imports

reflecting their very different behavioral specification both in theory and in the models we shall present. Government receives income from direct and indirect taxes (including tariffs), purchases commodities directly, and also saves. Households receive factor income, which they divide between consumption and savings. The specification of the behavioral rules for households and government provide, together with the behavioral rules for producers, the core of the specification of the planning models we shall discuss.

In our SAM, the "rest-of-the-world" account is set up to reflect the sources of foreign exchange (column) and its disposition (row). Foreign exchange receipts from exports and foreign borrowing are distributed to various actors: producers (24.5 billion) and households (19.7). These receipts are used to buy imports (33.7) or are held by the government as increased reserves (10.5). Foreign saving is not treated separately, but is included in the accounts of the three institutions. The foreign and domestic components of the institutional accounts are thus not shown directly in Tables 5.1 and 5.2.

The treatment of trade in the SAM is consistent with the approach we shall develop in the next two chapters describing how we open the core model behaviorally to include imports and exports. The approach is somewhat different from that used in most macro models, so it is helpful to compare the two. Tables 5.3 and 5.4 present a simpler, more aggregated SAM that distinguishes foreign and domestic saving, presenting the accounts in a form that is more familiar to those who work with national income accounts. The factor and commodity accounts have been eliminated, so activities are assumed to pay all of value added to institutions and import demand by each account is entered separately.

Table 5.4. *A macroeconomic SAM for Turkey, 1973 (billion TL)*

	Activities	Institutions	Capital account	Rest of world	Row sum
Activities	172.9	243.7	48.7	24.5	489.8
Institutions	294.1				294.1
Capital account		49.1		9.2	58.3
Rest of world	22.8	1.3	9.6		33.7
Column sum	489.8	294.1	58.3	33.7	

The rest-of-the-world account is different from that in Table 5.2 because there is no payment from the rest of the world to the institutional accounts. Instead, net foreign savings are entered as payment from the rest of the world to the capital account, and the sum of the rest-of-the-world account equals total imports (in border prices) rather than total foreign exchange inflow (as in Table 5.2).[19] Institutional income thus does not include any receipts from the rest of the world.

Finally, the "capital" account can be thought of as an investment bank. It collects all savings, domestic and foreign, and spends them on investment goods. In the input–output accounts, as in the SAM, the demand for investment goods (by sector of origin) is given. In addition, the SAM distinguishes the various sources of savings. However, neither account shows which sectors receive the increased capital (investment by sector of destination). The treatment of investment is discussed in more detail later.

The major usefulness of the SAM approach is that it brings together the accounts of each of the various economic actors whose behavior is to be modeled into a consistent framework. Such a data set, at least for a base year, is required for the implementation of such a model. Like the input–output accounts, the SAM provides a framework that requires the expanded set of data to be consistent. This consistency property provides a useful check in reconciling data from disparate sources.[20]

The presentation of the SAM has been based on a number of conventions that reflect the particular features of the models developed in

[19] From Table 5.2, net foreign savings equals the balance of trade or foreign capital inflow minus reserve accumulation; $33.7 - 24.5 = 19.7 - 10.5 = 9.2$ billion TL.

[20] See Methodological Appendix A for a description of how to construct a consistent set of data using the SAM framework.

Table 5.5. *Factor market and product supply equations*

	Number of equations	
Production functions:		
$\quad X_i^S = f(\overline{K}_i, L_i^a, V_{1i}, \ldots, V_{ni})$	n	(5.5.1)
Intermediate goods demand:		
$\quad V_{ij} = a_{ij}X_j$	$n \cdot n$	(5.5.2)
$\quad V_i = \sum_j V_{ij}$	n	(5.5.3)
Labor aggregation:		
$\quad L_i^a = L_i^a(L_{i1}, \ldots, L_{im})$	n	(5.5.4)
Net prices:		
$\quad PN_i = P_i - \sum_j a_{ji}P_j - td_iP_i$	n	(5.5.5)
Labor demand equations:		
$\quad PN_i \dfrac{\partial X_i}{\partial L_i^a} \dfrac{\partial L_i^a}{\partial L_{is}} = W_s$	$n \cdot m$	(5.5.6)
Aggregate labor demands:		
$\quad L_s^D = \sum_i L_{is}$	m	(5.5.7)
Aggregate labor supply:		
$\quad L_s^S = \overline{L}_s$	m	(5.5.8)
Excess demand for labor equations:		
$\quad L_s^D = L_s^S = 0$	m	(5.5.9)

Total: $4n + 3m + n \cdot m + n \cdot n$

	Endogenous variables	Number
X_i^S	Sectoral production	n
V_{ij}	Intermediate goods demand	$n \cdot n$
V_i	Aggregate intermediate goods demand	n
L_i^a	Aggregate labor by sector	n
PN_i	Net prices	n
L_{is}	Labor demand by sector and type	$n \cdot m$
L_s^D	Aggregate labor demand by type	m
L_s^S	Aggregate labor supply by type	m
W_s	Wage of labor by type	m

Total: $4n + 3m + n \cdot m + n \cdot n$

this book. It should be emphasized that there is as yet no such thing as a "standard" SAM. The definition of the different accounts, the degree of disaggregation, and the accounting conventions used should reflect the particular model and set of issues that are being considered.

5.5   Summary of the static CGE model

The complete set of equations

The complete set of equations for the model is collected together in Tables 5.5 and 5.6. Table 5.5 gives the equations for the factor markets that essentially underlie the aggregate supply or production transformation set considered earlier. The endogenous variables in these equations describe all the flows in the first column of the social accounting matrix. In real terms, they give employment, intermediate demand, and product supply. In terms of monetary flows, they give payments for intermediate goods, labor, capital, and indirect taxes. Table 5.6 gives the equations for the product markets in the model economy. The endogenous variables describe the flows in the last four columns of the social accounting matrix. They give the distribution of factor income to "institutions" (households and government); its allocation among taxes, consumption and saving; and finally the resulting demand for products.

The presentation in Tables 5.5 and 5.6 emphasizes the market-clearing role of wages and prices in the core model. For any given set of product prices P_i, there are as many equations in Table 5.5 as there are endogenous variables. The heart of the problem is to find a set of average wages such that, given the labor demands from Eq. (5.5.6), there is zero excess demand in the markets for labor of different skill categories. The solution of the excess demand equations for labor for different sets of product prices defines the summary numerical supply function given in Eq. (5.3.11).[21]

The product market equations in Table 5.6 can, by simple substitution, be reduced to the set of excess demand equations. Note that the number of equations is one greater than the number of variables. As we have discussed, the equations are not independent, so that the n excess demand equations can determine only $n - 1$ relative prices. The price normalization equation (5.5.23) is required to set the absolute price level.[22]

The product market equations, as we have noted, include the flow of funds among the various institutions in the economy. They thus include

---

[21] Note, as discussed earlier, that it is straightforward to assume that for some categories of labor, the (real) wage is fixed. The labor supply function for the skill category is simply dropped when the wage is set exogenously, and the excess demand for labor equation serves only to determine total employment.

[22] The question of existence of at least one general equilibrium solution with non-negative values of the endogenous variables was discussed earlier.

Table 5.6. *Product market equations*

	Number of equations	
Household, capitalist, and government income:		
$Y_s = \sum_i W_s L_{is}(1 - t_s)$	m	(5.5.10)
$Y_k = \left(\sum_i PM_i X_i - \sum_i \sum_s L_{is} \right)(1 - t_k)$	One	(5.5.11)
$Y_g = \sum_s \dfrac{t_s}{1 - t_s} Y_s + \dfrac{t_k}{1 - t_k} Y_k + \sum_i td_i P_i X_i$	One	(5.5.12)
Total saving:		
$TS = \sum_s \hat{S}_s Y_s + \hat{S}_k Y_k + \hat{S}_g Y_g$	One	(5.5.13)
Consumer demand:		
$C_{is}^D = C_{is}[P_1, \ldots, P_n, (1 - \hat{S}_s) Y_s]$	$n \cdot m$	(5.5.14)
$C_{ik}^D = C_{ik}[P_1, \ldots, P_n, (1 - \hat{S}_k) Y_k]$	n	(5.5.15)
$C_{ig}^D = C_{ig}[P_1, \ldots, P_n, (1 - \hat{S}_g) Y_g]$	n	(5.5.16)
$C_i^D = \sum_s C_{is}^D + C_{ik}^D + C_{ig}^D$	n	(5.5.17)
Investment demand:		
$U_i = \sum_j s_{ji} P_j$	n	(5.5.18)
$\Delta K_i = \overline{H}_i \dfrac{TS}{U_i}$	n	(5.5.19)
$Z_i = \sum_j s_{ij} \Delta K_j$	n	(5.5.20)
Aggregate excess demands:		
$X_i^D = C_i^D + Z_i + V_i$	n	(5.5.21)
$X_i^D - X_i^S = 0$	n	(5.5.22)
Price normalization:		
$\sum_i P_i \Omega_i = \overline{P}$	One	(5.5.23)

Total: $8n + m + n \cdot m + 4$

	Endogenous variables	Number
Y_s	Labor income by type	m
Y_k	Capital income	One
Y_g	Government revenue	One
TS	Total saving	One
C_{is}^D	Consumer demands by labor households	$n \cdot m$
C_{ik}^D	Consumer demands by capitalists	n
C_{ig}^D	Government consumption	n
C_i^D	Aggregate consumption demand	n
U_i	Capital goods price	n
ΔK_i	Real investment by sector of destination	n
Z_i	Investment goods demands by sector of origin	n
X_i^D	Aggregate demands by sector	n
P_i	Prices	n

Total: $8n + m + n \cdot m + 3$

the flows that are the focus of demand-driven macro models. As we have discussed, we are focusing on issues of sectoral structure, resource allocation, and trade, and so are not attempting to determine endogenously variables such as the price level. However, in any CGE model, the flow-of-funds accounts must specify the entire circular flow in the system – there are no leakages. Thus the macroeconomic problem of reconciling aggregate savings and investment is also an inherent part of the model. In the literature, this reconciliation is referred to as the "closure" problem because it involves closing the flow-of-funds accounts (see Adelman and Robinson, 1978; Lluch, 1979).

The treatment of investment

There are two modeling issues related to investment that are not dealt with in the social accounting framework: first, the determination of the volume of investment and, second, its sectoral allocation. We shall treat the second issue in our discussion of intertemporal linkages. In the model equations presented in Table 5.6, the sectoral share parameters for investment ($\overline{H}_i$) are simply assumed to be fixed. The level of total investment, however, is determined endogenously. In the capital account row in the SAM, total savings (and hence investment) are determined by applying exogenous savings rates to the income of each institution in the economy. Total investment is thus determined by savings behavior and is thus also a function of the distribution of income among the different households and the government (assuming that their savings rates differ). This model of total savings and investment is very classical in spirit, except that we have added government to the usual capitalist and labor classes.

The determination of aggregate investment is clearly a very important part of any dynamic planning model, and the classical approach we have presented is not the only reasonable way to treat investment in such a model. There is no shortage of theories of investment in economics – the problem is more that there is no widespread agreement on which theories are best. In a planning model such as our CGE model, a number of different choices seems reasonable. We shall give two alternative examples. First, in a model intended for policy planning, one might wish to specify the level of real investment exogenously. A planner might well wish to trace out the impact of alternative investment scenarios on the model economy and simply assume that policies can be chosen that will achieve the desired level of investment. The model can be adapted to embody this approach. Instead of being endogenous, real capital stock growth (usually measured in base-year prices) would be set exogenously. Some other parameters, such as the savings rates in Eq. (5.5.13), would then have to be adjusted endogenously so that sufficient savings are generated to finance the purchase of the capital goods. Alternatively, in "Kaldorian" fashion, one could argue that with fixed savings rates, the distribution of income will have to adjust to validate the exogenously specified investment.[23]

Second, a different savings-determined approach has some appeal. Instead of having savings be partly a function of the distribution of income among institutions, one might assume that the society determines aggregate savings by setting aside a fixed portion of total national income. The precise mechanism by which this fixed rate is determined and applied is left purposely vague. One might appeal to a complex interaction among government credit policy, the workings of the banking system, and inflation – all of which are not explicitly included in the planning model. The essential view is that society as a whole determines the savings rate – a view that might well be labeled neoclassical. Again, some parameters will have to adjust endogenously for the flow of funds to remain consistent.

The three investment theories we have discussed – the one actually modeled and the two alternatives – certainly do not represent an exhaustive list of possible approaches. However, they do represent an interesting range, and all have some appeal for inclusion in a planning model intended to be used for policy analysis in the medium to long run. In the next chapters, we shall have occasion to discuss some of the implications of using these approaches to investment when the model is extended to include international trade and the possibility of foreign capital inflows. In most of the book, however, we shall take the classical view and investment will be determined by the amount of savings generated by applying savings rates to the different institutions or income categories. Note that this approach leaves the solution homogeneous of degree zero in all prices.

Solution strategies

A number of different approaches have been used to solve CGE models such as the one we have presented.[24] As discussed in Methodological Appendix B, it is useful to distinguish between a solution strategy and

[23] For further discussion of such mechanisms, see Chapter 12.
[24] See Methodological Appendix B for a brief survey of solution strategies and a thorough discussion of the solution algorithms used to solve the CGE models used in this book.

a solution algorithm. A solution strategy refers to the way in which the equations of the model are substituted and rearranged so as to reduce the solution problem as much as possible before solving it on a computer. A solution algorithm refers to the actual numerical algorithm used to solve the reduced set of equations on the computer. In devising a solution strategy for CGE models, it is important to take advantage of our knowledge of the economic properties of the system of equations. In this section, we describe our basic solution strategy and use it as a framework for clarifying further the workings of the model.

Our basic solution strategy is, in fact, evident from the way in which the model equations were presented. The entire model can be reduced by substitution – either analytical or numerical – to sets of excess demand equations for the factor and product markets. The solution problem thus is reduced to that of finding a set of equilibrium wages and prices – a fixed-point problem.

In choosing a solution strategy, two criteria are most important. First, how hard is it to solve the reduced equations numerically? Second, how hard is it to reduce the model equations to the chosen set, especially when, as is often the case, one wants to be able to experiment with a variety of analytic formulations? Reducing a CGE model to sets of market excess demand equations is usually a straightforward procedure requiring, with one exception, simply the evaluation of the equations of the model in order. The only place where numerical techniques may have to be used is in the derivation of labor demands by firms given wages – the marginal revenue product equations. The resulting excess demand equations are, of course, extremely nonlinear, and it is virtually impossible even to write out their analytic representation. Numerically, however, they can be handled.

Given our solution strategy, all solution algorithms will follow the same general procedure. They will all start with some initial set of wages and prices (which satisfy the normalization rule), calculate the excess demands in both factor and product markets, and then revise wages and prices iteratively based on calculated excess demands. The iterations stop when equilibrium is reached; that is, a set of wages and prices is found such that all excess demands are sufficiently close to zero. Different algorithms use quite different techniques for revising wages and prices given the excess demands from the last iteration, and there are a variety of such algorithms from which to choose. A brief survey plus a detailed description of our particular choice is given in Methodological Appendix B. Note, however, that for models using more-or-less "standard" production functions and demand systems, the excess demand equations are quite well behaved (after some scaling transformations) and are solvable by the imaginative application of standard numerical algorithms for solving systems of nonlinear simultaneous equations.

Inherent in the general solution strategy described here is a "price-adjustment" rather than a "quantity-adjustment" specification. The problem is seen as that of adjusting prices and wages until equilibrium is reached. One might instead use a quantity-adjustment approach. For example, in the labor markets one might find it difficult or inconvenient to invert the marginal revenue product equations to solve for labor demands given fixed wages. One can use a quantity-adjustment solution strategy that avoids the problem. Instead of assuming fixed wages and solving for labor demands, one can start with a labor allocation and solve for marginal revenue products by sectors. The equilibrium condition for the labor markets is restated. Instead of being "demand equals supply for each category of labor," it becomes "marginal revenue products are equal across all sectors for the same labor category." The solution problem is then to find a physical allocation of labor such that all labor is employed and marginal revenue products are equal across sectors for each category of labor.[25]

In discussing solution strategies, one must be careful not to confuse properties of an algorithm with properties of an economy. For example, the choice between a "price-adjustment" and a "quantity-adjustment" solution strategy has nothing to do with how one views the behavior of an actual economy out of equilibrium. In the literature on decomposition algorithms for solving linear programming models, there has been some tendency to interpret the behavior of different algorithms as reflecting differences in actual economies. Kornai (in Goreux and Manne, 1973) has warned against making such interpretations, and his warning is equally valid in interpreting solution strategies for CGE models. The CGE model is formulated as an equilibrium model, and one should place no significance on the actual path the model economy follows during iterations designed to find the equilibrium.

In terms of solution strategy, it is convenient to separate the factor and product markets and solve them seriatim. For example, for a given set of product prices, it is possible to solve for a set of wages that will clear the factor markets. This solution will yield product supplies and factor incomes that are then used to determine excess demands in the product markets and hence leads to a new guess at prices. Solving the two markets separately reduces the number of endogenous variables that

---

[25] This technique has in fact been used for some models [see Derviş (1975), de Melo (1977), and de Melo and Derviş (1977)].

have to be solved at any one time, although it means that one set of markets must be solved more often (in this case, the factor market must be solved for each price iteration). In general, reducing the number of endogenous variables per iteration yields algorithmic improvements that outweigh the disadvantages of having to solve the markets more often.

5.6 Equilibrium, time, and market clearing

The CGE model presented so far is purely static. Time did not enter into its specification, and all endogenous variables are therefore viewed as simultaneously determined. The solution constitutes a simultaneous intersection of the sectoral supply and demand functions. In a very Walrasian fashion, prices play a parametric role in the sense that decision makers react passively to prices, and it is these reactions that determine the demand and supply schedules. But, assuming that uniqueness conditions hold, there is only one vector of prices at which all demand and supply decisions of the various agents in the economy are mutually compatible, and it is that price vector that defines the general equilibrium solution.

Such a description is extremely neoclassical in spirit, and the core model is so close to the Walrasian ideal that one may rightly question its relevance for the formulation of policy in economies where institutional features and structuralist characteristics result in behavior far removed from the idealized description given so far. The question then arises of how far one can accommodate non-neoclassical features in the CGE framework without giving up its basic characteristics and internal consistency.

First, there may be elements of imperfect competition that need to be included in the model. This will not fundamentally alter the character of the solution: Prices will remain market-clearing prices, although some of the supply functions will now reflect monopoly power. One could also extend the model to incorporate monopoly power in the factor or product markets. In either case, one needs to model the relevant perceived demand elasticities in the factor and/or product demand equations. Monopoly-pricing rules could be replaced by mark-up pricing rules, in which case the supply schedules will include profits as arguments. It would, of course, be far more difficult to model imperfect competition properly, because certain indeterminacies may occur. Aside from such problems of indeterminacy, however, these model extensions do not change the fundamental market-clearing nature of the model solution.

Second, as was discussed in connection with labor markets, there may be some markets that will not be allowed to clear. The solution of such an applied model can be characterized as a "constrained" general equilibrium, close in spirit to the Walrasian construct but incorporating quantity constraints. The question of which markets should be constrained in a CGE model is a difficult one. It is certainly far from evident that prices observed in the real world of developing countries are in fact market-clearing prices. We shall discuss further below how the solution prices should be interpreted, but it should be noted that the problem is present not only in factor markets but also in product markets. This aspect of market adjustment has been recently emphasized in the theoretical work on the micro foundations of macroeconomics. This work emphasizes non-tâtonnement processes and mixed quantity-cum-price-adjustment mechanisms that may have consequences more important than allowed for or foreseen by traditional Walrasian theory.

One would of course like to address these issues properly, incorporating disequilibrium and partial adjustment in the actual model formulation. But given the medium to long-term planning purposes served by CGE models, it would in our view be premature at the present time to give up the basic notion of Walrasian equilibrium for a generalized disequilibrium model. The reason that general equilibrium theory (and, indeed, partial equilibrium theory) is of any use at all is that the equilibrium solution does exert a certain "pull" on the economic system: Although the economy may never actually be at equilibrium, it should not be too far away from it. This is clearly our fundamental premise. It does mean that one gives up short-term "tracking" as well as short-term prediction. But this should not be upsetting. It is the equilibrium shifts over time due to fundamental trends in technology, tastes, policies, and other exogenous factors that one can analyze with an equilibrium model. For these purposes, the assumption of market-clearing prices is a valuable one to retain as the basic organizing principle in models focusing on medium to long-run change.[26]

It remains true, however, that certain constraints on prices – particularly factor prices – are of a permanent and structural kind. In a sense, they form part of the notion of equilibrium. Take, for instance, the Lewis labor surplus model with its roots in classical political economy. The fact that the real wage is fixed in the modern urban sector and that the labor market is not allowed to clear does not reflect disequilibrium in the usual sense. Instead, it reflects a long-run structural feature of the economy that should be incorporated in a planning model. In fact, taking real wage determination outside of the equilibrium model goes

---

[26] We do, however, consider quantity-adjustment mechanisms in the market for foreign exchange (see Chapter 9).

back to the Marxian-Ricardian foundations of general equilibrium theory as recently revived in England, most notably by Morishima (Morishima, 1973). Taking a more classical view, there is no real conflict between letting product prices clear product markets (thus regulating the supply and demand of commodities) and, at the same time, regarding the real wage (and hence the average rate of profit) as more exogenous, strongly influenced by factors that are not explicitly modeled.

A second area in which the concept of equilibrium and the notion of market clearing is not always clearly defined relates to investment and the determination of capital asset prices. When capital is treated as a stock of produced means of production that differs in composition among sectors, the assumption of perfect capital mobility cannot very well be maintained in a dynamic analysis. It is much better to assume that, once installed, capital cannot move from one sector to another within a given time period. As we saw earlier, this assumption leads to upward-sloping short-run supply curves. The assumption of heterogeneous and sector-specific capital greatly increases the importance of today's decisions on tomorrow's alternatives. Considering the question of how sectoral supply curves shift over time, one realizes that they shift essentially because of technical progress, which is usually considered exogenous, and because of sectoral capital accumulation, which is usually modeled endogenously. If labor supply constraints are binding, demographic change will also affect the supply schedules. But capital accumulation is the most important endogenous cause of change, and traditionally constitutes one of the most important areas of concern for the development planner.

What is meant by an equilibrium allocation of investment? Much depends on how one views the workings of capital markets. In perfect neoclassical intertemporal equilibrium, the market price and production price of capital will always be the same, the profit rate will be the same at any given moment of time in all sectors, and the economy will be traveling along an intertemporally efficient path where prices are correctly foreseen and no mistakes are made. It is perfect foresight or the intertemporal clearing of capital markets that is here the crucial assumption about linkage. A giant intertemporal tâtonnement process that determines capital prices and equalizes profit rates is assumed, so that if ever production costs were to exceed market prices, investment would be cut back, and conversely. This would be the mechanism that regulates capital accumulation.[27]

---

[27] Note that fixed sectoral capital stocks need not prevent the equalization of profit rates. They are equalized by an appropriate adjustment in the market prices of capital, i.e., share prices on the stock market.

Although it is perhaps possible to argue that intertemporally efficient paths exert a certain pull on the economy, just as static equilibrium is assumed to do, one is clearly here on much more slippery ground. First, it is clear that even in the most developed economies, futures markets operate only for a few commodities, and to assume some kind of giant intertemporal tâtonnement to reflect the actual workings of a market economy requires more than usual abstraction from reality. Second, even if one were willing to model such an intertemporal tâtonnement, the question of boundary conditions remains open.

An intertemporal equilibrium system can be reduced to a system of $2n$ difference equations in capital stocks and prices. Whereas one set of boundary conditions is provided by the n initial capital stocks, the remaining set of n boundary conditions constitutes a problem. If we were to give the system the base-period set of prices as n initial conditions, the resulting path can be shown to be highly unstable: The system, trying to validate the initial conditions, would soon attempt to achieve negative output values.[28] One therefore has to give it either a terminal capital stock vector or a terminal price vector to achieve a more reasonable solution. Still another alternative may be to assume capital mobility in the initial year so as to free the system from the necessity of validating the historical capital stock and combine an initial price vector with terminal growth requirement on the capital stocks. Whichever reasonable alternative one chooses, however, the system becomes indecomposable over time whenever boundary conditions are split, and one ends up with a very large system of intertemporal simultaneous equations. Even such systems can be solved by taking advantage of their sparse structure.[29] Most often, however, the concept of intertemporal equilibrium is abandoned, and profit rates – defined as the return to capital valued at production cost prices – remain unequal. This does reflect what can be observed in real-world economies. Such a specification does not necessarily reflect a belief that claims on existing capital stocks do not get revalued, but the stock valuation process is not being modeled. Given the extremely thin nature of equity markets in all developing countries, there is good reason for this neglect.

There remains, however, the problem of determining the allocation of investment by sector of destination. In an intertemporal equilibrium model, this allocation is determined by the requirement that production

[28] See Hahn (1966) for a discussion of this problem. Note the resemblance with the discussion of stability in linear models in Chapter 2.

[29] See Derviş (1975) for a model that achieves intertemporal efficiency and must therefore be solved simultaneously for all time periods. The alternative chosen there is to let capital be mobile in the initial period.

costs must equal the discounted sum of future returns. In a model that abandons the concept of intertemporal equilibrium, the allocation of investment remains open and must be governed by an alternative mechanism.

One way of solving this problem is to assume that the allocation of investment by sector of destination in any given period is determined by the prices, production costs, and profit rates of the previous period. One gives up the notion of an intertemporal equilibrium and settles for a time-recursive model where the only input needed to solve any one period's model is the exogenous parameters and the past history of the economy. It may be that investment is governed by expectations about the future, but one assumes that these expectations are formed purely on the basis of past experience, not on the basis of some kind of tâtonnement into the future where decision makers could test the consistency of their expectations. Because we no longer insist on validating the initial configuration by equalizing profit rates, the system is not necessarily unstable. How stable it will in fact be will, of course, depend on how the mechanism determining investment allocation is formulated dynamically.

A general two-stage dynamic formulation

What is really proposed is a two-stage specification of the overall dynamic model: In the first stage, all markets are assumed to clear subject to a number of restrictions on the ability of certain markets, such as capital and labor markets, to adjust. In a second stage, the dynamic adjustment of certain variables whose values were fixed in the first stage is explicitly modeled. The overall dynamic model is thus partitioned into a static within-period equilibrium model and a separate between-period model that provides the necessary intertemporal linkages and shifts the sectoral supply and demand functions. Both the problem of structural disequilibrium in the labor market and the pattern of investment determination are thus "taken out" of the core equilibrium model and put into a stage 2 dynamic adjustment model that links the sequence of years considered during a given planning exercise into a consistent whole.[30]

This solution to the dynamic linkage problem, which gives up the notion of intertemporal equilibrium, has been chosen by most general equilibrium model builders. Although it is a practical solution, long adopted by model builders in the advanced economies, it also represents

[30] See Adelman and Robinson (1978a, 1978b) for a formalization of this approach.

a retreat from the ambitious attempts of earlier planning models at determining intertemporally efficient or optimal growth paths. Because the "terminal conditions" problem has never really been satisfactorily solved (and probably cannot be given the inherent open endedness of the future), the paths proposed by optimizing models were never fully convincing.[31]

In a general, two-stage approach to dynamic formulation, the role of the stage 2 dynamic adjustment model is to update all the exogenous variables entering the static stage 1 model, which will then be solved for the next period. In turn, when various variables are updated for the following period, the dynamic adjustment model will take the solution of past-period stage 1 models as given.

Not all the updating equations will be of a behavioral kind. Some demographic and technological variables will be updated following some separately calculated or projected trends. Others will simply remain the same, as for instance is usually the case for input–output coefficients. Only subsets of the dynamic linkage equations will attempt to model economic behavior or government policies. Table 5.7 summarizes a typical set of variables likely to be updated by the dynamic linkage equations of a between-period model.

Although the classification given in Table 5.7 encompasses a wide range of variables, it is not meant to apply to all models. It provides examples of variables that have typically been included in dynamic CGE models, but other models have used different approaches. There are, for instance, models in which demographic variables such as population growth and dependency ratios are treated as functions of economic variables.[32] Other models may endogenize technological change (making it depend, for instance, on accumulated past investment) or attempt to model government behavior as endogenously reacting to a set of economic indicators determined by the equilibrium model. These more ambitious models remain exceptions, however. In most cases investment allocation and rural–urban migration are the only important economic mechanisms modeled in stage 2.

One could of course take a lot "out" of stage 1 and put it "into" stage 2. Indeed, price formation could be modeled dynamically as a disequilibrium adjustment process in the between-period model. This would dramatically reduce the degree of simultaneity in the stage 1 model! But

---

[31] See the discussion in Chapter 3 on terminal conditions in linear programming models.

[32] For example, the ILO Bachue models described in Rodgers, Hopkins, and Wery (1977).

Table 5.7. *The endogenous variables of a stage 2 dynamic model*

Variables and parameters that most often remain unchanged
Share parameters in the sectoral production functions
Input–output coefficients
Capital composition coefficients

Variables and parameters that are usually updated according to simple trends
Technological shift parameters in sectoral production functions
Total labor supply, sometimes by skill categories
Some variables determined in the "rest of the world" in open-economy models
Engel elasticities in the consumer demand functions

Variables that are seen as determined largely by government policy or political mechanisms
Money supply or the overall price index
Tax rates and government expenditure shares
Wages for some labor categories
Tariffs, quotas, and export subsidies in open-economy models

Variables that are updated by modeling economy behavior
Sector capital stocks
Labor supplies to subsets of sectors, in particular the rural urban composition of the labor force
Investment shares by sector of destination

---

we have already argued that for development planning purposes an attempt to set up a general disequilibrium model that would be focused on short-term adjustments and disequilibrium phenomena in the product markets might well be counterproductive. For our purposes, and for most empirical applications, what needs most to be included in the stage 2 between-period model are submodels of the sectoral allocation of investment and of rural–urban migration.

We shall therefore discuss a simple set of dynamic equations that can be used to describe investment allocation and rural–urban migration. They form the core of the between-period model and, together with trend equations and the updating of government policy variables, allow the model to be run forward in time.

Investment allocation

After determining the volume of investment, a multisector model must specify the structure of investment by sector of destination. In the presentation of the static model, we have so far treated these shares as predetermined. For some purposes, such as testing the feasibility, consistency, and/or desirability of otherwise formulated investment plans and growth targets, it may be best to treat them as predetermined and analyze the consequences of a specified set of investment shares. But in most cases one will want to model the determination of investment by sector of destination endogenously and thereby attempt to capture the effects of government policy on the structure of investment.

Theoretically, probably the most satisfying way to model sectoral investment allocation would be to split the process into two parts. First, determine the desired investment by each sector and, second, model the allocation process by which the supply of investable funds is reconciled with the demand. This explicit distinction of the demand and the supply side underlies much of the recent work on investment theory in macro models (see Jorgenson, 1963). In the multisector context, each sector would determine its desired capital stock according to various rules – such as accelerators, expected profitability, or expected sales. This demand for capital stock must then be translated into a demand for a flow of investment. Finally, this flow demand must be compared to the supply of funds available for investment to the particular sector. If the two do not match, the adjustment mechanism must be modeled. This approach necessitates a realistic specification of both the demand and supply relationships, including the explicit modeling of the loanable funds market and the banking system. Adelman and Robinson (1978) have used this general approach with a simple model of expectations and investment demand linked to a fairly elaborate model of the supply of loanable funds that distinguished among retained earnings, bank credit, and unorganized money market loans.

The data base and effort required for such a full specification makes it very difficult to achieve. For many purposes, a less ambitious approach will be sufficient, and we shall describe a simple formulation that can be regarded as a minimum core specification to be qualified and expanded in planning applications. An extreme specification would be to assume that money markets do not exist and allocate the investable funds in proportion to each sector's share in aggregate capital income (or profits). More realistically, one can adjust the proportions as a function of the relative profit rate of each sector compared to the average profit rate for the economy as a whole. Sectors with a higher-than-average profit rate would get a larger share of investible funds than their share in aggregate profits. We shall use this formulation for our simple dynamic model. The shares are given by[33]

---

[33] Note that because $\Sigma_i \, SP_{it} = 1$, then it is true that $\Sigma_i \, H_{it} = 1$ for any value of the parameter μ, because the average profit rate is equal to the sum of the sector profit rates weighted by the shares in total profits.

$$H_{it} = SP_{i,t-1} + \mu SP_{i,t-1} \left(\frac{R_{i,t-1} - AR_{t-1}}{AR_{t-1}} \right) \qquad (5.6.1)$$

where

SP_{it} = sectoral share in aggregate profits
μ = "mobility" of investable funds parameter
R_{it} = sectoral profit rate
AR_t = average profit rate

The profit rates are defined as returns to capital when the entire capital stock is valued in current prices and also includes capital gains. The equation is

$$R_{it} = \frac{PN_{it}X_{it} - \sum_s W_s L_{ist}}{U_{i,t-1}K_{i,t-1}} + \frac{U_{it} - (1 - \bar{d}_i)U_{i,t-1}}{U_{i,t-1}} \qquad (5.6.2)$$

where

$K_{i,t-1}$ = the capital stock at the end of the last period
(and which is used in production in this period)
$\bar{d}_i$ = fixed sectoral depreciation rates
U_i = the capital goods price in Eq. (5.3.24)

When the investment mobility parameter μ is zero in Eq. (5.6.1), there is no intersectoral mobility of investment funds. In essence, all investment is financed by retained profits (ignoring savings from government and labor income). When μ is positive, the sectoral allocation of investment will respond to profit-rate differentials and high-profit-rate sectors will attract funds from low-profit-rate sectors. Thus μ measures the intersectoral mobility of investment funds. It is *not*, however, an index of the degree of perfection of capital markets. Even if μ is zero, the system may move toward equalizing profit rates over time, and, if μ is too large, it is easy to make sectoral profit rates oscillate. The parameter μ is rather an indicator of the responsiveness of capital markets to static market signals, namely, current profit rates in the various sectors.

We have presented a lagged version of the simple investment model, but we could have let current profit shares and profit rates determine the investment shares. Not much would change, again on the assumption that there are no serious oscillations resulting from the underlying technological and taste parameters. Thus, once we abandon the concept of an intertemporal tâtonnement, we could in fact incorporate the determination of investment in the within-period model.

It is not necessary to define the SP_{it} variables as sectoral shares in aggregate profits. They could represent any measure of the "normal" allocation of investable funds. For example, one might argue that, in the absence of a money-market response to profit-rate differentials, investable funds would be allocated according to current sectoral shares in the capital stock. In practice, given the important role played by government investment, the simple investment theory we have described may in any case have to be seriously qualified in any specific application. Where the government controls a substantial proportion of total investment funds, the allocation of funds should reflect government policy objectives. Although we would argue that the simple theory outlined here is a good point of departure, it is clear that the realistic specification of investment allocation, even in a purely descriptive model and quite apart from problems or optimization, still represents a major challenge for modelers.

Rural–urban migration

Capturing the essence of structural dualism characterizing many developing economies represents another major problem for the model builder. Rapid urbanization, even in the face of urban unemployment and poverty, has accompanied growth in most developing countries. Efforts have been made to reconcile the observed simultaneous urban unemployment and migration from rural to urban areas. The popular model developed by Harris and Todaro (1970) explains migration from rural areas to cities in terms of the relation between the wage in rural areas, W_1, and the expected urban wage, W_2^e, which is the urban wage weighted by the rate of employment in the urban sector.

Migration models have been included in CGE models and have empirically turned out to be very important.[34] It is also possible to treat migration as a function of the differential between the rural and urban wages without assuming that equilibrium is reached, that is, that the rural wage equals the expected urban wage. In this approach, migration is seen as a disequilibrium adjustment mechanism and is modeled as part of stage 2.

Assume that labor category 1 is rural labor and that labor category

[34] See Ahmed (1974), de Melo and Derviş (1977), and Adelman and Robinson (1978a). Ahmed treated the distribution of the labor force such that the rural wage equaled the expected urban wage. Migration was thus treated exactly as in the Harris-Todaro model as the movement of labor required to bring about the equality between the rural wage and the expected urban wage.

2 is unskilled urban labor, the category that migrants will join. Alternatively, it is possible to spread the migrants among the different urban labor categories, but this will not be done here. Let the two labor categories have natural rates of growth $\hat{G}_1$ and $\hat{G}_2$. Thus, the labor supply equations for the two categories of labor become

$$\bar{L}_1^S(t + 1) = (1 + \hat{G}_1) \, \bar{L}_1^S(t) - MIG(t) \tag{5.6.3}$$

$$\bar{L}_2^S(t + 1) = (1 + \hat{G}_2) \, \bar{L}_2^S(t) + MIG(t) \tag{5.6.4}$$

$$MIG(t) = e \left(\frac{W_2^e}{W_1} - 1 \right) \bar{L}_1^S(t) \tag{5.6.5}$$

$$W_2^e = W_2 \left(\frac{L_2^D}{\bar{L}_2^S} \right) \tag{5.6.6}$$

This formulation is exactly the Harris-Todaro formulation except that there is no assumption that equilibrium is reached (i.e., $W_2^e = W_1$). As in the Harris-Todaro formulation, the definition of the expected wage in Eq. (5.6.6) makes sense only if there is urban unemployment. This implies that we are using the fixed-real-wage version for urban unskilled labor, because otherwise $L_2^D = \bar{L}_2^S$ and $W_2^e = W_2$. If, at the fixed wage, $L_1^D > \bar{L}_1^S$, then one should switch to a full-employment model in which the urban wage is determined endogenously and $W_2^e = W_2$.

Because the migration equations are part of the stage 2 model, migration is seen as a quantity-adjustment process that need not achieve full equilibrium. Harris and Todaro require that the urban wage W_2 be fixed and define migration by comparative statistics, imposing the condition that $W_2^e = W_1$. In the stage 2 model, however, it is not assumed that $W_2^e = W_1$ and, indeed, the model dynamics may be such that equality is never achieved. In this disequilibrium adjustment model, the definition of the expected wage is less important than in the Harris-Todaro comparative statics formulation. However, the response elasticity parameter (e) in Eq. (5.6.5) is correspondingly more important, because it determines the magnitude of the migration response during this period to a gap between the rural and expected urban wages.

Whether one wishes to model migration in stage 1 or stage 2 is partly a question of empirical realism. If it is modeled as part of stage 1, then there are assumed to be no constraints on the amount of migration that can take place within the period. If it is modeled as part of stage 2, one must specify a parameter such as e that gives the degree of responsiveness of the quantity-adjustment model. Although the Harris-Todaro model might be useful for exploring comparative statics questions of "equilibrium" migration, an explicitly dynamic model must deal with the adjustment process.

It should be clear from this discussion that there is considerable scope for flexibility in the choice of which variables are to be determined in each stage. Naturally, the outcome of this selection will determine how close the overall CGE model remains to the core Walrasian model. The specification of intertemporal linkages is a difficult but crucial element in the formulation of any planning model, and we shall see in later chapters how the outcome of specific policy experiments is profoundly affected by alternative specifications of dynamic linkages.

5.7   Conclusion

We saw at the outset how traditional linear models do not incorporate some of the important general equilibrium interactions present in any economic system. We then proceeded to build step by step the general equilibrium demand and supply curves of a simple core CGE model. The presentation emphasized the links and points of departure from the linear models of earlier chapters. We saw that the solution of the model resulted in the selection of price and wage vectors equating all product and factor market demands and supplies. We also examined briefly how one might solve such a model numerically.

The simple model developed in the early sections of the chapter was extremely Walrasian and neoclassical in spirit. With the exception of taxes on factor incomes and a brief allusion to fixed wages for certain labor categories, there was essentially no difference between the technologically feasible production possibility set and the resulting transformation set reflecting market behavior and institutional characteristics of the economy. All markets cleared. Applied models, however, although close in spirit to the Walrasian construct, can be characterized as reflecting a "constrained" general equilibrium. For example, the discussion of fragmented capital and labor markets in the two-stage formulation of the dynamic model indicated that the extent of factor mobility between time periods is affected by the degree of structural rigidities in the economy.

It should be clear, however, that an applied CGE model cannot be viewed as a short-run projections model and is not intended for that purpose. It is better suited to explain medium- to long-term trends and structural responses to changes in development policy. The analysis of short-run cyclical variations around basic trends requires a quite different approach. This is not to say that one is not entitled to expect good predictive performance from CGE models. On the contrary, they should be able to predict, conditional upon policy variables, trends in sectoral structure, intersectoral terms of trade, income distribution, trade performance, and government revenue – and do so better and more consistently than linear models or more informal methods. But the problems facing development policy are inherently longer-run problems, and the models thus naturally reflect an emphasis on the long run rather than on the short run, on growth rather than stabilization, and on trends rather than cyclical variation.

CHAPTER 6

Foreign trade and trade policy

6.1 Introduction

The general equilibrium model discussed so far deals with a closed economy. All commodities are produced and used at home, and the only income available in the community is derived from domestic production and sales. In fact, of course, foreign trade and international capital flows play a major role in all economies. In some countries exports constitute as much as a third of domestic production, with imports claiming an equivalent fraction of total expenditure. In only a few countries does the share of foreign trade fall below 10 percent of domestic product.

In developing economies, trade and international capital flows play perhaps an even more crucial role than in advanced industrial economies. Whereas in the latter the share of trade may often be higher, developing economies are dependent on trade as an important mechanism of real capital formation. Imported capital goods and the modern technology they embody constitute a crucial input into the development process.

More generally, problems of industrialization have almost always been linked to problems of trade. The instruments of trade policy have been used not only for purely trade-related goals, but also as tools of overall development policy. Trade policy variables such as exchange rates, tariffs, and quotas are relatively easily manipulated by governments and have the political advantage, for example, compared to tax rates, of generating real and obvious benefits for some groups, while imposing costs that are not as easily identifiable and the burdens of which are spread more thinly across society. A good deal of development policy is therefore trade policy. Any planning exercise that does not incorporate foreign trade and trade policy in the model-building effort in a way reflecting the instruments and trade-offs facing the policy maker is bound to be seriously deficient. It is also clear that trade mechanisms should be modeled in such a way that they do clearly interact with policy instruments that are in fact at the disposal of the policy maker.

The aim of this and the next chapter is to introduce foreign trade into the computable general equilibrium framework. We discuss how a general equilibrium model can be opened to trade and build up, step by step, a specification that allows a realistic and flexible representation of foreign trade and trade policy. A substantial part of the discussion is devoted to a brief survey of the relevant knowledge and insights available from the theoretical literature. This review is important if one is to relate numerical results obtained from empirical models to the qualitative results of theoretical reasoning. Computable general equilibrium models extend our capacity to understand and analyze reality by allowing us to escape from the restrictiveness of simple two-by-two or three-by-two general equilibrium models or from the limitations of partial equilibrium analysis. Unless we keep a firm grip on the causal mechanisms that determine particular numerical results, these models can easily degenerate into magic black boxes that yield a mass of quantitative results but do not really add to our understanding of the economic mechanism or to our capacity to improve its performance.

With this requirement in mind, we survey relevant parts of the "trade and welfare" literature and indicate in what sense alternative specifications in a planning model can be expected to lead to different results and policy conclusions. The next two sections are devoted to a discussion of exchange rate determination and trade policy instruments that constitute the new elements brought into the model presented in Chapter 5 as a result of the introduction of foreign trade. Section 6.4 reviews the role of trade policy and planning in the dynamic context of a growing economy. Finally, Section 6.5 summarizes and concludes the chapter.

6.2   The exchange rate, balance of trade, and normalization

The exchange rate with only traded commodities

When a general equilibrium model is opened to trade, the chain of causality it embodies usually changes dramatically. Whereas in a closed economy the basic technological and demand variables determine the price system, the situation is quite different in standard models of international trade. Whenever the domestic market is "small" in relation to the world market, prices are determined in the international market and the chain of causality runs from these world prices to domestic factor prices and production patterns. When the home country is a "large" country in the world market, domestic technological and taste parameters will influence world market prices, and one can no longer talk of a simple causal chain.

Many planning models that focus on foreign trade consider any one country taken on its own to be too small to affect the terms at which it trades. When the "small-country assumption" is made, any individual country becomes a price taker facing fixed exogenous world prices. The general equilibrium model is then essentially turned on its head: Whereas the relative price system was the final solution determined by the equations of the closed-economy model, it becomes exogenous in simple "small" open-economy models. The domestic economy must now adjust to the given prices, producing only those commodities that can earn a normal profit and exporting a fraction of them to pay for imports. It is substantially correct to say that whereas supply and demand determine relative prices in a closed economy, they adjust to world prices in a small open economy where transport costs and product differentiation are assumed to be negligible. The small-country assumption is important, and we shall return to a critical appraisal of it later. For the moment we turn to an analysis of its implications for the structure of a simple general equilibrium model.

Assume that there are n commodities, each associated with one sector of the economy and each at least potentially tradable in the international market. Any particular commodity has identical characteristics, whether it is produced at home or abroad. There are no transport costs or trade restrictions. Of course, not all commodities need to be produced at home, but we shall assume that at all relevant price configurations, all commodities are demanded at home. Under these circumstances, we may write

$$P_i = \overline{PW}_i ER \qquad (6.2.1)$$

where P_i are domestic prices, $\overline{PW}_i$ are world prices denoted in foreign currency, and ER is the exchange rate.[1]

The first thing to note about this specification is that all domestic prices are fixed in relative terms. We shall always have

$$\frac{P_i}{P_j} = \frac{\overline{PW}_i}{\overline{PW}_j} \qquad \text{for all } i \text{ and } j \qquad (6.2.2)$$

[1] Note that by exchange rate we mean the price of a "dollar" in terms of the local currency. This is standard in the trade-theory literature. It is not standard International Monetary Fund (IMF) practice, however: There the exchange rate is defined as the dollar price of local currency.

Consider the normalization rule adopted in Chapter 4, namely,

$$\sum_i P_i \Omega_i = \overline{P} \qquad (6.2.3)$$

Clearly this implies that

$$\sum_i \overline{PW}_i \Omega_i ER = \overline{P} \qquad (6.2.4)$$

and

$$ER = \frac{\overline{P}}{\sum_i \overline{PW}_i \Omega_i} \qquad (6.2.5)$$

The exchange rate in such a model is nothing but the domestic price level divided by the value, in world prices, of a fixed bundle of commodities. Setting the exchange rate or setting the price level is equivalent. In that sense the exchange rate is a purely macroeconomic phenomenon and has no significance in terms of relative domestic prices or structure of production.

At first glance one might worry that arbitrarily fixing the exchange rate (or price level) could lead to disequilibrium in the balance of trade. A moment's thought, however, will show that there cannot be an effective balance-of-trade disequilibrium in this model. To see this, consider a very simple economy, with no investment and no intermediate goods, in which all income is spent on consumer goods. We have

$$T_i = X_i - C_i \qquad (6.2.6)$$

where X_i denotes domestic production, C_i denotes domestic consumption, and T_i denotes quantity traded.

If $X_i > C_i$, $T_i > 0$ and the good in question is exported. On the contrary, if $X_i < C_i$, $T_i < 0$ and some of the good in question is imported. A balance-of-trade deficit would imply that

$$\sum_i \overline{PW}_i T_i < 0 \qquad (6.2.7)$$

and therefore, multiplying both sides by ER,

$$\sum_i P_i T_i < 0 \qquad (6.2.8)$$

But this could occur only if

$$\sum_i P_i(X_i - C_i) < 0 \qquad (6.2.9)$$

or

$$\sum_i P_i X_i < \sum_i P_i C_i \qquad (6.2.10)$$

violating the community's effective budget constraint. People would be spending $\sum_i P_i C_i$, more than they earn, $\sum_i P_i X_i$. Similarly, a balance-of-trade surplus would imply that $\sum_i P_i X_i > \sum_i P_i C_i$ and the community would therefore be hoarding. In a monetary model $\sum_i P_i C_i$ could temporarily be greater than $\sum_i P_i X_i$ if people were running down their money balances and somebody (the central bank or the rest of the world) was willing to accumulate them. But, as emphasized in Chapter 5, the CGE models discussed here do not include the specification of money-holding behavior, and although the price-normalization equation can be viewed as a stable demand function for a monetary asset, we implicitly assume full adjustment of the price level to any discrepancies between desired and actual money balances, and the equality between income and expenditure is therefore always preserved. In this framework, hoarding is impossible and Walras's law implies balance-of-trade equilibrium quite independently of the particular set of relative prices that happens to rule in the world market.

What does all this imply for the domestic labor market? Assuming sectoral capital stocks to be fixed and labor to be the only mobile factor of production within the economy, sectoral demand functions for labor under perfect competition are of the form

$$L_i = L_i \left(\frac{W}{P_i}, \overline{K}_i \right) \qquad (6.2.11)$$

where W is the nominal wage and hence W/P_i is the real wage in terms of sectoral output that the producer equates to the marginal physical product of labor. Because all prices are constant and proportional to the exchange rate, this function can be written as

$$L_i = L_i(W, ER, \overline{K}_i) \qquad (6.2.12)$$

with $\partial L_i / \partial W < 0$ and $\partial L_i / \partial ER > 0$ for all i.

Equilibrium in the labor market requires that the excess demand for labor equal zero:

$$EL = \sum_i L_i(W, ER, \overline{K}) - \overline{L} = 0 \tag{6.2.13}$$

With ER fixed, this equation can be solved for W. Fixing the exchange rate or the general price level thus determines the nominal wage. Alternatively, we could fix the nominal wage (i.e., normalize around the wage), which would determine the exchange rate and the general price level. In either case, we would simply be solving for the equilibrium real wage.

The exchange rate with nontraded commodities

The preceding discussion suggests that this model is really much too simple and fails to capture important aspects of reality in which over-valued exchange rates and distorted relative prices play an important role. Observation of the real world suggests that relative prices are far from equal across countries, and that domestic price systems have a great deal of independence from world prices even when there is substantial trade.

A first step toward more realism has traditionally been taken by introducing a class of "nontradable" commodities into open-economy models. Nontradable commodities, also called "home goods," are commodities that are not subject to international trade, usually because transportation costs would be prohibitive. Most services as well as housing and construction fit this category. Assume for the moment that all such nontradables have been aggregated into one sector, and let this sector be denoted by subscript H. For simplicity, assume that the home-goods sector is the last of our n sectors. The effective budget constraint now becomes

$$\sum_{i=1}^{n-1} P_i X_i + P_H X_H = \sum_{i=1}^{n-1} P_i C_i + P_H C_H \tag{6.2.14}$$

Therefore, from the budget constraint,

$$\sum_{i=1}^{n-1} P_i(X_i - C_i) < 0 \Rightarrow P_H(X_H - C_H) > 0 \tag{6.2.15}$$

$$\sum_{i=1}^{n-1} P_i(X_i - C_i) > 0 \Rightarrow P_H(X_H - C_H) < 0 \tag{6.2.16}$$

Remembering that $X_i - C_i = T_i$ and $P_i = PW_i ER$ for all $i \neq H$, it is clear that Walras's law no longer rules out balance-of-trade disequilibria. Equations (6.2.15) and (6.2.16) may be rewritten, assuming strictly positive prices, as

$$\sum_{i=1}^{n-1} \overline{PW_i} T_i < 0 \Rightarrow X_H > C_H \tag{6.2.17}$$

$$\sum_{i=1}^{n-1} \overline{PW_i} T_i > 0 \Rightarrow X_H < C_H \tag{6.2.18}$$

Given an arbitrary price system, an excess demand or supply of tradable commodities is offset by an excess supply or demand for home goods. Thus, we can no longer expect the balance of trade to clear for any relative price system. The relative price of nontradables in terms of tradables now appears as a new significant variable. Note that income continues to equal expenditure, and balance-of-payments disequilibrium manifests itself not as an overall (macroeconomic) excess demand phenomenon but as an excess demand for tradables compensated by an excess supply of nontradables. These real or microeconomic imbalances may have been *caused* by macroeconomic imbalances such as an excess of domestic inflation over world inflation leading to a relative price of home goods that is too high, but the macroeconomic processes remain exogenous to the model.

To gain a better understanding of the structure of models that include nontradables, consider a simple economy with $n - 1$ tradable commodities, one nontradable, and labor as the only variable factor of production. Sectoral output depends on the quantity of labor employed, and labor is employed up to the point where its marginal value product equals the wage. There is a fixed supply of labor. The domestic consumption demand for each sector's output depends on total income and commodity prices. As previously, sectoral capital stocks are fixed, and W is the nominal wage.

The domestic output supply functions may therefore be written as

$$X_i = X_i(ER, W, \overline{K}_i) \qquad i = 1, \ldots, n - 1 \tag{6.2.19}$$
$$\frac{\partial X_i}{\partial ER} > 0 \qquad \frac{\partial X_i}{\partial W} < 0$$

$$X_H = X_H(P_H, W, \overline{K}_H) \qquad \frac{\partial X_H}{\partial P_H} > 0 \qquad \frac{\partial X_H}{\partial W} < 0 \tag{6.2.20}$$

The effective demand functions are of the form

$$C_i = C_i(ER, P_H, W) \qquad i = 1, \ldots, n-1$$
$$\frac{\partial C_i}{\partial ER} < 0 \qquad \frac{\partial C_i}{\partial P_H} > 0 \qquad \frac{\partial C_i}{\partial W} < 0$$

$$(6.2.21)$$

and

$$C_H = C_H(ER, P_H, W) \qquad \frac{\partial C_H}{\partial ER} > 0 \qquad \frac{\partial C_H}{\partial P_H} < 0 \qquad \frac{\partial C_H}{\partial W} < 0$$

$$(6.2.22)$$

An increase in W will lead to a rise in the real wage, a fall in employment, a fall in output, and therefore a fall in effective income and effective demand. We also assume all goods to be gross substitutes in demand. Note that the supply and demand functions are similar to those described in Chapter 5. In particular, they are homogenous of degree zero in ER, P_H, and W. If (ER^e, P_H^e, W^e) is an equilibrium configuration, any multiple will also constitute an equilibrium.

Let us for the moment normalize around the wage and thus measure everything in wage units. This will ease the following discussion of the relation between the exchange rate and the price of home goods. Equilibrium in the market for foreign exchange requires that

$$EF = -\sum_{i=1}^{n-1} \overline{PW}_i(X_i - C_i) = 0 \qquad (6.2.23)$$

or

$$EF = \sum_{i=1}^{n-1} \overline{PW}_i[C_i(ER, P_H) - X_i(ER)] = 0 \qquad (6.2.24)$$

where EF represents the value of excess demand for tradables, that is, the trade deficit in world prices.

Equilibrium in the market for nontradables requires that

$$EH = (C_H - X_H) = 0 \qquad (6.2.25)$$

or

$$EH = [C_H(ER, P_H) - X_H(P_H)] = 0 \qquad (6.2.26)$$

where EH is the excess demand for home goods.

Finally, equilibrium in the labor market requires that the value of excess demand for labor, EL, be zero; that is,

$$EL = \sum_{i=1}^{n-1} L_i(ER) + L_H(P_H) - \bar{L} = 0 \tag{6.2.27}$$

Consider the configuration of ER and P_H that would yield equilibrium in the market for home goods. Totally differentiating (6.2.26), we get

$$dEH = \frac{\partial C_H}{\partial ER} dER + \left(\frac{\partial C_H}{\partial P_H} - \frac{\partial X_H}{\partial P_H} \right) dP_H \tag{6.2.28}$$

and therefore

$$\frac{dP_H}{dER} \bigg|_{dEH=0} = \frac{-(\partial C_H/\partial ER)}{(\partial C_H/\partial P_H) - (\partial X_H/\partial P_H)} > 0 \tag{6.2.29}$$

Expression (6.2.29) is positive, because the numerator and the denominator are negative.

Note that the effective budget constraint implies that

$$\sum_{i=1}^{n-1} P_i C_i + P_H C_H = \sum_{i=1}^{n-1} P_i X_i + P_H X_H \tag{6.2.30}$$

and therefore if $EH = 0$, we shall also have $\sum_{i=1}^{n-1} P_i(C_i - X_i) = 0$ and therefore $EF = 0$.

Let us, however, consider the labor market. Totally differentiating (6.2.27), we get

$$dEL = \left[\sum_{i=1}^{n-1} \left(\frac{\partial L_i}{\partial ER} \right) \right] dER + \left(\frac{\partial L_H}{\partial P_H} \right) dP_H \tag{6.2.31}$$

and therefore

$$\frac{dP_H}{dER} \bigg|_{dEL=0} = \frac{-\sum_{i=1}^{n-1} (\partial L_i/\partial ER)}{\partial L_H/\partial P_H} < 0 \tag{6.2.32}$$

where $\partial L_i/\partial ER > 0$ and $\partial L_H/\partial P_H > 0$. Because the numerator is negative and the denominator is positive, the expression is negative. Overall equilibrium can thus be depicted as the intersection of two

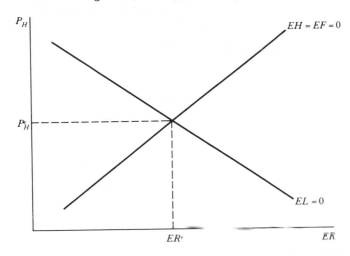

Figure 6.1. General equilibrium in a simple model with tradables, one home good, and labor.

curves in (P_H, ER) space as illustrated (with arbitrarily straight lines) in Figure 6.1.

The simple story behind Figure 6.1 can be told as follows. Given that W is our numéraire, there exist many combinations of ER and P_H that generate equilibrium in the markets for home goods and foreign exchange. What really matters is the ratio of ER to P_H, where ER determines the level of tradable goods prices and P_H the level of home goods prices. Balance-of-trade equilibrium is achieved when the value of tradables stands in the right ratio to the value of nontradables. But it is also clear that too high a combination of P_H and ER along the curve $EH = EF = 0$ will imply a very low real wage and therefore excess demand for labor. Similarly, too low a combination of P_H and ER implies too high a real wage and will lead to unemployment. There will normally exist only one combination of P_H and ER on $EH = EF = 0$ consistent with the real wage necessary for labor market clearing. This combination (P_H^e, ER^e) constitutes the general equilibrium solution of the system.

An exogenous net foreign capital inflow can easily be introduced into the model. Equation (6.2.24), giving the excess demand for foreign exchange, would then become

$$EF = \sum_{i=1}^{n-1} \overline{PW_i}[C_i(ER, P_H) - X_i(ER)] - \overline{F} = 0 \qquad (6.2.24a)$$

where $\overline{F}$ denotes the net flow of foreign resources in "dollars." Changes in $\overline{F}$ would shift the $EH = EF = 0$ curve in Figure 6.1 with ER^e/P_H^e falling with increases in $\overline{F}$.[2]

Normalization and definitions of the exchange rate

As already noted in Chapter 5, whereas normalizing around the wage rate is often convenient for theoretical discussion, in actual model building and planning exercises it is much more convenient to normalize around a price index. As long as no real relative price in the model is fixed, the precise normalization is of little consequence and one could conduct any experiment in terms of price ratios only. But as soon as one wants to fix any relative price in the system, the normalization rule takes on much greater significance. Thus one may want to fix the real wage and give up labor market clearing. If the wage was at the same time our numéraire, the fixing of the real wage would require the fixing of some additional variable or sets of variables such as an aggregate price index. Similarly, if one wanted to fix the exchange rate, it is not clear that fixing the exchange rate in terms of the wage would be a very meaningful way of modeling fixed exchange rates. If, on the other hand, it had been the exchange rate itself that we had normalized around, modeling fixed exchange rates would again require the fixing of some additional variable or price index.

Because, as discussed in Chapter 5, it is convenient to use a no-inflation benchmark, we normalize around an aggregate price index instead of setting a variable such as a wage rate, the exchange rate, or the price of any particular commodity equal to one. Returning to the normalization equation used in Chapter 5,

$$\sum_i P_i \Omega_i = \overline{P} \tag{6.2.33}$$

The choice of an overall price index instead of the wage as numéraire does not at all affect the nature of the model discussed above and illustrated in Figure 6.1. Substituting $PW_i ER$ for P_i in (6.2.33) yields

$$\sum_{i=1}^{n-1} \overline{PW}_i \cdot ER \cdot \Omega_i + P_H \Omega_H = \overline{P} \tag{6.2.34}$$

---

[2] Chapters 10, 11, and 13 explore the adjustment problems induced by exogenous changes in $\overline{F}$ in the framework of a more elaborate model.

Now suppose that the equilibrium configuration $P_H = P_H^e$, $ER = ER^e$, and $W^e = 1$ (numéraire) depicted in Figure 6.1 violated the price normalization (6.2.34). Suppose, for instance, that it yielded a price level twice as high as $\bar{P}$. We can divide P_H^e, ER^e, and W^e by 2 without affecting equilibrium in the product and labor markets and thus easily obtain a new equilibrium vector of product and factor prices that satisfies the price-level normalization. Given such a normalization, if we now set W, we are fixing the real wage rate and must expect disequilibrium, notably in the labor market. If we set ER, we are fixing the exchange rate and must expect disequilibrium, notably in the foreign exchange market. We shall usually prefer (6.2.33) as the normalization rule. The explicit introduction of money could also follow more naturally from this kind of price-level normalization because it can be interpreted as an appropriate argument in a demand function for money.

It is worth noting once more that the normalization equation is nothing more than a choice of numéraire. It does not affect the relative price system or real quantity variables. It must be stressed, however, that any particular applied model must be interpreted in light of the normalization chosen. We shall illustrate this necessity by discussing at some length the meaning of a change in the exchange rate.

From (6.2.34) we have

$$ER = \frac{\bar{P} - P_H \Omega_H}{\sum_{i=1}^{n-1} \overline{PW_i} \Omega_i} \tag{6.2.35}$$

It follows that the price of the home good is given by

$$P_H = \frac{\bar{P}}{\Omega_H} - \frac{\sum_{i=1}^{n-1} \overline{PW_i} \Omega_i}{\Omega_H} ER \tag{6.2.36}$$

so that

$$\frac{dP_H}{dER} = - \frac{\sum_{i=1}^{n-1} \overline{PW_i} \Omega_i}{\Omega_H} < 0 \tag{6.2.37}$$

Given our normalization rule, an increase in ER (i.e., a devaluation) will lead to a fall in the absolute price of home goods. The relationship between P_H and ER is linear, with a slope equal to $(\sum_{i=1}^{n-1} \overline{PW_i} \Omega_i / \Omega_H)$. Because the devaluation increases the price of all tradable commodities, the price of nontradables must fall if the overall price index is to remain at its predetermined value. The smaller the weight of home goods in the commodity basket defining the price level, the larger must be the decline in P_H. It is also clear that, given our normalization rule, an x percent devaluation will lead to a greater than x percent change in the price of tradables relative to that of nontradables. This should be noted because often in the literature on devaluation, the exchange rate is defined to be the ratio of the value of a basket of tradables to the value of a basket of home goods. In our notation, this would imply that

$$ER^r = \frac{\sum\limits_{i=1}^{n-1} P_i \Omega_i}{P_H \Omega_H} = \frac{\sum\limits_{i=1}^{n-1} \overline{PW}_i \Omega_i ER}{P_H \Omega_H} \tag{6.2.38}$$

where ER^r stands for what we call the "real" exchange rate. Setting $ER = ER^r$ would itself be a normalization! Whatever the particular value of ER^r may be, for (6.2.38) to hold we must have

$$\frac{\sum\limits_{i=1}^{n-1} \overline{PW}_i \Omega_i}{P_H \Omega_H} = 1 \tag{6.2.39}$$

which determines P_H,

$$P_H = \frac{\sum\limits_{i=1}^{n-1} \overline{PW}_i \Omega_i}{\Omega_H} \tag{6.2.40}$$

Therefore, defining the exchange rate as the ratio of the value of tradables to the value of nontradables fixes the price of home goods. Alternatively, the exchange rate is often required only to be proportional to the ratio of the value of tradables to the value of nontradables so that a given percentage change in the exchange rate always reflects the same percentage change in this ratio. Under those circumstances we would have

$$P_H = \lambda \frac{\sum\limits_{i=1}^{n-1} \overline{PW}_i \Omega_i}{\Omega_H} \tag{6.2.41}$$

where λ is an arbitrary but constant factor of proportionality. The particular value chosen for λ determines P_H, and, provided that it remained constant, the exchange rate would always be proportional to the ratio of the value of tradables to the value of nontradables. It is therefore clear that a given percentage change in the exchange rate, say, a 20 percent devaluation, will represent a different degree of relative price adjustment depending on whether we normalize by requiring the overall price level to remain constant (in which case the price of home goods must fall absolutely) or we normalize by fixing the price level of home goods only. In order to interpret the results of a model correctly, it is important to keep these distinctions in mind.

In applied models it is convenient to normalize around the overall price level and project it exogenously. Changes in the overall price level can be observed empirically, whereas changes in a home-goods price index are much more difficult to quantify. Thus, if an inflation rate is to be exogenously projected for a dynamic applied model, it is natural to project an overall inflation rather than home-goods inflation only. It is true that the exchange rate cannot in this case be defined both as the conversion factor that translates "dollars" into domestic currency *and* as the ratio of the value of a basket of tradables to the value of a basket of home goods. But it is easy to check from (6.2.35) that the exchange rate remains a linear monotonic function of the relative price of tradables to nontradables when we chose the overall price level as numéraire.

To summarize and facilitate further discussion, let us introduce some terminology. When we refer to the *nominal exchange rate* or simply the *exchange rate,* we shall always mean the number by which world prices (say, dollar prices) must be multiplied to obtain local prices net of all taxes. The exchange rate is simply the actual parity that translates "dollars" into local currency. The concept of the *effective exchange rate,* often used in the literature (see Bhagwati, 1978; Krueger, 1978), refers to the price of foreign currency inclusive of all taxes imposed on its purchase. Thus, in the case of imports, the effective exchange rate equals the exchange rate multiplied by one plus the rate of import duties.

The *real exchange rate* will be used to mean the relative price of a basket of tradables with respect to a basket of nontradables. A real devaluation will mean that tradables have become relatively more expensive, whereas a nominal devaluation simply means that the exchange rate has changed. A nominal devaluation will imply a greater, equivalent, or smaller real devaluation, depending on whether the price of home goods falls, remains constant, or increases.

A *price-level-deflated exchange rate,* also used in the literature, refers to the exchange rate deflated by a price index with some arbitrary base measuring domestic inflation. The purchasing-power parity or PPP price-level-deflated exchange rate is the exchange rate deflated not by a domestic price deflator, but by a deflator measuring the excess of domestic inflation over world inflation. Thus, if a country's exchange rate is 20 units of local currency to the dollar and if, in the reference period, the local price index has doubled with respect to the world price index, the PPP price-level-deflated exchange rate would be 10. For an identical choice of weights, changes in the real exchange rate are equivalent to changes in the PPP-PLD (price-level-deflated) exchange rate.

Finally, there is the concept of the *equilibrium exchange rate*. This is the exchange rate that equates the demand and supply of foreign exchange in a given period and for a given set of trade taxes and subsidies. The equilibrium exchange rate is not necessarily an optimal exchange rate or the appropriate shadow price of foreign exchange because there may be trade taxes and distortions and, even in their absence, free trade may not be an intertemporally optimal policy. Furthermore, it must be stressed that we implicitly assume equilibrium in money markets, so that the equilibrium exchange rate always fully adjusts to differential inflation rates as well as to changes in the real sphere, such as differential rates of technical progress, changes in tastes, and changes in real resource flows.

A good summary of some of the issues in exchange-rate analysis can be provided by discussing what causes the equilibrium exchange rate to change over time.[3] For simplicity, assume that all tradables have been aggregated both in the domestic country and in the rest of the world and denote ER^r simply by r. Let P_T and $\overline{PW}_T$ denote the domestic and world price of tradables, respectively, and let P_H and $\overline{PW}_H$ be the prices of nontradables at home and in the rest of the world. General equilibrium in the domestic economy at any particular moment implies an equilibrium price system and therefore an equilibrium real exchange rate:

$$r = \frac{P_T \Omega_T}{P_H \Omega_H} \tag{6.2.42}$$

or

$$P_H = \frac{P_T \Omega_T}{r \Omega_H} \tag{6.2.43}$$

Substituting (6.2.43) into the price-level equation yields

$$P_T \Omega_T + P_T \frac{\Omega_T}{r} = P \tag{6.2.44}$$

---

[3] The exposition in this section is based on and similar to that of Dornbusch (1978).

or

$$P_T = k \cdot P \qquad (6.2.45)$$

where $k = 1/\Omega_T (1 + 1/r)$.

Similarly, in the rest of the world,

$$\overline{PW}_T = l \cdot \overline{PW} \qquad (6.2.46)$$

where PW is the rest-of-the-world price level and l is a parameter analogous to k for the rest of the world.

Therefore, letting e denote ER^e, the equilibrium exchange rate is

$$e = \frac{P_T}{\overline{PW}_T} = \frac{k \cdot P}{l \cdot \overline{PW}} \qquad (6.2.47)$$

and

$$\hat{e} = (\hat{k} - \hat{l}) + (\hat{P} - \hat{PW}) \qquad (6.2.48)$$

where $(\hat{\ })$ denotes percentage changes over time.

Changes in the equilibrium exchange rate can be decomposed into changes due purely to real forces $(\hat{k} - \hat{l})$, such as differential rates of technical progress between tradables and nontradables, changes in tastes, differential rates of factor accumulation, and so on, and changes due to differential inflation $(\hat{P} - \hat{PW})$, caused by differences in domestic and foreign supplies and demands for money.[4] Changes in the exchange rate reflect both real and monetary phenomena. The general equilibrium models discussed in this book determine $\hat{k}$ endogenously. Events in the rest of the world that determine $\hat{l}$ and $\hat{PW}$ and domestic inflation $\hat{P}$ are treated as exogenous. The *effects* of changes in l (e.g., an OPEC oil price increase) and/or $\hat{P}$ and $\hat{PW}$ can and will be analyzed in the model framework.

6.3   Introducing trade policy

In the previous section we have seen how the introduction of the exchange rate and of exogenous world prices affects the structure of a general equilibrium model. The chain of causality is at least partly reversed, with world prices having a determining influence on domestic prices. Trade policy affects the domestic economy by entering this chain at its very beginning. The imposition of a tariff on a category of imports will raise not only the domestic price of the imports in question, but also

---

[4] For an application of this decomposition formula, see Chapter 10.

the price of the domestically produced import-competing commodities. Thus, under the small-country assumption, the government is seen as having direct control over the relative domestic prices of tradable commodities. This makes trade policy into a very powerful instrument affecting economic structure, growth, and income distribution.

The purpose of this section is to examine briefly how the main propositions of the theory of international trade and commercial policy can be carried over in the formulation of a CGE model. Particular emphasis will be put on those effects of trade policy that can be usefully captured in a CGE model and those that cannot. This will lead us to consider the effects of trade policy on resource allocation with a comparison of the results one would obtain with a partial equilibrium and with a general equilibrium model. Finally, the effects of trade policy on potential welfare are examined.

Tariffs, subsidies, and quantitative restrictions

Denote the *ad valorem* tariff, subsidy, or export tax for sector i by tm_i. Then domestic prices in a tariff-ridden economy are linked to world prices by

$$P_i = \overline{PW}_i(1 + tm_i)ER \qquad i \in T \tag{6.3.1}$$

where T denotes the set of tradable sectors. For a small open economy, world prices $\overline{PW}_i$ are exogenously fixed, so that trade policy fully determines the relative domestic price of tradables. For any pair of sectors,

$$\frac{P_i}{P_j} = \frac{\overline{PW}_i(1 + tm_i)}{\overline{PW}_j(1 + tm_j)} \tag{6.3.2}$$

because the exchange rate cancels out. Trade taxes are therefore crucial in a small, open-economy model. When sector i is an export sector, tm_i is an export subsidy (to be denoted as te_i) if it is positive or a tax if it is negative.

The effects of a tariff can be illustrated with Figure 6.2 for the case of two traded sectors and a standard model with no distortions in factor or commodity markets. Free-trade production takes place at A and consumption takes place at C_1. In free trade the world price ratio $\Pi = \overline{PW}_1/\overline{PW}_2$ is equal to the domestic price ratio. A tariff on importables (sector 2) lowers the relative domestic price below the world price, as indicated by the lines labeled P. This tariff results in the following well-known effects: (1) a production effect whereby producers shift toward

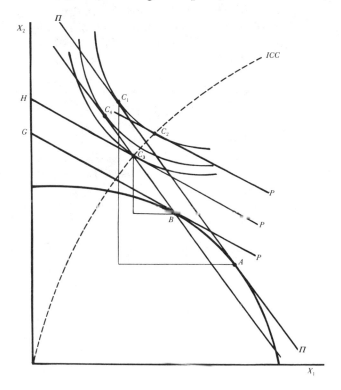

Figure 6.2. The effects of a tariff on production, consumption, and trade.

the production of importables $(A \rightarrow B)$; (2) a government revenue effect
GH, as the government now collects tariff revenue; (3) a reduction in
the volume of trade, indicated by the relative size of the two trade tri-
angles; (4) a welfare effect as the community moves onto a lower indifference curve and ends up consuming at C_3. The movement from C_1 to
C_3 can be determined with the help of the income consumption line
denoted by ICC; it is due to a substitution effect $(C_1 \rightarrow C_2)$ and an
income effect $(C_2 \rightarrow C_3)$.[5] Similar effects would result from the protection of exportables.

Note that the loss in welfare can be decomposed into two effects: a
production effect indicating the costs to the community of producing
inefficiently and a consumption effect resulting from consumption at

---

[5] It is assumed that the government has identical preferences with the private
sector or that it redistributes its revenues to the private sector.

distorted prices. The production effect is indicated by the movement from C_1 to C_4, which is where the community would end up if a subsidy were granted directly to producers, leaving consumer choice undistorted. The consumption effect is indicated by the movement from C_4 to C_3.

Trade policy, however, is not restricted entirely to the application of tariffs, subsidies, and export taxes. There are many other instruments used by governments to control the volume of trade.[6] One of them is import rationing, which is often used when a country faces an acute foreign exchange shortage and when foreign exchange revenues are allocated to importers according to some rule. We shall consider in Chapter 9 how an economy is likely to adjust under such circumstances.

Quantity restrictions (QRs) or quotas are another instrument that governments use to affect the allocation of resources. It is often noted in the literature that there are conditions under which quantitative restrictions can be related to price-mechanism devices by defining "equivalent" price devices that would result in the same effect on production. Although this is strictly true for the CGE models in this book, in practice it will turn out that such equivalences cannot be easily established either analytically or computationally because there are too many other effects, particularly distributional ones, which result in various instruments having a different impact on the economy.

Moreover, the analogy between different instruments is valid only provided that competition prevails before and after the imposition of the quota. In fact it assumes that import licenses are transferable between firms and that there is a market in licenses. In practice it is likely that the imposition of quotas will lead to the establishment of a monopolistic market structure, because quotas are often confined to existing firms or are distributed pro rata, that is, in proportion to existing production levels, and the market for licenses may be very imperfect. In this case, if the profit-maximizing level of imports is less than the quota level, imports will fall below the quota-imposed level, and an indirect effect of the imposition of the quota will be to raise profits above what they would have been in the absence of the quota. The point here is that a nonprohibitive tariff does not have the monopoly-creating effect of a quota, although it shares with it the import-replacing effect. Thus, a given reduction in imports when achieved by a tariff may be associated with a greater rise in domestic output than when achieved by a quota. It follows that there will be a smaller fall in consumption with a tariff

---

[6] For a description of the variety of direct measures to control the volume and composition of trade, see Bhagwati (1978, chap. 2). He also discusses the conditions under which the equivalences mentioned later hold.

than under a quota, so that the domestic price will rise less with a tariff. Moreover, even in the simplest possible case, this equivalence will hold only statically, because in a dynamic model a constant tariff through time will give rise to an increase in the volume of imports, whereas a constant quota will lead to higher premia (rents) to holders of licenses. It is therefore substantially incorrect to argue, even in a fairly simple multisector model, that the equivalence propositions referred to in the literature will continue to hold.

As soon as the assumption of perfect competition is dropped, or at least as soon as one recognizes that trade policy is likely to affect the degree of competition in the economy, it becomes necessary to consider the effects of trade policy in the presence of economies of scale, a phenomenon that will be ignored here but that deserves to be investigated. Changing market structures also give rise to the possibility that firms become less efficient when trade policy restricts the degree of competition in the economy. This is often referred to as a decline in X-efficiency (see Leibenstein, 1978). Finally, it is likely that in an environment where trade restrictions give rise to large quota profits to the holders of licenses, real resources will be expended to obtain these licenses. This will lead to further inefficiencies, because real resources will be diverted toward nonproductive activities, and the economy will become what Krueger has called a "rent-seeking society."[7] We shall consider later on how rent seeking can be incorporated into a CGE model.

Whether protection is achieved by the price mechanism or by quantitative restrictions, there are three areas of concern to the policy maker for which a CGE model can provide useful insights. First, a CGE model quantifies the effects of trade policy on resource allocation and economic structure and provides some information about the sectors in which the economy is likely to develop a comparative advantage. Second, it provides an estimate of the efficiency effects of alternative trade policy regimes, thereby giving an estimate of the effects of trade policy on welfare. Third, the choice of trade strategy is likely to affect the distribution of income among socioeconomic groups as well as between the public and the private sector.

At this point it is useful to discuss trade policy and resource allocation and illustrate some of the crucial ways in which results generated by a CGE model differ from those that one would obtain in a partial equilibrium setting. This discussion will indicate both where the two approaches differ and what are their data requirements.

---

[7] See Krueger (1974b). A detailed discussion of the effects of trade policy on market structure is provided by Corden (1974, chap. 8).

Partial and general equilibrium analysis

How, then, would one estimate the change in production pattern as the economy moves from A to B in Figure 6.2? In partial equilibrium analysis, one would use information on the elasticity of supply ϵ^s for each sector together with the rate of protection, which is measured by the nominal rate of protection ($NRP = tm$). Letting ^ denote a percentage change (e.g., $\hat{X} \equiv dX/X$), an expression for each sector's percentage change in output is given by

$$\hat{X} = \epsilon^s NRP \tag{6.3.3}$$

Resource pulls in any sector would therefore depend on its own supply elasticity and on the nominal rate of protection. This way of reasoning assumes that all trade takes place in final commodities or that only the tariff changes. However, there are important interindustry linkages embodied in a multisector model given the fact that commodities enter into the production of other commodities. It is thus necessary to estimate the protection accorded to a commodity at a given stage of production because one can no longer simply use the nominal rate of protection (NRP), which is the difference between a sector's domestic price and the world market price. Taking Ricardo's famous example of trade in cloth and wine between England and Portugal, one should not refer to a country's comparative advantage in clothing, but indicate separately its advantages and disadvantages in cotton growing, spinning, weaving, and clothing manufacturing.

Accordingly, one needs to distinguish between nominal protection and effective protection (protection to value added). The effective rate of protection (ERP), which expresses the margin of protection on value added (or net price) in the production process, recognizes the fact that a tariff provides a subsidy to the activity producing the product to which it applies, and imposes a tax on the product of other activities using that product as an input. Denoting by superscripts zero and one the situations before and after the change in tariffs, the general equilibrium ERP for sector j is defined as

$$ERP_j \equiv \frac{PN_j^1}{PN_j^0} - 1 \tag{6.3.4}$$

where

$$PN_j^k = [\overline{PW}_j (1 + tm_j^k) - \sum_i a_{ij} \overline{PW}_i (1 + tm_i^k)] ER^k$$
$$k = 0, 1 \tag{6.3.5}$$

under the assumption that intermediate inputs are purchased in fixed proportions.

It should be clear that a CGE model provides full ERP estimates together with the resulting reallocation of resources. However, the popularity of ERPs as indicators of resource pulls is based on the premise that they can be calculated in a partial equilibrium framework by making three important simplifying assumptions about (1) the treatment of the exchange-rate adjustment following a change in trade taxes; (2) the treatment of nontraded goods; and (3) factor price effects. We examine in turn the implications of these assumptions for the calculation of ERPs.

First, unless one has a general equilibrium model, it is difficult to estimate by how much a change in protective structure affects the exchange rate. Take the case of raising a tariff uniformly on all imported goods. For simplicity, assume that the tariff proceeds are redistributed to consumers via lump-sum subsidies and that the economy operates on its budget constraint. Then the tariff raises the domestic relative price of importables in terms of exportables by the amount of the tariff. At this point, if one can make the reasonable assumption that home goods are substitutes for both exportables and importables, there will be an excess demand for nontraded goods. As already shown in Section 6.2, the budget constraint and Walras's law ensure that this excess demand for home goods is exactly equal to the balance-of-trade surplus valued at domestic, undistorted prices. For the moment, let subscripts h, m, e denote the home goods, and import and export competing sectors. The income and expenditure identities are

$$I \equiv X_h P_h + P_m X_m + P_e X_e + tm\ \overline{PW}\ ER \qquad (6.3.6)$$
$$E \equiv C_h P_h + P_m C_m + P_e C_e \qquad (6.3.7)$$

Equating income and expenditure and defining $M \equiv C_m - X_m$ (imports) and $E \equiv X_e - C_e$ (exports), it follows that

$$ER(\overline{PWE} \cdot E - \overline{PW} \cdot M) = P_h(C_h - X_h) \qquad (6.3.8)$$

which equates the excess demand for home goods with the balance-of-trade surplus valued at domestic prices. To attain equilibrium, home goods have to appreciate in terms of both importables and exportables or, equivalently – as was demonstrated in the discussion on normalization – the price of both importables and exportables would have to fall equiproportionately in terms of home goods. Because we shall always use a normalization rule that maintains the aggregate price level constant [e.g., Eq. (6.2.3)], a tariff will appreciate (lower) the exchange rate so as to satisfy the normalization rule.

Because appreciation affects equally the price of both the exportables and importables, the ERP still correctly measures the protective margin of the importable relative to the exportable. However, net effective rates of protection (NERPs) are needed to take into account the appreciation of tradables relative to nontradables. Therefore, we have the following expression:

$$NERP_j = \frac{(1 + ERP_j^1)ER^1}{(1 + ERP_j^0)ER^0} - 1 \qquad (6.3.9)$$

where the definition of ERP_j no longer includes the exchange-rate change, which has to be estimated independently. Provided that this net rate is positive, resources will be attracted into the importable sector from the exportable sector and the home-good sector. If some estimates of sectoral supply elasticities are available, one can obtain an expression for the percentage increase in output for sector j in an analogous way to the simple case without intermediate inputs. The expression is

$$X_j = \epsilon_j^s NERP_j \qquad (6.3.10)$$

The second simplification underlying the use of effective protection measures to predict resource shifts is also related to the presence of non-traded goods. The absence of nontraded goods, coupled with the assumption that world prices are fixed, eliminates the impact of demand considerations so that it is easy to measure the production and consumption effects of a tariff separately. The former are given by (6.3.10) and the latter by the NRP discussed earlier. However, as soon as the presence of nontraded goods is recognized, this simple separation of production and consumption effects breaks down, because the production and consumption of each nontraded good has to be brought into equilibrium by a relative price adjustment among these goods. Therefore, in the presence of links among nontraded goods – through substitution effects in production and/or consumption – production and consumption effects may no longer be separated for the system as a whole. It follows that one cannot predict the relative price adjustments among nontraded goods resulting from a change in trade policy.

Finally, factor prices are assumed to be fixed. This simplification will also lead to a bias in the estimates based on a partial equilibrium methodology. To examine quantitative differences between the results obtained in a partial equilibrium analysis and those obtained from the model, suppose that sectoral technology is described by fixed intermediate input coefficients as assumed in Chapter 5 (and in the ERP methodology) and that output is described by a two-factor CES function of capital and labor with returns to scale, λ_i. A change in tariff structure will alter relative net prices, which in turn will affect the firm's demand for factors and hence output supplies. Totally differentiating the factor demand and production function equations yields, *after* allowing for factor substitution,

$$\hat{X}_i = \lambda_i(1 - \lambda_i)^{-1}(P\hat{N}_i - \theta_{iL}\hat{W} - \theta_{ik}\hat{r}) \tag{6.3.11}$$

where, as before, carets indicate percentage changes, and θ_{ik} and θ_{iL} are the shares of total product (adding up to λ_i) accruing to each factor.

Expression (6.3.11) provides a measure of comparative advantage in the long run when capital is mobile across sectors. The short-run impact effect of a change in trade policy assumes that sectoral capital stocks are fixed so that they drop out in the process of differentiation. Assume for simplicity that returns to scale are unity, so that factor payments exhaust the value of total product ($\theta_{ik} + \theta_{iL} = 1$). Then the supply response will be finite despite constant returns to scale, because in fact there are decreasing returns to scale to the variable factor of production, labor, and the expression corresponding to (6.3.11) is

$$\hat{X}_i = \sigma_i^X \frac{\theta_{iL}}{\theta_{ik}}(P\hat{N} - \hat{W}) \tag{6.3.12}$$

where σ_i^X is the elasticity of substitution between capital and labor. Equation (6.3.12) is the supply response taking into account changes in the wage rate that are omitted in a partial equilibrium estimation.

Sectoral output changes derived from (6.3.12) can be compared with an ERP-based prediction as expressed in Eq. (6.3.10). The main differences are the neglect of factor price changes in the partial equilibrium measure and the treatment of nontraded goods. Thus, $P\hat{N}$ is the percentage change in value added, inclusive of changes in relative prices among nontraded goods, which are not predicted correctly in the expression yielding $NERP_i$. Moreover, it is unlikely that the estimate of the exchange-rate adjustment calculated under partial equilibrium assumptions will correspond to that emerging from the CGE model. In general, estimates based on partial equilibrium assumptions are fairly accurate predictors of resource pulls for small changes in relative prices. As soon as substantial changes take place, even the refined ERP methodology (with data requirements close to those of CGE-based estimates) does not fare well. Given that the data requirements for a sophisticated study of protection and resource allocation are similar to the data requirements for a CGE model, it seems preferable to use the extended CGE model. Note also that the assumptions about how markets operate are also similar.[8]

The distinction between partial and general equilibrium estimates could also be highlighted by deriving an expression for consumption changes similar to (6.3.11). Consumption response to a change in tariff structure depends upon own-price, cross-price, and income elasticities of demand. Again, the partial equilibrium expression will not include the induced changes in relative prices among nontraded goods and would have to be based on separately provided estimates of income and exchange-rate changes.

Expressions (6.3.11) and (6.3.12) are also useful to highlight the difficulty of modeling a small open economy under perfect competition when the technology exhibits constant returns to scale (CRS) and the number of traded goods (n) is greater than the number of factors of production (m).[9] As long as the number of traded sectors and the number of commodities is the same, there is a simple correspondence between product prices and factor prices. What happens if $m < n$? Take as an example the case of three commodities and two factors. From the first-order conditions for profit maximization, only two commodity prices are needed to determine factor prices. Therefore, for each selected supply of commodity 3, a different supply pattern will result, each consistent with the given prices and input coefficients. There exists an infinity of possible supply patterns, all consistent with the same set of commodity prices. The production possibility set will be convex, but the surface will contain linear segments.[10] The simplest example is provided by the Ricardian model with two commodities and one input, labor. In the general case, the supply response to price changes will lead to specialization, because with exogenously determined product prices, at most m sectors will be able to cover costs.

In a multisector model, specialization will not occur, at least in the short run, because each sector has a specific factor of production, capital. The zero-profit conditions will always hold, because the rents accruing to capital are determined residually, precisely so as to satisfy Euler's equation. In the long run, however, the reallocation of capital across sectors will tend to equalize rental rates, so that only those sectors that cover costs will continue producing. The specialization problem, already

---

[8] Comparisons of partial and general equilibrium estimates of resources pulls are to be found in Taylor and Black (1974) and de Melo (1978a).

[9] For a formal discussion, see Samuelson (1948).

[10] Melvin (1968) provides a geometric exposition of the two-factor, three-good case.

discussed in Chapter 3 in a linear programming framework, remains an issue as long as we assume constant returns to scale and have the domestic price of tradables equal to exogenously fixed world prices.

6.4 Trade policy and efficiency

The most basic proposition in international trade is that free trade raises the level of potential welfare for a country above the level reached in autarchy. This increase in potential welfare can be further subdivided into the gains from exchange resulting from obtaining goods at a lower price from abroad, and the production gains from specialization in the commodities in which the country has a comparative advantage. Equally well known is the companion proposition that policy-induced distortions in the product markets, in the form of tariffs and quotas, and in the factor markets, in the form of wage distortions and imperfect mobility, reduce the potential welfare gain from free trade. Because government policy in the foreign trade sector will be typically very active, it is important to discuss in some detail how government policy affects welfare.

For a perfectly competitive economy with no monopoly power in trade and perfect factor mobility, *laissez faire* is Pareto optimal because the economy will operate efficiently; that is, the transformation curve coincides with the production possibilities frontier. Under these conditions, the first-order conditions for an economic maximum will hold for any pair of commodities: $DRT = DRS = FRT$ (where DRT represents the marginal rate of transformation in domestic production, DRS represents the marginal rate of substitution in consumption, and FRT represents the marginal foreign rate of transformation). Perhaps the simplest way to illustrate these marginal equivalences is to consider an economy consisting of two sectors (1 and 2) and two factors, capital and labor. Then the marginal equivalences can be obtained by totally differentiating the production functions, substituting into the resulting expressions the values for marginal products obtained from the first-order conditions, and using the factor endowments constraints to obtain

$$-\frac{dX_2}{dX_1} = \frac{P_1}{P_2}\left(\frac{r_2\,dK_1 + W_2\,dL_1}{r_1\,dK_1 + W_1\,dL_1}\right) = \frac{\overline{PW_1}}{\overline{PW_2}} \qquad (6.4.1)$$

In the absence of tariffs, monopoly power in trade, and different rates of return to capital or labor across sectors, the marginal equivalences will hold because $P_1/P_2 = \overline{PW_1}/\overline{PW_2}$, and the expression in parentheses in (6.4.1) will equal one.

Expression (6.4.1) can also be related to Figure 6.2. When there are no distortions in the system (i.e., when the economy is producing at A and consuming at C_1), the marginal rate of transformation indicated by the slope of the production possibility curve at A is equal to the marginal rate of substitution in consumption at C_1 and to the foreign marginal rate of transformation given by the ПIII line.

Following are some of the more important cases giving rise to a departure from the marginal equivalences described by (6.4.1). In addition to trade taxes mentioned earlier, there are various imperfections in factor markets and the case of monopoly power in trade.

It is virtually always the case that manufacturing (sector 2) pays a much higher wage than agriculture (sector 1). Then the term in parentheses in (6.4.1) will no longer be equal to unity and the economy will no longer be operating on its production possibility frontier. It will be operating on a contracted transformation curve reflecting the fact that the private marginal cost of production in manufacturing exceeds the social marginal cost of production.

The contribution of a CGE model with its emphasis on simulation of market behavior is that it allows an assessment of the effect of these distortions in a framework that is in close agreement with the theoretical model. Indeed, all that needs to be done is to extend the basic model in Chapter 5 and let the wage rates in each sector (W_{is}) differ by constants of proportionality (ϕ_{is}) reflecting the extent of distortion. Each sector will have its own wage, which will be related to the endogenously determined economy-wide wage for that category of labor by

$$W_{is} = \phi_{is} W_s \qquad (6.4.2)$$

For policy analysis, what is important is the distinction between differentials that are a cause of distortion and those that are not. Examples of nondistortionary differentials include capital specificity and industrial wages exceeding agricultural wages because of the higher costs of urban living or costs of migration. Even if the quality of labor is identical, which rules out higher urban wages as a result of returns on investment in human capital, money wages may not be a correct indication of true wages because there are nonmarket food supplies in agriculture. It is sometimes argued that a rough indicator of the social opportunity cost of labor in urban areas is the wage rate paid in the urban small-scale sector, so that the excess of wages over the amount paid in the manufacturing sector represents a distortion.

It is generally the case, however, that manufacturing pays a wage in excess of the opportunity cost of labor, thereby giving rise to a justification of protection for the manufacturing sector as a way of offsetting the high wage.[11] Similarly, cheaper capital for the modern large-scale sector than for small-scale industry and agriculture may be due to the greater risk from lending to small business or small farmers. Yet, on the whole, capital market imperfections caused by government policies tend to make credit to large-scale manufacturing unduly cheap. These distortions in the factor market call for policy intervention. It must nevertheless be stressed that before stating that the constants in Eq. (6.4.2) can be set to one by policy intervention, one has to be fairly confident that they do indeed represent removable distortions.[12]

An important cause of factor market distortions in some developing countries is the tendency for labor in large-scale manufacturing to secure a minimum wage well above the full-employment wage. In this case, too, the market transformation frontier will lie inside the production possibility frontier. A model specification with a fixed real wage was presented in Chapter 5. In such an economy, the level of employment depends not only on the real wage, but also on relative product prices. The relationship depends on the relative factor intensity of production in the various sectors.[13]

Because the total level of employment is variable, the welfare implications of this model will differ from those in the standard neoclassical model in the following sense. If trade leads the country to export the capital-intensive good, employment and welfare will decrease. Hence, there would be an argument for restricting trade to increase aggregate employment and output. On the other hand, if exports are labor intensive, as is typically the case in developing countries, a reduction in trade barriers leading to increased specialization will raise employment and welfare.

Another important deviation from marginal conditions that is relevant for developing countries occurs when the country has some monopoly power in trade, that is, when $FRT \neq DRT$. This is (often) the case on the export side, either because exports consist of highly differentiated products for which the elasticity of demand is not infinite or, in the case

---

[11] See Hagen (1958). Note that the first-best policy would be to subsidize the use of labor in manufacturing. In the case where unemployment coexists with a high wage in the manufacturing sector as in the Harris-Todaro model, the policy prescriptions are reversed. See Bhagwati and Srinivasan (1974) or Corden (1974, chap. 6).

[12] For an example where these differentials are interpreted as distortionary, see de Melo (1977).

[13] See Brecher (1974), who examines the relationships in a two-factor, two-commodity model.

of homogeneous primary products, because the country is a substantial supplier of a product on world markets. Then, if foreign retaliation can be ignored, it is optimal to restrict the volume of exports below the level they would reach under free trade because, with a downward-sloping demand curve, marginal revenue will fall short of marginal cost in free trade. Also important to note is that an export subsidy would in this case lead to a deterioration in the terms of trade and welfare.

The optimal export tax will be the tax rate that results in a volume of exports such that the marginal revenue from an extra unit of exports is equal to the marginal cost of supplying it. If the elasticity of demand for exports is constant, then it can be shown that the optimal export tax should be set equal to the inverse of that elasticity.[14]

To summarize: The central proposition of the theory of domestic distortions is that the optimal policy intervention involves making the appropriate correction at the point of divergence (first-best). If there are constraints in the choice of policies, one is compelled to move down the hierarchy, adding at each step an additional distortion as one moves down the sequence of policies away from first-best. Similarly, when distortions must be introduced into the economy because the values of certain variables are constrained, the optimal method of doing so is to choose that policy intervention which creates the distortion affecting directly the constrained variable.[15]

It would, however, be a serious mistake to construe these propositions to imply that development policy consists solely of trying to attain a distortion-free economy. On the contrary, the situation facing developing countries is often one that requires second-, third-, or fourth-best choices. The functioning of markets is quite imperfect, income distribution is of paramount importance, and government revenue is a binding constraint that cannot be ignored. Under those circumstances, designing development policy no longer reduces to the pursuit of a first-best policy, because there are too many factors that prevent the implementation of such a policy. Policy design becomes an exploration of

[14] See Corden (1974, chap. 7). It is tempting to use a CGE model to determine the optimal export tax, but one must keep in mind the possibility of foreign retaliation, possible lags in the adjustment of foreign demand to changes in taxes or subsidies, and the need to consider transport and market development costs that would result from a drive to expand exports.

[15] For a summary of the propositions underlying the theory of domestic distortions, see Bhagwati (1971). For a perceptive discussion of the assumptions on which the theory is built, see Corden (1974). Corden uses many examples relevant for policy making in a developing economy.

alternatives over time, where the costs and benefits of each alternative must be carefully weighed.

As a simple example, consider again the case of protection of the manufacturing sector. According to the theory of domestic distortions, it would be preferable to use a subsidy to producers rather than a tariff, because the former avoids the consumption cost caused by distorting consumer preferences. In terms of Figure 6.2, a subsidy to producers instead of a tariff would allow the community to reach a higher level of welfare (C_4 instead of C_3). But policy makers in developing countries face budgetary constraints in the form of collection and disbursement costs, which prevent them from having the option of choosing the better policy. Their situation is a second-best one, and they operate in an environment characterized by other distortions.

With limited options and many distortions there are no obvious policy recommendations. Indeed, it is well known that reducing the degree of one distortion in the presence of another may not be welfare increasing. The point here is not to note that anything can happen; rather it is to recognize the complexity of the policy environment and the need for careful analysis. A CGE model allows comparison among various alternatives that may all reflect second- or third-best situations. Its strength lies in the fact that the comparisons are not restricted to "small" policy changes, and that a great deal of general equilibrium interaction can be taken into account. Although precise quantification may be impossible, the CGE framework can help in formulating the right questions and can stimulate empirical work designed to increase our knowledge of the relevant trade-offs.

6.5 Trade policy and planning in a dynamic context

So far we have discussed the specification of trade and trade policy in a static framework without introducing time. But some of the most interesting aspects of the debate over the appropriate trade strategy for developing countries are related to dynamic problems. For example, the argument for protection in developing countries has relied primarily on dynamic considerations based mostly on some variant of the "infant industry" argument.

In Chapter 5 we discussed some of the difficulties of building truly dynamic models. The essence of the problem relates to differential speeds of adjustment of quantity and price variables, and the problem only gets more difficult when we include foreign trade in the analysis. It should be quite clear that the various trade-substitution and export-demand elasticities we have discussed are not "timeless" concepts. The values they take should depend on whether one is engaged, say, in a five-year planning exercise and constructs a model that attempts to trace the behavior of the economy in each year of a five-year period, or whether one is doing a comparative statics exercise for some target year that may be five or ten years into the future. Quite apart from these empirical issues relating to speeds of adjustment, the building of a dynamic general equilibrium model including foreign trade raises some issues that do not arise in a purely static context. The most important of these relates to the determination of aggregate investment and the extent to which trade policy can affect the pace of capital accumulation.

Recall the discussion of the alternative stylized versions of the determinants of aggregate investment presented in Chapter 5. Let us now see how trade policy can affect the rate of growth by considering each one of these versions in turn. Suppose first that the rate of growth of capital stock is somehow determined exogenously, perhaps by the government always being ready to save just enough for a real-capital-accumulation target to be fulfilled. In this case, there is interaction among trade policy, aggregate investment, and growth, because the growth rate of the capital stock is not affected by either the aggregate level of real income or by the different saving propensities of the factors of production. The rate of growth of the economy is independent of trade policy.

Alternatively, assume that a constant fraction of national income is saved. Then real investment will rise and fall with real income, and any change in trade policy that affects real income will affect the pace of capital accumulation. Thus an increase in trade distortions lowers real investment by lowering real income.

Moreover, trade policy can lead to a change in real investment not only through this income effect but also through a relative price or substitution effect. When the proportion of expenditure on investment is constant, a policy that leads to a change in the relative price of investment goods in terms of consumption goods will alter the real amount of investment obtained from a given nominal amount of savings. A trade policy that, for example, succeeds in cheapening imports of capital goods will increase the real amount of investment and hence raise the rate of capital formation. This cheapening is often one of the aims of trying to keep an overvalued exchange rate. In this case a restrictive trade policy would increase the rate of capital accumulation if the substitution effect more than outweighed the loss in real income resulting from a restrictive trade policy. Such a policy may be justified if the socially desired savings propensity is higher than the private one and if, furthermore, first-best policies for raising investment are not feasible. The opposite is of course true for a policy that tries to *protect* the domestic capital goods industries. By raising the relative price of capital goods, it will depress real investment.

The substitution effect just described is further complicated by the presence of home goods. Given that construction activities usually account for between one-third and one-half of total investment, it is important to consider what happens in a model where a portion of capital goods are nontraded. An attempt at depressing the price of imported capital goods may well result in increasing the price of home goods. In the typical CGE model there are no substitution possibilities among different types of investment goods, and hence the potentially positive effect of restrictive trade policy just described will be weakened, because it is likely to lead to a rise in the price of nontraded construction goods.

Finally, consider a third case where investment is determined by the propensities to save out of labor and capital income. Then trade policy may affect capital accumulation through redistribution effects; if capitalists and wage earners each have constant propensities to save out of income, and provided that these propensities are different, a change in trade policy will affect total savings and therefore capital accumulation. If capitalists have a much higher propensity to save than wage earners, and if investment goods are capital intensive, then a policy that lowers the price of investment goods may reduce investment by reducing the share of capitalist income. This distribution effect has to be added to the income and substitution effects when we consider the effect of trade policy on capital accumulation and the rate of growth of the economy.[16]

Employment growth and capital accumulation jointly determine the growth of total factor inputs in an economy. Trade policy may affect the rate of growth, not only by affecting capital accumulation but also by affecting total employment. Of course, this can be so only if total employment is a variable responsive to changes in relative prices, which is the case in models with fixed wages. We have already summarized, in Section 6.4, the relationship between trade policy and employment. In fixed-wage models with unemployment, it is possible for trade policy to increase employment and output by stimulating more labor-intensive production activities. Whether it is expansionary or restrictive trade policy that yields this effect depends on the relative factor intensities of exportables and import substitutes. In a dynamic context, trade policy in the form, for example, of gradual trade liberalization, may lead to an increase in the rate of growth of total productive employment for a given

---

[16] For an application of these cases in a three-sector model, see de Melo and Derviş (1977).

path of the real wage. This establishes another link between overall growth and trade policy.

Total factor accumulation is, however, only part of what determines economic growth. As is by now well established, the total growth in at least conventionally measured inputs falls substantially short of explaining the growth in output over time. (see Solow, 1957; Denison, 1967; Jorgenson and Nishimizu, 1978). The residual is usually attributed to "technical progress."

The possible links between trade policy and technical progress remain probably the most ardently debated topic in the development literature. On the one hand, there is the belief that protection of industry is a precondition for rapid industrialization and that technical progress depends directly on the growth of industry through the spread of industrial techniques and industrial attitudes. On the other hand, there is the belief that protection stifles competitive innovation, prevents the introduction of new products and methods, and reduces contact with the world market and hence slows down the pace of technical progress in an economy. Needless to say, we are as yet far from being able to incorporate these considerations formally in multisector planning models.

Some questions can be clarified by formal modeling and simulation of alternatives. Consider, for example, the potential conflict between static efficiency considerations and the kind of dynamic considerations that are loosely referred to as "infant industry" arguments. The "infant industry" argument is based on a divergence between static and dynamic effects of trade policy and emphasizes dynamic considerations. Although it is generally recognized that trade distortions have static welfare costs, it is then argued that the dynamic benefits associated with a protectionist trade policy are well worth the static costs. Thus investment should proceed, not according to static comparative advantage, but according to long-run dynamic comparative advantage.

Assume that all factors including capital are perfectly homogeneous and mobile across sectors. Suppose at the same time that the production possibility curve of the country in question is shifting in such a way as to lead to shifts in comparative advantage as a result of differential sectoral rates of technical progress and/or factor accumulation. For example, the country in question may start with a comparative advantage in cotton textiles, but as capital accumulation and technological progress take place, it may enter a phase where its comparative advantage lies in electrical machinery. Is the fact that a country will develop a comparative advantage in electrical machinery ten years from now a reason to shift present investment away from textiles into electrical machinery and to produce more such machinery today? If capital and other factors are mobile, the answer is clearly no. When and if comparative advantage changes, capital and production should be shifted to the machinery sector, but there is no reason to do it or encourage it before the change in comparative advantage occurs. Current prices still provide the best allocation signals.

But now, in accordance with the basic CGE model presented in Chapter 5, assume that capital once installed is immobile between sectors for the period under consideration and that people have static expectations and do not correctly predict the future, basing their investment decisions on current profit rates. If comparative advantage shifts in an unforeseen fashion, a sequence of investment allocations based on static comparative advantage will turn out to be intertemporally inefficient. Welfare would increase if capital could be shifted into the machinery sector at an earlier stage in anticipation of the coming shift in comparative advantage. The energy crisis may serve as a suggestive and somewhat extreme example of the effects of unforeseen shifts in price and cost structures. Clearly, if somebody had foreseen present oil prices in the early 1960s, a lot more capital could have been shifted into alternative sources of energy and, although this would not have been justified at the "static" prices of the 1960s, it would have turned out to be intertemporally efficient.

Although the suddenness of the change and the partly political mechanisms involved make oil and energy an extreme example, it helps to underline the issue. When capital is heterogeneous and imperfectly mobile and when the frictionless future markets of general equilibrium theory are absent, market mechanisms cannot be expected to lead to intertemporally efficient growth paths. In a dynamic context, efficiency and comparative advantage must be redefined in dynamic terms. The necessity of minimizing misallocations of investments will be an extremely important policy task in an environment where change is rapid and where structuralist constraints make it extremely difficult to "undo" unforeseen errors. In our example relating to cotton textiles and electrical machinery, one should give up utility today by shifting out of textiles and into machinery until the marginal static cost of doing so equals the marginal dynamic benefit of reallocating the capital stock in anticipation of a new structure of comparative advantage. One may learn a lot about just how and when to shift investment priorities by exploring alternative growth paths with a CGE model.

The dynamic inefficiency of myopic markets has always provided one major argument for central planning and government action. The existence of foreign trade does not, per se, add a new qualitative element to the argument. It may, however, increase the degree of uncertainty that is likely to prevail and the extent of dynamic resource misallocation that might occur. Whether government action is in fact likely to be less myopic than the sum of the expectations of private entrepreneurs is of course an open and often-debated question. In developing economies with rudimentary capital markets, a very strong argument can be made for the government to provide the long-run perspective that is essential for dynamic efficiency. Even in countries with highly developed capital markets, the limitations inherent in futures markets, and important differences between the social and the private evaluation of risk, have led many authors to rest the case for central indicative planning on arguments of dynamic efficiency.

Thus, dynamic considerations do provide a strong justification for policy intervention to stimulate investment in sectors expected to gain comparative advantage in the future. Note that one does not need to assume the existence of "learning" externalities as usually discussed in the context of the "infant industry" argument. We have so far stressed only the role of imperfect foresight, which is alone sufficient for an allocation of investment based on the present structure of comparative advantage to be intertemporally inefficient. "Learning" externalities that would be hard to internalize even with perfect foresight constitute an additional argument.

The most common learning externalities emphasized in the infant industry argument relate first to labor training and the returns from which accrue to the workers themselves while the costs are borne by firms and, second, to accumulation of technical know-how that cannot be internalized and kept by individual firms, as well as more general notions of knowledge diffusion and the creation of "modern attitudes" that are taken to benefit society. These effects are much more difficult to quantify. They may, however, be very important, perhaps more important than the more easily modeled effects of differential rates of technical progress and factor accumulation. There is little doubt that general considerations stressing the need for "modern" attitudes and general diffusion of knowledge have often provided the single strongest impetus for an interventionist trade policy.

It is very important to stress that "interventionism" need not imply inward-looking, protectionist trade strategies. The dynamic infant industry arguments apply as much or more to infant export industries as they do to infant import-competing industries. In the case of export industries, a very important "infant marketing" argument should in fact be added to the traditional "learning-by-doing" arguments. The situation is quite symmetric – export promotion beyond the static limits of comparative advantage definitely has the same kind of static resource allocation costs as import restrictions. It may also be expected to have the same, or perhaps even more important, dynamic benefits if the sectors emphasized are indeed those that will exhibit comparative advantage in the longer run. Furthermore, the "learning" that takes place through competition in international markets may have benefits that have no counterpart in purely domestic economic activity. Finally, the discipline and competition imposed by a more export- and world market-oriented strategy may have beneficial effects not only on efficiency but also on the distribution of domestic income.

6.6 Conclusion

The development of empirically realistic models tends to lead far away from the simple models of trade theory. It is clear that it is very difficult for some of the dynamic considerations we have discussed to be incorporated explicitly into multisector planning models. But a greater degree of realism and flexibility than is common in pure theory models can be achieved. In the next chapter we shall present a CGE model that incorporates a number of extensions to the basic model presented in Chapter 5 and is designed to capture more realistically the impact of different trade policies on domestic prices and resource allocation. These extensions will not alter the qualitative impact of policies that operate through causal mechanisms highlighted by trade theory. For example, one can still talk about the static consumption and production costs of protection. Tariffs on relatively capital-intensive import-substituting industries will still lower total employment in a fixed-wage setting and will also alter income distribution. As we shall see in succeeding chapters, the mechanisms that have been discussed in this chapter will still operate but will be somewhat harder to trace and quantitatively weaker than in the simpler and purer models of trade theory.

The discussion in this and later chapters focuses on models of a single country. The terms-of-trade issue, so crucial in the long debate on global trade and development, cannot, however, be analyzed properly with single-country models. For this reason, little space has been devoted to the optimum tariff argument, which is best examined in a multicountry setting where the impact of multilateral trade negotiations and tariff agreements can be analyzed. Whereas one country's big export push may lead to only a very moderate decline in the terms of trade, the same strategy centered on the same kind of products adopted by a large number of countries may lead to a large deterioration in their terms of trade and perhaps even a reduction in their collective welfare. Single-country models thus are not the proper framework in which to discuss worldwide trade and development strategies. The best we can hope to achieve with the kind of single-country models discussed in this book is to specify trade and particularly the determination of exports in a way that is consistent with expected overall trends in the world economy. To do more, in a formal way, would imply an attempt at modeling the world economy as a whole, which is well beyond the scope of our effort. It is important, however, to remember that what may be good policy for a particular developing country may not be good policy for all developing countries taken as a group. Recent developments in the world economy have again demonstrated the potential gains and losses that may arise from joint action undertaken by groups of countries. In focusing on a single country, one should not forget the worldwide implications of particular strategies and the scope for international action.

CHAPTER 7

A CGE model for an open economy

7.1　Introduction

In Chapter 6 we followed the standard small-country assumption often made in international trade theory. When the share of a country in the world market is very small, and when users do not differentiate products by country or region of origin, a country is like a small firm in a competitive market: It is a price taker and cannot affect the terms at which it trades. The small-country assumption is a useful point of departure that allows a clear-cut analysis of the links between foreign trade and the domestic economy. But it is very hard to reconcile it with observed facts and to use it in its pure form in multisector planning efforts.

The discussion on supply functions has already stressed that the small-country assumption coupled with an assumption of constant returns to scale on the production side leads to a tendency toward extreme specialization in production that does not fit the empirical evidence. We also stressed in Section 6.3 that the assumption of perfect substitutability in use between foreign and domestic goods rules out the possibility of two-way trade if one abstracts from intercountry transportation and storage costs. A good is either imported or exported but never both. What was true for linear programming models remains true for the simple model presented in Chapter 6.

In fact, two-way trade has been observed in trade statistics even when products are classified in extremely disaggregated form.[1] Furthermore, perfect substitutability implies "the law of one price" reflected in Eqs. (6.2.1) and (6.2.2). World prices determine the domestic price of tradables, and a given product has the same price whether it is imported or produced domestically. Recent empirical evidence by Isard (1978), for example, indicates that for the most narrowly defined domestic and foreign goods for which prices can be matched (four- and five-digit SITC categories), disparities among the common currency prices of goods from

---

[1] Grubel and Lloyd (1975) found significant two-way trade even at a seven-digit standard industrial trade classification (SITC) level.

different countries are systematically correlated with exchange rates rather than randomly fluctuating over time.[2]

From the point of view of building applied multisector planning models, the problem increases with the degree of aggregation. Most applied planning models have to be fairly aggregated, distinguishing at most among three-digit SITC categories. Aggregation errors are not too serious as long as relative prices and relative shares remain fairly constant. But in models focusing on trade policy and its effects, the responsiveness of the shares of domestic and foreign goods in various markets to changes in relative prices is the heart of the problem. Assuming perfect substitutability within a particular sector – say, textiles – implies that there is no product differentiation between imports and domestic products, that textiles will either be exported or imported but never both, and that changes in world prices, exchange rates, and tariffs are *fully* translated into changes in domestic prices. Thus, in a country where textile imports consist largely of synthetic fiber and domestic production consists of cotton cloth, the small-country assumption implies that a 50 percent increase in the import price of synthetic fiber will lead to a 50 percent increase in the price of domestic cotton cloth.

The perfect-substitutability assumption greatly exaggerates the power that trade policy has over the domestic price system and domestic economic structure and is quite untenable as a workable approximation, particularly in the context of building applied, fairly aggregated, multisector planning models. Note that although disaggregation definitely helps, it is quite impossible empirically to implement economy-wide general equilibrium models distinguishing a few hundred sectors with, for example, cotton cloth and synthetic fibers or tractors and woodworking machinery appearing as individual items. And even at that level of disaggregation, perfect substitutability would be only a rough approximation.[3]

The opposite assumption has often been made in the development planning literature, particularly in "two-gap" models. In "structuralist" models, imports are treated as "noncompetitive," and the degree of substitutability between domestic and foreign goods is assumed to be zero. Instead of perfect substitutes, imports become perfect complements of

---

[2] Even for a specific primary commodity such as wheat, prices at a common import point at a given point in time vary by supplier.

[3] For sectors such as machinery, it is unreasonable to assume perfect substitutability even at the commodity level. The problem is not only one of aggregation but also depends on the characteristics of the commodities produced in each sector. See Lancaster (1966).

domestic products. This introduces a great deal of rigidity into these models. In particular, trade policy-induced changes in relative prices such as the exchange rate can have no, or only very indirect, effect on the structure of the domestic economy. This rigidity leads to foreign exchange "gaps" that cannot be alleviated by trade and exchange rate policy.

Reality is obviously somewhere in between. For any given level of aggregation, foreign and domestic goods in a given SITC category are not identical, may have different prices, and may be characterized by a degree of substitutability that varies across sectors. To capture these features, we shall formally introduce product differentiation by country of origin into the structure of demand for commodities in any given country. This allows a flexible and intermediate specification representing a useful compromise between the extreme assumptions of perfect substitution and perfect complementarity.

In Section 7.2 we discuss the treatment of imports as imperfect substitutes of domestically produced commodities. In Section 7.3 we turn to exports and the implications of aggregation and product differentiation. Section 7.4 draws together the discussion on imports and exports and shows how the change in specification affects the general equilibrium solution. In Section 7.5 we analyze the role of trade policy in the presence of product differentiation. Finally, before concluding in Section 7.7, Section 7.6 describes a decomposition methodology that allows analysis and measurement of real income changes resulting from changes in trade policy within the framework of a multisector general equilibrium model.

7.2 Product differentiation and the treatment of imports

A formulation that allows one to keep aggregative commodity categories across countries but specifies product differentiation by country of origin into the structure of demand was proposed in a partial equilibrium framework by Armington (1969). It is based on a two-level CES formulation that has been extremely useful in much of the empirical literature on estimating import demand functions.[4] It is also a very useful specification for building trade-oriented applied general equilibrium models for single economies.

---

[4] See, for instance, Leamer and Stern (1970). For applications in multisector planning models, see, among others, Dixon et al. (1977), Petri (1976), and Whalley (1977).

Let us define for each tradable commodity category an aggregate or composite commodity Q_i, which is a CES function of commodities produced abroad (imports, M_i) and commodities produced domestically, D_i. The aggregation is given by

$$Q_i = \overline{B}_i \,[\delta_i M_i^{-\rho_i} + (1 - \delta_i) D_i^{-\rho_i}]^{-1/\rho_i} = f(M_i, D_i) \qquad (7.2.1)$$

where $\overline{B}_i$, δ_i, and ρ_i are parameters and M_i and D_i are like inputs "producing" the aggregate output. The demands for imports and domestically produced commodities become derived demands, in just the same way as the demand for factor inputs is a derived demand in a traditional production model.

Given the specified prices for the imported and domestic goods, the problem facing the user or buyer is mathematically equivalent to that facing the firm wishing to produce a specified level of output at minimum cost. The solution is to find a ratio of "inputs" (M_i to D_i) so that the marginal rate of substitution (the slope of the iso-output curve for the composite good) equals the ratio of the price of the domestically produced commodity to the price of the imported commodity. Letting PD_i denote the domestic good price and PM_i the domestic currency price of imports, the familiar first-order conditions for cost minimization yield

$$m_i = \frac{M_i}{D_i} = \left(\frac{PD_i}{PM_i}\right)^{\sigma_i} \left(\frac{\delta_i}{1 - \delta_i}\right)^{\sigma_i} \qquad (7.2.2)$$

where $\sigma_i = 1/(1 + \rho_i)$ is the "trade-substitution" elasticity.

Let us denote by θ_{im} and θ_{id} the "value shares" of imports and domestically produced goods in total domestic expenditure. We have

$$\frac{\theta_{im}}{\theta_{id}} = \frac{PM_i\,M_i}{PD_i\,D_i} = \left(\frac{\delta_i}{1 - \delta_i}\right)^{\sigma_i} \left(\frac{PD_i}{PM_i}\right)^{\sigma_i - 1} \qquad (7.2.3)$$

If and only if the trade substitution elasticities σ_i equal unity, the last term in (7.2.3) disappears and the value shares remain constant irrespective of relative prices. In that case the CES aggregation reduces to a Cobb-Douglas function. The magnitude of σ_i determines the responsiveness of domestic demand to changes in the relative price of imported goods brought about by trade and exchange-rate policy or exogenous events. If σ_i is very high, the responsiveness of M_i/D_i to small changes in PD_i/PM_i will be so great that PD_i/PM_i will never change much from its base value and we approximate the case where $PM_i = PD_i$. If, on the other hand, σ_i is very low, very large changes in PM_i/PD_i may take place. In the extreme case where $\sigma_i = 0$, M_i/D_i would be fixed and we would be back in the fixed-coefficients, two-gap models, where relative price changes cannot directly affect the demand for imports.

Rather than working with the import-to-domestic-goods ratio, it is often convenient to work with the ratio of domestic goods in total composite commodity use. We shall call this ratio the "domestic use ratio" and denote it by d_i. Because the aggregation function is linearly homogeneous in M_i and D_i, it can be rewritten as

$$Q_i = f_i(m_i, 1)D_i \tag{7.2.4}$$

where f_i represents the function in (7.2.1). We then have

$$d_i = \frac{D_i}{Q_i} = f_i^{-1}(m_i, 1) \tag{7.2.5}$$

With m_i a function of PD_i/PM_i only, it is clear that d_i will also depend uniquely on PD_i/PM_i. The demand for the composite good Q_i itself will, of course, depend on the whole relative price system.

Using d_i, we can go from composite commodity demand to the (derived) demand for the domestically produced commodity. If V_i, C_i, and Z_i denote, respectively, intermediate demand, consumption demand, and investment demand for composite commodity i, then the demand functions for the domestically produced components will be

$$\begin{aligned}
V_i^d &= d_i V_i \\
C_i^d &= d_i C_i \\
Z_i^d &= d_i Z_i
\end{aligned} \tag{7.2.6}$$

These domestically produced goods combine with imports to produce the aggregate good, Q_i. Total demand for domestic production is obtained by adding export demand.[5]

There are many places where further substitution could have been introduced into the model formulation. For instance, one could allow for different aggregation functions according to functional use, just as one could allow for substitution among intermediate goods. However, such extensions require many more estimated parameters and further

---

[5] The domestic use ratio discussed here is analogous to the one discussed in Chapter 2 on input–output models except that here we describe a theory of how it is determined.

complicate the linkage mechanisms in the model. It is not clear that the gains offset the costs in a fairly aggregated model.

7.3   The small-country assumption and the treatment of exports

Two things are ordinarily implicit in the small-country assumption: fixed international terms of trade and domestic tradables prices rigidly linked to import prices. Recognition of aggregation problems and product differentiation leads us to drop the assumption of perfect substitutability between imported and domestically produced commodities which, in turn, leads to a domestic price system that is no longer rigidly linked to world prices. Introducing product differentiation violates the small-country assumption if the latter is interpreted as requiring equality between domestic and world prices of tradables adjusted for tariffs. But if all we mean by the small-country assumption is that the terms of trade of a country are fixed because the "dollar" prices of both its imports and exports are fixed, this weaker form of the small-country assumption need not be violated by introducing product differentiation and differences between the price of imports and domestically produced commodities. If world prices of imports remain fixed and exogenous and if the dollar prices of exports also remain exogenous, the small-country assumption holds in the sense that the terms of trade are fixed.

On the import side, the small-country assumption is a statement about the rest of the world's supply curves. Being small on the import side means constituting a small fraction of the market for commodities produced in other countries. Product differentiation does not affect this kind of "smallness," and the usual assumption of infinitely elastic foreign *supply* curves is a reasonable one. We shall therefore always maintain the assumption of exogenously fixed import prices. But when it comes to maintaining the small-country assumption on the export side, the situation is quite different. When a country is selling a differentiated product, it may no longer be small in the market for that product. If we treat the rest of the world symmetrically with a single country, we must recognize that the demand for exports produced in a particular country will be less than infinitely elastic. This implies that export prices are no longer fixed, and the small-country assumption, even in its weak form requiring only fixed terms of trade, may no longer hold.

If the small-country assumption were to hold, a country's export prices would be fixed in the world market independently of the quantities exported. Letting PE_i denote domestic currency receipts of exporters per unit of exports from sector i and $\overline{PWE_i}$ denote the world "dollar" price of exports, we would have Eq. (7.3.1), analogous to Eq. (7.2.1), to determine PE_i:

$$PE_i = PWE_i(1 + te_i)ER \qquad (7.3.1)$$

where te_i is the rate of export subsidy. If $PE_i > PD_i$, no domestic sales would take place and whatever is produced domestically would be exported. This would clearly exert upward pressure on the domestic price. Because no domestic sales would take place until $PE_i = PD_i$, the domestic price would rise until at least the equality is satisfied and we would never observe a situation in which $PE_i > PD_i$. It would, of course, be conceivable that all domestic production is exported while domestic demand is being satisfied by imports. We could, in principle, have $PE_i > PD_i$ and $D_i = 0$ so that PD_i would have no more function in the model. Assuming that in practice, such extreme behavior can be ruled out, the constraints implied by the model on the export side can be summarized as follows:

$$\text{If } PE_i = PD_i, \qquad E_i \geq 0 \qquad (7.3.2)$$
$$\text{If } PE_i < PD_i, \qquad E_i = 0$$

This treatment of exports would remain faithful to the small-country assumption. But, as noted above, it is quite inconsistent with the view that products are differentiated by country of origin and imperfect substitutes for one another. The assumption of product differentiation naturally leads to less than infinitely elastic demand functions for a country's exports. These demand functions then take the general form

$$E_i = E_i (\Pi_i, PWE_i) \qquad (7.3.3)$$

where Π_i is an "aggregate" world price for products in category i and reflects a weighted average of production costs and trade policies in *all* countries. The fact that our country is small allows us to treat Π_i as exogenously fixed. But PWE_i, which is the dollar price of a particular country's exports, is *endogenously* determined by its domestic production costs, export incentives, and exchange rate policy. We have

$$PWE_i = \frac{PD_i}{(1 + te_i)ER} \qquad (7.3.4)$$

An increase in domestic production costs increases PD_i and leads to an increase in the dollar price of exports, PWE_i. An increase in export subsidies or a devaluation of the exchange rate leads to a fall in PWE_i. Such a fall in PWE_i, with constant Π_i, leads to an increase in the demand for exports from sector i. If a country wants to increase its market share in commodity category i, it must lower the dollar price of its own product. Assuming that the world as a whole behaves in a manner similar to the single country modeled and consumes products according to the rules of cost-minimization subject to a generalized CES formulation that specifies "composite" world commodities, the world demand functions for a given country's product are of the following simple constant elasticity form, similar to a single country's import demand functions:

$$E_i = \overline{E}_0 \left(\frac{\Pi_i}{PWE_i} \right)^{\eta_i} \tag{7.3.5}$$

where η_i is the price elasticity of export demand and E_0 is a constant term reflecting total world demand for commodity category i and the country's market share when $\Pi_i = PWE_i$. The fact that the country is small means that we can neglect effects of changes in PWE_i on Π_i and on world demand for aggregate commodity category i. But we cannot always neglect the effect changes in PWE_i have on our country's market share. For example, we can safely neglect the effect that an increase in the price of Turkish ceramics has on the world demand for ceramics. But Turkey's market share in the world market for ceramics is sensitive to changes in Turkish prices relative to all other countries' prices. Turkey cannot, all other factors held constant, increase its market share simply by making more output available. It also has to lower price. Conversely, if Turkish prices increase, Turkey will not all of a sudden lose its export market completely, but its market share will decline.

There are clearly many problems and qualifications that must be discussed in this context. For some very homogeneous products, where style, quality, brand names, durability, and so on, do not count, the strict small-country assumption may in fact hold. But there are not many such products. In general, and even when market shares are quite small, it is not reasonable to assume that export prices are fixed independently of quantities exported. It may be better, instead, to recognize the existence of downward-sloping demand curves for a country's exports.

What determines the price elasticities along these demand curves? Traditionally it has been argued that a country's market share is the major determinant of the price elasticity of demand for its exports. The model underlying the traditional argument is the one based on assumptions of product homogeneity and perfect substitutability. If, on the contrary, we treat the world's demand for a country's products symmetrically with a single country's demand for the world's products, it is clear that the export demand functions would be derived similarly to the import demand functions. If, in addition, we were to assume, following Armington, that shares in the world market are governed by cost minimization subject to the same CES aggregation function on a world scale, the price elasticities would be equal to the trade substitution elasticities that appear in the CES aggregation functions. This would imply that η_i in Eq. (7.3.5) would be equal to σ_i in Eq. (7.2.1). It is not, however, reasonable or practical to insist on this degree of symmetry. The CES formulation on the import side is a convenient approximation, and it is neither necessary nor useful to view it as derived from a generalized CES formulation governing behavior in the world market as a whole. Substitution elasticities are not in fact constant over wide ranges of factor or commodity ratios, and a CES formulation is probably a good approximation over only a particular range. Thus, although the price elasticities characterizing the export demand functions are themselves derived from substitution elasticities, these need not be equal to the substitution elasticities between imported and domestic goods within one country. Instead, they might be thought of as characterizing a different region of a generalized variable elasticity of substitution aggregation function that governs behavior in the world market. In particular, it is reasonable to assume that the export demand elasticities η_i have much higher values than the trade substitution elasticities σ_i, on the presumption that substitution elasticities vary inversely with the value shares in total cost.[6]

Several further considerations are relevant to the specification of exports. A country's market share may be affected by variables other than relative prices. Thus, if a country wants to expand exports significantly, it may have to break into new markets, advertise its products, and establish appropriate information and marketing channels. Transportation costs are also relevant, because an increase in exports may involve selling in more distant markets. These considerations may not directly affect the price elasticity of demand for exports. But if we think of PWE_i as the export price net of marketing, information, and transportation costs, the case for a significant inverse relationship between PWE_i and export volume is further strengthened.[7] Note that marketing and transportation costs may imply an asymmetry in the relationship

---

[6] In the applications, we do not explicitly link the values taken by σ_i to value shares in total costs.

[7] Moreover, the value taken by the price elasticity of demand for exports is likely to depend significantly on the time period over which equilibrium is defined.

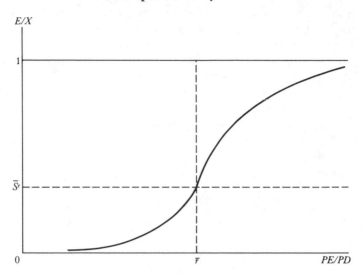

Figure 7.1. The export supply function.

between PWE_i and E_i: The average revenue curves may be less elastic when exports expand than when they contract.

Turning from export demand to export supply, the supply of exports from any sector is equal to total domestic production minus domestic use. An increase in the domestic price PD_i will normally lead to a rise in exports from sector i, because domestic supply expands and domestic use contracts. The price elasticity of export supply is determined, therefore, by the price elasticity of total domestic production and the price elasticity of domestic demand.

As long as we consider domestically produced commodities belonging to any category i as identical, whether they are exported or consumed domestically, this is the only logically valid specification for export supply. It may lead to problems, however, if the exports in a large aggregate sector are in fact quite distinct products from the domestically consumed basket of goods. Consider, for example, mining. A country may export copper, but copper may constitute a small fraction of total mining output, which is dominated by coal. The assumption that the supply of exports is simply the difference between total domestic production and domestic absorption may in such a case greatly overestimate the possible responsiveness of export supply to the "average" price in the mining sector.

It is hard to deal with this problem without increasing the complexity of the model.[8] A possible way out is to consider the following specification:

$$\frac{E_i}{X_i} = f_i \left(\frac{PE_i}{PD_i} \right) \tag{7.3.6}$$

with $PE_i = PWE_i (1 + te_i) ER$. The share of exports in total domestic production is a function of the ratio of the per-unit receipts that a domestic producer receives for exports, PE_i, to the domestic price, PD_i, which now must be reinterpreted as applying to domestic sales only. This extra constraint reflecting aggregation problems prevents the model from providing overestimates of the export supply response to trade policy measures. More specifically, the function form adopted for the export function is an asymmetric logistic function as depicted in Figure 7.1.

Dropping subscripts, the equation of this function reduces to

$$\frac{E}{X} = \frac{\overline{A}_1}{1 + \exp[\overline{B}_1 (r - \overline{r})]} + \overline{C}_1 \qquad r \geq \overline{r}$$

$$\frac{E}{X} = \frac{\overline{A}_2}{1 + \exp[\overline{B}_2 (r - \overline{r})]} + \overline{C}_2 \qquad r \leq \overline{r} \tag{7.3.7}$$

where $r = PE/PD$ and $\overline{A}, \overline{B},$ and $\overline{C}$ are parameters of the function.

Given that we impose an upper asymptote of one and a lower asymptote of zero, the only parameters to be chosen are $\overline{B}_1$ and $\overline{B}_2$, which determine the "rate of response" of the export ratio to a change in the domestic price ratio. $\overline{B}_1$ and $\overline{B}_2$ are determined together, so that given $\overline{B}_1$, $\overline{B}_2$ is set and the slope of the curve at the inflection point $(\overline{r}, \overline{S}^e)$ is the same in both directions. The parameters $\overline{S}^e$ and $\overline{r}$ are set from the base-year data. The asymmetric specification has the flexibility of allowing a different supply response depending on whether r falls or rises. In general, however, we shall adopt a symmetric form for the function.

When export demand functions [Eq. (7.3.5)] are combined with export supply functions of this form [Eq. (7.3.6)], or indeed any kind of separate export supply functions, the "clearing" of export markets in sector i no longer takes place as part of market clearing in sector i. We have in effect added as many markets to the CGE model as there are exported products. The domestic price PD_i will now clear the domestic market for commodity i. The export price PE_i (or PWE_i) will have to

[8] Ideally, one would resolve this problem with a highly disaggregated model.

clear the export market and $PD_i \neq PE_i$. In terms of Figure 7.1, PE would be determined by the intersection of a demand curve for exports expressed in domestic currency units (not drawn in the figure) and the export supply function.

Thus, going over to a formulation that separately specifies supply functions for exports is costly not only in terms of additional parameter values to be estimated but also because of the increased size of the model when it is used in conjunction with export demand functions. Nevertheless, in applied and fairly aggregated models an extra supply restraint on exports may be required at least in some sectors. Otherwise, the model will tend to overestimate the responsiveness of export supply to trade policy measures.

To summarize, we propose the following treatment of exports. On the demand side, the elasticity of demand for the export demand functions will be of the constant-elasticity type. The magnitude of the export demand elasticities will then depend both on the country's market share and on the degree of product differentiation. If the products in a given category are quite homogeneous and if the market share is small, it is reasonable to make the small-country assumption and assume infinitely elastic export demand. On the supply side, export supply is usually derived residually by subtracting domestic demand from total domestic production. But in some cases, when exports substantially differ from domestic production in the same sector, a logistic supply function determining the ratio of exports to total supply as a function of relative profitability of production will be added to the specification.[9]

7.4   The general equilibrium solution

It is now time to pull the various pieces of the discussion together and summarize the structure of a computable general equilibrium model of an open economy where domestic goods are imperfect substitutes for imports. This section is comparable to Section 5.3. A complete list of equations is given in the appendix to this chapter. The most compact summary can be provided by writing down the excess demand equations of the model as functions of the endogenous variables.

On the demand side, relative prices and incomes determine total demands for each composite commodity. Part of this demand will be satisfied by imports, part of it will be satisfied by domestic production. The domestic use ratio d_i in each sector is determined by the relative

---

[9] An alternative is to assume that exports are simply exogenous. See the application in Chapter 13.

costs of imports and domestic goods [see (7.2.5)]. We can therefore write down the demand functions for domestically produced commodities as follows:[10]

$$X_i^D = d_i V_i + d_i C_i + d_i Z_i + E_i \tag{7.4.1}$$

where V_i, C_i, Z_i are, respectively, intermediate demands, consumption demand, and investment demand for the composite commodities in each commodity category. The domestic use ratio d_i transforms these demands for composite commodities into demands for domestically produced commodities. Exports, E_i, are produced domestically and must be added to intermediate, consumption, and investment demand to obtain total demand for domestically produced commodities. Because each component of demand and the domestic use ratio itself depend on domestic prices, the exchange rate, and the exogenous values of world prices and tariffs, we can rewrite the demand equation as a vector function:

$$X^D = D(PD_1, \ldots, PD_n, ER) \tag{7.4.2}$$

On the supply side, we assume as in Chapter 5 that for any commodity price vector we find the factor price vector that clears labor markets and substitute the result into the aggregate supply functions. We then get, similar to equations in Chapter 5, vector supply functions of the form

$$X^S = X(PD_1, \ldots, PD_n, ER) \tag{7.4.3}$$

and sectoral excess demands are given by

$$EX_i = X_i^D - X_i^S = 0 \tag{7.4.4}$$

This gives us n equations in $n + 1$ variables: the n domestic commodity prices and the exchange rate. We also have the balance-of-payments constraint:

$$EF = \sum_{i=1}^{n} \overline{PW}_i M_i - \sum_{i=1}^{n} PWE_i E_i - \overline{F} - 0 \tag{7.4.5}$$

where M_i and E_i are imports and exports, respectively, and $\overline{F}$ stands for the exogenous value of the net foreign resource inflow. In all, there are $n + 1$ equations in $n + 1$ variables. But again the excess demand equations are not independent (by Walras's law), and we require a

[10] Without using a superscript to distinguish domestically produced goods from imports and composite goods.

price-normalization equation to close the system. The normalization equation will now take the form

$$\sum_{i=1}^{n} \Omega_i P_i(PD_i, ER) = \overline{P} \tag{7.4.6}$$

where P_i are the composite commodity prices that depend on PD_i and ER. Under the assumption of cost minimization by the users of imports and domestic goods, the values of P_i are given by the cost function corresponding to the CES aggregation function:

$$P_i = \frac{1}{B_i} [\delta_i^{\sigma_i} PM_i^{(1-\sigma_i)} + (1 - \delta_i)^{\sigma_i} PD_i^{(1-\sigma_i)}]^{1/(1-\sigma_i)} \tag{7.4.7}$$

where $PM_i = \overline{PW}_i (1 + tm_i) ER$, so that the only endogenous variables that appear in (7.4.7) are again PD_i and ER. The normalization closes the system and, in principle, allows us to solve the model for n domestic commodity prices and the exchange rate as a function of the exogenous parameters and government policy variables. The standard solution strategy is the same as for a closed-economy model. One can start by guessing domestic prices, but must now add an initial guess at the exchange rate. By first solving the labor markets (with or without fixed wages) and substituting the result into the sectoral demand and supply functions, numerical estimates of excess demands in each sector can be obtained. The iteration then proceeds by revising the initial price and exchange rate guesses until a general equilibrium is reached.

7.5   Trade policy and resource allocation in the presence of product differentiation

Trade policy and domestic prices

We saw in Section 6.3 that the effect of trade policy on resource allocation depends crucially on the elasticity of supply of the product and the extent to which the change in trade policy affects the domestic price. In particular, it was shown that if the country is small, then an x percent increase in the import price resulted in an x percent increase in the domestic price, so that the domestic price system was determined entirely by trade policy. It was also seen that, in the presence of intermediate products, the resource-pull effects of a change in the whole tariff structure could be approximated, in partial equilibrium, by the structure of effective rates of protection across sectors.

A question that naturally arises when one introduces imperfect substitution into the CGE model is the extent to which trade policy protects domestic producers, that is, the extent to which the imposition of a tariff raises the price of goods produced domestically. Now that the arguments of the demand and supply functions of domestically produced goods have been determined, it is possible to investigate the protective effect of trade policies along the same partial equilibrium lines as in Chapter 6, and to contrast the results obtained in the presence of product differentiation and intraindustry trade with those resulting from the more standard trade specification where domestically produced and foreign produced goods are perfect substitutes.

The equilibrium condition in the market for the domestically produced good in sector i is

$$X_i^n = X_i^S \tag{7.5.1}$$

where, in a partial equilibrium setting,

$$X_i^D = D_i(PD_i, PM_i) + E_i(PWE_i) \tag{7.5.2}$$

and

$$X_i^S = X_i^S(PD_i) \tag{7.5.3}$$

The arguments in the demand and supply functions are those discussed in Sections 7.2 and 7.3, and the functional forms are also the same. For exports, a downward-sloping demand curve is assumed along the lines described in Section 7.3 [see Eq. (7.4.11)]. What, then, are the effects of a subsidy on exports of sector i, and what are the effects of a tariff on import substitutes competing with domestically produced goods in that sector?

A subsidy to exports shifts outward the supply curve for exports expressed in foreign currency units.[11] Whether foreign exchange earnings rise or fall depends on whether the foreign elasticity of demand for exports is greater than or less than unity. In domestic currency units, the subsidy leads to windfall profits that accrue to domestic suppliers who find it momentarily more profitable to sell their output abroad. The resulting shortage in supply for domestic use leads to a rise in the domestic price PD until it is equal to the export price PE [see Eq. (7.3.1)]. The resulting rise in the domestic price leads to an increase in total domestic supply, a fall in the demand for the domestically produced

---

[11] The supply curve of exports is obtained as the difference between the total domestic supply curve and the domestic demand curve. For convenience, assume that $PD = PE$.

good entering the aggregation function, and a substitution toward imports. The net result is an outward shift of the supply curve for exports expressed in foreign currency units, so that the equilibrium foreign exchange price of exports, PWE_i, falls as a result of the subsidy.

Consider now the effect of raising a tariff, tm_i, on imports and its effect on the demand for the domestically produced good for domestic use, that is, excluding exports. If the domestically produced good is a substitute for the imported good, there will be an outward shift in the demand curve for the domestically produced good. For a given supply for domestic use, this leads to a rise in the domestic price, which has a secondary repercussion on the demand for exports, which will fall as the export price (expressed in foreign exchange units) rises. This leads to an outward shift of the supply curve of the domestic good for domestic use following the decline in demand for exports. As a result, the net effect of a tariff on the domestic price will be less than it would have been if there had been no feedback via the demand for exports.

Figure 7.2 provides a useful way of summarizing the effects of trade policy on the equilibrium domestic price. Quadrant I depicts the demand curve for the domestically produced good entering the aggregation function for a given import price (reflected by a given tariff tm). Quadrant II transforms the export price PE (which must be equal in equilibrium to the domestic price PD) into foreign exchange units by multiplying it by the exchange rate ER times one plus the *ad valorem* subsidy rate te. In turn, quadrant III shows the foreign demand E for domestic exports as a function of the foreign currency price of those exports, PWE. With this apparatus we can trace out in quadrant IV the locus of points depicting domestic and foreign demand for various domestic prices. For instance, given a domestic price PD_0, we can find in the usual way the corresponding domestic demand D_0 and the corresponding export demand E_0. The curve DE_0 in quadrant IV is the locus of points describing combinations of domestic and foreign demand, each point being consistent with a different domestic price.

To complete the diagram, we must introduce domestic supply, which is an increasing function of the domestic price. A family of 45° lines, each corresponding to a different domestic price, indicates how domestic supply can be divided between domestic and export demand. Suppose that domestic supply corresponding to domestic price PD_0 is OS_0. Then at that price there is an excess supply ES_0, which will lower the domestic price. As the domestic price falls and one moves to a 45° line closer to the origin, total demand increases, which means a movement along the DE_0 curve away from the origin. This adjustment process will continue until an equilibrium is reached. It is also clear that – given the shapes of the demand curves – equilibrium will exist and be unique.

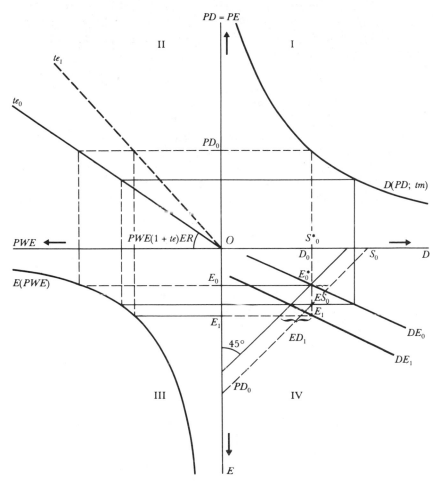

Figure 7.2. Export demand, domestic demand, and the equilibrium price for a domestically produced good.

Now consider the effect of a subsidy. For simplicity, suppose that OS_0^* is the supply corresponding to domestic price PD_0. Then E_0^* is an equilibrium point. A subsidy shifts the Ote_0 curve in quadrant II clockwise to Ote_1. At the previously established equilibrium price, PD_0, there will be an increase in export demand indicated by $E_0^* E_1$ in quadrant IV, because the export price in foreign exchange units is lowered as a result of the subsidy. There is therefore an increase in demand at any given domestic price, reflected in a downward shift of DE_0 to DE_1. As we have explained, there will be an increase in the domestic price until excess demand is eliminated.

The effects of a tariff can be likewise examined. If domestically produced goods are substitutes for imported ones, the domestic demand curve in quadrant I will shift outward, which will result in an upward shift of the DE_0 curve in quadrant IV, reflecting this time an increase in domestic demand. Again there will be an excess demand leading to a corresponding price adjustment. A similar outcome leading to an excess demand for domestic goods will result if there is an outward shift of the foreign demand curve due, for instance, to a fall in supply of foreign producers competing with domestic exports or to an increase in the average world price of goods falling in that sector's classification.

Finally, note that this diagram is useful in verifying the well-known proposition that a devaluation (leading to a clockwise shift in quadrant II and an outward shift in the demand curve for imports in quadrant I) is equivalent to combining a tariff on imports with a subsidy on exports at the same rate. Note, however, that although the subsidy and the tariff are granted at the same rate, that rate will be different from the percentage change in the exchange rate when domestic and foreign goods are imperfect substitutes.

Although this graphical presentation is useful in indicating how trade policy affects the demand for domestically produced goods and indicates what are the major influences in determining how the domestic price is affected by trade policy, a more formal analysis, using the functional forms described in the previous sections, is necessary to determine more precisely how trade policy affects resource allocation between sectors, and within sectors, between exports and domestic use. Because the effects of trade policy on sectoral resource allocation depend crucially on how the domestic price is affected by the policy change, we confine ourselves to determining how the domestic price changes as a result of a change in trade policy.

Consider the change in the domestic price brought about by a change in the export price. Totally differentiate (7.5.1), drop the sector subscript, and rearrange to obtain the ratio of the differentials:

$$\frac{dPD}{dPWE} = \frac{\partial E / \partial PWE}{\partial X / \partial PD - \partial D / \partial PD} < 0 \qquad (7.5.4)$$

The term in the numerator is the change in export demand resulting from the change in the foreign currency price, and is negative by assumption. The first term in the denominator is the total supply response, which is positive, whereas the second term is the change in demand for domestic use holding the import price constant. It is negative, so the denominator is positive. Because the numerator and denominator are of opposite signs, a fall in the foreign currency price of exports raises the domestic price.

A similar expression can be obtained for a change in the import price *PM*. It is given by

$$\frac{dPD}{dPM} = \frac{\partial D/\partial PM}{\partial X/\partial PD - \partial D/\partial PD - \partial E/\partial PWE} \tag{7.5.5}$$

which is slightly more complicated than the corresponding expression for an export subsidy because of the feedback effect on the export side noted earlier. The sign of this expression is ambiguous, and it is intuitively easy to understand why. Because we know that the denominator will be positive, we need only consider the term in the numerator which indicates the change in the demand for the domestic good for a change in the import price, again holding the domestic price constant. Clearly, if the foreign and the domestic goods are gross complements, this term will be negative and the domestic price will fall.

How can this happen given our functional forms? Recall that domestic and foreign goods substitute for one another with the same elasticity in all uses, namely, σ. The demand for the domestically produced good is a derived demand, because it enters the CES aggregation function [(Eq. 7.4.1)]. As a result of the rise in the import price, the price of the composite good will increase. Suppose, then, that the price elasticity of demand for the composite good, ϵ^d, is large. Then the increase in the composite good price will lead to a substantial fall in the demand for that good, which in turn implies that the demand for the domestic good will fall. If this price effect outweighs the substitution effect, the net demand for the domestic good will fall and one can say that foreign and domestic goods are complements.

A little algebra will provide a condition for the functional forms described in the previous sections.[12] Under cost minimization, the following conditions hold:

$$D = (1 - \delta)^\sigma \left(\frac{P}{PD}\right)^\sigma Q \tag{7.5.6}$$

$$M = \delta^\sigma \left(\frac{P}{PM}\right)^\sigma Q \tag{7.5.7}$$

$$P = [\delta^\sigma PM^{(1-\sigma)} + (1 - \delta)^\sigma PD^{(1-\sigma)}]^{1/(1-\sigma)} \tag{7.5.8}$$

where (7.5.6)–(7.5.7) are the first-order conditions and (7.5.8) is the cost function derived from the CES aggregation function. Totally dif-

[12] See de Melo and Robinson (1978) for the derivations.

ferentiating the equilibrium condition yields (with a caret indicating a log differential)

$$\hat{X}^s X^s = \hat{D} D + \hat{E} E \tag{7.5.9}$$

To obtain expressions in terms of elasticities and shares, define the following:

$$\hat{X}^s \equiv \epsilon^s \hat{PD} \qquad \hat{Q} \equiv -\epsilon^d \hat{P} \qquad \hat{E} \equiv -\eta P \hat{W} E \tag{7.5.10}$$

$$\theta_m = \frac{PM \cdot M}{PQ} = \delta^\sigma \left(\frac{P}{PM}\right)^{\sigma-1} \tag{7.5.11}$$

The import share θ_m can be expressed only as a function of prices and the elasticity of substitution under conditions of cost minimization. It will vary when relative prices change, but at times we shall take it to be constant because we are restricting ourselves to small changes around equilibrium, given partial equilibrium assumptions.

Now totally differentiate (7.5.6)–(7.5.8) to obtain

$$\hat{D} = \sigma(\hat{P} - \hat{PD}) - \epsilon^d \hat{P} \tag{7.5.12}$$
$$\hat{M} = \sigma(\hat{P} - \hat{PM}) - \epsilon^d \hat{P} \tag{7.5.13}$$

$$\hat{P} = \delta^\sigma \left(\frac{P}{PM}\right)^{\sigma-1} \hat{PM} + (1 - \delta)^\sigma \left(\frac{P}{PD}\right)^{\sigma-1} \hat{PD}$$
$$= \theta_m \hat{PM} + (1 - \theta_m)\hat{PD} \tag{7.5.14}$$

Substitution of (7.5.12)–(7.5.14) into (7.5.10) and use of (7.5.10) provides us with expressions for a change in the domestic price given changes in tariffs and/or subsidies.

After some manipulation, the expressions for the percentage change in the domestic price for a small change in the rate of subsidy, *te,* is

$$\hat{PD} = \frac{\eta}{(\epsilon^s + \eta)/D + [\epsilon^s + \epsilon^d(1 - \theta_m)]/E} \lambda_e \hat{te} \tag{7.5.15}$$

The corresponding expression for the case of a small change in the tariff rate is

$$\hat{PD} = \frac{(\sigma - \epsilon^d)\theta_m}{(\epsilon^s + \eta)(E/D) + \epsilon^s + \epsilon^d + (\sigma - \epsilon^d)\theta_m} \lambda_m \hat{tm} \tag{7.5.16}$$

where

$$\lambda_m = \frac{tm}{1 + tm} \quad \text{and} \quad \lambda_e = \frac{te}{1 + te} \tag{7.5.17}$$

Note that the import share, θ_m, defined in (7.5.11) is taken to be constant.

What, then, can we learn from these expressions? First, the derived nature of demand for the domestic good is shown by the presence of the elasticity of supply in both expressions. Thus, other things being equal, the higher the elasticity of supply, the smaller the adjustment in the domestic price necessary to bring back equilibrium in the market. The same can be said of the role of the price elasticity of demand for the composite good, ϵ^d.

Second, the role of the elasticity of demand for exports is important in determining the extent to which a change in trade policy affects the domestic price. In the case of an export subsidy, the dominating effect of its value is quite obvious, because the higher its value, the larger will be the corresponding domestic price change. Note, however, that it is also important when there is a change in the tariff rate, especially when the share of domestically produced goods being exported is large. The higher the elasticity of demand for exports, the smaller will be the domestic price change resulting from a change in tariff policy. What this implies is that a tariff will lead to a fall in exports as domestic output is taken away from foreign markets toward domestic use, and the easier this substitution process, the smaller will be the price increase.

Third, from Eq. (7.5.16), it can be seen that for any elasticity of substitution, the responsiveness of domestic prices depends on the import share. Thus, even if a sector is tradable in the sense that θ_m is not zero, the response of the domestic price to a change in the import price will be small if the import share is low.

Fourth, expression (7.5.16) provides a necessary condition for a rise in the import price to lead to a fall in the domestic price. Because the denominator is always positive ($\epsilon^d > \epsilon^d \theta_m$) and all elasticities are defined as positive numbers), a necessary condition is that the elasticity of substitution in use be less than the elasticity of demand for the composite good. It is difficult to say when this will be the case, because in general the elasticity of substitution tends to be low for sectors such as intermediates with a fair degree of processing, which also tend to have a low elasticity of demand because they enter into intermediate production with a zero price elasticity of demand. For capital goods, however, the situation depends on how responsive aggregate investment is to price changes, because imported capital goods generally have a very low elasticity of substitution with foreign produced substitutes.[13]

[13] For an examination of limiting cases for various parameters, see de Melo and Robinson (1978).

A classification of sectors by degree of tradability

The implication of this specification in a multisector framework is that it allows for a richer and more realistic description of sectors with respect to their role in foreign trade. We are no longer faced with the traditional specification where sectors are either traded, with their prices entirely determined outside the model, or nontraded, with their prices entirely determined endogenously. Instead there is a continuum of sectors characterized by different degrees of "tradability." For most purposes it is useful to distinguish four groups of sectors: nontradables, exportables, import substitutes, and import complements.

A sector can be characterized as producing nontradables if the share of exports in total production and the share of imports in domestic use are very small. Construction and services provide the best examples.

A sector producing exportables is characterized by a high ratio of exports in domestic production. Just how high the export ratio has to be for the sector to behave as an exportables-producing sector remains at this point an open question.

Commodities characterized by high shares of imports in total domestic use can be divided into import substitutes and import complements depending on the ease of substitution between domestic and foreign goods as well as on the sectoral own-demand elasticities for the composite good. This distinction between import substitutes and import complements reflects the traditional distinction between competitive imports and noncompetitive imports, but it allows for variations in the degree of substitutability rather than the simple and extreme classification that treats imports as either perfect substitutes or perfect complements for domestic goods. A good dividing line between import substitutes and import complements is given by expression (7.5.5), with sectors classified as import substitutes whenever $dPD/dPM > 0$ and as import complements when $dPD/dPM < 0$. We have seen that the sign of $(\sigma - \epsilon^d)$ determines the sign of dPD/dPM, so that import substitutes are sectors for which the trade-substitution elasticity exceeds the own-composite good demand elasticity. As σ gets very large, these sectors behave as traditional perfect substitutes for competitive imports.

If, on the contrary, the elasticity of substitution in use between domestic and foreign goods is lower than the own-demand elasticity, the relevant sector will behave as if sectoral imports were noncompetitive. In a traditional model distinguishing noncompetitive from competitive imports, a tariff on noncompetitive imports would not protect any specific domestic sector. Similarly, imposing tariffs on imports characterized by very low trade-substitution elasticities will not protect domestic industry in the same sector. For example, in many developing countries, imported and domestic machinery tend to be noncompetitive in this sense. What is classified under machinery in the domestic economy and what is included in machinery imports tends to be a set of quite different goods with very little substitutability. Although some subsets may in fact be competitive, the sectoral aggregate will be dominated by noncompeting products.

Apart from the four-way classification into nontradables, exportables, import substitutes, and import complements, a further useful characterization of sectors is to rank them by their degree of *import dependence*. This distinction is necessary to capture interindustry linkages so far neglected. Thus, a sector will be defined as very import dependent if its production processes are characterized by a heavy use of imported intermediate inputs. Thus, particular sectors may be very tradable (i.e., characterized by high export or import shares), but this need not imply that they are import dependent on the input side. For instance, food processing may be characterized by a high export share and therefore be quite tradable, but domestic production may show little need for imported inputs and the sector would not be import dependent. Production costs would not be directly affected by a devaluation, and import rationing would not create major difficulties for continued production. Sectors should therefore be distinguished not only by the degree of tradability of their output but also by their dependence on imported inputs.

7.6 Trade policy, real income, and welfare

We have seen how changes in trade policy will affect prices, incentives, and resource allocation in an economy represented by a computable general equilibrium model. These changes will in turn affect real income and welfare. Ultimately, we are interested in resource allocation and incentives because they affect welfare. The models described in this book are designed to help the policy maker analyze and quantify the effects that various policies have on the economy and, in particular, on real income in the community. It is therefore very important to compare the welfare or real income of an economy in alternative situations, each characterized by different policies and/or exogenous parameters. To the extent that we can make such comparisons, the design of optimal policy packages becomes possible and one set of policy measures can be said to lead to a "better" outcome than another.

Index numbers and welfare comparisons

Consider first an economy with only one consumer or, equivalently, an economy with many identical consumers, where identical refers not only to tastes but also to endowments. Consider situations 1 and 2, characterized by consumption or "absorption" vectors $Q^1 = (Q^1_1, \ldots, Q^1_n)$ and $Q^2 = (Q^2_1, \ldots, Q^2_n)$. It is easiest at this stage to think of these as consumption bundles, although they may in fact include investment. Situation 1 represents the initial or base solution, whereas situation 2 reflects a particular policy change. We want to be able to compare Q^1 and Q^2 and assess whether one is an improvement on the other.

If $Q^2_i > Q^1_i$, for $i = 1, n$, there is more of every single commodity in situation 2 and, if there is only a single representative consumer, Q^2 is an unambiguous improvement on Q^1. But even in that simple case it is not clear how much of an improvement Q^2 is over Q^1. If, moreover, $Q^2_i > Q^1_i$ for some i but $Q^2_i < Q^1_i$ for others, we cannot immediately rank the two vectors.

Assume that the price vectors $P^1 = (P^1_1, \ldots, P^1_n)$ and $P^2 = (P^2_1, \ldots, P^2_n)$ ruled in a competitive market when Q^1 and Q^2 turned out to be the commodity bundles chosen by the representative consumer. Then these prices contain information that can help us compare physical commodity bundles. Suppose, for example, that we have

$$\sum_{i=1}^{n} P^2_i Q^2_i > \sum_{i=1}^{n} P^2_i Q^1_i \qquad (7.6.1)$$

The equation states that a Paasche index of quantities increased when we moved from Q^1 to Q^2. We can infer from such an increase that Q^2 is preferred to Q^1 using the theory of revealed preference. The inequality indicates that at prices P^2, Q^1 was less expensive than Q^2 and therefore could have been chosen. The fact that it was not chosen implies that Q^2 must be preferred to Q^1. An increase in a Paasche index of real income is therefore a sufficient condition for welfare to have increased.

Now suppose that the inequality was reversed, using a Laspeyres index (with base prices P^1):

$$\sum_{i=1}^{n} P^1_i Q^2_i > \sum_{i=1}^{n} P^1_i Q^1_i \qquad (7.6.2)$$

This indicates that commodity bundle Q^2 and something more could have been purchased in situation 1 (with prices P^1). The fact that it was not implies that the movement from Q^1 to Q^2 represents a definite loss of welfare. Therefore, a necessary condition for welfare to have improved is that a Laspeyres index of real income increases between situations 1 and 2:

$$\sum_{i=1}^{n} P_i^1 Q_i^2 > \sum_{i=1}^{n} P_i^1 Q_i^1 \tag{7.6.3}$$

Note that it is quite possible, as illustrated in Figure 7.3C, that a Laspeyres index increases while a Paasche index decreases. In such cases we cannot reach a conclusion about the direction of change in welfare. On the other hand, with a single representative consumer it is not possible to have a Paasche index increase and a Laspeyres index decrease. The situation depicted in Figure 7.3D cannot arise.

In all cases depicted in Figure 7.3, there is more of one commodity and less of another, so that it is only by using price weights that we can attempt to rank different bundles. Consider the situation described in Figure 7.3A. Commodity bundle Q^2 is definitely preferred to commodity bundle Q^1. But by how much? The Laspeyres index of real income has almost doubled, but the Paasche index has increased by much less.

Depending on the particular shape of the underlying utility or welfare function, either the Paasche or the Laspeyres index may be a better approximation to the "true" change in welfare. In general, the Paasche index will constitute a "lower bound" and the Laspeyres index will constitute an "upper bound" to the underlying change in welfare.[14] It may therefore be reasonable to take some average of the two indices to measure the change in welfare. Although this averaging hides some information, it is often a convenient way of reporting results, particularly when there is no major disagreement between the Paasche and Laspeyres indices. Some information is clearly lost, but we shall in general use the arithmetic average of the Paasche and Laspeyres indices or an indicator of real income or absorption. Unless the two indices conflict, this is a reasonable compromise and allows a more compact presentation of results.

In the presence of more than one consumer, the problem of ranking alternative consumption or "absorption" vectors becomes much more difficult. Suffice it here to note that as soon as there is more than one consumer, changes in prices alter, through their income effects, the distribution of income. This implies that observed economy-wide consumption choices need no longer be consistent with any particular ratio-

---

[14] A sufficient condition for this to be true is that the utility function be homothetic. See Samuelson and Swamy (1974) for a good comprehensive discussion. They also discuss various averages of the two indices.

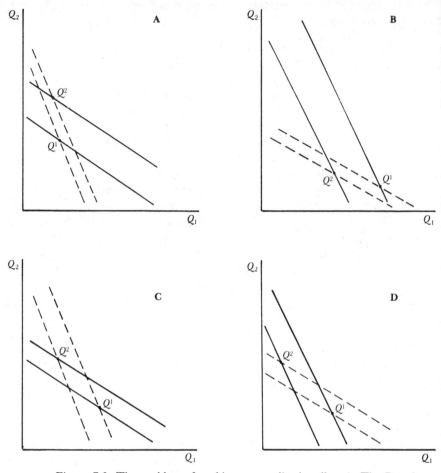

Figure 7.3. The problem of ranking commodity bundles. A. The Paasche and Laspeyres indexes both increase. Q^2 is preferred to Q^1. B. The Paasche and Laspeyres indexes both decrease. Q^2 is inferior to Q^1. C. The Laspeyres index increases, but the Paasche index decreases: We cannot rank Q^1 and Q^2. D. The Laspeyres index decreases, but the Paasche index increases. This situation cannot arise with consistent maximizing behavior.

nal preference ordering. Unless very stringent conditions are satisfied by the preferences of all individuals and groups (see Samuelson and Swamy, 1974), an increase in the Paasche index is no longer a sufficient condition, and an increase in the Laspeyres index is no longer a necessary condition for an improvement in welfare. We shall follow much of traditional trade theory in assuming a representative consumer, or, what is equivalent, a community indifference map.[15]

Decomposing changes in real income

Real income changes between periods and/or across situations as a result of various underlying economic mechanisms. Consider, for instance, the effect of imposing tariffs on an economy with variable terms of trade. An improvement in the terms of trade will tend to increase real income. But the wedge driven by tariffs between domestic and international rates of transformation will tend to reduce real income. When comparing two situations, say, one with and the other without tariffs, we would like not only to rank the two situations but also to decompose the total change in real income into the component changes due to, for example, changes in the terms of trade and changes in the efficiency of consumption and production. Such a decomposition methodology based on revealed preference and index number theory has been developed by M. Ohyama (Ohyama, 1972; Caves and Jones, 1977). We summarize it here, adapting it to the general equilibrium model with differentiated commodities.

Consider two solutions characterized by superscripts 1 and 2, where 1 denotes the initial or base solution and 2 denotes a particular policy experiment. We shall not make a distinction between consumption and investment and define real income as total domestic absorption, that is, as the sum of consumption and investment. Real income is thus equal to domestic production plus imports minus intermediate use minus exports. A sufficient condition for solution 2 to constitute an increase in welfare over solution 1 is that the Paasche index of income has increased. In vector notation, we must have

$$PM^2(M^2 - M_v^2) + PD^2(X^2 - X_v^2 - E^2)$$
$$> PM^2(M^1 - M_v^1) + PD^2(X^1 - X_v^1 - E^1) \quad (7.6.4)$$

where M and M_v denote total and intermediate import vectors and X, X_v, and E denote total domestic production, domestic intermediate input, and export vectors, respectively. Rearranging, we get

$$PM^2(M^2 - M^1) - PM^2(M_v^2 - M_v^1) - PD^2(E^2 - E^1)$$
$$+ PD^2(X^2 - X^1) - PD^2(X_v^2 - X_v^1) > 0 \quad (7.6.5)$$

as a sufficient condition for an improvement in welfare. Furthermore,

[15] In the empirical examples presented in the next chapter, there is only one aggregate private consumer. The distribution-focused model of Chapter 13, however, specifies a number of consumers.

assuming that the expression on the left-hand side can itself be taken as a "measure" of the change in real income between solutions 1 and 2, it is instructive to decompose it further by using the fact that

$$PM^2 = (I + \hat{T})PW^2ER^2 \tag{7.6.6}$$

and

$$PE^2 = PD^2 = (I + \hat{T}e)PWE^2ER^2 \tag{7.6.7}$$

where $\hat{T}^2$ and $\hat{T}e^2$ are diagonal matrices of differences between the world prices of imports and exports and their domestic prices. When there are no quantitative restrictions, $\hat{T}$ and $\hat{T}e$ simply reflect tariffs and export subsidies. Substituting (7.6.6) and (7.6.7) into (7.6.5) and rearranging terms, we get

$$\begin{aligned}
(PW^2M^2 &- PWE^2E^2)ER^2 - PW^2M^1ER^2 \\
&+ PWE^2E^1ER^2 + \hat{T}^2PW^2ER^2[(M^2 - M^1) - (M_v^2 \\
&- M_v^1)] - \hat{T}e^2PWE^2(E^2 - E^1)ER^2 + PD^2(X^2 - X^1) \\
&- PD^2(X_v^2 - X_v^1) - PW^2(M_v^2 - M_v^1)ER^2 > 0 \tag{7.6.8}
\end{aligned}$$

The first term in expression (7.6.8), $(PW^2M^2 - PWE^2E^2)ER^2$, is simply equal to the balance-of-trade deficit in domestic currency prices and can be replaced by F^2ER^2, the value of net resource transfers, because by the balance-of-payments constraint characterizing solution 2, it must be true that

$$PW^2M^2 - PWE^2E^2 - F^2 = 0 \tag{7.6.9}$$

Similarly, we must have

$$PW^1M^1 - PWE^1E^1 - F^1 = 0 \tag{7.6.10}$$

and therefore

$$(PW^1M^1 - PWE^1E^1 - F^1)ER^2 = 0 \tag{7.6.11}$$

Given that (7.6.11) equals zero, we can add it to expression (7.6.8) without affecting its value. Rearranging terms, we obtain the following decomposition of the change in real income, ΔR_P, expressed as the change in a Paasche quantity index:

$$\Delta R_P = (F^2 - F^1)ER^2 \qquad \text{foreign resource effect}$$

$$+ (PW^2 - PW^1)M^1ER^2 + (PWE^2 - PWE^1)E^1ER^2$$
$$\text{terms-of-trade effect}$$

$$+ \hat{T}^2PW^2\,[(M^2 - M^1) - (M_v^2 - M_v^1)]\,ER^2$$
$$\text{tariff distortion effect}$$

$$- \hat{T}e^2PWE^2(E^2 - E^1)ER^2 \qquad \text{export subsidy distortion effect}$$

$$+ PD^2(X^2 - X^1) - PD^2(X_v^2 - X_v^1)$$
$$- PW^2(M_v^2 - M_v^1)ER^2 \qquad \text{net production effect} \qquad (7.6.12)$$

Consider each element of the decomposition given in (7.6.12). The foreign resource effect reflects the direct impact that a change in the availability of net foreign resources has on domestic absorption. The terms-of-trade effect has two components reflecting import prices and export prices. We shall always make the small-country assumption on the import side, so $PW^2 - PW^1$ will always be zero. But when the small-country assumption is dropped on the export side, we can get nonzero terms-of-trade effects whenever $PWE^2 \neq PWE^1$.

The tariff distortion effect arises because, with positive tariffs, the benefit derived by domestic consumers from incremental imports exceeds their social cost given by world prices not inclusive of tariffs. Similarly, the export subsidy distortion effect reflects the fact that exports are more costly to society than to exporters when there are positive export subsidies. Jointly the tariff and export subsidy effects constitute a consumption distortion effect that captures changes in real income due to changes in the degree and pattern of distortions affecting the final use of commodities.

The last term in (7.6.12) is the net production effect itself, obtained by subtracting changes in domestic and imported intermediate inputs from changes in total domestic production.

This decomposition has many advantages. It does not depend on the two situations being in any sense "close." It applies to large as well as small changes, and is close to traditional national income accounts. When the economy can be viewed as maximizing utility subject only to its budget constraint and technological parameters, $\Delta R_P > 0$ is a sufficient condition for welfare to have improved. The terms that make up ΔR_P are additive and each, taken separately, isolates an interesting aspect of trade policy.

The decomposition methodology also has important weaknesses and disadvantages. It cannot be treated as a quantity index of real income or welfare. We have the usual index number problem, and there is nothing ideal about a Paasche index. We can, of course, compute the Laspeyres version of the decomposition. Denoting it by ΔR_L, we get

$$\begin{aligned}
\Delta R_L = {} & (F^2 - F^1)ER^1 + (PW^2 - PW^1)M^2ER^1 \\
& + (PWE^2 - PWE^1)E^2ER^1 + \hat{T}^1PW^1\,[(M^2 - M^1) \\
& - (M_v^2 - M_v^1)]\,ER^1 - \hat{T}e^1PWE^1(E^2 - E^1)ER^1 \\
& + PD^1\,(X^2 - X^1) - PD^1(X_v^2 - X_v^1) \\
& - PW^1(M_v^2 - M_v^1)ER^1 \qquad\qquad\qquad\qquad (7.6.13)
\end{aligned}$$

There is nothing ideal about a Laspeyres index either, except that, as we argued before, $\Delta R_L > 0$ does normally constitute a necessary condition for welfare to have increased. If we impose further restrictions and assume a homothetic utility function, then it is also true that the "unobservable" true percentage change in welfare lies between ΔR_p (the lower bound) and ΔR_L (the upper bound). In this case, taking some kind of average is reasonable. We shall usually take the arithmetic average, because it preserves additivity of the decomposition. Although this may be reasonable, it must be admitted that there is no hard justification for it. Thus, although the Paasche and Laspeyres indices do allow us to rank some situations and help us get a feel for the quantitative importance of individual elements underlying a change in real income, the methodology must be used with care, keeping in mind its limitations. It is nevertheless very useful, and in development planning where GDP calculations and their unqualified use have dominated discussion and policy applications, one should not, perhaps, be too much of a purist.

Before concluding this section, it is important to stress that, for some applications and some policy experiments, it may be desirable to use a particular utility function or social welfare function. One can, for example, assume that

$$\text{Welfare} = U(C_1, \ldots, C_n)$$

with the particular intertemporal form

$$\text{Welfare} = \sum_{t=1}^{T} \left(\frac{1}{1 + \rho} \right)^t U(C_{1t}, \ldots, C_{nt}) \tag{7.6.14}$$

Provided that one agrees on an origin such as $U = 0$ when $(C_1, \ldots, C_n) = 0$, the explicit use of a utility or welfare function allows a complete ranking of all possible situations and policy packages and a quantitative comparison between any two alternatives. The practice is well established in the linear programming and optimizing literature (where most welfare functions are linear!)

7.7   Conclusion

In this chapter we have outlined a specification that represents a substantial step forward in the building of applied multisector general equilibrium models of open economies. Instead of restricting choice to either a fixed-coefficients specification treating traded goods as rigid complements to domestic goods or a specification that rules out two-way trade by treating domestic and foreign goods as perfect substitutes, the introduction of trade-substitution and export-demand elasticities allows an intermediate position between these two extremes. This in turn allows distinction between sectors such as machinery, characterized by low substitution elasticities, and sectors such as paper or petroleum, where substitutability in use is high. More realistic behavior of quantities and prices can also be expected, with the tendency to specialization much diminished and the domestic price system more autonomous than in neoclassical theory but less isolated from world prices than in fixed-coefficients models. On the export side, specifying very high demand elasticities will approximate the small-country assumption. But one is no longer forced to make this assumption, and for many categories of products, it is more realistic to assume moderate export demand elasticities and thus have the country face downward-sloping demand curves for its exports. All this is, of course, made possible and easy by the nonlinear nature of the general equilibrium model. Although piecewise linearization can often achieve the same results, it is much easier to formulate the model in nonlinear form to start, provided that a solution can be obtained numerically at reasonable cost.

There remain, however, the problems of parameter estimation and validation. Although it may be much better to set trade-substitution elasticities at values *between* zero and infinity than at these extreme boundary values, there may be strong disagreement as to their exact magnitude. This disagreement was never allowed to surface in the traditional models except in the form of wholesale rejection of "neoclassical" models by "structuralists" and vice versa. Introducing the new set of elasticities explicitly raises the empirical question of their magnitude for particular kinds of commodities and countries of particular size and levels of development. It thus has the virtue of creating the need for better data and econometric work. In the meantime, as the data and econometric evidence are not yet available,[16] it is important to develop a feel for the range of magnitudes involved and for the sensitivity of the results to parameter values. We turn to such an investigation in Chapters 8 and 9.

7.A   Appendix: Equations of the flexible exchange rate model

This appendix presents the flexible exchange rate version of the model in complete equation form. Endogenous variables are denoted by capital

---

[16] Some studies do, of course, exist, but they refer mostly to trade between industrialized countries. See, for example, Leamer and Stern (1970), as well as Dixon (1975) and the studies cited therein.

letters. Lowercase letters, Greek letters, and letters with bars ($^-$) are exogenous variables or parameters (with the exception of d_i).

Import price equations

$$PM_i = \overline{PW}_i(1 + tm_i)ER \qquad\qquad n$$

where $\overline{PW}_i$ is the world price of imports in "dollars," tm_i is the tariff rate, and ER is the exchange rate.

Export price equations

$$PWE_i = \frac{PD_i}{(1 + te_i)ER} \qquad\qquad n$$

where PD_i is the domestic price (in local currency) and te_i is the export subsidy rate.

Composite price equations

$$P_i = \frac{PD_i + PM_i \cdot M_i/D_i}{f_i(M_i/D_i, 1)} \qquad\qquad n$$

where M_i is imports, D_i is domestic demand for domestic production, PD_i is the price of domestically produced commodities, and $f_i(-)$ is the CES trade aggregation function for aggregating domestic and imported goods. This equation is an alternative to Eq. (7.4.7).

Net price equations

$$PN_i = PD_i - \sum_j P_j a_{ji} - td_i PD_i \qquad\qquad n$$

where a_{ji} are the fixed input–output coefficients and td_i is the indirect tax rate.

Price-level equation

$$\Sigma\, \Omega_i P_i = \overline{P} \qquad\qquad \text{One}$$

where Ω_i are the weights for the price index ($\Sigma_i \Omega_i = 1$) and $\overline{P}$ is the price level.

Production functions

$$X_i^S = \overline{A}_i g_i(\overline{K}_i, L_i) \hspace{6cm} n$$

where X_i^S is total domestic production (supply), $\overline{A}$ is the productivity parameter, $\overline{K}_i$ and L_i are (aggregate) sectoral capital and labor, and $g_i(-)$ is the CES production function.

Labor aggregation functions

$$L_i = \lambda_i(L_{1i}, \ldots, L_{mi}) \hspace{5cm} n$$

where L_{ki} is labor of category k in sector i and $\lambda_i(-)$ is the CES labor aggregation function.

Labor market equilibrium

$$PN_i \frac{\partial X_i}{\partial L_{ki}} = W_k \hspace{5cm} m \cdot n$$

$$L_k^D = \sum_i^n L_{ki} \hspace{5.5cm} m$$

$$L_k^D - \overline{L}_k^S = 0 \hspace{5.5cm} m$$

where L_k^D and L_k^S are the demand and supply of labor of category k, and W_k are equilibrium wages, $k = 1, m$. Wage distortions can be specified as discussed in Chapter 6, Eq. (6.4.2).

Export demand functions

$$E_i = \overline{E}_i \left(\frac{\Pi_i}{PWE_i} \right)^{\eta_i} \hspace{4.5cm} n$$

where PWE_i is the supply price of domestic exports in dollars and Π_i is an average world price for that market.

Import demand functions

$$M_i = \left(\frac{\delta_i}{1 - \delta_i} \right)^{\sigma_i} \left(\frac{PD_i}{PM_i} \right)^{\sigma_i} D_i \hspace{3cm} n$$

where σ_i is the trade-substitution elasticity and δ_i is the share parameter in the CES trade aggregation function.

Balance-of-payments equilibrium

$$\sum_i \overline{PW} \cdot M_i - \sum_i PWE \cdot E_i - \overline{F} = 0 \qquad \text{One}$$

where $\overline{F}$ is the exogenous value of net foreign capital inflow.

Income equations

Net labor income is given by

$$R_L = \sum_i \sum_k W_k \cdot L_{ki} (1 - t_k) \qquad \text{One}$$

where t_k is the direct tax rate on labor income category k.
  Net nonlabor factor income is given by

$$R_K = \sum_i (PN_i X_i - \sum_k W_k L_{ki}) \cdot (1 - tk_i) \qquad \text{One}$$

where tk_i is the direct tax rate on sectoral nonlabor income.
  Government income is given by

$$R_G = \sum_i \sum_k t_k W_k L_{ki} + \sum_i tk_i \cdot (PV_i X_i - \sum_k W_k L_{ki})$$

$$+ \sum_i tm_i \overline{PW}_i ER \cdot M_i \qquad \text{One}$$

$$- \sum_i te_i PWE_i ER \cdot E_i + \sum_i td_i X_i^S PD_i + \overline{F} \cdot ER$$

Alternative treatments of $\overline{F}$ are easily specified (see Chapter 5), and various specifications are used in the application.

Investment equations

$$TINV = \overline{S}_L R_L + \overline{S}_K R_K + \overline{S}_G R_G \qquad \text{One}$$

where $TINV$ is the value of total investment and $\overline{S}_L$, $\overline{S}_K$, , and $\overline{S}_G$ are the savings rates out of labor income, capital income, and government income.

$$Y_i = \theta_i \cdot TINV \qquad n$$

where θ_i are exogenous sectoral investment shares and Y_i is investment by sector of destination.

Investment by sector of destination is then translated into investment by sector of origin by the capital composition coefficients, s_{ij}:

$$Z_i = \sum_j s_{ij} Y_j \qquad\qquad n$$

Consumption demand equations

$$C_i = C_{iL} + C_{iK} + C_{iG} \qquad\qquad n$$

$$C_{ij} = \overline{q}_{ij}(1 - \overline{S}_j) \frac{R_j}{P_i} \qquad j = L, K, G \qquad\qquad 3n$$

where C_i is total consumer demand for composite commodity i, equal to the sum of the demands coming from wage earners, capitalists, and the government. Each of these groups spends their income net of savings according to a set of constant expenditure shares $\overline{q}_{ij}$. In the application in Chapter 13, the linear expenditure system is used instead.

Intermediate demand equations

$$V_i = \sum_j a_{ij} X_j \qquad\qquad n$$

where V_i is the demand for composite intermediate inputs derived from sectoral production levels and the input–output coefficients.

Product market equilibrium

$$D_i = d_i \cdot (Y_i + C_i + V_i) \qquad\qquad n$$

where d_i, the domestic use ratio, is given by

$$d_i = \frac{1}{f_i(M_i/D_i, 1)} \qquad\qquad n$$

where f_i is the CES trade aggregation function.

Total demand for domestically produced goods is therefore

$$X_i^D = D_i + E_i \qquad\qquad n$$

Product market equilibrium is defined by

$$X_i^D - X_i^S = 0 \qquad\qquad n$$

$$Total: 19n + m \cdot n + 2m + 6$$

Of these equations, only $19n + m \cdot n + 2m + 5$ are, however, independent. There are thus as many endogenous variables as independent equations.

Endogenous variables

PM_i	n	Import prices
PWE_i	n	Export prices
ER	one	The exchange rate
PD_i	n	Domestic prices
P_i	n	Composite commodity prices
PN_i	n	Net or value-added prices
X_i^S	n	Domestic production by sector
L_i	n	Aggregate labor by sector
L_{ik}	$m \cdot n$	Labor by category and sector
W_k	m	Wages by category
L_k^D	m	Total employment by labor category
E_i	n	Exports
M_i	n	Imports
R_L	one	Labor income
R_K	one	Capital income
R_G	one	Government income
$TINV$	one	Total investment
Y_i	n	Investment by sector of destination
Z_i	n	Investment by sector of origin
C_i	n	Total sectoral consumption
C_{ij}	$3n$	Consumption by category of consumer
V_i	n	Intermediate demand
D_i	n	Total demand for domestic use
d_i	n	Domestic use ratio
X_i^D	n	Total demand
	$19n + m \cdot n + 2m + 5$	

PART III

Trade policy and resource allocation: a quantitative analysis

CHAPTER 8

Protection, prices, and resource pulls

8.1 Introduction

Chapter 6 discussed in qualitative terms how to introduce foreign trade and trade policy into a CGE model. Chapter 7 presented a specific model with product differentiation between imported and domestically produced goods and argued that this approach is the best way of handling foreign trade within the framework of fairly aggregated multisector planning models. The purpose of this and the next chapter is to provide both examples of foreign trade issues that can be usefully investigated with a CGE model and an examination of the sensitivity of the model to systematic variation in key trade elasticities. Both chapters are applications of the material presented in Chapters 6 and 7 and are intended to prepare the ground for the more detailed policy applications presented in Chapter 10 and 11.

The focus in Chapter 9 is on the macroeconomic impact of alternative policies. This chapter emphasizes microeconomic effects by providing a detailed quantitative examination of the price and quantity linkages captured by a CGE model featuring product differentiation. These linkages are examined by exploring the quantitative effects on resource allocation of varying tariffs, subsidies, and the exchange rate. It is particularly important to stress the importance of carrying out an exercise where trade taxes are varied systematically because, as we saw in Chapter 7, product differentiation modifies the nature of the mechanism and the linkages that lead from trade policy variables to prices, incentives, and resource allocation. Also, a systematic examination of how the various elasticities in the models determine the magnitude of relative price changes is crucial in order to understand and interpret the policy results in Chapters 10, 11, and 13.

The investigation proceeds with the use of a "stylized" nineteen-sector model of a semi-industrialized economy. In manufacturing, the level of disaggregation corresponds closely to the standard two-digit SITC breakdown. The nonmanufacturing sectors are more aggregated (five sectors in all). The focus is therefore clearly on the industrial sector. Although a much finer sectoral detail would be necessary for an in-depth investigation of trade policy on resource allocation at the micro level, the two-digit breakdown provides useful insights and provides a basis for a dialogue between the macro planner and the sector specialist.

The data for the application are based on Turkish statistics, and Chapters 8 and 9 set the stage for the more specific, policy-oriented discussion of Turkish foreign trade and industrialization in Chapters 10 and 11. In order to focus on the essential linkages in a core CGE model, we here simplify the model, abstracting from some of the institutional characteristics of the Turkish economy in order to bring out more clearly the mechanisms at work. This "stylized" version is also useful in helping to explore the sensitivity of the model to the values assumed by some of its key parameters. At the present stage of data availability, formal econometric estimation of many model parameters is largely beyond reach, and one must often make educated guesses of the values of important parameters in any given application. It is therefore important to investigate the sensitivity of modeled behavior and policy prescriptions to different assumptions about key parameter values. Although we have to be selective and cannot present an exhaustive set of sensitivity experiments, Chapters 8 and 9 provide information on the mechanisms at work in different policy simulations and the sensitivity of results to parameter specification. In the process, we hope to clarify the debate between "elasticity pessimists" and "elasticity optimists" by quantifying the impact of different parameter assumptions in the context of selected policy experiments.

The chapter is divided into three parts. Section 8.2 is devoted to an examination of how the constellation of elasticities reflecting the characteristics of different sectors accounts for the differential impact on domestic prices and resource allocation of equal percentage changes in single tariffs and subsidies. The question to be answered is the following: Why does a 50 percent tariff on, for example, petroleum imports raise the price of domestically produced petroleum products more than a 50 percent tariff on clothing raises the price of domestically produced clothing? Although the analysis rests on the full solution of the model, the fact that trade taxes are altered one at a time gives the analysis a partial equilibrium flavor, which allows us to take full advantage of the discussion on trade policy and resource allocation presented in Chapter 7.

Section 8.3 defines and contrasts effective rates of protection (ERPs) and domestic resource costs (DRCs) in a model with product differentiation. The relationship that is known to hold between these two measures is shown not to be affected by the presence of product differentiation. Finally, Section 8.4 extends the analysis of Section 8.2 by examining quantitatively the impact on resource allocation of across-the-board changes in trade taxes. Throughout, experiments are chosen so as to make the interpretation of results easier to understand rather than to attempt to replicate trade tax reforms that are likely to take place in a semi-industrial country. Indeed, it is this tailored selection of experiments that makes it possible to discuss meaningfully in Section 8.4 how partial equilibrium estimates of the impact of trade taxes on resource allocation are likely to differ from estimates obtained with a general equilibrium model.

8.2 The price mechanism and resource allocation

We saw in Section 7.5 that, even when viewed in partial equilibrium, a sector's response to a change in trade policy incentives is the result of many factors involving supply, demand, and trade substitution elasticities. The analysis pointed in particular to the need for an examination of the model's sensitivity to a systematic variation in the elasticities that determine the behavior of the foreign trade sector. To explore how trade policy affects resource allocation and the composition of imports and exports in the manufacturing sector, we examine sector by sector the impact of changes in single sectoral tariff and subsidy rates. These experiments are carried out under a range of values for the export demand and trade substitution elasticities.

Model outline and reference run

The benchmark year for the experiments is 1973, a year during which trade restrictions were minimal in Turkey. It is thus reasonable to associate the parameters of the model calibrated to the benchmark year with those representing an "equilibrium" in the economy. In fact, this section uses a "free-trade" reference solution. This is largely a matter of convenience, and has the distinct advantage of providing an easier way of comparing our results with other estimates of the effects of protection, most of which select free trade as the norm against which interferences in the foreign trade sector are evaluated. The basic structure of the model used in this chapter and in Chapter 9 follows closely the specification of the core CGE model extended to include product differentiation and export demand functions as described in Chapter 7. The following description sketches only the particular characteristics of the model not already discussed.

On the demand side, sectoral consumption and investment demands are given by constant expenditure proportions. For consumption demand, this specification implies that the uncompensated own-price

elasticity of demand for sectoral composite outputs is unity. This specification has the advantage of simplifying the interpretation of results in
two ways: First, the elasticity of the response of private final demand to
a change in sectoral price, itself due to a change in trade policy, is the
same across the economy; and second, the effects of trade policy on the
factoral distribution of income, which are quite substantial in some
experiments, are not permitted to feed back through the demand system,
because all consumers share the same representative demand system.
For investment demand there will be a zero (unitary) own-price elasticity of demand for each of the sectors producing investment goods if
aggregate investment is held fixed in real (nominal) terms. Because
investment goods are distinguished both by sector of origin and by sector
of destination, capital is heterogeneous in the sense that the composition
of a unit of capital differs across sectors, so that the price of capital in
each sector is the weighted sum of the prices of its components.

Following the formulation in Chapter 5, capital stocks are sectorally
fixed within periods, reflecting the fact that capital is less mobile than
labor in the short run. In the comparative static experiments reported
here, the results may therefore be interpreted as a relatively short-run
response of the economy to a policy change. In a trade-oriented and
industry-focused model, it is sensible to view agriculture as an exogenous sector, because no attempts are made at modeling its behavior. To
reflect this exogeneity, which may be interpreted as a form of dualism,
the labor supply in agriculture is fixed within periods so that the short-
run supply response in agriculture to a change in price is zero.

The urban labor force, which cannot be employed in agriculture, is
perfectly mobile across urban sectors and is composed of two labor categories: organized and unorganized (or skilled and unskilled). The supply of both categories of labor is assumed fixed, so their respective wages
adjust to equate total demand with total supply for each category. There
are no wage differentials for the same category of labor across sectors,
so labor in each category moves across sectors until the value of its marginal product is everywhere the same.[1] Such a specification of factor
markets, while unrealistic for policy analysis, is convenient for exploring
the efficiency aspects of resource movements captured by the model
because the resulting free-trade reference solution has well-understood

[1] This specification eases the welfare interpretation of some of the experiments
in Chapter 9, because it precludes the possibility of interpreting the reference
solution as a second-best solution due to a distortion in the labor market
caused by wage differentials.

efficiency characteristics that would not hold in the presence of a more elaborate specification of labor markets.

Finally, production technology is given by a two-level CES production function. Aggregate labor and capital substitute for one another with a constant elasticity of substitution, whereas at a lower level aggregate labor is itself a CES aggregation function of the two categories of labor.[2]

Labor and capitalists save a constant fraction of their aftertax income, so the model is savings driven. Given the fixed sectoral composition of aggregate capital, the own-price elasticities of demand for investment goods are determined by their value shares in total investment. Also, to abstract from any policy-induced redistribution of income between the private and public sectors, the government's budgetary revenues are maintained at their base-year level. To maintain a fixed level of revenues in real terms, the government performs a set of transfers to and from the private sector according to whether a change in policy gives rise to a net receipt from or a net disbursement to the private sector. Because each factor of production is assumed to have a fixed propensity to save, government consumption is determined residually. This information allows us to focus on the price mechanism and resource allocation and ignore the distributional aspects of trade policies (which are discussed in later chapters).

The sectoral characteristics of the economy in the "free-trade" reference run are given in Table 8.1. The solution is the one corresponding to the set of high trade elasticities given in Table 8.2.[3] Of the nineteen sectors in the model, fourteen are in manufacturing. These manufacturing sectors can be roughly divided into three categories: consumer goods (food, textiles, clothing, wood, and paper); intermediates (chemicals, rubber and plastics, petroleum products, nonmetallic mineral products, and basic metals); and capital goods (metal products, nonelectrical machinery, electrical machinery, and transportation equipment).

The first three columns of Table 8.1 provide the essential production characteristics for each sector. The gross outputs in column (1) reveal

---

[2] In the experiments we describe, we assume the elasticity of substitution between the two labor categories to be one, i.e., a Cobb-Douglas labor aggregation function. Aggregate capital is a fixed-coefficients aggregation of different capital goods.

[3] Equilibrium solutions and the structure of the economy are slightly different under the two sets of trade elasticities. We use the term "trade elasticities" to refer collectively to both the trade-substitution and export-demand elasticities.

Table 8.1. *Structure of the manufacturing sector in the reference solution*

	(1) X	(2) PN/PD	(3) K/L	(4) E/X	(5) RMQ	(6) IMD
1. Agriculture	103.2	71.7	15.2	2.2	2.6	7.6
2. Mining	3.8	67.7	85.6	3.8	7.0	19.6
3. Food	44.9	20.5	79.5	9.7	1.4	1.5
4. Textiles	24.7	21.8	81.4	18.6	4.2	7.2
5. Clothing	7.6	49.1	16.8	1.9	2.5	3.5
6. Wood and wood products	6.6	31.7	32.7	0.2	0.5	3.0
7. Paper and printing	5.2	32.7	190.5	0.4	10.9	9.4
8. Chemicals	10.7	37.9	245.0	2.5	48.0	28.3
9. Rubber and plastics	5.2	27.1	98.1	1.5	19.0	20.2
10. Petroleum and petroleum products	16.1	41.3	2,526.0	4.4	58.3	20.3
11. Nonmetallic mineral products	6.7	38.6	179.5	3.4	7.7	9.8
12. Basic metals	14.5	23.9	638.2	2.8	24.2	15.4
13. Metal products	6.3	37.8	32.4	1.2	16.0	17.1
14. Nonelectrical machinery	9.4	43.0	108.0	1.1	55.6	39.8
15. Electrical machinery	5.0	40.8	60.5	0.3	38.5	22.5
16. Transportation equipment	11.9	37.3	60.5	0.1	28.6	19.0
17. Construction	28.9	57.9	24.9	—	—	13.8
18. Infrastructure	59.7	71.4	694.7	7.2	1.6	15.8
19. Services	109.9	81.7	33.0	5.6	1.4	3.9

Notes: This solution corresponds to the set of trade elasticities denoted as "high" in Table 8.2.
   Column (1): Gross output: billions of 1973 TL.
   Column (2): Sectoral value-added as a percent of domestic price.
   Column (3): Capital to aggregate labor ratio: (million TL/man-year).
   Column (4): Ratio of exports to domestic output (%).
   Column (5): Ratio of imports to total domestic demand (%).
   Column (6): Share of imported intermediate inputs in total intermediate inputs.
   Classification of sectors: consumer goods: sectors 3–7; intermediate goods: sectors 8–12; capital goods: sectors 13–16.

a typical composition of output found in a semi-industrial country where agriculture and services provide more than 40 percent of gross domestic production. Within the manufacturing sector, the traditional nondurable food and textile industries dominate, but a few key intermediate and capital goods sectors such as chemical, petroleum products, basic metals, and transportation equipment are significant and indicate that the economy is indeed in the "semi-industrial" category. The importance of intermediate inputs for each sector is indicated by the per-unit ratio of net price to gross domestic price in column (2). Column (3) gives the capital–labor ratio in each sector. Consumer goods are

Table 8.2. *Trade substitution and price elasticities (%)*

	Trade substitution		Export demand		Output supply	Composite demand
	(1) Low	(2) High	(3) Low	(4) High	(5) ϵ^s	(6) ϵ^d
1. Agriculture	2.00	6.00	2.0	4.0	1.57	0.55
2. Mining	0.33	1.00	2.0	4.0	2.59	0.17
3. Food	0.75	2.25	2.0	4.0	0.63	0.74
4. Textiles	0.75	2.25	2.0	4.0	2.12	0.61
5. Clothing	0.75	2.25	3.0	6.0	1.88	0.79
6. Wood and wood products	0.75	2.25	3.0	6.0	1.87	0.38
7. Paper and printing	0.33	1.00	3.0	6.0	0.81	0.38
8. Chemicals	0.33	1.00	3.0	6.0	0.24	0.43
9. Rubber and plastics	0.33	1.00	3.0	6.0	0.69	0.50
10. Petroleum and petroleum products	1.50	4.50	3.0	6.0	0.02	0.15
11. Nonmetallic mineral products	0.33	1.00	3.0	6.0	0.66	0.43
12. Basic metals	0.33	1.00	3.0	6.0	0.36	0.00
13. Metal products	0.33	1.00	3.0	6.0	1.59	0.68
14. Nonelectrical machinery	0.25	0.75	3.0	6.0	0.34	0.36
15. Electrical machinery	0.25	0.75	3.0	6.0	0.57	0.46
16. Transportation equipment	0.25	0.75	3.0	6.0	0.70	0.25
17. Construction	—	—	—	—	1.40	—
18. Infrastructure	0.25	0.75	2.0	4.0	0.23	0.69
19. Services	0.25	0.75	2.0	4.0	1.37	0.50

Notes: Columns (1) and (2): σ, trade substitution elasticities [defined in Eq. (7.2.1)].
Columns (3) and (4): η, price elasticity of export demand [defined in Eq. (7.3.5)].
Column (5): ϵ^s, price elasticity of output supply [defined in Eq. (8.2.1)].
Column (6): ϵ^d, own-price elasticity of composite demand [defined in Eq. (8.2.2)].

labor intensive, and intermediate goods as a whole are the most capital intensive, with capital goods industries somewhere in between.[4]

The next three columns in Table 8.1 provide information about each sector's trade orientation. Column (4) indicates that only four sectors in the economy export more than 5 percent of their production, with food and textiles, being the most export-oriented sectors in the economy. These export ratios are quite low by international standards, and reflect a country that has followed an inward-looking development strategy.[5] On the import side, the typical picture emerges when one considers both the share of imports in aggregate composite expenditures [column (5)]

[4] Because these are direct capital–labor ratios, they provide only a rough indication of sectoral capital intensity.

[5] A comparison of the extent of openness for a set of semi-industrial countries is provided in Balassa and Associates (1980b, chap. 3).

and the share of imported intermediates in total intermediate inputs [column (6)]. With the exception of nonmetallic products, intermediates and capital goods are both import oriented (in the sense of a large share of imports) and import dependent (in the sense of a large share of imported intermediate inputs). It should be noted, however, that although it is generally the case that import-dependent sectors are also import oriented, there are some notable exceptions. Chemicals, petroleum products, transportation equipment, and the machinery sectors all have much higher import shares in final demand than in intermediate inputs. The opposite is the case for mining and infrastructure, which are fairly intensive in their use of imported intermediate inputs but show a small import share in final use. Construction also falls in the same category as mining and infrastructure. It is the only "pure" nontraded sector in the economy, yet 17 percent of its intermediate inputs are imported.

The range of elasticities chosen to explore the sensitivity of the model to key parameter values is shown in Table 8.2. On the import side, the high substitution elasticities are three times the low set. On the export side, the high export demand elasticities are twice the low set. Given the paucity of econometric estimates, we attempt to establish "bounds" by exploring the range of variation in the response of endogenous variables to changes in exogenous variables conditional on the parameters in Table 8.2. In particular, the sectoral variation in the elasticities of substitution between domestic and imported goods is a rough estimate of the extent of product differentiation due to differences in quality and degree of product homogeneity. Thus, agricultural and petroleum products are viewed as the most homogeneous products, together with the more traditional nondurable consumer goods (which are assumed to be more substitutable in use than other manufactures). Similarly, on the export side, it is assumed that the price elasticity of export demand for primary products and services is lower than for manufactured products.

Finally, because they are important in determining the ultimate impact of changes in tariffs and subsidies, estimates of partial equilibrium sectoral elasticities of supply and elasticities of composite demand are reported in columns (5) and (6). Sectoral price elasticities of supply are defined as

$$\epsilon_i^s \equiv \sigma_i^X \frac{\theta_{iL}}{\theta_{iK}} \tag{8.2.1}$$

where σ_i^X is the elasticity of substitution in production between capital and labor and $\theta_{ij}(j = K, L)$ are the factor shares for capital and labor.

Thus, supply elasticities are greatest in labor intensive sectors with high substitution elasticities between capital and labor.

Given the model specification, the demand for intermediate goods is given by fixed input–output coefficients and hence is not price sensitive. Consumer demand functions are specified with constant expenditure shares, which implies an uncompensated own-price elasticity of one for every commodity. Aggregate investment demand is fixed nominally, but the sectoral composition of aggregate real investment is given by fixed coefficients. The demand for the aggregate capital good has an own (aggregate) price elasticity of one, but the price elasticity of demand for investment by sector of origin depends on the value shares in aggregate nominal investment. Considering all the three sources of demand – intermediate, consumption, and investment – the partial equilibrium own-price elasticity of demand for the composite good in each sector is given by

$$\epsilon_i^d \equiv \frac{C_i + \theta_i Z_i}{Q_i} \tag{8.2.2}$$

where

$$\theta_i = \frac{Z_i P_i}{\sum_j Z_j P_j} \tag{8.2.3}$$

These partial equilibrium estimates are given in column (6). Although general equilibrium interactions are in fact empirically significant, we report them to provide a feel for the pattern of responsiveness of composite demands across sectors and as an approximation of the elasticity of composite demand defined in Eq. (7.5.10).

The effects of single tariff and subsidy changes on domestic prices

We are now in a position to investigate numerically the sensitivity of the model to the range of elasticities given in Table 8.2 by considering the range of domestic price responses to single changes in tariffs (Table 8.3) and in export subsidies (Table 8.4).

In analyzing the results, the discussion of protection and resource allocation given in Chapter 7 is especially relevant given the partial equilibrium assumptions made there. Starting with the effect of a change in the tariff rate on imports, recall that the resulting percentage change in domestic price is an increasing function of the cross-elasticity

Table 8.3. Resource pull effects of single 50% tariff changes under high and low trade elasticities (%)

	(1) $\hat{PD}_H$	(2) $\hat{PD}_L$	(3) $\hat{P}_H$	(4) $\hat{P}_L$	(5) $(PN/\hat{W})_H$	(6) $(PN/\hat{W})_L$	(7) $\hat{XD}_H$	(8) $\hat{XD}_L$	(9) $\hat{EM}_H$	(10) $\hat{EM}_L$
1. Agriculture	1.9	-0.2	2.3	0.3	0.0	-0.3	0.0	0.0	-88.4	-53.4
2. Mining	0.8	-0.1	3.6	2.9	1.2	-0.1	2.7	-0.2	-33.4	-12.7
3. Food	0.1	0.0	0.6	0.6	0.3	0.1	0.1	-0.1	-55.3	-26.0
4. Textiles	0.5	0.2	1.9	1.2	1.0	0.1	1.9	0.0	-57.7	-25.7
5. Clothing	0.7	0.1	1.5	1.0	0.5	0.0	1.0	0.3	-58.5	-26.4
6. Wood and wood products	0.2	0.1	0.3	0.2	0.1	0.2	0.3	0.1	-59.4	-26.2
7. Paper and printing	2.5	0.5	6.8	5.0	2.7	-1.8	2.1	-1.4	-32.6	-13.6
8. Chemicals	11.5	0.0	27.0	20.3	11.7	-12.0	2.6	-3.1	-22.8	-14.2
9. Rubber and plastics	2.3	-0.2	9.7	7.7	4.7	-2.5	3.1	-1.8	-31.9	-14.1
10. Petroleum and petroleum products	18.6	20.4	31.9	28.6	13.0	15.1	0.2	0.2	-43.0	-20.9
11. Nonmetallic mineral products	1.2	0.2	4.3	3.1	2.2	0.4	1.4	-0.2	-33.6	-12.6
12. Basic metals	14.4	9.1	11.3	18.7	19.7	4.0	6.4	1.4	-18.6	-7.6
13. Metal products	0.9	-0.7	7.4	0.6	1.3	-1.3	1.9	-2.4	-33.7	-14.8
14. Nonelectrical machinery	5.8	-2.8	26.4	21.7	4.1	-13.0	1.3	-4.6	-19.7	-13.4
15. Electrical machinery	4.2	-1.1	19.9	16.8	5.2	-5.7	2.8	-3.2	-21.0	-12.5
16. Transportation equipment	6.8	3.0	8.2	15.0	6.0	-1.7	4.2	-1.1	-18.3	-9.7
17. Construction	—	—	—	—	—	—	—	—	—	—
18. Infrastructure	-0.2	-0.7	0.6	7.3	-0.1	-0.7	-0.1	-0.1	-18.3	-9.9
19. Services	-0.3	-0.3	-0.3	-1.1	-0.2	-1.7	-0.4	-0.6	-18.5	-6.4

Notes: Subscripts H and L refer to "high" and "low" trade elasticity specification (see Table 8.2). PD = domestic price, W = wage, P = composite good price, XD = domestic production, PN = net price (value added), EM = imports.

Table 8.4. *Resource pull effects of single 50% subsidy changes under high and low trade elasticities (%)*

	(1) $\hat{PD}_H$	(2) $\hat{PD}_L$	(3) $\hat{P}_H$	(4) $\hat{P}_L$	(5) $\hat{XD}_H$	(6) $\hat{XD}_L$	(7) $\hat{ED}_H$	(8) $\hat{ED}_L$
1. Agriculture	6.6	3.5	6.2	3.4	0.0	0.0	248.7	101.9
2. Mining	4.2	1.6	3.8	1.5	12.8	6.1	323.7	117.0
3. Food	7.1	3.6	7.0	3.6	17.9	8.9	191.1	86.6
4. Textiles	6.0	2.9	5.5	2.7	48.6	21.5	207.2	93.0
5. Clothing	5.2	2.8	4.9	2.6	13.6	7.0	186.7	203.3
6. Wood and wood products	0.8	0.4	0.8	0.3	2.8	0.9	966.1	234.5
7. Paper and printing	2.3	0.5	2.1	0.4	4.3	0.9	861.3	233.1
8. Chemicals	11.5	4.3	5.4	2.1	5.3	2.2	464.7	193.3
9. Rubber and plastics	5.0	1.0	3.9	0.8	10.3	2.4	736.5	226.7
10. Petroleum and petroleum products	35.1	23.6	9.8	13.4	0.7	0.5	89.7	81.8
11. Nonmetallic mineral products	11.0	4.2	10.0	3.9	14.9	5.9	470.4	192.7
12. Basic metals	14.7	7.0	10.7	5.0	11.9	6.6	380.0	170.7
13. Metal products	2.9	1.0	2.4	0.9	9.6	3.4	831.8	226.1
14. Nonelectrical machinery	6.5	2.3	2.5	0.9	4.5	1.6	656.2	214.7
15. Electrical machinery	1.9	0.3	1.2	0.2	2.0	0.4	912.0	234.9
16. Transportation equipment	0.9	0.0	0.7	0.0	1.2	0.0	963.4	238.0
17. Construction	—	—	—	—	—	—	—	—
18. Infrastructure	11.9	5.8	11.6	5.4	3.8	2.0	145.5	82.4
19. Services	5.3	2.3	5.1	2.2	2.8	1.2	166.5	87.3

Notes: Subscripts H and L refer to "high" and "low" trade elasticity specification (see Table 8.2). PD = domestic production, P = composite good price, ED = exports. PD = domestic price, XD = domestic of demand for the domestic good, which in turn is associated with a large spread between the elasticity of demand for the composite good (ϵ^d) and the elasticity of substitution in use between the domestically produced and foreign goods (σ). The imposition of a tariff on imports will, other things being equal, lead to a large increase in demand for the domestically produced good if it is easy to substitute it for the foreign-produced good (a high value of σ), if the sector has a large import share, and/or if the demand for the composite good is relatively insensitive to a change in its (composite) price. Given the model specification, sectors with low elasticities of demand are those for which the ratio of consumption and investment to total composite output [see Table 8.1, column (6)] is low. Finally, note that because the demand for the domestic good is a derived demand, the extent of the increase in the domestic price is a *decreasing* function of the elasticity of domestic supply (ϵ^s).

It was also shown that the percentage change in the domestic price for a given change in the tariff will be lower, the larger the ratio of exports to domestic use (E/D) and the higher the foreign elasticity of demand for exports (η). Thus, as one increases σ and η simultaneously, there are two countervailing effects on the responsiveness of the domestic price to a change in the tariff rate. However, one would expect the influence of σ to be dominant partly because the ratio E/D falls as σ increases.[6]

These are the main effects that were identified in Section 7.5 as the determining influences of a small change in tariff on the domestic price. The allocation consequences of this change in price would then be linked directly to the sectoral elasticity of supply. When we move toward an actual experiment with the model, however, we must be aware of the simplifications made in this analysis.

Starting first with the general equilibrium effects of lesser magnitude, note that the formula for the change in the domestic price [Eq. (7.5.16)] neglects the effect of the exchange-rate adjustment on the final change in the tariff rate. We shall consider the effect of a 50 percent change in a single tariff, but the net change in import prices will be less than 50 percent by an amount equal to the resulting revaluation of the exchange rate to maintain equilibrium in the balance of trade. This exchange-rate adjustment depends on the share of total imports in the sector to which the tariff is applied, but is usually negligible for a single tariff change.[7]

---

[6] The same countervailing effects are at work on the export side. In that case, the dominant effect of η is obvious.

[7] There will also be a change in the wage rate, which is also usually insignificant.

Second, we must take into account the presence of intermediate products, in particular intrasectoral flows, which are often significant.[8] An estimate of the resource-pull effects of a change in tariffs has to be based on net prices PN rather than on gross prices PD. Sector i's net price (ignoring indirect taxes) is given by

$$PN_i = PD_j - \sum_j \bar{a}_{ji} P_j \tag{8.2.4}$$

where P_i is the price of the composite good. Therefore, the percentage change in the net price of a sector due to a change in the sectoral tariff is given by

$$\hat{PN}_i = \left(\frac{PD_i}{PN_i} \right) \hat{PD}_i - \bar{a}_{ii} \left(\frac{P_i}{PN_i} \right) \hat{P}_i \tag{8.2.5}$$

under the assumption that the prices of other composite goods are unaffected; that is, $\hat{P}_j = 0$ for $j \neq i$. Recall that the change in the price of the composite good is itself given by

$$\hat{P}_i = \theta_{im} \hat{PM}_i + (1 - \theta_{im}) \hat{PD}_i \tag{8.2.6}$$

where θ_{im}, the share of imports in total composite expenditures, is again assumed to remain constant for small changes. Therefore, the cost of purchasing commodities from sectors with large import shares such as intermediates and capital goods will rise substantially with the increase in import prices.[9] For sectors that have substantial intrasectoral purchases, it may well turn out that net prices fall even if an increase in the import price raises the gross price. This result is analogous to the case where a sector has a negative effective rate of protection, because the weighted sum of tariffs on intermediate goods exceeds the tariff rate on the final commodity. We return in Section 8.4 to a discussion of the notion of effective protection in the presence of product differentiation.

It is now easier to interpret the results of the one-by-one imposition of a 50 percent tariff on domestic prices and resource allocation that are reported in Table 8.3.[10] Consider first the percentage change in the

---

[8] Of the fourteen sectors experiencing changes, nine have own input–output coefficients of 0.20 or more, with two sectors having coefficients of above 0.40; only two sectors have coefficients below 0.10.

[9] Note that the change in the composite good price is always between the change in the domestic price and the change in the import price.

[10] Note that the convergence criterion of the solution algorithm is that the excess demand in each sector be less than 1 percent. The "standard error" of the reported number is probably around one percentage point, although we did not try to investigate the issue empirically.

domestic price, PD_i, corresponding to the set of high elasticities given in column (2). Primary goods and consumer goods that have low import shares and export a relatively large amount of their output show virtually no price increase at all (less than 1 percent). This is so because they behave either as nontradables (e.g., wood) or as exportables (e.g., textiles and food). Intermediates, as a rule, behave as import substitutes because they generally have fairly large import shares. The exceptions are rubber and plastics and nonmetallic mineral products, both of which have low import shares so that their prices do not change much.

To see the mechanisms at work, trace out, for an example, the causes behind the 18.6 percent increase in the domestic price of petroleum products, which dominates the other figures in that column. From the information provided in Tables 8.1 and 8.2, it is clear that the major factors are a high import share in combination with a low elasticity of final demand (because of the fact that petroleum products are used mostly as intermediates and, of course, the fact that these products are good substitutes in use regardless of origin). These factors, in conjunction with the extremely low elasticity of domestic supply, result in a dramatic rise in the domestic price of petroleum products. This result is to be expected, because it is difficult to find substitutes for these products on the demand side and it is difficult to increase their output, at least in the short run. A similar but less dramatic combination of shares and elasticities underlies the large price increases registered for chemicals and basic metals.

Are the results substantially affected by the values of σ_i and η_i? Clearly, the rise in domestic prices is substantially less, and some sectors become import complements when the elasticities are lowered. What is important to note is that there is no simple rule of thumb that gives the domestic price response as trade elasticities are uniformly and systematically varied. For instance, in the case of chemicals, the domestic price increase falls from 11.5 percent to zero as one goes from high to low trade elasticities, a result that stands out in contrast with the pattern in other sectors. The reason is that when the trade-substitution elasticity is low, it is close to the estimated value of the elasticity of final demand, so that the two effects cancel each other out and the fact that chemicals has a high import share becomes unimportant.

With the exception of transportation equipment, all capital goods sectors become import complements when trade elasticities are lowered. Thus, in a low-elasticity "structuralist" environment, tariff protection may have an effect opposite to the one intended. If there are no close substitutes for foreign goods and if investment demand is moderately sensitive to the price of investment goods, then a capital-goods sector will not benefit from protection. Thus, quite apart from the political economy arguments for tariff setting, these results provide a possible explanation as to why many developing countries provide increasing tariff protection to their industries or protect very selectively on the basis of domestic availability. A possible scenario might be the following. First, "modest" initial protection is granted to a sector or a group of sectors. As it becomes apparent that these sectors are not protected, tariffs are raised further, and so on. As we shall see in Chapter 9, under such circumstances, only forced substitution toward domestically produced goods via protection by rationing can provide positive protection to domestic industries – which may help explain the observed preference for protection by quantity restrictions (QRs) in many semi-industrialized countries.

The final impact on resource allocation of a tariff-induced change in the import price depends on how the costs of intermediate inputs have been affected. Recall that producers make their production decisions based on net prices. Because producers cannot substitute among intermediate inputs, the cost of higher input prices (reflected by a rise in the own-composite price) is fully passed on to them. As indicated by Eq. (8.2.4), the increase in the composite good price will be substantial for intermediates and capital goods because these sectors have high import shares. This is confirmed in columns (3) and (4) of Table 8.3, which also verify that the increase in composite good prices falls between the change in the price of the domestically produced goods and the domestic currency price of import substitutes. Because of the rise in the cost of intrasectoral purchases, it is generally the case that net price changes are less than changes in gross prices.[11]

To summarize, the sectors that benefit most from tariff protection, in the sense of a rise in net price, are the import-oriented sectors that have already been identified when discussing changes in gross prices. However, it is worth reiterating that the final general equilibrium resource-pull effect of an increase in the tariff is not necessarily reflected by the

---

[11] There are some instances when this is not the case. Net prices may rise more than gross prices because the normalization rule requires that a weighted sum of changes in composite prices be zero [see Eq. (8.4.1)]. Therefore, if a sector's composite price goes up substantially and that sector has a large share in total aggregate expenditures, all other composite goods prices will have to fall. Thus, for large sectors that do not have substantial intrasectoral purchases, this general equilibrium effect via the normalization rule may be the dominant factor in explaining the difference between changes in gross prices and changes in net prices.

size of the change in the net price because the two are jointly determined and inversely related to one another. It is often the case that sectors which have large increases in net prices do not expand much (e.g., petroleum products) because, other things being equal, a large domestic price response to a tariff is associated with a low supply elasticity. As can be seen from columns (7) and (8), the short-run allocational effects are small, and no sector experiences more than a 5 percent change in output. A comparison of output changes under both sets of trade elasticities indicates that, although the range of domestic price response is not very sensitive to a fairly wide range of elasticities, the behavior of sectors is sensitive because they switch fairly easily from import substitutes to import complements when trade elasticities are lowered.

It is interesting to relate the resource shifts with those that would obtain under a more neoclassical trade specification where domestic and foreign goods would be perfect substitutes. To do this, multiply the supply elasticities in Table 8.2 [column (5)] by one-half, because in that case the domestic price would increase by the full amount of the tariff and $\hat{PD}_i = \hat{PM}_i = 0.5$. This would provide a rough estimate of the increase in sectoral outputs, which could then be compared with the results in column (7).[12] These resource pulls would still be larger than those that would be obtained in the very long run with product differentiation – but not by much. In that case, letting $\epsilon_i^s = \infty$, the output response to a change in tariffs would be given by $\hat{X}_i = (\sigma_i - \epsilon_i^d)\theta_{im}\hat{PM}_i$, which turns out to be usually less than the short-run response with perfect substitution.[13]

Finally, the effects on imports are reported in the last two columns of Table 8.3. These will be later compared with the response on the export side. As expected, this response is quite sensitive to the selected values of σ_i, which in turn suggests that the extent of exchange-rate adjustment necessary to maintain balance of trade in the face of across-the-board changes in trade incentives is fairly sensitive to the values selected for σ_i and η_i.

The effects of changes in tariffs on the domestic price system require careful interpretation because of the indirect effects caused by imperfect substitution. On the export side, however, the linkages are much easier to follow: The effect of an export subsidy on the domestic price system depends mostly on the sectoral elasticity of demand for exports. More-

---

[12] This estimate neglects the increase in costs associated with intrasectoral purchases, which, however, tends to be small.

[13] The expression for $\hat{X}$ is obtained from Eqs. (7.5.9) and (7.5.14) after noting that $\epsilon^s = \infty$, $\hat{PD} = 0$, and hence $\hat{E} = 0$.

over, this link is a direct one and, given that the pattern of export demand elasticities is fairly similar across sectors (see Table 8.2), one would expect the main determinant of the response of domestic prices to a change in subsidies to be the sectoral share of production that is exported. Thus, one would expect that the sectors whose prices rise the most following the imposition of a 50 percent subsidy would be the export-oriented sectors.

The results in Table 8.4 confirm this expectation. The sectors that export a large share of domestic production show the largest increase in prices [see column (1)].[14] Because the increases in domestic prices are much greater than in the case of a similar change in tariff, the output response is also greater [column (5)]. This is, of course, due to the fact that in this case the links are direct, which also accounts for the fact that the domestic price system is more sensitive to the elasticities of demand on the export side than to the elasticities of substitution on the import side.

The sensitivity of the domestic price system to the specified values of η is also reflected in the sectoral export response to a 50 percent export subsidy. Given that the elasticities of export demand are constant, the percentage change in exports can be approximated by

$$\hat{E}_i = \eta_i(\hat{te}_i + \hat{ER} - \hat{PD}_i) \tag{8.2.7}$$

Therefore, for given values of η_i and $\hat{te}_i$, an increase in the domestic price raises the foreign currency price of exports, which in turn lowers the quantity of exports demanded; a devaluation has the opposite effect. Because the values of η_i and $\hat{te}_i$ are the same for most sectors, those sectors whose domestic prices increase the most experience the smallest increase in exports. This result is apparent in comparing the export response in columns (7) and (8) with the domestic price response in columns (1) and (2).

The magnitude of the export response in columns (7) and (8) confirms the greater sensitivity of the model to the specification of export demands than to the specification of import demands, again because the effects are direct. The question then is whether such a difference between the import demand and the export demand response to equal

[14] Naturally, there are some minor exceptions that are revealed by a closer scrutiny. For instance, clothing and basic metals have the same export demand elasticities, and clothing exports a larger share of its output than basic metals, yet basic metals register almost twice as large an increase in price. Here the clue is to be found in the relative value of ϵ^s in both sectors. [See Eq. (7.5.15) and Table 8.2.]

changes in incentives is an adequate approximation of actual behavior. We would argue that the export responses in Table 8.4 are overestimates for the reasons given in Chapter 7, and we shall explore in the next chapter the implications of introducing export supply constraints in the model. We believe, however, and empirical evidence suggests, that there is a greater response to incentives on the export side than on the import side (see Balassa and Associates, 1980b, chap. 3).

8.3   Project evaluation and resource allocation: DRCs and ERPs

Much effort during recent years has been devoted to answering the following questions: (1) How would the structure of the economy be affected by a change in tariffs and/or export susdidies; and (2) how can one measure the welfare costs of distortions and construct criteria for future resource allocation? We have discussed in Chapter 6 how effective rates of protection (ERPs) can be used as predictors of resource pulls. Domestic resource costs (DRCs), on the other hand, are suggested as criteria for project evaluation.[15] The virtue of both measures, which partly accounts for their popularity, is that their application does not require the use of a general equilibrium model. Thus ERPs require only sectoral supply elasticities together with an estimate of the exchange-rate adjustment that would accompany the change in trade policy, and DRCs would call for a set of shadow prices for domestic primary factors and for foreign exchange.

Naturally, a general equilibrium model makes the use of ERPs completely redundant, because it accurately generates the impact on resource allocation of any change in trade policy that can be handled within the framework of the model. Similarly, DRCs lose much of their appeal as criteria for estimating the cost of distortions, because these too are computed within the model. Finally, a major advantage of a well-specified CGE model is that it can simulate different policy alternatives facing policy makers and provide the relevant second-best shadow prices to serve as inputs into the evaluation of future projects. However, because ERPs and DRCs are widely used by policy makers, it is important to relate them to one another and to understand how they are usually computed. To clarify the similarities and distinctions between the

---

[15] For a synthesis and review of work on the relative merits of DRCs and ERPs, see Bhagwati and Srinivasan (1978) and references therein.

two sets of measures, we examine them in the context of the CGE model used in this chapter.

We start with domestic resource costs and examine how they emerge from the model. Net prices per unit of output (inclusive of indirect taxes) are exhausted by total factor payments. Because domestic and foreign goods are imperfect substitutes, the resulting marginal cost pricing equations ensure that, in equilibrium, the vector of domestic prices satisfies the following equality:

$$PD = (I - A^T \hat{d})^{-1}(\hat{w}l + \hat{q}k) + \hat{td}PD \qquad \text{Part1}$$
$$+ (I - A^T \hat{d})^{-1} (A^T \hat{dm})PM \qquad \text{Part2} \quad (8.3.1)$$

where

I = identity matrix
T = superscript indicating a transpose
$\hat{}$ = a diagonal matrix
A = matrix of composite good input–output coefficients with elements (a_{ji})
d = vector of domestic to composite good ratios with elements
$$d_i = \frac{D_i}{Q_i}$$
m = the vector of import to domestic good ratios with elements
$$m_i = \frac{M_i}{D_i}$$
td = vector of indirect taxes on output
l, k = vectors of labor and capital to output ratios

From (8.3.1), the cost of producing a unit of output in each sector can be broken down into two components: (1) a domestic component (Part 1) that reflects the direct and indirect labor and capital costs of producing the commodities that enter as intermediate inputs into the production of a unit of output of that sector augmented by the indirect tax and (2) a foreign component (Part 2) that reflects the direct and indirect import-related costs associated with producing a unit of output of that sector. This decomposition can be made even clearer if we further note that $A^T \hat{d}$ is the transpose matrix of domestic input–output coefficients, $A^T \hat{dm}$ is the transpose matrix of import coefficients with elements (m_{ji}), and $R^T = (I - A^T \hat{d})^{-1}$. Then

$$PD = R^T(\hat{w}l + \hat{q}k) + \hat{td}PD + R^T A^T \hat{dm} PM \qquad (8.3.2)$$

For each sector i,

$$PD_i = \sum_j r_{ji}w_jl_j + \sum_j r_{ji}q_jk_j + td_iPD_i$$

$$+ \left(\sum_j r_{ji}m_{ji}\right)\overline{PW}_j(1 + tm_j)ER \quad (8.3.3)$$

where r_{ji} and m_{ji} are the elements of the matrices R and $A^T{}_{dm}$.

We can now state the equilibrium conditions that hold under cost minimization. A producer in sector i must be indifferent between selling a marginal unit on the domestic market or exporting it. As a buyer, the producer must equate the marginal products of domestic and foreign goods in producing composite commodities. If a unit produced in sector i is exported, it will earn $PWE_i (1 + te_i)ER$ in domestic currency units. Equating the net return with the net cost of production yields

$$[PWE_i(1 - td_i)(1 + te_i)$$

$$- \sum_j r_{ji}m_{ji}\overline{PW}_j(1 + tm_j)]ER = \sum_j r_{ji}(w_il_i + q_ik_i) \quad (8.3.4)$$

Users of domestic and foreign commodities equate the marginal rates of substitution to the price ratios, which implies that

$$\frac{dM_i}{dD_i} = \frac{(1 - \delta_i)}{\delta_i}(m_i)^{(1+\rho_i)} = \frac{PD_i}{PM_i} \quad (8.3.5)$$

Substituting the expression for PD_i from (8.3.3) yields

$$\left[\frac{(1 - \delta_i)}{\delta_i}M_i^{(1+\rho_i)}\overline{PW}_i(1 + tm_i)(1 - td_i) - \sum_j r_{ji}m_{ji}\overline{PW}_j(1 + tm_j)\right]ER$$

$$= \sum_j r_{ji}(w_il_i + q_ik_i) \quad (8.3.6)$$

Of course, the marginal conditions required for the equilibrium to be efficient are satisfied only if wages for identical categories of labor are the same across sectors (i.e., there are no wage differentials) and there are no trade or output taxes.[16]

In the presence of distortions, there is a deviation between private and social profitability. For project evaluation, one wishes to compare the social opportunity costs of production with the social benefits from a project. The issue then is to determine what are the prices that represent

[16] See the discussion in Chapter 6.

social costs and benefits. Suppose that we are considering future projects in the economy and that the present set of tariffs, subsidies, indirect tax rates, and differential factor rewards are to remain in effect. Then the equilibrium (i.e., market-clearing) value of the exchange rate that satisfies (8.3.4) and (8.3.6) represents the opportunity cost of foreign exchange. The net social benefits from exporting or import substituting are given by the net earnings or savings in terms of foreign exchange. This approach leads to the DRC criterion, namely, that a project in sector i should be accepted only if the domestic resource costs per unit of foreign exchange earned (or saved) do not exceed the value of the equilibrium exchange rate. For an import-substituting activity the criterion is $DRC_i^m \leq ER$, and for an export activity it is $DRC_i^e \leq ER$, where

$$DRC_i^m \equiv \frac{\sum r_{ji}(w_j l_j + q_j k_j)}{[(1 - \delta_i)/\delta_i]\, m_i^{(1 + \rho_i)}\, \overline{PW}_i - \sum_j r_{ji} m_{ji} \overline{PW}_j} \qquad (8.3.7)$$

and

$$DRC_i^e \equiv \frac{\sum r_{ji}(w_j l_j + q_j k_j)}{PWE_i - \sum_j r_{ji} m_{ji} \overline{PW}_j} \qquad (8.3.8)$$

Now, the condition for $DRC_i^m = DRC_i^e$ is that $te_i = tm_i$.[17] Similarly, for DRCs to be equated across sectors requires in addition that wages and indirect taxes be equal across sectors, $td_i = td_j$ and $w_i = w_j$.

Expressions (8.3.7) and (8.3.8) can also be used to show the relationship between ERPs and DRCs. Note that, as stated, DRC_i^e and DRC_i^m are defined as the ratio of value added at domestic prices to value added expressed in foreign currency prices. From the definition of the

---

[17] To see this, note that the condition requires the first terms in the denominator to be equal. Because $dM_i/dD_i = PD_i/PM_i$ and $PD_i = PE_i$, the condition is

$$PWE_i ER = \frac{PWE_i(1 + te_i)ER}{\overline{PW}_i(1 + tm_i)ER} \cdot \overline{PW}_i ER$$

which holds only if $te_i = tm_i$. Note also that in the case of rationing discussed in Chapter 9, even if $te_i = tm_i$, $DRC_i^e \neq DRC_i^m$ because $dm_i/dD_i \neq PD_i/PM_i$. A similar situation occurs if there are export supply constraints, because $PE_i \neq PD_i$.

ERP, it is clear that, so long as the prices at which domestic resources are valued are market prices, the two measures are related to each other, and

$$ERP_i^d = 1 + DRC_i^m \qquad ERP_i^e = 1 + DRC_i^e \qquad (8.3.9)$$

where superscripts d and e indicate that effective protection is for domestic and export sales, respectively.[18]

8.4   Analyzing across-the-board changes in trade taxes

Just as DRCs are the appropriate criteria for project evaluation because they are based on shadow prices, ERPs are useful as indicators of resource pulls resulting from changes in trade taxes because they rely on market prices. In Section 8.2 we saw how trade policy affects resource allocation when general equilibrium repercussions can be safely neglected. It is natural to push the investigation one step further and see how the economy responds to across-the-board changes in tariffs and subsidies. Such an examination is useful for several reasons. First, it brings out the importance of general equilibrium repercussions of policy packages. One can explore the extent to which estimates based on partial equilibrium analysis are likely to be misleading when there are substantial changes in trade policy. Second, simultaneous equal changes in tariffs and/or subsidies across the board are similar to an adjustment in the exchange rate, so we are preparing the ground for the analysis of the effects of devaluation on resource allocation to follow in Chapter 9.

Price normalization, ERPs, and product differentiation

The introduction of across-the-board changes in incentives forces us to take into account the exchange-rate adjustment necessary to maintain equilibrium in the balance of trade. As discussed in Chapter 6, the magnitude of the exchange-rate adjustment is linked to the selection of the normalization rule. The price-normalization rule is given by

$$\sum_i P_i \Omega_i = \overline{P} \qquad (8.4.1)$$

which amounts to fixing an aggregate price index of composite goods.

---

[18] We shall present an example of the use of DRCs in Chapter 10.

This normalization implies that a weighted sum of changes in composite good prices must always be zero. More precisely,

$$\sum_i \delta_i \hat{P}_i = 0 \qquad \sum_i \delta_i = 1 \qquad\qquad (8.4.2)$$

where $\delta_i = (\Omega_i P_i)/\bar{P}$ and Ω_i are the weights in the aggregate price index. An across-the-board tariff resulting in an increase in composite good prices must lead to a fall in the price of domestic goods. The reasoning is parallel to that followed earlier when there was perfect substitution, except that we are now referring to domestic goods instead of nontraded goods.

Start first with across-the-board subsidies, holding tariffs constant. Combining (8.2.7) and (8.4.2) provides an expression for the relationship that must hold between changes in domestic prices and the exchange rate so as to satisfy the normalization rule:

$$\hat{ER} = -\frac{\sum_i (1 - \theta_{im})\delta_i \hat{PD}_i}{\sum_i \delta_i \theta_{im}} \qquad\qquad (8.4.3)$$

Assuming that the share of domestic goods in total expenditures can be approximately taken to be fixed, the larger the policy-induced change in domestic prices, the larger will be the necessary adjustment in the exchange rate. Thus, an across-the-board subsidy will raise domestic prices, which in turn will lead to a fall in the value of the exchange rate.

For the case of an across-the-board change in tariffs, or in the case of simultaneous changes in tariffs and subsidies, the normalization rule requires that

$$\hat{ER} = \frac{\sum_i \delta_i(1 - \theta_{im})\hat{PD}_i + \sum_i \delta_i \theta_{im}\lambda_{im}\hat{tm}_i}{\sum_i \delta_i \theta_{im}} \qquad\qquad (8.4.4)$$

which states that a weighted sum of tariff changes must be equal to a weighted combination of changes in domestic prices and the exchange rate.[19] Unless the change in export subsidies is much greater than the change in import tariffs, the major effect on the exchange-rate adjust-

---

[19] The role of exchange rate changes in shifting the relative price between domestic goods on the one hand and imports and exports on the other, so as to eliminate trade imbalances, is explained in Chapter 6. The parameter λ is defined by Eq. (7.5.17).

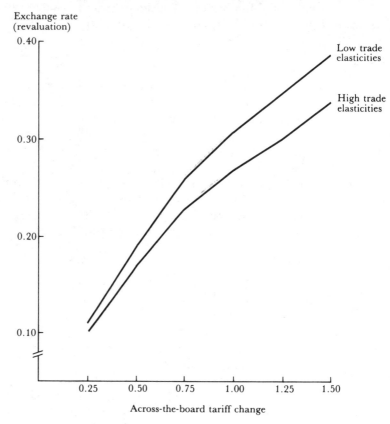

Figure 8.1. Exchange-rate elasticity to tariff changes.

ment will be the second term in the numerator of (8.4.4), which is the weighted sum of tariff changes. Again, the larger the increase in tariffs, the greater the accompanying exchange-rate adjustment.

To get a sense of the magnitude of the exchange-rate adjustment to a change in trade policy for the normalization rule adopted in the model, Figure 8.1 plots the percentage revaluation that occurs for a set of across-the-board tariff rates ranging from 25 to 150 percent. The two lines correspond to the adjustment under the set of high and low trade elasticities provided in Table 8.2.

Several points emerge from Figure 8.1. First, of course, it confirms the prediction of Eq. (8.4.4), namely, that the elasticity of the exchange rate with respect to changes in tariffs is positive. Second, it shows that the elasticity falls as the tariff increases, which is due to the convex shape of the export demand curves and of the iso-level curves between domestic and imported goods. In both cases, the quantity response to price changes becomes small as one approaches the axes; that is, it becomes more and more difficult to substitute domestic goods for imported ones, and to increase exports.

In addition, Figure 8.1 shows that, for a given change in tariffs, the exchange response is greater the lower are the trade elasticities. Thus, for instance, the revaluation associated with a set of 50 percent across-the-board tariffs, increases from 15 percent to 21 percent as one moves from the high set to the low set of trade elasticities. This is so because the rise in domestic prices needed to reduce exports (in order to eliminate the balance-of-trade surplus) is greater the lower the export elasticity of demand. Another way of looking at it is to note that as export-demand and trade-substitution elasticities tend to infinity, the economy becomes "small" both on the export side and on the import side. In this case, as discussed in Chapter 6, in the absence of nontraded goods, Walras's law always implies balance-of-trade equilibrium independently of relative prices in the world (and therefore domestic) markets. Thus the exchange-rate adjustment tends to zero as trade elasticities increase.

In addition to the exchange-rate adjustment, with the simultaneous change of incentives across sectors the domestic price change is no longer a guide to the extent of protection accorded to a sector. To measure the effects of changes in trade policy on resource allocation, it is necessary to consider ERPs that express the protection to value added accorded by a change in trade taxes. The effective rate of protection to a sector is defined as

$$ERP_i \equiv \frac{PN_i^1}{PN_i^0} - 1 \tag{8.4.5}$$

where PN_i^1 and PN_i^0 are the value added in that sector before and after the change in trade policy. To simplify the notation, assume that units are defined so that prices are equal to unity in the reference free-trade solution. Then $PN_i = 1 - \Sigma_j\, a_{ji}$ and the effective rate of protection (ERP) is given by

$$ERP_i = \frac{\hat{PD}_i - \sum_j a_{ji}\hat{P}_j}{1 - \sum_j a_{ji}} \tag{8.4.6}$$

It is desirable to relate the ERP directly to the change in trade policy, which can be done by substituting (8.2.6) into (8.4.6). Then the expression for the ERP reduces to

$$ERP_i = \frac{\hat{PD}_i - \sum_j a_{ji}[\theta_{jm}\lambda_{jm}tm_j + (1 - \theta_{jm})\hat{PD}_j]}{1 - \sum_j a_{ji}} \tag{8.4.7}$$

It is evident that, in the presence of product differentiation, an across-the-board change in tariff structure will not lead to a proportional change in value added across sectors unless changes in both tariff rates and domestic prices are identical across sectors ($\hat{tm}_j = \hat{PD}_j$ for all j). But we know that, with a few notable exceptions, the changes in domestic prices resulting from single changes in tariffs are not very large (especially when they are weighted by the share of domestic goods). Therefore, we may neglect the second term in brackets in Eq. (8.4.7).[20] It then becomes clear that the sectors that have a lower ERP when there is an equal across-the-board change in tariffs are those sectors for which the share of imported intermediate inputs ($\sum_j a_{ji}\theta_{jm}$) is high. Those are the sectors that are classified as import dependent [see Table 8.1, column (6)]. Therefore, other things being equal, the sectors that will suffer most from a uniform across-the-board tariff are those sectors that are most import dependent. In the spirit of the traditional measure of effective protection, the presence of tariffs on imported intermediate inputs lowers the ERP accorded to a sector.

Resource shifts: partial versus general equilibrium analysis

What, then, are the differences in impact on resource allocation between single tariff and subsidy changes and "equivalent" across-the-board changes in tariffs and subsidies? Can one at least expect that the rank-

---

[20] Note that if domestic and foreign goods were perfect substitutes, equal tariffs would lead to equal ERPs because, given that $tm_i = tm_j$ for all i and all j and $\hat{PM}_i = \hat{tm}_i\lambda_i$, it would always be true that

$$ERP_i = \frac{tm_i - \sum_j a_{ji}tm_j}{1 - \sum_j a_{ji}} = \frac{tm_i - tm_i\left(\sum_j a_{ji}\right)}{1 - \sum_j a_{ji}} = tm_i$$

In this expression it is assumed that all goods are traded and that the small-country assumption holds for both imports and exports.

ing of output changes in the one-by-one cases is maintained when all sectors receive protection simultaneously? To answer this question, two experiments have been selected for contrast with the one-by-one results reported in Section 8.2. Both experiments are conducted with a set of high trade elasticities. The first experiment (A-1) consists of providing a set of uniform across-the-board tariffs that result in an increase in the domestic currency price of imports of 50 percent. Given the accompanying exchange-rate revaluation, this requires that tariffs be set equal to 110 percent for all sectors. Therefore, this experiment results in the same increase in the domestic currency price of imports as in the one-by-one case discussed earlier when the tariff was set equal to 50 percent and the exchange-rate adjustment was negligible. The other experiment (A-2) consists of providing a set of 50 percent across-the-board subsidies to exports. It, too, is designed to be compared with the corresponding one-by-one export subsidy discussed earlier, although one cannot easily design an experiment that results in the same effect on the foreign currency price of exports because this depends on the value of domestic prices, which cannot be determined before the experiment.

Start with Experiment A-1. It increases the domestic currency price of imports by 50 percent, which leads to a fall in the aggregate volume of imports. On the export side, matters are somewhat more complicated because the foreign currency price of exports – unlike that of imports – is not fixed. Indeed, the percentage change in the foreign currency price for sector i's exports is given by

$$P\hat{W}E_i = -\lambda_{ie}\hat{te}_i - \hat{ER} + \hat{PD}_i \tag{8.4.8}$$

Therefore, the foreign currency price of exports will rise by the extent of exchange-rate revaluation adjusted for any change in domestic prices. Thus, the foreign terms of trade, which is an export-share weighted-average change in sectoral foreign currency prices, rises by 16 percent in Experiment A-1.

Whereas an across-the-board tariff improves the terms of trade because exports are restricted, an across-the-board subsidy that encourages exports worsens the terms of trade. Thus, a 50 percent subsidy to exports leads to a 13 percent worsening in the terms of trade in spite of a 12 percent revaluation. This is due to the depressing effect of the subsidy on the export price represented by the first terms on the right-hand side of (8.4.8), which states that a 50 percent subsidy lowers the export price by roughly 33 percent. These results, which indicate that the export response to a change in export subsidies is greater than the import response to a change in tariffs, confirm the one-by-one results reported in Section 8.2.

The macroeconomic effects just described are substantial. Indeed, they may be expected to have an impact on economic structure. It is precisely because these effects are quantitatively significant that the model was kept as simple as possible so as to make the task of comparing single changes in trade policy with across-the-board changes easier. What, then, are the new dimensions resulting from moving from a policy that raises the domestic currency price of imports of, say, transportation equipment by 50 percent to a policy that raises the domestic currency price of imports in all sectors by 50 percent?

On aggregation grounds alone, one would expect that the resource shifts would be smaller when there is an across-the-board change in trade policy because of the dampening impact of cross-effects in production and demand (see Jones and Berglas, 1977). For instance, we saw in the one-by-one subsidy case that all sectors would expand. Clearly this cannot be the case when all sectors receive export subsidies simultaneously. Indeed, some sectors have to contract to release resources to be used in the expanding sectors, and it is even possible that some other sectors will expand more when there is an across-the-board change in tariffs or subsidies.

Table 8.5 ranks sectors for single changes in trade policy and for across-the-board changes in trade policy. In each column, the sectors are ranked by the percentage change in sectoral output from the level reached in the base solution. For example, domestic output in the transportation equipment sector expands by 4.2 percent when the domestic currency price of imports of transportation equipment increases by 50 percent, the domestic currency price of all other imports being held constant. When the domestic currency price of all imports rises by 50 percent (i.e., when there is a 110 percent tariff across the board), the output expansion in the transportation equipment sector is only 2.0 percent.

In the across-the-board tariff experiment, despite cross-substitution effects in supply and demand, the four or five sectors that expand the most gain almost as much as in the case of single tariff changes. This is so because the economy-wide change in tariff structure improves the terms of trade by 16 percent. On the other hand, an across-the-board change in export subsidies leads to a deterioration in the terms of trade of 13 percent. The resulting decline in disposable income accounts for the fact that in this case the sectors that expand the most expand much less than when subsidies are granted on a one-by-one basis. However, such income effects cannot explain why there is a substantial change in the rankings among sectors (indicated by the criss-crossing of lines joining sectors in the two sets of experiments) because income elasticities of demand are unity for all sectors. Moreover, the change in rankings is

Table 8.5. *Comparison of rankings of output responses to changes in tariffs and subsidies*

Tariff rankings

Sector	50% tariff (one-by-one) Output change (%)	50% tariff Sector no.	110% tariff (across-the-board) Sector no.	110% tariff Output change (%)
Basic metals	6.4	12	12	6.4
Transportation equipment	4.2	16	7	3.4
Rubber and plastics	3.1	9	19	3.4
Electrical machinery	2.8	15	16	2.0
Mining	2.7	2	8	1.7
Chemicals	2.6	8	10	0.2
Paper and printing	2.1	7	1	0.0
Textiles	1.9	4	6	−0.5
Metal products	1.9	13	2	−0.7
Nonmetallic mineral products	1.4	11	14	−0.9
Construction	1.3	1	17	−1.0
Nonelectrical machinery	1.0	14	9	−2.7
Clothing	0.3	5	15	−2.8
Wood products	0.2	6	18	−3.4
Petroleum products	0.1	10	11	−4.5
Food	0.0	3	3	−4.9
Agriculture	−0.1	17	5	−5.1
Infrastructure		18	13	−7.8
Services	−0.4	19	4	−14.8

Subsidy rankings

Sector	50% subsidy (one-by-one) Output change (%)	50% subsidy Sector no.	110% subsidy (across-the-board) Sector no.	110% subsidy Output change (%)
Textiles	48.6	4	4	23.6
Food	17.9	3	3	9.5
Nonmetallic mineral products	14.9	11	11	3.2
Clothing	13.6	5	5	2.2
Mining	12.8	2	13	2.2
Basic metals	11.9	12	9	1.4
Rubber and plastic	10.3	9	18	1.4
Metal products	9.6	13	12	0.9
Chemicals	5.3	8	6	0.5
Nonelectrical machinery	4.5	14	2	0.4
Paper and printing	4.3	7	8	0.2
Infrastructure	3.8	18	1	0.0
Wood products	2.8	6	10	−0.6
Services	2.8	19	14	−1.5
Electrical machinery	2.0	15	7	−2.0
Transportation equipment	1.2	16	15	−2.4
Petroleum products	0.7	10	19	−2.5
Construction		1	17	−4.0
Agriculture	0.0	17	16	−4.3

Notes: Sectors are ranked by the percentage change in output from the base solution.

not due to a redistribution of income between the private and public sectors caused by the collection and disbursement of trade taxes, because these have been carefully neutralized by lump-sum transfers.

Consider the comparison of rankings for the case of tariff changes. Agriculture (sector 1) is not included because it has by assumption a zero elasticity of supply to net price changes, because both capital stock and labor are fixed. Also note that construction (sector 17), which is a pure nontraded sector, does not figure in the one-by-one experiments because there cannot be a direct tariff or subsidy on a nontraded sector. It appears in the across-the-board experiments and with a contraction in output as one would expect, because across-the-board tariffs raise the price of traded sectors vis-à-vis nontraded ones and result in shifts of resources toward the more tradable sectors. However, this is not the case for some of the other less tradable sectors such as clothing, wood, and services (sectors 5, 6, and 19). All three of these sectors not only improve their ranking but also expand absolutely more when there is an across-the-board tariff. The reason is that all of them are among the least import-dependent sectors in the economy, which means that they enjoy relatively high ERPs. Import-dependent sectors such as rubber, metal products, and electrical machinery (sectors 9, 13, and 15) suffer from the increased purchasing costs of imported inputs. As a consequence, they have low ERPs, and their relative ranking deteriorates. Finally, some of the more export-oriented sectors such as textiles (sector 4) experience a large decrease in output because of the revaluation, which lowers export demand. The same applies for food (sector 3), although its ranking does not change.[21]

Similar effects are evident in a comparison of the rankings of single export subsidies with those of across-the-board export subsidies. However, the change in rankings is less pronounced because the effects on the export side are more direct than on the import side. The correlation coefficient for the tariff experiments is 0.28 compared to 0.95 for the export subsidy experiments. The cross-effects are not so strong on the export side because the pattern of increase in composite good prices shows much less variation than in the case of changes in tariffs [see Table 8.4, columns (3) and (4)].

---

[21] One could, of course, compare the predictive ability of ERP-based partial equilibrium estimates with those obtained from the full general equilibrium model. For such a comparison in a more disaggregated model where domestic and foreign goods are perfect substitutes, see de Melo (1980).

8.5 Conclusion

The mechanisms whereby a change in policy ultimately affects resource allocation are complicated. In particular, the extent to which policy makers can expect to confer protection to domestic production by means of traditional instruments such as tariffs and subsidies is likely to depend crucially on certain characteristics such as export-demand and trade-substitution elasticities, market shares of imported goods and exports, as well as the more conventional sectoral elasticities of supply and demand.

In addition to its usefulness as a tool for quantifying the effects of changes in policy on resource allocation, a CGE model can also provide a framework for dialogue between macro planners and sector specialists. Here its strength is twofold: First, it provides a set of shadow prices for domestic inputs and foreign exchange; second, and more important, it is particularly well suited for investment analysis in the second-best environment characteristic of virtually all developing countries. It should be clear that the practical relevance of shadow prices for project evaluation is closely linked to the characteristics of the model that generates them, in particular, its ability to capture the institutional constraints facing policy makers in product and factor markets.

CHAPTER 9

Foreign exchange shortages and adjustment policies

9.1 Introduction

The thrust of Chapter 8 was an exploration of the effects of trade taxes and subsidies on resource allocation. It was also made clear that to any particular set of trade taxes corresponds an "equilibrium"exchange rate such that the demand for foreign exchange equals the supply of foreign exchange at that exchange rate. With this kind of flexible exchange rate, a foreign payments imbalance cannot arise. Just as commodity prices are allowed to clear commodity markets, the exchange rate is allowed to clear the foreign exchange market. In a flexible exchange-rate model, it is not really possible to consider a "foreign exchange gap" or a "binding" foreign exchange constraint. Foreign exchange is a resource like any other, and it is, of course, better to have more of it rather than less. In that sense, there is always a foreign exchange "constraint." But with a flexible exchange rate the demand for foreign exchange always equals its supply.

However, acute foreign exchange shortages have been a recurring problem for many developing countries. In the development planning literature, the problem has been discussed within the framework of the "two-gap" or "multigap" models developed and elaborated during the 1960s. These models assume fixed import–output coefficients and limited possibilities for export expansion. As a result, a foreign exchange shortage becomes an almost absolute constraint on growth in the sense that even if domestic savings were available in sufficient amounts to allow an increase in investment, the absence of the required complementary foreign exchange makes such an increase impossible. The neoclassical answer to this "structuralist" view has always been to stress the role of relative prices and, in particular, exchange-rate adjustment as a means of overcoming any foreign exchange shortage. Stated simply, this view amounts to treating the alleged foreign exchange gap as reflecting an overvalued real exchange rate. If the exchange rate were allowed to clear the foreign exchange market, there would be no foreign exchange gap.

The experience of developing countries, however, indicates that it is extremely difficult to achieve the necessary rise in the effective exchange

288

rate to restore equilibrium in the foreign exchange market. As Krueger (1978) has documented for a group of developing countries, the typical pattern of adjustment policies often involves an unsuccessful devaluation followed by a return to various forms of foreign exchange rationing. The reasons why devaluations are often unsuccessful are myriad and much discussed in the literature (see Krueger, 1978; Bruno, 1979; Diaz-Alejandro et al., 1979), but the main point we wish to pursue in this chapter is that countries often rely on other policies whose quantitative impacts need to be systematically explored. In understanding different adjustment mechanisms, all students of trade and exchange-rate policy in developing countries agree that the elimination of persistent foreign exchange imbalances requires substantial adjustments in the real sphere of the economy. Macroeconomic phenomena may be important, but there must also be a reallocation of resources toward sectors where there is scope for import substitution and/or where exports can be expanded. The relationship between different policy regimes and these necessary structural adjustments provides the major focus of our analysis.

The policy regimes or adjustment mechanisms we consider include import rationing and exchange-rate adjustment. These are explained and contrasted with one another in Section 9.2, with numerical results reported in Section 9.3. The model and data base used are the same as those described in Chapter 8, although the reference solutions are slightly different. To provide continuity with the analysis carried out in the last chapter, the same set of trade elasticities are carried over to the quantitative analysis in this chapter. This selection of elasticities allows us to reexamine the issue of the foreign exchange gap and to bring out the adjustment implications of foreign exchange shortages under both "structuralist" and "neoclassical" views of the world.

Whereas Chapter 8 focused mostly on microeconomic aspects, this chapter is oriented more toward the macroeconomic implications and welfare effects of different adjustment mechanisms or policies. Therefore the effects on economic structure of the different adjustment mechanisms are reported at a more aggregated level, with the manufacturing sector broken down into consumer goods, intermediate goods, and capital goods.

In Section 9.2 we describe the simplest forms of the various adjustment mechanisms, including two import-rationing schemes. Realistically, such policies are likely to have various side effects that should also be considered. For example, in an economy characterized by acute rationing, resources are likely to be diverted away from productive uses toward activities pursuing the rents associated with rationing. Section 9.4 discusses an approach to incorporating such effects in a CGE model.

We have also argued in Chapter 7 that the standard treatment of exports, where the supply of exports is defined as the difference between sectoral production and domestic use, is likely to lead to an overestimation of export response to export price changes in a fairly aggregated model. This was confirmed by the experiments reported in Chapter 8. Accordingly, in Section 9.5 we consider the alternative specification proposed in Chapter 7, namely, to use a logistic function for export supply to provide a more realistic specification of the export supply response to trade policy measures.

Finally, Section 9.6 goes into a detailed examination of the welfare implications of the different adjustment mechanisms considered in the chapter. That section brings together in a summary fashion the welfare loss caused by the shortfall of foreign exchange under each of the adjustment mechanisms. These losses are further decomposed by considering the share of each of the components (foreign resource, terms of trade, trade distortions, and net production) that account for the total loss in welfare. This procedure is an application of the decomposition methodology developed in Chapter 7. Conclusions about the policy implications of foreign exchange shortages in a developing economy close the chapter.

9.2   Exchange-rate flexibility and import rationing

Until recently, most developing (as well as developed) countries kept fixed exchange rates that were periodically adjusted only in the face of major imbalances. Despite a widespread movement toward a regime of more continuous adjustments in exchange rates, many countries still keep fixed exchange rates. We shall therefore discuss the role of different exchange-rate regimes in a general equilibrium model and, in particular, the different ways the economy can adjust to foreign exchange imbalances when the exchange rate is fixed.

To explore the role of exchange-rate policy and other adjustment mechanisms and to relate our discussion to the literature on foreign exchange "gaps" in development, it is useful to assume a sudden shortfall in the "normal" flow of foreign resources to which a country is accustomed. Let us, for example, assume that, as a result of a political realignment, a country no longer receives a flow of grant aid to which it was accustomed. If prices were to remain constant, there would be an excess demand for foreign exchange, because at given prices and exchange rates, the supply of foreign exchange inclusive of foreign aid was just equal to demand. Eliminating aid will disturb this equality and create a need for adjustment. Note that there are many other reasons why a country may find itself facing a foreign exchange "crisis." It may have pursued inflationary fiscal and monetary policies resulting in domestic price rises well above world inflation, which will result in an appreciation of the real exchange rate leading to excess demand for foreign exchange. The resulting balance-of-payments deficit may be temporarily financed by running down reserves or borrowing on international money markets. When these sources are exhausted, the country faces a foreign exchange crisis and will, in one way or another, have to adjust to it.

Alternatively, the sudden shortage of foreign exchange may be caused by exogenous changes in the country's terms of trade: declines in its export prices or increases in its import prices as a result of changed conditions on international markets. But a crisis induced by a price change – such as OPEC's oil price increase – is different from one that appears in the form of an exogenous shortfall of net foreign resources. In the latter case, the process of adjustment involves changes in the structure of relative prices as a consequence of the foreign exchange crisis, whereas in the former, it is relative price changes that are the cause rather than the consequence of the crisis. We shall therefore concentrate on analyzing a foreign exchange shortage caused by an exogenous decline in the "normal" flow of foreign resources. Changes in relative domestic prices and/or the terms of trade will be induced changes that are part of the adjustment mechanism.

Faced with a sudden shortage of foreign exchange, a country may let its exchange rate float until the excess demand for foreign exchange disappears. This is what would happen if we exogenously changed $\bar{F}$ in the open-economy model discussed in Chapter 6. The nominal exchange rate ER would rise endogenously until equilibrium is restored. Given our normalization requiring a constant overall price level, the prices of the less tradable commodities would have to fall, allowing the real exchange rate to change and inducing a new structure of production and consumption that corresponds to the new, diminished, availability of foreign resources.

A country may not, in fact, allow this exchange-rate adjustment to proceed. It may instead keep its exchange rate fixed and attempt to adjust in different ways. If the country can borrow on international money markets, it can replace the lost flow of foreign resources by borrowed funds and, at least in the short run, the need for adjustment would disappear. Let us therefore rule out this possibility. Not being able to borrow and not willing to devalue, a country may decide to *ration* foreign exchange expenditures. Rationing is a very common reaction to a shortage and has characterized many crisis situations. It thus deserves careful analysis as an alternative to exchange-rate adjustment. Why have many countries preferred massive import rationing to exchange-rate adjustment? How can one model import rationing at fixed exchange rates in a CGE model? These issues will be explored.

Although less prevalent than in the 1960s, trade regimes based on exchange control and some degree of overall import rationing characterize many developing countries. We are not referring here to specific quotas designed for specific sectors, although these also abound, but to restrictive licensing and general import rationing as a mechanism to manage the balance of payments. Although there was a movement away from extremely restrictive import regimes in the 1970s, it is interesting to note that even a country as "outward looking" as Brazil used a comprehensive system of "import denials" as part of its response to the oil price increase and ensuing trade imbalance.

What happens when imports are rationed? There is no general answer to this question, because what happens to prices, incentives, and resource allocation under rationing depends crucially on the exact form of the rationing scheme and on the legal and/or extralegal methods of adjusting to rationing. We shall distinguish two extreme cases: fixprice rationing and premium rationing. Let us first define fixprice rationing.

Recall the demand for import equations when imports and domestic goods are treated as imperfect substitutes. Consumers and producers demand the composite commodity Q_i that is a CES aggregation of imports and domestically produced goods. In the absence of rationing, the first-order conditions yield import demand functions of the form

$$ M_i^* = \delta_i^{\sigma_i} \left(\frac{P_i}{PM_i} \right)^{\sigma_i} \gamma_i^{\sigma_i \rho_i} Q_i \tag{9.2.1} $$

where P_i is the price of the composite commodity and M_i^* denotes *desired* imports. The sum of desired imports in dollars is given by

$$ \sum_{i=1}^{n} \overline{PW}_i \cdot M_i^* \tag{9.2.2} $$

With a fixed exchange rate, there is nothing that guarantees that this sum is equal to the sum of export earnings and net foreign resource inflows. Usually what is assumed in fixed-exchange-rate models is that changes in foreign exchange reserves or additional short-term borrowing make up any excess of desired expenditure over foreign exchange earnings. But we assume that the country can no longer find additional funds and has run out of reserves. Therefore, the trade balance in dollars remains fixed across experiments. For simplicity, assume that it is zero.

Actual realized imports then amount to whatever is allowed by available export revenues. Desired imports, as determined by the customs clearance price (c.i.f. + tariffs) and the usual cost-minimization procedure, may add up to a much larger magnitude than export earnings. A rationing mechanism is then introduced to bring about an ex post equality between receipts and expenditures of foreign exchange.

Let RM denote the ratio of total available foreign exchange, $TFEX$, to total desired imports:

$$RM = \frac{TFEX}{\sum_{i=1}^{n} \overline{PW}_i \cdot M_i^*} \tag{9.2.3}$$

A simple rationing rule is to allocate foreign exchange to the various sectors in proportion to desired imports M_i^*. Actual realized imports are then obtained by multiplying desired imports in each sector by the overall excess demand parameter RM:

$$M_i = M_i^* \cdot RM \tag{9.2.4}$$

The quantity adjustment mechanism we have outlined is clearly a stylized and simplified story. We shall refer to it as "fixprice" rationing to underline the fact that the user price of imports remains fixed in spite of an overall shortage. It is appropriate for countries where imports of producer goods are tied to user specific quotas and licenses, where resale is prohibited, and where consumer goods imports are insignificant. In such countries there is some justification for adopting a stylized model that specifies that realized sectoral imports are proportional to desired sectoral imports and that desired sectoral imports are based on the customs clearance price with the rents due to the restrictive import regime accruing directly to the users of the imported producer goods. What is crucial here is the assumption that the users of imports do not have to pay more than the tariff-inclusive c.i.f. price, so quantity allocations are channeled directly to users without going through some kind of auction or market system. The exchange rate is truly fixed: Except for (fixed) tariffs and export subsidies, both exporters and importers pay ER units of domestic currency for one dollar's worth of imports. They do not get the amount of imports they would like to get. But, for the imports that they do get, they pay only the official exchange rate.

In the fixprice rationing scheme, consumers are forced off their demand curves for imports. It is also true that the price of the composite good in each sector, which reflects the rationed price of imports, will no longer equal the marginal cost of acquiring the composite good. Behaviorally, each demander should solve his or her particular constrained maximization problem, and we can no longer maintain the simple two-stage formulation. In the empirical experiments reported later, we in fact retain the two-stage formulation and assume that consumers remain on their demand function for the composite good given the actual rationed composite good price, even though they are off their demand function for imports. This specification is much simpler and does little damage because empirically the sectors with large import ratios (intermediate and capital goods) are largely demanded in fixed proportions and hence there is little scope for changing demand proportions in response to changes in relative composite prices. If there were major imports of consumer goods, this simplification would be much less justifiable.[1]

Alternatively, it is possible that under rationing a legal or semilegal parallel "green" market develops for the scarce imports, or, more directly, for the scarce foreign exchange. Let us define such a system as rationing by premium. Assume again that the demand for imports exceeds the supply of foreign exchange necessary to buy those imports at a given fixed exchange rate. But, contrary to the case of fixprice rationing, assume that the government tolerates the emergence of a parallel or "free" market for foreign exchange allocations. In that case, those who demand foreign exchange will bid up its price until at the new price demand again equals supply. If PR is the premium rate that emerges in this parallel market and ER is the official exchange rate, the user cost of imports will now be

$$PM_i = \underbrace{\overline{PW_i} \cdot ER}_{} + \underbrace{\overline{PW_i}ER \cdot tm_i}_{} + \underbrace{\overline{PW_i}ER \cdot PR}_{} \qquad (9.2.5)$$

Price of imports in domestic currency	Value of the tariff	Value of the premium due to rationing

or, collecting terms,

$$PM_i = \overline{PW_i}(1 + tm_i + PR)ER \qquad (9.2.6)$$

Viewed in this way, the premium acts as a variable, but sectorally uniform, import surcharge. Under rationing with premium, producers

---

[1] We wish to thank Jean Waelbroeck for helpful discussions on this issue. For further analysis of price rationing, see also Derviş (1979).

adjust by cost minimizing given domestic prices and premium-inclusive import prices. Neglecting distribution effects between the government and the private sector, such a mechanism works as if the exchange rate were flexible on the import side. Desired imports are again equal to actual imports, because the price mechanism has been allowed to adjust the demand of imports to the supply of foreign exchange.

Fixprice rationing and rationing with a uniform premium are two simple, easy-to-understand, but somewhat extreme cases. Reality will usually contain elements of both. Often, for example, the public sector is subject to fixprice rationing while the private sector bids for a residual allocation of foreign exchange. On the whole, fixprice rationing is commonly observed for bulky investment goods imported under user-specific licenses, whereas import premia are the rule for light consumer goods and intermediates. Note that sometimes the state has an import monopoly. The extent to which premia emerge may then depend on the state's distribution network and its capacity to deliver the goods to final users. Finally, it is clear that premia may also emerge on the export side if exporters are allowed to keep part of the foreign exchange they earn. For the moment we assume that this is not the case and that the foreign exchange authorities are successful in preventing exporters from holding on to the dollar revenues of their exports.[2]

9.3 An empirical comparison of devaluation and import rationing

Let us now compare a policy of allowing the exchange rate to adjust to import rationing of the two kinds described earlier as alternative adjustment mechanisms to a foreign exchange crisis taking the form of a shortfall in the flow of foreign resources. In all cases, we continue to assume that the monetary authorities keep the overall price level at an exogenously specified value.

A devaluation or flexible exchange-rate policy simply consists of allowing the exchange rate (i.e., the price of foreign exchange) to float up until equilibrium is restored. Because the overall price level is fixed, this implies that domestic prices must in general fall, behaving in the aggregate like the nontradables of the standard model. In fact, there are no "pure" tradables or nontradables. Instead, as we have discussed, the sectors distinguished in the model can be ranked by degrees of tradability, depending basically on their import shares and the magnitude of some key elasticities. Starting from a position of equilibrium, a deval-

[2] In Chapters 10 and 11 we discuss the effects of letting export premia emerge alongside import premia.

uation induced by a shortfall of foreign exchange will tend to raise the relative price of close import substitutes and exportables and lower the price of essentially nontraded commodities or commodities that behave as import complements. The resulting reallocation of resources will lead to an expansion in the production of exports and import substitutes and a contraction in the production of nontradables and import complements. This reallocation of resources will combine with expenditure switching on the demand side to reestablish equilibrium. Unless one makes the small-country assumption on the export side, there will also be a terms-of-trade effect: For exports to expand, their dollar price must decline. With fixed import prices, this decline leads to a deterioration in the country's foreign terms of trade.

To sum up, the shortfall leads to a "neutral" contraction of the country's consumption and investment possibility frontier due directly to the decline in net foreign resources and to devaluation-induced changes in relative prices leading to a new pattern of production and consumption and a further terms-of-trade-induced reduction in domestic real income. The same result could be achieved by domestic price deflation with a fixed nominal exchange rate. For equilibrium to be restored, the real exchange rate (i.e., the relative price of an aggregate of domestic goods to an aggregate of foreign goods) must fall. Whatever the necessary rate of real devaluation, it can be achieved by many different combinations of changes in the nominal exchange rate and the overall price level. The disequilibrium dynamics may, of course, be very different in each case but, as noted before, such problems are beyond the scope of our discussion.

Consider now the effect of import rationing. Whether premia appear or not, the whole burden of adjustment falls on the import side. Exports do not expand directly as part of the adjustment mechanism. There is therefore no terms-of-trade effect. Dramatic adjustments happen, however, on the import side. First, consider the case with a premium. Because the entire burden of adjustment is on imports, and because trade-substitution elasticities are much lower than export demand elasticities, the magnitude of the premium required to equate the demand and supply of foreign exchange will be much larger than the exchange-rate adjustment required in the flexible exchange-rate case. Premia of 100 percent or more can often emerge. The resource-allocation effects of such premia are similar to the effects of very high uniform tariffs, of the form discussed in Chapter 8. Import substitutes and nontradables benefit at the expense of exportables and import complements. Furthermore, sectors that are very import dependent in their intermediate input requirements suffer from the very high premia.

In contrast with adjustment by devaluation or by premia, adjustment by fixprice rationing falls entirely on domestic prices, because both the exchange rate and the user price of imports are held fixed. With fixprice rationing, the ratio of actual to desired imports falls substantially below unity and, as a consequence, producers are forced into using domestic goods. Because rationing forces users to increase their purchases of domestic goods, the situation is quite different from one where adjustment takes place via premia. In that case, for sectors that are poor substitutes for imports, the increasing premium-inclusive price of imports will not significantly affect import demand and the imports-to-domestic goods ratio in such sectors will fall much less than in sectors with high trade-substitution elasticities. Although demand for the now much more expensive composite commodity may fall, the composition of demand will not change much. There is therefore no great increase in the demand for the imperfect domestic substitutes. On the contrary, the protective effect of fixprice rationing is stronger in sectors with low trade-substitution elasticities. These sectors will expand and will be forced to move up their increasingly steeper supply curves. The large producer surplus so created is equivalent to the premium created in the alternative case, but its sectoral distributional impact is different.

We now turn to a quantitative illustration of the alternative adjustment policies described earlier. Start from an equilibrium position where expenditures on imports are equal to $2,600 million while foreign exchange earnings from exports are $1,400 million so that the foreign resource inflow is $1,200 million. To illustrate the differential impact of alternative adjustment mechanisms, we have carried out the following six experiments, assuming for each experiment an exogenous $600 million decline in net foreign resources:

E-1: Devaluation, low trade elasticities
E-2: Premium rationing, low trade elasticities
E-3: Fixprice rationing, low trade elasticities
E-4: Devaluation, high trade elasticities
E-5: Premium rationing, high trade elasticities
E-6: Fixprice rationing, high trade elasticities

This 50 percent decline in net foreign resource inflow corresponds to 3 percent of GDP. Thus we are dealing with a sizable foreign exchange "crisis."

Macroeconomic effects of alternative adjustment mechanisms

Consider first the basic macroeconomic results reported in Table 9.1. There is a 21.5 percent devaluation when we assume low trade elasticities and a much smaller 8.7 percent devaluation with high trade elas-

Table 9.1. *The macroeconomic impact of alternative adjustment mechanisms (% changes from base run)*

Experiment[a]	Devaluation		Premium rationing		Fixprice rationing	
	Low (E-1)	High (E-4)	Low (E-2)	High (E-4)	Low (E-3)	High (E-5)
Exchange rate	21.5	8.7	0.0	0.0	0.0	0.0
User price of imports[b]	21.5	8.7	71.6	32.0	0.0	0.0
Dollar price of exports[b]	−17.1	−6.6	−2.7	−1.2	−0.7	−0.4
Imports (volume and $ value)	−9.3	−8.2	−19.6	−20.4	−21.5	−22.4
Export (volume)	44.6	37.0	5.6	4.8	0.7	0.9
Exports ($ value)	21.5	27.1	2.7	3.8	0.2	1.0
Nonagricultural wage	−1.1	−0.5	−9.7	−5.0	−2.3	−1.2
GDP	−0.4	−0.3	−1.3	−1.0	−2.4	−1.3

[a]"Low" and "high" refer to the two sets of trade elasticities.
[b]Weighted average, where the weights are the volumes traded.

ticities. Because the values of the high set of elasticities are about three times the values of the low set, the rate of exchange-rate adjustment responds nonlinearly to changes in the values of these parameters in the same way that it does to across-the-board changes in tariffs (see Figure 8.1). Thus, if the response were linear, a tripling of trade elasticities would reduce the extent of devaluation to 7.1 percent instead of the observed 8.7 percent. In a sense there are "diminishing returns" to increases in the values of the trade elasticities. The reduced need for relative price adjustment when elasticities are high is also reflected in the smaller change in import and export prices.

Under either kind of rationing the official exchange rate remains fixed. However, under rationing with premium, the user price of imports rises by 71.6 and 32 percent, respectively, with low and high elasticities. This rise is between three and four times greater than the rise in import prices that occurs with devaluation, reflecting the fact that the entire burden of adjustment has shifted to the import side. Thus imports become much more expensive to domestic users when there is rationing with premium than with devaluation, a fact that is not always appreciated. What this also illustrates is that the "black market" (i.e., the official rate plus the premium) exchange rate should not be taken to be equal to the underlying equilibrium exchange rate. Quite apart from considerations of risk that may stem from the extralegal nature of the black (or parallel) market, the fact that exports do not usually benefit from the parallel market premium implies that the equilibrium exchange rate that would rule if adjustment were permitted on both the import and the export sides must be significantly below the parallel market rate that rules for imports when there is premium rationing.

In the case of fixprice rationing, the user cost of imports is kept constant by forcing users off their demand curves. The necessary reduction in the volume of imports is reached solely by an adjustment in relative domestic prices, leading to a substantial reallocation of resources that will be discussed shortly. From the point of view of the user price of imports, fixprice rationing and premium rationing represent the two extreme cases, with devaluation in between. Fixprice rationing does, in fact, often reflect a desire to avoid any rise in import prices. For instance, public enterprises that may already be in a precarious financial situation may press for some form of fixprice rationing. Who exactly is forced off his demand curve and to what extent may, of course, vary widely from case to case. Our experiments reflect only one possible formula to distribute the burden of adjustment.

The change in the terms of trade is determined entirely by the change in the dollar price of exports. Because the average domestic price level of exports (not reported in Table 9.1) does not change much, changes in the terms of trade are determined almost entirely by changes in the exchange rate. Thus, the decline in the terms of trade is 6.6 percent for devaluation with high elasticities and 17.1 percent with low elasticities, and there is a sizable income effect associated with adjustment by devaluation.

Corresponding to the average change in the user price of imports, there is a change in the volume of imports and exports that is shown in Table 9.1. Not surprisingly, the reduction in the volume of imports is greater when there is no expansion of exports, and it reaches more than 20 percent under fixprice rationing. It is also interesting to note the wide range in the implied aggregate import and export demand elasticities (with respect to the average user price of imports and the average dollar price of exports) under each of the adjustment mechanisms. In the case of a devaluation, the import demand elasticity varies between 0.4 and 0.9, whereas the export demand elasticity varies between 2.6 and 5.6. In the case of premium rationing, the import demand elasticity varies between 0.3 and 0.6, whereas the export demand elasticity varies between 2.1 and 3.9. Finally, in the case of fixprice rationing, the adjustment is due entirely to the changes in domestic prices. Cross-section regression estimates of import and export responses to trade incen-

Table 9.2. *Aggregation scheme*

1. Agriculture	1. Agriculture
2. Consumer goods	3. Food
	4. Textiles
	5. Clothing
	6. Wood and wood products
	7. Paper and printing
3. Intermediate goods	3. Mining
	8. Chemicals
	9. Rubber and plastics
	10. Petroleum and petroleum products
	11. Nonmetallic mineral products
	12. Basic metals
	13. Metal products
4. Capital goods	14. Nonelectrical machinery
	15. Electrical machinery
	16. Transportation equipment
5. Construction	17. Construction
6. Infrastructure and services	18. Infrastructure
	19. Services

tives combining tariffs, subsidies, and exchange-rate adjustments indicate import elasticities of 0.4 and export elasticities of 1.3.[3] It is noteworthy that these estimates stand roughly in the same ratio to each other as our analysis suggests. Indeed, our results indicate that one must be careful when speaking of such aggregate elasticities, because their values are likely to vary widely depending on what is held fixed (and it is not always clear from these statistical estimates which variables are held fixed).

The relative labor intensity of the expanding nonagricultural sectors is indicated by the change in the nonagricultural average wage. In all cases there is a fall in the wage. It is most significant in the case of adjustment by premia, indicating that the import-substituting sectors that are protected by premia are relatively capital intensive.

Finally, note that GDP declines in all three cases. The decline is always greater when elasticities are low (i.e., the economy has more difficulty adapting to a shortfall of foreign exchange). In terms of minimizing GDP changes, devaluation is the best and fixprice rationing the worst adjustment policy. This result reflects the increasing violation of marginal efficiency conditions as we move from devaluation to fixprice

[3] See Balassa and Associates (1981b, chap. 3) for a summary of the evidence.

Table 9.3. *Structure of the economy in the base run (solution with high elasticities)*

	Sectoral shares in total output (%) (1)	Ratio of imports to domestic goods (%) (2)	Ratio of imports to total intermediate inputs (%) (3)	Ratio of exports to total output (%) (4)	Trade substitution elasticities (high) (5)	Export demand elasticities (high) (6)
Agriculture	21.5	1.6	8.4	1.6	6.0	4.0
Consumer goods	17.2	1.5	3.8	10.9	2.0	4.0
Intermediate goods	14.4	26.5	19.5	3.8	1.5	6.0
Capital goods	5.5	56.7	29.6	0.8	0.75	6.0
Construction	6.1	—	15.3	—	—	—
Infrastructure and services	35.3	1.6	8.4	5.0	0.5	4.0

rationing. Premium rationing introduces a gap between the domestic resource costs of exports and import substitutes, whereas fixprice rationing goes further by interfering with the equalization of the marginal productivity of imports across sectors. We shall see in Section 9.6 how one can decompose the welfare losses associated with the declines in GDP reported in Table 9.1.

Structural impact of alternative adjustment mechanisms

We turn now to an examination of how the sectoral composition of output is affected by the different adjustment policies to a foreign exchange crisis. The mechanisms by which sectoral structure is affected are those described at length in Chapter 0, namely, relative gross and net prices. It is therefore possible to simplify the presentation of the results by aggregating the nineteen sectors distinguished so far into six sectors. Table 9.2 indicates the aggregation scheme whereby the nineteen sectors are collapsed into six sectors.

The structure of the economy in the base run prior to the $600 million decline in net foreign resources is given in Table 9.3. That table is an aggregation of the information already provided in Tables 8.1 and 8.2, except that the base-run solution in this chapter is not identical to the base-run solution in Chapter 8 because here we are starting from the trade tax structure that was actually observed in 1973, rather than from a solution without those trade taxes. However, the tax rates were quite low in 1973, so the two base runs are quite similar.

To understand how the structure of the economy is affected by the various adjustment mechanisms, one must keep in mind that, on the one hand, an adjustment via devaluation is neutral in the sense that it affects *both* exports and imports in each sector, whereas, on the other hand, adjustments via premium and fixprice rationing are asymmetric because the foreign currency price of exports is not affected directly as it is by a devaluation. It is therefore important to note the trade orientation of the sectors in the economy as described in Table 9.3.

Consumer goods and, to a lesser extent, services are exportables (i.e., they have a high ratio of exports to domestic supply). Construction is the most nontradable sector, followed by services. Intermediate goods, capital goods, and construction are all import dependent in that they have a high ratio of imported to total intermediate inputs. Sectors characterized by significant shares of imports in total domestic demand can be divided into import substitutes and import complements, depending on the trade-substitution elasticity (see Chapter 8). A sector that will be most strongly protected by a devaluation or premium on imports is one that is an import substitute and is not import dependent. Protection will always attract resources into such a sector. In the six-sector aggregation, the two sectors that have the highest import shares (intermediate and capital goods) are also the most import dependent. Intermediate goods have a higher trade-substitution elasticity and are less import dependent than capital goods, and so should be more protected by a devaluation or import premium. Construction, which is import dependent but nontradable, will be adversely affected by any policy that raises import prices.

Table 9.4 indicates the effects on relative domestic prices and net prices of the three adjustment mechanisms. Adjustment by devaluation raises the relative price of close import substitutes and exportables at the expense of import complements and less tradable sectors. The extent of relative price changes is greater the lower are the set of trade elasticities because, as seen earlier, the exchange-rate adjustment is greater. This is confirmed in columns (1) and (2) of Table 9.4, which indicate that intermediate and consumer goods show the largest relative price increase. What happens to sectoral output is of course determined by the change in relative net prices. The pattern of changes in net prices is in turn determined by the degree of each sector's dependence on imported intermediate inputs. Thus the most import dependent sectors

Table 9.4. The impact of adjustment mechanisms on gross and net prices (% changes from base solution)

| | Devaluation | | | | Premium rationing | | | | Fixprice rationing | | | |
| | Domestic prices | | Net prices | | Domestic prices | | Net prices | | Domestic prices | | Net prices | |
	Low (1)	High (2)	Low (3)	High (4)	Low (5)	High (6)	Low (7)	High (8)	Low (9)	High (10)	Low (11)	High (12)
Agriculture	0.2	−0.1	−0.7	−0.6	−1.6	−1.1	−3.0	−1.9	−4.1	−2.6	−5.5	−3.5
Consumer goods	1.5	0.6	1.2	0.4	−2.9	−1.7	−9.3	−5.0	−2.2	−1.5	−3.3	−2.1
Intermediate goods	5.5	3.4	2.0	2.8	5.0	5.1	−7.2	1.9	12.1	7.5	17.8	12.2
Capital goods	0.7	1.2	−8.2	−2.0	0.1	2.8	−21.9	−5.4	15.9	12.8	21.4	21.2
Construction	0.1	−0.1	−3.2	−1.8	−3.7	−1.9	−11.7	−6.5	−1.0	−0.4	−6.3	−3.4
Infrastructure and services	0.2	0.0	−1.2	−0.7	−6.9	−3.8	−10.0	−5.6	−2.6	−1.7	−4.1	−2.5

(capital goods, intermediate goods, and construction) are the sectors whose relative position deteriorates the most because they are adversely affected by the increase in intermediate input costs caused by the devaluation-induced increase in import costs. Again, the effect is greater for the set of low trade elasticities because of the necessary devaluation to restore equilibrium in the foreign exchange market. Thus, in the end, devaluation draws resources toward the consumer goods and the intermediate goods sectors and away from the rest of the economy.

With adjustment by premium rationing, one would expect the more export-oriented sectors not to fare as well as under adjustment by devaluation, because they do not benefit directly from a lowering of their price expressed in foreign currency units. This is indeed the case, as consumer goods and infrastructure and services, the two most export-oriented sectors, experience a fall in both relative gross and net prices. Because the whole burden of adjustment is borne on the import side when trade elasticities are low, the increase in the user price of imports is so great (71.6 percent in Table 9.1) that net prices fall in all sectors [Table 9.4, column (7)]. However, there is also a 9.7 percent fall in nonagricultural wage costs as a result of the fact that construction is both a large labor-intensive sector and an import-dependent sector. Thus, as the cost of its imported intermediate inputs rise, it releases labor and leads to a fall in the wage rate. Thus, in the final analysis, adjustment by premium rationing leads to a shift of resources toward the more labor-intensive sectors.

We now come to the more difficult case of adjustment by fixprice rationing, which amounts to forcing domestic users to increase their use of domestic goods. The question then is to determine which are the sectors that experience the greatest increase in demand, that is, which are the sectors whose domestic prices increase the most. A useful way of visualizing the resulting adjustment mechanism is to return to the graphical presentation of the determination of the equilibrium domestic price in Section 7.5. In terms of Figure 7.2, fixprice rationing is equivalent to an outward shift of the domestic demand curve in quadrant 1, because it forces users to increase their demand for domestic goods. Note two things about the outward shift of the demand curve. First, the extent of the shift is greater the larger the ratio of imports to domestic goods. From Table 9.3, column (2), it is clear that the dominating shifts are those of the capital goods and the intermediate goods sectors, which have respectively import-to-domestic use ratios of 57 and 27 percent. Second, the slope of the demand curve depends on the trade-substitution elasticity, and the more substitutable domestic goods are for imports the flatter is the demand curve, and, therefore, the smaller the rise in the equilibrium domestic price for a given outward shift of the demand curve.

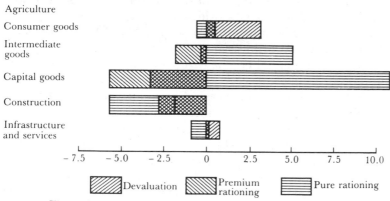

Figure 9.1. Output changes under alternative adjustment mechanisms.

Working through the effects of an outward shift of the demand curve on the equilibrium price (and hence domestic supply), it becomes clear that intermediate goods and especially capital goods are the sectors toward which resources are drawn from the rest of the economy. Moreover, the extent of the increase in the relative price of these two sectors will be greater when trade elasticities are low. Indeed, looking at columns (9) and (10) of Table 9.4 not only confirms this, but also reveals the strikingly strong effect of adjustment by fixprice rationing on the structure of the economy. Thus, for the low (high) elasticity case, the relative price of intermediate goods rises by 12.1 percent (7.5 percent) and the relative price of the capital goods sector by 15.9 percent (12.8 percent).

Perhaps the best way to summarize the impact the different adjustment mechanisms have on sectoral structure is to consider them side by side as in Figure 9.1, which shows the percentage change in each sector's output under each of the adjustment mechanisms. Scanning that figure confirms our result, namely, that premium rationing is a magnification of devaluation as the import-dependent sectors (intermediates, capital goods, and to a lesser extent construction) contract more as a result of the greater increase of imported input prices. Fixprice rationing leads to strong protection of intermediates and capital goods at the expense of the less tradable sectors of the economy.

9.4 Rationing with rent seeking

So far we have analyzed rationing as an adjustment mechanism that works without diverting resources from their normal productive use. Labor and capital in each sector produce output, and the rationing mechanism as such affects output only by the impact it has on relative prices and hence on the economy-wide allocation of resources.

But, as first formally argued by Anne Krueger (1974b) and elaborated by Bhagwati and Srinivasan (1979), rationing is likely to divert resources from their normal productive use into activities necessitated or made profitable by the existence of rationing. Rationing gives rise to special rents, explicitly, as in the case of premium rationing, or implicitly, with fixprice rationing. When there is rationing, it becomes worthwhile to spend real resources in the pursuit of these rents. Labor that might otherwise be used to produce commodities may now be used in activities such as lobbying for quantity allocations, negotiating with government officials, and so on. Part of the existing capital stock may also be used for such activities. Less resources are devoted to the production of commodities and services, and the net production possibility set of the economy will contract as a consequence of this diversion of resources into what Krueger calls "rent seeking." Note that resource diversion may occur as a result of rationing not only because of rent seeking à la Krueger but also because rationing as an allocation mechanism may simply impose unavoidable resource costs. Thus, waiting in gasoline lines is not really a rent-seeking activity but leads to much the same resource diversion as rent seeking. We shall therefore define all such diversions resulting from rationing as rent-seeking activities. The resources diverted from production by rent seeking constitute an additional burden of adjustment through rationing that one should take into account when analyzing alternative adjustment mechanisms.

How much resources will be devoted to rent seeking in any particular situation? One possible answer to this important question is to say that in equilibrium the total value of rents resulting from rationing must equal the total value of resources devoted to rent seeking. This is the position taken by Krueger and elaborated by Bhagwati and Srinivasan (1979). But it is probably an extreme position. It is possible that equilibrium under certain kinds of rationing would not yield large "windfall" rents to anybody. At most, factors "specialized" in rent-seeking activities would see their incomes increase at the expense of other factors. However, when one observes rationed systems in the real world, it is striking how much pure rent appears to be created and how effortlessly some profits seem to be achieved. It is reasonable, therefore, to argue that whereas the magnitude of resource diversion to rent seeking depends on the magnitude of rationing rents, the value of rent-seeking resources is less than the value of these rents. In other words, a certain part of the rents arising from rationing are "pure" rents with no resource costs.

Modeling rent-seeking activities is obviously a very difficult undertaking. What is really needed is some knowledge about the "technology" of rent seeking. Given the absence of such knowledge, we shall use a simplified specification and measure the resource diversion resulting from rent seeking in units of output from each sector. This amounts to assuming that each sector combines factors of production in rent-seeking activities in the same way as it combines them in production. Let PRM_i be the total value of rationing rents in sector i. Let r_i be the ratio of pure rents (i.e., rents that do not require resource diversion) to total rents. Finally, let VR_i be the value of resources diverted to rent seeking in sector i. We postulate the following:

$$VR_i = (1 - r_i)PRM_i \tag{9.4.1}$$

Assuming some particular value for r_i, we can calculate the loss of output resulting from rationing in each sector provided that we can calculate PRM_i, the rationing rents in that sector. When $r_i = 1$, we get the Krueger-Bhagwati-Srinivasan rule that equates the value of rents to the value of resources diverted to rent seeking. With $r_i = 0$, there is no resource cost arising from rent seeking and we are back to where we were before; with $0 < r_i < 1$, we have partial rent seeking as the general case.

Calculating PRM_i is straightforward in the case of rationing with premium. We simply calculate the value of import premia in each import-purchasing sector. Imports purchased by sector i are the sum of consumer goods imports of category i, investment goods imports required in the particular proportions required for aggregate capital, and intermediate goods imports governed by input–output coefficients. Once the volume of imports is calculated, the total "rent" attached to the imports is obtained by multiplying the local currency value of these imports at the official exchange rate by the import premium rate resulting from rationing. This gives us PRM_i. Multiplying it by r_i gives us VR_i, the value of rent-seeking resources or the value of output lost because of rent seeking. Letting U_i denote the ratio of the value of output lost because of rent seeking to the total value of sectoral production, we can rewrite the sectoral production functions in the form

$$X_i = (1 - U_i)f_i(\overline{K}_i, L_i) \tag{9.4.2}$$

where $U_i = VR_i/PD_iX_i$. Note again that if $r_i = 0$, $VR_i = 0$ and $U_i = 0$, so that we are back to the more traditional formulation. For a given r_i, the more the official exchange rate is overvalued, the greater will be the import premium, the greater will be the value of rents, and the greater will be the value of output lost as a result of rent-seeking activities.

The situation is more complicated when there is fixprice rationing. The value of sectoral rents is given by the difference between total expenditure on imports at fixed prices and total expenditure on the same imports priced at their marginal value to users. Given knowledge of the trade aggregation functions, one can compute the marginal value of imports at the rationed solution. The procedure is analogous to computing the value of rents under premium rationing. Given that nothing fundamentally different is involved, we restrict our empirical discussion of rent seeking to the case of premium rationing where the rents are an explicit part of the model solution.

Rent seeking in one form or another does form an integral part of the functioning of rationed markets. Its inclusion in theoretical or applied models is still very new, and little empirical work has been done on understanding the "technology" of rent seeking. On the other hand, it is a very important phenomenon, and an analysis of adjustment with rationing that does not include rent seeking is likely to be misleading.

What, then, are the effects of taking into account rent-seeking activities in the case of adjustment with premium rationing? The macroeconomic impact is mostly reflected in a further fall in GDP resulting from the diversion of resources away from productive uses. Thus, for low trade elasticities, whereas without rent seeking the decline in GDP is 1.3 percent, with rent seeking the decline in GDP becomes 2.9 percent. This of course is a sizable decline if one recalls that the original decline in net foreign resources itself amounted to about 3.0 percent of GDP. For high trade elasticities, adding rent seeking raises the adjustment cost in terms of GDP from 1.0 to 1.8 percent.

In addition to this extra burden of adjustment, rent seeking results in a slightly lower increase in the user price of imports, especially in the case of low trade elasticities. In that case, with rent seeking the user price of imports rises by 61.4 percent instead of 71.6 percent when there is no rent seeking. This a result of the fact that the contractionary effect on output of rent seeking lowers the demand for imports and hence for foreign exchange so that the adjustment of the effective exchange rate is smaller.

Table 9.5 summarizes the net average effect of rent seeking, as well as the distribution of its effects across the economy. For the economy as a whole, for low (high) trade elasticities, premia payments amount to 7.0 percent (3.6 percent) of value added and 4.1 percent (2.1 percent) of total cost. Premia payments as a share of both total cost and value added are highest for the import-dependent sectors, intermediates, and

Table 9.5. *The effect of rent seeking on resource use and production*

	Premia payments as percent of value added		Premia payments as percent of total cost		Output loss due to rent seeking	
	Low	High	Low	High	Low	High
Agriculture	3.0	1.4	2.1	1.0	1.0	0.5
Consumer goods	9.0	4.8	2.1	1.0	1.1	0.5
Intermediate goods	31.8	15.0	10.5	5.2	5.3	2.6
Capital goods	46.0	22.0	16.4	8.3	8.2	4.1
Construction goods	7.0	3.5	3.8	1.9	1.9	0.9
Infrastructure and services	3.2	1.6	2.4	1.2	1.2	0.6
Total	7.0	3.6	4.1	2.1	2.1	1.1

capital goods. Correspondingly, these are the sectors that suffer the greatest output loss. Whereas the average output loss for the economy varies between 1.1 and 2.1 percent depending on trade elasticities, output losses in the capital goods sector ranges between 4.1 and 8.2 percent and for intermediate goods, between 2.6 and 5.3 percent.

To summarize, rent seeking results in output loss for all sectors in the economy and also leads to an exaggeration of the effect of adjustment to foreign exchange shortages on the composition of sectoral output. Thus capital goods, which is already the sector that suffers most from adjustment by premium rationing, is also the sector that is most adversely affected by rent seeking.

9.5 Export supply constraints

In the experiments discussed earlier, the supply of exports in any sector is determined by subtracting domestic use (consumption + investment demand) from total sectoral production. The sensitivity of export supply to export price changes, therefore, varies directly with the sensitivity of domestic production levels and the sensitivity of domestic demand to price changes. When the domestic price in a sector goes up, total supply expands and domestic demand contracts, leaving a greater exportable surplus. As discussed in Chapter 7, this treatment of export supply may encounter problems in fairly aggregated applied models where exports in any particular sector will tend to be quite distinct products from the domestically consumed basket of goods. In cases like this, we proposed

Table 9.6. *Devaluation with and without export supply constraints (% changes from base solution)*

	Devaluation: no export supply constraints		Devaluation: with export supply constraints	
	Low	High	Low	High
Exchange rate	21.5	8.7	30.0	10.7
Domestic price of exports	1.7	0.9	11.0	4.6
Dollar price of exports	−17.6	−6.6	−13.2	−5.4
Imports (volume and $ value)	−9.3	−8.2	−11.2	−10.2
Export (volume)	44.6	37.0	35.1	30.7
Exports ($ value)	21.5	27.1	17.3	23.8
GDP	−0.4	−0.3	−0.7	−0.4

to specify separate sectoral export supply functions to prevent the models from overestimating the export supply response to trade policy measures. To illustrate the effect of such constraints, we have rerun the devaluation experiments with logistic export supply functions in every sector. This specification probably overestimates export supply rigidity, but it is interesting to test the effect of imposing the additional supply constraints.

The effects of imposing additional export supply constraints are easy to understand. For a given percent devaluation, the increase in the supply of exports diminishes substantially. At given domestic export prices, foreign demand has increased by the same amount that it did without the extra supply constraints. Two forces are therefore operating. On the one hand, there is further pressure on the exchange rate because of the lack of sufficient export response. On the other hand, there is upward pressure on export prices as foreign demand exceeds domestic supply.

The macroeconomic results of devaluation with export supply constraints are contrasted with devaluation without export supply constraints in Table 9.6. The result is a greater exchange-rate adjustment and a significant increase in the domestic price of exports. This increase in the domestic price of exports stands out in contrast to all the other adjustment mechanisms, including the case of devaluation, where the domestic price of exports remains largely unaffected. It is also interesting to note that the dollar price of exports falls less with the export supply constraints despite the greater devaluation. This is of course due to the countervailing and dominating effect of the increase in the domes-

Table 9.7. *The effects of export supply constraints on export volumes (% changes from base run)*

	Devaluation: no export supply constraints		Devaluation: with export supply constraints	
	Low	High	Low	High
Agriculture	47.3	40.4	36.2	31.5
Consumer goods	43.9	36.0	38.2	37.1
Intermediate goods	44.2	29.7	8.2	−3.7
Capital goods	80.9	52.7	−2.9	−30.0
Construction	0.0	0.0	0.0	0.0
Infrastructure and services	16.8	39.8	40.7	37.0

tic price of exports. As a consequence, both the volume and the value of exports rise less when there are export supply constraints. Imports, therefore, decline by a greater percentage than in the absence of export constraints.

Adjustment is also more costly in terms of GDP. GDP loss is greater because the economy has greater difficulty adjusting, necessitating a greater change in the relative price system including the exchange rate. Thus, with low trade elasticities, the fall in GDP increases from 0.4 to 0.7 percent when there are export supply constraints. It is precisely situations such as these that are espoused by structuralists when they characterize the productive sphere of the economy as unbalanced or as ridden by bottlenecks.[4]

The pattern of sectoral export response to devaluation with and without export supply constraints is reported in Table 9.7. The pattern is easy to understand in the case of no export supply constraints, because the same forces are at work here as those described in Chapter 8. Export expansion is greater the larger the value of the export demand elasticities and the greater the extent of devaluation. These effects work in opposite directions as trade elasticities are increased, and it can be seen from the first two columns of Table 9.7 that it is the exchange-rate effect that dominates, because sectoral export expansions are larger with low trade elasticities.

When there are export supply constraints, the pattern of export

[4] See Diamand (1978) for an extensive discussion of bottlenecks and what he calls "unbalanced production structures" (UPS).

responses is smaller and shows greater diversity across sectors even though the parameters of the logistic function describing the supply constraints are the same for all sectors. In this case, the ratio of exports to domestic supply is an increasing function of the ratio of the domestic currency price of exports to the domestic price. The domestic currency price of exports is determined so that, given the exchange rate and the foreign currency price of exports, it clears the export market. It is clear that because the pattern of export demand elasticities is fairly uniform across sectors and changes in the exchange rate affect all sectors equally, changes in domestic prices are now important. Thus sectors experiencing the largest relative price increases, such as intermediates and capital goods, are those sectors that have the lowest export supply ratios. Indeed, it turns out that, for these sectors, the increase in domestic prices is sufficient to direct goods away from the export market despite a substantial devaluation.

9.6   Welfare effects of different adjustment mechanisms

In assessing the total effects of adjustment to a reduction in net foreign resource inflow, we have so far referred only to changes in real GDP measured in terms of base-year prices. Because that measure excludes the initial shortfall of foreign exchange, it has the advantage of focusing directly on the *extra* cost to the economy of having to restore equilibrium after the shortfall in foreign exchange. Unfortunately, GDP is not an altogether satisfactory measure of changes in potential welfare because, as international economists have often pointed out, the opportunities facing the economy should be considered at "world" or "foreign" currency prices.

However, in a model where traded goods are imperfect substitutes in use, there is no easy way to evaluate GDP at "world" prices. As an alternative, we proposed in Chapter 7 to use a welfare index. This approach allows us to decompose the change in welfare into its various components and thereby to measure the contribution of each component. Yet, like other measures, it has some drawbacks. In particular, it cannot be used for the case where adjustment takes place by fixprice rationing, because then it is not possible to say if an observed consumption bundle would have indeed been selected over another one at the prevailing prices. We therefore cannot use the decomposition measure meaningfully in the case of fixprice rationing.

Table 9.8 provides a ranking in descending order of welfare losses in terms of changes in both GDP and total absorption using an arithmetic

Table 9.8. *Ranking adjustment mechansims in terms of welfare losses*

Percent decrease in GDP		Percent decrease in absorption (arithmetic average)	
Low	High	Low	High
Premium rationing with rent seeking (2.9)	Premium rationing with rent seeking (1.8)	Premium rationing with rent seeking (5.5)	Premium rationing with rent seeking (4.5)
Pure rationing (2.4)	Pure rationing (1.3)	Devaluation (4.3)	Premium rationing (3.7)
Premium rationing (1.3)	Premium rationing (1.0)	Devaluation with export supply constraints (4.3)	Devaluation (3.5)
Devaluation with export supply constraints (0.7)	Devaluation with export supply constraints (0.4)	Premium rationing (4.0)	Devaluation with export supply constraints (3.5)
Devaluation (0.3)	Devaluation (0.3)		

average of the Laspeyre and Paasche indices. In comparing the two sets of measures, there are several points that must be kept in mind. First, the GDP measure yields significantly lower figures because it does not include the foreign capital inflow decline as a loss, whereas the absorption measure does. Second, the absorption measure does not include figures for the case of fixprice rationing for the reasons stated above. Finally, the absorption measure includes as a loss the deterioration in the terms of trade, which is not directly taken into account in the GDP measure. It is in fact the sensitivity of the magnitude of the contribution of changes in the terms of trade that accounts for the changes in rankings in the total absorption measure.

Comparing the two sets of measures yields a ranking of adjustment mechanisms that conforms with expectations that would lead us to believe premium rationing with rent seeking and fixprice rationing are the most costly adjustment mechanisms. Indeed, in all cases, premium rationing with rent seeking is the most costly adjustment mechanism because of the extra loss inflicted by the diversion of resources away from productive uses toward rent-seeking activities. It is followed by fixprice rationing and, in the case of low trade elasticities, both these mechanisms are approximately twice as costly in terms of percentage GDP loss as any of the other alternatives. Also, as expected, devaluation is the least costly way to adjust in terms of GDP loss.

When we turn to the figures indicating the percent decrease in absorption, we must contend with the concomitant terms-of-trade-induced decline in absorption caused by an increase in exports. This means that devaluation, which is the policy that induces the greatest increase in export volume, is accompanied by a decline in the foreign currency price of exports. Moreover, the magnitude of that decline is greater the lower are the values of the foreign demand elasticities. As a result of the importance of this terms-of-trade-induced decline in absorption, it turns out that devaluation both without and with export supply constraints leads to a greater decline in total absorption than adjustment by premium rationing when trade elasticities are low. However, as can be seen from Table 9.8, the situation is reversed when the trade elasticities are high, in which case the rankings are similar to those in terms of GDP.

To isolate further the factors that account for the decline in total absorption, Table 9.9 identifies the contribution of each of the components that add up to the total decline in absorption. The components include the decline in net foreign capital inflow; the decline in the terms of trade; the tariff and export subsidy effects; and finally, the net production effect. As can be seen from column (7), the foreign resource effect accounts for more than 60 percent of the total decline in absorption in all cases except adjustment with rent seeking under low elasticities. The variation in the contribution of the resource effect when the exchange rate is held fixed [column (2)] is due to the fact that with low trade elasticities the equilibrium base exchange rate is 6.5 percent lower than with high trade elasticities.

That the adjustment costs to foreign exchange imbalances are greater when the economy is characterized by low trade elasticities has already been noted when discussing the percentage decline in GDP under the various adjustment mechanisms. It is quite clear from column (7) that this is also true in terms of absorption. Thus, within each adjustment mechanism, the share of the decline in absorption that is accounted for by the foreign resource effect is always greater when elasticities are high than when elasticities are low. Because the absolute contribution of the foreign resource effect does not change much, this implies that there is substantial variation in the contribution of the other effects depending on the values taken by the trade elasticities.

A comparison of devaluation with premium rationing tends to indicate that they have offsetting advantages and disadvantages. Devalua-

Table 9.9. *Decomposition of the decline in absorption under selected adjustment mechanisms*

| | | | Percent decline in absorption, of which:[a] | | | | | |
	Trade elasticities	Percent decline in absorption (1)	Foreign resource effect (2)	Terms-of-trade effect (3)	Tariff effect (4)	Export subsidy effect (5)	Net production effect (6)	(2) ÷ (1) (7)
Experiment								
Devaluation	Low	4.3	2.6	1.3	0.3	0.2	0.0	0.60
	High	3.5	2.6	0.5	0.2	0.1	0.1	0.74
Devaluation with export constraint	Low	4.3	2.6	1.1	0.3	0.1	0.1	0.60
	High	3.5	2.6	0.4	0.2	0.1	0.2	0.74
Premium rationing	Low	4.0	2.3	0.2	1.0	0.0	0.5	0.58
	High	3.7	2.5	0.1	0.7	0.0	0.4	0.68
Premium rationing with rent seeking	Low	5.5	2.3	0.2	1.0	0.0	2.0	0.42
	High	4.5	2.5	0.1	0.7	0.0	1.2	0.72

[a]Totals may not add up because of rounding.

tion does not generate allocative inefficiency, as it allows the economy to remain on its production possibility frontier. On the contrary, the allocative inefficiency losses are notable when adjustment takes place by premium rationing, particularly when there is rent seeking. In that case, the allocative inefficiency loss reaches 2.0 percent with low trade elasticities [column (6)]. There is also quite a difference in the consumption distortion effect that results from the joint effect of tariffs and subsidies that drive a wedge between the marginal benefits and the marginal costs of consumption. Here, too, devaluation imposes less of a reduction in real income than premium rationing. There is up to a 1 percent decline in real absorption caused simply by adjustment via premia, which is quite a substantial loss to the economy if one considers it in the context of a 3 percent decline in GDP. There are therefore gains to adopting adjustment policies that are neutral with respect to import substituting and exporting activities. Note also that the small export subsidy effect and the small tariff effect in the case of devaluation are due to the presence of the existing trade tax structure, which yields an average tariff rate of 34 percent and an average subsidy rate of 7 percent.

However, the disadvantage in terms of a greater decline in absorption caused by the consumption and production losses that accompany adjustment by premium rationing are mostly offset by the reduction in absorption due to a decline in the terms of trade that goes along with adjustment by devaluation. With low trade elasticities, devaluation causes a decline in absorption of 1.3 percent. Thus, when export demand elasticities are low, a large devaluation is needed to correct even moderate shortfalls in foreign resource flows, and real income will be severely affected by adverse terms-of-trade movements that result in a transfer of welfare out of the devaluing country to the rest of the world. Indeed, the choice of rationing over devaluation as an adjustment mechanism has often been rationalized in these terms by economists and policy makers in developing countries. Our analysis suggests that there is considerable support for this view, especially if one considers that even with high export demand elasticities (around 5), there is still a reduction in real income of 0.5 percent.

9.7   Conclusion

On the basis of the detailed analysis of alternative adjustment mechanisms to a shortfall in foreign resource inflow, it is quite obvious that policy choices are much more difficult to make than one would be led to believe on the basis of simpler macroeconomic models, particularly those in the tradition of two-gap analysis. Alternative adjustment mechanisms have substantially different impacts on resource allocation between sectors, which must be evaluated in the framework of development plans that often focus on the structure of production. These alternative mechanisms also have different welfare implications. Policy makers choosing a particular approach must take into account as much as possible information about the flexibility of the economy.

It is important to stress that when the economy has little flexibility, it has more difficulty adjusting which, in turn, necessitates a greater change in the relative price system (including the exchange rate if it is allowed to adjust). Elasticity pessimism, whether on the demand side or on the supply side, implies the need for a large change in relative prices to achieve a small quantity adjustment. Statements declaring that devaluation "won't work" because of low elasticities often really reflect the belief that the kind of relative price adjustment required is impossible to achieve. Prices not only allocate resources, but also generate income, and the change in the relative position of different income groups implicit in a particular change in relative prices may be very difficult to achieve if potential losers are able to protect their income shares. To assume that relative *prices* can, in fact, change is to assume that relative *incomes* can, in fact, change. We discuss these "structuralist" issues further in Chapters 12 and 13.

PART IV

Trade policy, growth, and industrial strategy: Turkey, 1973–1985

CHAPTER 10

The anatomy of a foreign exchange crisis: 1973–1977

10.1 Introduction

The next two chapters provide policy focused real-world applications of the modeling methodology developed in Chapters 5 and 7. Their purpose is to analyze the very serious foreign exchange crisis that emerged in Turkey in 1977 and to explore the impact of alternative policies on the growth path of the economy. The analysis of this chapter illustrates how a multisector, general equilibrium growth model can be used as a tool to help us understand past developments. Chapter 11 provides an example of how such a model can be used as an instrument of planning and policy choice for the medium term.

The model, which we call the TGT model (Turkey, growth, and trade), is a nineteen-sector computable general equilibrium model incorporating foreign trade in the manner described at length in preceding chapters. Imports and domestic commodities are imperfect substitutes. Export demand elasticities vary between 3, in sectors such as food and tobacco products, and 6, in sectors such as clothing, wood products, and nonmetallic mineral products. In a few sectors, such as agriculture, mining, and nonfactor services, a separate logistic supply function limits the capactiy to expand the share of exports in total production. (See the discussion in Section 7.3.)

Quantity restrictions and import rationing of the type discussed in Chapter 9 have played a major role in Turkey. Throughout the postwar period, Turkey followed a fixed exchange-rate policy, with import rationing as the adjustment mechanism equating ex post demands and supplies of foreign exchange. There were major devaluations but always to a new, fixed parity. When the exchange rate is fixed, the TGT model specifies economy-wide import rationing. Of course, rationing becomes effective only when the demand for foreign exchange at a given exchange rate exceeds its supply. From the mid-1960s until about 1978, the sale of import licenses or the resale of imports was difficult in the case of most producer goods. With producer goods constituting about 90 percent of total imports, it would have been reasonable to assume "fix-price" rationing rather than explicit import premia as the basic adjustment mechanism. Between 1978 and 1980, however, a large parallel market for foreign exchange finally emerged, and the government did not seriously try to prevent, and even started to encourage, the resale of imports and foreign exchange. The system thus changed in character to one much closer to premium rationing.

The TGT model includes a set of macroeconomic and government accounts that summarize and reproduce the aggregate flow of funds in the economy. The government collects income taxes, indirect taxes, and tariffs and spends revenue on consumption, investment, and transfers. It then saves a certain proportion of its revenue, makes some transfers to the private sector, and spends the rest on consumption according to predetermined consumption shares. In the forward-looking experiments described in Chapter 11, it is sometimes government consumption that is set at exogenous target values, with government investment computed as a residual after total government revenue is determined endogenously.

In the factor markets we distinguish between rural and urban labor. The latter category is further subdivided between "organized" or "modern" sector labor and "unorganized" or "traditional" sector labor. The traditional sector absorbs all urban labor that is not employed by the modern sector. Between periods, rural–urban migration à la Harris-Todaro and natural population growth determine changes in the supply of labor.

Capital accumulation is determined by savings behavior. As in Chapters 8 and 9, private savings are governed by savings functions of the simple proportional type. Four categories of private income are distinguished: rural wages, urban organized sector wages, urban unorganized sector wages, and capital income. Each is characterized by a specific savings rate, with the bulk of private savings coming from capital income. The sum of private savings is then added to government savings to determine the value of total economy-wide investment. The Turkey model, is therefore, savings driven. It is a multisector growth and trade model with a set of consistent macroeconomic accounts, designed to analyze trade policy, industrial structure, and the role and nature of the foreign exchange constraint in Turkey's recent economic history.

All the essential features of this type of general equilibrium model have been discussed at length in Chapters 5, 6, and 7, and the TGT model is a real-world application of the core model developed in these chapters. The numerical applications in Chapters 8 and 9 are based on the same data, and the essential structure of the model is the same. For a complete description of the specification and data base, the reader should refer to Derviş and Robinson (1978).

The remainder of this chapter is devoted to a detailed analysis of the factors that led to the 1977 "crisis" and its immediate sectoral impact. Section 10.2 provides a brief review of Turkey's recent economic performance, particularly over the period immediately preceding the crisis, that is, from 1973 to 1977. Having isolated the main factors that contributed to the crisis, Section 10.3 shows how the TGT model can be used to estimate an equilibrium exchange rate for that period and hence to decompose the change in its value in terms of the major factors singled out earlier. The welfare costs of postponing adjustment are examined in Section 10.4, whereas Section 10.5 indicates the sectoral impact of the rationing that took place during the crisis.

10.2 The making of a crisis: Turkey, 1973–1977

Historical background

Turkey's growth rate has been impressive throughout the postwar period, averaging 6.2 percent over three decades (1947–77). This relatively high growth rate was achieved without the availability of particularly valuable resources such as oil, and with only a moderate amount of foreign aid. Finally, although income is quite unequally distributed (with a very large rural–urban gap and a Gini coefficient above 0.5), basic needs are reasonably well met and problems of malnutrition, basic health care, basic education, and shelter are less acute than in many countries with equal or even higher per-capita incomes.[1]

The initial conditions from which Turkey started after World War I were not favorable. For example, in terms of both physical infrastructure and human resources, Egypt was significantly ahead of Turkey at the beginning of the century (see Issawi, 1980). Particularly in terms of human resources, all the Southern European countries, including Bulgaria, Greece, Serbia, Croatia, Spain, and Portugal, were far ahead of Turkey before and after World War I. Furthermore, the rate of population growth in Turkey remained between 2.5 and 3.0 percent throughout the century and, while on a declining trend, it is still more than double that in the rest of Southern Europe. With a per-capita income around $1,000 in the late 1970s, Turkey remains poorer than many semi-industrial countries.

Growth, although rapid on average, has not proceeded at a steady pace. The foundations of Turkish industrialization were laid in the decade before World War II and, in spite of the world depression, Tur-

---

[1] See Derviş and Robinson (1980) for an analysis of Turkish income distribution.

Percentage growth rate
of industrial sector

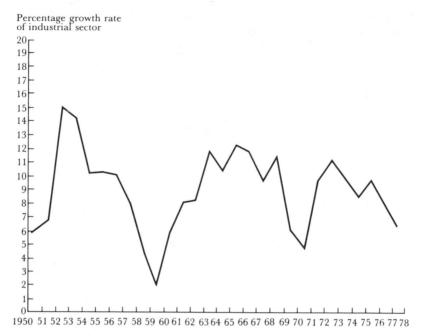

Figure 10.1. Industrial growth in Turkey, 1950–78 (two-year moving averages).

key achieved substantial growth in the 1930s with important invest-ments in infrastructure and the creation of state economic enterprises that successfully led to the beginnings of industrial growth. The war and the diversion of resources and change of priorities it created in spite of Turkey's neutrality were probably the major causes of the complete economic standstill that followed in the 1940s.[2]

Since 1950, which marks the beginning of regular national account-ing as well as an important political turning point, Turkey seems to have gone through three rather similar cycles. Each starts with a period of quite rapid industrial growth and ends with a major foreign exchange crisis, a large devaluation, and a transitory slowdown in industrial growth.[3] In Figure 10.1, two-year moving averages of industrial growth

[2] See Bulutay et al. (1975) for estimates of national income in the 1930s and 1940s. See also Herschlag (1968) and Land (1970).

[3] Economy-wide growth has not always followed the movements of industrial growth because of the extreme volatility of agricultural growth, heavily dependent on weather conditions.

rates[4] have been plotted against time. The three cycles are quite apparent from the graph. Each downswing is associated with an acute foreign exchange crisis and a major effective devaluation, close to 100 percent in 1958, about 50 percent in 1970, and again about 50 percent in the period from September 1977 to March 1978.[5]

Although a clear cyclical pattern emerges from Figure 10.1, one has to be careful in interpreting the cycles in too mechanistic a fashion. Common factors and aspects did exist, but one crisis has not been a simple repetition of its predecessor. Thus, whereas the 1958–60 crisis followed a period of almost hyperinflation and was followed by a period of remarkable price stability, exactly the opposite is true of the 1970 crisis. It followed a period of relative price stability but was followed by a period of substantial inflation. The impact on export performance has also varied. The 1958 de facto devaluation was not followed by a major upward surge of exports. Between 1957–8 and 1961–2, exports increased by only 23 percent in real terms. In contrast, export revenues increased by 153 percent between 1969–70 and 1973–4.

There was reason for much optimism in the early 1970s. The foreign exchange constraint that plagued the Turkish economy throughout the 1950s and 1960s disappeared all of a sudden. For the first time ever in postwar history, the current account deficit declined to zero in 1972 and turned into a $484 million surplus in 1973. Foreign exchange reserves reached $2 billion (American billion) at the end of 1973, a figure equal to annual merchandise imports.

The situation seemed to point to an increase in the possible trend growth rate of the Turkish economy from about 6.5 percent to about 8.0 percent. In fact, between 1970 and 1976, GDP grew at an annual average rate of 7.7 percent. It was even on an accelerating trend after 1973, seemingly in spite of the oil crisis and the world depression that followed. There was general agreement in Turkey that the Fourth Five-Year Plan due to start in 1978 should aim at an annual growth rate of at least 8.0 percent. This kind of growth rate was perceived to be a necessary minimum for the absorption of underemployment and for a significant narrowing of the absolute income gap that separates Turkey from other Southern European countries, an objective planners have always hoped to achieve by the end of this century.

[4] Note that by "industrial" we are here referring to the nonagricultural sector, including services.

[5] See Krueger (1974a) for the computation of changes in effective exchange rates in 1958 and 1970. Further devaluations occurred, cumulating to more than 100% for the period between March 1978 and January 1980.

But the optimism of the early 1970s was shattered by an acute foreign exchange crisis that emerged in 1977 and continues at the date of writing. The cumulative current account deficit since 1974 had reached $8 billion by the end of 1977, with the 1977 deficit alone about $3 billion. Although the foreign exchange crisis of the late 1970s is similar in many ways to the 1958 crisis, it has been deeper, with a much greater percentage resource gap. The debt–service ratio climbed from 11.4 percent of exports and workers' remittances in 1976 to 15.6 percent in 1977, and it will exceed 30 percent in the 1980s. Payments for imports were delayed on a wide scale, foreign exchange reserves declined to a level of only one month's worth of imports, industry began to lack crucial imported inputs as well as energy, and growth in per-capita income came to a halt in the latter half of 1977.

Predictions and projections for the future vary widely. In the short run, that is, in the early 1980s, it seems clear that only a very substantial new inflow of foreign resources can allow a resumption of adequate growth and prevent mass unemployment and stagnation. But before attempting to provide projections for the future and evaluating possible alternative policy packages, it is necessary to analyze the nature of the crisis that emerged in 1977. How did Turkey move from a $0.5 billion current account surplus to a $3.2 billion deficit in four years? Did the crisis develop largely because of factors endogenous to Turkey's development policies, or can it be explained by exogenous shocks coming from the world economy? Would a policy of maintaining a constant purchasing-power-parity-deflated exchange rate have sufficed to avoid the crisis? Are the problems that emerged in 1977 the necessary outcome of Turkey's inward-looking, import-substituting development strategy, or would the crisis never have occurred had it not been for the oil price increase and unfavorable external circumstances? With a quantitative general equilibrium model, it is possible to provide some answers to these questions and assign approximate weights to the various factors that lead to the 1977 collapse. This chapter presents a detailed quantitative analysis of the emergence of the 1977 crisis, providing some background on the 1970s as a whole, but concentrating on the 1973–7 period immediately preceding what has proved to be the most serious economic and social crisis Turkey has faced in half a century.

Summary of events and policy reactions

The period from 1970 to 1977 marks the third cycle in Turkey's postwar path of industrialization (see Figure 10.1). We shall briefly describe events in this period that started with the 1970 devaluation and led to the 1977 crisis.

The latter half of the 1960s was characterized by severe foreign exchange shortages and consequently increasingly severe import rationing. Although growth performance, particularly in the industrial sector, was impressive, exports virtually stagnated. Between 1960–61 and 1969–70, exports increased at an annual rate of only 5.9 percent in current-dollar value, which reflects near stagnation in real terms. Over the same period, imports grew by only 6.7 percent in current dollar value, or about 3 percent in real terms, compared to an average annual growth of real GDP above 6 percent and an annual industrial growth rate of about 10 percent.

Although foreign exchange shortages were chronic and net incentives had drifted more and more against exports, the situation in 1970 was far less serious than it had been in 1958. The main reason was probably a still small but significant flow of workers' remittances, averaging about $100 million a year since 1965, which compensated for about 40 percent of the trade deficit. Import substitution was also proceeding relatively successfully, particularly in transportation equipment and machinery, and the foreign exchange situation was not really deteriorating rapidly. The timing of the devaluation that occurred in August 1970 must be explained as much by political as by purely economic factors. To quote Anne Krueger, "the fact that a foreign exchange shortage had continued for so long meant that it could continue longer" (Krueger, 1974a, p. 312).

It is quite possible that it was the dismal performance of exports in general and of manufactured exports in particular that constituted the single most important factor leading to the 1970 devaluation. At the State Planning Organization in particular, the failure of any manufactured exports to materialize was perceived as a serious bottleneck to further growth and as an indication that Turkey's industrial development was lacking an important dimension. The 1970 policy adjustment was a substantial one, increasing the effective exchange rate for imports by about 50 percent, for traditional agricultural exports by 28 percent (tobacco, hazelnuts, dried fruits, raw cotton), and for manufactured exports by 57 percent (see Krueger, 1974a). The devaluation was followed by three years of extremely rapid increase in foreign exchange receipts, which made possible not only an unprecedented increase in imports but also an even more dramatic accumulation of foreign exchange reserves.

Exports, in sharp contrast to what had happened after 1958, responded vigorously to the 1970 exchange-rate adjustment. Their total value increased from $537 million in 1969 to $588 million in 1970, $677 million in 1971, $885 million in 1972, and $1,317 million in 1973, representing an annual average growth of 25 percent. Turkish exports had been close to $300 million in 1950 and 1951. Thus, in the two decades from 1950 to 1969, total export value failed to double, increasing by only 80 percent over nineteen years, a growth of only 3 percent per annum. In contrast, the near tripling of export earnings between 1969 and 1973 constituted an unprecedented achievement. It is true that the world economy was booming, cotton prices were high, and the external environment was favorable. But Turkey significantly increased her market share, which means that domestic supply conditions and incentives must be part of the explanation for the dramatic growth of exports.

The overwhelming source of export expansion in the early 1970s was in the food processing and textile sectors. Exports of processed food products increased from $200 million in 1969 to $390 million in 1973, whereas exports of textiles, including ginned cotton, increased from $127 million to $391 million in the same period. What is equally important is that from a base close to zero, significant exports appeared in the following categories of manufactured products: clothing, footwear, inorganic chemicals, cement, glass and glassware, and metal products. The 1970–3 period can be taken as an indication that the potential for export expansion in a wide range of manufactured products exists in Turkey, provided that the structure of incentives is conducive to such an expansion and provided that foreign market conditions are appropriate. Unfortunately, neither the structure of incentives nor foreign market conditions remained conducive to export expansion for more than a few years.

In addition to increased exports, Turkey acquired foreign exchange from workers' remittances, which increased from $141 million in 1969 to $273 million in 1970, $471 million in 1971, $740 million in 1972, and $1,183 million in 1973. This represents an annual average growth rate of 70 percent. By 1973, the flow of remittances was financing half of imports. The increase of remittances was only partly a reaction to devaluation. Between 1969 and 1973, the number of workers abroad itself grew at an average annual rate of about 35 percent. On the rough assumption that remittances are proportional to total income earned abroad, and noting that nominal income per worker measured in dollars grew at an annual rate of at least 10 percent, one would estimate a 50 percent annual growth rate. To this was added the redirection into official channels that no doubt followed the devaluation, as well as some repatriation of accumulated savings that constituted a direct response to the exchange rate adjustment. The great surge in remittances was dramatic and largely unexpected.[6]

Inflation was moderate in the 1960s, accelerating somewhat toward the end of the decade, but averaging only about 5 percent per annum from 1960 to 1970. The situation changed sharply after 1970. The wholesale price index rose by 16 percent in 1971, 18 percent in 1972, and 20.5 percent in 1973, making for an average inflation rate of 18.2 percent per year in the 1970–3 period. During the same period, worldwide inflation, expressed in dollars, also increased substantially, but did not average more than 10 percent per year.[7] Relative incentives had thus significantly drifted against exports by 1973, and the price-deflated exchange rate had appreciated by about 30 percent.[8]

Between 1973 and 1976, the annual spread between Turkey's domestic inflation rate and the worldwide inflation rate remained between 8 and 10 percentage points. Turkey did start a series of minor exchange-rate adjustments in this period, devaluing the Turkish lira against the dollar by an average of 5 percentage points a year, which did not fully compensate for the inflation differential. The upward drift in the purchasing-power parity price-deflated exchange rate thus continued, slowly but steadily, and by the end of 1976 the real exchange rate was therefore again close to what it had been before the 1970 devaluation.

After 1974, export revenues increased only very slowly and erratically, officially recorded workers' remittances even declined by about 40 percent, whereas imports almost tripled between 1973 and 1977. Figure 10.2 illustrates these divergent trends. As can be observed from Figure 10.2, exports and imports were growing at about the same rate between 1970 and 1973, whereas workers' remittances grew somewhat more rapidly, with the sum of exports and remittances actually overtaking the value of imports in 1972 and producing a sizable current account surplus in 1973. Imports jumped from $2.1 billion in 1973 to $3.8 billion in 1974, growing by 80 percent in one year. The foreign exchange gap created by this sharp increase in imports in 1974 was still, however, moderate, consisting of $819 million or about 2.8 percent of GDP. It is in 1975 that the danger of a major foreign exchange crisis became

[6] The Third Five-Year Plan, prepared in 1972, underestimated remittances in 1973 and 1974, projecting them at one-third of their actual value.

[7] See "Historical Rates of Change in US$ GDP Deflators: 1961–1975" (World Bank, 1978).

[8] The Turkish lira was actually formally revalued by 6% against the dollar between 1970 and 1973. For the definitions of the various exchange rates used here, see Section 6.2.

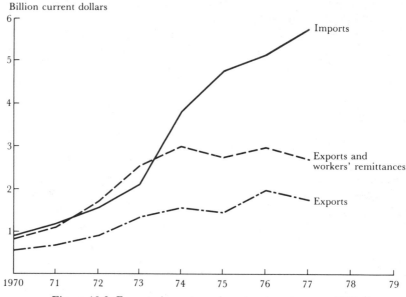

Figure 10.2. Exports, imports, and workers' remittances: 1970-7.

apparent. In that year, both exports and remittances declined while imports continued to grow rapidly, increasing by 25 percent over 1974. The foreign exchange gap (imports — exports — remittances) reached $2 billion or about 5.4 percent of GDP.

It is thus quite clear that the crisis was already apparent in 1975 and that the level and growth rate of imports experienced in 1974 and 1975 were inconsistent with the amount of export earnings and remittances that materialized. The situation did not improve in 1976 or 1977. On the contrary, in 1977 the foreign exchange gap reached $3 billion which, at the March 1978 exchange rate of 25 TL to the dollar, constituted about 9 percent of GDP. The gap was temporarily closed by massive international borrowing and the running down of the substantial foreign exchange reserves that had accumulated in 1972 and 1973. In the early 1970s, Turkey had remarkably low debt-to-GDP and debt–service ratios, which initially made massive borrowing possible.[9] But by the end of 1977, there were no more reserves to be run down, and Tur-

[9] In the 1965–74 period, Turkey's debt–GDP ratio did not exceed 5%. In turn, debt–service payments were never greater than 10% of total foreign exchange earnings.

key's borrowing capacity had reached its limits. The situation was no longer tenable, and a major readjustment had become inevitable.

Although the upward drift in the price-deflated exchange rate and the antiexport-biased shift in incentives resulting from Turkey's high inflation rate constitute one major element explaining the foreign exchange crisis, there have been other important developments. A significant part of the 1974 upward jump in imports that is apparent in Figure 10.2 can be attributed to the oil price increase. Turkey imported about 70 percent of its oil needs during the 1974–7 period, and there is no doubt that the oil price rise has had a major adverse impact on the balance of payments and the economy. Moreover, the supply price of imported capital goods and intermediates increased dramatically during 1974 and 1975, with the price index of OECD manufactured exports rising by a massive 36 percent between 1973 and 1975. Turkey was thus caught in a double squeeze between rising oil prices and rising industrial product prices. In fact, the Turkish government tried to insulate the domestic economy from the crisis and the effects of the oil price increase by setting up a special fund to subsidize the price of gasoline in the domestic market. Although this probably helped keep up real wages and profits domestically, at least for an interim period, it heightened the impact of the oil crisis on the balance of payments because it weakened any possible substitution effect against oil-intensive activities. By 1977, oil imports were almost equal in value to total merchandise exports! But how important have terms-of-trade effects and the oil price increase really been in explaining the present crisis? Have they been the major cause of the great widening in the foreign exchange gap?

Another development in the middle 1970s that has been suggested as one of the contributing causes of the current crisis is the major investment program undertaken by the government. The aggregate investment rate (as a proportion of GDP) increased steadily during the period, from about 18 to 23.5 percent. Because investment is relatively import intensive, this increase no doubt led to additional strain on the balance of payments. Again, one would like to know if a significant portion of the emerging "foreign exchange gap" was due to the increased investment share.

Another important factor was the stagnation and decline of remittance earnings. Finally, there were other factors, such as a general decline in the rate of growth of world trade and increased protectionist tendencies in the OECD. On the other hand, the Middle East market was booming, and Turkey could presumably have benefited from its proximity had domestic policies been aimed at such a target.

10.3   Decomposing the change in the equilibrium exchange rate

One way of analyzing the emergence of a foreign exchange crisis is to analyze what happens to the underlying "equilibrium" exchange rate over the period considered. As shown in Chapter 6, the change in an equilibrium exchange rate $\hat{e}$ over time can be written as

$$\hat{e} = (\hat{k} - \hat{l})(\hat{P} - \hat{PW}) \tag{10.3.1}$$

where $\hat{k}$ and $\hat{l}$ refer to changes in the real sphere and $\hat{P}$ and $\hat{PW}$ stand for domestic and world inflation. Factors such as the oil price rise and the rise in OECD export prices would have led to a rise in the equilibrium price of foreign exchange for Turkey even if Turkish inflation had been equal to world inflation and the purchasing-power-parity price-deflated exchange rate had remained constant. But what was the relative importance of the oil price, differential inflation, and other factors?

To formulate approximate answers to these questions, one can run the TGT model over the 1973-7 period with a flexible exchange rate, allowing ER to adjust in each year so as to equate total demand for foreign exchange to total supply. The historical inflation rates experienced by Turkey as well as world inflation are given exogenously to the model.[10] In a flexible exchange-rate experiment the exchange rate is then allowed to adjust to this exogenously specified inflation.

However, the "equilibrium" exchange rate determined by equating the annual demand and supply flows of foreign exchange will be sensitive to the exogenous flows of foreign capital and reserve accumulation. For example, in 1976 and 1977, Turkey borrowed large amounts of foreign exchange, which in no way reflect some "normal" or "equilibrium" amount of borrowing. The result was that there was little import rationing until 1977. Running the model with a flexible exchange rate but assuming the same massive borrowing that actually occurred yields a market-clearing exchange rate in 1977 only about 6-7 percent higher than the fixed rate of 18.2 in the rationing-constrained basic run.

To arrive at an "equilibrium" exchange rate, one thus has to assume an amount of borrowing and a level of reserves that can be sustained over time. It is not obvious what such a "normal" or "sustainable" level of reserves and borrowing would have been, but one can make certain reasonable assumptions. Regarding the stock of reserves, we assume that

[10] See World Bank (1978) for information on world inflation.

it should equal about 30 percent of annual imports.[11] At the end of 1972, Turkey's foreign exchange reserves stood at $1.2 billion compared to an import bill in 1972 of $1.6 billion. The stock of reserves was already too high. But another $700 million were allowed to accumulate during 1973, leading, at the end of 1973, to one of the highest reserves-to-imports ratios in the world. Thereafter, beginning in 1974, Turkey started running down its reserves, arriving in 1977 at a reserves-to-imports ratio below 10 percent.

For the equilibrium exchange-rate experiments, we assume that instead of first accumulating and then decumulating reserves, Turkey keeps its 1972 stock of $1.2 billion until the end of 1975. By that time, the reserve-to-imports ratio reaches 30 percent and, to preserve that ratio, reserves have to be slowly accumulated from 1976 onwards.

With respect to borrowing, it is more difficult to define a normal level. In Turkey's case, it is possible to argue that until 1974, the total amount of debt and the levels of annual borrowing were too low rather than too large given Turkey's size and total foreign exchange earnings. The situation was reversed quite dramatically in 1976 and 1977, with massive borrowing leading to a debt–GDP ratio close to 40 percent by the spring of 1978. Taking the 1973–7 period as a whole, Turkey borrowed at levels that could not be sustained over time given the trend increase in exports and the flow of workers' remittances. To compute an "equilibrium" exchange rate, we therefore assume that a "normal" level of borrowing would have implied a total cumulative net flow of $3.5 billion instead of the $6 billion that were actually realized. Starting from $500 million in 1973, the net foreign capital inflow is assumed to grow at 17 percent annually, about 8 percent in constant dollars, which is close to the 7 percent trend growth rate of Turkish GDP.[12] Under this "equilibrium" assumption, net foreign capital inflow would have reached $940 million in 1977 and summed to a total cumulative flow of $3.5 billion. Table 10.1 compares capital inflow and reserve decumulation in the basic run, which reflects the actual events over the 1973–7 period, with the figures assumed for the equilibrium experiments.

One may, of course, disagree with the exact magnitudes that appear

[11] In 1973 this ratio was 35% for Greece, 31% for Yugoslavia, 69% for Spain, 61% for Germany, 23% for India, and 50% for Mexico. (*Source:* IMF International Financial Statistics.)

[12] We assume a somewhat more rapid growth of net borrowing, reflecting what we believe is still a very moderate reliance on external resources given Turkey's initially low debt–GDP ratio.

Table 10.1. *Flexible-exchange-rate experiments: reserve decumulation and net capital inflow (millions of dollars)*

Basic run	1973	1974	1975	1976	1977	Cumulative
Basic run						
Reserve decumulation	−728	431	417	112	566	798
Net capital inflow	137	202	1,339	2,011	2,337	6,021
Sum	−591	633	1,756	2,123	2,898	6,819
All experiments						
Reserve decumulation	0	0	0	−200	−250	−450
Net capital inflow	500	585	685	800	940	3,510
Sum	500	585	685	600	690	3,060

in the lower part of Table 10.1. Instead of $3.5 billion, Turkey could probably have received $4.0 or $4.5 billion of net foreign resources without endangering its debt–service position. On the other hand, for national security and independence reasons, a higher level of reserves may be desirable. On the whole, the figures assumed represent reasonable orders of magnitude, and small variations in them do not affect the results.

Note that "equilibrium" has here been specified in terms of sustainable annual inflows of foreign exchange to compensate for a current account deficit. For an economy as closed as was Turkey's throughout the 1960s and 1970s, with capital account transactions strictly regulated, specifying such a flow equilibrium is quite reasonable. Any attempt to specify equilibrium in terms of very thin asset markets would clearly be misplaced.

Once the path of what is considered to be an equilibrium level of reserves and foreign borrowing is specified, it is possible to use the flexible exchange-rate version of the TGT model to explore the values that the market-clearing or "equilibrium" exchange rate would have taken if it had been allowed to move to equilibrate the supply of and demand for foreign exchange. We are not here referring to a shadow rate in the sense of a free-trade exchange rate, but to the rate that would have been an equilibrium rate given Turkey's structure of tariffs and in the absence of quantity rationing.

In a "basic run," which is used as a reference point for comparisons, the exchange rate is fixed at the official parity levels in each year, as are also the levels of capital inflow, remittances, and reserve decumulation. The intent of the basic run is to approximate as closely as possible the

Table 10.2. *Summary of price-index movements affecting the Turkish economy, 1973–7*

	(1) US dollar GDP deflator OECD North	(2) Turkish lira GDP deflator	(3) OECD manufactured exports price index ($)	(4) Oil price index ($)	(5) World price index in Turkish export markets ($)
1973	100.0	100.0	100.0	100.0	100.0
1974	110.0	128.0	120.9	386.0	130.0
1975	123.6	148.6	135.7	440.0	122.2
1976	127.6	174.0	140.2	455.2	128.3
1977	138.4	218.5	148.5	481.4	136.0
1973–7 average annual growth	8.5%	21.6%	10.4%	36.9%	8.0%

Source: "Commodity Price Forecasts," World Bank, Economic Analysis and Projections Department, May 1979, for columns (1), (3), (4), and (5). Turkish National Accounts for column (2).

actual path the economy followed in the 1973–78 period. Table 10.2 assembles some of the most important information about the exogenous variables that characterize the base run and that together set the stage for a major "crisis."

In Table 10.2, the first four indices were easy to obtain. It should be noted that everything is expressed in "dollars," so that the movement of the indices reflects the progressive depreciation of the dollar in the period considered. Column (5) refers to what we call a world export market price index. It is *not* the Turkish export price index, because the latter is endogenous in the TGT model. Recall the export demand functions:

$$E_i = \overline{E}_i \left(\frac{\Pi_i}{PWE_i} \right)^{\eta_i}$$

(10.3.2)

The index shown in column (5) is a weighted average of exogenous changes in world prices of products competing with Turkish exports, Π_i. These will, of course, have a strong impact on the endogenously determined prices of exports originating in Turkey, PWE_i. But because we do not make the small-country assumption on the export side, the PWE_i do not move in strict unison with Π_i. To arrive at the index

Table 10.3. *Experiment E-1: equilibrium exchange rates,
1973–7*

	Experiment E-1: equilibrium rates	Basic run: official parity
1973	10.1	14.0
1974	12.9	13.5
1975	18.5	14.5
1976	23.3	16.0
1977	27.7	18.2

shown in column (5), we constructed a weighted average of world price indices for the commodities that Turkey exports.[13]

The flexible-exchange-rate experiments were conducted with the assumptions about normal levels of foreign borrowing and reserve decumulation discussed above. In the first experiment (E-1), there are no other changes. It thus provides a reference path of equilibrium exchange rates given the shocks that the economy actually underwent, but assuming a flexible-exchange-rate policy and more normal capital flow and reserve behavior. The equilibrium exchange rates in each year derived from this experiment are compared with the actual rates in Table 10.3.

According to the TGT model, the equilibrium exchange rate was 10.1 in 1973, substantially *lower* than the official parity of 14 TL to the dollar. Thus, in terms of flow-equilibrium conditions, Turkey seems to have had a significantly undervalued exchange rate in 1973. Although this may, at first, seem surprising, one should remember that Turkey accumulated $1.5 billion of reserves between 1971 and 1973. The reserves-to-imports ratio rose to above 100 percent, far in excess of what can be considered normal or required. Furthermore, net borrowing in that period was minimal. The explanation for this dramatic reversal of the chronic foreign exchange shortage that had characterized the postwar period is primarily to be found in the massive increase of workers' remittances. To this must be added the very good export performance in the early 1970s. However, the situation did not last. Starting in 1974, the downward trend in the equilibrium value of the Turkish lira was very steep, and the degree of overvaluation steadily increased. By 1977, the TGT model results indicate that the Turkish lira was overvalued by more than 50 percent.

[13] For the manufacturing sectors, which represent a very small fraction of total exports, we simply took the OECD manufactured exports price index again.

Table 10.4. *Flexible-exchange-rate experiments: summary description and 1977 equilibrium exchange rate*

Experiment	Description	Exchange rate in 1977
Basic run	Fixed exchange rate, historical run, massive borrowing, loss of reserves and some import rationing after 1976	18.2
E-1	Basic run + flexible exchange rate + moderate borrowing + normal reserve behavior	27.7
E-2	E-1 + moderate inflation	19.1
E-3	E-2 + no oil price increase	15.4
E-4	E-3 + no other terms-of-trade changes	13.8
E-5	E-4 + continued moderate growth of workers' remittances	11.6

In Experiments E-2 through E-5, we progressively take out the major causal factors in order to explore their separate contribution to the spectacular decline of the equilibrium exchange rate. Table 10.4 presents a summary description of the experiments and gives the value that the equilibrium exchange rate would have reached in 1977 with the alternative assumptions characterizing each experiment.

Experiment E-2 is the same as Experiment E-1 except that domestic inflation is set equal to world inflation through the period.[14] This experiment isolates the effect of differential inflation rates in explaining the depreciation of the equilibrium exchange rate. The third experiment (E-3) is the same as E-2, except that there is no special rise in the world price of oil. It thus isolates the impact of the "oil crisis," defined narrowly as the quadrupling of the price of oil that occurred between 1973 and 1975. The fourth experiment (E-4) assumes that the rise in world prices in Turkey's export markets was, year by year, equal to the rise in the price index of OECD manufactured exports that constitute the supply price of Turkish imports. Together E-2 and E-3 thus isolate the effect of the exogenous changes in world prices to which Turkey had to adjust. Finally, Experiment E-4 is the same as Experiment E-3, except that workers' remittances, which stagnated after 1974, are assumed to grow in real terms at a rate equal to growth in GDP.

[14] Inflation is measured here by the OECD North and Turkish GDP deflators given in Table 10.2.

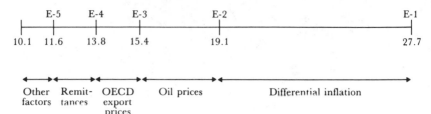

Figure 10.3. Contribution of factors to the total change in the equilibrium exchange rate.

These experiments enable us to decompose the change in the equilibrium exchange rate that occurred between 1973 and 1977. There is a question of "order," however. One could, for example, start by first taking out the oil price rise rather than the differential inflation. Fortunately, our results do not depend on order. We ran the same experiments in different sequences and found that the final decomposition was not affected significantly. This reflects the nature of the particular set of experiments and certainly need not be true generally. Empirically, there is hardly any "interaction" between the effects of, say, higher remittances and the oil price. These two exogenous factors have distinct *independent* effects on the exchange rate, and the magnitude of one effect does not depend on the magnitude of the other.

Figure 10.3 plots the equilibrium exchange rates in 1977 for Experiments E-1, E-2, E-3, E-4, and E-5 along a line whose origin is the equilibrium rate in 1973. The change in the final exchange rate between adjacent points is attributable to the single effect between the corresponding experiments.

Reading from right to left, one can compare the devaluations resulting from

Differential inflation: $\dfrac{27.7}{19.1} = 1.45$

Oil price rise: $\dfrac{19.1}{15.4} = 1.24$

High OECD export prices: $\dfrac{15.4}{13.8} = 1.12$

Low remittances: $\dfrac{13.8}{11.6} = 1.19$

Other factors: $\dfrac{11.6}{10.1} = 1.15$

Table 10.5. *The relative contribution of various causal factors to the total change in the equilibrium exchange rate*

Differential inflation	37%
Oil price rise	21
OECD exports price rise	11
Lower remittances	18
Other factors	13
Total	100%

Or, to express the relationship in a more useful way, the equilibrium exchange rate in 1977 is given by the expression

$$ER_{1977} = [(1.45)(1.24)(1.12)(1.19)(1.15)]ER_{1973} = 2.75 ER_{1973}$$

and

$$\log ER_{1977} - \log ER_{1973}$$
$$= \log 1.45 + \log 1.24 + \log 1.12 + \log 1.19 + \log 1.15$$

The percent change in the exchange rate is given by taking the logarithm of both sides of this expression and subtracting the log of ER_{1973} from both sides. The shares of the logarithms of the five terms in parentheses as a percent of the logarithm of their product (log of 2.75) provide an additive decomposition of the total change in the equilibrium exchange rate into the different causal factors. The percent shares of the five factors are given in Table 10.5.

In the experiments, we have succeeded in explaining $100 - 13 = 87$ percent of the total change in the equilibrium value of the exchange rate. Differential domestic inflation remains the single most important cause, yet it explains only 37 percent of the total change. Exogenous terms-of-trade changes explain another 32 percent, with the oil price alone responsible for about one-fifth of the total change. Another way of looking at it is to note that the oil price rise *in itself* led to a 36 percent depreciation of the equilibrium rate.

We could continue to try to isolate other factors that contributed to the crisis and further reduce the residual. One factor that did play a role was the otherwise desirable increase in the investment rate. Several things should be noted in this connection. First, the increase in the investment rate from 18 percent to about 23.5 percent that occurred during 1973–7 would, in itself, have led to some depreciation of the exchange rate. But the relative contribution of this factor is less than the contribution of any one of the factors analyzed above. When we add an Experiment E-6 that incorporates all the characteristics of E-5 and a constant investment rate, we reduce the 1977 equilibrium exchange rate from 11.6 to 10.9. This represents a 5 percent contribution in Table 10.5 and reduces the residual to 8 percent. Thus the change in the composition of final demand does not, in itself, play an important role. In a more complete macroeconomic analysis one may, of course, want to relate the surge in the investment rate to the increasing inflation, which we treat as exogenous. It is possible that, in that sense, the "investment boom" was a much more important factor. All we can establish here is that a rise in the proportion of investment in final demand does not have a very substantial impact on the equilibrium exchange rate, *if* it can be financed in a noninflationary way. Finally, it is interesting to note that there is a significant interaction effect, as one would expect given Turkey's reliance on imported machinery, between the effect of the OECD exports price rise and the effects of changes in the investment rate. Order here does matter, at least somewhat. If we take out the special rise in OECD export prices *after* having lowered the investment rate, the relative contribution of the OECD exports price rise declines from 11 to a little below 10 percent. Nothing dramatic, but enough to provide an example of a significant interaction effect.

The story that emerges from the decomposition of the equilibrium exchange rate is very interesting. Once it is realized how rapid and dramatic the change in the underlying equilibrium price of foreign exchange has been, it is easier to understand how Turkey, within only five years, moved from being an economy accumulating substantial resources to one facing a serious and threatening foreign exchange crisis. Furthermore, differential inflation, while an important explanation of the underlying change, explains less than 40 percent of the change in the equilibrium exchange rate. Given these changes, it is again easier to understand why many, in Turkey as well as outside, were caught by surprise. At the International Monetary Fund, for example, pure purchasing-power-parity calculations were made on a routine basis, and the magnitude of the disequilibrium that was developing was not recognized at an early stage. Between mid-1977 and early 1978, as part of a stand-by agreement with the IMF, Turkey devalued its currency by 37 percent. If differential inflation had been the only cause of disequilibrium, this should have been enough to restore foreign balance, at least initially. Instead, within less than a year, renewed pressure developed on the Turkish lira, with the free or "black market" exchange rate soaring to values between 50 and 60 TL per dollar before the end of 1978, while the official rate was kept at 25. Although part of this enormous spread can again be explained by differential inflation (which amounted to 35 or 40 percentage points in 1978), it is clear that the new parity of 25 that had been reached at the beginning of the year represented very serious overvaluation of the Turkish lira at the very time it was agreed upon. Our estimates indicate that 28 represented an equilibrium parity for 1977 (average over the year or at mid-year) and that the equilibrium value for 1978 (again at mid-year) was 38, not 25. Thus, one important component of the "failure" of policy in Turkey, as well as of policy advice to Turkey, can be traced to the simplistic estimates implicit in equilibrium exchange-rate calculations based purely on differential inflation and neglecting the real sphere. Had the magnitude of the required adjustment been recognized earlier, fewer mistakes might have been made in the attempts to restore equilibrium.

Concluding this section, it must be emphasized that an exchange-rate policy aimed at continuous annual flow equilibrium may not necessarily be the best policy to follow at all times. It may well be better for a country to try to isolate its economy from *transitory* shocks in the world economy or transitory capital flows. On the other hand, in the Turkish case, neither the oil price rise nor the decline in the growth of workers' remittances were transitory factors. Consider, for example, workers' remittances. If everything in the economy, including exports and imports, were growing at around 7 percent annually, but workers' remittances remained stationary, it is clear that the foreign exchange gap would steadily grow. In a situation like this, *exports must grow more rapidly than imports* to preserve equilibrium. In turn, real effective exchange rates will have to change continously to generate this more rapid growth of exports, which is the fundamental requirement that was ignored during the 1970s.

A better knowledge of what is the equilibrium rate and a better understanding of the factors that cause its change over time would seem to be prerequisites for adequate planning and policy formulation. The steep downward trend in the equilibrium value of the Turkish lira was seriously underestimated by those using informal, back-of-the-envelope calculations, a deficiency that affected policy formulation and discussions about the future. Building and operating a general equilibrium model is more costly and is certainly no safeguard against bad judgment. But it can be a great help in generating more careful estimates and can be useful in the formulation of better policies.

10.4   The macroeconomic and welfare effects of postponing adjustment

Our analysis focusing on the equilibrium exchange rate shows that a major crisis was in the making by 1975 and that a rather dramatic adjustment had become necessary at that time. The oil crisis, the increase in OECD export prices, and the deceleration of remittance income led to a situation requiring a substantial increase in exports and import-substituting production. Turkey could have started to ration imports – which would have led to increased import substitution – or it could have devalued – which would have led to more import substitution *and* more exports. Instead Turkey started to borrow in a really big way. Euro-currency borrowing was made particularly attractive to domestic borrowers by the government guaranteeing exchange risk. In that way producers or traders able to obtain a foreign loan paid interest rates much lower than those on domestic loans. This, in turn, allowed giving foreign lenders front-end fees of various sorts so that on both sides there were substantial incentives. Foreign lenders did in fact come forward with not less than $7 billion in two years (1976 and 1977), a rather staggering figure given that Turkish exports did not exceed $4 billion in the same two years. In the meantime, domestic inflation gathered steam, so that the real exchange rate, instead of depreciating, appreciated significantly. As we estimated, the degree of overvaluation of the Turkish lira reached about 50 percent by the middle of 1977.

But all this should not cloud the fact that by delaying adjustment, Turkish policy makers were able to postpone the welfare loss and cut in real domestic absorption that would have come with the adjustment. 1977 was an election year, and political competition was fierce. There were therefore great political incentives to postpone the adjustment – at the cost of making the burden even greater in the future. Policy makers in the 1975–7 period may not have been fully aware of the magnitude of the oncoming crisis, but there is little doubt that a conscious effort was made to delay its effects and postpone adjustment. And indeed, until late in 1977, growth proceeded at about 8 percent per annum, there was little import rationing, imports were financed by borrowing and provided cheaply to users, there were no significant shortages, and the price of gasoline was kept below 40 percent of the average price in Europe.

There is thus a fascinating "political economy" aspect to the Turkish crisis. It provides an extreme example of "election economics," with foreign lenders playing a crucial role in the domestic power play. Without attempting to analyze these political questions, we shall instead discuss *how much* of a real cut in absorption was being postponed and in what form the postponement was achieved. Table 10.6 summarizes some of the important economy-wide magnitudes characterizing the basic run (reflecting actual developments) and the various flexible-exchange-rate experiments.

Consider first GDP growth and its components. As can be seen from the first two columns in Table 10.6, adjusting to the exogenous events by allowing the exchange rate to depreciate instead of engaging in massive borrowing would have lowered GDP growth in the period by more than one percentage point, from 8.1 to 6.9 percent. The difference is much more dramatic when we consider domestic absorption, that is, consumption and investment. Consumption would have grown by only 4.3 percent instead of 8.0 percent, and investment growth would have fallen from 14.2 to 6.7 percent. The short-term gain achieved by postponing the crisis was, as these figures show, quite substantial. Turning to the trade figures, note that constant price exports did not increase at all in the 1973–7 period for the basic run, whereas they would have had to grow at almost 25 percent per annum in the flexible-exchange-rate case. This dramatic difference in export behavior is also reflected in the terms-of-trade index. In the basic run, terms-of-trade deteriorate by 24 percent between 1973 and 1977. With a flexible-exchange-rate policy, the deterioration of the terms of trade is twice as bad, with a total change of more than 50 percent. This is part of the "cost" of the dramatic expansion in exports that characterize a flexible exchange rate, immediate adjustment policy.

Columns 3, 4, 5, and 6 of Table 10.6 turn to a summary description of the various flexible-exchange-rate experiments already described in Section 10.3. Each experiment takes "out" one component of the crisis, and so we can expect to see improved performance indicators as we move to the right when reading the table.

The first experiment, moderate inflation, does not have any noticeable effects. This must obviously be so, because real variables in the model are not affected by changes in the price level, provided that the exchange rate is flexible and no other nominal variables are fixed. Except for a few small numbers in the government accounts, this is indeed the case in the TGT model, so very little changes when inflation is lowered except, of course, that the nominal exchange rate is now also lower.[15]

Column 4 reports on the effect of "taking out" the oil price increase from the historical run. The effect is substantial. GDP growth increases

[15] See Table 10.4 for the impact of lowering inflation on the equilibrium exchange rate.

Table 10.6. *The basic run and flexible-exchange-rate experiments: some economy-wide magnitudes*

	Basic run: fixed ER, massive borrowing	E-1: flexible ER, moderate borrowing	E-2: moderate inflation	E-3: no oil crisis	E-4: no other terms-of-trade effects	E-5: higher remittances
1973–7 cumulative flows (billion $)						
Total net foreign						
resource flow (including reserve decumulation)	6.8	3.0	3.0	3.0	3.0	3.0
Workers' remittances	6.1	6.1	6.1	6.1	6.1	8.5
Petroleum imports	5.5	4.7	4.7	2.2	2.3	2.5
Total merchandise imports	20.9	19.4	19.5	18.2	18.6	19.3
Total merchandise exports	7.7	9.8	9.9	8.6	9.0	7.8

1973–7 growth rates (constant 1973 TL)						
GDP	8.1%	6.9%	7.0%	8.0%	8.2%	8.5%
Consumption	8.0%	4.3%	4.3%	5.7%	6.0%	7.0%
Investment	14.2%	6.7%	6.7%	10.2%	11.1%	12.6%
Exports	−0.1%	24.9%	25.1%	20.2%	20.0%	13.4%
1977 values and indexes						
Export/import ratio (current $)	30%	60%	62%	55%	57%	40%
Real GDP index (1973 = 100)	137	130	131	136	137	139
Real export index (1973 = 100)	99	243	245	208	207	160
Real consumption index (1973 = 100)	136	118	118	125	126	131
Real capital stock index (1973 = 100)	120	118	118	121	122	123
Foreign terms of trade (1973 = 100)	124	151	151	120	111	106

by a full percentage point, from 7 to 8 percent. Interestingly enough, the economy achieves the growth rate of the massive borrowing (basic run) case with only moderate borrowing, if there is no oil crisis. Domestic absorption is still much lower, however, because exports have to grow much faster and, of course, the net foreign resource inflow is much lower. Note also that the oil crisis costs Turkey 30 percentage points in the foreign terms-of-trade index.

Moving farther to the right on Table 10.6, we first eliminate the terms-of-trade effect due to the special rise in OECD export prices and finally allow remittances to grow rather than stagnate. With Experiment E-5 we are again close to the magnitude of the basic run. We can thus conclude that the massive borrowing strategy pursued by policy makers allowed growth and absorption to proceed *as if* there had been no oil crisis, no worsening of Turkey's terms of trade, and no stagnation in remittances. This is, in a rough way, what emerges from Table 10.6.

A more systematic way of analyzing and comparing the impact of the various causal factors that led to the 1977 crisis is to use the welfare decomposition analysis described in Chapter 7 and already illustrated in Chapter 9. There are problems in using the decomposition in applied models, because there may be more than one consumer and the weak axiom of revealed preference does not necessarily hold. In the Turkey model the problem does not arise, because the consumer demand functions are identical across groups in the private economy. Only the government is assumed to have different consumption shares. There is also some mild import rationing that occurs in the basic run in 1976 and 1977, but the degree of fixprice rationing does not exceed 15 percent and there is, of course, no rationing in the flexible-exchange-rate runs. On the whole, therefore, the decomposition procedure can be used without fear of getting misleading answers. Table 10.7 summarizes the results of the analysis.

Consider the first five rows of Table 10.7, which refer to the percent change in domestic absorption that occurs with "normal" (moderate) borrowing and a flexible-exchange-rate policy instead of massive borrowing and a fixed-exchange-rate policy. A plus (+) indicates that domestic absorption increases and a minus (−) indicates a decrease.[16]

In 1973 there is a 6.4 percentage point increase in absorption as a result of the fact that the "normal" net foreign resource transfer would

---

[16] As discussed in Chapter 7, we report the arithmetic average of the Paasche and Laspeyres indices. Although relative weights sometimes change significantly, there are no sign changes between the Laspeyres and Paasche formulas in the present set of experiments.

Table 10.7. Decomposition of the percent difference in real absorption between the basic run and alternative experiments

		Total % change in absorption	Of which:	Foreign resource effect	Terms-of-trade effect	Trade distortions effect	Net production effect
E-1: flexible ER, moderate borrowing	1973	6.4		4.3	0.7	0.9	0.5
	1974	−0.6		−0.1	0.2	−0.6	−0.1
	1975	−5.3		−3.3	−0.5	−0.2	−1.3
	1976	−6.9		−4.1	−1.1	−0.7	−1.0
	1977	−9.7		−5.1	−1.1	−0.9	−2.6
E-2: moderate inflation	1973	6.4		4.3	0.7	0.9	0.5
	1974	−0.6		−0.1	0.2	−0.6	−0.1
	1975	−5.3		−3.3	−0.5	−0.2	−1.3
	1976	−7.1		−4.1	−1.2	−0.7	−1.1
	1977	−9.9		−5.1	−1.3	−0.8	−2.6
E-3: no oil crisis	1973	6.4		4.3	0.7	0.9	0.5
	1974	3.4		−0.1	2.8	0.3	0.3
	1975	0.3		−2.6	2.3	−0.1	0.7
	1976	−0.5		−3.8	2.1	−0.2	1.4
	1977	−2.9		−4.7	2.0	−0.3	0.1
E-4: no other terms-of-trade effects	1973	6.4		4.3	0.7	0.9	0.5
	1974	2.7		−0.1	2.6	0.1	0.0
	1975	1.3		−2.7	3.1	−0.0	0.9
	1976	0.9		−3.7	2.9	−0.1	1.8
	1977	−1.4		−4.5	2.6	−0.2	0.7
E-5: higher remittances	1973	6.4		4.3	0.7	0.9	0.5
	1974	2.7		−0.1	2.6	0.1	0.0
	1975	2.7		−1.8	3.3	0.2	1.0
	1976	4.5		−1.2	3.0	0.3	2.4
	1977	2.8		−2.0	3.0	0.2	1.6

have been greater than the "actual" one in the first year. But thereafter there are losses, increasing with each year. These losses are, of course, fundamentally due to the decrease in borrowing, and therefore, net foreign resources, assumed for E-1. They are thus losses of the same kind as those analyzed in the previous chapter. They are triggered by a contraction of net foreign resources, and the foreign resource effect reflects this direct loss. But there are secondary burdens. The ensuing devaluation leads to greater exports and less imports which, in turn, leads to negative terms-of-trade effects, changes in the trade distortions burden, and changes in net production. Thus in 1977, there is a total loss of 9.7 percent, of which 5.1 percentage points are due to the lower value of net foreign resources, 1.1 percentage points reflect lower export prices due to devaluation, 0.9 percentage points are due to the increased burden of trade distortions due to higher exports and lower import volumes, and 2.6 percentage points reflect a net production loss due essentially to the reduced quantity of intermediate imports. These figures illustrate how significant the short-term gains of postponing adjustment were in the Turkish case. They also again illustrate the "transfer" problem: Lower net foreign resources generate a substantial secondary burden. Exports must increase and imports must contract enough to allow the "transfer" to take place. In the process, the terms of trade deteriorate, the burden of existing trade distortions becomes larger, and the net production set of the economy, dependent on imported inputs, contracts.

Consider now the next four sets of rows in Table 10.7. Comparing the numbers appearing there with those appearing in set 1 allows an assessment of the impact of each causal factor on real absorption in the 1973–7 period. In Experiment E-2, assuming moderate inflation cannot lead to results significantly different from Experiment E-1, because lower prices compensated by lower exchange rates leave the real magnitudes of the system constant. Except for some small numbers in the government accounts, the model is homogeneous of degree zero in the price level and the exchange rate. The interesting comparison concerns, therefore, Experiments E-3, E-4, and E-5. For convenience we reproduce and rearrange in Table 10.8 the percentages referring to 1977 for E-1, E-3, E-4, and E-5.

As indicated below, assuming away the oil price increase reduces the welfare loss required in 1977 from 9.7 percentage points to 2.9 percentage points: a gain of 6.8 percentage points. The foreign resource effect is somewhat lower because of the lower exchange rate, essentially equal to that in E-1, but there is a 2.0 percentage points compensating positive terms-of-trade gain. The combined effect of a smaller trade deficit but better terms of trade results in approximately a zero net change

Table 10.8. *Decomposition of the percent difference in real absorption between the basic run and alternative experiments, 1977*

	Total	Foreign resource effect	Terms-of-trade effect	Trade distortions effect	Net production effect
E-1: moderate borrowing	−9.7	−5.1	−1.1	−0.9	−2.6
E-2: no oil crisis	−2.9	−4.7	+2.0	−0.3	+0.1
E-3: no other terms-of-trade effects	−1.4	−4.5	+2.6	−0.2	+0.7
E-4: higher remittances	+2.8	−2.0	+3.0	+0.2	+1.6

in the distortions and net production effects. As a result, the total loss in real absorption is reduced to 2.9 percentage points.

Removing the additional terms-of-trade burden imposed by the surge in OECD export prices leads, in Experiment E-3, to a further reduction of the percentage change in absorption to only 1.4 percentage points. Finally, normally growing remittances, no OECD export price surge, and no oil crisis leads to 2.8 percent *more* domestic absorption in 1977 with a flexible exchange rate and moderate borrowing than with the massive borrowing actually undertaken. The welfare decomposition procedure thus provides us with another way of analyzing and weighing the elements that led to the 1977 crisis in Turkey. It underlines perhaps somewhat more forcefully than the decomposition of the equilibrium exchange rate the importance of the oil crisis and also provides an interesting example of transfer-problem analysis.

To summarize, there are a number of lessons to be drawn from the analysis of the 1973–7 period. Given the variety and magnitude of the shocks that Turkey has undergone, and the speed with which they developed, it is perhaps understandable why Turkish policy makers and other observers were to some extent caught by surprise. The oil price rise, the 1974–5 surge in OECD export prices, the swing in remittances, and the fact that all these factors coincided in time, contributed to confusing the picture. Perhaps the most important lesson for those concerned with exchange-rate analysis is that simple purchasing-power-parity calculations can miss the truth by a very large margin. In the Turkish case this appears to have had some very unfortunate consequences, because the magnitude of the required adjustment was initially seriously underestimated. When a new government undertook an effort at adjustment in early 1978, in concert with the international financial institutions, the magnitude of the adjustment measures fell very much short of what would have been necessary. In the next section, we turn to a discussion of the crisis period and an analysis of the behavior of an economy under severe import rationing.

10.5   Import rationing and rent seeking: the crisis in 1978

The beginning of 1978 marked the full emergence of the crisis that had been developing since 1975. Turkey was no longer able to service her debt or to transfer foreign exchange for even the most essential imports. Real investment in 1978 declined by about 20 percent over 1977, and per-capita GDP growth came to a halt. In this section we discuss the massive import rationing that occurred and the resulting resource allocation and distribution effects on the economy.

In March 1978 Turkey had formally devalued its currency, setting the new parity at 25 TL to the dollar. This represented a depreciation of about 38 percent over the average value of the exchange rate in 1977. Except for a minor adjustment to 26.5 TL, the price of the dollar was officially kept constant until the summer of 1979. In the same 1977–9 period domestic inflation exploded. The GDP deflator went up by about 40 percent in 1978 and by more than 50 percent in 1979. Between mid-1977 and mid-1979, the wholesale price index went up by 130 percent, casting some doubt on the more conservative GDP deflator estimates. In any case, it is clear that the real exchange rate appreciated very substantially during the two years. Taking 100 percent as a conservative estimate for the excess of domestic over world inflation between mid-1977 and mid-1979, and comparing that with the $(26.5 - 18.2)/18.2 = 45$ percent devaluation that occurred in the same period, one can estimate that the PPP-price-level-deflated exchange rate went up by more than 50 percent in this period. To this must be added that the initial exchange rate in mid-1977 was already overvalued by about 50 percent, as shown earlier. Assuming that differential inflation was the only factor affecting the equilibrium exchange rate between 1977 and 1979, one can conclude that by mid-1979 the exchange rate of 26.5 represented a 100 percent overvaluation of the Turkish lira. In fact, the further surge in oil prices in early 1979 because of the Iranian crisis and a new worldwide shortage also affected the equilibrium exchange rate. Running the TGT model for 1978 and 1979 with a flexible exchange rate yields the results shown in Table 10.9. These numbers give some indication of the order of magnitude of the disequilibrium

Table 10.9. *TGT Model: equilibrium exchange rates, 1978–9*

	Official parity	Equilibrium exchange rate	Degree of overvaluation (%)
1978	25.0	34.0	36
1979:			
Until June 12	26.5	50.4	90
After June 12	47.1		7

characterizing the situation until mid-1979. In June 1979, after a new interim agreement with the IMF and Turkey's creditors, the lira was further devalued and overvaluation was almost eliminated, at least at that point in time.

Import rationing of some form has been a more or less permanent feature of the Turkish economy since the early 1950s. One must, however, distinguish conceptually between commodity-specific quotas and across-the-board, economy-wide import rationing used as a mechanism to manage the balance of payments. The former type of selective quantity restrictions, important in particular for consumer goods, has existed in various forms throughout the postwar period. Such quotas have often been circumvented quite openly through smuggling, and their real impact on the economy is hard to assess. In contrast, import rationing as an adjustment mechanism to foreign exchange shortages essentially took the form of either long delays in the foreign exchange transfers that importers have to make through the Central Bank or of simple refusals to grant import licenses. It became massive during each of the three crisis periods that affected Turkish postwar growth. Very important in 1956–60, and 1966–70, such general rationing was dramatic at the outset of the crisis toward the end of 1977.

Although it is important to distinguish conceptually between commodity- and sector-specific quantity restrictions and overall import rationing, in practice this distinction is not easy to maintain. Quota lists are periodically updated, and their degree of restrictiveness often reflects the "bite" of import rationing and overall foreign exchange shortages. Overall rationing for balance-of-payments purposes thus spills over into the administration of quota lists. Furthermore, whenever the shortage of foreign exchange becomes severe, the fact of being able in principle to import a product may become irrelevant if in practice the Central Bank does not transfer the foreign exchange to pay for it. In such periods the massive foreign exchange rationing caused by acute shortage swamps all other specific quantity restrictions in the system. This is precisely what happened in the late 1970s: The effective constraint on imports was simply the ability to find enough foreign exchange to pay for them. All other restrictions were secondary.

Until mid-1978 the government did, in fact, attempt to administer a system of fixprice rationing. The importation and distribution of steel and steel products were, for instance, nationalized early in 1978, and the state attempted to allocate available steel to final users directly, "in proportion to need" charging only the c.i.f. + tariff price. Use of the same system was attempted for fertilizers and some other basic intermediate imports. In fact, excess demand was much too strong, and the state's administrative capability much too weak, for fixprice rationing to work, except perhaps for a small fraction of imports. Quickly a parallel market for foreign exchange developed, with an effective exchange rate fluctuating from day to day. By the end of 1978 the system was therefore much closer to rationing with a premium through the market rather than to the fixprice rationing mechanism the government was trying to implement. In effect, user costs increased on the import side, while the price of foreign exchange was kept fixed on the export side at the low official parity. The nature of a large part of Turkish exports (agricultural commodities) and the institutional channels for these exports (semipublic cooperatives) made exchange control much easier on the export side.

The emergence of massive rationing and stringent import shortages also led to a substantial increase in the real resource costs of activities related to the rationing mechanism we call "rent-seeking activities" (following Krueger, 1974b). Competition for available imports became fierce, and it is fair to assume that substantial resources were diverted from direct productive use into activities aimed at obtaining imports and the rents associated with those imports.

There is no doubt that the complexity of the situation was such that no model can really hope to capture the full story with all its details and sectoral and distributional ramifications. The experiments we shall conduct with the TGT model must therefore be regarded as "stylized stories" that capture some important elements of the situation created by acute foreign exchange shortage, without being able to capture others. What we shall do is to assume rationing with premium for 1978 and solve the TGT model under that assumption. We also assume that 50 percent of the "rent" due to rationing is pure rent (that is, channeled to import users without additional resource costs), whereas 50 percent of the value of import premia goes to pay the real resources diverted from production and spent in the effort to obtain scarce foreign exchange and imports. The 50 percent ratio is arbitrary and reflects a compromise between assuming "pure premia" obtained costlessly and pure rent seeking, where the value of premia equals the value of resources spent trying to get them.[17]

The premium rate that emerges from the TGT model in 1978 is 90 percent. Given the official exchange rate of 25 TL to the dollar, this implies an effective exchange rate of 47.5 for imports in 1978. This value is quite consistent with the so-called free or black market rate that actually was experienced in Turkey. The latter appears to have fluctuated between 42 TL and 60 TL to the dollar during 1978, with the average value of transactions probably occurring around a rate of 50 TL to the dollar. It is important to stress that the premium-inclusive exchange rate is not equal to the equilibrium exchange rate that would have ruled under a flexible-exchange-rate regime. The equilibrium exchange rate in 1978 would have been 34 TL to the dollar according to the TGT model. The reason for this difference is, of course, the export-expansion effect that occurs under a flexible-exchange-rate regime but does not occur under a premium rationing regime.

Thus rationing raises the user costs of imports by 90 percent, whereas full adjustment by a devaluation would increase the user costs of imports by only 36 percent. Compared with a flexible-exchange-rate regime, rationing with premia tends to favor import-substituting sectors at the expense of export-oriented sectors.[18] Under import rationing, the user costs of imports increase 2.5 times more than when the adjustment takes place simultaneously by import reduction and export expansion.

In addition to this effect, there is a loss in output because of resources that are diverted toward rent seeking. What makes the loss in output differ across sectors is both the share of intermediate inputs in the total costs of production and the share of imported inputs in total intermediate inputs. Thus sectors where both these ratios are high will be sectors that suffer the greatest losses because of the diversion of real resources toward rent-seeking activities. For a better understanding of the microeconomic impact of premium rationing, we first discuss the sectoral impact of import premia. We then discuss the extent of bias between production for export and production for internal use using domestic resource costs (DRCs) within each sector between exporting and import-substituting activities.

[17] For a more complete discussion of rationing and rent seeking and how they are included in the model, see Chapter 9.

[18] For a definition of what characterizes import-substituting sectors, see Chapters 7 and 8.

Table 10.10. *The sectoral impact of import premia in 1978*

Sector	Ratio of imported to total intermediate inputs	Premia payments as percent of value added	Premia payments as percent of total cost	Output loss due to rent seeking (%)
1. Agriculture	9.9	4.4	3.0	1.5
2. Mining	18.3	16.1	8.3	4.1
3. Food	1.9	14.0	2.1	1.1
4. Textiles	9.5	27.8	4.5	2.3
5. Clothing	4.2	9.9	3.6	1.8
6. Wood	4.1	12.7	2.8	1.4
7. Paper	11.0	29.4	8.7	4.3
8. Chemicals	33.1	123.9	27.6	13.8
9. Rubber	24.1	80.7	14.7	7.3
10. Petroleum products[a]	15.9	16.4	9.3	4.7
11. Non metallic mineral products	10.6	32.8	9.0	4.5
12. Basic metals	17.6	47.5	9.3	4.7
13. Metal products	19.4	67.3	15.6	7.8
14. Nonelectrical machinery	41.3	131.9	25.5	12.7
15. Electrical machinery	24.6	83.3	21.8	10.9
16. Transportation equipment	18.4	35.5	10.6	5.3
17. Construction	16.0	12.4	5.6	2.8
18. Infrastructure	13.9	23.6	9.0	4.5
19. Services	4.5	2.1	1.6	0.8
Total	11.5	10.0	5.9	3.1

[a] "Petroleum and petroleum products" includes refining.

Table 10.10 summarizes both the net average effect of the massive rationing that occurred on the economy as well as the distribution of these effects across sectors. Column 1 indicates that, for the economy as a whole, the ratio of imported to total intermediate inputs is 11.5 percent. Premia payments amount to 10 percent of value added (column 2), and to 5.9 percent of total cost (column 3). Although we do not have enough information to analyze the distributional consequences of the premia, it is clear that they are major. It is, for example, worth noting that the total value of import premia in 1978 (128 billion TL) is approximately equal to the total value of direct taxes and is three times the value of tariff collections!

In addition to this substantial impact in aggregate terms, one must also take account of the very uneven distribution of premia payments across sectors, both as a percentage of total cost and as a percentage of value added. The net result is that whereas the average output loss for the economy is 3.1 percent (column 4), the variation in output losses across sectors varies from 0.8 percent in services to 13.8 percent in chemicals.

To get a better understanding of what accounts for this loss in output, consider some of the sectors whose output losses due to rent seeking are among the largest: chemicals, rubber, nonelectrical machinery, and electrical machinery. At first glance, one would expect that the output loss in nonelectric machinery would be higher than the loss in chemicals, because column 1 indicates that the former has a ratio of imported to total intermediate inputs of 41.3 percent, whereas the latter's ratio is only 33.1 percent. It turns out, however, that the output loss due to rent seeking is 13.8 percent in chemicals, whereas in machinery it is only 12.7 percent. The reason for this reversal in rankings is that the premia payments are a larger percentage of total cost (column 3) for chemicals (27.6 percent) than for nonelectrical machinery (25.5 percent), because the value-added ratio is higher in nonelectrical machinery than in chemicals. Next consider rubber and electrical machinery, both of which have a ratio of imported inputs to total intermediate inputs of about 24 percent. Here again one can ascribe the greater loss in output of electrical machinery to the fact that premia payments are a larger share of total costs than for rubber (column 3). In general, one can conclude that the hardest-hit sectors are, in order: capital goods sectors, intermediate goods sectors, and then the consumer goods and nontradables sectors. There are, of course, some notable exceptions, such as chemicals. As one would expect, the hardest-hit sectors are generally the sectors that are the most import dependent (as shown in column 1).

Next, we consider the extent of bias, both within and between sectors, in incentives for producing for exporting and for import substituting. The measure we use to analyze the bias is the domestic resource cost (DRC), which is defined as the marginal domestic costs in a sector (direct and indirect) in domestic currency divided by the net foreign exchange earned from a unit of production. The foreign exchange is earned either from directly exporting the good or from using it to substitute for imports and is measured net of direct and indirect intermediate import costs. The sectoral DRCs thus have the units of an exchange rate and can be compared to the economy-wide exchange rate.

Within a sector, the DRC for exporting and import-substituting activities will be the same if the effective exchange rate is the same for intermediate inputs and for exports and imports in that sector. That is, the nominal exchange rate augmented by tariffs and premia on the import side equals the rate augmented by export subsidies on the export side. This equality and the fact that producers are indifferent between producing for the export or domestic markets implies that the net foreign exchange earnings from both export and import-substituting activities are the same. Because the costs of production are the same, the exporting and import-substituting DRCs must also be the same. When comparing DRCs for exports or import substitutes across sectors, differences may arise as a result of differences in the marginal foreign exchange cost and/or to intersectoral differences in the costs of inputs. Such intersectoral differences in input costs may be due to differences in wage rates across sectors for the same category of labor or to intersectoral differences in indirect tax rates.

As shown in Chapter 8, the DRC for exporting or import substituting in each sector measures the effective exchange rate for that activity. DRCs thus can be compared to a properly defined shadow exchange rate to see if a particular sector can "profitably" engage in exporting or import substituting. Sectors with DRCs lower than the shadow exchange rate should expand, because they can earn foreign exchange at lower domestic cost. Thus a sector's DRC gives information on the minimum value that the effective exchange rate must have for the activity to be profitable.

The sectoral DRCs for 1978 are given in Table 10.11. The equilibrium exchange rate is 34.0. At that rate almost all exporting activities are profitable, whereas virtually none of the import-substituting activities is profitable. The major reason for the difference is that the user price of imports (including premia) is 90 percent above the value given by the official exchange rate. There is thus an across-the-board bias against export activities and in favor of import-substituting activities. In the manufacturing sectors, the bias averages 26 TL to the dollar, which is itself equal to more than the official exchange rate!

The first two columns in Table 10.11 use market wages and actual profit rates to value domestic factor inputs. Strictly speaking, they reflect a ranking by effective protection rather than domestic resource cost, because the latter presupposes shadow pricing of domestic resources. As discussed in Chapter 5, fully satisfactory shadow pricing really would require a dynamic optimizing model. In its absence, we have used the *average* economy-wide rental rate and the sectoral wage rates derived from an equilibrium exchange rate run as shadow prices of capital and labor and have recomputed sectoral domestic resource costs on this basis. Columns 3 and 4 in Table 10.11 give the results. Sectors with above-

Table 10.11. *Domestic resource costs (DRCs) by sectors in 1978*

	Market prices		Shadow prices	
	Export	Import	Export	Import
1. Agriculture	27.1	52.0	24.6	47.2
2. Mining	22.5	46.9	29.0	60.5
3. Food	22.8	46.6	20.8	42.5
4. Textiles	24.3	52.5	25.3	54.5
5. Clothing	26.2	46.0	24.0	42.2
6. Wood	24.9	48.9	25.8	50.7
7. Paper	23.3	55.1	24.2	57.2
8. Chemicals	22.5	53.6	19.7	50.0
9 Rubber	21.1	53.8	21.2	53.9
10. Petroleum products	27.1	50.3	9.1	16.9
11. Nonmetallic mineral products	23.4	53.7	27.0	61.9
12. Basic metals	22.2	46.1	26.9	56.0
13. Metal products	22.9	50.4	24.8	55.7
14. Nonelectrical machinery	22.7	55.0	18.7	45.5
15. Electrical machinery	22.9	48.1	19.9	41.9
16. Transportation equipment	21.8	50.2	17.4	40.2

Notes: Units are TL per dollar. The equilibrium exchange rate is 34.0, TL/$. "Market prices": actual wage and profit rates used in the computation. "Shadow prices": shadow wage and profit rates used in the computation.

average profit rates now fare better than sectors with below-average profit rates. Given the massive premium, it is still true that at the margin there is need for reduction in all import-substituting activities except petroleum and expansion in all export activities. But the rankings change when domestic inputs are shadow priced. Nonelectrical machinery, for example, substantially improves its ranking, whereas mining loses out, reflecting the fact that the former enjoys a very high profit rate and the latter a very low one. Only the shadow-priced domestic resource costs carry any normative significance because, if the shadow prices are correct, the DRCs reflect social opportunity cost.

The DRC calculations underline the costs to Turkey of dealing with the emerging foreign exchange crisis through a regime of import rationing rather than through adjustment in relative prices, including the exchange rate. The emergence of very large import premia causes major distributional shifts among sectors and leads to rent-seeking activities that clearly waste real resources. The bias against exports implicit in the premia system are enormous, and are clearly reflected in the DRC calculations. The net effect is to reduce the ability of the economy to earn scarce foreign exchange through expanded exports.

10.6   Conclusion

The analysis presented in the preceding sections illustrates the use of a CGE modeling framework in improving our knowledge of past events and in weighing the importance of various causal factors that affect the course of events. Starting in 1974, Turkey suffered major exogenous shocks coming from the world economy. These shocks were greater for Turkey than for almost any other middle-income country because of the initial conditions characterizing the Turkish situation, especially the excessive reliance on remittance income, a small export base, and heavy dependence on imported fuel. Many countries had at least one of these disadvantages but few, if any, had all three simultaneously. The oil crisis and its repercussions would have created a slowdown in Turkish economic growth even under the best possible economic management, and it is also true that, in contrast to some countries, no great flow of timely foreign help was made available to Turkey. But the magnitude of the crisis that emerged and the extent of the hardship it created are due largely to the lack of planning, decisiveness, and rationality in domestic economic policy during that period.

Concluding, it is worth stressing again that the CGE model used was able to deal with real factors, medium-term trends, and equilibrium values. A considerable amount of insight was gained through the analysis. But one must be aware of the fact that neither short-run disequilibrium behavior nor the sociopolitical variables that lie behind the explosion of money supply and inflation characterizing the post-1977 period can easily be fitted into any multisector planning model. Reality is extremely complex, and no single model or framework of analysis can by itself provide "the whole story." Different tools and approaches should be viewed as complementary and used jointly in the economic and political analysis of socioeconomic events.

CHAPTER 11

Growth and structural change: alternative scenarios, 1978–1985

11.1   Introduction

In this chapter we turn to a forward-looking analysis of alternative growth paths for the Turkish economy. Instead of being used as a tool for analyzing past events, the TGT model is used here as a planning model: a device that generates consistent sets of alternative projections, each depending on a specific set of policy choices. The fundamental premise behind a CGE-based planning exercise is that growth paths depend on the structure of prices and incentives and that these in turn can be strongly influenced by government policy. In particular, tariffs, export subsidies, and exchange-rate policy will help determine the relative importance of export expansion, import substitution, and nontradables production in overall growth. These policy variables will, of course, interact with truly exogenous variables such as international prices, rates of growth of world demand, and so on, in determining the pattern of incentives and growth. But they do have a determining influence on the characteristics of growth in economies where markets matter, and planning in a market economy must take this into account.

The TGT model has been used to provide an analysis of Turkey's growth prospects in the 1980s as part of a World Bank review of Turkey's fourth five-year plan (see World Bank, 1980, chap. 7). In this chapter, we present three experiments that illustrate how the model can be used to provide such an analysis. Each experiment or "run" of the model is based on a different set of policy assumptions, and each will lead to a different growth path. We then compare and analyze the properties of these growth paths.

Experiment E-1 assumes that after a transitory movement to more neutral incentive structures, the real exchange rate is again allowed to drift, leading to a progressively increasing bias against the production of exportables and the reemergence of a substantial premium on imports. Specifically, we shall assume that the purchasing-power-parity price-level-deflated exchange rate is allowed to drift down by 5 percent every year starting in 1980. This leads to increasing foreign exchange shortage and continued growth in the value of the premium rate. We assume, furthermore, that exporters are not allowed to keep any of the foreign exchange they earn, and that the effective exchange rate on the export side is kept at the official parity adjusted for existing and constant export subsidies. The experiment is therefore characterized by continued and growing premium rationing of the type described in Chapter 9.

Experiment E-2 describes a quite different scenario. Although Turkey does not move immediately to a fully flexible exchange rate, the parallel market existing for imports is progressively extended to exports by an export earnings retention scheme that increases from 50 percent in 1980 to 100 percent in 1985. At that point, the parallel market "takes over" all foreign exchange transactions, so that effectively there is a flexible exchange rate.[1] This experiment reflects a scenario in which Turkey abandons strict exchange controls and allows the market to determine the effective equilibrium value of foreign exchange. This would mark a shift toward an outward-looking phase in Turkey's industrialization efforts. As we shall see, such a shift would have very important effects not only on overall economic performance but also on the pattern of sectoral growth.

Experiment E-3 is a variant on E-2 where the export earnings retention scheme is not applied to traditional agriculture-based exports, which amounts to imposing a special agricultural exports tax, and where there is also a government resource mobilization effort that succeeds in raising the investment rate from 20 percent of GDP in 1979 to about 25 percent in 1985. This experiment thus reflects a package that emphasizes manufactured exports and combines the shift in trade policy with an increasing overall investment effort. Table 11.1 summarizes the characteristics of the three experiments.

The experiments are designed to reflect some of the basic options and decisions facing Turkish planners in the 1980s. Given the huge foreign exchange gap that emerged in the late 1970s, the dominant question is whether Turkey can move toward more outward-looking export-oriented development policies. However, our emphasis on trade policy should not lead to neglect of the importance of resource mobilization in determining development performance. Moreover, export orientation based on a unified exchange rate may not reflect the desire of planners for rapid growth in nontraditional manufacturing sectors and in struc-

---

[1] Note, however, that there is still rent seeking, as discussed in Chapter 9, as long as there is rationing. The premium now applies to both exports and imports, and its magnitude declines.

Table 11.1. *Forward-looking planning experiments for Turkey*

Experiment	Characteristics
E-1	Real exchange rate drifts back down. Increasing antiexport bias.
E-2	Movement toward more neutral trade policies. Effectively, a flexible exchange rate extends to all foreign exchange transactions by 1985.
E-3	Same as E-2 but there is also a resource mobilization drive that increases the investment rate five percentage points over seven years and a special tax on traditional agricultural exports.

tural transformation of the economy. Experiment E-3 thus represents an investment-oriented and manufactured-exports-biased variant of E-2.

11.2 Macroeconomic alternatives

The basic macroeconomic results obtained for each alternative policy package are summarized in Tables 11.2 and 11.3. These tables taken together show the impact of policy on Turkey's growth path and the various trade-offs involved. First, compare E-1 to E-2 in terms of growth performance. With a gradual shift toward a floating exchange rate that removes the antiexport biases of the past, the volume of exports is projected to grow at 17.1 percent annually over the plan period. This allows real import growth of 7.5 percent and GDP growth of 6.8 percent. Contrast this to the 4.4 percent GDP growth achieved with E-1 under severe rationing. The implied average import–GDP elasticity, an elasticity that the IMF, for example, often uses in its projections, is slightly above unity for E-2 but only 0.3 for the "bad" trade policy run which, as we shall see, implies rather dramatic import substitution.

The import-dependent industrial sector is most severely affected by restrictive trade policy. Under E-2, it loses 3.4 percentage points in growth compared to 2.1 percentage points lost in services and 0.8 percentage points lost in agriculture. Similarly, fixed investment suffers a much greater decline in growth than does consumption. Finally, note the impact of trade policy on real wage growth: A restrictive trade policy cuts rural and urban wage growth by almost 4 percentage points.

Although the impact of trade policy appears substantial, the results should almost certainly be regarded as "minimum differences." The

Table 11.2. *Macroeconomic effects of alternative policies on growth in Turkey: average annual growth rates, 1978– 85 (%)*

	E-1	E-2	E-3
GDP (real):			
Average, 1978–85	4.4	6.8	6.9
Terminal year, 1985	4.4	6.9	7.5
Value added (real):			
Agriculture	2.9	3.7	3.5
Industry	5.4	8.8	9.4
Services	4.6	6.7	6.4
Consumption (real)	4.3	5.8	5.0
Fixed investment (real)	3.6	6.6	9.1
Economy-wide capital stock (real)	4.2	4.7	5.1
Real wage in agriculture	3.5	7.1	5.8
Average real urban wage	0.0	3.8	4.5
Exports:			
Volume (real)	3.8	17.1	16.9
Value (dollars)	11.4	20.5	20.2
Imports:			
Volume (real)	1.4	7.5	7.3
Value (dollars)	7.7	14.6	14.2

true costs of a return to restrictive trade policies may well be larger because the average net annual resource inflow has been kept constant across the experiments. Note, as a result, the very different debt–service ratios arrived at by 1985: 52 percent in E-1 versus 33–34 percent in E-2 and E-3. Although special political and strategic circumstances may allow a very high debt burden, it is likely that foreign resource flows would dwindle if the debt–service ratio were to rise too much. To explore the impact of even a tighter foreign exchange constraint, we ran a variant of E-1 in which the net foreign resource flow was set to zero after 1980. This variant yielded a growth rate of only 3.5 percent instead of the 4.4 percent achieved in E-1. Even a zero foreign resource flow, however, would *not* reduce the debt–service ratio below 36 percent given the dismal export performance achieved in E-1. Though computationally cumbersome because it involves back-and-forth iterations between separate runs, it is possible to adjust the net foreign resource flow until the debt–service ratio is reduced to a target level. In Turkey's case and given the assumptions of E-1, this would involve early repayments of principal and negative net resource transfers abroad – an unlikely event. Nevertheless, it is important to realize that the debt-

Table 11.3. *Macroeconomic effects of alternative policies on growth: some 1985, terminal-year values*

	E-1	E-2	E-3
Composition of GDP (%):			
Agriculture	24.4	26.2	23.2
Industry	38.1	31.7	36.1
Services	37.5	42.1	40.7
Investment rate (%)	22.4	19.3	24.8
ICOR	4.6	3.1	3.2
Economy-wide profit rate (%)	14.2	21.7	19.8
Capital goods price index (1978 = 100)	582	460	510
GDP deflator (1978 = 100)	525	525	525
Foreign terms-of-trade index	93.4	127.5	126.7
Agricultural terms-of-trade index	110.6	130.5	117.4
Exports–GDP (%)	6.1	11.5	11.2
Imports–GDP (%)	8.3	14.1	13.6
Debt–service ratio (%)[a]	52.0	35.5	34.1
Average annual net foreign resources inflow[b]	342.2	342.2	342.2

[a]Defined as amortization plus interest divided by exports plus remittances.
[b]"Foreign resources" here refer to what is below the current account line; i.e., they do not include workers' remittances.

service ratio constitutes an important constraint on the feasibility of any particular scenario, and that very high ratios require very particular political circumstances if they can be achieved at all.

Although a restrictive trade policy inflicts the greatest loss of real growth on the industrial sector, the share of industry in GDP in current prices reaches 38.1 percent in E-1 against 31.7 percent in E-2. With rationing, industrialization proceeds in current prices, whereas it almost stagnates in constant prices! The same kind of relative price phenomenon is responsible for the fact that the investment rate in 1985 is 3 percentage points higher with a restrictive trade policy than with a flexible exchange rate. In fact, real 1985 investment is 23 percent higher in E-2, reflecting not only the 17 percent higher level of GDP, but also the fact that the relative user price of capital goods is much lower with a flexible exchange rate, so that any given nominal amount of savings buys more real investment goods.

Returning to the export projections, note that whereas the rate of growth of export volume rises from 3.8 to 17.1 percent, the export value growth rate rises only from 11.4 to 20.5 percent between E-1 and E-2.

The spread between the volume and value growth rates reflects a substantial adverse terms-of-trade effect inherent in a flexible-exchange-rate policy. Indeed, as can be seen from Table 11.3, there is a 27.5 percent deterioration in the terms of trade over the seven-year period considered, which is due to the downward-sloping export demand curves that characterize most sectors in the TGT model. Increased export orientation also implies a movement in the internal terms of trade favoring agriculture. This reflects the heavy weight of agriculture and agriculture-based products in Turkey's exports.

Now turn to E-3, where agricultural exports are taxed and there is a substantial increase in government savings leading to a 1985 investment rate of 24.8 instead of 19.3 in E-2. The impact of this composite experiment is significant on the growth rate of fixed investment ($+2.5$ percentage points) and on the spread between agricultural and urban wage growth (reduced from 3.3 to 1.3 percentage points). Note also that the composite of 1985 GDP in current prices changes significantly as a result of a combined relative price and volume growth effect favoring the industrial sector. On the other hand, overall GDP growth is not much affected. This reflects the fact that the agricultural export tax hurts export performance, whereas increased investment demand generates a higher level of demand for imports. As a result, there is not only more rationing and output loss but also more rapid capital accumulation and therefore greater output growth. On balance, average aggregate export, import, and GDP growth remain about the same. It remains true, however, that the increasing rate does raise GDP growth substantially in the final years of the plan (7.5 in 1985 instead of 6.9 for E-2), but too late to have a significant impact on the seven-year average. Furthermore, as we shall see, it is at the micro level that E-3 has its most interesting impact.

In conjunction with the investment rates, it is instructive to consider the economy-wide ICORs implied by the projection, because the investment rate–ICOR ratio yields the GDP growth rate. The trade-liberalization strategy leads to an ICOR of only 3.1 in 1985 compared to 4.6 under restrictive trade policy. This is a considerable achievement, which essentially reflects two things: a shift in resource allocation toward less capital-intensive sectors, and a progressive elimination of the resource waste associated with massive rent seeking.

A convenient macroeconomic summary of the real-income implications of our three alternative policy packages can be provided by using the real-income decomposition procedure presented in Chapter 7. Table 11.4 describes the results for three selected years, providing percent differences in real absorption achieved in E-2 and E-3, taking E-1 as the base.

Table 11.4. *Decomposition of the percent difference in real absorption between the restrictive trade policy run, E-1, and experiments E-2 and E-3*

Experiment	Year	Total percent change in absorption, of which:	Terms-of-trade effect	Consumption distortions effect	Net production effect
E-2	1981	+ 3.9	−1.0	+0.5	+ 4.4
	1983	+ 8.1	−1.7	+0.7	+ 9.1
	1985	+12.5	−2.3	+1.3	+13.5
E-3	1981	+ 3.2	−0.6	+0.4	+ 3.4
	1983	+ 7.8	−1.3	+0.6	+ 8.5
	1985	+13.5	−2.0	+1.2	+14.3

The net production effect dominates both the negative terms-of-trade effect and the positive consumption distortions effect, particularly toward the end of the plan period. The net production effect itself is composed of four effects that are not, however, simply additive. There is a standard static neoclassical resource allocation effect. There is a dynamic resource reallocation effect stemming from a reallocation of investment. There is a resource growth effect due to increased real capital accumulation. And finally, there is the rent-seeking effect: With exchange liberalization, resources formerly devoted to rent seeking start producing real output. In the terminal year of the plan, real domestic absorption is 13.5 percent higher in E-2 and 14.3 percent in E-3. When we consider that the debt–service ratio is 34 percent instead of 52 percent with restrictive trade policies, the results provide a powerful illustration of the benefits of exchange liberalization, at least at the macroeconomic level. Note again that what has been held constant across experiments is the net foreign resource transfer. If instead the debt–service ratio were treated as an effective constraint – which for Turkey would imply net transfers abroad – the difference under scenario E-1 in real income and growth would be much larger.

11.3   Relative prices and the sectoral pattern of growth

The economy-wide perspective and the alternative scenarios presented so far rely on developments in each of the nineteen sectors distinguished in the TGT model. Although the macroeconomic results provide an overview and underline the most essential differences in the alternative scenarios, a real understanding of the nature of the alternative growth paths must also be based on an analysis of sectoral developments. Although a nineteen-sector disaggregation is not enough to allow a real link between economy-wide analysis and analysis at the microeconomic project level, consideration of sectoral developments implicit in the macro perspectives is important in evaluating the macro results. The reasonableness of the overall growth projections depends on the reasonableness of the underlying sectoral growth rates, and nineteen sectors represent enough disaggregation to provide a useful framework for more detailed sectoral analysis. Evaluation of sectoral growth must focus not only on the rise in domestic production as such, but also on the pace of import substitution and/or export expansion that is implicit in the sectoral growth projections.

Relative prices and relative price effects play a very important role in determining the resource allocation and growth that in turn determine the structure of sectoral growth. The restrictive trade policy experiment (E-1) that assumes a falling price-deflated exchange rate leads to quite different relative price effects than those of the higher exchange-rate strategies of Experiments E-2 and E-3. Severe import rationing exerts upward pressure on the price of import substitutes and adversely affects the price of exportables and nontradables.

Although rationing leads to higher final output prices of import substitutes, it is important to remember that sectors such as chemicals and basic metals are also extremely import dependent and will suffer when there is severe rationing from having to buy imported inputs at the very high premium-inclusive price. In addition, these are the sectors that will devote large fractions of their resources to rent-seeking activities. Thus, although the price of their output may go up, this may not, in fact, lead to increased production even in a purely static context. Dynamically, capital accumulation and capital goods price effects further complicate the picture. Thus, as discussed at length in Chapters 8 and 9, the mechanisms at work here are quite different from the simpler mechanisms stressed by pure trade theory, and the introduction of rent seeking makes the analysis different even from that appropriate to premium-absorbing devaluation as such. Note, finally, that throughout the forward-looking experiments, we are essentially comparing premium rationing to exchange liberalization, that is, devaluation. A comparison between fixprice rationing and devaluation would generate different results.[2]

---

[2] See Derviş and Robinson (1978) for an analysis of forward projections with fixprice rationing. After 1979, Turkey abandoned the extensive use of fixprice rationing, and seems unlikely to revert to it.

Sectoral characteristics in the TGT model

The TGT model distinguishes nineteen sectors that are aggregations of the sectors distinguished in the 1973 State Institute of Statistics Input–Output Table. There are differences in sectoral definitions between input–output and foreign trade data, and it is important to note that lightly processed agriculture commodities appear in the manufacturing sectors, not in agriculture. Thus, preserved fruits and vegetables, olive oil, and tobacco are included in the food sector, and cotton ginning is included in the textile sector. Second, crude oil and natural gas are aggregated with refining in an integrated petroleum and petroleum products sector.

Table 11.5 summarizes some important data that characterize the individual sectors' role in trade in 1978, the base year. These characteristics change over time, but Table 11.5 nevertheless provides a good overview of what is important. The first column presents the ratio of imports to domestic goods in domestic use of each category of commodities. This RMD ratio is measured in constant base-year (1978) prices. The second column presents the proportion, IMD, of imported intermediates in total intermediate input use for each sector, measured in 1978 prices, and measures sectoral import dependence. The third column tabulates the model estimates of premia payments by sectors as a percent of total costs (in 1978). Column 4 provides the ratio E/X of exports to total domestic production, again in constant prices. Finally, columns 5 and 6 give, respectively, the assumed export demand and trade-substitution elasticities, which fall somewhere between the "high" and "low" values used as upper and lower bounds in Chapters 8 and 9.

Several things should be noted in Table 11.5. Turkey did not in 1978 import significant amounts of finished consumer goods or agricultural products, and the proportion of imports in total domestic demand for "light" manufactured goods such as processed food, textiles, clothing, and wood products is very small. But Turkey imported a large share of its nonelectrical machinery and was also heavily dependent on imports of chemicals, electrical machinery, basic metals, and transportation equipment. Turkey was also dependent on imports of crude petroleum, but most refining is done domestically and the import ratio in sector 10, which aggregates crude petroleum with petroleum and coal products, remains moderate.

The degree of import dependence and the degree to which output is lost as a result of rent seeking are reflected in the proportion of imported intermediates in total intermediate inputs and the ratio of premia to

Table 11.5. *Sectoral trade data, 1978*

	Ratio of imports to domestically produced goods in domestic use, RMD	Share of imported intermediates in total intermediate inputs, IMD	Premia share of sectoral costs, PREMIA	Share of exports in total domestic production, E/X	Sectoral export demand elasticities, η_i	Sectoral trade substitution elasticities, σ_i
1. Agriculture	0.6	9.9	3.0	1.9	∞^a	2.00
2. Mining	5.3	18.3	8.3	9.5	∞^a	0.56
3. Food	0.7	1.9	2.1	10.9	3.0	0.66
4. Textiles	1.3	9.5	4.5	18.1	∞^a	0.66
5. Clothing	1.3	4.2	3.6	6.9	6.0	0.66
6. Wood	0.2	4.1	2.8	0.3	6.0	0.66
7. Paper	6.3	11.0	8.7	0.2	4.0	0.66
8. Chemicals	58.1	33.1	27.6	1.4	4.0	0.33
9. Rubber	14.5	24.1	14.7	0.9	4.0	0.33
10. Petroleum products	16.2	15.9	9.3	0.0	6.0	2.00
11. Nonmetallic mineral products	4.5	10.6	9.0	1.9	6.0	0.66
12. Basic metals	23.2	17.6	9.3	0.9	4.0	0.50
13. Metal products	12.5	19.4	15.6	1.3	4.0	0.50
14. Nonelectrical machinery	80.2	41.3	25.5	0.9	4.0	0.33
15. Electrical machinery	46.2	24.6	21.8	0.2	4.0	0.33
16. Transportation equipment	21.7	18.4	10.6	0.0	4.0	0.75
17. Construction	0.0	16.0	5.6	0.0	—	—
18. Infrastructure[b]	0.9	13.9	9.0	7.1	3.0	0.20
19. Services[b]	0.8	4.5	1.6	4.4	3.0	0.20
Average	7.5	11.5	6.0	4.2	—	—

[a] Fixed world price.
[b] Following the 1973 SIS Input–Output Table, trade and transportation margins are not distributed to the individual sectors but appear in the

sectoral costs. Note that the IMD_i ratios provide only "first-round" direct estimates of import dependence, because they do not take into account the indirect dependence created through input–output linkages, capital requirements, and general equilibrium price effects. Food, clothing, wood products, and services are the sectors that appear least dependent on imports, followed by textiles and agriculture. The average IMD_i ratio in industry (including construction) is 14.9 percent, and the economy-wide ratio is 11.5 percent. The sectors most dependent on imported intermediate inputs are nonelectrical machinery, with an IMD_i ratio of 41 percent, followed by chemicals, 33 percent, and electrical machinery, 25 percent.

Column 3 provides estimates of the share of premia in total costs of each sector in 1978. The sectoral distribution roughly follows that of intermediate import dependence given in column 2, with some excep tions in sectors such as construction and transportation equipment where the ratio of intermediate to total costs is relatively low. As discussed earlier, their magnitude indicates the high degree of import rationing in 1978, with the model generating an import premium rate of 90 percent (see Section 10.5).

Column 4 in Table 11.5 gives the share of exports in total domestic output. There are really only three sectors that have a substantial export ratio: mining (excluding crude petroleum), textiles, and food. Trade and transportation margins, as well as tourism revenues and revenues from air travel, lead to significant E/X ratios also in infrastructure and services. The export ratio is very low in most manufacturing sectors. The bulk of Turkish exports still consists of only lightly processed agricultural products: tobacco, hazelnuts, dried fruits, ginned cotton, cotton cloth, and, in recent years, wheat. To this must be added a small amount of mineral products, principally raw borates and chromium.

Although manufactured exports have always been small, they showed the first signs of life in the 1970–73 period with the appearance of exports in clothing, leatherware, cement, building materials, glass and glass products, fabricated metal products, and light electrical machinery (see Section 10.2). With appropriate policy support, these exports could probably have grown rapidly in the 1973–7 period, taking advantage of the proximity of the booming Middle East market. Their very small base should also have allowed rapid expansion in the markets of industrialized countries. But in real terms, manufactured exports declined over the 1973–7 period, reflecting the increasing overvaluation of the Turkish lira and the extreme domestic market orientation of economic policies, relative prices, and incentives.

The last columns in Table 11.5 present the assumed trade elasticities.

In agriculture, mining, and textiles the small-country assumption was made for exports, Turkey essentially being a price taker for such homogeneous products as cotton, wheat, and mining products, which dominate trade in these sectors. The other export demand elasticities range from 3 to 6, reflecting an intermediate position between the extreme elasticity pessimism common in Turkey and the more optimistic view of many outside researchers such as Krueger. The trade-substitution elasticities range from 2.0 for agriculture to 0.2 for infrastructure and services. It is important to stress, in the light of the results to be discussed later, that these are conservatively low values.

Microeconomic results

Figure 11.1 shows the results obtained for gross and net prices early in the plan period (1981) and in the terminal year (1985). As expected, the results for gross prices are very different from those for net prices. Exchange liberalization leads to a rise in both the gross and the net price of exportables. But whereas the gross price of importables tends to fall, their net price rises, indicating that premium rationing fails to provide effective protection to the intermediate and capital goods industries. Consider, for example, basic metals, a typical import-substituting sector. The decline in its gross price as a result of exchange liberalization is 4.2 percent in 1981 and more than 8 percent in 1985. But the net price in this sector rises by 11.7 percent in 1981 and by almost 30.0 percent in 1985.

Table 11.6 describes the impact of exchange liberalization and of the resource-mobilizing policy package on the levels of sectoral output reached by 1985. Note that, given the dramatic nature of the rationing that constitutes our base of comparison, not a single sector suffers a loss of output. Production expands throughout the economy, though not in an even way. The sectors that expand most under scenario E-2 are, in decreasing order, clothing (48.6 percent), nonmetallic, mineral products (45.2 percent), chemicals (43.3 percent), nonelectrical machinery (37.7 percent), and textiles (36.7 percent). These sectors are either export oriented (clothing, mineral products, and textiles), or they are import-dependent sectors that suffer considerable negative effective protection and diversion of resources to rent seeking in the case of continued trade restrictions. The supply elasticities inherent in the degree of labor intensity and the capital–labor substitution elasticities also affect the degree of output expansion. Clothing tops the list because it is a sector that does not need to wait for lengthy investment projects to be completed

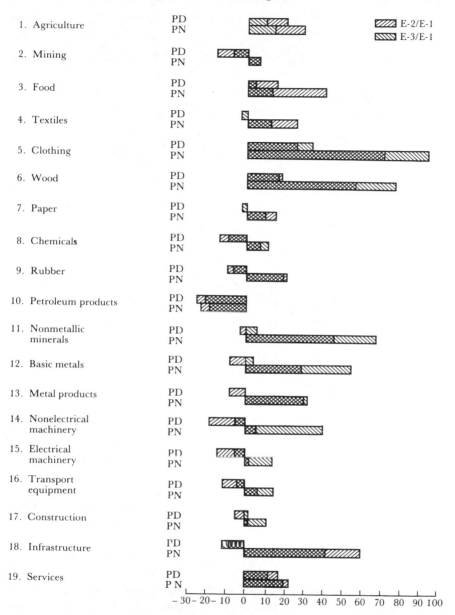

Figure 11.1. The behavior of gross and net prices.

Table 11.6. *Percent increase in 1985 output over E-1 levels*

Sector	E-2	E-3
1. Agriculture	3.3	2.6
2. Mining	30.8	32.2
3. Food	25.3	8.1
4. Textiles	36.7	18.5
5. Clothing	48.6	84.3
6. Wood	9.4	21.5
7. Paper	22.3	18.7
8. Chemicals	43.3	42.3
9. Rubber	35.0	33.7
10. Petroleum products	8.7	10.5
11. Nonmetallic mineral products	45.2	64.0
12. Basic metals	23.5	35.1
13. Metal products	35.6	29.5
14. Nonelectrical machinery	37.7	52.6
15. Electrical machinery	28.4	36.0
16. Transportation equipment	12.9	19.7
17. Construction	18.5	38.8
18. Infrastructure	24.5	22.5
19. Services	8.4	7.5
Total	17.0	17.7

before output can expand. When we turn to E-3, the ranking becomes clothing (84.3 percent), nonmetallic mineral products (64.0 percent), nonelectrical machinery (52.6 percent), chemicals (42.3 percent), and construction (38.8 percent). Textiles no longer appear among the top five sectors because they suffer from an export tax. Machinery and construction move up, reflecting the increased investment effort.

Tables 11.7, 11.8, and 11.9 provide more detailed statistics at the nineteen-sector level on the impact of policy changes on the structure of the economy. Table 11.7, which gives the share of exports in total production, indicates that for E-2 the overall share of exports rises from 4.2 to 7.8 over the seven-year period. This significant but moderate increase conceals, however, quite dramatic export share surges in nontraditional manufactured exports, particularly in clothing, but also in chemicals, nonmetallic mineral products, and nonelectrical machinery. In clothing the export ratio goes from 6.9 to 35.9, radically transforming that sector and turning it into the most export-oriented sector in the economy. We shall return later to a discussion of the behavior of export shares.

Table 11.7. *Share of exports in total production, 1978 and 1985 (%)*

Sectors	1978	Experiment E-1, 1985	Experiment E-2, 1985	Experiment E-3, 1985
1. Agriculture	1.9	1.9	2.3	2.1
2. Mining	9.5	10.4	15.0	12.0
3. Food	10.9	8.8	24.2	14.5
4. Textiles	18.1	17.4	21.2	19.2
5. Clothing	6.9	8.4	35.9	48.5
6. Wood	0.3	0.3	3.0	7.5
7. Paper	0.2	0.2	1.4	2.8
8. Chemicals	1.4	0.9	9.8	14.9
9. Rubber	0.9	0.6	5.8	9.3
10. Petroleum products	0.0	0.0	0.5	0.7
11. Nonmetallic mineral products	1.9	0.9	18.9	25.2
12. Basic metals	0.9	0.5	5.4	5.6
13. Metal products	1.3	0.9	8.1	11.5
14. Nonelectrical machinery	0.9	0.7	9.0	8.2
15. Electrical machinery	0.2	0.2	2.0	2.3
16. Transportation equipment	0.0	0.0	0.4	0.6
17. Construction	0.0	0.0	0.0	0.0
18. Infrastructure	7.1	7.1	8.1	8.5
19. Services	4.4	4.5	5.0	5.2
Average	4.2	3.9	7.8	7.7

Although they appear dramatic, they are not unprecedented in other countries that started with similarly small initial ratios.[3] It is also worth stressing that the potential for export expansion in the more traditional food and textiles sectors is limited, so that if the kind of overall export revenue growth rate projected by E-1 is to be achieved, nontraditional manufactured exports must perform exceedingly well. Finally, it must be remembered that even with such outstanding export performance, Turkey's debt–service ratio is still projected to be 34 percent by 1985.

Table 11.8 gives average sectoral growth rates as well as terminal-year growth rates for each of the nineteen sectors. It is interesting to note the impact of the increasing investment rate on terminal-year growth rates. Nonelectrical machinery grows at 12.2 in E-3 as compared to 8.9 percent in E-2, whereas construction reaches a growth rate

[3] See Chapter 4 for a historical overview of a selected group of semi-industrial countries.

Table 11.8. *The pattern of sectoral growth*

Sectors	Average annual growth rate 1978–85			Growth rate in terminal year 1985		
	E-1	E-2	E-3	E-1	E-2	E-3
1. Agriculture	3.4	3.9	3.8	3.6	4.3	4.2
2. Mining	4.9	9.0	9.1	5.0	7.7	10.1
3. Food products	4.2	7.5	5.2	4.7	5.7	4.7
4. Textiles	4.0	8.5	6.3	3.4	8.2	5.2
5. Clothing	6.7	12.9	16.4	4.1	10.8	12.3
6. Wood products	4.8	6.1	7.7	5.5	6.6	9.3
7. Paper	4.6	7.6	7.2	4.2	6.6	7.3
8. Chemicals	3.8	9.4	9.3	3.8	7.0	8.9
9. Rubber and plastics	3.9	8.4	8.3	3.2	7.6	8.0
10. Petroleum and petroleum products	10.9	12.3	12.5	10.9	12.3	13.9
11. Nonmetallic mineral products	4.0	9.7	11.6	4.5	9.4	12.3
12. Basic metals	5.0	8.3	9.7	4.8	8.8	11.5
13. Metal products	3.6	8.3	7.6	3.2	7.5	7.5
14. Nonelectrical machinery	3.3	8.2	9.7	3.9	8.9	12.2
15. Electrical machinery	3.8	7.6	8.5	4.3	8.7	11.2
16. Transportation equipment	5.4	7.2	8.1	5.9	7.7	11.2
17. Construction	4.1	6.6	9.1	5.6	8.7	14.0
18. Infrastructure	4.5	7.9	7.6	4.6	7.6	8.4
19. Services	5.3	6.6	6.4	4.7	6.0	6.3
Total	4.9	7.3	7.4	5.0	7.7	8.4

of 14.0 percent instead of 8.7. This reflects the substantial impact of increasing investment on sectoral production patterns.

Table 11.9 describes the total (direct and indirect) shares of wages, profits, indirect taxes, and imports in total sectoral prices. The table is obtained by inverting the input–output matrix and therefore distributes domestic intermediate input costs to their underlying labor, and capital and imported input cost elements. Figure 11.2 illustrates the change in the structure of total cost for two important sectors: chemicals and nonelectrical machinery. The basic story holds for all sectors – the share of imports in total cost (price) is uniformly and significantly lower with exchange liberalization. This result should be emphasized, because one of the common arguments against devaluation is that it pushes up the

Table 11.9. Components of domestic price by sector in 1985 (%,

Sectors	E-1				E-2				E-3			
	Imports	Indirect tax	Profits	Wages	Imports	Indirect tax	Profits	Wages	Imports	Indirect tax	Profits	Wages
1	7.4	1.6	38.4	52.7	4.3	1.5	38.7	55.8	5.1	1.5	38.7	55.0
2	17.8	2.5	25.2	54.5	12.5	2.6	26.2	59.5	13.8	2.6	26.6	57.9
3	10.5	11.3	37.7	40.3	7.0	11.2	39.0	44.1	8.0	11.3	39.5	43.2
4	18.5	13.4	29.2	37.9	11.9	13.4	32.1	44.6	13.6	13.4	31.1	42.7
5	14.3	5.0	33.4	46.4	7.8	4.3	35.5	54.0	8.1	3.9	35.0	53.8
6	14.2	3.3	37.0	45.4	8.6	3.1	38.0	31.5	9.4	3.1	37.8	50.9
7	22.2	6.7	40.5	30.5	15.3	6.8	43.0	35.9	17.0	6.8	42.8	34.8
8	40.1	5.4	35.0	19.5	29.0	5.8	41.5	24.7	31.4	5.7	40.8	23.4
9	39.5	6.4	28.3	25.4	27.5	6.7	34.5	32.8	30.2	6.6	33.5	31.0
10	18.6	0.2	77.2	3.9	19.6	0.3	75.2	5.1	19.3	0.3	75.9	4.8
11	23.4	9.8	43.2	23.7	17.4	9.8	45.0	29.9	17.4	9.7	45.9	28.8
12	36.6	6.7	35.0	21.8	26.4	6.7	42.6	26.6	26.6	6.5	43.6	24.8
13	41.3	3.9	28.9	25.9	29.3	3.8	34.6	33.7	31.0	3.8	34.7	31.8
14	52.2	2.7	29.9	15.2	40.0	2.9	37.6	20.4	39.7	2.7	39.1	19.5
15	41.0	6.1	32.4	20.6	30.5	6.2	38.6	25.8	31.7	6.1	38.7	24.6
16	34.8	9.5	32.6	23.1	26.1	9.4	37.6	27.9	27.3	9.3	37.5	26.9
17	24.1	3.3	35.9	36.7	17.0	3.3	38.8	42.0	17.8	3.3	38.9	41.0
18	25.7	4.9	54.5	14.8	19.8	4.9	56.8	19.2	21.4	5.0	56.2	18.2
19	3.3	6.7	40.0	49.9	2.0	6.6	40.1	51.6	2.2	6.6	40.2	51.4

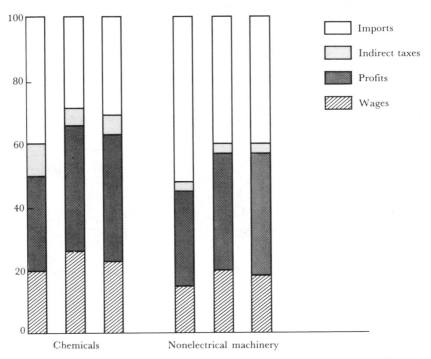

Figure 11.2. Components of domestic price in chemicals and nonelectrical machinery (1985).

user price of imports. This is simply not true if the alternative is premium rationing. It *is* true if the alternative is receiving or borrowing more money from abroad. As long as that is feasible, particularly the former, it may fruitfully be pursued; but the situation changes when the choice is between tight rationing and allowing exchange liberalization. It is quite clearly this latter choice that Turkey faces in the 1980s.

Table 11.10 provides a summary of the microeconomic results by describing the structure of gross output and capital stock (both in constant 1978 prices) and employment reached under alternatives E-1, E-2, and E-3. What changes most dramatically is the structure of employment, while the structure of capital remains much more stable, reflecting the relative immobility of that factor in the short and medium run. Note again that, far from promoting a more "advanced" industrial structure, restrictive trade policies based on premium rationing hurt not only the growth but also the relative shares of the basic intermediate goods and capital goods producing industries.

Table 11.10. *The structure of the economy in 1985*

	E-1			E-2			E-3		
	Output	Capital stock	Employment	Output	Capital stock	Employment	Output	Capital stock	Employment
1	17.6	14.4	53.5	15.6	14.5	53.4	15.4	14.3	52.9
2	0.8	1.1	0.6	0.9	1.1	0.8	0.9	1.2	0.8
3	7.8	2.4	0.9	8.4	2.5	1.2	7.2	2.4	0.8
4	4.4	2.0	1.2	5.1	2.1	1.5	4.4	2.0	1.2
5	2.0	0.7	3.3	2.5	0.7	4.8	3.1	0.7	6.4
6	1.2	0.6	0.9	1.1	0.6	1.0	1.2	0.6	1.1
7	1.0	0.9	0.2	1.0	0.9	0.2	1.0	0.9	0.2
8	2.2	1.3	0.2	2.8	1.4	0.2	2.7	1.3	0.2
9	1.0	0.5	0.2	1.1	0.5	0.3	1.1	0.5	0.3
10	9.4	5.2	0.2	8.7	5.3	0.2	8.8	5.3	0.2
11	1.2	1.4	0.3	1.5	1.4	0.4	1.7	1.4	0.6
12	4.4	3.4	0.3	4.6	3.4	0.4	5.0	3.5	0.5
13	1.2	0.5	0.8	1.4	0.5	0.8	1.3	0.5	0.7
14	2.2	0.8	0.2	2.6	0.8	0.2	2.8	0.9	0.3
15	1.1	0.4	0.2	1.2	0.4	0.2	1.2	0.4	0.2
16	2.8	0.9	0.8	2.7	0.9	0.6	2.9	0.9	0.7
17	5.8	2.0	2.6	5.9	2.2	3.0	6.9	2.2	4.0
18	10.8	43.3	1.3	11.5	42.5	2.2	11.3	42.7	2.0
19	23.1	18.2	32.3	21.4	18.3	28.6	21.1	18.3	26.9
20	100.0	100.0	100.0	100.0	100.0	100.0	100.0	100.0	100.0

11.4   Export expansion, import substitution, and the sources of growth

In this section we continue the analysis of the underlying sectoral developments implied by the various scenario experiments undertaken with the TGT model by using the methodology discussed in Chapter 4 to decompose sectoral growth into three components due to domestic demand expansion, export growth, and import substitution.[4] In Chapter 4 this decomposition analysis is used to compare historical growth in a selection of countries. Here we use it in a forward-looking planning exercise to complement the preceding analysis of sectoral developments and to give a comparative view of what is implied by different policies and growth paths. We briefly summarize the methodology below. A complete description is given in Chapter 4.

The material balance equations for the supply of and demand for domestically produced goods can be written as

$$X_i = d_i (F_i + V_i) + E_i$$

where

X_i = domestic production in sector i
d_i = domestic use ratio
F_i = final domestic use demand for composite goods
V_i = intermediate domestic use demand for composite goods
E_i = export demand for the domestically produced commodity

Intermediate demands are determined by the fixed input–output coefficients, a_{ij}. In matrix notation, the material balance equation can thus be written as

$$X = (I - \hat{D}A)^{-1} (\hat{D}F + E)$$

where $\hat{D}$ is a diagonal matrix of the d_i ratios, A is the matrix of input–output coefficients, and X, F, and E are vectors. The matrix $\hat{D}A$ is the matrix of domestic goods input–output coefficients. Denoting the change in a variable by Δ [$\Delta X = X(t + 1) - X(t)$], the change in total domestic demand can be written as

$$\begin{aligned} \Delta X = \ &R\hat{D}(\Delta F) &&\text{domestic demand expansion} \\ &+ R(\Delta E) &&\text{export expansion} \\ &+ R(\Delta \hat{D})(F + V) &&\text{import substitution} \end{aligned}$$

[4] A fourth component due to changes in input–output coefficients is always zero in this application, because the input–output coefficients are assumed to be constant in the TGT model.

Table 11.11. *Sources of growth of total gross production (%)*

		Average annual growth rate	Domestic demand expansion	Export expansion	Import substitution	Changes in IO coefficients
Korea	1955–63	5.8	74.5	10.0	21.4	−6.0
	1963–70	15.7	81.8	21.9	−1.8	−1.9
	1970–73	16.0	51.9	55.7	−3.2	−4.4
Turkey	1953–63	5.3	92.3	2.5	1.8	3.3
	1963–68	6.6	83.6	4.9	8.3	3.2
	1968–73	6.8	81.8	16.3	−1.4	3.3
Mexico	1950–60	6.2	85.5	1.0	5.4	8.1
	1960–70	7.2	94.1	3.1	6.0	−3.2
	1970–75	6.1	89.8	5.9	−1.3	5.6
Colombia	1953–66	5.8	76.1	10.0	6.9	7.0
	1966–70	5.9	69.5	21.8	6.6	2.1
Yugoslavia	1962–66	11.6	87.6	23.9	−6.2	−5.3
	1966–72	6.9	82.0	30.2	−18.4	6.1

Note: Column 1 shows the average annual growth rates of total gross output. Columns 2–5 contain the contributions of each causal factor to output growth expressed as percentages of the change in total gross output in each subperiod, and add up to 100% except for rounding errors.
Source: Table 4.3.

where $R = (I - \hat{D}A)^{-1}$. Sectoral growth is thus allocated among three sources: domestic demand expansion, export expansion, and import substitution.[5]

When evaluating the decomposition measures derived from the TGT model for Turkey, it is important to be able to place them in a wider context and to compare our projections to the experience of other countries as well as to the performance of Turkey in the past. Table 4.3 summarized the percentage decomposition by different sources of manufacturing growth (obtained by summing algebraically over the sectoral changes) for eight countries. In Table 11.11 we present the results for Turkey and four countries of comparable size of the decomposition of the sources of total gross output growth (summing over all sectors).

It is especially interesting to compare the projections for the 1978–85

[5] As discussed in Chapter 4, there is an index number problem implicit in the decomposition equation, because the decomposition can be defined using combinations of initial and terminal-year weights analogous to Paasche and Laypeyres price indices. In the tables, we present the averages of the two types of indices. Note also that we are analyzing the change in output rather than the deviation from balanced growth.

period with Turkey's performance in the past. Unfortunately, 1953–63 is the first period for which we have Turkish data. The first part of that period (1953–8) was one of tight import rationing and significant import substitution. It was followed after the 1958 devaluation by a period of increasing imports. The net effect is that the 1953–63 period is characterized by a very small contribution of both import substitution and export expansion to growth. In the 1963–8 period, when there was again significant import rationing, the contribution of import substitution to growth was significant and much larger than that of export expansion. In the 1968–73 period, the role of exports increased and that of import substitution became slightly negative (indicating that import coefficients actually rose). Although the benchmark year in our data for the switch to export expansion is 1968, the actual turning point was closer to 1970, when there was a major devaluation.

It is somewhat surprising, given Turkey's consistently and strongly inward-oriented development strategy, that the relative contribution of import substitution has not been very great in two of the three subperiods. But the first period includes a complete cycle, with a foreign exchange crisis in 1958, and the terminal year, 1973, was the only year in the last two decades in which Turkey accumulated a massive amount of foreign exchange. It is therefore more interesting to focus on the 1963–8 period, characterized by a chronic shortage of foreign exchange. The contribution of import substitution was 8.3 percent during those years, which is substantial but not enormous. It is a smaller contribution than that experienced by Korea in the late 1950s and early 1960s, but larger than in similar periods in Colombia and Mexico.

Historically, the role of exports in growth has also varied. From the end of the war to about 1970, export expansion contributed little to growth. However, the substantial expansion of exports after the exchange-rate adjustment in 1970 contributed significantly to aggregate growth. From Table 11.11, export expansion constituted 16.3 percent of total growth in the 1968–73 period, much greater than in any previous subperiod, higher than in Mexico, but lower than in Yugoslavia. The rapid expansion of exports in the 1968–73 period seems to indicate that, with proper policies, exports can play an increasingly important role in generating growth. After 1973, with the drift in incentives against exports discussed earlier, their role diminished.

Table 11.12 presents the decomposition of aggregate growth for the various experiments with the TGT model. In analyzing the forward runs, it is important to be aware of the problems created by choosing different starting points. The base year, 1978, represents with 1979 the depth of the foreign exchange crisis. It is far from being a "normal" year, and is characterized by extreme import rationing.

Table 11.12. *TGT model experiments: decomposition of aggregate growth, percentage composition by source*

TGT model run	Period	Domestic demand expansion	Export expansion	Import substitution
Historical run	1973–77	100.4	−1.0	0.6
	1977–78	−32.6	36.0	96.6
E-1	1978–85	78.3	5.2	16.5
E-2	1978–85	71.8	25.9	2.3
E-3	1978–85	71.3	24.5	4.2

We have done a historical run of the TGT model for the 1973–8 period, whose results are also tabulated in Table 11.12. In that run, the depth of the crisis in 1978 is clearly evident. Domestic demand falls and, with severe rationing, the squeeze on imports is severe. The contribution of import substitution to growth in 1977–8 is enorrmous. Given this result, further import substitution in the 1978–85 period would be difficult to achieve, a point that should be remembered in judging the forward-run experiments. The historical run also clearly shows the negligible contribution of export expansion to growth in the 1973–7 period.

It is interesting to compare the projected sources of growth in Table 11.12 with those from other countries and from recent Turkish history given in Table 11.11. The restrictive exchange policy scenario projects a contribution of export expansion to growth of only 5.2 percent. In Experiments E-2 and E-3, the contribution of exports rises to around 25 percent, which is higher than Turkey achieved in the 1968–73 period (16.3 percent). However, these higher shares are not extreme by international standards. They are comparable to the rates in Korea and Yugoslavia and to what was achieved in Colombia after 1966.

The contribution of import substitution to growth is very small under our export-oriented scenarios, below historical rates in Turkey and elsewhere. Though low, these rates are realistic given the high degree of import rationing present in the base year (1978). Experiment E-1 (with extreme import rationing and increased bias against exports) yields a 16 percent contribution of import substitution to growth.

Table 11.13 gives the contributions to growth at the six-sector level for the three experiments. Note that all runs involve a significant amount of import substitution in the manufacturing sectors. In general, the results of Experiments E-2 and E-3 are broadly similar, with the only major difference occurring in the role of export expansion in the agricultural sector. Experiment E-3, with somewhat less expansion of

Table 11.13. *Contributions to growth: aggregate sectors*

	Domestic demand expansion	Export expansion	Import substitution
Experiment E-1			
Agriculture	93.8	0.8	5.4
Consumer goods	98.0	−2.4	4.4
Intermediate goods	56.6	−0.8	44.2
Capital goods	44.9	−0.3	55.4
Construction	100.0	0.0	0.0
Infrastructure and services	91.4	4.9	3.7
Experiment E-2			
Agriculture	68.8	37.7	−6.5
Consumer goods	50.4	50.5	−0.9
Intermediate goods	59.5	33.4	7.1
Capital goods	90.1	12.7	−2.8
Construction	100.0	0.0	0.0
Infrastructure and services	85.1	15.1	−0.2
Experiment E-3			
Agriculture	84.2	20.4	−4.6
Consumer goods	56.0	44.8	−0.8
Intermediate goods	58.9	31.8	9.3
Capital goods	85.6	14.9	−0.5
Construction	100.0	0.0	0.0
Infrastructure and services	85.2	14.7	0.1

exports, yields a somewhat greater contribution to growth from import substitution, concentrated in the manufacturing sector. Both experiments yield higher contributions of export expansion in every sector compared to E-1 and lower contributions of import substitution.

The sectoral results for Experiment E-1 reveal a largely autarchic development strategy. In mining and manufacturing, import substitution is very important. In all other sectors, domestic demand expansion, and hence reliance on domestic markets, is the major driving force of growth. The degree of import substitution required within the manufacturing sector appears to be dramatic.

Because Table 11.13 gives only the relative contributions of the separate effects in each sector, it cannot tell much about the intersectoral linkages at work and the actual magnitudes of the different effects in each sector. It is thus useful to consider the contributions of the different effects on the change in physical output by sectors. We have selected nine sectors to analyze: food processing, textiles, clothing, chemicals,

Table 11.14. *Deviation in 1985 of domestic and net prices in E-2 and E-3 from those in E-1 (%)*

Sector	Domestic prices		Net Prices	
	E-2	E-3	E-2	E-3
Food	15.4	5.4	40.7	10.8
Textiles	−3.3	−2.1	25.0	12.0
Clothing	26.0	34.3	70.2	95.8
Chemicals	−13.0	−8.8	6.9	10.7
Basic metals	−8.1	3.7	29.2	55.2
Metal products	17.5	−0.4	30.8	32.2
Nonelectrical machinery	−18.1	−5.3	6.5	40.4
Electrical machinery	−13.8	−5.1	1.8	13.9
Transportation equipment	−11.1	−3.7	6.3	14.7

Notes: Net prices are defined as the weighted average of the domestic and export price minus the cost of intermediate inputs and indirect taxes.

basic metals, metal products, nonelectrical machinery, electrical machinery, and transportation equipment. Figures 11.3 to 11.11 present the total output change in each of these sectors for the three experiments, and its decomposition into changes due to domestic demand expansion, export expansion, and import substitution. The unit is millions of 1978 TL. The value of projected output in 1985 is also given in the figures for each of the nine sectors in the basic run.

Processed food and textiles include the bulk of Turkish exports and, no matter what happens in other sectors, they will continue to dominate exports over the plan period by virtue of their large initial base. (Note that the sectors include ginned cotton and tobacco products.) Together, they account for about two-thirds of total merchandise exports in 1978. From Figures 11.3 and 11.4, it is clear that the various experiments have significantly different impacts on the sectors. Consider first the two export promotion experiments, E-2 and E-3. In the case of food processing, the differences are due almost entirely to the different role of export expansion, whereas for textiles, domestic demand expansion also varies. Import substitution is negligible in both sectors in all the runs.

The reason for the different impact of domestic demand expansion in the two sectors can be deduced from an examination of the behavior of prices in the two sectors that are reproduced in Table 11.14. Although net prices rise in both sectors (compared to E-1), the gross domestic

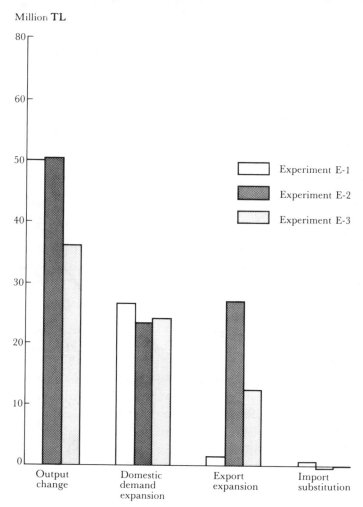

Million **TL**

Figure 11.3. Sources of growth, 1978–85, for processed food.

price actually falls in the textiles sector. The fall in domestic price induces an increase in domestic demand and hence more of a contribution of domestic demand expansion to growth in textiles. One of the reasons for the much greater deviation between gross price and net price behavior in the textiles sector is that the net price is a weighted average of net receipts from both domestic and export sales. In the case of textiles, the world price is assumed not to be affected by the volume of

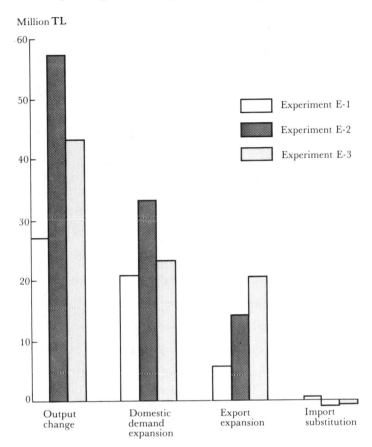

Million TL

Figure 11.4. Sources of growth, 1978–85, for textiles.

Turkish exports. Thus, with export subsidies, the export price remains fixed at the higher level and the net price rises even though the domestic price falls. In the case of processed food, the export price is sensitive to the volume of Turkish exports, and so the domestic and export prices are more closely linked. Another factor explaining the difference between textiles and food is that whereas food is dependent on agriculture, whose gross price increases with exchange liberalization, the textiles sector is dependent on chemicals, whose price declines when import rationing is relaxed, positively affecting the net price of textiles.

It is also important to note that in both textiles and food processing, exports expand in Experiments E-2 and E-3 through increases in pro-

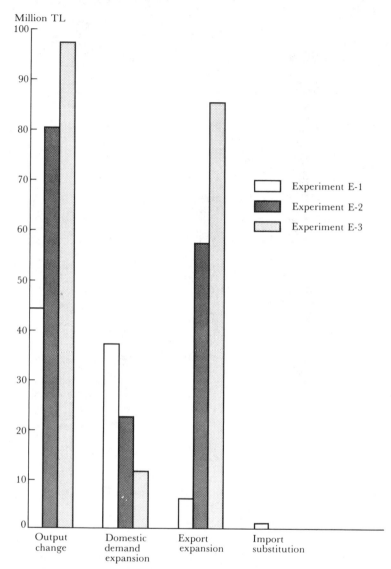

Figure 11.5. Sources of growth, 1978–85, for clothing.

duction and not through squeezing domestic demand. In Experiment E-
1, on the other hand, the lower output change in textiles is due both to
lower domestic demand expansion and to lower export expansion.

Figure 11.5 refers to the clothing sector. The story is essentially the
same as for processed food, but the role of exports is more important.

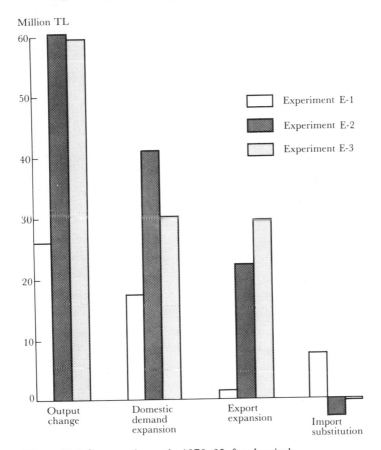

Figure 11.6. Sources of growth, 1978–85, for chemicals.

Because textiles represent an important input into clothing, the two sectors are closely linked. Textile exports were higher in Experiment E-2 than in E-3, as was total textile production. The opposite was true for the clothing sector, with production and exports being higher in Experiment E-3. In Experiment E-2, the removal of the bias against textile exports led to higher exports, diverting supplies from the domestic clothing sector. In Experiment E-3, the policy regime favors the domestic sales of textiles. The clothing sector purchases them as inputs and embodies them in clothing exports.

Figures 11.6 and 11.7 give the results for two important intermediate goods sectors, chemicals and basic metals. Experiment E-1 shows slow growth, negative export expansion, and significant import substitution. The two export-promotion experiments (E-2 and E-3) show much

Million TL

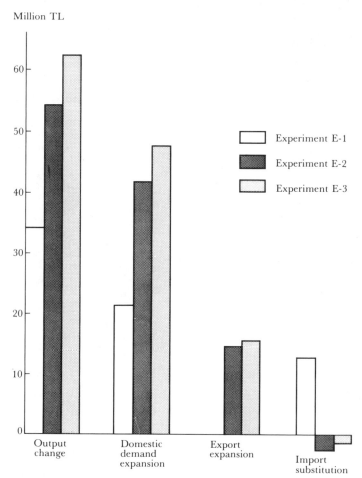

Figure 11.7. Sources of growth, 1978–85, for basic metals.

higher growth than in the basic run, particularly for chemicals, with the increase coming from increased exports and domestic expansion. In the latter two experiments, there is negative import substitution.

Historically, chemicals has been a sector in which the import ratio has steadily increased. In the 1977–8 period, extreme import rationing forced a significant decline in the ratio of imports to domestic use in the sector, so the forward runs are starting from a base where the import ratios are lower than in earlier periods. Table 11.15 gives the ratios for 1973 and 1978 and clearly shows the impact of import rationing. It

Table 11.15. *Ratio of imports to domestically produced goods in total domestic use, 1973 and 1978 (%)*

	1973	1978
Chemicals	59.1	38.2
Basic metals	29.7	18.1
Metal products	15.4	8.9
Nonelectrical machinery	86.1	54.8
Electrical machinery	50.3	30.0
Transportation equipment	29.1	17.1

Notes: Based on real data in 1973 prices. Values for 1978 are estimated based on model results.

should be noted, however, that 1973 was a year of extremely high imports, so it is difficult to judge without a more detailed examination of the sectors whether the 1978 ratios are wildly distorted or can be taken to represent a sustainable base. Considering the heterogeneous nature of the two sectors, the low-export Experiment (E-1), in which output grows slowly, with import substitution being a large source of growth, does seem unrealistic. Although significant import-substituting investment is planned for both sectors in the future, it would seem difficult for it to account for one-third of the change in output in the plan period. The slightly negative contributions in Experiments E-2 and E-3 seem much more reasonable.

In the two export-promotion experiments, export expansion plays a significant role in both sectors, particularly in chemicals. Chemicals is a large and diversified sector, dominated by high-cost, import-substituting activities, but it also contains subsectors that process low-cost domestic minerals and can provide a base for future exports. The relative role of exports is projected to be smaller in basic metals, dominated by the iron and steel industry.

Figures 11.8 to 11.11 show the impact of the experiments on four sectors "downstream" from basic metals. Although the relative magnitudes of the different sources of growth vary among the experiments, the pattern is similar – and is the same as that in the chemicals and basic metals sectors. Domestic demand expansion is the most important source of growth in all the sectors. Export expansion is significant in metal products and nonelectrical machinery and is relatively smaller for electrical machinery and transportation equipment. As for chemicals

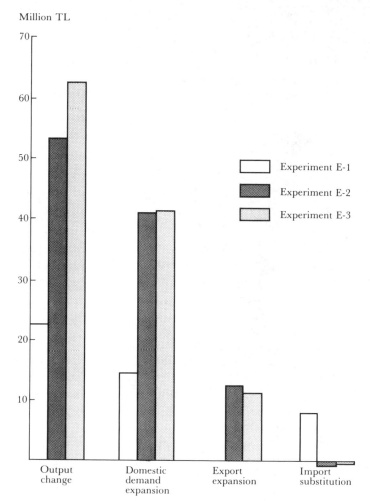

Figure 11.8. Sources of growth, 1978–85, for nonelectrical machinery.

and basic metals, there has already been a significant decrease in the import ratios (see Table 11.15), so further significant import substitution is not projected, even in Experiment E-1.

Note also that in the restrictive exchange policy experiment (E-1), domestic demand expansion in the metal products and the electrical and nonelectrical machinery sectors is very low. This result reflects the slow growth of real investment that occurs in that experiment.

Million TL

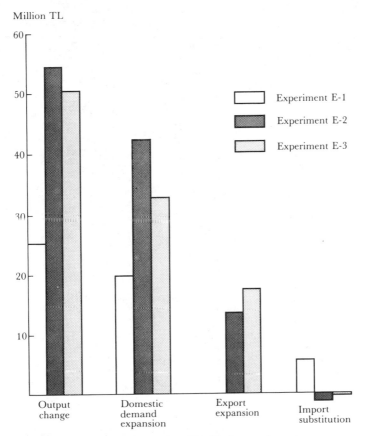

Figure 11.9. Sources of growth, 1978–85, for metal products.

11.5 Conclusion

The microeconomic analysis of the sources of growth for selected sectors indicates first and foremost that in the early 1980s import substitution cannot be a substantial source of output expansion in Turkey. The basic reason is that the economy has already reached extremely low import-to-output ratios in the late 1970s and further reductions would be very difficult and costly. The choice is essentially between an autarchic strategy where almost the entire source of growth is domestic demand expansion and an outward-looking strategy where export expansion becomes a very substantial source of growth. What must be stressed in this context is that the decomposition analysis we have conducted refers to a

Million TL

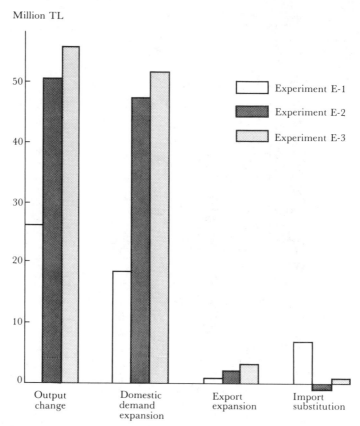

Figure 11.10. Sources of growth, 1978–85, for electrical machinery.

specific period in a particular country. Once equilibrium is restored and a certain balance again exists between the domestic resource costs of import-substituting and export-expanding activities, import substitution may again become an important source of output expansion. But in Turkey in the first half of the 1980s, this is not going to be the case. If import ratios were kept constant at their 1978–9 levels, and if the economy could adjust to those low levels, that in itself would constitute a major achievement. The source of expansion will have to be overall demand growth and improved export performance. The relative share of these two factors will in turn depend on the structure of incentives and trade policies.

The last section of this chapter illustrates how the general equilibrium modeling framework can be used to link what has so far been a

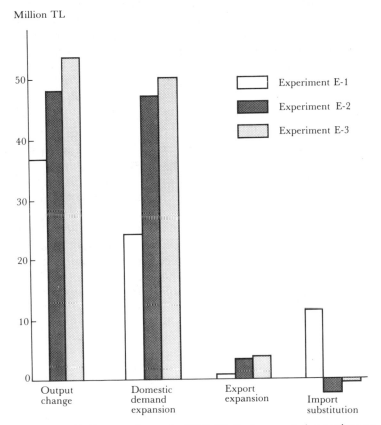

Figure 11.11. Sources of growth, 1978–85, for transportation equipment.

purely descriptive decomposition methodology to explicit policy measures. What makes this linkage possible is, of course, the explicit modeling of the market mechanism, for it is through the impact on relative prices and the structure of incentives that government policy affects real variables and the pace and pattern of growth.

Concluding, it is worth emphasizing that the TGT model attempts to capture medium-term mechanisms and does not include an analysis of macroeconomic monetary mechanisms and very short-term adjustment processes. Nevertheless, to reach the longer run, a country must bridge the short run. Although the CGE model has nothing to say about the interaction between monetary policy and real magnitudes, the relationship is clearly important. A monetary squeeze that is too severe may have strong negative effects on production and capacity utilization. On the other hand, monetary expansion may prevent any real change in the structure of incentives. It is important to weigh the gains from lower inflation rates against the losses in potential output, employment, and perhaps even exports. A strongly deflationary approach to crisis management may make the beginning of an export-led growth effort more difficult to achieve. In our opinion, a gentle approach, including adjustments and indexation in exchange rate and interest rates, and special support for "infant" export industries, coupled with a substantial injection of new foreign borrowing made possible by the introduction of more export-oriented policies, constitutes a more successful policy package for crisis management than severe deflation policies. Unfortunately, the time required for this "gentle" approach to work may often not be available through hesitation and indecisiveness. Foreign help may not be available in adequate amounts at the time of greatest need. A more drastic and difficult transition may be the only alternative. The choice depends on the specifics of a particular country's situation. Although a CGE model helps in elaborating medium-term strategies, these must always be linked to an analysis of short-term tactics which, in turn, depend crucially on the relevant political circumstances in any given case.

PART V

Income distribution and multisector planning models

CHAPTER 12

Modeling distributional mechanisms

12.1 Introduction

So far, the distribution of income, though an important aspect of the specification of a CGE model, has remained in the background of the discussion. The core model discussed in Chapter 5 will generate the distribution to factors of production, but a much more detailed analysis of income distribution and of the relationships between policy and distribution is often possible and desirable. Distributional issues have increasingly asserted themselves as a major concern of economic analysis and public policy. Perhaps more than any other issue, the distribution of income results from a complex set of relationships that requires a general equilibrium rather than a partial equilibrium analysis. A model where prices and incomes are truly endogenous is therefore all the more useful in this context. Are certain development strategies more conducive to equitable growth than others? What are the relationships between a country's foreign trade regime and its income distribution? How do alternative policy packages compare from the point of view of distribution? These are the kinds of questions faced by the development planner, and a general equilibrium analysis of the economy is essential to understand the linkages involved and to help design adequate national policies.

The distribution of income in any economy is as much a sociopolitical process as a purely economic one, and any economic approach to distributional issues is bound to have political and social implications. One ought to be aware of these implications, and we try in the next section to capture some of the flavor of the debate about alternative approaches to the analysis of the distribution of income. We then discuss different approaches to the specification of distributional mechanisms in economy-wide models. Finally, we consider in some detail how a multisector CGE model can be extended to emphasize distributional mechanisms and to generate a number of different income distributions that are relevant for policy analysis.

12.2   Normative and positive approaches to income distribution

In considering questions about the distribution of income, it is important to remember how deeply neoclassical economics is rooted in utilitarian philosophy with its atomistic view of society. From the beginning of the science, there has been a major analytic dichotomy between the utilitarian view of society as essentially individualistic and the classical (and Marxian) view of society as composed of a few competing social classes. This dichotomy has resulted in the growth of two quite different approaches within the field of economics to the analysis of income distribution. The first focuses on both the normative and positive analysis of the distribution of income to atomistic individuals or households – the "size distribution." The second focuses on the distribution of income to a few aggregate groups. In the classical and Marxist traditions, these groups control or own aggregate factors of production (labor, capital, and land) and are defined by their function in the economy; hence, the "functional distribution."

The welfare analysis of income distribution is the most strongly rooted in utilitarian philosophy. Although much of the work has sought to free economics from some of the perceived weaknesses of utilitarianism, the analysis has retained a narrow view of society as essentially individualistic. Welfare economics has thus concentrated largely on the size distribution and has not been particularly concerned with the distribution of income among groups, no matter how defined.

The major modern work in this tradition has sought to separate questions of equity from those of efficiency. The notion of a Pareto-optimal point – that is, a position from which the economy cannot move without making someone worse off – has been used to separate equity questions and so judge them by normative criteria that are completely independent from criteria by which questions of efficiency are judged. In a sense, this work sought to purge questions of income distribution from economics. According to this view, economics should be concerned with "efficiency," and equity questions should be left to sociologists or philosophers. Normative judgments require interpersonal comparisons of utility, something economists should scrupulously avoid. Let fools rush in where angels fear to tread![1]

More recently, there has been active work explicitly trying to incor-

---

[1] Perhaps the most eloquent, and one of the earliest, statements of this view is in Robbins (1932). For a radical critique of Robbins' view, see Gintis (1972).

porate equity judgments into economic analysis and to explore the impact of different equity judgements. In the development literature, for example, there is a major debate about whether or not one should include equity criteria directly in benefit–cost analysis by giving different weights to benefits depending on who receives them. One side argues that this approach unnecessarily mixes separable criteria, resulting only in confusion. The other side sees it as a practical way to incorporate equity judgments into policy analysis (see Squire and Van Der Tak, 1975; Harberger, 1971).

Recent work in welfare economics and the theory of social choice, while remaining in the utilitarian and atomistic tradition, has brought into question the extreme separation between considerations of equity and efficiency that has characterized modern neoclassical theory. This work, especially that inspired by Rawls (1971), can be seen as an attempt to bring back into economics some of the normative analysis that neoclassical writers have tried to separate from the science.[2] In any case, those in the utilitarian tradition all agree on the priority of the individualistic focus of welfare economics.[3] Given an individualistic focus, attention turns to how one measures the distribution of income to individuals, because different aggregate measures reflect different value judgments about the distribution. There has been an active literature recently on the relationship between different social welfare functions and different aggregate measures of inequality (see Sen, 1973). There has also been a lot of work describing the properties of different measures of inequality and proposing new measures. The appendix to this chapter surveys the properties of different measures and discusses some of the empirical and welfare issues involved in measuring the distribution.

Another major strand of work on income distribution in economics has also concentrated on the size distribution, but has sought to explain it rather than judge it. Under the general heading of size distribution theories, one can distinguish a number of different approaches. For example, human capital theorists have sought to explain the distribution of earnings, whereas others, such as Champernowne, have dealt with the distribution of unearned income (see Champernowne, 1953; Min-

[2] See Sen (1970, 1973), Rawls (1971), and Phelps (1965, 1973), for recent examples. Fields (1980) has attempted to use formal welfare criteria to support the recent emphasis on poverty alleviation in developing countries.

[3] There is some work, however, on what is the appropriate "individual" for welfare analysis: persons, households, per-capita households, or even per-adult-equivalent households. For a discussion of some of the issues and an application analyzing fiscal incidence, see Meerman (1979).

cer, 1970; Becker, 1970). One can also distinguish theories of the distribution of assets (both human and nonhuman) from theories of the distribution of income. What economists working in this general approach have in common, however, is a tendency to take the economic system as given. A person's income is assumed to depend on individual characteristics rather than on structural characteristics of the aggregate economy. Thus, the distribution of income is implicitly assumed to be determined by an aggregation of atomistic decisions, particularly about education, savings, marriage, and bequests.[4]

Such size distribution theories tend to have rather limited policy implications. Logical policy conclusions have a long-run focus and involve things such as encouraging education, reducing prejudice, and discouraging assortative mating within income classes. The problem is not only the individualistic theoretical orientation, but also the tendency to assume that the economic system is given. Such analyses thus tend to neglect the production side of the economy and questions of the supply of income-earning opportunities in a society. Work in the size distribution tradition thus ignores both the importance of macroeconomic fluctuations and their impact on incomes in the short run, and the dynamic economic forces that affect growth and structural change in the medium and long term. The empirical work supporting the view that education and human capital variables are important determinants of the distribution of earnings is very strong, but rather than leading to a separation of human capital analysis from other fields of economic research, it should lead to closer integration of this approach into the general theory of capital formation, social mobility and growth.

The caveat for planners implicit in this work is that any economy-wide model that does not include a detailed analysis of human capital formation can only hope to capture a few of the forces that affect the distribution of income. As we shall see, the sorts of macroeconomic policies that are a large part of a country's development strategy do have a significant impact on the distribution of income, and it is important to consider how to capture the relevant interactions in planning models. However, such models cannot and do not claim to provide a comprehensive explanation of what determines the distribution of income in a society. Providing such an explanation is certainly beyond their scope, and, indeed, is probably beyond the scope of economics as a science. It

---

[4] Perhaps the most fully articulated model in this tradition is that of Blinder (1975). See also Tinbergen (1959b) for a more general analysis associating income with various individual characteristics.

is difficult and controversial enough to try to capture the most important economic mechanisms affecting distribution in the medium term without trying to explain the social, political, and economic forces that underlie the existing pattern of ownership of assets, both physical and human, and their evolution over time. Furthermore, while important in its own right for policy analysis, an understanding of the relationships between income distribution and the policy elements of a country's medium-term development strategy are an important part of any wider explanation of the processes at work.

Concern with the functional distribution – the distribution of income to aggregate factors of production – goes back at least to Smith, Ricardo, and Marx and persists in the Marxist tradition and in the work of the neo-Keynesian Cambridge school (e.g., Robinson, Sraffa, Kaldor, and Pasinetti). The Latin American "structuralist" school, which in many ways can be considered to be part of the Cambridge tradition, also focuses on factor shares. There is a strong tendency to assume that increasing the income share of aggregate labor "improves" the distribution (i.e., reduces poverty and/or reduces inequality), an assumption the neoclassicists tend to reject. For example, if organized labor is the only group strong enough to challenge the status quo and reduce the share of the capitalist elite, an increase in its share will be welcomed by neo-Marxians, structuralists, and social democrats. Neoclassicists and conservatives, in contrast, tend to argue that an increased share of organized labor need not improve the size distribution and may hurt groups with incomes below that of organized labor.

Factor shares are also interesting because they reflect a fundamental division of society into socioeconomic classes with distinct political interests and power. The division of society into distinct classes that can easily be associated with aggregate factors of production is not important in neoclassical theory, and concern immediately reverts to the size distribution via an atomistic decomposition of society into individuals or households. This neglects the fact that in a world where aggregate factors do reflect coherent, significant political and economic entities, the functional distribution is of interest in its own right.

It is difficult to reconcile the different perspectives on income distribution. To those who regard the private ownership of capital as the overriding cause of maldistribution, it is frivolous to analyze redistribution policies within the size distribution framework. On the other hand, neoclassical economists have trouble understanding why, if some notion of overall equality is the basis for distributional concern, the problem should not be tackled directly by attempts to reduce some measure of "distance" between individuals. To neoclassicists, casting the problem into an aggregated conflict between capital and labor embodies an unwarranted a priori assumption about what is important in the income distribution mechanism.

In every society, the distribution of income is a politically sensitive topic – indeed, it is probably the most important political issue and underlies most political conflicts in society. In analyzing the relationship between policy regimes and the distribution of income, it is important to go beyond the rather narrow economic views of the process and consider explicitly the way in which a society and polity view distributional issues. If all members of society identify themselves as either "capitalists" or "labor," then the narrow functional distribution is all that the economist may need to consider. If society is made up of individuals who can, for purposes of social and political analysis, be treated atomistically as a collection of unconnected units, then one need be concerned only with the pure size distribution of income. Neither extreme seems either theoretically or empirically reasonable. We feel, therefore, that it is necessary to seek a middle ground and reconcile the two approaches in order to achieve a balanced framework for policy analysis.

The definition of an appropriate socioeconomic decomposition of society represents a difficult problem, one without a general solution appropriate for all countries. For modern political scientists concerned with "interest groups" or "constituencies," a variegated classification is required that might, for example, distinguish groups by ethnic origin, location, age, sex, status, or education as well as by the traditional economic classification by occupation or source of income. Such a detailed breakdown is not really feasible for an economic model that concentrates on the workings of various markets. Some compromise is required that defines groups and institutions in a way that is useful for political analysis but is nonetheless closely related to the variables determined by a planning model. In this way, although one will probably not completely satisfy either political scientists or economists, one may hope to succeed in capturing some of the complexity of a socioeconomic system.

Empirically, then, to reconcile the pure "size distribution" and "functional distribution" approaches to analyzing the distribution of income, and to include intermediate distributions, one must build more complete models that generate both. Such models are necessary if planners are to consider both the welfare implications of their policies for members of society considered individualistically and the political implications of policies that will differentially affect important institutions and socioeconomic groups. However, before discussing the technical problem of including the functional, institutional, socioeconomic, and size distributions within a single model, it is important to consider the nature of different types of models and the causal factors they include.

12.3 Distributional mechanisms and economy-wide models

The use of a multisector, general equilibrium model focusing on resource allocation mechanisms as a framework for analyzing income distribution issues carries with it some implicit convictions about what are "important" mechanisms affecting the distribution of income to individuals, factors, or socioeconomic groups. To begin with, one must believe that the sectoral structure of production, employment, and prices has a significant impact on distribution. In addition, the operation of factor and product markets represents significant transmission mechanisms by which policy changes or external shocks affect income distribution. Third, factors that work through market mechanisms have significant indirect as well as direct effects, implying the need for a general equilibrium framework.

These propositions seem rather uncontroversial, but they do tend to focus attention on a particular set of mechanisms that may not always be considered as the most important affecting distribution. At one extreme, to those working in what we have loosely termed the human capital approach, the economic system is assumed given and attention is focused on the link between the size distribution of income and the distribution of individual characteristics. In this individualistic, positive analysis, income is determined by savings propensities, inheritance, education defined broadly, genetics, and chance. If these mechanisms are all that is important, then multisector models are not an appropriate tool of analysis, and it is not useful to worry about how such models capture distributional mechanisms.

At the other extreme are models where macroeconomic mechanisms are viewed as the fundamental determinants of the distribution of income. A key feature of such models is that causality runs from investment to savings to the distribution of income.[5] Assume, for example, that as a result of an external disturbance, such as a shortfall in foreign capital inflow, the overall balance between savings and investment is disturbed. In a CGE model of the type described in the preceding chapters, this imbalance will lead to *relative* price changes, notably a change

---

[5] See Kaldor (1955) for the seminal work on a macroeconomic theory of income distribution.

in the real exchange rate, to reestablish foreign balance. There will also be a decline in investment because it passively adjusts to the sum of foreign and domestic savings and, also, there will be a decline in the relative price of capital goods. Finally, as a result of these relative price changes, there will be changes in wages and profits and in the distribution of income.

By contrast, consider a model where investment is fixed in real terms. A decline in foreign savings will create a macroeconomic disequilibrium between nominal savings and investment. We shall use the term "Kaldorian" to describe models in which the adjustment mechanism to such an imbalance is seen to be the most important influence on the distribution of income. A decline in real investment being ruled out, something else in the system has to give. Following Kaldor and assuming that the savings rate out of profit income is much higher than out of wage income, it is possible to reestablish equilibrium if the share of profits in national income increases sufficiently to generate an increase in domestic savings sufficient, in turn, to offset the decline in foreign savings. For such a rise in the share of profits to materialize, the real wage must decline. Whether this decline is achieved in the model by a fall in the nominal wage with a constant price level or by a rise in the price level with a constant nominal wage is of secondary importance. If the nominal wage is chosen as numéraire in the model, it is the aggregate price level that must rise, adding an apparent inflationary adjustment mechanism – although money-holding behavior is usually not modeled explicitly.[6]

The distinction between Kaldorian and relative-price-adjustment mechanisms depends on a model's "closure" rule, that is, the way in which equilibrium between savings and investment is achieved.[7] These Kaldorian models were originally developed for Latin American countries in which, according to the "structuralist" school, relative-price-adjustment mechanisms do not work. It should be intuitively clear that this kind of Kaldorian closure has the potential for greater swings in the distribution of income than a classical closure that lets investment adjust to savings and where the distribution of income is affected only indi-

[6] See Taylor (1979) and the references therein for various examples of Kaldorian macro models. These models typically assume fixed investment coupled with a fixed nominal wage and a fixed exchange rate and so rely on an inflation mechanism to change the real wage.

[7] See Chapter 5 for a discussion of closure rules. For further discussion of their distribution implications in macro models, see the recent symposium in the *Journal of Development Economics* led off by Bruno (1979).

rectly through a chain of causality that runs from commodity prices to factor prices via changes in sectoral production structure and sectorally different factor intensities and factor mobility.

The relationship and direction of causality between investment and savings is clearly a crucial problem when building policy models for developing countries. Models that allow investment to adjust to savings treat the demand for investment goods more or less like a demand for any other set of goods. Fixed savings rates imply a unit-elastic demand for aggregate capital goods and, in a sense, there is no special problem of closure. This specification allows attention to be focused on the microeconomic determinants of income distribution that work through relative factor intensities in production and the interaction between the structure of demand and the structure of production and employment. Thus, for example, if the more tradable commodities are relatively labor intensive, a foreign exchange shortfall may lead to a rise in the wage-rental ratio as a consequence of a relative rise in the price of the more tradable commodities.

If one wants to focus on and analyze this kind of intersectoral mechanism, it is important to specify a macroeconomic closure rule that is as neutral as possible in its effect on the distribution of income. A Kaldorian mechanism working through adjustments in the real wage would tend to swamp the microeconomic mechanisms working through multisector relationships, and the result becomes much more difficult to interpret. There are, of course, alternatives to the classical or Kaldorian closure rules. It is possible, for example, to let the government play an active compensating role, generating enough savings to validate any given investment target without necessarily altering the wage-rental ratio or the relative shares of private capital and labor.[8]

These problems will be illustrated further in the next chapter. Our starting point will always be to specify a fixed aggregate price level and to treat the demand for investment as determined by savings so that the microeconomic mechanisms can be isolated and analyzed. But we shall see how important compensating behavior - for example, by the government - can be. Furthermore, as emphasized in the writings of the Latin American structuralist school, precisely because changes in relative commodity price affect the distribution of income, there may be countervailing forces against such changes (see Diamand, 1978). For example, if a real devaluation implies a decline in the relative share

---

[8] See, for example, de Melo and Robinson (1980), who specify such a mechanism in a CGE model for Colombia that focuses on the distributional impact of trade policies.

and/or real income of a particular socioeconomic group that happens to be very powerful, the political economy of the situation may be such that a real devaluation is practically impossible. In this context, it is crucial to understand who, in fact, would suffer from a real devaluation. A multisector CGE model that focuses on relative price mechanisms can provide a useful framework for analyzing such questions, and can also be used for exploring what kind of action by the government could compensate the losers and thus make a needed adjustment politically feasible.

The first effort to incorporate the distribution of income in the framework of a CGE model is the Adelman-Robinson model of Korea. More recent efforts are the Lysy-Taylor model of Brazil and the Ahluwalia-Lysy model of Malaysia (see Adelman and Robinson, 1978; Ahluwalia and Lysy, 1979; Lysy and Taylor, 1980). It is perhaps a pity that these first models all mixed macroeconomic and relative price relationships in the CGE framework, because it has led to some confusion in interpreting their results. In all three models, the aggregate price level is endogenous; in the Adelman-Robinson model, through a simple quantity-theory demand-for-money function and in the other two models through the kind of Kaldorian macroeconomic relationships described above. Within periods, the Adelman-Robinson model assumes that nominal investment is fixed but does not specify a fixed nominal wage, and so relies largely on relative-price-adjustment mechanisms.

All three models find that the overall size distribution of income is quite stable and difficult to change through policy intervention. Taylor and Lysy feel that this stability is due to their particular specification of a closure rule (Taylor and Lysy, 1979). Although their macroeconomic analysis of their own model is quite persuasive, it should be noted that other models with quite different macroeconomic specifications also show empirical stability of the overall size distribution.[9] Closure rules are important, but they are not the whole story. Also important is the fact that, as discussed in the previous section, any medium-term planning model can capture only some of the important factors affecting the distribution. By construction, the endogenous relationships in such models affect only part of the total variation in incomes, which implies that the overall distribution will be insensitive to moderate changes in model parameters and exogenous variables.[10]

---

[9] See, for example, the Bachue model of Rodgers, Hopkins, and Wery (1977) and also de Melo (1979).

[10] The details of how the overall distribution is specified in such models are given later.

Within the generally stable overall distribution, the models all show a great deal of variation and sensitivity to policies of the relative and absolute incomes of different socioeconomic groups. As we have discussed, a strong argument for the use of multisector CGE models is precisely that they permit the analysis of distributional effects that go beyond the narrow functional distribution that is the focus of macroeconomic models. We shall discuss later the appropriate definition of interesting socioeconomic groups and how their income is determined within the models. The important point to note here is that the types of policies considered in these models do have a significant impact on the socioeconomic distribution.[1] Adelman and Robinson focused especially on the distribution to socioeconomic groups and on the socioeconomic composition of quantiles of the overall distribution. Taylor, Lysy, and Ahluwalia appear to focus more on the aggregate functional distribution, which is consistent with their emphasis on the Kaldorian macro mechanism imposed on their multisector models.[12] However, the wider definition of socioeconomic groups characteristic of the multisector CGE models is also perfectly consistent with a more general structuralist view of the importance of considering distributional mechanisms in policy analysis.

Thus, in analyzing distributional issues, multisector planning models can be placed along a continuum that ranges from extreme micro to extreme macro. It is also important to consider a second continuum, that of time horizon. In their assumptions of various rigidities in nominal magnitudes such as wages, the exchange rate, or expenditure categories such as investment, the Kaldorian specifications tend to focus on relatively short-run adjustment mechanisms. The models with savings-determined investment, in contrast, focus on the medium term, anywhere from two to ten years. They thus tend to assume fewer or somewhat different structural rigidities than do the macro models. However, as we have seen, many of the factors determining the distribution of income are really long run in nature.

Taking a long-run perspective on income distribution changes one's view both of how income is measured and how to model the processes affecting the distribution. In a long-run analysis, and perhaps for all

[11] Extending the earlier work, more recent models, such as those of de Melo and Robinson (1980) and de Melo (1979), also focus on the socioeconomic distribution and emphasize relative-price-adjustment mechanisms such as changes in the exchange rate and the agricultural terms of trade.

[12] And may also explain why they emphasize one-sector special versions of their models. See Taylor and Lysy (1979) and Ahluwalia and Lysy (1979).

welfare analysis, the concept of income that should be used is that of permanent or lifetime income. The difference is quite important. For example, it has often been noted that a society in which lifetime income is exactly the same for all people will show a significant amount of inequality in current income because the society consists of people of different ages and hence who are at different points in the life-cycle income profile. Static measures of inequality applied to current income such as those discussed in the appendix to this chapter will fail to capture these demographic effects and are clearly not adequate measures of the distribution of permanent income. More generally, static inequality measures will be unable to distinguish among societies with different degrees of mobility between socioeconomic classes. Thus a socially very mobile society that may be characterized by quite unequal incomes at any given point in time would be ranked equally with a society in which not only is there inequality but also in which the same people remain poor and socioeconomic mobility is minimal.

It is obvious that there are great difficulties in empirically modeling long-run cumulative processes and we are still far from having an adequate integration in a unified model framework of factors affecting the distribution and factors affecting growth and structural change.[13] Processes connected with demographic change, education, health, nutrition, technological change, investment, and asset accumulation are certainly not well understood and hence cannot be easily captured in empirical models. It is also clearly important to consider the dynamic elements both of economic change and of socioeconomic mobility. A focus on lifetime income requires that one keep track of individual mobility – a model of net changes will not suffice – and it is very difficult to capture the mechanisms leading to socioeconomic mobility with a purely economic model. A number of different mechanisms are likely to be important in affecting the relative structure of, and movement among, different socioeconomic groups. A list would include: (1) rural-urban migration, (2) movements within the urban labor market, (3)

---

[13] See Kelley, Williamson, and Cheetham (1972) for a two-sector, long-run dualistic model, and Chenery and Syrquin (1979) for an input–output model. For an example of empirical economic–demographic models, see Rodgers et al. (1977). For a critical survey of these models, see Arthur and McNicoll (1975) and reply by Rodgers, Wery, and Hopkins (1976). A comparison of the Bachue-Phillipines model with the Adelman-Robinson model of Korea is given in Adelman, Hopkins, Robinson, Rodgers, and Wery (1979). Sanderson (1980) also surveys recent economic-demographic models.

demographic trends, (4) movement through the educational system, (5) savings and asset creation, both physical and human, and (6) asset redistribution.

A multisector planning model can capture the first two mechanisms of social mobility and can also include demographic effects, given a specified demographic submodel. However, it is more difficult to incorporate mobility through education, asset creation, or asset redistribution. A lot depends on how far one can go in specifying the ownership of human and physical capital by various socioeconomic groups. But even with a full specification of ownership patterns and household income formation, one would still be far away from a model able to predict the probability that a member of one group will break out and enter another group. One framework available for developing such a model is that of a "mobility matrix," which is mathematically akin to a Markov transition matrix. The elements of such an intergroup mobility matrix would be partly generated by the model (for example, through endogenous migration) and partly estimated exogenously from longitudinal data.[14]

In Chapter 5 we discussed a two-stage framework for a dynamic model in which the first stage is a static CGE model and the second stage is a model of intertemporal linkages that "updates" the exogenous variables of the static CGE model for the next period. Any attempt at modeling socioeconomic mobility would require a much more elaborate stage 2 model than has usually been specified. Demographic and educational submodels would become much more important, with the static within-period CGE model being only one component, and perhaps not the most important, of a much more elaborate dynamic model. Such an attempt at modeling mobility is beyond the scope of our discussion and would be the subject of a book in itself.[15]

From this discussion, it is apparent that the use of multisector planning models for the analysis of distributional issues represents an uneasy middle ground between various extremes. There is no one choice either of degree of aggregation or of time frame that will suit all purposes. In evaluating the particular choices made by past and future modelers, one must always remember the problems that a model is designed to illuminate. The principle of Occam's razor is also relevant – one should

[14] For an attempt at exploring the properties of such a model, see Robinson and Derviş (1977).

[15] See Robinson (1976c) for a sketch of what the structure of such a long-run model might look like.

always seek the simplest model that serves the purpose. However, it is important not to confuse size and complexity; the two properties are quite distinct. Large models may be very simple in structure, and even one-sector models may be very complex. The lesson is not that small models are better, for they often are not, but that one should not expect a single model to serve all purposes. The determinants of the distribution of income and the mechanisms by which it changes represent one of the most difficult theoretical and empirical problems facing the science of economics. We are certainly far from having any adequate general theory of the processes involved, if such a theory is even possible. Modesty and a willingness to consider a variety of approaches seem to us to be required of all those who would either do research or make policy concerning problems of income distribution.

12.4   Generating income distributions in a planning model

Virtually any economy-wide model will generate the distribution of income to aggregate factors of production. For further analysis of the interaction between income distribution and social and political forces, one is interested in the distributions among "institutions" (e.g., government, households, and public and private corporations) and among socioeconomic groups. Exactly how these distributions ought to be defined depends on the particular social and institutional structure of the country in question, as well as on the particular problems motivating the work. Finally, for neoclassical welfare analysis, one is interested in the size distribution.

Thus, in general, in the context of planning models, one can distinguish five different distributions that might be of interest to policy makers, the distributions to: (1) factors of production, (2) institutions, (3) socioeconomic groups, (4) individuals, (5) households. Figure 12.1 presents a schematic picture of how a planning model might generate all these distributions. We shall discuss them in order and shall consider the first three within the framework of a social accounting matrix (SAM).[16] Social accounting matrices provide an invaluable statistical framework for the analysis of the mappings between the different kinds of distributions one may want to consider.

[16] Although the discussion will focus on behavioral models, it is feasible to use the SAM approach to analyze income distribution using static multipliers analogous to those from an input–output model. For example, see Cline (1972), Weisskoff (1972), and Pyatt and Round (1979).

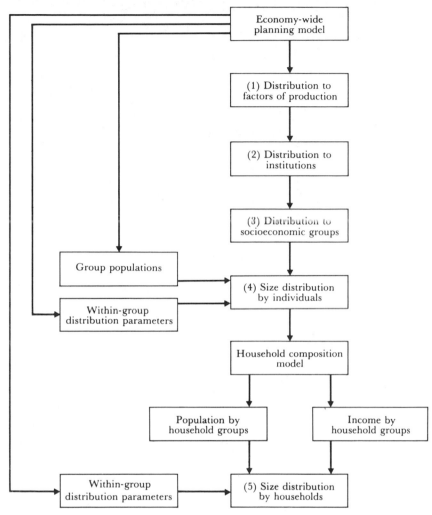

Figure 12.1. The distribution of income in planning models.

*Factors, institutions, and socioeconomic groups in a
SAM framework*

Table 12.1 presents the structure of a social accounting matrix that
focuses on the factor and institutional accounts. It is an extension of the
SAM discussed in Chapter 5. In the SAM, the functional distribution
is given in rows (3) and (4) of column (1), which give the division of
total value added at factor cost (excluding indirect taxes) between labor

Table 12.1. *Structure of a social accounting matrix*

			Factors		Institutions			Capital account (8)	Rest of world (9)
Receipts	Expenditures Activities (1)	Commodities (2)	Labor (3)	Capital (4)	Households (5)	Enterprises (6)	Government (7)	Capital account (8)	Rest of world (9)
Activities (1)		Domestic sales							
Commodities (2)	Intermediate inputs				Private consumption		Export subsidy Government consumption	Investment	Exports
Factors: Labor (3)	Wages				Labor income				
Capital (4)	Rentals					Capital income			
Institutions: Households (5)					Transfers	Distributed profits	Transfers,		Net factor income
Enterprises (6)							Transfers		Net private flows
Government (7)	Indirect taxes	Tariffs			Direct taxes	Direct taxes			Net public flows
Capital account (8)					Private saving	Retained earnings	Government saving		Reserve decumulation
Rest of world (9)		Imports							
Totals (10)	Total costs	Total absorption	Wages	Rentals	Household income	Enterprise income	Government income	Investment	Total imports

and capital. In a multisector model, the "activities" consist of all the producing sectors, so the functional distribution can be disaggregated by sector. In a model focusing on income distribution, it is also important to distinguish among a number of different types of labor. For example, the model used in the next chapter distinguishes four categories of labor, each with its own separate labor market: agricultural labor tied to the land, marginal labor mobile across all sectors, industrial labor, and service-sector labor. This classification represents probably the minimum necessary to capture the stylized structure of the labor markets in a developing country and also reflect a useful socioeconomic classification.

Total value added at market prices, which includes indirect taxes, is distributed to the various institutions in the economy: households, enterprises, and government. These institutions represent the basic "actors" whose behavior must be modeled. Households will be discussed in more detail later. In models in which there is no joint production, enterprises are classified by sectors of production (or activities). They are the entities that "own" the capital stock and hence receive all capital income. Out of their income, they are assumed to pay some in (corporate) taxes to the government, retain some to buy investment goods, and distribute the rest to the household sector (distributed profits). In the empirical models discussed in this book, enterprise behavior has been modeled very simply, without any really separate behavioral rules, and in Chapter 5 the enterprise and household accounts were simply lumped together. Of the existing CGE models, only the Adelman-Robinson model of Korea keeps the enterprise accounts separate and gives them a real behavioral role (for example, in their specification of sectoral investment allocation and retained earnings rates).

The government receives all taxes and expends funds on export subsidies, government consumption, saving, and transfers to the household sector and to enterprises. In all the models in this book, the government is an active agent in that it operates according to specified behavioral rules. Note that, as in Chapter 5, indirect taxes are assumed to be paid at the factory gate and so are entered only as a payment by activities to the government. Data permitting, different treatments are certainly possible. For example, one technique is to create a separate indirect tax account that differentiates taxes paid by different categories of purchasers, such as retail sales taxes, taxes on wholesale purchases, and so on (see King, 1981). Such a differentiation might be important in particular applications.

Government and the consolidated capital account are not shown as being closely linked. The various flows of funds that relate to central bank activities, such as credit policies, money creation, and interest-rate policies, are not reflected in the SAM. The modeling of such flows is one central focus of macro models, and although they may have important effects on the distribution of income, we have argued that it is useful in the first instance to concentrate on multisector rather than macroeconomic mechanisms.[17]

The rest of the world is treated somewhat differently in the SAM in Table 12.1 than in Chapter 5. In focusing on the distribution of income, it may be important to keep track of the separate flows between specific institutions and the rest of the world. Thus, the SAM shows separate entries for net factor income from abroad and public and private net capital flows (net also of interest, amortization, and profit repatriation). In the SAM presented in Chapter 5, these flows were lumped into one aggregate flow. Note that in the treatment here, the savings by institutions include both domestic and foreign components.[18] Also, the total of the rest-of-the-world account equals the value of total imports, as in Chapter 5. As with the other accounts, more elaborate treatments are certainly feasible and might be important in specific applications.[19]

In the SAM, the institution titled "households" really represents all the people in the society. Indeed, what really distinguishes the functional and institutional distributions from the other three (socioeconomic, personal, and household) is precisely that one need not associate individuals with the categorization of income recipients. They do not reflect a classification of individuals, but of different flows of funds that reflect the basic functional and institutional structure of society. "Households," on the other hand, represents a categorization of individuals. The distributions by socioeconomic groups, individuals, and households all represent different ways of describing the distribution *within* the "households" institution.

Before discussing different ways to characterize the distribution of income within the "households" institution, it is worth noting some of the problems associated with the definition of the income flows that accrue to it. For example, following standard accounting practice, cor-

[17]   There are a variety of ways of trying to capture such monetary mechanisms in a CGE model. Derviş and Robinson (1978), for example, incorporate a seigniorage transfer mechanism in their model, but do not pursue its distributional implications. Adelman and Robinson (1978), as we have discussed, explicitly incorporate a demand-for-money function in their model.

[18]   The reconciliation of this approach with that of the national income accounts was discussed in Chapter 5.

[19]   For example, one might separate the current and capital accounts and/or separate inflows and outflows (i.e., enter gross flows from institutions to the rest of the world).

Table 12.2. *A socioeconomic classification of households*

Type	Income sources
Small farmers	Wages, profits, transfers, foreign remittances
Marginal laborers	Wages, transfers, foreign remittances
Industrial laborers	Wages, transfers, foreign remittances
Service-sector laborers	Wages, transfers, foreign remittances
Agricultural capitalists	Profits, rent, transfers
Industrial capitalists	Profits, transfers, net foreign inflow
Service-sector capitalists	Profits, transfers

porate income taxes and retained earnings are not counted as part of the income of individuals in the society. This practice leads to serious problems when making international comparisons between countries in which the distinction between owners of enterprises and legal entities such as corporations are not similar. Particularly in developing countries, the distinction is quite fuzzy.

A second problem area is the treatment of government spending. In the field of public finance, there is an active literature on how one can allocate the benefits of government spending to different groups in the society. In terms of the SAM, this work can be seen as a kind of transfer account that allocates government consumption into the "household" institution. Although potentially important, such an expenditure incidence exercise is largely independent of the kinds of problems that have provided the focus of planning models, and we do not discuss it.[20]

For policy analysis it is important to consider a division of society into socioeconomic groups that are both economically and politically relevant. As we have discussed, the definition of appropriate groups represents a difficult problem, and a compromise is required that defines groups in a way that is useful for political analysis but is nonetheless closely related to the variables generated by a planning model. Given the nature of a CGE planning model, the easiest classification scheme is to differentiate groups by type and sector of origin of income.

Table 12.2 presents a disaggregation of the household accounts that gives one example of a classification of households by socioeconomic groups. We shall use it as an example to discuss the problems of devis-

[20] See Meerman (1979) and Selowsky (1979) for studies of fiscal incidence in Malaysia and Colombia. The problem is discussed in a SAM framework in Pyatt and Thorbecke (1976).

ing a "good" socioeconomic decomposition of households. There are seven groups, four types of labor differentiated by skill category, and three kinds of recipients of capital income differentiated by sector. This is the classification used in the empirical application in the next chapter and is rather closely tied to the functional distribution.

The "small farmers" are assumed to earn most of their income from labor and also to be tied to the land so that they are immobile. Subsistence farmers, share croppers, small landowners burdened with debt, and rural workers without access to the transportation and communications network would all fall in this category. "Marginal labor" is unskilled and/or unorganized labor that is assumed to be mobile across all sectors in the economy. The overwhelming source of employment for this category would be provided by the agricultural and urban traditional sectors. "Industrial labor" constitutes organized and/or skilled labor, including technical and managerial workers, and is assumed to be employed largely in the industrial sectors, although it might also include most government workers. "Service-sector labor" is assumed to be the urban counterpart of small farmers. It is made up of workers in the urban traditional sector most of whose income comes from their labor but who are immobile for a variety of reasons. The three "capitalist" categories are assumed to receive most of their income from profits and/or rent rather than from wages and salaries. They are here categorized by sector, because their income will be sensitive to shifts in relative product prices.

Along with a socioeconomic classification of income is a classification of all income-earning individuals in a society. In fact, many individuals have multiple sources of income. For example, capitalists usually also earn salary income, and farmers in developing countries often earn a significant fraction of their income from nonagricultural activities. With data on such multiple sources, it is relatively easy to classify individuals into socioeconomic groups according to their major source of income and then allocate to them income from more than one source. The allocation involves a mapping from factor income and/or transfers among socioeconomic categories. It is difficult, however, to have a very sophisticated model of such multiple income sources, and there are clear benefits to keeping the classification of socioeconomic groups relatively simple.

The choice of socioeconomic groups in Table 12.2 could certainly easily be expanded.[21] It is intended to represent the simplest categorization that adequately captures the economic dualism and structural rigidities

---

[21] Adelman and Robinson (1978), for example, distinguish fifteen different categories of income recipients.

characterizing many developing countries. As we shall discuss in more detail in the next chapter, the model in which these groups are embedded is designed to explore the distributional impact of trade policies in a "structuralist" environment characterized by a relatively segmented labor market and various rigidities in the ability of the economy to respond to external shocks. The choice of appropriate groups represents a compromise between our desire on the one hand to keep the model simple and so tie the groups closely to factor and sectoral income and, on the other, to provide an interesting division for policy analysis that includes an appreciation of political forces. For models with a different focus, a different compromise is required.

The size distribution by individuals

From the schema in Figure 12.1, we are now ready to consider the size distribution by individuals. The result of the previous steps is a division of all individuals into different socioeconomic groups constituting a complete and mutually exclusive decomposition of society. In addition, the aggregate income of each group is derived from the model. In order to calculate the overall size distribution of income by individuals, it is necessary to describe the distribution of income within each group and then consider the collection of groups taken together. One approach to deriving the overall distribution is to assume that the distribution of income within each group can be represented by a distribution function of the form

$$f_i(y \mid \theta_i) \tag{12.4.1}$$

where y refers to the income variable, θ_i is a vector of parameters in the distribution function, and f_i reflects a particular form of the frequency function characterizing the distribution within group i. The overall distribution of income in society is a linear weighted sum of the individual group distributions:

$$f(y \mid \theta) = \sum_{i=1}^{n} n_i f_i(y \mid \theta_i) \tag{12.4.2}$$

The weights n_i represent population shares, and the vector θ is the set of all within-group parameters θ_i. If we denote the mean income in each group by μ_i, the economy-wide average income by μ, and the within group variances by σ_i^2, the overall variance of incomes in society is given by the formula

$$\sigma^2 = \sum_{i=1}^{n} n_i \sigma_i^2 + \sum_{i=1}^{n} n_i (\mu_i - \mu)^2 \qquad (12.4.3)$$

Intuitively, it is clear that overall inequality in a society is a function of inequality *within* specified socioeconomic groups, inequality *between* these same groups, and finally the numerical weights these groups carry in the society. This is reflected in Eq. (12.4.3), which is essentially a statistical decomposition of variance.

The variance of income is not usually used as a summary measure of inequality – the log variance is a much more commonly used measure. One reason is that the log variance is a measure of *relative* inequality. A proportional change in all incomes leaves the log variance unchanged, whereas such a proportional change will alter the variance. The decomposition-of-variance formula can also be used for log variances by simply defining σ_i^2 as the within-group log variance and μ_i as the within-group log mean income.

Suppose for an instant that all groups were perfectly homogeneous with no within-group variances in incomes. We would thus have

$$\sigma^2 = \sum_{i=1}^{n} n_i (\mu_i - \mu)^2 \qquad (12.4.4)$$

Overall inequality would increase whenever one group's income moved further away from the economy-wide average and/or whenever the weight of a group characterized by greater distance from the mean increased with respect to the weight of a group closer to the economy-wide average.

If, on the other hand, we assumed that all groups were characterized by an identical mean income, and within-group variances were positive, we would have

$$\sigma^2 = \sum_{i=1}^{n} n_i \sigma_i^2 \qquad (12.4.5)$$

Overall inequality would now increase whenever inequality within one group increased and/or whenever the weight of a group characterized by relatively high variance increased relative to the weight of a group displaying lower variance.

In the general case of different mean incomes and positive within-group variances, it is still true that, all other things held constant, an increase in inequality within any one group, as well as an increase in the distance between any one group's mean income and the economy-wide average, will increase overall inequality. The impact of changes in group weights is more difficult to analyze, because the "within-group-variance" effect must be analyzed in conjunction with the "distance-between-groups"effect.[22]

Note that the overall distribution function $f(y|\theta)$ is the sum of distribution functions, not the distribution of a sum of random variables. Thus central limit theorems do not apply, and the overall function may, in principle, have any shape. Given specified within-group distribution functions, it is feasible to generate the overall distribution empirically even though it is analytically an intractable function.[23]

The approach to deriving the distribution of income described here enables one to decompose the entire distribution given knowledge of the parameters of the within-group distributions. The analysis is based on a decomposition of the overall distribution into a collection of within-group distributions and does not rely on the decomposition of any particular measure of inequality. The overall distribution is specified empirically, and one can thus generate any desired measures numerically, without being restricted to a particular measure and its associated decomposition.[24]

Assume for the moment that each within-group distribution is given by a two-parameter lognormal frequency function. The two parameters are the log mean and the log variance, that is, the mean and variance of the logarithms of individual incomes within each group. The lognormal distribution is often used to describe the distribution of income, although it is commonly found that it does not provide a good description of the distribution at the upper tail. However, in the formulation here, the function is not used to describe the entire distribution, but to describe a collection of within-group distributions. Alternative distribution functions could also be used, such as the three-parameter lognormal or the Pareto if it seemed desirable. Indeed, because the overall function is formed by summing the separate functions numerically, it would be perfectly feasible to specify a different function for every within-group distribution.

For the two-parameter lognormal distribution, it is necessary to specify the log mean and log variance. The CGE model will provide the

---

[22] See Robinson (1976a) and Fields (1980) for examples of the analysis of the distributional impact of changes in group shares in population and income.

[23] Robinson (1976b) describes the technique in detail and gives a computer program for doing the computations.

[24] This approach can also provide a useful framework for incorporating and reconciling distributional data from disparate sources and for analyzing the sources of inequality. For an application to Turkey, see Dervis and Robinson (1980).

arithmetic mean income for each group. If the log variances are known, then the log means can be calculated from the following relationship, which holds for the lognormal distribution:

$$\mu = \ln(\bar{y}) - \tfrac{1}{2}\sigma^2 \tag{12.4.6}$$

where $\bar{y}$ is the arithmetic mean income, μ is the log mean, and σ^2 is the log variance.[25]

One procedure for generating the overall size distribution would be to specify the within-group log variances exogenously, use the CGE model to solve for the group mean incomes, and then use the above relationship to calculate the log mean incomes. The overall size distribution is then constructed numerically by summing the within-group distributions. A fact that must of course be kept in mind is that if the within-group log variances are specified exogenously, then the model will generate only a part of overall inequality endogenously – that arising from between-group differences in mean incomes. Given that, in most empirical applications, between-group differences seldom account for more than half of the overall log variance of incomes, any policy experiments with the model that are assumed to leave within-group variances unchanged can have only a fairly limited impact on the overall size distribution. As discussed earlier, this specification may, in fact, be quite realistic, because many policy changes will not affect within-group relative distributions in the short to medium term.

In certain cases, it may be worthwhile to try to make the log variances (or some measure of the within-group dispersion of incomes) endogenous variables. In fact, a typical multisector model generates some income dispersion endogenously. For example, profit receipts are differentiated by sector and, in some models, wages are also permitted to vary among sectors. It is possible to use this information to estimate within-group log variances for those groups for which the model generates a number of different incomes.[26]

Another approach would be to have the log variance parameter itself be a function of other endogenous variables.[27] However, specifying the

---

[25] See Aitchinson and Brown (1957) for a thorough discussion of the properties and uses of the lognormal distribution.

[26] This is what Adelman and Robinson did with the wage-earning groups in their model. Lysy and Taylor (1980) also use this approach to estimate the overall size distribution in their model, without differentiating among subgroups in the population and without specifying different within-group distributions.

[27] See, for example, Metcalf (1972), who uses this approach in an aggregate econometric model of the United States.

appropriate function and estimating its parameters represents a major challenge. In any case, as we have discussed, the factors affecting the within-group dispersion seem, in general, to be more long run in nature. Thus, the fact that a proportion of total inequality in the model is exogenous is a reasonable specification for the time frame usually considered in a medium-term planning model.

Household composition and the household distribution

Referring to the schema in Figure 12.1, the previous steps yield the size distribution of income by individual recipients. Each category of recipients has been enumerated, and their average income has been determined in the model. Individuals who do not receive income, such as unpaid family workers, children, retired people, and other dependents, are not considered at all. There is no consideration of households consisting of workers and dependents either as income-receiving or as behavioral units.

It is important to consider the household as an institutional unit in an economic model for a number of reasons. Households are often considered to be behaviorally distinct units that make economic decisions about consumption expenditure and the supply of labor. The simple CGE model presented earlier treated the individual as the relevant decision-making unit – a more realistic model might well distinguish between workers and households. Empirical studies indicate that consumption and savings decisions are a function of household size, number of children, and other demographic variables as well as of income. Furthermore, definitions of poverty or economic welfare are often expressed in terms of per-capita or per-adult-equivalent household income and consumption. The household thus becomes the natural focus of analysis.

To go from per-worker income to household income requires an explicit specification of household composition. Households typically have more than one worker in more than one occupation and also differ in size, age composition, and dependency ratios. A complete model should capture these differences in household compositions. We shall present a very simple linear model that combines workers and worker income into households.

The technique we use is based on knowledge of the average number of workers in each household category, their occupational distribution, and the average household size.[28] Assume that households are classified according to the occupation of the head of the household. Thus there

---

[28] This presentation follows Adelman and Robinson (1978).

are exactly as many household categories as there are categories of income recipients.[29] Assuming that the average number and occupational composition of workers in each household category is constant, and given the population and average income of all income-recipient groups, it is possible to derive the total number of households and average income in each household category.

Define the following matrices:

H = matrix such that H_{ij} is the share of "other workers" of category j in household category i. Note that $\sum_j H_{ij} = 1$ for all i.

n = column vector such that n_i is the average number of "other workers" in households of category i.

N = diagonal matrix such that $N_{ii} = n_i$ and $N_{ij} = 0, i \neq j$.

w = column vector such that w_i equals the average income of workers in category i.

y = column vector such that y_i equals the average total income of households in category i.

h = column vector such that h_i is the total number of households in category i.

p = column vector such that p_i is the total number of workers in occupational category i.

Note that n_iH_{ij} is the number of "other workers" in category j in household i. The total income of a household is the sum of the income of the head and of the incomes of all "other workers." Thus, $y = w + NHw$, or

$$y = Qw \tag{12.4.7}$$

where $Q = I + NH$. Here Q_{ij} is the total number of workers in category j in household i.

It must be true that total household income be identically equal to total worker income. Therefore [where (') indicates the transpose],

$$h'y \equiv p'w \tag{12.4.8}$$

Substituting from (12.4.7), we get $h'Qw = p'w$. Because this must be true for any w, it follows that

$$h'Q = p' \tag{12.4.9}$$
$$h' = p'Q^{-1} \tag{12.4.10}$$

We estimate Q from survey data and, given Eqs. (12.4.7) and (12.4.10),

---

[29] One might specify a category of "unemployed" households whose income derives from secondary workers and/or transfers.

we can calculate both average incomes and household numbers by household category. Note that there is no restriction on the sign of the elements of Q^{-1}, and it is theoretically possible to have negative elements in h. This implies that so many workers of a given category are needed as "other workers" that the household category must generate such workers ex nihilo by having a negative entry.

Given the parameter n, the average number of "other workers" in different household categories, the model accounts for the economically active population and for the number of households. It does not account for the entire population including dependents. To do so requires separate information on the demographic characteristics of each household category. Demographic parameters relating to each household category, such as total size, number of workers, age structure, and so forth, would be specified exogenously. Such a specification is perhaps reasonable in the short to medium term. In the longer run, however, household formation and composition should be viewed as an endogenous process, interacting with economic variables.

The household composition model yields the number and average income of households in each category. We thus have a new set of household groups corresponding to the income-recipient groups defined by the model. One can use the same technique to generate the overall size distribution of income by households as was used to generate the size distribution for individuals. One must specify the within-group log variances, compute the within-group log means under the assumption of lognormality, and then generate the overall size distribution numerically. All the steps required in the schema of Figure 12.1 to move from factor payments to the size distribution by households are now complete.

In translating from factor income to household income, it was assumed that all workers in each household received the average income of their occupational category. Also, it was assumed that the within-household-group log variances were to be specified exogenously, independently of the within-occupational-group log variances. These assumptions could be relaxed in a more sophisticated model that incorporated a stochastic specification of worker composition of households. It seems likely that there is a correlation between the income of the head of the household and that of other workers in the household. For example, a household in which the head has above-average white-collar income will probably have other workers with above-average incomes in their occupations. Thus, the household composition process is likely to group people in a way that yields greater relative inequality in household income, because it will associate people from the upper and lower tails of the within-occupation distributions.

If, in the household composition process, the correlations between the relative income of the head of the household in his within-group distribution and the relative incomes of other workers in their respective within-group distributions were known, it would be possible to derive the parameters of the within-household-group distributions. The data requirements for this approach are significant, however, because one must specify the entire correlation matrix between occupational and household categories.

It is also important to note that this simple linear technique is to be used to translate unidirectionally from the functional to the household distribution. It certainly does not represent an adequate theory of household formation and thus cannot be used in a dynamic situation in which, for example, the skill composition of workers within households changes over time. In longer-run analysis, one must face directly the problem of adequately modeling the dynamic process of household formation.

12.5   Conclusion

As emphasized throughout the discussion, there are many facets to the analysis of income distribution beyond strictly economic considerations. The distribution of income within a society is the outcome of sociopolitical forces as well as economic ones. It was stressed that, in analyzing the relationship between policy and the distribution of income, the planner ought to attempt to consider explicitly the way society views distributional issues. It would seem that a balanced framework for policy analysis must attempt to reconcile the extreme views whereby on the one side society is viewed as made up of either capitalists or labor, and on the other as a collection of unconnected individuals.

This chapter has also investigated the various levels at which distributional issues can be incorporated into a CGE model. Any formulation from a purely functional one according to factor shares to a detailed specification of household formation will also involve normative issues. Once the difficult selection of how to incorporate income distribution has been made, the model provides a useful laboratory to investigate the distributional consequences of alternative policies. The next chapter provides applications of the approaches presented in this chapter.

The model specification that can be used in a given country depends partly on data availability and partly on the purposes for which the model is to be used. In the short to medium term, it is reasonable to specify a number of demographic parameters exogenously. It is important, however, to differentiate among different socioeconomic groups, because that is an important part of the policy relevance of the model. It is also important to distinguish the within-group and between-group distributions, because this points up the limitations of the model in "explaining" overall inequality. In general, it has been found to be the case that the overall size distribution of income can be substantially affected only by major shocks. However, the distribution among socio-economic groups is much more unstable and can be very policy responsive.

The empirical sensitivity of the distribution of income among socio-economic groups to policy shocks emphasizes the importance of attempting to integrate political and economic analysis when considering the distribution of income. Changes in the distribution among socioeconomic groups are politically very important even if such changes do not have substantial effects on the overall size distribution (and hence on the level of welfare as usually considered by economists). Thus different policies that have, for example, the same impact on overall poverty may have dramatically different effects on the composition of the poor (and of the rich) by socioeconomic groups. These differences may determine the political impact or feasibility of different policy packages and may well be more important in choosing among different policy packages than questions of narrowly defined economic impact or efficiency.

12.A   Appendix: Measures of income distribution

Useful summary descriptions of the distribution of income are based on two general principles. First, welfare economics has traditionally considered individuals to be the important units of analysis. Thus, one should consider and measure the properties of the overall size distribution of income. Second, we have argued that the division of society into socioeconomic groups is useful for both policy and welfare analysis. Thus, one should measure the properties of the between-group and within-group distributions.

The measures of the overall size distribution should, at root, reflect properties of the distribution that are important for making welfare judgments. Thus, it is important to evaluate descriptive statistics of the overall distribution in terms of the value judgments they implicitly or explicitly embody. Descriptive statistics of the between-group distribution, on the other hand, serve more as tools of policy analysis. Although people may well have normative value judgments with regard to the between-group distribution, analyzing and measuring changes in the distribution are more important for tracing out political and structural implications than for making welfare judgments. Thus, for example, it is useful to decompose the total log variance into between- and within-group parts not for welfare analysis but in order to understand the relationship between the economic structure and the distribution.

Because descriptive measures of the overall distribution are to be used in evaluating the distribution, it is useful to consider some of the normative equity judgments that are at least often proposed, if not widely acceptable.[30]

First, more equality of income distribution is preferable to less, given the initial situation. This is not usually carried so far as to imply that perfect equality is best, but only that a decrease in relative inequality is better.

Second, the existence of a group of people living in poverty is inherently a bad thing. Welfare is improved by reducing the extent of poverty (however defined) without regard to the rest of the distribution.

Third, the existence of a group of very rich people – a power elite – is a bad thing. This judgment is clearly more controversial and also depends on how one defines "very rich." Whereas poverty is usually defined in absolute terms, "very rich" is usually defined relatively. The rich might be considered to be too rich if the top 10 percent of the population controlled, say, 50 percent of total income instead of the more usual 25 to 40 percent.

Fourth, the existence of a group of chronically poor or chronically rich people is a bad thing. "Chronic poverty" is defined as a situation in which the same individuals (or, alternatively, their children) remain in poverty period after period. The case where not only the same individuals but also their children remain in poverty – chronic intergenerational poverty – is perhaps the worst of all. "Chronic wealth" is defined analogously.

The first and third value judgments lead naturally to descriptive measures that concentrate on the relative distribution of income. Measures such as the Gini coefficient, the log variance, and the Theil index are not affected by proportional changes in all incomes. The second value judgment, however, focuses attention on the lower tail of the distribution and leads to measures that are sensitive to the definition of the poverty line. For example, given a poverty line Y_p, one poverty measure is simply the share of the population with income less than Y_p. Fishlow (1972) has suggested a slightly more sophisticated measure defined as the share of total aggregate income that must be transferred from those above the poverty level to those below so that everyone in the poverty population receives Y_p.

Recent work, especially relating to "basic needs," has focused attention on the poor and especially on the appropriate definition of poverty. In general, a focus on poverty implies the use of measures of absolute income levels rather than of measures of the relative distribution. It is

---

[30] Our list follows Szal and Robinson (1977), although a similar discussion can be found in Sen (1973), and in Champernowne (1974).

important to distinguish carefully between the two kinds of measures because, especially when average income is growing and there is structural change, they give very different pictures of what is happening in a society. Focusing exclusively on either kind of measure is liable to give a distorted picture.[31]

The last value judgment – that chronic poverty and chronic wealth are bad – reflects the notion that more equality of opportunity is a good thing. Society is better off when there is more economic mobility – a dynamic concept that cannot be captured by descriptive statistics of the distribution at a point in time. Most measures currently used to describe the distribution are static measures in the sense that they neglect mobility aspects of the distributional mechanisms. However, there are possible trade-offs in welfare terms between static and dynamic notions of income inequality. For example, a highly unequal static distribution might be considered acceptable or even desirable if there were in addition a great deal of socioeconomic mobility over time. The problems of analyzing socioeconomic mobility were discussed briefly in the chapter.[32]

Because our approach to modeling income distribution generates the entire distribution numerically, it is also possible to generate any descriptive statistics one might desire. There are a number of different descriptive measures of the static distribution that have been suggested. We shall present only a brief summary survey, concentrating on the measures that fit best into the framework of planning models.

Based on our discussion of welfare judgments, statistics describing the distribution should reflect the degree of inequality in the distribution. In fact, the measures usually used are all "inequality" measures; that is, they are increasing functions of the degree of inequality, however defined. There has recently been much discussion about the nature of the social welfare function implied by various inequality measures. We shall not survey that literature, although it is clearly important to understand the properties of different measures so that one can understand how they define "inequality." Given our emphasis on the distribution of income between and within groups defined in socioeconomic terms, we shall concentrate on those overall measures that are relatively easy to decompose into within-group and between-group contributions to total inequality.

There are two common ways to represent a distribution.[33] The first

---

[31] See Fields (1980) for a good discussion of the different impact on relative and absolute distribution measures of different growth paths.

[32] See Szal and Robinson (1977) for a discussion of measures of mobility.

[33] Champernowne (1974) presents four types of diagrams. In addition to the "population" frequency function and the Lorenz curve, he presents an "income" frequency function and a Pareto diagram.

is to graph the frequency function with income on the horizontal axis and percent frequency of the population on the vertical axis. The area under the frequency function must equal one. The second common way to picture an income distribution is to graph the Lorenz curve. A point on a Lorenz curve indicates the percentage of total aggregate income (on the vertical axis) held by a percentage of the total population (on the horizontal axis). Reading from left to right, the population is arrayed in order of increasing income. Examples of a frequency function and a Lorenz curve are given in Figures 12.A.1 and 12.A.2.

If everyone has the same income, then the Lorenz curve is a straight 45° line. In this case, the frequency function collapses to a point at the mean income. The more unequal is the distribution, the farther is the Lorenz curve from the diagonal line and the more spread out is the frequency function from the mean.

We shall consider four summary measures of the distribution: (1) the coefficient of variation of income; (2) the log variance, (3) the Gini coefficient, and (4) the Theil coefficient.[34] Decomposition equations are available for all four of these measures. The first two measure the degree of relative dispersion of the frequency function. The Gini coefficient measures the shape of the Lorenz curve, and the Theil coefficient is a measure based on information theory.

The coefficient of variation is defined as the standard deviation of income divided by the mean. The log variance is the variance of the logarithm of income. The Gini coefficient is defined as the area between the Lorenz curve and the diagonal line divided by the total area under the diagonal. The Theil measure is defined as

$$T = \log(N) - \sum_{i=1}^{N} Y_i \log\left(\frac{1}{Y_i}\right)$$

where Y_i is the share of aggregate income going to person i and N is the total number of people.

All four measures are relative measures in that they are unaffected by proportional changes in all incomes. The Theil index has the odd property that it is bounded above by $\log(N)$, so that the larger is N the greater is the amount of possible inequality. It is possible to scale the index so that it is bounded by zero and one, changing somewhat the notion of inequality being measured.

Champernowne (1974) has compared six standard measures (including the four we are considering) and a number of special measures in

[34] There are, of course, other measures. See Szal and Robinson (1977) and Sen (1973) for more complete surveys.

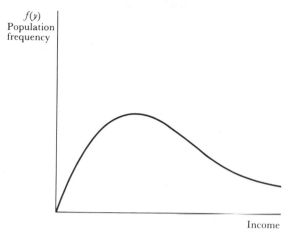

Figure 12.A.1. Frequency function.

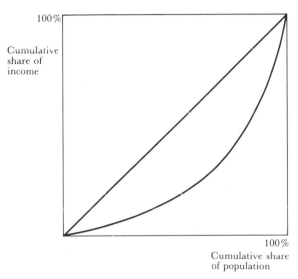

Figure 12.A.2. Lorenz curve.

terms of their sensitivity to different types of inequality exhibited by different income distributions. He distinguishes three different types of inequality: alpha, due to extreme relative wealth; beta, due to variations in less extreme incomes; and gamma, due to extreme poverty. He has generated a number of distributions exhibiting the different kinds of inequality and has compared the descriptive qualities of the various

Table 12.A.1. *A comparison of the sensitivity of four inequality indices to different types of inequality*

	Inequality type		
Inequality index	Alpha (wealth)	Beta (middle)	Gamma (poverty)
Coefficient of variation	Sensitive (1)	Insensitive (4)	Insensitive (4)
Log variance	Insensitive (4)	Sensitive (1)	Sensitive (1)
Gini coefficient	Insensitive (3)	Sensitive (2)	Sensitive (2)
Theil index	Sensitive (2)	Insensitive (3)	Insensitive (3)

Notes: The numbers in parentheses represent rankings. The types of inequality are as follows: alpha, due to extreme relative wealth; beta, due to inequality among the less extreme incomes; gamma, due to extreme poverty.
Source: Based on Champernowne (1974).

measures.[35] Champernowne discusses a number of different ways of comparing the sensitivity of the various indices to different types of inequality. Table 12.A.1 summarizes his results. It should be noted that the table is somewhat oversimplified, because it is based on a number of different kinds of pairwise comparisons discussed in the article. It is, however, consistent with the conclusions he states.

It is clear from Table 12.A.1 that if one is especially interested in the bottom end of the distribution – the extent of poverty – the best measures to use are the log variance and the Gini coefficient. They are also the most sensitive measures when inequality is due to variation among the less extreme incomes. If one is interested in the top end of the distribution – extreme wealth – the coefficient of variation and the Theil index are relatively more sensitive indices.

Because we are interested in separating the overall income distribution into within- and between-group distributions, it is important to consider the decomposition properties of the various measures. The decompositions of the log variance and of the coefficient of variation are based on the standard statistical decomposition of variance equations and are straightforward. The decomposition of the Theil index is also

[35] In addition to the four measures we are considering, he also considers two special cases of Atkinson's index of inequality based on a specific form of the social welfare function. Sen (1973) has an excellent discussion of the social welfare approach to measuring inequality and of Atkinson's measure in particular.

simple and straightforward. There are a number of different decompositions of the Gini coefficient that have been developed. Examples are to be found in Mangahas (1974), Fei and Ranis (1974), and Pyatt (1976). None of them is particularly straightforward, and all have special data requirements. For example, Mangahas defines a decomposition of the total Gini coefficient into the sum of two terms. The first is a weighted average of the within-group Gini coefficients. The second term is a weighted sum (weights add to zero) of all possible Gini coefficients between paired groups. The weights are functions of group size, population size, group mean income, and total mean income. The calculation of the between-group Gini coefficients requires comparable data on the income frequency functions for each subgroup – data that are often not available. The other decompositions are somewhat different in purpose, but also require more data than group mean incomes, group sizes, and within-group summary statistics.

We tend to favor using the log variance when decomposing the overall statistic into between-group and within-group contributions. It is sensitive to inequality at the low end of the distribution but is much easier to decompose than the Gini coefficient. It is also a natural choice given that we specify that the within-group distributions are lognormal. In the applications in the next chapter, we also calculate the Gini coefficient as well as measures of the extent of poverty.

CHAPTER 13

External shocks, trade adjustment policies, and the distribution of income in three archetype economies

13.1 Introduction

This chapter explores empirically certain distributional issues that can be fruitfully examined within the context of a CGE model. As discussed in Chapter 12, economy-wide models provide a useful framework to analyze how the workings of the market mechanism, in conjunction with public policy, determine the returns to factors of production and the purchasing power of income. Changes in product and factor prices brought about either by government policy or by changes in market conditions alter the distribution of income among socioeconomic groups. In turn, the attempts of different socioeconomic groups to improve their relative position in society affects the choice of government policy. We shall investigate quantitatively the links among trade policy, economic structure, and the distribution of income both to socioeconomic groups and to individuals.

The application in this chapter departs from earlier ones in two important respects. First, although the model structure remains fundamentally the same as that described in Chapters 5 to 7, considerably more attention is devoted here to the factor markets and to differences in consumption patterns among demanders. There are more labor categories and, in addition, there is some experimentation with alternative specifications of the labor market. On the consumption side, a different demand system is implemented, which allows for cross-price effects and also differs by socioeconomic groups.

The second important point of departure concerns the application itself. Rather than basing the model on the historical, political, and economic circumstances in a particular country, we have sought to investigate how a common external shock and trade policy response might have different effects in alternative environments. We create three representative, or archetype, economies and subject them to the same set of policy reactions to an identical external shock. To keep the analysis and interpretation of results manageable, we emphasize distinguishing characteristics of our archetype economies and make them quite similar in

432

other nonessential aspects. How the data sets are constructed is described in Methodological Appendix A.

The approach followed here has some important implications for the analysis of development policy. First, it provides limited, but systematic, evidence of the extent to which differences in resource endowments and initial conditions reflected in differing economic structures affect the impact of a given economic policy. For instance, is an adverse movement in foreign terms of trade likely to affect more adversely a closed or an open economy and, if the economy is open, will it require a greater adjustment if it is a manufacturing exporter or if it is a primary exporter? One can also investigate whether, in different economic environments, similar or different policies are preferable from the point of view of their impact on the distribution of income.

A second interesting set of questions relates to political economy issues. By investigating the effects of policies on the distribution of income across a typology of countries, one can draw inferences about the likely course of action policy makers will take on the basis of pressures from the most influential groups in society. In a primary exporting economy, for example, how the income of large landowners is affected may be more important than in an economy that exports manufactures, where instead the impact on industrialists may well determine the political feasibility of a particular policy choice.

The next section considers recent external shocks that have had, and will continue to have, an important impact on the growth prospects of developing countries. The need to adjust to these shocks and the difficulty of accomplishing that adjustment because of structural rigidities are also discussed. Section 13.3 describes the archetype economies chosen for the analysis, along with the selected set of experiments. The following two sections describe the impact of alternative adjustment mechanisms on the distribution of income in each economy and contrast the effects of each policy response across the three representative economies. Section 13.6 discusses how the economic and political struggle between socioeconomic groups is likely to influence policy selection. Conclusions follow in Section 13.7.

13.2   External shocks and macroeconomic adjustment

Changes in the international economy in the decade of the 1970s have resulted in great structural changes in developing and developed countries. In the two decades before 1973, world trade grew at an unprecedented rate of 8 percent a year. Since 1973, the rate of growth has halved (Lewis, 1980). The reasons for this decline are clearly linked to the shocks that have occurred in the world economy since 1973, including the recession in developed countries.

Developing countries have been severely hurt by these events in a number of ways. They have experienced, together with other oil-importing countries, a substantial increase in the relative price of a crucial intermediate input for which no alternatives are available in the medium term. However, this price increase was also accompanied by an increase in the price of other essential industrial imports, such as capital goods, as a result of the general increase in the rate of inflation experienced by industrialized countries. Moreover, the world recession and the restrictionist policies pursued by industrialized countries have resulted in a decline in their foreign exchange price. Thus, the developing countries were caught between rising costs on the import side and relative stagnation of export markets.

Whether the events of the last few years represent a major change in the world economy such that trade will no longer be an important "engine of growth" for developing countries is a crucial question for policy makers. Lewis (1980) is pessimistic, whereas Balassa (1980a) is still optimistic. In any case, the shock was severe, and developing countries were forced to attempt major adjustments in order to restore equilibrium. The changes in relative prices that accompany such adjustments affect the distribution of income in a number of important ways. The first, and by no means least painful, adjustment requires that aggregate expenditure be cut to reflect the fall in the foreign terms of trade. Second, restoring equilibrium calls for expenditure switching and a reallocation of resources among sectors.

The extent and ease with which these adjustments take place depend on a number of factors. Above all, they depend on how the various socioeconomic groups will react to their perceived change in relative and absolute income. In addition, the nature and extent of disequilibrium caused by these shocks depends very much on the structure of the economy (as we shall see). Finally, the extent to which the decline in absorption can be cushioned by timely external borrowing and by the use of short-term stabilization policies will affect the ease with which the transition can be achieved.

To explore the range of possible adjustments, consider the standard model with tradables and home goods. Prior to the shock, the economy satisfies its budget constraint and is in a state of external and internal balance. For simplicity, assume a shock consisting only of a rise in the world price of imports, holding the price of home goods constant. The shock reduces income measured in terms of tradables, leading to a decline in income as a result of the decline in the terms of trade, the size of which depends on the openness of the economy.

With the increase in the price of imports, consumers would attempt to substitute home goods for tradables, creating an excess demand for home goods. Eventually, resources would shift to increase production of tradables. There would still, however, be macroeconomic disequilibrium requiring a permanent change in the real exchange rate. Achieving such a change, however, is a difficult task for policy makers. If the price adjustment cannot be maintained (perhaps, for example, because of sticky real wages), the economy will eventually be forced to deflate. One could, for instance, imagine that nominal wages rise with the price of imports, which in turn causes the price of home goods to rise, and so on.[1] The outcome then is permanent structural disequilibrium with successive rounds of devaluation accompanied by domestic inflation. If equilibrium is eventually reached, it is clear that both a reduction and a switch in expenditures must be achieved if the economy is to avoid unemployment of resources. However difficult it may be to carry out expenditure-switching policies, the costs of failure can be large in macroeconomic terms.

This is not to say that the distribution of income, broadly defined, is affected only by the structural changes we have described. However, the recent external shocks suffered by developing countries are structural rather than monetary and, in spite of their monetary consequences, they call for structural adjustments in the economy. It is the distributional consequences of these structural adjustments on which we focus in this chapter.

13.3   The three archetype economies

As discussed in Chapter 4, the pattern of growth across countries varies greatly. An important source of the variation is the degree of openness of the economy, which is itself influenced by country size, factor endowments, and past government policies. In their work analyzing the pattern of development across a large number of developing countries, Chenery and Syrquin constructed a typology of developing countries based on trade orientation and related to policy choices of a country as well as to its natural endowments. Much of our inspiration in the construction of the three archetype economies described here comes from their work

---

[1] Findlay (1973, chap. 12) presents a similar model where home goods prices are determined on a mark-up basis and real wages are fixed.

and more recent work based on comparative input–output data for a number of countries (see Chenery and Syrquin, 1975; Chenery, 1979, chaps. 1–3; Kubo and Robinson, 1979).

The three economies are all assumed to be "semi-industrial" countries with an income per capita around $1,000 (1980 US$). Such countries are in a transitional phase, with their economic structure closer to that of the industrialized countries than to the very poor low-income countries, in which the overwhelming bulk of economic activity is in the primary sector. Thus, although the different patterns of international trade in the three countries result in considerable variation in economic structure, they all generate well over 20 percent of GDP in the manufacturing sector.

Although they have quite different structures of trade, production, and employment, we have also assumed them to be similar in a number of other important respects. First, they are identical in size, with the same total physical output and size of the labor force. This simplification is particularly useful when comparing the number of people in poverty and various other macroeconomic changes. Second, they share virtually the same technology.[2] This assumption is common in cross-country analysis where universal access to a common technology is often assumed. The input–output coefficients differ very little across the three countries, the capital structure (S) matrices are identical, and sectoral capital–output ratios are the same. We do assume different labor endowments by skill categories, which implies that labor–output and hence capital–labor ratios differ.

The final area in which we have imposed uniformity across the archetypes relates to the choice of parameters describing consumer and producer responses to relative price changes. Trade elasticities, elasticities of substitution in production, and income and price elasticities of demand for consumption by socioeconomic groups are the same. Each socioeconomic group makes expenditure decisions according to the linear expenditure system (LES). The parameters of the LES vary across socioeconomic groups, but are the same for a given type of group across countries.[3] To simplify further, production functions are assumed to be Cobb-Douglas in capital and labor, with fixed input–output coefficients for intermediate inputs. Finally, the log variances describing the distribution of income within socioeconomic groups are the same for a given socioeconomic group in all three archetype economies.

The model has eight sectors. The primary sector (1) includes agri-

---

[2] For a discussion of how this was done, see Methodological Appendix A.

[3] See Methodological Appendix A for a description of the expenditure system.

Table 13.1. *Socioeconomic classification of individuals*

Type	Sectors of activity	Income source	Within-group log variance
Farmers	1	Wages + profits[a]	0.50
Marginal laborers	1–8	Wages	0.20
Industrial laborers	2–7	Wages	0.40
Service-sector laborers	8	Wages	0.25
Agricultural capitalists	1	Profits[a]	0.60
Industrial capitalists	2–7	Profits	0.60
Service-sector capitalists	8	Profits	0.50

[a] 25% of agricultural profits go to farmers, the rest to agricultural capitalists.

culture and mining, whereas the food sector (2) includes processing and manufacturing of food, beverages, and tobacco. Consumer goods (3) might also be called "light" industry and does involve some vertical aggregations, for example, textiles and clothing, wood and wood products. Intermediates (4) and capital goods (5) are demanded only by producers, whereas construction (6) is a pure investment good. Social overhead (7) includes utilities, transportation, and housing. Services (8) includes retail and wholesale trade, government services, banking, insurance, and so on. Furthermore, we assume that sectors 6–8 are pure nontraded sectors and that all government noninvestment expenditure is concentrated in services.

The discussion in Chapter 12 indicated how difficult it is to come up with a satisfactory definition of socioeconomic groups that is useful both for economic and political analysis and is also closely related to the variables generated endogenously by a CGE model. The socioeconomic classification described in Table 12.2 is one such compromise, which we have adapted for this application. Table 13.1 summarizes the socioeconomic classification of households, the sectors from which their income is derived, and whether that income is wage or profit income. Finally, it provides the assumed within-group log variance of the distribution of income within each socioeconomic group.[4]

By "farmers" we mean agricultural workers and small landowners or "minifundistas" who own a plot of land that provides enough income to support a family. What distinguishes them from marginal labor,

---

[4] See Section 12.4 for a discussion of the technique of generating the overall distribution by numerically aggregating different within-group distributions.

besides their slightly higher income, is that they are tied to the land and earn, in addition to their wage income, a share of agricultural profits. Because there is considerable variation in the size and quality of land owned by small farmers, we have assumed that this group has a fairly high within-group log variance. By contrast, marginal or mobile labor – the only group that is mobile across all sectors – is fairly homogeneous. With an income a shade above half of the economy-wide mean income, they are the largest and poorest group in society, and their income is fairly equally distributed. Industrial laborers, or organized labor, are employed only in the manufacturing sectors. The smallest wage-earning group in society, they are fairly disparate in composition and include white-collar workers, clerical workers, technicians, and engineers. Their income is about 1.5 times that of marginal labor. Service-sector laborers include government workers and, finally, we have the three capitalist groups, who get their income from profits. Their number is fixed exogenously, with the income of industrial capitalists about ten times the economy-wide mean income and about 30 percent above that of agricultural capitalists. Service-sector capitalists include a large group of self-employed (such as retail traders, etc.) and have an income about five times the mean income.[5]

These groups whose incomes are determined by the model represent the minimum necessary to capture the diversity of socioeconomic groups found in semi-industrial countries. Clearly there is a considerable range of variation in mean income and, at this level of aggregation, a considerable degree of heterogeneity within socioeconomic groups. The countries are characterized by a fairly high degree of inequality, with Gini coefficients of approximately 0.50 (or overall log variance of 0.60).[6] About 45 percent of the overall log variance is due to between-group variation and corresponds to that part of total inequality which is endogenous to the model.

We now come to the distinguishing characteristics built into the production side of the three archetype economies. The distinctions introduced into the otherwise similar structures fall under three categories. First, the economies are distinguished by their volume of trade. Two of the economies are open in the sense that the volume of exports as a

---

[5] Group and economy-wide mean incomes in the base run are given in Table 13.9.

[6] Gini coefficients of this magnitude are higher than those reported for Asian countries, where the distribution of land is fairly equal, but lower than those of most Latin American countries. See Jain (1975).

proportion of gross output is large (10 percent). Second, they are distinguished by their structure of production and trade. Of the two open economies, one is a primary exporter and the other is a manufacturing exporter. Accordingly, the structure of production is biased toward the primary sector in the first and toward manufacturing in the second. The third distinguishing characteristic, which provides the basis for the structural differences, are variations in factor endowments, tariffs, and subsidies that are assumed to account for the differences in production and trade structures among the three economies.

There are thus three archetype economies: primary exporter (PE), manufacturing exporter (ME), and closed economy (CL).[7] They differ in sectoral structure of production, employment, and capital; volume of trade; sectoral composition of exports and imports; skill composition of the labor force; and past trade policies as reflected in different sets of tariffs and subsidies. These differences are summarized in Tables 13.2 to 13.4.

Table 13.2 compares the structure of production and trade in the base run (prior to any shock) across the three archetypes. All of the variation in structure comes from the relative sizes of the industrial and primary sectors, and from variations within the manufacturing sector itself.

The PE economy, with a larger primary sector (and hence a smaller manufacturing sector), has a distinctively different gross output structure. The difference between the CL and ME structures are less pronounced, although the ME economy has a much larger consumer goods sector, which provides its main source of foreign exchange, whereas the CL economy has larger primary and food sectors to assure self-sufficiency.

The overall export and import ratios (see also Table 13.3) indicate the sharp differences in volume of trade between the closed and open economies. Note that with world prices exogenous and equal to unity, the foreign capital inflow is the same for all three economies and is maintained at its base-run level throughout the experiments. The variation in exports and imports is obvious even at the three-sector level of aggregation. The PE and ME economics have opposite structures and the CL economy resembles the PE economy on the importing side, whereas on the export side it has a balanced structure with half of its exports originating from the primary sector. Within the manufacturing

---

[7] Note that the structure of imports describing the closed economy in Table 13.2 corresponds more closely to that found in countries such as Mexico and Turkey than to that prevailing in larger countries such as Brazil or India.

Table 13.2. *Three archetype economies: structure of production and trade in the base run* (%)

Sectors		Gross production			Imports			Exports		
		CL	PE	ME	CL	PE	ME	CL	PE	ME
Primary	(1)	20.7	27.2	19.6	6.6	8.7	17.3	48.2	80.9	9.9
Food	(2)	13.4	11.5	12.0	4.0	13.4	14.2	12.8	4.5	6.2
Consumer	(3)	11.7	9.2	14.4	5.0	12.9	7.4	22.5	9.3	52.9
Intermediate	(4)	11.6	9.1	11.1	51.2	34.4	36.8	13.9	4.5	23.2
Capital goods	(5)	5.4	3.9	4.9	33.2	30.6	24.3	2.6	0.8	7.8
Construction	(6)	5.8	7.0	6.9	—	—	—	—	—	—
Social overhead	(7)	8.9	10.2	9.7	—	—	—	—	—	—
Services	(8)	22.5	21.9	21.4	—	—	—	—	—	—
Aggregates										
Primary	(1)	20.7	27.2	19.6	6.6	8.7	17.3	48.2	80.9	9.9
Industry	(2–7)	56.8	50.9	59.0	93.4	91.3	82.7	51.8	19.1	90.1
Services	(8)	22.5	21.9	21.4	—	—	—	—	—	—
Total		100.0	100.0	100.0	100.0	100.0	100.0	100.0	100.0	100.0
Ratio to GDP		175.3	150.3	159.5	11.2	18.7	19.0	7.4	15.2	15.5

sector, note that the CL economy is almost as dependent on imports of intermediates and capital goods as the other economies.[8]

Table 13.3 provides information on the sectoral trade orientation of the three archetype economies. It is crucial for understanding how the common external shock gets transmitted across sectors and across archetypes. We have already examined the sectoral classification of sectors according to their degree of tradability in the earlier applications, so suffice it to note again that although there are three pure nontraded sectors in each economy, these are among the most import-dependent sectors because of the high import content in total intermediate inputs.

The final distinction among the three archetypes relates to factor endowments, which are given in Table 13.4. All three economies have a total labor force of 10 million. As one would expect on the basis of the factor endowment theory of international trade, the pattern of trade is closely related to each archetype's factor endowments. Thus the PE economy has the largest supply of farmers, whereas the ME economy has the greatest supply of marginal labor and especially of organized labor, which are used intensively in the manufacturing sector. As is the case with most other indicators, the CL economy, which has the most balanced trade and production structures, has a pattern of factor endowments in between those of the two open economies.

13.4 The macroeconomic impact of an external shock

The external shock we impose on each of the archetype economies has two components. On the import side, the exogenous world prices of imports are raised by 25 percent across the board. On the export side, the volume of exports is lowered by 25 percent in all sectors.[9] World prices of exports, however, remain fixed. This experiment is intended

---

[8] Accompanying, and responsible for, this foreign trade structure are the following trade incentives: tariffs of 25%, 35%, and 20% for consumer goods, intermediates, and capital goods for ME and PE; 15% across-the-board export subsidies for PE and 75% export subsidies for manufacturing in ME; no export subsidies for CL and the following tariffs: consumer goods (75%), intermediates (75%), and capital goods (20%). All three economies have the following trade substitution elasticities: primary (3.0), food (1.5), consumer goods (1.25), intermediates (0.75), capital goods (0.25).

[9] In the model, it is convenient to cut exports by lowering all the sectoral export supply ratios (see Table 13.3). This, however, does permit a slight export supply response through changes in the sectoral composition and level of output. In the experiments, this effect is very small.

Table 13.3. *Three archetype economies: sectoral trade ratios in the base run* (%)

Sector	Imports/domestic supply[a]			Imported inputs/total intermediate inputs			Exports/domestic production		
	CL	PE	ME	CL	PE	ME	CL	PE	ME
Primary	2.3	5.7	11.0	9.7	13.7	14.7	9.8	30.3	4.9
Food	2.0	15.1	14.8	6.1	9.9	12.2	4.0	4.0	5.0
Consumer	3.0	19.2	9.5	12.0	19.2	15.7	8.1	10.2	35.7
Intermediates	29.8	49.3	49.2	17.1	25.1	23.5	5.0	5.1	20.2
Capital goods	39.8	98.8	69.2	28.0	38.5	32.2	2.0	2.0	15.4
Construction	—	—	—	24.8	30.9	27.3	—	—	—
Social overhead	—	—	—	25.1	31.6	27.4	—	—	—
Services	—	—	—	17.0	20.5	17.8	—	—	—
Average	6.7	13.8	13.2	15.8	20.7	19.5	4.2	10.2	9.7

[a] Domestic supply = domestic production – exports.

Table 13.4. *Three archetype economies:
composition of the labor force (%)*

	CL	PE	ME
Farmers	30	40	25
Marginal laborers	30	27	33
Organized labor	10	9	15
Service-sector labor	30	24	27
Total	100	100	100

to capture the essence of the events that occurred in the second half of the seventies. First, the increase in the purchase price of developing countries' imports spurred by the rise in energy prices and compounded by the inflationary situation that developed in the industrialized countries; second, the world recession that led to restrictionist policies in industrialized countries (including quantitative restrictions) and to a relative decline in world trade. We have deliberately chosen to ignore any additional terms-of-trade losses that occurred because developing countries face downward-sloping demand curves for their exports. Rather, we have emphasized the effects associated with export quantity restrictions coupled with an exogenous change in the foreign terms of trade.

In selecting the external shock we have tried to facilitate the comparison across archetypes by the following simplifications. First, combining equal across-the-board rises in import prices with equal across-the-board reductions in export volumes yields an undifferentiated external shock for all three economies so that the impact effect depends only on the total volume of trade in the economy. Second, by fixing the world price of exports, the decline in the foreign terms of trade is the same for all three economies so that the resulting income loss depends on the initial volume of trade and not on its composition.

To study the interactions between adjustment policies and the distribution of income, we compare the following three adjustment policies: devaluation, premium rationing, and premium rationing with a fixed real wage for marginal labor. There are important political as well as economic differences among the three adjustment mechanisms. A policy of devaluation, because of its fairly even spread across sectors, could be viewed as a political compromise reflecting some minimal degree of consensus among socioeconomic groups. A policy of granting import licenses giving rise to premia reflects a situation where political power is concentrated in the hands of capitalists and would accentuate income concentration. Finally, a policy of premia on imports coupled with fixed real wages for marginal or mobile labor reflects a situation where no socioeconomic group is firmly in control of policy making. Businessmen manage to appropriate the premia associated with a system of import control by licensing but, on the other hand, workers are sufficiently well organized to prevent a fall in real wages.

What, then, is the macroeconomic impact of alternative adjustments to the external shock? Table 13.5 contrasts the magnitudes of changes in the major components of GDP at constant prices across the three countries for each of the alternative adjustment mechanisms. Consider first the case of devaluation. At constant prices, the fall in real GDP ranges between 3.7 percent for CL to 2.3 percent for PE. At first sight, this result seems counterintuitive, because the economy that trades the least is the most severely affected. The result is due to the different structures of production and trade in the three economies. The CL economy has the highest ratio of intermediate input requirements to total production and, moreover, its imports are concentrated in the intermediate sector with a low trade-substitution elasticity. After the shock, the ratio of the value of intermediate inputs (both domestic and imported) to total absorption rises the most in the CL economy (up 4.9 percentage points compared to 4.2 and 2.9 for the PE and ME economies). The result is that the adjustment is much more painful for CL than for the other two economies. The required devaluation in the open economies is around 35 percent, whereas in the closed economy it is over 60 percent.

With a real GDP loss of 3.2 percent, the ME economy is hit harder than the PE economy. The reason is that the latter has a production structure biased toward the primary sector, which, next to food, is the least import-dependent sector in the economy. Although the ratio of imported to total intermediate inputs is about the same in the PE economy, the ratio of total intermediate inputs to total production is lower. The PE economy thus depends less on imported goods to maintain production levels.

It is also interesting to compare how the major final demand aggregates are affected by the shock. Private consumption falls the least in the PE economy, which is what one would expect because agricultural and food exports are now supplied to the domestic market, dampening the cut in aggregate consumption expenditure. With a 7.5 percent decline, the fall in private consumption expenditures is highest in the ME economy, which has to bear the brunt of higher prices for food imports. Government consumption rises by approximately 10 percent

Table 13.5. *The macroeconomic impact of the external shock*

	Experiment								
	Devaluation			Premium rationing			Premium rationing with fixed real wage		
	CL	PE	ME	CL	PE	ME	CL	PE	ME
Change from base run (%)[a]									
GDP	−3.7	−2.3	−3.2	−3.3	−2.0	−3.2	−4.9	−2.9	−6.5
Private consumption	−7.7	−4.2	−7.5	−4.4	−4.0	−6.6	−5.7	−5.0	−10.4
Government consumption	11.6	9.3	8.8	5.3	10.7	7.4	5.3	10.7	7.4
Investment	−12.8	−16.7	−7.1	−18.3	−16.7	−9.5	−19.3	−17.4	−12.7
Exports	−23.8	−22.8	−27.8	−23.8	−22.8	−28.9	−26.2	−23.8	−33.0
Imports	−32.9	−35.5	−37.8	−32.8	−35.5	−39.5	−34.4	−36.3	−41.2
Exchange rate	62.0	37.4	33.9	0.0	0.0	0.0	0.0	0.0	0.0
Selected ratios (%)									
Unemployment rate	—	—	—	—	—	—	3.6	1.6	7.1
Premium rate	—	—	—	86.8	57.0	42.7	84.1	50.4	41.6
Total premia/GDP	—	—	—	9.2	8.3	6.6	9.0	8.2	6.5

[a] All variables are real except the exchange rate.

across all three economies, largely because government domestic currency revenues from tariffs increase both because they are levied on higher foreign prices and because the currency has devalued.

Under devaluation, the differences in adjustments among countries are not great for exports and imports, but they are quite significant for investment. In the model, fixed savings rates are assumed for the government and for each socioeconomic group, which implies that the model is "savings driven." Foreign capital inflows are assumed to be part of savings. To understand why real investment falls by more than 16 percent in PE but by only 7 percent in ME, we need more information about the composition of investment and the sources of savings. First, note that one expects to find variations in relative prices and, hence, differences in the prices of capital goods. The same nominal investment will, after the shock, yield different real investment. As can be seen from Table 13.6, the investment goods price deflator varies widely across the three economies, changing least for the ME economy (because of the increased availability of capital goods on the domestic market).

There is also a second effect, which can be seen by examining the composition of savings (in current prices) provided in Table 13.6. The trade deficit, measured in world prices, is identical and remains fixed across the three economies and also is assumed to be part of saving. For further details, see Methodological Appendix A. But this saving takes place in domestic prices and hence varies with devaluation. The foreign component of domestic savings – 22 percent in the base run – rises dramatically across all three economies with devaluation. And of course it rises most in CL, where devaluation is greatest. Thus real investment falls less in CL than in PE, even though both economies experience essentially the same rise in capital goods prices.[10]

Whether and to what extent foreign capital inflows are channeled into investment is an issue that has often been debated in the literature. After having been much discussed in the context of two-gap models, the issue has resurfaced in the debate on the role of alternative closure rules on the distribution of income (see Papenek, 1972; Bhagwati and Grinols, 1975; and Chapter 12). As we have already noted in Chapter 12, how investment is determined may have a significant impact on the distribution of income. For example, had real investment been fixed, with increases in the prices of capital goods ranging from 6 to 19 percent,

[10] This effect, often referred to as the Hirschman (1948) effect, has been noted and investigated in the context of developing countries by, among others, Cooper (1971) and Krugman and Taylor (1978).

Table 13.6. *Volume and composition of investment*

| | Base-run values [a] | | | Ratios to base run (%) | | | | | | | | |
| | | | | Devaluation | | | Premium rationing | | | Premium rationing with fixed real wage | | |
	CL	PE	ME	CL	PE	ME	CL	PE	ME	CL	PE	ME
Foreign savings	22.0	22.0	22.0	159	141	136	130	100	100	100	100	100
Labor savings	20.0	23.0	21.0	80	87	90	80	83	86	80	83	81
Capitalist savings	38.0	49.0	30.0	82	88	87	103	102	97	100	102	93
Government	28.0	37.0	53.0	100	100	91	96	108	94	96	108	92
Total	108.0	132.0	126.0	103	99	98	96	100	94	95	99	92
Investment goods price deflator	100	100	100	118	119	106	118	120	104	118	120	105

[a] Nominal savings.

there would have been significant forced savings, which might have worsened the distribution of income depending on the nature of the forced-savings mechanism assumed.

Because exports are essentially fixed, the main difference between adjustment by devaluation and adjustment by premium rationing is the income transfer to capitalists. Also, devaluation has no inherent efficiency advantage over a uniform import premium. In other experiments not reported here, we allowed an export response to the policy shock by specifying logistic export functions (described in Chapter 7). When compared with adjustment by premium rationing, devaluation is more attractive in the case where some export response is allowed than in the version adopted here.

Many of the differences in the pattern of adjustment among the three economies remain when adjustment takes place by premium rationing. It is interesting, however, to note that the GDP loss is slightly less than in the case of devaluation for two economies, CL and PE. This effect is due largely to the distortion-removing effect of adding premia to tariffs. Thus CL and PE, which have the most uneven tariff structures, end up with tariff structures that are much more uniform as a result of the imposition of premia.[11] Also note that the pattern of changes in real investment is now almost entirely accounted for by the differential impact of the shock on capital good prices.

Premium payments as a percent of GDP range from 6.6 percent for ME to 9.2 percent for CL. The potential rents accruing to the private sector from a system of licenses can therefore be enormous, and it is no surprise that it is important what method of adjustment is used. Although more sensitivity analysis would be needed before one could establish a correspondence between devaluation and associated premia, these results are consistent with the often-made observation that huge rents are commonplace in economies that choose to maintain external balance with a system of import controls.[12]

Finally, we come to adjustment by premia combined with fixed real

[11] See Johnson (1960) for an analysis of the welfare effects of tariffs that takes into account the variance of tariffs across sectors.

[12] Note that the premium rate is higher than the devaluation rate even though the composition and volume of imports and exports are similar. This is entirely because of the normalization rule, which maintains a weighted sum of composite prices constant. Thus the domestic currency price of exports does not rise in the case of premia rationing, whereas it does in the case of devaluation. It follows that, to maintain the same price level, the domestic price of imports must rise more with premium adjustment, because domestic prices do not rise as much.

wages. The fall in GDP due to the contractionary impact of the external
shock is exacerbated by induced unemployment ranging from 1.6 percent for PE to 7.1 percent for ME. As a result, GDP falls substantially
more, except in the primary exporter. The PE economy is least affected
for two reasons. First, the cost of living rises less in the economies that
export rather than import food. This effect is important, because the
weight of food in the consumer basket of marginal labor is about 60
percent. Second, the PE economy has the smallest supply of marginal
labor (see Table 13.4), so that, other things being equal, aggregate
employment will not fall as much.

It is important to note that if we had instead made the short-run
assumption that nominal rather than real wages remain fixed, the
impact of adjustment on the distribution of income would have been
quite different. Indeed, with real wages falling, the demand for labor
would have increased. Such an assumption is not justified in a medium-
term model and, in any case, would require an analysis of inflationary
mechanisms that is beyond the scope of the present analysis.

13.5 Policy choice and the distribution of income

The impact of the external shock results in a decline in real income and
the extent of that decline depends on the choice of adjustment policy. In
addition, the composition of imports determines to a large extent
whether the burden of adjustment falls on consumption or on investment. Thus, for the ME economy, which is a food importer, the consumption loss tends to be high. For the CL and PE economies, which
import capital goods, the decline in GDP falls most heavily on investment. The rate of real investment, which is around 20 percent of GDP
in the base run for the three economies, falls to 17 percent in both the
CL and PE economies.

In addition to variations in real investment, the different policy
adjustments have important variations in incidence among socioeconomic groups. Which groups bear the brunt of adjustment across the
three economies, and is it the same groups that lose the most under both
devaluation and premium rationing? Can any group benefit in absolute
terms and experience a rise in real income? We explore these questions
in this section.

Before examining the magnitudes of distributional shifts, it is useful
to review the various mechanisms whereby the external shock affects
the distribution of earned income. First, on the supply side, the change
in relative net prices affects the distribution of value added between sectors and, within sectors, the distribution of value added between wages

and rents. These shifts determine, after taxes, the distribution of earned nominal income among the socioeconomic groups. Second, the distribution of income is affected by differential changes in the cost of living across groups. The relevant prices are those of composite goods (which include imports). Third, the distribution of income is affected by transfers, which here arise from the distribution of import licenses and hence premia.

Consider first the distributional shifts associated with changes in net prices. As a first approximation, divide the economy into two sectors, agriculture and manufacturing, and assume that labor is perfectly mobile between them whereas capital is immobile. Furthermore, assume a fixed wage differential CD between agriculture (A) and manufacturing (M). In Figure 13.1, $O_A O_M$ represents the total labor force in the economy, the vertical axes measure the wage of labor in the two sectors, and the two curves indicate the marginal revenue product of labor. Prior to the shock, the equilibrium distribution of the labor force is given by L_0 with labor income given by the sum of the two rectangles under wage lines W_A^0 and W_M^0, and capitalists' income given by the triangular region between the wage lines and the respective marginal revenue product (MRP) curves.

Now suppose that the external shock raises the net price agricultural terms of trade to PN^1, thereby shifting the VMP curve in agriculture. Clearly, capitalists in the manufacturing sector lose. On the other hand, the per-unit rents of capitalists in agriculture rise by more than the percentage increase in the agricultural net price.[13] Finally, the increase in the wage rate (W_A^0 to W_A^1) is less than the increase in the agricultural net price terms of trade, so labor gains in terms of manufacturing but loses in terms of agriculture. Hence, to determine what happens to labor's real income, we must consider its cost of living.

As can be seen from Figure 13.1, the magnitude of income changes depends on the elasticity of substitution between labor and capital (σ) in the two sectors and on the intensity with which the two factors are used in both sectors. A large value for σ_A combined with a small value for σ_M and/or a high labor share in agriculture and a low labor share in manufacturing would lead to a flat MRP_A and to a steep MRP_M curve, which in turn would imply that labor's income in terms of agriculture would rise. Because we assume the same (unitary) elasticities of

---

[13] Because the percent increase in net price is the weighted sum of the percent increase in the wage rate (which is less than the increase in the price) and rate of return to capital. For a discussion of this magnification effect, and of the importance of factor specificity, see Mussa (1974).

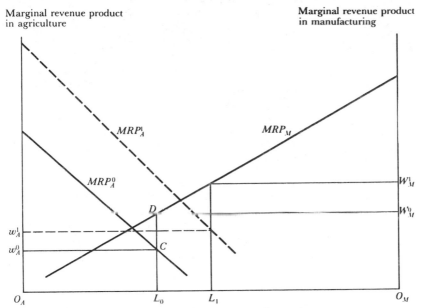

Figure 13.1. Factor mobility and the distribution of income.

substitution between capital and labor across all sectors, it is only differences in labor intensity between sectors that influence the distributional outcome. Introducing organized labor, which is mobile within manufacturing, does not alter the above mechanisms except that they share the manufacturing capitalists' losses, the extent of sharing being inversely related to the elasticity of substitution between the two labor categories (again assumed for simplicity to be everywhere unity).

Table 13.7 compares the impact of the external shock on selected relative price indices for the three economies. Regardless of the selected adjustment mechanism, the foreign terms of trade is assumed to rise by 25 percent. The impact on the net price agricultural terms of trade shows considerable variation across economies and adjustment mechanisms. Under devaluation, it rises substantially in the ME economy (41 percent), which must replace agricultural products that were previously imported. There is no change for the PE economy, whereas there is a 5 percent fall in the CL economy caused by the increased intermediate input costs in agriculture, which have a high import cost component. The composite price agricultural terms of trade, which are important in determining real income, follow the opposite course of the capital goods price deflator. This movement explains why real consumption

Table 13.7. *The impact of the external shock on selected relative price indices (ratios to base run, %)*

| | Experiment | | | | | | | | |
| | Devaluation | | | Premium rationing | | | Premium rationing with fixed real wages | | |
	CL	PE	ME	CL	PE	ME	CL	PE	ME
Foreign TOT[a]	125	125	125	125	125	125	125	125	125
Net price agricultural TOT	95	100	141	87	78	137	83	76	127
Composite price agricultural TOT	74	71	117	74	64	111	72	63	106

[a]TOT = terms of trade.

falls so much in the ME economy. With premium rationing, there is an income transfer to capitalists, whose expenditure shares on agricultural-based products are lowest, so that both price indices rise less for the ME economy and fall more for the PE and CL economies. On the basis of an examination of price indices, one would conjecture that the distributional shifts will be most pronounced in the ME economy.

Although there is much variation in shifts in price indices, which contribute to shifts in the functional distribution of earned income, relative shifts in cost of living indices among socioeconomic groups are equally important in determining changes in real incomes. Table 13.8 provides ratios of cost-of-living indices to their values in the base run for each socioeconomic group. The spread across groups is quite wide. Thus, for instance, the cost of living of farmers in the ME economy rises by 3 percentage points with devaluation, whereas that of capitalists falls by 9 percentage points.

Table 13.9 provides the group mean real incomes in the base run together with the percent changes from the values in the base run. It thus indicates which groups gain or lose in absolute terms. Table 13.10 provides information on the relative distribution of income by giving changes in group shares in total income. It is noteworthy that some groups gain in absolute terms after the external shock in spite of the sizable fall in the economy-wide mean income. Some striking patterns emerge: For the manufacturing exporter, regardless of the adjustment

Table 13.8. *Cost-of-living indices (ratios to the base run, %)*

| | Experiment | | | | | | | | |
| | Devaluation | | | Premium rationing | | | Premium rationing with fixed real wages | | |
	CL	PE	ME	CL	PE	ME	CL	PE	ME
Farmers	84	86	103	85	83	102	85	83	100
Marginal laborers	86	89	100	87	87	99	87	87	99
Organized labor	88	93	96	90	92	96	90	92	97
Service-sector labor	87	92	99	88	90	98	88	90	99
Agricultural capital	90	95	92	92	95	93	92	96	94
Industrial capital	90	95	91	92	96	93	92	96	94
Service-sector capital	90	95	91	92	96	93	92	96	94
Total	88	91	97	89	90	97	89	90	97

mechanism, farmers and agricultural capitalists always gain in absolute terms relative to the base run. In the other two economies, no group gains significantly when adjustment is by devaluation.[14] However, when there is adjustment by premium rationing, industrial capitalists gain absolutely along with service-sector capitalists and, to a lesser extent, service-sector labor.

What emerges from these figures is that, starting from a reasonable spread in mean incomes among groups in the base run (see Table 13.9, columns 1–3), the distribution of premia, amounting to close to 10 percent of GDP, raises the mean income of some recipient groups by up to 25 percent. No wonder that the choice of policy instrument is such a politically sensitive topic.

Consider, for example, service-sector capitalists. They are the largest and least well off of the capitalist groups. With adjustment by devaluation, even their relative position in society is likely to deteriorate as a result of the increase in the relative price of traded goods. However, when they receive the premia associated with the licenses they are granted for importing consumer goods, their mean income rises by almost 10 percent in the PE economy and by 7 percent in the CL economy. But in the ME economy, where import substitution in the primary sector is assumed achievable in the medium run, farmers and agricul-

[14] The only exception is the 0.7% increase for farmers in the PE economy.

Table 13.9. *Group mean real incomes*

| | Values: base run | | | Change from base run (%) | | | | | | | | | | |
| | | | | Devaluation | | | Premium rationing | | | Premium rationing with fixed real wages[a] | | |
	CL	PE	ME	CL	PE	ME	CL	PE	ME	CL	PE	ME
Farmers	2.5	2.9	2.9	−6.9	0.7	12.3	−13.5	−16.0	8.1	−16.7	−17.7	1.8
Marginal labor	2.3	3.2	2.6	−8.2	−1.9	−16.4	−9.9	−4.4	−20.6	−4.3	−1.0	−13.0
Organized labor	4.1	5.3	4.4	−7.2	−2.1	−17.0	−11.6	−3.6	−26.2	−10.4	−3.2	−26.9
Service-sector labor	3.2	3.7	3.2	−2.2	−7.0	−21.6	0.6	4.1	−15.9	−1.6	2.2	−20.0
Agricultural capital	31.7	40.5	37.1	−13.3	−7.9	26.8	−15.6	−21.2	22.8	−19.7	−23.1	13.9
Industrial capital	46.1	55.0	50.1	−11.8	−6.7	−13.3	23.7	24.4	−2.1	23.3	24.3	−3.8
Service-sector capital	23.1	28.3	25.9	−5.8	−13.0	−14.7	7.1	9.8	−1.0	3.9	7.0	−6.0
Mean income	4.1	5.1	4.7	−7.5	−4.7	−7.4	−3.4	−4.1	−6.4	−5.3	−5.3	−10.0

[a] Unemployed marginal labor has mean incomes of 1.2, 1.6, and 1.3 for CL, PE, and ME economies. Their mean income is assumed to be 0.5 that of employed marginal labor.

Table 13.10. *Group shares in total income*

| | Shares: base run | | | Change from base run (%) | | | | | | | | |
| | | | | Devaluation | | | Premium rationing | | | Premium rationing with fixed real wages | | |
	CL	PE	ME	CL	PE	ME	CL	PE	ME	CL	PE	ME
Farmers	17.0	21.8	14.4	0.1	1.3	3.1	−1.8	−2.6	2.2	−2.1	−2.8	1.9
Marginal labor	16.1	15.9	17.5	−0.2	0.4	−1.7	−1.1	−0.1	−2.6	−1.9	−0.5	−4.4
Unemployed	—	—	—	—	—	—	—	—	—	1.1	0.6	2.2
Organized labor	0.4	8.9	13.2	0.0	0.2	−1.0	−0.8	0.0	−2.8	−0.5	0.2	−2.5
Service-sector labor	21.8	16.5	17.5	1.3	−0.4	−2.7	0.9	1.4	−1.8	0.8	1.3	−1.9
Agricultural capital	15.7	17.8	11.7	−0.9	−0.6	4.3	−1.7	−3.2	3.7	−2.1	−3.4	3.1
Industrial capital	12.1	11.5	17.7	−0.5	−0.2	−1.1	3.4	3.4	0.8	3.7	3.6	1.2
Service-sector capital	9.9	7.6	8.0	0.2	−0.7	−0.6	1.1	1.1	0.5	1.0	1.0	0.4
All capital	35.7	36.9	37.4	−1.2	−1.5	2.6	2.8	1.3	5.0	2.6	1.2	4.7
Total	100.0	100.0	100.0	0.0	0.0	0.0	0.0	0.0	0.0	0.0	0.0	0.0
Gini coefficient	0.51	0.52	0.52	−0.01	−0.01	0.02	0.02	0.01	0.03	0.02	0.01	0.03
Theil index	0.59	0.62	0.63	−0.02	−0.03	0.07	0.07	0.04	0.12	0.07	0.04	0.11

tural capitalists appropriate these rents through higher domestic agricultural prices. In that economy, service-sector capitalists gain little from a system of import licenses, because imports of consumer goods become effectively replaced by domestic substitutes.

Finally, one can take a more aggregate view of the distribution of income along broad functional lines and lump all capitalists together in one group. Table 13.10 indicates that, taken as a group, capitalists always improve their relative position when they get premia, but in the case of devaluation they lose. It would appear that devaluation is not a politically easy adjustment policy to implement in a semi-industrial country.

The relative position of marginal labor, the largest labor group in each of the economies, declines in virtually all instances. Again, the swing in its relative position is most pronounced in the ME economy, where real income losses associated with increases in the cost of living lead to a loss of 1.7 to 4.4 percentage points in total (economy-wide) income. As is typical in developing countries, we assume that the employed support the unemployed by direct income transfers. In the model, this is done through transfers, so that the unemployed receive half the mean income of the employed. Struggling to maintain real wages leads the marginal or mobile labor group as a whole (including the unemployed) to mitigate their relative income loss (4.4 − 2.2 = 2.2 percent loss) compared to premium rationing (2.6 percent loss). With or without fixed real wages, the alternatives facing the poorest are gloomy indeed.

In these experiments, aggregate measures of income inequality such as the Gini coefficient hide more than they reveal. Even when the share of marginal labor falls more than 4 percentage points relative to capitalists, the Gini coefficient never changes by more than 3 percentage points.

More revealing from a distributional standpoint is an analysis of the composition of poverty. The results are given in Table 13.11, which shows the proportion of total population in poverty, as well as the group composition of people in poverty. The cutoff point taken here is a mean income of 1.5 which, in the base run, implies that 14 to 21 percent of the population is in poverty.[15] Consider the ME economy: It starts out with 15.6 percent of its population in poverty; after the adjustment, between 21.7 percent and 25.5 percent of its population is in poverty. Given a population of 10 million in each of the archetypes, it is easy to

---

[15] This corresponds approximately to $300 per capita in 1980.

Table 13.11. Analysis of poverty (percent shares)

	Base run			Devaluation			Premium rationing			Premium rationing with fixed real wages		
	CL	PE	ME	CL	PE	ME	CL	PE	ME	CL	PE	ME
Group shares in poverty												
Farmers	36.6	27.6	29.0	40.6	27.1	23.0	44.7	36.3	25.4	46.9	37.3	28.2
Marginal laborers	22.5	7.5	15.3	28.9	8.1	26.8	30.3	9.0	30.6	25.7	7.7	23.7
Unemployed	—	—	—	—	—	—	—	—	—	80.9	45.9	70.1
Organized labor	10.5	4.6	8.6	12.8	5.0	14.2	14.5	5.3	18.8	14.0	5.2	19.2
Service-sector labor	10.9	6.0	15.3	11.8	7.9	21.3	10.6	5.1	18.0	11.5	5.5	20.6
Overall	21.0	14.2	15.6	24.5	14.7	21.7	25.9	17.8	23.0	27.4	18.6	25.5
Group composition of poverty population												
Farmers	49.8	74.1	44.3	47.4	70.5	26.3	49.4	77.8	26.3	49.0	76.4	26.3
Marginal laborers	30.6	13.5	30.8	33.8	14.2	38.7	33.6	13.1	41.9	23.5	10.0	22.7
Unemployed	—	—	—	—	—	—	—	—	—	10.6	4.5	19.5
Organized labor	4.8	2.8	7.9	5.0	2.9	9.4	5.3	2.5	11.7	4.8	2.4	10.7
Service-sector labor	14.8	9.6	17.0	13.8	12.4	25.9	11.7	6.6	20.1	12.1	6.7	20.8
Total	100.0	100.0	100.0	100.0	100.0	100.0	100.0	100.0	100.0	100.0	100.0	100.0

Note: Poverty is defined as an income of less than 1.5 in the base year.

see that a large fraction of society can be adversely affected, even when aggregate measures of the relative distribution show little variation. An examination of the bottom half of the table indicates that there is a considerable change in the group composition of the poverty population as a result of the external shock. In the ME economy, in addition to a greater number of people in poverty, there is a large shift in the composition of poverty away from the primary sector toward the urban sector. Although for all three economies there is an increase in the number of people in poverty as a result of the deterioration in the foreign terms of trade, the composition of poverty varies depending on the selection of adjustment mechanism. Thus, under devaluation, the proportion of farmers among those that are in poverty declines, whereas the opposite occurs under premium rationing for the PE economy.

13.6   Class conflict and policy choice

The picture that emerges from comparing the impact of alternative adjustment mechanisms on the distribution of income in different economic environments is complex. There are certainly significant changes in the relative distribution among socioeconomic groups, with some groups gaining in absolute terms in spite of an overall decline in real income as a result of the external shock. Differences in economic environment alone suffice to make different groups gain or lose, even with the same adjustment policy. Different adjustment policies also have quite different effects on the distribution.

The fact that the choice of policies has a significant impact on the distribution of income leads to a number of political questions that go beyond the usual economic analysis of policy choice. Given the changes in the distribution of income among socioeconomic groups induced by both the external shock and the policy response, how is the distribution of political power affected? How will the political struggle between the gainers and losers decide the final choice of policy? Finally, assuming that one can analyze how policies are selected when there are conflicting group interests, is it likely that the same policy will be selected in different economic environments?

To explore these questions, we start from a number of simple assumptions about the way the social and political systems are structured. First, assume that each group realizes how its income would be affected under each policy regime. Second, assume that socioeconomic groups are distinct and care only about their own interests. We thus assume that we have partitioned the society into the important or politically relevant power groups, each pursuing its own interests with perfect knowledge. Third, assume that the intensity with which any group cares about a given policy change is measured by the relative difference in its income between the two situations. Define $Y_i(P)$ as the mean income of group i under policy regime P. In our experiments, P can be the following: B (base run), D (devaluation), P (premium rationing), and $P, \overline{W}$ (premium rationing with fixed real wage). For example, the intensity with which group i is for $(+)$ or against $(-)$ devaluation compared to premium rationing is a function of its relative change in income defined by

$$R_i(D; P) = \frac{Y_i(D) - Y_i(P)}{Y_i(B)} \tag{13.6.1}$$

In order to evaluate the political feasibility of any policy choice, we must be able to compare the gains and losses between groups according to some measure of their relative influence or political power. Thus, although a group may have a large gain or loss, and so care a lot about a particular policy choice, it may have little influence and so be unable to affect the final choice. We need some weighting scheme reflecting relative influence to aggregate the gains and losses across different socio-economic groups. There is certainly little agreement about how to derive such weights, so we have specified three different schemes that are consistent with different theories of the sources of political influence and that should provide a reasonable range of values. The analysis is not concerned with the more fundamental and difficult issues relating to the theory of how the political process works. Rather, given a political system, we are trying to capture in a stylized manner some of the elements that are likely to determine the course of policy selection by those who are already in power. The mechanisms by which political power is exercised are not explicitly considered.

The first scheme assumes that relative influence is given by shares in total population – "one person, one vote." The second scheme assumes that relative influence is measured by relative shares in total income – "one rupee, one vote." The third scheme assumes that the political system is dominated by the economic elite and hence that the relative influence of different groups is measured by their share in the elite. In this third case, we assume that the elite is defined as the top 5 percent of the overall personal income distribution and that relative influence is measured by the socioeconomic composition of this group.

The first scheme is rather naive but appealing to utilitarian welfare economists, if not to cynical political scientists. The second scheme is a kind of "effective demand" theory of the distribution of political power, with groups able to buy influence in proportion to their shares in total income. Large groups are still important, even if they have a relatively low mean income. The third scheme is really a simple oligarchy that corresponds reasonably well to a naive Marxist view of how a capitalist society works. This last measure, though somewhat extreme, is intended to provide a first approximation of how policy decisions are made in countries where power is concentrated in the hands of the capitalist class.[16]

Table 13.12 gives the three measures of relative political influence for the different groups in the base run. As one moves from group shares in total population to shares in total income to shares in the elite population, the relative influence of capitalists increases. Of the other groups, only organized labor essentially maintains its relative share of political influence in all three measures. All others lose, with marginal labor and service-sector labor having almost no representation in the elite in spite of their large shares of the total population.

Under the three different policy regimes, population shares, of course, do not change, but there are significant changes in the relative positions of the different socioeconomic groups by the two other measures. Table 13.12 also gives the average of the absolute values of change in group shares for the different archetypes and different policy regimes. Except in the ME economy, devaluation leads to much less change in group shares than either premium rationing or premium rationing with a fixed real wage. The two premia policy regimes have a similar impact on the relative position of different groups. One might argue that the average absolute change in group shares is a rough indicator of the extent of social and political disruption caused by a particular policy, because socioeconomic groups can be expected to resist any change in their relative power in the polity. Thus, in the CL and PE economies, devaluation is the policy regime that is the least disruptive of the existing political order. Whether this fact makes devaluation more or less desirable is a question that cannot be answered without considering the desirability of the existing order, an analysis well beyond our scope.[12]

Given the "political influence" shares in Table 13.12 and the infor-

[16] Note that the choice of the top 5% of the overall distribution is completely arbitrary. In general, the smaller the elite, the more relative political power is ascribed to capitalists. Given the way we generate the overall distribution, it is a simple matter computationally to change the definition of the elite. See Chapter 12 for further discussion of the technique.

[17] There is an active literature in political science analyzing the political strains that accompany economic development. For an entry into this literature, see Huntington and Nelson (1976).

Table 13.12. *Measures of the distribution of political power*

| | Base-run shares (%) in: | | | | | | | | |
| | Total population | | | Total income | | | Economic elite[a] | | |
Groups	CL	PE	ME	CL	FE	ME	CL	PE	ME
Farmers	28.6	38.1	23.8	17.0	21.8	14.4	6.5	7.1	5.8
Marginal labor and unemployed	28.6	25.7	31.5	16.1	15.9	17.5	0.2	0.3	0.2
Organized labor	9.5	8.6	14.3	9.4	8.9	13.2	8.9	9.0	11.1
Service-sector labor	28.6	22.9	25.7	21.8	16.5	17.5	3.8	2.0	1.8
Agricultural capital	1.8	2.2	1.5	13.7	17.8	11.7	31.2	39.5	26.3
Industrial capital	1.1	1.1	1.7	12.1	11.5	17.7	20.6	20.1	31.2
Service-sector capital	1.8	1.4	1.5	9.9	7.6	8.0	28.8	22.0	23.6
Sum	100.0	100.0	100.0	100.0	00.0	100.0	100.0	100.0	100.0
Policy regime	Average absolute change in group shares								
Devaluation	0.0	0.0	0.0	0.4	0.6	2.1	0.3	0.6	2.0
Premium rationing	0.0	0.0	0.0	1.5	1.7	2.1	1.2	1.3	2.0
Premium rationing with fixed wages	0.0	0.0	0.0	1.6	1.8	1.9	1.2	1.4	1.8

[a] The economic elite is defined as the top 5% of income recipients in the overall distribution of personal income.

mation on changes in the mean incomes of the socioeconomic groups, we can undertake an analysis of the political feasibility of different policy regimes. Equation (13.6.1) defines $R_i(P_1; P_2)$, which measures the relative gain or loss for group i between policy regimes P_1 and P_2. Expressions for the average gain of the gainers and the average loss of the losers, weighting by political influence shares, are given by

$$G(P_1; P_2) = \frac{\sum_i W_i R_i (P_1; P_2)}{\sum_i W_i} \qquad \text{for all } R_i > 0$$

$$L(P_1; P_2) = \frac{\sum_i W_i R_i(P_1; P_2)}{\sum_i W_i} \qquad \text{for all } R_i < 0$$

$$(13.6.2)$$

where

$$P_1, P_2 = \text{policy regimes}$$
$$W_i = \text{the relative influence weight of group } i$$
$$R_i = \text{is the relative gain of group } i \text{ from eq. (13.6.1)}$$

The average gain and loss functions reflect the intensity with which different groups support or reject one policy compared to another. The political feasibility of one policy compared to another depends, in addition, on the relative political influence of the gainers compared to the losers. Given that relative influence weights are used in defining the average gains and losses, G and L, the political feasibility of a particular policy choice depends on whether the weighted difference between G and L is positive or negative. We can thus define an index of political feasibility F, which is equal to this weighted difference. It is also just equal to the weighted average of the relative gains, R_i, over all groups, gainers and losers:

$$F(P_1; P_2) = \sum_i W_i R_i(P_1; P_2) \qquad (13.6.3)$$

Note that because we have three different political weighting schemes, there are three different feasibility indices for pairwise comparisons of policy regimes.

Table 13.13 presents the average gains and losses of the gainers and losers, G and L, as well as the index of political feasibility, F, for all pairwise comparisons of the three different policy regimes. In each pairwise comparison of policies, the first column gives the relative political influence of the gainers. We have already discussed which groups gain

Table 13.13. *Policy comparisons*

Archetype economy	Weighting scheme	Devaluation vs. premium rationing				Devaluation vs. premium with fixed wages				Premium vs. premium with fixed wages			
		Political weight of gainers	Average gain G	Average loss L	Feasibility index F	Political weight of gainers	Average gain G	Average Loss L	Feasibility index F	Political weight of gainers	Average gain G	Average loss L	Feasibility index F
CL	Population shares	68.5	4.1	4.6	1.4	39.9	8.1	2.9	1.4	61.9	2.9	4.5	0.1
CL	Income shares	56.1	3.8	14.2	−4.1	40.0	7.1	10.0	−3.0	74.6	2.7	4.0	1.0
CL	Elite shares	46.8	15.6	14.0	−0.2	46.6	6.3	18.8	−7.2	90.9	2.8	1.3	2.5
PE	Population shares	74.7	10.0	12.6	4.2	49.0	15.2	5.8	4.6	65.7	1.8	2.7	0.3
PE	Income shares	64.4	10.2	20.0	−0.6	48.6	14.1	13.1	0.1	73.2	1.6	2.4	0.6
PE	Elite shares	55.9	11.8	26.0	−5.1	55.6	13.3	24.3	−3.4	90.6	1.7	0.5	1.5
ME	Population shares	71.1	5.2	6.3	1.9	39.6	10.4	2.9	2.3	68.5	4.2	7.6	0.5
ME	Income shares	56.8	5.3	9.4	−1.1	39.3	11.0	5.4	−1.0	82.5	4.2	7.6	2.2
ME	Elite shares	43.3	5.3	12.1	−4.5	43.2	11.8	8.9	0.0	99.8	4.6	7.6	4.6

Note: See text for definition of G, L, and F.

and lose, and it is important to remember here that the group composition of the gainers and losers does vary across archetype economies and policy regimes. However, within each archetype and pairwise comparison, the differences in G, and L, and F are due only to the different political weighting schemes used.

Consider, for example, the comparison of devaluation with premium rationing. As the political weighting scheme goes from population shares to elite shares – democracy to oligarchy – the relative influence of the gainers declines substantially. In the comparison of premium rationing with and without a fixed real wage (the last four columns), the effect is reversed, with the political weight of the gainers increasing with the more oligarchic weights. In the first comparison, the gainers tend to be the small farmers and laborers, whose population share is high but whose representation in the top 5 percent is small. In the last comparison, the gainers are everybody but marginal and organized labor, so their weight is high under all three schemes, but especially so for elite shares.

The average gains and losses, G and L, measure the intensity with which the gainers and losers care about the outcome. For the first two policy comparisons, with a few exceptions (six out of eighteen, given the different weighting schemes and archetypes), the feasibility index indicates that those who care the most will determine the policy choice.[18] In the third pairwise comparison, between premium rationing with and without a fixed real wage, the opposite is the case in all three archetypes for the first two weighting schemes. Even though the losers lose more than the gainers gain, their weight is so low that the feasibility index is always positive.

Table 13.14 summarizes the ranking of different policies based on the pairwise comparisons in Table 13.13. It is interesting to note that the various pairwise comparisons never violate transitivity. That is, if policy P_1 is preferred to P_2 and P_2 is preferred to P_3, it is always true that the pairwise comparison shows that P_1 is preferred to P_3, as would be predicted by assuming transitivity.

Across all three economies, devaluation is the most preferred policy under the democratic weighting scheme, whereas premium rationing is the most preferred under both of the other weighting schemes. Indeed, with one exception (PE economy, income share weights), devaluation

---

[18] Note, however, that the measures of intensity also reflect the relative political power of different socioeconomic groups, because they use the political power weights in defining the average gains and losses.

Table 13.14. *Policy rankings*

Archetype economy	Weighting scheme	Policy ranking
CL	Population shares	$(D) > (P) > (P, \overline{W})$
CL	Income shares	$(P) > (P, \overline{W}) > (D)$
CL	Elite shares	$(P) > (P, \overline{W}) > (D)$
PE	Population shares	$(D) > (P) > (P, \overline{W})$
PE	Income shares	$(P) > (D) > (\overline{P}, W)$
PE	Elite shares	$(P) > (P, \overline{W}) > (D)$
ME	Population shares	$(D) > (P) > (P, \overline{W})$
ME	Income shares	$(P) > (P, \overline{W}) > (D)$
ME	Elite shares	$(P) > (P, \overline{W}) = (D)$

Notes: (D): devaluation; (P): premium rationing; $(P, \overline{W})$: premium rationing with fixed real wages; $>$: preferred to; $=$: indifferent to.

is the least preferred policy under the other schemes. It is interesting that devaluation, which skews the distribution of income the least, always prevails in a more democratic political system. Noting that historically more democratic political processes tend to emerge in the more developed countries, one might speculate that the Kuznets U hypothesis (that the distribution of income first becomes worse and then improves as the process of development unfolds) is at least partly related to changing policy choices as political power shifts over time.

There is remarkable agreement in policy rankings, given the choice of weights, across the three archetype economies. This is true in spite of the fact that the particular groups that gain or lose, and the magnitudes of their gains and losses, vary widely. Although our particular choices of policy regimes to compare were purposely made to enhance their differences, it is tempting to conclude that there are generalizations about the political feasibility of different policies that are valid for a wide variety of economic environments. The universal dominance of devaluation under a democratic weighting scheme and of premium rationing under the other schemes is certainly consistent with casual observation of a wide variety of countries, although our three simple weighting schemes do not capture adequately the wide variety of political systems represented in the world.

13.7   Conclusion

By constructing three archetype economies, we have been able to investigate quantitatively the importance of different initial conditions – resource endowments, past trade policies, and economic structure – affecting the impact of different policy regimes. It is striking how important differences in the initial structure of trade, employment, and production can be. For example, one surprising result is that the particular external shock we simulate (a decline in export markets and an adverse movement in the international terms of trade) generally has the most severe impact on the closed economy. This result is due to the relative importance of imported intermediate inputs in the closed economy. Once one sees the empirical result, it is easy to trace out the causal links by which it is manifested and to understand the qualitative economic forces at work. However, in traditional a priori qualitative theoretical analysis, it is easy to assume away what turned out to be empirically important differences and hence it is important to use empirical analysis to find such surprises. Indeed, the importance of such empirical analysis is one of the major arguments for using multisector planning models. In policy analysis, qualitative theoretical results would often suffice if only we were sure that we had captured all the important mechanisms at work. The various applications discussed throughout this book indicate that such confidence is often misplaced.

The analysis of the three archetype economies indicates that differences in economic structure between typical developing countries are very important to an understanding of the differential impact of similar policy regimes. In the analysis of these differences, the CGE model provides a common framework that is rich enough to accommodate a wide variety of market and nonmarket mechanisms that a priori theorizing indicates should be important. The model thus provides a good framework for tracing out the importance of differences in economic environment on the impact of an external shock and associated policy responses.

Another theme that runs through this book is that if planning models are to be useful for policy analysis, they should incorporate the variables that policy makers actually manipulate. As one progresses from static input–output models to CGE models, the range of issues that can be addressed increases enormously. Although all of our applications have focused on issues of foreign trade and trade policy, the usefulness of planning models is by no means so restricted. A multisector model is useful whenever structural differences and general equilibrium repercussions are likely to be important.[19]

Finally, the applications discussed in this chapter have emphasized that policy analysis is a political as well as an economic exercise. In analyzing the impact of a particular choice of policy, one must be aware of its distributional impact and of the political forces it is likely to set in motion. Planning models can provide a useful tool for such policy analysis if they can be extended to trace out the impact of different policy regimes on socioeconomic groups that reflect important political divisions in the society. As our applications clearly indicate, such interdisciplinary analysis represents a major challenge. The simple assumptions we have made certainly do not do justice to the relevant theories of political or economic conflict. However, we hope our study represents a useful first step and indicates one important direction for future research in the application of planning models for policy analysis.

[19] An interesting application in a developed country is Hudson and Jorgenson (1978), who use a CGE model of the United States to explore the impact of higher energy prices on the distribution of real income.

PART VI

Methodological appendixes

Constructing social accounting matrices

A.1   Introduction

Constructing a consistent data base for an economy-wide model is a nightmare with which every model builder is all too familiar. Perseverance and a strong dose of ingenuity are usually both required. The greater the extent of disaggregation across sectors, factors, institutions, and households, the more difficult is the task of reconciliation. As disaggregation increases, so does the number of separate accounts that must balance in the accounting framework.

This appendix describes the method used to generate the three archetype data sets used in Chapter 13. Our approach is to work within the framework of the social accounting matrix (SAM) described in Chapter 12 and to use a variety of techniques to impose consistency at different stages of the generation of the data. Although the method is applied to archetypal, made-up data sets based on "representative" countries, the approach has been used in dealing with disparate data for particular countries.

In assembling any economy-wide data base, whether real or representative, inconsistencies emerge that require one to make decisions about the relative reliability and accuracy of different data sources. For example, it is usually the case that the national income and product figures that emerge from input–output data are different from the official national accounts. The foreign trade statistics in the input–output accounts, the national product accounts, and the trade accounts are often quite different. Savings estimated from institutional flow-of-funds data are often different from investment estimated from production accounts. Finally, for example, government flow-of-funds data are hard to reconcile among the different accounts. Such inconsistencies are sometimes due to variations in definitions among the different accounts, but, more often, they arise from differences in coverage and accuracy. In practice, one is thus forced to assemble an economy-wide data base in sequence, starting with what are considered to be the more reliable data and forcing data assembled at later steps to be consistent with control totals from former steps.

471

The method we describe represents one such approach, with a definite sequence of steps in which consistency is forced, applied to constructing the data sets for the three archetype economies. There is, however, nothing sacred about the particular sequence we have chosen, and one might well change it in particular applications. Also, in practice, one generally iterates informally across the steps rather than following a simple sequence. If data at a later step reveal glaring inconsistencies, one often questions the reliability of the data at earlier steps and goes back to reconsider them as well.

The flow charts in Figures A.1 and A.2 present the adjustment procedure in schematic form.[1] The steps are given by Roman numerals and the additional data required at each stage are described in boxes at the left of the figures. There are ten steps in all, and forced reconciliation in which input parameters are changed is done at three steps (indicated by diamonds). The data that are distinctively different across the three archetype economies are marked by asterisks.

The adjustment is done in two distinct stages. First, in steps I to IV in Figure A.1, the production accounts based on an input–output table are reconciled. Second, in steps V to X in Figure A.2, the income and expenditure accounts are reconciled with the production accounts. Thus, in this procedure, the input–output accounts provide the starting point and are considered to be the controlling data source.

A.2   Production accounts

Starting from the input–output accounts, steps I to III in Figure A.1 generate the final demand columns and the total sectoral value-added row. Given total final demand and production by sectors, the available supply of goods by sector for intermediate use is determined as a residual. Given an initial set of input–output coefficients, sectoral demand for intermediate goods is determined. Unless we started with a consistent set of accounts, these demands will not equal supply, and some reconciliation procedure is required.

The procedure we use is called the RAS method and consists of iteratively adjusting the rows and columns of the matrix of intermediate inputs (the input–output coefficients) until the matrix converges on the specified row and column control totals.[2] The control row totals are

---

[1] A computer program is available to do the procedure.

[2] For a description of the algorithm and a discussion of its convergence properties, see Bacharach (1970). The sum of the control column and control row must be the same. In this case, the requirement is that total value added equal total final demand (i.e., that national income equal national product).

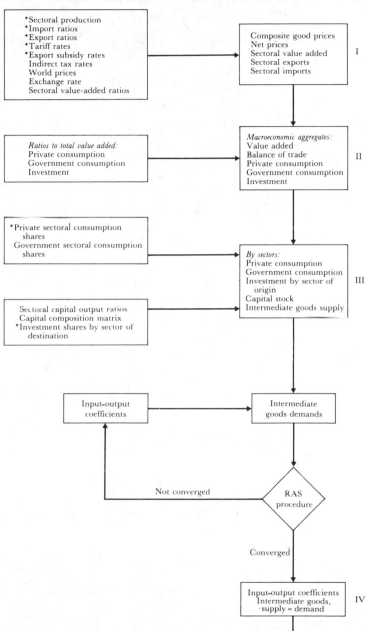

Figure A.1. Reconciliation of the production accounts. Asterisk indicates input variables that differ across the three archetype economies.

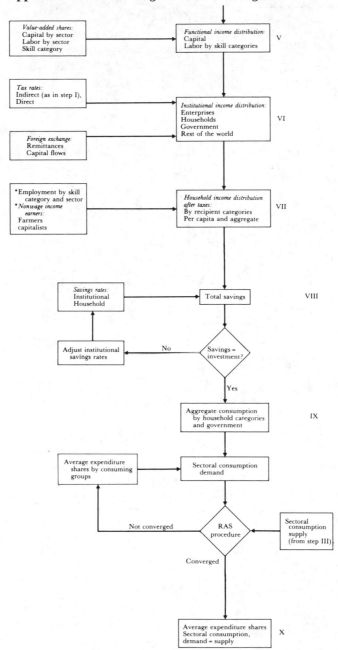

Figure A.2. Reconciliation of the income and expenditure accounts. Asterisk indicates input variables that differ across the three archetype economies.

given by the total supply of intermediate inputs by sectors, given the specified sectoral production and final demand. The column control totals are total purchases of intermediate inputs by sectors and are given by the total value of sectoral production minus sectoral value added.

If one started with a consistent input–output table, steps I to IV would not be necessary. However, our intent was to build three distinctively different data sets for three archetype economies. The major differences in the three archetype economies are in their production, consumption, trade, and employment structures. Tables 13.1 to 13.3 indicate the major differences. In addition to variations in the structure and volume of trade, we also assumed that tariffs and subsidies differed, reflecting historical differences in trade policies. We thus did not start with three sets of consistent accounts. Instead, we started with three different sets of structural data and a common set of input–output coefficients and used the procedure summarized in Figure A.1 to create three consistent data sets. The result is that the input–output tables are slightly different for the three economies.[3]

The input variables that are significantly different across the three archetype economies are marked by asterisks. There was some adjustment of input data required to achieve similar input–output structures and also to achieve a similar balance of trade. Such adjustments were relatively minor, but did provide a check of the "reasonableness" and consistency of the quite different production and trade structures characteristic of the archetype economies.

A.3   Income and expenditure accounts

Steps I to IV yield a consistent set of production and aggregate income (value-added) accounts. The next stage is to generate a consistent set of disaggregated income and expenditure accounts. The procedure we use is given in Figure A.2, steps V to X, and is essentially to generate the functional, institutional, and household distributions by disaggregating value added. Receipt and expenditure balances are maintained for each account, with forced adjustment required at two steps to ensure consistency with the production accounts.

The total labor force is assumed to be the same across the three economies, and the shares of sectoral value added by different skill categories of labor and by capital are also assumed to be the same. However, the skill composition of the labor force and the sectoral structure of employ-

---

[3] The sectoral value-added ratios are the same across the countries, having been specified to give the control column totals.

ment differ across the economies, reflecting the very different structures of production. The sectoral structure of employment was adjusted informally so that wage differentials by skill categories and sectors would be similar across the three economies. The result, in step V, is the functional distribution of income.

From the functional distribution, we move to the institutional distribution in step VI by generating the government and rest-of-the-world accounts, in addition to the household and enterprise accounts. Tax rates, both direct and indirect, are assumed to be the same. Given the different tax bases, the total size of the government sector differs, but not dramatically. Inputs for foreign remittances and capital inflow are shown to indicate where they would enter, but they are assumed to be zero in the three archetype economies.

The household distribution by socioeconomic groups is really a rearranging of the "household" institutional distribution because, in both, households are classified by source of income. The only new data are the number of people in each household category. The labor households correspond to employment by skill category; the numbers of farmers and capitalists have been estimated so as to achieve similar relative per-capita mean group incomes across the three economies.

In step VIII, total savings are generated by applying fixed savings rates (the same across the three economies) to institutional and household incomes. Total savings so generated are compared to total investment from step II in the production accounts. If they differ, then the savings rates of institutions (i.e., corporate saving) are adjusted to achieve consistency. Given savings, step IX generates aggregate expenditure by households and government.

Finally, in step X, given average expenditure shares by consuming groups, total demand for products by sector is calculated. If this demand does not equal the sectoral supply of goods for consumption computed in step III, an adjustment procedure is required. A rectangular expenditure matrix is calculated with rows referring to sectors and columns to household groups.[4] Each entry is the expenditure on good i (row) by household category j (column). The column control totals are aggregate expenditure by household groups, and the row control totals are total private consumption by sectors from step III. The matrix of expenditures is then adjusted by the RAS procedure so that it satisfies the column and row control totals.[5] The results yield new average expenditure shares by household groups.

[4] Government expenditure shares are not adjusted, so the expenditure matrix is defined to include only private consumption.
[5] Note that the procedure can be applied to a rectangular matrix.

The result of step X is a set of average expenditure shares by household groups such that consistency is achieved between the sectoral expenditures from the demand side and sectoral supplies of consumer goods from the production side. If the RAS procedure yielded dramatically different expenditure shares for the same socioeconomic group across the archetype economies, the specification of the structure of aggregate consumption in the production accounts would be suspect. In fact, we did do some informal adjustment of the structure of consumption in the production accounts so that there were no major differences in the structure of demand by the same socioeconomic group across the three economies.

A.1 Archetype country social accounting matrices

Tables A.1 to A.3 give the SAMs for the three archetype economies (for the base runs described in Chapter 13). Because production accounts are discussed in some detail in the chapter, no sectoral disaggregation is provided in the SAMs. Instead, the focus is on the institutional and household accounts. To make the presentation more compact, various accounts have been combined in the SAMs. Because capital income is all assumed to accrue to "enterprises," there is no separate institutional account for enterprises. Note that enterprise savings are shown as a payment by the factor "capital" to the capital account (row 15, column 4). Also, in the factor account for "labor," receipts by the four different skill categories have been aggregated. Separate wage payments to different categories can be seen in the first four household categories, which correspond to the four skill categories of labor. Similarly, capital income in sectors has been aggregated in the factor accounts and somewhat disaggregated in the household accounts. The "small farmers" category of households receives a fraction (25 percent) of capital income from agriculture, which reflects the fact that they are landowners. The "agricultural capital" category thus represents larger farmers all of whose incomes are assumed to come from land ownership.

With the exception of the treatment of enterprises, the SAMs correspond to the framework discussed in Chapter 12 (see Section 12.4 and Table 12.1). Note that in the archetype economies, there are no remittances or foreign capital inflows, which accrue directly to households. Instead, the balance of trade enters directly into the capital account and is thus assumed to be saved. This treatment is simple, but is justified for our purposes because we hold the balance of trade constant in the three economies and across all experiments in Chapter 13.

A comparison of the three archetype SAMs indicates a number of

Table A.1. *Social accounting matrix: closed economy (CL)*

Receipts	Expenditures															
	1	2	3	4	5	6	7	8	9	10	11	12	13	14	15	16
1. Activities		956														42
2. Commodities	461					69	71	37	86	47	42	37	389	93	108	
Factors																
3. Labor	265															
4. Capital	229															
5. Sum (3 + 4)	494															
Households																
6. Small farmers			54	21	75											
7. Marginal laborers			71		71											
8. Organized labor			45		45											
9. Service-sector labor			95		95											
10. Agricultural capital				62	62											
11. Industrial capital				87	87											
12. Service-sector capital				47	47											
13. Sum (6–12)			265	217	482	75	71	45	95	62	87	47	482			
14. Government	43	31				6		4		4	34	5	47			
15. Capital account				12	12			4	9	11	11	5	46	28		22
16. Rest of the world		64														
17. Totals	998	1051	265	229	494	75	71	45	95	62	87	47	482	121	108	64

Table A.2. *Social accounting matrix: primary exporter (PE)*

		Expenditures														
Receipts	1	2	3	4	5	6	7	8	9	10	11	12	13	14	15	16
1. Activities		971												15		103
2. Commodities	438					110	86	43	81	78	48	35	481	72	132	
Factors																
3. Labor	316															
4. Capital	292															
5. Sum (3 + 4)	608															
Households																
6. Small farmers			87	33	120											
7. Marginal laborers			86		86											
8. Organized labor			53		53											
9. Service-sector labor			90		90											
10. Agricultural capital				100	100											
11. Industrial capital				101	101											
12. Service-sector capital				44	44											
13. Sum (6–12)			316	278	594											
14. Government	43	27						5		5	39	5	54			
15. Capital account				14	14	10		5	9	17	14	4	59	37		22
16. Rest of the world		125														
17. Total	1,089	1,123	316	292	608	120	86	53	90	100	101	44	594	124	132	125

Table A.3. *Social accounting matrix: manufacturing exporter (ME)*

Receipts	Expenditures															
	1	2	3	4	5	6	7	8	9	10	11	12	13	14	15	16
1. Activities		973												22		98
2. Commodities	472					67	87	59	78	51	76	37	455	65	126	
Factors																
3. Labor	300															
4. Capital	273															
5. Sum (3 + 4)	573															
Households																
6. Small farmers			53	20	73											
7. Marginal laborers			87		87											
8. Organized labor			73		73											
9. Service-sector labor			87		87											
10. Agricultural capital				60	60											
11. Industrial capital				138	138											
12. Service-sector capital				44	44											
13. Sum (6–12)			300	262	562											
14. Government	49	24				6		7	9	3	52	5	67			
15. Capital account				11	11			7		6	10	2	40	53		22
16. Rest of the world		121														
17. Total	1,094	1,118	300	273	573	73	87	73	87	60	138	44	562	140	126	121

Table A.4. *Group shares in nominal household income (%)*

	CL	PE	ME
Small farmers	15.6	20.2	13.0
Marginal laborers	14.7	14.5	15.5
Organized labor	9.3	8.9	13.0
Service-sector labor	19.7	15.2	15.5
Agricultural capital	12.9	16.8	10.7
Industrial capital	18.0	17.0	24.5
Service-sector capital	9.8	7.4	7.8
Total	100.0	100.0	100.0

Notes: CL = closed economy; PE = primary exporter; ME = manufacturing exporter.

interesting contrasts. First, note that the price-normalization rule used in the CGE model is expressed in terms of composite good prices (see Chapter 13). However, because tariffs and export subsidies differ among the three economies, so do domestic prices of imports and domestically produced goods. The result is that, although gross production is virtually the same across the three economies, the nominal receipts of "activities" are different, being higher in the more open economies, which have significant export subsidies and hence higher domestic prices. The commodity accounts (total absorption) follow a similar pattern.

Given their quite different production structures (and slightly different relative prices), the three economies also have different aggregate value-added ratios. The ratio is lowest for the closed economy (CL) and highest for the primary exporter (PE) – 54 percent and 60 percent, with the manufacturing exporter (ME) having a ratio of 57 percent, in market prices. These differences, of course, lead to significant differences in GDP among the three economies.

Columns 3 to 5 show the distribution of factor income to households (rows 6 to 13). Table A.4 gives the percent distribution of nominal household income by socioeconomic groups. The quite different structures of the three economies are clearly evident, with small farmers and agricultural capital having smaller shares in the manufacturing exporter (ME), followed by the closed economy (CL) and primary exporter (PE). Industrial capitalists have by far the largest share in the ME economy.

Columns 6 to 13 give the distribution of household income among consumption, savings, and government (taxes). The aggregate rates of direct taxation are similar across the three economies, being slightly higher in the ME economy (12 percent, compared to 10 and 9 percent in the CL and PE economies, respectively). The aggregate household savings rates are essentially the same in the CL and PE economies (11 percent), but are much lower in the ME economy (8 percent). This result comes from the fact that in the ME economy, government saving is much more important and hence corporate saving and private saving, especially for capitalists, are lower. Government saving is 42 percent of investment in the ME economy compared to 26 and 28 percent in the CL and PE economies, respectively.[6]

Note finally that the different volumes of trade are evident in the three SAMs by comparing the rest-of-the-world columns. The volume of trade in the CL economy is about half that in the other two. As noted above, the PE and ME economies have significant export subsidies (shown as an entry from government to activities; row 1, column 14). The average tariff rates are also quite different, more than double in the CL economy compared to the other two.

A.5   Consumption: the linear expenditure system

In the construction of the three archetype SAMs, average expenditure shares by the different classes of consumers were given exogenously and then adjusted to achieve consistency with the production accounts. The CGE model requires the specification of a complete set of expenditure equations and, as discussed in Chapter 5, a variety of expenditure systems has been used in various models. In the model used in Chapter 13, we have specified the Stone-Geary linear expenditure system (LES). For each socioeconomic group, consumer demand is given by (omitting a group subscript)

$$C_i = \gamma_i + \frac{\beta_i}{P_i}\left(Y - \sum_j P_j \gamma_j\right) \tag{A.5.1}$$

where Y is total nominal expenditure for the group, γ_i are the committed expenditures or "subsistence minima" in physical terms, and β_i are the marginal budget shares that determine the allocation of supernu-

---

[6] Government saving is higher because, given the larger capitalist income in the ME economy, the direct tax take is higher (given that the tax rate is highest on capital income). The effect is to shift savings from capitalists and enterprises to government.

merary income (i.e., expenditure above that required for purchasing the subsistence minima).[7]

Given the average budget shares, there are a variety of ways to estimate the parameters of the system depending on the extent and quality of available data. For our archetype data sets, we have chosen to compute the parameters of the LES for each group given exogenously specified average budget shares, income elasticities of demand, and a parameter measuring the elasticity of the marginal utility of income with respect to income (often called the "Frisch parameter") (Frisch, 1959; Brown and Deaton, 1972). In the LES, the Frisch parameter is equal to the ratio of total expenditure to supernumerary expenditure:

$$\psi - \frac{-Y}{Y - S} \qquad S - \sum_j P_j \gamma_j \qquad (A.5.2)$$

Given the average budget shares and expenditure elasticities, the marginal budget shares are given by

$$\beta_1 = \epsilon_i \alpha_i \qquad (A.5.3)$$

where ϵ_i are the expenditure elasticities and α_i are average budget shares. Note that the marginal budget shares must sum to one, which is equivalent to imposing the condition, known as Engel aggregation, that the sum of the expenditure elasticities weighted by average budget shares must equal one.

The subsistence minima γ_i are related to the other parameters according to the following equation:

$$\gamma_i = \left(\frac{Y}{P_i} \right) \left(\alpha_i + \frac{\beta_i}{\phi} \right) \qquad (A.5.4)$$

Our estimates of the average budget shares, income elasticities, and Frisch parameters are based on various cross-country studies, especially that of Lluch, Powell, and Williams (1977) (see Chenery and Syrquin, 1975; Chenery 1979). They estimate that the Frisch parameter rises from -7.5 to -2.0 as per-capita income rises from \$100 to \$3,000 (in 1970 US dollars) (see Lluch et al., 1977; pp. 54–55). Our archetype countries are assumed to have a per-capita GDP of about \$500, which, given the various group mean incomes, implies that the Frisch parameter ranges from -5.0 to -1.6. The estimates we have used are given

---

[7] The expenditure equations are often given in per-capita terms. See Brown and Deaton (1972) for a survey of different systems.

Table A.5. *Expenditures shares and elasticities by groups*

	Small farmers	Marginal laborers	Organized labor	Service-sector labor	Agricultural capital	Industrial capital	Service-sector capital
Average expenditure shares (%)							
Primary	50.2	35.2	20.1	25.1	15.2	10.1	10.1
Food	20.4	25.5	30.7	35.7	15.5	20.6	20.6
Other consumer	9.8	9.8	14.8	9.8	19.8	19.8	19.8
Social overhead	9.8	14.8	14.8	14.7	19.9	19.9	19.9
Services	9.8	14.7	19.6	14.6	29.6	29.6	29.6
Total	100.0	100.0	100.0	100.0	100.0	100.0	100.0
Income elasticities							
Primary	0.92	0.90	0.74	0.82	0.43	0.43	0.43
Food	0.92	0.90	0.74	0.82	0.43	0.43	0.43
Other consumer	1.19	1.16	1.19	1.20	1.20	1.20	1.20
Social overhead	1.19	1.16	1.19	1.31	1.12	1.12	1.12
Services	1.19	1.16	1.39	1.31	1.38	1.38	1.38
Frisch parameter	−4.0	−5.0	−4.0	−4.0	−1.6	−1.6	−1.6

in Table A.5, along with the average budget shares and income elasticities.

Given the parameters of the LES, the own and cross-price elasticities of demand can be computed from the following equations:

$$\eta_{ii} = -\epsilon_i\left(\frac{P_i\gamma_i}{Y} - \frac{1}{\phi}\right) \tag{A.5.5}$$

$$\eta_{ij} = -\epsilon_i\left(\frac{P_j\gamma_j}{Y}\right) \qquad i \neq j \tag{A.5.6}$$

In our eight-sector model, there is consumer demand for only five sectors. No distinction is made between durables and nondurables. The own-price elasticities of demand for food range from -0.35 to -0.55 across the groups, whereas that for services range from -0.35 to -1.07. These values are within the ranges reported by Lluch et al. (p. 248) for households with mean incomes ranging from \$500 to \$1,500.

Solution strategies and algorithms

B.1 Introduction

This appendix briefly surveys the existing techniques used to solve computable general equilibrium models and discusses our particular approach in detail. Given the existing state of the art, there is no "canned" program that one can use to solve all CGE models – no simple equivalent to the simplex method in linear programming. The modeler must therefore exploit the mathematical (and economic) properties of the system in order to reduce the number of nonlinear equations that must eventually be solved. The modeler then must choose among existing algorithms of varying complexity and applicability, no one of which dominates for all models. Although much progress has been made in the last decade in solving CGE models, to the point that any reasonably competent graduate student can be trained to handle quite sophisticated and interesting models, it is not yet a feasible task for someone who is unfamiliar with computers.

Following Adelman and Robinson (1978), we distinguish between a "solution strategy" and a "solution algorithm." The purpose of a solution strategy is to establish numerically a set of simultaneous nonlinear functions (generally excess demand equations) whose solution will provide the equilibrium values of all the endogenous variables in the model. A solution algorithm is a computational technique for solving the set of simultaneous nonlinear equations numerically. The solution strategy sets up the problem; the solution algorithm finds the answer. We first examine briefly two examples of strategies for solving CGE models. After that we review some of the algorithms that have been used to solve such models and then discuss in detail the approach we have used to solve the models presented in this book.

B.2 Solution strategies

As discussed in Chapter 5, the equations of any general equilibrium model can usually be reduced by substitution to a set of nonlinear excess demand equations. In our models, there are three sets of markets that must be cleared: factor markets, product markets, and the foreign

486

exchange market. Although it is possible to attack all three sets of markets simultaneously, it is usually more efficient computationally to separate them. We consider two solution strategies that separate the different sets of markets: (1) the factor market strategy and (2) the product market strategy.[1] They are presented schematically in Figures B.1 and B.2.

Figure B.1 gives an example of the factor market strategy in a closed-economy model in which all factors of production, both labor and capital, are assumed to be mobile across sectors. In this case, equilibrium requires that wages of labor by skill category and capital rentals be equalized across all sectors. This model is quite different from the model presented in Chapter 5, in which capital was assumed to be immobile across sectors within a given period. Although we have not used this specification, it has been used for a number of models and is worth reviewing.[2] It also leads to a significantly simpler solution problem because, under some circumstances, it is feasible to substitute out the excess demand equations for the product markets.

Starting with a guess at factor prices – average wages by skill category and the average rental of capital – one can use sectoral cost functions and the assumption of perfect competition to generate cost prices for each sector. Given production functions with constant returns to scale, these cost prices are independent of the level of production. Given supplies of the different factors, one can then generate factor incomes. If the expenditure functions depend only on factor incomes (and not, for example, on sectoral income or rural–urban income), it is possible to solve for the demand for commodities. Setting sectoral production equal to demand, the production functions can be used to generate the sectoral demand for capital and labor. Aggregating, one gets total demand for factors and hence excess demands. If these excess demands are zero, the model is solved. If not, the solution algorithm generates a new guess at factor prices and starts the next iteration.

This variant of the factor market strategy has the major advantage that the product markets are essentially substituted out and there is no need to compute excess demands for products. The strategy greatly reduces the dimensionality of the solution problem and is thus desirable when using algorithms that are very sensitive to the number of equations being solved. However, it cannot be used in this variant in models in which some factor such as capital is sectorally fixed, because cost

---

[1] In the discussion that follows, we present one variant of each strategy. For a more wide-ranging discussion, see Adelman and Robinson (1978).

[2] Examples of different applications are given in a later section.

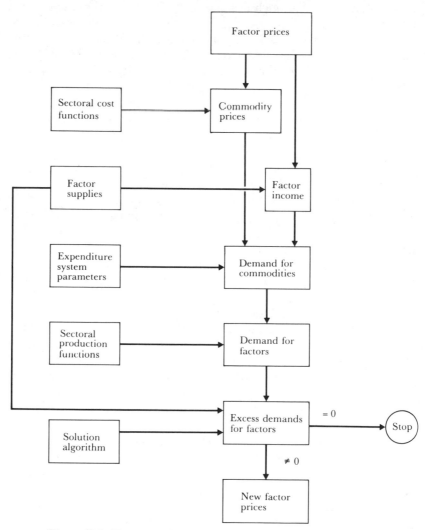

Figure B.1. Factor market solution strategy: closed-economy model with mobile factors.

prices will not then be independent of production levels. It also cannot be used easily if the demand for products depends in any way on the sectoral structure of production. In our models, for example, government tax revenues depend on the structure of production, and hence the demand for products cannot be solved given only factor incomes. In such

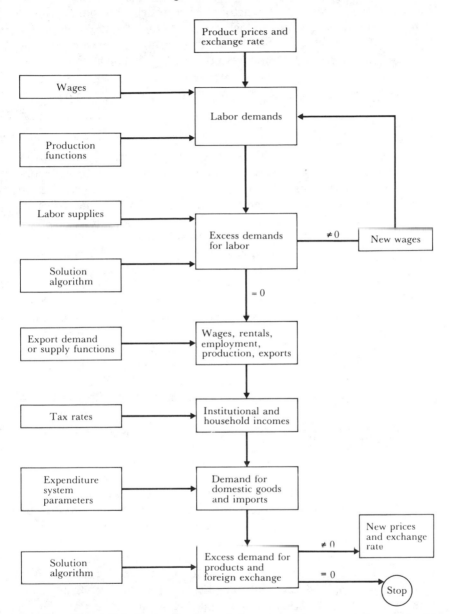

Figure B.2. Product market solution strategy: open-economy model with fixed sectoral capital stocks.

cases it is possible to adapt the factor market strategy, but only by introducing excess demands for products (see Lysy and Taylor, 1980).

Figure B.2 presents the flow chart for the product market solution strategy that is used for the models presented in this book. The particular strategy presented assumes that the exchange rate varies to clear the market for foreign exchange. Variations on this mechanism are discussed in more detail later.

Essentially, the solution strategy follows the order in which the equations of the CGE model are presented in Chapter 5. Assume an initial guess at product prices and the exchange rate. The strategy then works on the labor market. Given sectoral production functions, the assumption of profit-maximizing behavior on the part of producers, and an initial guess at wages of different skill categories of labor, one solves for the demand for labor in each sector. Given labor supplies (or labor-supply functions), one computes excess demands for labor of different skill categories. If these demands are zero, the labor market is solved. If not, the solution algorithm generates a new guess at wages and starts a new iteration.

When the labor market is solved, the model generates wages, capital rentals, employment, production, and exports (the latter based on some specification of the export market). One then has enough information to generate the functional, institutional, and household income distributions – the entire flow of funds in the SAM. Then, given the parameters of the household expenditure functions, one can generate the demand for products and imports. Given the product supplies solved earlier, one generates the excess demands for products. If they are zero, the model is solved. If not, the solution algorithm generates a new guess at prices and the exchange rate and starts a new iteration.

The product market strategy has the disadvantage that one cannot substitute out the product markets as was done in the particular variant of the factor market strategy we have sketched. However, the assumptions required to achieve such a reduction in the dimensionality of the solution problem are really not feasible for models of developing countries. The product market strategy provides a flexible framework for solving CGE models and, as described in Chapters 5 to 7, allows a wide variety of behavioral specifications to be easily incorporated. Once it is no longer possible to devise a strategy that reduces the size of the problem, convenience in computation and specification are important criteria to consider.

As the discussion of these two strategies indicates, there is a kind of loose trade-off between choice of strategy and degree of flexibility in model specification. For instance, it is considerably easier to solve a model with a fixed rather than a flexible exchange rate because of the significant interdependence between the foreign exchange market and the product markets.[3] It may well be worthwhile to sacrifice some model flexibility if it is then possible to use a simpler or more robust solution algorithm. The next section briefly reviews a number of algorithms that have been used to solve CGE models and the solution strategies to which they are applicable.

B.3   Solution algorithms

Our original inspiration for solving economy-wide, general equilibrium models numerically comes from the work of Johansen (1960). His solution strategy was to reduce the CGE model to a set of log-linear equations (linear in growth rates) in all the endogenous variables. The system of linear equations can be solved by inverting the resulting matrix of coefficients, which is the simplest possible solution algorithm.[4] The gain in using a simple solution algorithm must be weighed against the limitation in flexibility of model specification inherent in being required to reduce the equations to a log-linear system.[5]

Another approach is to note that most economic models of competitive general equilibrium can be expressed as a maximization problem. Once in this form, the resulting system can be attacked using programming algorithms designed for constrained-maximization problems.[6] This approach is a natural extension of linear programming models and has the advantage that one can easily specify inequality constraints in the model. However, it may well not be at all convenient, analytically or empirically, to express the model in terms of activity analysis.

Finally, there are a variety of solution algorithms that work directly with the various excess demand equations, using the kind of solution strategies described in the last section. These algorithms can be divided into three types: (1) those based on fixed-point theorems, (2) those based

[3] The extent and nature of this interdependence is discussed in Section B.5.

[4] Johansen's model was applied to Norway and later updated. See Johansen et al. (1968). His original approach was essentially replicated for Chile by Taylor and Black (1974).

[5] Although it is interesting to see how much flexibility in specification is possible. See, for example, Dixon et al. (1977), who have built a very large CGE model for Australia with a rich behavioral specification and have solved it by log linearization.

[6] See Takayama and Judge (1971), Chenery and Raduchel (1971), Goreux and Manne (1973), Dixon (1975), Ginsburgh and Waelbroeck (1978), and Manne et al. (1978).

on a tâtonnement process, and (3) those exploiting information about the derivatives of the excess demand functions.

Algorithms based on fixed-point theorems are truly elegant mathematically and have been applied to a number of economy-wide models.[7] A major advantage of this approach is that for models that satisfy the conditions of the fixed-point theorem, the algorithms are guaranteed to find a solution. A major disadvantage is that, even with recent advances, they get very expensive to implement as the number of excess demand equations increases. As of this writing, fixed-point algorithms would not be the best method to use to solve a model of even moderate size, say, twenty to thirty excess demand equations. It is not surprising that modelers in this tradition have tended to restrict themselves to specifications that permit the use of the factor market strategy described in the last section. Finally, strictly speaking, fixed-point algorithms are not applicable to models that do not satisfy the assumptions of the fixed-point theorems – for example, a model not homogeneous of degree zero in prices.

Algorithms based on a tâtonnement process simply adjust the price in each sector in response to that sector's excess demand. If sectoral excess demand is positive, raise the price; if negative, lower the price. This technique is a special version of the Gauss-Seidel iteration procedure and does not require any evaluation of derivatives of the excess demand equations. It is thus easy to implement and has been used in a number of models.[8] Another major advantage is that once the algorithm is "tuned" to a particular model, it is generally very efficient.[9] However, the requirement that a tâtonnement algorithm be tuned to the model also presents a problem because the algorithm can be implemented only by a user who thoroughly understands its properties – i.e., it cannot be used as a "canned" program. Another disadvantage is that the algorithm becomes finicky and/or inefficient in models in which there are significant interactions among markets. For example, a tâtonnement algorithm is hard to implement and inefficient for the flexible-exchange-rate

---

[7] The seminal work is by Scarf and Hansen (1973). For examples of particular models, see Shoven and Whalley (1974); Whalley (1977); and Feltenstein (1980).

[8] Adelman and Robinson (1978) used this technique to solve their twenty-nine-sector model. Other examples are Derviş (1975), Ahluwalia and Lysy (1979), Dungan (1980), and Lysy and Taylor (1980). Ginsburgh and Waelbroeck (1980) discuss the mathematical properties of tâtonnement algorithms in some detail.

[9] For example, Adelman and Robinson (1978) usually required only fifteen to twenty-five "function evaluations" (computations of the set of excess demand equations) to solve their twenty-nine-sector model.

models in this book. Therefore, we have used instead an algorithm that requires information about derivatives of the excess demand functions.

The third class of algorithms that deals directly with the set of algebraic excess demand equations is defined by their use of derivatives of the functions.[10] We shall call them "Jacobian algorithms," because their performance is sensitive to the determinant of the matrix of numerical derivatives – the Jacobian. Consider a set of nonlinear functions, $f_i(P_1, \ldots, P_n)$, which, in matrix terms, yields the following solution problem:

$$f(P) = 0 \qquad (B.3.1)$$

where P is the vector of variables and f is the vector of functions. In general, any iteration procedure for solving this set of equations can be written as

$$P^{(k+1)} = P^{(k)} + \alpha^{(k)} d^{(k)} \qquad (D.3.2)$$

where the superscript k refers to the iteration, $d^{(k)}$ is a direction vector, and $\alpha^{(k)}$ is a scalar giving the size of the step to be taken in direction $d^{(k)}$.

In the tâtonnement algorithm, the direction vector is given simply by the sign of $f(P)$, and the step size is tuned by the user for the particular model. In Jacobian algorithms, the direction vector depends on the matrix of derivatives of the functions $f(P)$. Define this matrix as D:

$$D_{ij} = \frac{\partial f_i}{\partial P_j} \qquad (B.3.3)$$

A classic approach to solving Eq. (B.3.1) is to use the linear Taylor series expansion for $f(P)$:

$$f(P) \simeq f(P^{(k)}) + D(P^{(k)})(P - P^{(k)}) \qquad (B.3.4)$$

Setting $f(P) = 0$ and solving for $P = P^{(k+1)}$ yields

$$P^{(k+1)} = P^{(k)} - D^{-1}f(P^{(k)}) \qquad (B.3.5)$$

This is the Newton or Newton-Raphson method, with the direction vector d given by $-D^{-1}f$ and the step size α equal to 1.

A second approach is to set up the solution problem as a minimization problem of a special kind. Let

$$\Phi(P) = \sum_i [f_i(P)]^2 = [f(P)]' f(P) \qquad (B.3.6)$$

where the prime (′) indicates the transpose. $\Phi(P)$ is a scalar function that has a minimum when $f(P) = 0$. Thus, minimizing the function

---

[10] For an elementary discussion of such techniques, see Conte and de Boor (1972).

$\Phi(P)$ will yield a solution to $f(P) = 0$. In seeking a P that will minimize $\Phi(P)$, it makes sense to search in the direction in which the function decreases the fastest, that is, the steepest. Consider the Taylor series expansion of $\Phi(P + d)$,

$$\Phi(P + d) - \Phi(P) \simeq d'\nabla\Phi \tag{B.3.7}$$

where d represents a small step and $\nabla\Phi$ is the gradient vector of Φ:

$$\nabla\Phi = \frac{\partial\Phi}{\partial P} \tag{B.3.8}$$

Note that

$$d'\nabla\Phi = ||d|| \cdot ||\nabla\Phi|| \cdot \cos\theta \tag{B.3.9}$$

where $||d||$ and $||\nabla\Phi||$ are Euclidean norms and θ is the angle between the two vectors.[11] For a normalized small step d, Eq. (B.3.9) suggests that the direction of steepest descent, which minimizes the left-hand side of (B.3.7), occurs when $\cos\theta$ equals -1, or $d = -\nabla\Phi$.

Differentiating (B.3.6), $\nabla\Phi$ is given by

$$\nabla\Phi = 2D'f \tag{B.3.10}$$

and, hence, using the method of steepest descent yields the iteration formula

$$P^{(k+1)} = P^{(k)} - 2\alpha^{(k)}D'f(P^{(k)}) \tag{B.3.11}$$

In general, the Newton-Raphson method given in Eq. (B.3.5) has quadratic convergence properties provided that the initial guess is sufficiently close to the solution. The method of steepest descent is preferred when the initial guess of P is far from the solution, but it is slower to converge. A number of algorithms have been developed that interpolate between the Newton-Raphson and steepest descent directions. These algorithms differ in how they do the interpolation, how they choose the step size $\alpha^{(k)}$, and how they compute the derivatives of $f(P)$.[12] We have chosen a method due to Powell that does not require the analytic specification of the derivatives of $f(P)$.[13] The Powell algorithm estimates the matrix of derivatives by numerical approximation (requiring $n + 1$

---

[11] For a discussion of norms, see the appendix to Chapter 2.
[12] The basic techniques are discussed in standard texts on numerical analysis. See, for example, Dahlquist and Bjorck (1974).
[13] The method and the associated computer algorithm are described in Powell (1970a, 1970b).

function evaluations) and then updates the approximation using a technique that does not generally involve extra function evaluations.[14]

A major disadvantage of techniques that require the numerical approximation of derivatives is that such methods require $n + 1$ function evaluations before they even start to search for the solution P's. A tuned tâtonnement method can easily converge in ten to twenty iterations and would thus clearly dominate any technique that requires $n + 1$ iterations just to get started. Even for a model in which tâtonnement is inefficient, the trade-off in moving to a Jacobian technique appears to be quite serious.

In order to avoid having to recompute the derivatives numerically for every solution, we have adapted the Powell algorithm so that it can save and reuse the matrix of derivatives generated from a previous solution. Although it is true that the performance of the algorithm is sensitive to the initial guess of the derivatives, the robustness of the procedure is quite surprising. It is a common observation in numerical analysis that derivatives are tricky – much harder, for example, than integrals – and our experience probably has much to do with how we specified the functions to be solved. The details of our solution strategy, particularly how we scaled the endogenous variables and the functions, are discussed in the next section.

Use of the Newton-Raphson technique requires that the matrix of derivatives, D, be inverted, and thus the method fails if the determinant of D is zero. This determinant is the Jacobian of the vector function $f(P)$, for which the matrix of partial derivatives is computed; we write it as $J(f)$. Algorithms that use any variant of the Newton-Raphson technique, such as the Powell algorithm, become very sensitive and may fail if the Jacobian is small, but nonetheless different from zero because Eq. (B.3.5) then generates a nonsensically large step. Such algorithms usually incorporate some test of singularity of $J(f)$ and change direction if it becomes too small.

Computable general equilibrium models have excess demand equations with a number of special properties, so it is important to explore analytically the nature of the Jacobian of such systems. The next section discusses these properties in some detail in the context of our particular solution strategies. A useful mathematical theorem in this context defines the notion of "functional dependence" in a system of equations. We state the theorem below (without proof).[15]

---

[14] The technique, due to Broyden, is described in Powell (1970a) and Dahlquist and Bjorck (1974, p. 443).

[15] For further discussion, and a proof, see Kaplan (1952, pp. 132–6).

A set of functions $f_i(P_1, \ldots, P_n)$ is called "functionally dependent" if they are related in a given domain by an identity of the form

$$\psi(f_1, \ldots, f_n) \equiv 0 \tag{B.3.12}$$

To rule out degenerate cases, assume that $\nabla\psi \neq 0$ for the range of f_i over the given domain.

If the f_i functions are differentiable in the domain and are functionally dependent, then the Jacobian of f is identically equal to zero in that domain:

$$J(f) \equiv 0 \tag{B.3.13}$$

Conversely, if $J(f) \equiv 0$ and $\nabla f_i \neq 0$ for all i, then, in some neighborhood of each point in the domain, the set of functions f_i is functionally dependent.

Note that the definition of functional dependence can be extended to the case where the number of variables P_i differs from the number of equations f_i. If the number of equations exceeds the number of variables, there is always some form of functional dependence, because the rank of the matrix of derivatives cannot exceed the number of variables.

In the next two sections, we discuss the details of the particular solution algorithms used to solve the models presented in this book. The product market solution strategy discussed in Section B.2 assumes that at every price iteration the factor markets have been solved. In the discussion that follows, we can thus always assume that, for every set of prices, a set of wages has been calculated that gives equilibrium employment and production in every sector.[16] We need only write down the excess demand equations for the product markets and for the foreign exchange market. Before discussing the open-economy solution strategy in Section B.5, we consider at some length the simpler closed-economy model, which captures the major features of our solution approach.

B.4   The closed-economy model

Consider a model of a closed economy that, after numerically substituting out the factor markets, yields the following $n + 1$ equations, which must be solved to find n equilibrium prices.

$$f_i(P_1, \ldots, P_n) = P_i(X_i^D - X_i^S) = 0 \qquad i = 1, \ldots, n \tag{B.4.1}$$
$$g(P_1, \ldots, P_n) - \overline{P} = 0 \tag{B4.2}$$

[16] Note that we need not, and generally do not, assume that these are market-clearing wages. As discussed in Chapter 5, it is relatively easy to specify different assumptions about how the labor markets operate.

where

P_i = price of good i
X_i^D = demand for sector i
X_i^S = supply for sector i
$\bar{P}$ = exogenous aggregate price level

The equations f_i are the nominal sectoral excess demands, and g is the price-normalization rule. In the standard Walrasian system, the excess demand equations have two properties that are essentially independent but are often confused: (1) They satisfy Walras's law, and (2) they are homogeneous of degree zero in prices. First, consider Walras's law, which can be written as

$$\sum_i P_i(X_i^D \quad X_i^S) - \sum_i f_i = 0 \tag{B.4.3}$$

Walras's law is written as an identity because it arises from the fact that the system must satisfy the budget constraint even when it is out of equilibrium. In terms of social accounting matrices, the system must satisfy Walras's law if every account (row and column) balances, even if there are nonzero excess demands.[17]

If Walras's law holds, then the set of excess demand equations f_i are not all independent. Given any $n - 1$ of them, we can use Eq. (B.4.3) to solve for the nth. For our purposes, there are two important points to note about Walras's law. First, it is not a necessary property for the system of equations f_i to have, either for a solution to exist or for the use of particular solution algorithms.[18] Second, although Walras's law suffices to prove that the system of excess demand equations f_i is functionally dependent [in the sense that the Jacobian vanishes identically, $J(f)$ $\equiv 0$], it is also possible to write an equivalent set of excess demand equations whose Jacobian does not vanish. Consider, for example, the real excess demand equations e_i:

$$e_i = X_i^D - X_i^S = 0 \tag{B.4.4}$$

Walras's law is now written as $\sum P_i e_i \equiv 0$.

Assuming positive equilibrium prices (or at least complementary slackness), the two sets of equations e_i and f_i will have the same solution.

---

[17] Note that Eq. (B.4.3) must hold in equilibrium, and that it is possible to write down a set of excess demand equations that does not satisfy Walras's law (as an identity) but nonetheless yields the same equilibrium solution. We present such a system later.

[18] For a discussion of the role of Walras's law in existence proofs, see Lancaster (1968, chap. 9).

However, the set e_i does not satisfy the requirements of the functional dependence theorem discussed in the previous section and, hence, from Walras's law alone, one cannot conclude that $J(e) = 0$. Of course, the equations e_i are still not independent in the sense that it is always possible to solve $n - 1$ of them and use Walras's law to solve for the nth. But for certain numerical solution algorithms, as we have discussed, the fact that the Jacobian does not vanish is important. It might well be numerically convenient to work with the set of equations e_i rather than the set f_i. Scaling the equations can make a major difference in the operation of a given algorithm.

The second important point to note about the set of excess demand equations e_i of a standard general equilibrium model is that they are homogeneous of degree zero in prices. This property is extremely important for proving that the general equilibrium system has at least one solution because the proofs require that one be able to work with the set of normalized price vectors. If the system is not homogeneous of degree zero in prices, it may still have a solution, but it is difficult to prove it. However, we and others have worked with nonhomogeneous systems and have always found solutions empirically.

If the system is homogeneous of degree zero, then it is obvious that only relative prices matter. In this case, regardless of whether or not Walras's law holds, the set of excess demand equations is functionally dependent and the Jacobian is zero.[19] Thus, one cannot work directly on the set of n excess demand equations using a solution algorithm that requires a nonzero Jacobian.

The obvious solution if one wishes to work with an algorithm requiring a nonzero Jacobian is to drop one of the excess demand equations and replace it with the price-normalization rule. Consider the following system of n equations in n prices, in which the price-normalization rule is written as an equilibrium condition:

$$f_i^*(P_1, \ldots, P_n) = f_i(P_1, \ldots, P_n) = 0 \qquad i = 1, \ldots, n - 1$$
$$f_n^*(P_1, \ldots, P_n) = g(P_1, \ldots, P_n) - \overline{P} = 0 \qquad \text{(B.4.5)}$$

The Jacobian of this system, $J(f^*)$, is nonzero, and we rely on Walras's law to guarantee that the nth excess demand will be zero once we have found a set of prices that yields zero excess demands for the other $n - 1$ markets.

[19] Consider, for example, the normalization rule $P_n = 1$. Then the system can be written as n equations in $n - 1$ variables, $f_i(P_1, \ldots, P_{n-1}, 1)$. As noted earlier, any set of equations in which there are more equations than unknowns is functionally dependent. See Kaplan (1952, pp. 132–6).

The system of equations (B.4.5) can be attacked directly, but its asymmetric treatment of the markets may give rise to problems. The fact that the omitted market is solved residually means that its excess demand is the algebraic sum of the excess demands in the other markets. Although each of those markets may converge within an acceptable criterion, their sum may yield an unacceptable level of excess demand in the omitted market. There is a way to deal with this scaling problem but, as we shall discuss, there are also ways to retain the symmetric treatment of the markets, and both approaches seem to be robust.

B.5   The open-economy model

The open economy adds a market for foreign exchange to the n product markets, and an extra variable: the exchange rate ER. This is the core model described in Chapter 7 and provides the starting point for all the empirical applications. Domestically produced and imported goods are specified as imperfect substitutes, so there are three sets of prices in the system: domestic prices (PD_i), world prices of imports $(\overline{PW}_i)$, and composite good prices (P_i).[20] However, world prices of imports are assumed to be fixed exogenously and hence the composite goods prices can be written as functions of the domestic prices and the exchange rate. The solution problem, then, is to find a set of domestic prices PD_i and an exchange rate (or some other equilibrating variable) that yield zero excess demands in the n product markets and in the foreign exchange market. As before, we assume that for every set of prices one can solve for equilibrium factor prices and so numerically substitute out the factor markets.

Following are the equations whose solution yields equilibrium prices. Consider the model in which the exchange rate is the equilibrating variable for the foreign exchange market. The extension to premium or fixprice rationing is straightforward. The equations, including various scaling factors, are

$$F_i(\pi_1, \ldots, \pi_{n+1}) = \frac{X_i^D - X_i^S}{X_i^S} = 0 \qquad i = 1, \ldots, n \quad (B.5.1)$$

$$F_{n+1}(\pi_1, \ldots, \pi_{n+1}) = \frac{\overline{\sigma}_B(B - \overline{FK})}{FT} = 0 \qquad (B.5.2)$$

$$PD_i = \lambda \pi_i \overline{\sigma}_i \qquad i = 1, \ldots, n \qquad (B.5.3)$$

$$ER = \pi_{n+1} \overline{\sigma}_{n+1} \qquad (B.5.4)$$

$$G(PD_1, \ldots, PD_n, ER) - \overline{P} = 0 \qquad (B.5.5)$$

[20] In some variants of the model, we also allow for a difference between the domestic and world prices of exports. See Chapter 7 for further discussion.

where

$$PD_i = \text{domestic prices}$$
$$ER = \text{the exchange rate}$$
$$X_i^D = \text{sectoral demand}$$
$$X_i^S = \text{sectoral supply}$$
$$\overline{B} = \text{balance of trade in dollars}$$
$$\overline{FK} = \text{exogenous foreign capital inflow}$$
$$\overline{FT} = \text{average foreign trade (exports plus imports divided by 2) in dollars}$$
$$\lambda = \text{price-normalization parameter}$$
$$\overline{\sigma}_i, \overline{\sigma}_{n+1}, \overline{\sigma}_B = \text{exogenous scaling parameters}$$
$$\overline{P} = \text{exogenously set aggregate price level}$$

In this system, the solution problem is to find a set of $n + 1$ π's so that the $n + 1$ excess demand equations and the price-normalization rule are all satisfied. All the excess demands are written in terms of shares. The $\overline{\sigma}_i$ and $\overline{\sigma}_{n+1}$ are usually set to the base-year prices and exchange rate (or to solution values in the previous period for the dynamic model), so the π variables are expressed as multipliers scaled around one. The scaling parameter $\overline{\sigma}_B$ is set so that the convergence criterion guarantees acceptable accuracy in the balance-of-trade equation when the other excess demand equations have converged ($\overline{\sigma}_B$ is usually set equal to 2). Such scaling of the variables and of the excess demand equations is important and has a significant effect on the efficiency of the solution algorithm.

The parameter λ appears in Eq. (B.5.3) because we always scale the PD_i's so that the price-normalization equation is satisfied. Thus, whereas the π_i's are unrestricted, λ is set so that the domestic prices and the exchange rate are restricted to the normalized set. This approach is convenient because solution algorithms designed for general systems of algebraic equations are usually not designed to search over a restricted or normalized domain of the endogenous variables.[21]

Equations (B.5.1) to (B.5.5) represent $n + 2$ equations ($n + 1$ excess demands and price normalization) in $n + 1$ variables (PD_1, ..., PD_n and ER). The system satisfies Walras's law (properly formulated in nominal terms), and the complete set of $n + 1$ excess demand equations is homogeneous of degree zero in all prices (PD_1 and ER). Note, however, that because of the way in which price normalization is imposed, the excess demand functions are not homogeneous of

---

[21] We experimented with restricting the algorithm directly, but our experience indicates that this approach is much easier and performs as well.

degree zero in the π's. Because the price-normalization scaling variable, λ, is applied only to the PD_i in Eq. (B.5.3), a doubling of all the π's will lead to a change in relative prices – in particular, the real exchange rate.

Given the scaling of the excess demand functions and that they are not homogeneous of degree zero in the π's, the Jacobian of the functions, $J(F)$, is not equal to zero. It is thus feasible to attack the system of excess demand equations directly, treating all markets symmetrically and using the scaling variable λ to map changes in the π's into changes in normalized prices. We have in fact used this approach for the flexible-exchange-rate model, and it has generally worked quite well. There are, however, some numerical pitfalls that sometimes cause problems and can thus offset the advantages of treating all markets symmetrically.

Although the Jacobian $J(F)$ does not equal zero, the property of the system that yields this result is our particular way of imposing price normalization. With a reasonably large number of sectors, say, more than ten, the indirect impact on other relative prices of a change in a given π_i, working through the normalization equation, is of a lower order of magnitude than the direct effect on the given price. For very small changes in π_i, the Jacobian empirically becomes relatively small and the solution algorithm suffers.[22] The use of an updating procedure for recomputing the matrix of first partial derivatives may, in some cases, drift toward singularity of the Jacobian.

As discussed in the previous section, the obvious way to avoid such problems is to abandon the symmetric treatment of all markets and to replace one of the product market excess demand equations with the price-normalization equation. In our treatment, one simply uses the variable λ as a measure of the extent to which the π's do not satisfy the price-normalization equation. The convergence criterion is that λ equal one. Walras's law guarantees that the omitted market will be in equilibrium when all the other excess demands go to zero.[23] This asymmetric technique also appears to work quite efficiently and robustly.

---

[22] We confirmed this property by computing the numerical Jacobian using a variety of step sizes. As the step size decreased, the determinant decreased and the elements of the inverse of the matrix of first derivatives became relatively large. In the Powell algorithm we have described, this situation need not be fatal because the algorithm then moves away from the Newton method and toward the method of steepest descent.

[23] We also use a scaling factor, so the price-normalization "excess demand" equation is written $\bar{\sigma}(\lambda - 1)$. A value for $\bar{\sigma}$ of n seems to achieve a reasonable balance in convergence in the omitted market relative to the other markets.

In addition to the flexible-exchange-rate model, we also have used three models with a fixed exchange rate that (1) allow the balance of trade to be unconstrained, (2) achieve foreign balance by premium rationing, and (3) achieve foreign balance by fixprice rationing. In the second and third cases, one simply replaces the exchange rate on the left-hand side of Eq. (B.5.4) with the appropriate variable – either the premium rate or the rationing rate. In the first case, one simply drops the foreign balance Eq. (B.5.2) from the system, as well as the associated price equation (B.5.4), and works only with the n product market excess demand equations and the n prices, PD_i. Because the exchange rate is fixed in all three cases, the resulting system is not homogeneous of degree zero in either prices or π's. Thus one can treat the excess demand equations symmetrically, and we have tended to use this approach in the applications.[24]

Table B.1 gives the matrix of derivatives of the excess demand equations for the ME archetype economy discussed in Chapter 13. Given the scaling parameters, the derivatives are essentially elasticities and measure the change in percent excess demand (as measured by F_i) for a percent change in the corresponding price. The scaling factor for the balance of trade, $\bar{\sigma}_B$, was set to one.[25]

The diagonal elements in the derivative matrix – the own-price excess demand elasticities – are generally larger than the off-diagonal elements. However, there are a number of relatively large off-diagonal elements, and the matrix is not at all diagonally dominant. Cross-market effects clearly are quite significant, and hence a Jacobian algorithm that takes the cross-derivatives into account should be more efficient than a tâtonnement algorithm. Note especially the linkages between the primary and food sectors, between construction and the rest, and between the foreign exchange and product markets.[26]

---

[24] Both versions appear to work quite efficiently. The eight-sector model usually solves in ten to fifteen price iterations, and the nineteen-sector model in fifteen to twenty-five price iterations, using either the symmetric or asymmetric approach.

[25] The matrix was generated numerically, using a step size of 0.10. The computed derivatives are quite similar for a wide range of step sizes and, as we noted before, the Jacobian gets dangerously small only for a step size of 0.01 or less.

[26] The derivative matrices for the other archetype economies are similar but with some significant differences, especially in the foreign exchange market. The general properties of the matrix – large diagonal elements with some significant off-diagonals – also hold for the nineteen-sector models of Turkey used in earlier chapters.

Table B.1. *Matrix of derivatives of the excess demand equations*

Market	1	2	3	4	5	6	7	8	9
Primary	−0.5	0.4	0.1	0.0	0.0	0.0	0.0	0.1	0.3
Food	0.8	−1.6	0.2	0.1	0.0	0.5	0.2	0.4	0.3
Consumer	0.1	0.1	−0.7	0.1	0.0	0.4	0.1	0.1	0.0
Intermediate	0.0	0.2	0.2	−1.0	0.0	0.6	0.1	0.0	0.2
Capital goods	0.1	0.3	0.0	0.4	−0.7	0.1	0.1	−0.2	−1.0
Construction	0.3	1.3	0.8	2.1	0.5	−3.3	0.5	0.1	−0.9
Social overhead	0.0	0.3	0.1	0.2	0.1	0.5	−1.1	0.3	0.1
Services	0.0	0.2	0.1	0.1	0.1	0.1	0.1	−0.5	−0.1
Foreign exchange	−0.2	−0.1	0.3	−0.3	−0.1	0.0	0.2	0.8	2.3

Notes: The matrix is computed for the ME archetype economy evaluated at the base solution using a step size of 0.10. The derivatives are expressed as elasticities, and measure the effect of a change in a price (column) on the excess demand in a market (row).

B.6   Conclusion

The survey of solution strategies and algorithms presented here gives some indication of the wide range of approaches used to solve CGE models. The advances made in the last ten years or so are impressive, and the published literature is only just starting to reflect the volume and variety of work in this area. The current state of the work with CGE models and ways of solving them is reminiscent of the ferment in the early days of work with linear programming models. As in that period, there is a need for more work on the relationships between the economic and mathematical properties of the applied models.

It should be clear that there is as yet no "best" way to solve CGE models. The approach developed here appears to be a step toward the use of algorithms that require a minimum of "tuning" by the user, but that can still be applied to relatively large models that allow a wide scope for behavioral specification. However, we are still far from eliminating the need to specify a solution strategy. Modelers cannot simply write down their equations any way they like. Although there is work being done that seeks to automate the translation from a set of equations to a solution strategy, it is not yet far enough advanced to help those who are applying CGE models (see Bisschop and Meeraus, 1980). For a while, at least, there will remain serious trade-offs among model specification, solution strategy, and solution algorithm that will constrain applied modelers.

References

Adelman, I. (1969), *Practical Approaches to Development Planning: The Case of Korea,* Baltimore, Md.: Johns Hopkins Press.

Adelman, I., M. Hopkins, S. Robinson, G. Rodgers, and R. Wery (1979), "A Comparison of Two Models for Income Distribution Planning," *Journal of Policy Modeling,* vol. 1, pp. 37–82.

Adelman, I., and S. Robinson (1978a), *Income Distribution Policies in Developing Countries,* Stanford, Calif.: Stanford University Press.

  (1978b), "Income Distribution, Import Substitution, and Growth Strategies in a Developing Country," in Day and Cigno, *Modelling Economic Change: The Recursive Programming Approach.*

Adelman, I., and E. Thorbecke, eds. (1966), *The Theory and Design of Economic Development,* Baltimore, Md.: Johns Hopkins Press.

Ahluwalia, M., and F. Lysy (1979), "Welfare Effects of Demand Management Policies: Impact Multipliers Under Alternative Model Structures," *Journal of Policy Modeling,* vol. 1, no. 3, pp. 317–43.

Ahmed, F. (1974), "Migration and Employment in a Multi-Sector Model: An Application to Bangladesh," Unpublished Ph.D. dissertation, Princeton University.

Aitchison, J., and J. Brown (1957), *The Lognormal Distribution,* Cambridge: Cambridge University Press.

Allen, R. G. D. (1960), *Mathematical Economics,* London: Macmillan.

Almon, C. (1967), *Matrix Methods in Economics,* Reading, Mass.: Addison-Wesley.

  (1966), *The American Economy to 1975,* New York: Harper & Row.

Armington, P. (1969), "A Theory of Demand for Products Distinguished by Place of Production," *IMF Staff Papers,* vol. 16, pp. 159–78.

Arrow, K., and F. Hahn (1971), *General Competitive Analysis,* San Francisco: Holden-Day.

Arrow, K. J., L. Hurwicz, and H. Uzawa, eds. (1958), *Studies in Linear and Nonlinear Programming,* Stanford, Calif.: Stanford University Press.

Arrow, K., S. Karlin, and P. Suppes, eds. (1960), *Mathematical Methods in the Social Sciences,* Stanford, Calif.: Stanford University Press.

Arthur, W. B., and G. McNicoll (1975), "Large-Scale Simulation Models in Population and Development: What Use to Planners?" *Population and Development Review,* vol. 1, no. 2, pp. 251–266.

Bacharach, M. (1970), *Biproportional Matrices and Input Output Change,* Cambridge: Cambridge University Press.

Balassa, B. (1980), "The Process of Industrial Development and Alternative Development Strategies," World Bank Staff Working Paper No. 438, Washington, D.C.: The World Bank.

Balassa, B., and Associates (1980), *Development Strategies in Semi-Industrial Countries,* Baltimore, Md.: Johns Hopkins Press.

504

Becker, G. (1970), *Human Capital*, New York: Columbia University Press.

Bergsman, J., and A. Manne (1966), "An Almost Consistent Intertemporal Model for India's Fourth and Fifth Plans," in Adelman and Thorbecke, *The Theory and Design of Economic Development.*

Bhagwati, J. (1978), *Foreign Trade Regimes and Economic Development: Anatomy and Consequences of Exchange Control Regimes*, Cambridge, Mass.: Ballinger.

(1971), "The Generalized Theory of Distortions and Welfare," in Bhagwati et al., *Trade, Balance of Payments and Growth.*

Bhagwati, J., and E. Grinols (1975), "Foreign Capital, Dependence, Destabilization and Feasibility of Transition to Socialism," *Journal of Development Economics*, vol. 2, pp. 85–98.

Bhagwati, J., R. W. Jones, R. A. Mundell, and J. Vanek, eds. (1971), *Trade, Balance of Payments and Growth*, Amsterdam: North-Holland.

Bhagwati, J., and T. N. Srinivasan (1979), "Revenue-Seeking: A Generalization of the Theory of Tariffs," Washington, D.C.: The World Bank (mimeo).

(1978), "Shadow Prices for Project Selection in the Presence of Distortions: Effective Rates of Protection and Domestic Resource Costs," *Journal of Political Economy*, vol. 86, no. 1, pp. 97–116.

(1974), "On Reanalyzing the Harris-Todaro Model: Policy Rankings in the Case of Sector-Specific Wages," *American Economic Review*, vol. 64, pp. 502–8.

Bisschop, J., and A. Meeraus (1980), "Toward Successful Modeling Applications in a Strategic Planning Environment," Washington, D.C.: The World Bank (mimeo).

Blinder, A. (1975), *Towards an Economic Theory of Income Distribution*, Cambridge, Mass.: M.I.T. Press.

Blitzer, C. (1975), "Employment and Human Capital Formation," in Blitzer, Clark, and Taylor, *Economy-Wide Models and Development Planning*, chap. 7.

Blitzer, C., P. Clark, and L. Taylor (1975), *Economy-Wide Models and Development Planning*, London: Oxford University Press.

Brecher, R. (1974), "Minimum Wage Rates and the Pure Theory of International Trade," *Quarterly Journal of Economics*, vol. 88, pp. 98–116.

Brody, A. (1970), *Proportions, Prices and Planning*, Amsterdam: North-Holland.

Brown, A., and A. Deaton (1972), "Surveys in Applied Economics: Models of Consumer Behaviour," *Economic Journal*, vol. 82, pp. 1145–1236.

Bruno, M. (1979), "Income Distribution and the Neoclassical Paradigm: Introduction to a Symposium," *Journal of Development Economics*, vol. 6, pp. 3–10.

(1966), "A Programming Model for Israel," in Adelman and Thorbecke, *The Theory and Design of Economic Development.*

Bulutay, et al. (1975), *Turkiyinin Milli Geliri, 1923–48*, Ankara: S.B.F., Yayinlari.

Burmeister, E., and A. Dobell (1970), *Mathematical Theories of Economic Growth*, London: Macmillan.

Carter, A., and A. Brody, eds. (1970), *Contribution to Input–Output Analysis*, Amsterdam: North-Holland.

Caves, R., and R. Jones (1977), *World Trade and Payments: An Introduction*, 2nd ed., Boston: Little, Brown.

Celásun, M. (1978), "A Computable General Equilibrium Model for the Analysis of Structural Transformation and Relative Price Changes," *METU Studies in Development*, no. 20, pp. 1–24.

Chakravarty, Sukhamoy (1969), *Capital and Development Planning*, Cambridge, Mass.: M.I.T. Press.

Champernowne, D. (1974), "A Comparison of Measures of Inequality of Income Distribution," *Economic Journal,* vol. 84, pp. 787–816.

(1953), "A Model of Income Distribution," *Economic Journal,* vol. 63, pp. 318–51.

Chenery, H. B. (1960), "Patterns of Industrial Growth," *American Economic Review,* vol. 50, pp. 624–54.

Chenery, H. B. (1979), *Structural Change and Development Policy,* London: Oxford University Press.

ed. (1971), *Studies in Development Planning,* Cambridge, Mass.: Harvard University Press.

Chenery, H. B., and M. Bruno (1962), "Development Alternatives in an Open Economy: The Case of Israel," *Economic Journal,* vol. 52, pp. 79–103.

Chenery, H. B., and P. G. Clark (1959), *Interindustry Economics,* New York: Wiley.

Chenery, H., and W. J. Raduchel (1971), "Substitution in Planning Models," in Chenery, *Studies in Development Planning.*

Chenery, H. B., S. Shishido, and T. Watanabe (1962), "The Pattern of Japanese Growth, 1914–1954," *Econometrica,* vol. 30, pp. 98–139.

Chenery, H. B., and M. Syrquin (1979), "A Comparative Analysis of Industrial Growth," in Matthews, *Economic Growth and Resources: Trends and Factors.*

(1975), *Patterns of Development 1950–1970,* London: Oxford University Press.

Chenery, H., and H. Uzawa (1958), "Non-linear Programming in Economic Development," in Arrow, Hurwicz, and Uzawa, *Studies in Linear and Non-linear Programming.*

Cline, William R. (1972), *Potential Effects of Income Redistribution on Economic Growth: Latin American Cases,* New York: Praeger.

Cole, D. C., and P. N. Lyman (1971), *Korean Development: The Interplay of Politics and Economics,* Cambridge, Mass.: Harvard University Press.

Conte, S., and C. de Boor (1972), *Elementary Numerical Analysis: An Algorithmic Approach,* New York: McGraw-Hill.

Cooper, R. N. (1971), *Currency Devaluation in Developing Countries,* Princeton, N.J.: Princeton Essays in International Finance.

Corden, W. M. (1974), *Trade Policy and Economic Welfare,* London: Oxford University Press.

Dahlquist, G., and A. Bjorck (1974), *Numerical Methods,* Englewood Cliffs, N.J.: Prentice-Hall.

Day, R., and A. Cigno (1978), *Modelling Economic Change: The Recursive Programming Approach,* New York: North-Holland.

Deardorff, A. V., and R. M. Stern (1979), "An Economic Analysis of the Effects of the Tokyo Round of Multilateral Trade Negotiations on the United States and Other Major Industrialized Countries," MTN Studies No. 5, Committee on Finances, Washington, D.C.: U.S. Government Printing Office.

Debreu, G. (1959), *The Theory of Value,* New York: Wiley.

Denison, E. F. (1967), *Why Growth Rates Differ,* Washington, D.C.: Brookings Institution.

Derviş, K. (1975), "Substitution, Employment, and Intertemporal Equilibrium in a Non-Linear Multi-Sector Planning Model for Turkey," *European Economic Review,* vol. 6, pp. 77–96.

Derviş, K., and S. Robinson (1980), "The Sources and Structure of Inequality in Turkey (1950–73)," in Ozbudun and Ulusan, *The Political Economy of Income Distribution in Turkey.*

(1978), "The Foreign Exchange Gap, Growth and Industrial Strategy in Turkey:

1973–83," World Bank Staff Working Paper No. 306, Washington, D.C.: The World Bank.

Desai, P. (1969), "Alternative Measures of Import Substitution," *Oxford Economic Papers,* vol. 21, no. 3, pp. 344–59.

Diamand, M. (1978), "Towards a Change in the Economic Paradigm Through the Experience of Developing Countries, *Journal of Development Economics,* vol. 5, pp. 19–53.

Diaz-Alejandro, C., et al. (1979), "Exchange Rate Policy in Semi-industrialized Countries: A Symposium," *Journal of Development Economics,* vol. 6, no. 4, pp. 459–548.

Dixon, P. B. (1975), *The Theory of Joint Maximization,* Amsterdam: North-Holland.

Dixon, P. B., B. Parmenter, G. Ryland, and J. Sutton (1977), *Orani, A General Equilibrium Model of the Australian Economy,* vol. 2, Canberra: Government Publishing Service.

Dorfman, R., P. A. Samuelson, and R. M. Solow (1958), *Linear Programming and Economic Analysis,* New York: McGraw-Hill.

Dornbusch, R. (1978), "The Theory of Flexible Exchange Rates, Regimes and Macroeconomic Policy," in Frenkel and Johnson, *The Economics of Exchange Rates.*

Dungan, P. D. (1980), "An Empirical, Multi-Sectoral Walrasian-Keynesian Model of the Canadian Economy," Unpublished Ph.D. dissertation, Princeton University.

Eckaus, R., F. D. McCarthy, and A. Mohieldin (1979), "Multisector General Equilibrium Models for Egypt," Cambridge, Mass.: M.I.T. Department of Economics Working Paper No. 233.

Evans, H. D. (1972), *A General Equilibrium Analysis of Protection: The Effects of Protection in Australia,* Amsterdam: North-Holland.

Eysenback, M. L. (1969), "A Note on Growth and Structural Change in Pakistan's Manufacturing Industry," *Pakistan Development Review,* vol. 11, no. 1, pp. 58–65.

Fane, G. (1973), "Consistent Measures of Import Substitution," *Oxford Economic Papers,* vol. 25, no. 2, pp. 251–61.

 (1971), "Import Substitution and Export Expansion: Their Measurement and an Example of Their Application," *Pakistan Development Review,* vol. 11, no. 1, pp. 1–17.

Fei, J., and G. Ranis (1974), "Income Inequality by Additive Components," Discussion Paper 207, Economic Growth Center, New Haven: Yale University.

Feltenstein, A. (1980), "A General Equilibrium Approach to the Analysis of Trade Restrictions with an Application to Argentina," *IMF Staff Papers,* vol. 27, no. 4, pp. 749–84.

Fields, G. (1980), *Poverty, Inequality and Development,* Cambridge: Cambridge University Press.

Findlay, R. E. (1973), *International Trade and Development Theory,* New York: Columbia University Press.

Fisher, F. (1965), "Choice of Units, Column Sums and Stability in Linear Dynamic Systems with Nonnegative Square Matrices," *Econometrica,* vol. 33, no. 2, pp. 445–50.

Fishlow, A. (1972), "Brazilian Size Distribution of Income," *Papers and Proceedings of the American Economic Association,* vol. 62, pp. 391–402.

Frank, C. R., Jr., K. S. Kim, and L. Westphal (1975), *Foreign Trade Regimes and Economic Development: South Korea,* New York: National Bureau of Economic Research.

Frank, C. R., Jr., and R. Webb, eds. (1977), *Income Distribution: Policy Alternatives in Developing Countries,* Washington, D.C.: Brookings Institution.

Frenkel, J. A., and H. G. Johnson, eds. (1978), *The Economics of Exchange Rates,* Reading, Mass.: Addison-Wesley.

Frisch, R. (1959), "A Complete Scheme for Computing All Direct and Cross Demand Elasticities in a Model with Many Sectors," *Econometrica,* vol. 27, pp. 177–96.

Fullerton, D., A. T. King, J. Shoven, and J. Whalley, "Tax Integration in the U.S.: A General Equilibrium Approach," *American Economic Review* (in press).

Gale, D. (1960), *The Theory of Linear Economic Models,* New York: McGraw-Hill.

Gerschenkron, A. (1952), "Economic Backwardness in Historical Perspective," in Hoselitz, *The Progress of Underdeveloped Areas.*

Ginsburgh, V., and J. Waelbroeck (1980), *Activity Analysis and General Equilibrium Modeling,* Amsterdam: North-Holland.

(1978), "Computational Experience with a Large General Equilibrium Model," in J. Los, ed., *Computing Equilibria: How and Why.*

Gintis, H. (1972), "Welfare Economics and Individual Development," *Quarterly Journal of Economics,* vol. 86, no. 4.

Goreux, L. M. (1977), *Interdependence in Planning: Multilevel Programming Studies of the Ivory Coast,* Baltimore, Md.: Johns Hopkins Press.

Goreux, L. M., and A. S. Manne, eds. (1973), *Multi-level Planning: Case Studies in Mexico,* Amsterdam: North-Holland.

Grubel, H. G., and P. J. Lloyd (1975), *Intra-Industry Trade: The Theory and Measurement of International Trade in Differentiated Products,* London: Macmillan and Halsted.

Gupta, S. (1977), "A Model for Income Distribution, Employment, and Growth: A Case Study of Indonesia," World Bank Occasional Staff Papers No. 24, Baltimore, Md.: Johns Hopkins Press.

Hadley, G. (1962), *Linear Programming,* Reading, Mass.: Addison-Wesley.

Hagen, E. (1958), "An Economic Justification of Protectionism," *Quarterly Journal of Economics,* vol. 72, pp. 496–514.

Hahn, F. (1966), "Equilibrium Dynamics with Heterogeneous Capital Goods," *Quarterly Journal of Economics,* vol. 80, pp. 633–46.

Harberger, A. C. (1971), "Three Basic Postulates for Applied Welfare Economics: An Interpretative Essay," *Journal of Economic Literature,* vol. 9, no. 3, pp. 785–97.

Harcourt, G. (1972), *Some Cambridge Controversies in the Theory of Capital,* Cambridge: Cambridge University Press.

Harris, J., and M. Todaro (1970), "Migration Unemployment and Development: A Two-Sector Analysis," *American Economic Review,* vol. 60., pp. 126–42.

Heal, G. (1973), *The Theory of Economic Planning,* Amsterdam: North-Holland.

Herschlag, Z. (1968), *Turkey: The Challenge of Growth,* Leiden: E. J. Brill.

Hirschman, A. (1948), "Devaluation and Trade Balance: A Note," *Review of Economics and Statistics,* vol. 31, pp. 50–53.

Hoselitz, B., ed. (1952), *The Progress of Underdeveloped Areas,* Chicago: University of Chicago Press.

Hudson E., and D. Jorgenson (1978), "Energy Prices and the U.S. Economy, 1972–76," *Natural Resources Journal,* vol. 18, no. 4, pp. 877–97.

Huntington, S., and J. Nelson (1976), *No Easy Choice: Political Participation in Developing Countries,* Cambridge, Mass.: Harvard University Press.

Isard, P. (1978), "How Far Can One Push the Law of One Price?" *American Economic Review,* vol. 67, no. 5, pp. 942–8.

Issawi, C., (1980), *An Economic History of Turkey,* Chicago: University of Chicago Press.

Jain, S. (1975), "Size Distribution of Income: A Compilation of Data," Washington, D.C.: The World Bank (mimeo).

Johansen, L. (1960), *A Multi-Sectoral Study of Economic Growth,* Amsterdam: North-Holland.

Johansen, L., H. Alstadtheim, and A. Langsether (1968), "Explorations in Long-Term Projections for the Norwegian Economy," *Economics of Planning,* vol. 8, no. 1-2, pp. 70-117.

Johnson, H. G. (1960), "The Costs of Protection and the Scientific Tariff," *Journal of Political Economy,* vol. 68, no. 4, pp. 327-45.

Jones, R. W., and E. Berglas (1977), "Import Demand and Export Supply: An Aggregation Theorem," *American Economic Review,* vol. 67, no. 2, pp. 183-7.

Jorgenson, D. (1963), "Capital Theory and Investment Behavior," *American Economic Review,* vol. 53, pp. 247-59.

(1960), "A Dual Stability Theorem," *Econometrica,* vol. 28, pp. 892-9.

Jorgenson, D., and M. Nishimizu (1978), "U.S. and Japanese Economic Growth, 1952-1974: An International Comparison," *Economic Journal,* vol. 88, no. 352, pp. 707-26.

Kaldor, N. (1955), "Alternative Theories of Distribution," *Review of Economic Studies,* vol. 23, pp. 83-100.

Kaplan, W. (1958), *Ordinary Differential Equations,* Reading, Mass.: Addison-Wesley.

(1952), *Advanced Calculus,* Reading, Mass.: Addison-Wesley.

Karlin, S. (1959), *Mathematical Methods and Theories in Games, Programming and Economics,* vol. 1, Reading, Mass.: Addison-Wesley.

Kehoe, T. J. (1980), "An Index Theorem for General Equilibrium Models with Production," *Econometrica,* vol. 48, pp. 1211-32.

Keller, W. J. (1980), *Tax Incidence: A General Equilibrium Approach.* Amsterdam: North-Holland.

Kelley, A., J. Williamson, and R. Cheetham (1972), *Dualistic Economic Development: Theory and History,* Chicago: University of Chicago Press.

Kendrick, D. (1972), "On the Leontief Dynamic Inverse," *Quarterly Journal of Economics,* vol. 86, pp. 693-6.

King, B., (1981), "What Is a SAM?, A Layman's Guide to Social Accounting Matrices," World Bank Staff Working Paper No. 463, Washington, D.C.: The World Bank.

Kmenta, J., and J. B. Ramsey, eds. (1981), *Large Scale Econometric Models: Theory and Practice,* Amsterdam: North-Holland.

Kornai, J. (1972), *Rush Versus Harmonic Growth,* Amsterdam: North Holland.

Krueger, A. (1979), "Interactions Between Inflation and Trade Regime Objectives in Stabilization Programs," Minneapolis: University of Minnesota (mimeo).

(1978), *Foreign Trade Regimes and Economic Development: Liberalization Attempts and Consequences,* Ballinger Publishing Co.

(1974a), *Foreign Trade Regimes and Economic Development: Turkey,* New York: Columbia University Press.

(1974b), "The Political Economy of the Rent-Seeking Society," *American Economic Review,* vol. 64, no. 3, pp. 291-303.

Krugman, P., and L. Taylor (1978), "Contractionary Effects of Devaluation," *Journal of International Economics,* vol. 8, pp. 445-56.

Kubo, Y., and S. Robinson (1979), "Sources of Industrial Growth and Structural

510   **References**

Change: A Comparative Analysis of Eight Countries," Washington, D.C.: The World Bank (mimeo).

Kuhn, H. W., and A. W. Tucker (1956), "Linear Inequalities and Related Systems," *Annals of Mathematics Studies,* vol. 38, Princeton, N.J.: Princeton University Press.

Kuyvenhoven, A. (1978), *Planning with the Semi-Input–Output Method,* Leiden: Martinus Nijhoff.

Kuznets, S. (1966), *Modern Economic Growth: Rate, Structure, and Spread,* New Haven, Conn.: Yale University Press.

Lancaster, K. (1968), *Mathematical Economics,* New York: Macmillan.

    (1966), "A New Approach to Consumer Theory," *Journal of Political Economy,* vol. 74, pp. 132–57.

Land, J. (1970), "The Role of Government in the Economic Development of Turkey, 1923 to 1963," Rice University Program of Development Studies, Paper No. 8, Houston, Tex.: Rice University.

Leamer, E., and R. M. Stern (1970), *Quantitative International Economics,* Boston: Allyn & Bacon.

Leibenstein, H. (1978), *General X-Efficiency Theory and Economic Development,* London: Oxford University Press.

Leontief, W. (1970), "The Dynamic Inverse," in Carter and Brody, *Contribution of Input–Output Analysis.*

    (1953), "Domestic Production and Foreign Trade: The American Capital Position Re-examined," *Proceedings of the American Philosophical Society,* vol. 97.

Leontief, W., et al. (1953), *Studies in the Structure of the American Economy,* New York: Oxford University Press.

Lewis, W. A. (1980), "The Slowing Down of the Engine of Growth," *American Economic Review,* vol. 70, no. 4, pp. 535–64.

    (1954), "Development with Unlimited Supplies of Labour," *Manchester School of Economic and Social Studies,* vol. 20, pp. 189–92.

Lluch, C. (1979), "Models of Employment and Income Distribution," *Journal of Development Economics,* vol. 6, no. 1, pp. 31–47.

    (1973), "The Extended Linear Expenditure System," *European Economic Review,* vol. 4, pp. 21–32.

Lluch, C., A. Powell, and R. Williams (1977), *Patterns in Household Demand and Saving,* London: Oxford University Press.

Los, J., ed. (1978), *Computing Equilibria: How and Why,* Amsterdam: North-Holland.

Lysy, F., and L. Taylor (1980), "A Computable General Equilibrium Model for the Functional Distribution of Income: Experiments for Brazil, 1959–71," in Taylor et al., *Models of Growth and Distribution for Brazil.*

Malinvaud, E. (1977), *The Theory of Unemployment Reconsidered,* London: Oxford University Press.

Mangahas, M. (1974), "A Note on Decomposition of the Gini Ratio Across Regions," Research Discussion Paper 74-2, Institute of Economic Development and Research, School of Economics, Manila: University of Philippines.

Manne, A. (1974), "Multi-Sectoral Models for Development Planning: A Survey," *Journal of Development Economics,* vol. 1, pp. 574–95.

Manne, A., H. Chao, and R. Wilson (1978), "Computation of Competitive Equilibria by a Sequence of Linear Programs," Stanford, Calif.: Stanford University (mimeo).

Manne, A., S. Kim, and T. F. Wilson (1980), "A Three-Region Model of Energy, International Trade and Economic Growth," Stanford, Calif.: Stanford University Department of Operations Research (mimeo).

Mathur, P. N. (1964), "Output and Investment for Exponential Growth in Consumption–An Alternative Formulation; and Derivation of Their Technological Upper Limits," *Review of Economic Studies,* vol. 31, pp. 73–82.

Matthews, R. C. O., ed. (1979), *Economic Growth and Resources: Trends and Factors,* New York: Macmillan.

McKenzie, L. (1960), "Matrices with Dominant Diagonals and Economic Theory," in Arrow et al., *Mathematical Methods in the Social Sciences.*

Meerman, J. (1979), *Public Expenditure in Malaysia: Who Benefits and Why?* London: Oxford University Press.

Melo, J. de (1980), "Tariffs and Resource Allocation in Partial and in General Equilibrium," *Welwirtschaftliches Archiv,* Band 116, pp. 114–30.

(1978a), "Tariffs and Resource Allocation in a Walrasian Trade Model," *International Economic Review,* vol. 19, no. 1, pp. 25–45.

(1978b), "Estimating the Costs of Protection: A General Equilibrium Approach," *Quarterly Journal of Economics,* vol. 92, no. 2, pp. 209–27.

(1977), "Distortions in the Factor Market: Some General Equilibrium Estimates," *The Review of Economics and Statistics,* vol. 54, no. 4, pp. 398–405.

Melo, J. de, and K. Derviş (1977), "Modelling the Effects of Protection in a Dynamic Framework," *Journal of Development Economics,* vol. 4, pp. 149–72.

Melo, J. de, and S. Robinson (1980), "The Impact of Trade Policies on Income Distribution in a Planning Model for Colombia," *Journal of Policy Modeling,* vol. 2, pp. 81–100.

(1978), "Tradability in Trade Theory," Washington, D.C.: The World Bank (mimeo).

Melo, M. de (1979), "Agricultural Policies and Development: A Socioeconomic Investigation Applied to Sri Lanka," *Journal of Policy Modeling,* vol. 1, no. 2, pp. 201–16.

Melvin, J. (1968), "Production and Trade with Two Factors and Three Goods," *American Economic Review,* vol. 58, no. 5, pp. 1249–68.

Metcalf, C. (1972), *An Econometric Model of the Income Distribution,* Chicago: Markham.

Michalopoulos, C. (1975), "Production and Substitution in Two-Gap Models," *Journal of Development Studies,* vol. 11, no. 4, pp. 343–56.

Mincer, J. (1970), "The Distribution of Labor Incomes: A Survey with Special Reference to the Human Capital Approach," *Journal of Economic Literature,* vol. 8, no. 1, pp. 1–26.

Morishima, M., (1977), *Walras' Economics: A Pure Theory of Capital and Money,* Cambridge: Cambridge University Press.

(1973), *Marx's Economics: A Dual Theory of Value and Growth,* Cambridge: Cambridge University Press.

Morley, S. A., and G. W. Smith (1970), "On the Measurement of Import Substitution," *American Economic Review,* vol. 60, no. 4, pp. 728–35.

Mussa, M. (1974), "Tariffs and the Distribution of Income: The Importance of Factor Specificity, Substitutability and Intensity in the Short and Long Run," *Journal of Political Economy,* vol. 82, no. 6, pp. 1191–1203.

Nikaido, H. (1970), *Introduction to Sets and Mappings in Modern Economics,* Amsterdam: North-Holland.

(1968), *Convex Structures and Economic Theory,* New York: Academic Press.

512   **References**

Ohyama, M. (1972), "Stability and Welfare in General Equilibrium," Ph.D. thesis, University of Rochester.

Ozbudun, E., and A. Ulusan, eds. (1980), *The Political Economy of Income Distribution in Turkey,* New York: Holmes and Meier.

Pack, H. (1971), *Structural Change and Economic Policy in Israel,* New Haven, Conn.: Yale University Press.

Papanek, G. (1972), "The Effect of Aid and Other Resource Transfers on Saving and Growth in Less Developed Countries," *Economic Journal,* vol. 82, pp. 934–50.

Petri, P. (1976), "A Multilateral Model of Japanese-American Trade," in Polenske and Skolka, *Advances in Input–Output Analysis.*

Phelps, E. S., ed. (1973), *Economic Justice,* Harmondsworth, Baltimore: Penguin Educational.

(1965), *Private Wants and Public Needs,* New York: Norton.

Polenske, K. R. and J. Skolka, eds. (1976), *Advances in Input–Output Analysis,* Cambridge, Mass.: Ballinger.

Powell, A. A. (1981), "The Major Streams of Economy-Wide Modelling: Is Rapprochement Possible?," in Kmenta and Ramsey, *Large Scale Econometric Models: Theory and Practice.*

Powell, M. J. D. (1970a), "A Fortran Subroutine for Solving Systems of Nonlinear Algebraic Equations," in Rabinowitz, *Numerical Methods for Non-linear Algebraic Equations.*

(1970b), "A Hybrid Method for Nonlinear Equations," in Rabinowitz, *Numerical Methods for Non-linear Algebraic Equations.*

Pyatt, G. (1976), "On the Interpretation and Disaggregation of Gini Coefficients," *The Economic Journal,* vol. 86, no. 342, pp. 243–55.

Pyatt, G., and J. Round (1979a), "Social Accounting Matrices for Development Planning," *The Review of Income and Wealth,* series 23, no. 4, pp. 339–64.

(1979b), "Accounting and Fixed Price Multipliers in a Social Accounting Matrix Framework," *Economic Journal,* vol. 89, pp. 850–73.

Pyatt, G., and E. Thorbecke (1976), *Planning Techniques for a Better Future,* Geneva: International Labour Office.

Rabinowitz, P., ed. (1970), *Numerical Methods for Non-Linear Algebraic Equations,* London: Gordon & Breach.

Rawls, J. (1971), *A Theory of Justice,* Cambridge, Mass.: Harvard University Press.

Robbins, L. (1932), *The Nature and Significance of Economic Science,* London.

Robinson, S. (1976a), "A Note on the *U* Hypothesis Relating Income Inequality and Economic Development," *American Economic Review,* vol. 66, pp. 437–40.

(1976b), "Income Distribution Within Groups, Among Groups, and Overall: A Technique of Analysis," Discussion Paper No. 65, Research Program in Development Studies, Princeton, N.J.: Princeton University.

(1976c), "Toward an Adequate Long-Run Model of Income Distribution and Economic Development," *American Economic Review,* vol. 66, no. 2, pp. 122–7.

(1972), "Sources of Growth in Less Developed Countries: A Cross-Section Study," *Quarterly Journal of Economics,* vol. 85, pp. 391–408.

Robinson, S., and Byung-Nak Song (1972), "A Dynamic Input–Output Model of the Korean Economy," Research Program in Economic Development, Discussion Paper No. 30, Princeton, N.J.: Princeton University.

Robinson, S., and K. Derviş (1977), "Income Distribution and Socioeconomic Mobility: A Framework for Analysis and Planning," *Journal of Development Studies,* vol. 13, no. 4, pp. 347–64.

Rodgers, G. B., M. Hopkins, and R. Wery (1977), *"Population, Employment and Inequality: Bachue-Philippines,"* Geneva: International Labour Office.

Rodgers, G. B., R. Wery, and M. Hopkins (1976), "The Myth of the Cave Revisited: Are Large-Scale Behavioral Models Useful?" *Population and Development Review,* vol. 2, nos 3–4, pp. 395–411.

Samuelson, P. (1953), "Prices of Factors and Goods in General Equilibrium," *Review of Economic Studies,* vol. 21, no. 54, pp. 1–20.

Samuelson, P., and S. Swamy (1974), "Invariant Economic Index Numbers and Canonical Duality: Survey and Synthesis," *American Economic Review,* vol. 64, no. 4, pp. 566–93.

Sanderson, W. C. (1980), "Economic-Demographic Simulation Models: A Review of Their Usefulness for Policy Analysis," Laxenburg, Austria: International Institute for Applied Systems Analysis, RM-80-14.

Scarf, H., and T. Hansen (1973), *The Computation of Economic Equilibria,* New Haven, Conn.: Yale University Press.

Sekerka, B., O. Kyn, and L. Hejl (1970), "Price Systems Computable from Input–Output Coefficients," in Carter and Brody, *Contribution to Input–Output Analysis.*

Selowsky, M. (1979), *Who Benefits from Government Expenditure? A Case Study of Colombia,* London: Oxford University Press.

Sen, A. K., (1973), *On Economic Inequality,* New York: Norton.

(1970), *Collective Choice and Individual Welfare,* San Francisco: Holden-Day.

Shoven, J., and J. Whalley (1974), "On the Computation of Competitive Equilibria on International Markets with Tariffs," *Journal of International Economics,* vol. 4, pp. 341–54.

Solow, R. (1957), "Technical Change and the Aggregate Production Function," *Review of Economics and Statistics,* vol. 39, pp. 312–20.

(1956), "A Contribution to the Theory of Economic Growth," *Quarterly Journal of Economics,* vol. 70, pp. 65–94.

Squire, L., and H. Van Der Tak (1975), *Economic Analysis of Projects,* Baltimore, Md.: Johns Hopkins Press.

Srinivasan, T. N. (1975), "The Foreign Trade Sector in Planning Models," in Blitzer et al., *Economy-Wide Models and Development Planning.*

Stewart, G. W. (1973), *Introduction to Matrix Computations,* New York: Academic Press.

Stone, R. (1970), *Mathematical Models of the Economy and Other Essays,* London: Chapman & Hall.

Stone, R., and J. A. C. Brown (1962), "Output and Investment for Exponential Growth in Consumption," *Review of Economic Studies,* vol. 29, no. 80, pp. 241–5.

Syrquin, M. (1976), "Sources of Industrial Growth and Change: An Alternative Measure," Washington, D.C.: The World Bank (mimeo).

Szal, R., and S. Robinson (1977), "Measuring Income Inequality," in Frank and Webb, *Income Distribution: Policy Alternatives in Developing Countries.*

Takayama, T. and G. C. Judge (1971), *Spatial and Temporal Price and Allocation Models,* Amsterdam: North-Holland.

Taylor, L. (1979), *Macro Models for Developing Countries,* New York: McGraw-Hill.

(1975), "Theoretical Foundations and Technical Implications," in Blitzer et al., *Economy-Wide Models and Development Planning.*

514   References

Taylor, L., E. Bacha, E. Cardoso, and F. Lysy (1980), *Models of Growth and Distribution for Brazil,* London: Oxford University Press.

Taylor, L., and S. Black (1974), "Practical General Equilibrium Estimation of Resource Pulls Under Trade Liberalization," *Journal of International Economics,* vol. 4, no. 1, pp. 37–58.

Taylor, L., and F. Lysy (1979), "Vanishing Income Redistributions: Keynesian Clues About Model Surprises in the Short Run," *Journal of Development Economics,* vol. 6, pp. 17–30.

Tinbergen, J. (1959a), *Selected Papers,* edited by L. H. Klaassen, L. M. Koyck, and H. J. Witteveen, Amsterdam: North-Holland.

(1959b), "On the Theory of Income Distribution," in Tinbergen, *Selected Papers.*

United Nations Statistical Office (1975), *Towards a System of Social and Demographic Statistics,* Department of Economic and Social Affairs, ST/ESA/STAT/SER.F/18, New York: United Nations.

(1968), *A System of National Accounts,* series F, no. 2, rev. 3, New York: United Nations.

Weisskoff, Richard (1972), "A Multi-Sector Simulation Model of Employment, Growth, and Income Distribution in Puerto Rico: A Re-Evaluation of 'Successful' Development Strategy," New Haven, Conn.: Yale University (mimeo).

Westphal, L. E. (1978), "The Republic of Korea's Experience with Export-Led Industrial Development," *World Development,* vol. 6, no. 3, pp. 347–82.

(1971), *Planning Investments with Economies of Scale,* Amsterdam: North-Holland.

Whalley, J. (1977), "The U.K. Tax System 1968–1970: Some Fixed Point Indications of Its Economic Impact," *Econometrica,* vol. 45, no. 8, pp. 1837–58.

Woods, J. E. (1978), *Mathematical Economics,* London, New York: Longman.

World Bank (1980), *Turkey: Policies and Prospects for Growth,* Washington, D.C.: The World Bank.

(1978), "Historical Rates of Change in U.S. $ GDP Deflators: 1961–1975," Economic Analysis and Projections Department, Washington, D.C.: The World Bank.

(1976), *World Tables 1976,* Baltimore, Md.: Johns Hopkins Press.

Index

accounting framework: CGE model and, 155-62; of dynamic input-output models, 45; input-output matrix and, 57; multisector analysis and, 6-7; social accounting matrix (SAM) and, 155-62, 410, 411-17, 471-85; of static input-output models, 17, 21, 26, 27; TGT model, 322

Adelman, I., 46, 176

Adelman-Robinson model of Korea, 406, 407, 413

adjustment function, 11; dynamic input-output model, 34, 35, 36, 39-41, 59; of forward-running model, 61; growth rate and, 61

aggregation: exchange rate and, scheme for, 301-5; export substitution of domestic products and, 225; import substitution of domestic products and, 224

agriculture, 121, 208, 260, 262, 286; CGE model/income distribution and, 437-8, 450, 452, 453; export tax, growth and, 360; exports/TGT growth and, 364; inward-looking strategy and, 117; structural change and, 110; in TGT model, 367

Ahluwalia-Lysy model of Malaysia, 406

Almon, Clopper, 46

Armington, P., 221, 227

Arrow, Kenneth, 155 n13

backward-running model, 40-1, 59-60

balance of payments, 80, 86; equation, flexible exchange rate model and, 252; exchange rate adjustment and, 291; Turkish foreign exchange crisis and, 331, 351

balance of trade: exchange rate/ normalization and, 183-92; Korean growth example and, 114-17; *see also* foreign trade; trade

Balassa, B., 434

barter model, 151, 152

Bhagwati, J., 306

borrowing: exchange rate adjustment and, 291; foreign, SAM/CGE and, 160; Turkish foreign exchange crisis and, 331, 333, 342, 346-8

British economic models, 46

budget constraint problem (linear programming), 133

capacity: constraints in linear programming models, 66-7; full, multisector input-output model and, 40; Korean growth example and, 117; terminal, linear programming and, 87; trade policy/linear programming and, 84-5

capacity utilization (linear programming), 62

capital, 64; account in SAM/CGE, 161; accumulation/savings and TGT model, 322; basic structure of CGE model and, 141, 148; capacity constraints/linear programming and, 66-7; constant composition of, per sector, 37, 61; dynamic input-output model and, 37-41; dynamic model building and, 212, 213, 215; elasticities, "free-trade" solution and, 260, 261; foreign, exchange rate and, 191; foreign, Korean growth and, 112, 117; market clearing/CGE and, 171, 172; terminal conditions of linear programming and, 87-90; trade policy/linear programming and, 84; updating, linear programming model and, 67

capital account, income distribution and, 413

capital goods, 139; prices/linear programming and, 74-5

capital inflow, TGT model and, 333-4

capitalists, CGE model/income distribution and, 438, 453-6

central planning, 131, 132, 215; *see also* planning

Champernowne, D., 399, 430

515

Chenery, Hollis, 25, 27, 28, 91, 93, 94, 110, 435
circular flow (economy-wide), *see* economy-wide circular flow
Clark, P.G., 25, 27, 28
class conflict, income distribution policy and, 458-66
closed economy, 433; computable general equilibrium model and, 131-81, 496-9
closure, income distribution mechanisms and, 404-5, 406
Colombia, 96, 107, 370
commodities: demand for/income generation (CGE model), 145-8; excess demand equations for CGE model and, 148-50; nontraded, exchange rate and, 187-92; SAM and, 157-9; supply of/factor markets (CGE model) and, 139-45; traded, exchange rate and, 183-7
Comparative Study of the Sources of Industrial Growth and Structural Change, (A) (World Bank research project), 96 n3
competition: imperfect, CGE model and, 169; introduction of trade into CGE model and, 200, 201; perfect, CGE model and, 143, 201; quotas and, 200
computable general equilibrium model (CGE): basic structure of one-period, 138-55; change of specification effect, exports/imports and, 230-2; class conflict/distributional policy choice and, 458-66; closed economy and, 131-81, 496-8; development planning and, 131-3; distributional mechanism/economy-wide models and, 403-10; distribution of income/archetype economies and, 435-41; distribution of income/policy and, 449-58; excess demand equation for commodities and, 148-50; exchange rate adjustment/devaluation vs. imports and, 295-305; exchange rate adjustment/import rationing with rent seeking and, 305-9; exchange rate definitions/price-normalization and, 192-7; exchange rate flexibility/import rationing and, 290-5; exchange rate/nontradables and, 187-92; exchange rate/tradables and, 183-7; existence proof and, 153-5; export/small-country assumption and, 224-30; export supply/exchange rate adjustment and, 309-12; external shocks/macroeconomic distributional

adjustment and, 433-5, 441-9; factor markets/supply of commodities and, 139-45; foreign exchange shortages and adjustment in, 288-317; "free trade" reference solution and, 259-65; generating income distribution in, 410-24; income generation/demand for commodities and, 145-8; intertemporal linkages/market clearing and, 169-80; introducing trade policy into, 197-207; investment allocation and, 175-8; investment treatment in, 165-6; measuring income distribution in, 425-31; normative/positive approaches to income distribution and, 389-403; open economy and, 219-54; optimal/market solutions and, 133-8; overview of, 10-13; planning/dynamic context and, 211-17; price mechanism/resource allocation and, 259-74; price-normalization and, 150-3; product differentiation/imports and, 221-4; resource allocation/DRCs-ERPs and, 274-8; resource allocation policy and, 287; rural-urban migration and, 178-80; social accounts and, 155-62; solution algorithms and, 491-6; solution strategies and, 486-91; solving, 503; static, summary of/solutions and, 163-9; tariff/subsidy change effects in, domestic prices and, 265-74; TGT model and, 358; trade policy efficiencies and, 207-11; trade tax changes in, 278-86; two-stage formulation and, 173-5; welfare effects of exchange rate adjustment and, 312-16; *see also* Turkey, growth, and trade model
consumer: defined, 245 n15; SAM and, 482; welfare comparisons and, 242, 243
consumer goods, exchange rate adjustment and, 302, 304
consumption: adjustment function/growth rate and, 61; basic structure of CGE model and, 147; CGE model/distribution and, 444-6, 449; demand (sectoral), price mechanism/resource allocation and, 259-60; Korean growth and, 113, 117, 118, 121; linear programming and, 70-1; multisector input-output model and, 38, 40, 41; objective function/linear programming and, 65-6; one-sector input-output model and, 31-6; patterns, distribution of income and,

516

432; SAM and, 482-5; target equilibrium paths/dynamic input-output model and, 42-4, 46
cost equations (linear programming), 74
cost of living, CGE model/distribution and, 450, 452
credit, 209
cross-country comparisons, 483; static input-output model and, 92-110
currency, Turkish, overvaluation of, 342
Czechoslovakia, 52-3

debt, TGT model/growth and, 362-3, 365, 373
decomposition: analysis (methodology) of real income, 245-8; of change in the equilibrium exchange rate (TGT model), 332-41; of changing demand patterns, static input-output model and, 92, 96-110; growth rate and, 110; income distribution/size distribution by individuals and, 419; methodology, domestic demand and, 93-6; TGT model/growth and, 379, 380
deflation, domestic price/exchange rate adjustment and, 296
demand: CGE model and, 135-6, 167-8; CGE model, distribution and, 444-6; changing patterns in, eight-country comparison, 93-6, 101; for commodities, income generation/CGE model and, 145-8; consumption, equation in flexible exchange rate model and, 253; domestic goods as substitute for imports and, 230-1; elasticities of, price mechanism/resource allocation and, 259-74; excess, equation for commodities/CGE model and, 148-50; excess, tradables/nontradables/supply and, 188, 189; export, elasticities of, 226-7; export/import elasticities in, exchange rate adjustment and, 299-300; export/import function equation, flexible exchange rate model and, 251; for exports, small-country assumption and, 224-8, 230; growth and, 121; immediate, equation in flexible exchange rate model and, 253; labor, CGE model and, 144, 163; product differentiation by country of origin and, 221-3; see also domestic demand; final demand
Derviş, K., 322

devaluation, 11, 236; distributional mechanisms and, 406; exchange rate adjustment and, 289, 295-305, 310-11, 314-16; TGT model/growth and, 374, 380; trade adjustment/income distribution and, 443, 446-8, 451, 460, 464-5; Turkish foreign exchange and, 321, 324-5, 327, 342, 348, 350-1
developed countries, 137; restrictionist policies and, 434
developing countries: economic structure and differences in, 466; foreign exchange shortages and, 288-9; growth decline and, 433-5; models and, 137-8; policy analysis/models and, 2
development policies: analysis of, application of CGE model and, 432-3; choices in, income distribution and, 449-58; class conflict/distribution and, 158-66; distortion free economy and, 210; dynamic considerations and, 216; multisector models and, 4-8; trade adjustment policy/distribution of income and, 433-5, 441-9; see also policy; trade adjustment policies
development process, income and, 91
development strategies, 8; CGE model and, 131-3; input-output models and, 91; inward-looking, 114-21; models and, 137-8; outward-looking, 112; trade policies and, 182-3
diagonalization of a matrix, 53-5
domestic demand: decomposition/static input-output model and, 93-6, 104; growth and, 93; imports/TGT model and, 367, 382, 383; input-output material balance equation and, 27, 28; manufacturing growth and, 105, 123; see also demand; final demand
domestic goods: exports substituted for, 76; foreign goods substituted for, 184; as imperfect substitute for imported goods, 221-4, 230-2; introduction of trade into CGE/foreign goods and, 203; static input-output models and, 24-9; as substitute for imported goods, 24, 29, 76, 184, 203; TGT model and, 378, 382
domestic resource costs (DRCs): project evaluation/resource allocation and, 274-8; TGT model and, 353, 355-7
duality theorem, 63 n2; multipliers/ "prices" and, 64, 72, 73; shadow prices/resources and, 134
"dual stability," 41, 60; see also stability

517

economic growth, *see* growth; growth paths; growth prospects

economy-wide circular flow, 18-19

economy-wide models, income distribution and, 403-10

education, Korean manufacturing growth and, 112

effective protection, 11; ERP/project evaluation/resource allocation and, 274-8; trade policy/CGE model and, 202-4, 205; trade tax changes and, 281-2, 286; *see also* nominal protection; protection

efficiency: competition/trade policy and, 201; dynamic, 216; income distribution and, 398-9; trade policy and, 207-11

elasticities, 258; export demand, 226-7, 249; of export/import demand, exchange rate adjustment and, 299-300; reflection of different sector accounts and price mechanism/ resource allocation, 259-74; trade, defined, 261 n3; trade-substitution, 249

empirical economic-demographic models, 408

employment, 466; dynamic models and, 213; Korean growth example and, 120-1; static input-output model factor requirements and, 30; tariffs and, 217; TGT model/growth and, 376, 394; welfare implications of CGE model and, 209

enterprise account, income distribution and, 413

equity, income distribution and, 398-9, 426

exchange rate: devaluation vs. import rationing and, 295-305; export supply constraints and, 309-12; flexible, equations of model for, 249-54; import rationing with rent seeking and, 305-9; Korean manufacturing growth and, 111; linear programming and, 76; non-commodities and, 187-92; protection and, 203; tariffs and, 204; tariffs/adjustment and, 268; TGT model growth experiment and, 359, 360, 370, 376, 381; TGT model used to estimate an exchange rate for 1973-1977 and, 332-41, 343; traded commodities and, 183-7; trade tax changes and, 278-81, 283; welfare effects of adjustment of, 312-16

existence proof, core model of CGE and, 153-5, 163 n22

expenditure accounts (SAM), 475-7

export expansion, 126, 311; decomposition methodology of static input-output model and, 93, 94; dynamic input-output model (Korean example) and, 110, 111-12, 123; exchange rate adjustment and, 289; growth and, 126; marketing/ transportation costs and, 227-8; static input-output model (manufacturing growth) and, 104, 107-10; TGT model/growth and, 378-94; *see also* exports; export subsidies

exports, 218, 219, 466; CGE model/ income distribution and, 438, 439, 441-3, 448, 452; demand elasticities and, 226-7, 249; demand function equation/flexible exchange rate model and, 251; domestic price increases and, 281; domestic prices and, 233, 234, 236; dynamic input-output models and, 46, 47, 117, 120-1, 123; employment/welfare and, 209-10; exchange rate adjustment and, 290, 296, 299, 302; foreign exchange constraints/linear programming and, 68; infant industry argument and, 216; manufacturing, resource allocation/trade policy and, 259, 263, 273, 274; price equation, flexible exchange rate model and, 250; primary exporting economy and, 433; SAM/CGE model and, 159, 160; sector tradability classification and, 240; small-country assumption and, 224-30; static input-output model and, 24-9, 30, 96, 101-4; as substitute for domestic goods, 76, 203; supply of, exchange rate adjustment and, 309-12; terminal year/linear programming and, 89; TGT model and, 325, 327-30, 331, 333, 337, 340, 342, 343, 352, 353; TGT model/ growth prospects and, 359-60, 363-4, 369-73; trade policy/linear programming and, 80, 81, 83; trade theory and, 31; *see also* export expansion; export subsidies

export subsidies, 359; across-the-board changes in, 278-9, 282-6; domestic prices and, 235, 236, 238, 239, 272-4; Korean manufacturing growth and, 111; SAM and, 481; small-country assumption and, 225; TGT model/ growth and, 385; variation in elasticities/trade policy and, 233; *see also* export expansion; exports

external shocks, 458, 466;
macroeconomic adjustment and, 433-5; macroeconomic impact and, 441-9

factor markets: CGE model and, 139-45; distortion of, in CGE, 209; distribution of income and, 432; TGT model and, 322
factor requirements (primary), of static input-output models, 29-31
factors of production, income distribution and, 401, 410
farmers (CGE model), income distribution and, 437-8, 452, 453; *see also* agriculture
feasibility, 63 n2; linear programming and, 64, 69, 71; target equilibrium paths and, 44-5, 56
Fei, J., 431
final demand: dynamic input-output models and, 31, 36-7; growth and, 126, 127; interindustry model and, 101; static input-output models and, 23, 25, 30; *see also* demand; domestic demand
Findlay, R. E., 435 n1
firms, 143; linear programming budget constraint problem and, 134, 135
fixprice rationing, *see* import rationing, fixprice
forecasting, 3; CGE model and, 180-1
foreign exchange: constraints in linear programming model, 67-9; Korean growth and, 112; shortages of, adjustment policies and, 288-317
foreign exchange crisis (Turkey/1973-1977): adjustment postponement of, welfare costs/macroeconomic effects of, 342-50; estimation of an equilibrium exchange rate and, 332-41; historical background to, 323-6; import rationing/rent seeking (1978) and, 350-8; overview/sources of, 321-3; policy reaction to, 326-31
foreign trade, 10, 11; computable general equilibrium model and, 182-3; definitions of, 195-6; dynamic input-output models and, 46-7; exchange rate and, 183-97; linear programming model and, 80-7; realism in speculation of, CGE model and, 219-21, 240; sectors and, 240; shadow price/linear programming and, 76; static input-output models and, 19, 24-9; *see also* balance of trade; trade

forward-running model, 40-1, 59, 60; adjustment function of, 61
"free-trade" reference solution (CGE model), 259-65

general equilibrium models: dynamic, trade policy and, 211-17; empirical, 2, 3; usefulness of, 7; *see also* computable general equilibrium model
Gerschenkron, A., 100 n5
government: basic CGE model and, 145-6; credit/capital markets and, 209; dynamic efficiency and, 216; income distribution mechanisms and, 413, 415; policy of, welfare and, 207; SAM/CGE model and, 159-60
gross domestic product (GDP): Korean growth example and, 114; national accounts and, 21; Turkish foreign exchange and, 343, 350
growth: changes in technology and, 46; decline in (since 1973), 433-5; dynamic input-output model (Korean example) and, 110-26; industrial, Turkey and, 323-5; one-sector/multisector model comparison and, 61; static input-output model and, 92-110; target equilibrium and, 35; terminal year/linear programming and, 88, 89; trade policy and, 213-14; *see also* growth prospects
growth paths, 34, 36; alternative long-range, 112; manufacturing (Korea) and, 111-14; price structure and, 359; sectoral growth rates and, 43-4
growth prospects (TGT model): experiments in, 259-60; export expansion/import substitution and, 378-94; macroeconomic alternatives and, 361-5; relative price/sectoral growth and, 367-76; *see also* growth
Grubel, H.G., 219 n1

Hahn, F., 155 n13
Harcourt, G., 52
Harris, J., 178, 179
Heckscher-Ohlin trade theory, 31
horizontal axis graphing of income distribution, 428
households: basic CGE model and, 145-6; income distribution and, 410, 413, 414-15, 421-4; linear programming budget constraint problem and, 135, 136; SAM/CGE model and, 159-60, 476, 481-2
Hudson, E., 467 n19

human capital theory, income
distribution and, 399, 400
Hungary, 53

import complements, 240
import licenses, 200, 201, 321, 351, 443,
453
import rationing, 200; vs. devaluation in
exchange rate adjustment, 295-305;
exchange rate adjustment and, 290-5;
fixprice, 11, 292-4, 297, 299-301,
302, 304, 308, 312, 313, 352;
premium, 11, 294-5, 296-7, 298-9,
300, 302, 304, 307-8, 366, 369, 443-
4, 448, 452, 453, 456, 460, 464, 465;
rent seeking/exchange rate
adjustment and, 305-9; TGT model
and, 321, 342, 346, 350-8; TGT
model/growth and, 366, 369, 380-1;
see also imports; import substitution
imports, 217, 219, 283; CGE model/
income distribution and, 439, 441-3,
444, 448; change in specification
effects on equilibrium solution and,
230-2; demand function equation of
flexible exchange rate and, 251;
domestic prices and, 237-9; dynamic
input-output models and, 46-7, 114,
117; foreign exchange constraints/
linear programming and, 68; as
imperfect substitute for domestic
goods, 221-4, 230-2; introduction of
trade into CGE model and, 197, 200;
manufacturing, resource allocation/
trade policy and, 264, 268, 269, 270,
272; price equation, flexible exchange
rate and, 250; sector tradability
classification and, 224; small-country
assumption and, 224; static input-
output model and, 21, 24-9; as
substitute for domestic goods, 24, 29,
76, 203, 220; terminal year/linear
programming and, 89; TGT model
and, 321, 325, 327, 329, 330, 331,
340; TGT model/growth prospects
and, 359, 361, 366-9, 374-6; trade
policy/linear programming and, 80;
see also import rationing; import
substitution
import substitution, 126, 359;
decomposition methodology of static
input-output model and, 93, 94-5;
dynamic input-output model (Korean
example) and, 111, 113, 121-6;
exchange rate adjustment and, 289;
growth and, 126; import complements
and difference in, 240; industries

using, tariffs and, 217; static input-
output model (manufacturing growth)
and, 104, 107-10; TGT model and,
327, 342, 353, 355-7, 366; TGT
model/growth and, 378-94; see also
import rationing; imports
income: cross-country growth
comparisons and, 96; development
process and, 91; dynamic model and,
213; equation, flexible exchange rate
model and, 252; generation, demand
for commodities (CGE model), 145-8;
linear programming budget constraint
problem and, 135; SAM/CGE model
and, 159-60; TGT model/growth
and, 364, 365; trade policy and, 245-
8; Turkish foreign exchange crisis
and, 323; see also income distribution
income accounts (SAM), 475-7
income distribution: application of CGE
model and, 432-3; archetype
economies and, 435-41; class conflict/
policy choice and, 458-66; economic/
sociopolitical process and, 397;
economy-wide models and, 403-10;
external shocks/macroeconomic
adjustment and, 433-5, 441-9;
generating, in a planning model, 410-
24; measures of, 425-31; normative/
positive approaches to, 398-403;
policy choice and, 449-58; tariffs and,
217; see also income
index numbers: decomposition
methodology and, 247-8; exchange
rate adjustment/welfare and, 312-13;
TGT model and, 379 n5; welfare
comparisons and, 242-5
individuals: income distribution and,
410, 415, 416, 425; size distribution
by, 417-21
industrialization, 96, 110, 182; infant
industry argument and, 216;
protection and, 214; Turkish, 258,
323-5
infant industry argument, 216
inflation: foreign exchange and, 291;
TGT model/growth and, 394;
Turkish foreign exchange crisis and,
329, 331, 332, 337, 338, 339, 340,
348, 350
input-output models: accounts in, static
models and, 17-21; diagonalization
and, 53-5; dynamic, 9; empirical
application of, 91-127; factor
requirements of static, 29-31; foreign
trade in static, 24-9; industrial
growth/structural change in static,

92-110; material balance equation of static, 21-4; multisector dynamic, 36-42; one-sector dynamic, 31-6; one-sector and multisector compared, 60-1; price system in, 9; relative prices and, 48-53; semipositive matrices and, 55-8; stability of dynamic system and, 59-60; static, 9; system, policy analysis/linear programming and, 62-90; target equilibrium paths in dynamic, 42-6; technological change/foreign trade in dynamic, 46-7; trade strategy and structural change/growth in dynamic, 110-26; viability and, 23, 58

institutions, income distribution and, 410, 413

interindustry model, 101

investment: adjustment function/growth rate and, 61; allocation in CGE model, 175-8; CGE model/distribution and, 446, 449; demand (sectoral), price mechanism/resource allocation and, 259-60, 261; dynamic model and, 212-13, 213-14, 215, 216; equation, flexible exchange rate model, 252-3; income distribution models and, 403-5, 407; Korean manufacturing growth and, 112, 114, 117, 121; multisector dynamic input-output models and, 37-41; objective function/linear programming and, 66; one-sector dynamic input-output models and, 31-6; terminal year/linear programming and, 87; TGT model/growth and, 363, 364; trade policy/linear programming and, 84-5; treatment in CGE model and, 142, 147, 148, 165-6, 171, 172-3; Turkish foreign exchange crisis and, 331, 339-40, 353; updating of, linear programming model and, 67

Isard, P., 219

Israel, 96, 101, 104, 105, 108

Japan, 96, 100, 104, 105, 107, 123
Johansen, L. H., 150
Jorgenson, D., 41 n10, 60 n31, 214, 467 n19

Kaldor, N., 404
Korea: *see* South Korea
Korean five-year plan: *see* South Korea, five-year plan
Kornai, J., 91, 168
Krueger, Anne, 152, 289, 306, 370
Kubo, Y., 92 n1
Kuznets, Simon, 1, 18

labor: basic structure of CGE model and,140-1, 142, 144-5, 163, 167, 169; categories, "free-trade" reference solution and, 260, 261; constraints in linear programming model, 69, 70-1; equation, flexible exchange rate model, 251; exchange rate/balance of trade and, 186, 190; income distribution and, 416, 438, 441, 450, 451; Korean manufacturing growth and, 114; rural-urban migration in CGE model and, 178-9; SAM and, 475-6; static input-output model primary factor requirements and, 30, 31

labor training, 216

Laspeyres index, 379 n5; decomposition methodology and, 248; exchange rate adjustment/welfare and, 313; welfare comparisons and, 243-6

Leontief, Wassily, 6, 18, 31, 40

Lewis, W.A., 434

linear programming models, 9, 133; basic structure of dynamic, 63-71; capacity constraints in, 66-7; capital/investment updating and, 67; development planning and, 62-3; foreign exchange constraints in, 67-9; labor constraints in, 69; material balance equation in, 65-6; objective function in, 65; shadow prices in, 71-80; terminal conditions in, 80-7; terminal conditions problem of, 87-90; trade policy/comparative advantage in, 80-7

literacy, Korean manufacturing growth and, 112

Lloyd, P.J., 219 n1

Lluch, C., 483

loans, 176

Lorenz curve graphing of income distribution, 428

Lysy-Taylor model of Brazil, 406

macroeconomic forecasting models, 3
Malinvaud, E., 3
Mangahas, M., 431
manufacturing gross output, cross-country comparison and, 97-101
manufacturing sector, 257, 436, 452; expansion in, comparative study and, 101-4; output of, growth and, 97-101; protection of, 211, 214; resource allocation/manufacturing imports-exports and, trade policy effects of, 259-74; TGT model/growth and, 363, 367; trade strategy and growth in, 105-10; wages/trade policy and, 208

522

definitions and, 192-7; trade tax changes, and, 278-82

prices: basic structure of CGE model and, 141, 143-4, 148, 150, 167-8, 169-71; devaluation of domestic, exchange rate adjustment and, 296, 299; distribution of income and changes in, 432; domestic, tariffs/subsidies and, 265-74; domestic, trade policy and, 232-9; elasticities of, trade substitution and, 264-5; equations for, in flexible exchange rate model, 250; existence proof of core CGE model and, 153-5; exports/small-country assumption and, 224-6, 227; export supply/exchange rate adjustment and, 290; factor, introducing trade into CGE model and, 204, 206; foreign exchange and changes in, 291; gross/net, exchange rate adjustment and, 302-5, 317; growth decline and increases in, 434; growth path and, 359; income distribution mechanisms and, 405-6; index movement of, TGT model and, 335-6; linear programming and, 64; linear programming budget constraint problem and, 134-5, 136; mechanism, resource allocation (CGE model) and, 259-74; multichannel systems of, 52-3; policy for, models and, 132; relative, CGE model/distribution and, 436, 450-2; relative, input-output models and, 48-53; relative, TGT model and, 367-76; social costs-benefits, project evaluation/resource allocation and, 276-7; static input-output models and, 21-2; substitution of foreign and domestic goods and, 219-20; substitution of imported and domestic goods and, 222; see also market prices; shadow prices

price system, input-output models and, 9

product accounting (static input-output models), 17, 18, 19-21

product differentiation, 257, 259; exports/small-country assumption and, 224-5; imports and, 221-4; trade policy/resource allocation and, 232-41; trade tax changes and, 282

production: accounts, SAM and, 472-5, 481; budget constraint problem (LP) and, 133-4; CGE model/income distribution and, 438-9, 466; possibility frontier, 45; primary, manufacturing growth and, 100, 101;

static input-output models and, 21, 23; technology, 261; TGT model/growth and, 365

production function: basic structure of CGE model and, 139, 141, 145, 167; flexible exchange rate equation for, 251

product market equilibrium (flexible exchange rate model), 253-4

profits: basic structure of CGE model and, 143, 145, 176-8; income, savings rate/distribution and, 404; maximization of, 50, 51, 143, 145; rate equation for (linear programming), 77-8; rates of, 49, 176-8; TGT model and, 356, 357, 374

project evaluation, resource allocation/DRCs-ERPs and, 274-8

protection, 302; of exportables, 199; policy-making concerns of, 201; resource allocation and, 201, 202; tariff/domestic prices and, 271; tariff/noncompetitive imports and, 240; trade policy/CGE model and, 202-5; see also effective protection; nominal protection

purchasing-power-parity computations, Turkish foreign exchange crisis and, 340, 349

Pyatt, G., 431

quantity variables (CGE model), 132, 168

quotas, 200-1, 207, 351; exchange control and, 292

Ranis, G., 431

rationing: see import rationing

Rawls, J., 399

reasonableness (target equilibrium), 44

reference run (CGE model), 259-65

remittances, Turkish foreign exchange crisis and (TGT model), 327, 328, 329, 330, 331, 333, 334, 336, 337, 338, 341, 349

rent seeking: CGE model/distribution and, 448; import rationing/exchange rate adjustment and, 305-9, 313; sectoral impact of rationing/TGT model and, 352, 355; TGT model/growth and, 365

reserve decumulation (TGT model), 333-4

resource allocation: exchange rate adjustment and, 289, 296, 306, 317; input-output model and, 92; policy change and, 287; product

523

resource allocation (*cont.*)
  differentiation/trade policy and, 232-41; protection and, 201, 202; shadow prices/linear programming and, 75; TGT model/growth and, 365; trade policy/linear programming and, 85; trade policy/manufacturing imports-exports and, 259-74; trade taxes and, 278, 282-6; welfare and, 241
Robinson, S., 92 n1, 176, 322
rural-urban migration (CGE model), 178-80

Samuelson, P., 84
savings, 261; basic structure of CGE model and, 146, 147, 166; CGE model/distribution and, 446-8; defining rate of, in input-output model, 33, 35; dynamic model building and, 212, 213; income distribution/models and, 403-5, 407; SAM/CGE and, 160-1, 476, 482; TGT model and, 322
sectors, 67; CGE model/distribution and, 436-7, 441; exchange rate adjustment and, 302-5, 317; growth in, trade strategy and, 105-10; growth rates/growth path and, 43-4; Korean growth pattern and, 114, 121; tariff/subsidy rates and, 259-74; TGT model/growth and, 367-70, 383; tradability classification and, 240-1; trade-substitution/export demand elasticities and, 249; trade tax changes and, 284; Turkish foreign exchange/sectoral impact of rationing and, 350-8
semipositive matrices, mathematical properties of, 55-8
service sector, 110, 117, 121, 262; exchange rate adjustment and, 302, 304
shadow prices, 9, 134; DRCs and, 278; in linear programming model, 71-80; trade policy/linear programming and, 81, 82-3, 86; *see also* market prices; prices
Shishido, S., 93
size distribution: by individuals, 417-21; theories of, income distribution and, 399-400, 401, 402, 406, 425
small-country assumption, 219; CGE model/exports and, 224-30; exchange rate/price system and, 184; introduction of trade into CGE and, 198
social accounting matrix (SAM): computable general equilibrium

model and, 155-62; construction of, 471-85; income distribution and, 410, 411-17; *see also* accounting framework
social mobility, 409
socioeconomic groups: archetype economies/income distribution and, 437-8; income distribution and, 410, 415-16, 423, 458-9, 460, 462-4
Solow, R., 60 n31
South Korea, 96, 100, 101-104, 107, 108, 370; dynamic input-output model example and, 110-26; five year plan, 46
specification effects, change in, imports/exports and, 230-2
Srinivasan, T. N., 306
stability: of dynamic system, 59-60; long-run equilibrium growth path and, 32; one-sector/multisector models and, 61; *see also* "dual stability"
stagnation, Turkish foreign exchange crisis and, 331
Stone, Richard, 46
structural change, 400; dynamic input-output model (Korean example) and, 110-26; export expansion/import substitution (TGT model) and, 378-94; growth experiments and, 259-60; macroeconomic alternatives in TGT model and, 361-5; multisector models and, 1; relative price/sectoral growth (TGT model) and, 367-76; static input-output model and, 92-110
subsidies, 198; to producers, protection and, 211; *see also* export subsidies
substitutability: elasticities (export demand/trade substitution), prices/resource allocation and, 259-74; exchange rate adjustment and, 302; exports and domestic goods, 76, 224; of foreign and domestic goods, 184, 219-21, 237, 248, 272, 275; imports and domestic goods, 24, 29, 76, 220; imports as imperfect substitutes for domestic commodities, 221-4, 230-2; introduction of trade into CGE model, foreign/domestic goods and, 203
supply: of commodities, factor markets/CGE model and, 139-45; curve for exports, 233-4; domestic goods as imperfect substitute for imports and, 231-2; export, small-country assumption and, 228-30
Syrquin, M., 91, 110, 435

unemployment, 213
uniqueness in CGE analysis, 155
United States, 31, 46, 467 n19
urban sector, 260

value composition equation (linear programming), 75-7
value judgement, income distribution and, 425-7
viability, input-output models and, 23, 58

wages: basic structure of CGE model and, 144, 145, 163, 167, 170; CGE model/distribution and, 449; differentials, "free-trade" reference solution and, 260; exchange rate/nontradables and, 189; exchange rate/price level and, 187; income, savings/distribution and, 404; introduction of trade into CGE and,

208-9; rates of, 49; tariffs and, 217; TGT model and, 356, 374
Watanabe, T., 93
welfare: analysis of income distribution and, 398, 399, 425-7; comparisons, index numbers and, 242-5; costs, adjustment postponement/Turkish foreign exchange and, 342-50; costs, project evaluation/resource allocation and, 274, 276, 277; decomposition methodology and, 248-9; effects of exchange rate adjustment, 312-16; government policy/trade policy and, 207; implication of CGE model/employment and, 209; trade policy and, 241-8
Williams, R., 483
workers' remittances: see remittances, Turkish foreign exchange crisis and (TGT model)